# POWER, POLITICS AND PEOPLE

## BOOKS BY C. WRIGHT MILLS

Listen, Yankee: The Revolution in Cuba (1960)

Images of Man (1960)
(Edited with an Introduction)

The Sociological Imagination (1959)

The Causes of World War Three (1958)

The Power Elite (1956)

Character and Social Structure (1953)
(with H. Gerth)

White Collar (1951)

The Puerto Rican Journey (1950)
(with C. Senior and R. Goldsen)

The New Men of Power (1948)

From Max Weber: Essays in Sociology (1946)
(Ed. and Tr. with H. Gerth)

## BOOKS BY IRVING LOUIS HOROWITZ

The War Game: Studies of the New Civilian Militarists (1963)

Radicalism and the Revolt Against Reason (1961)

Philosophy, Science and the Sociology of Knowledge (1960)

C. WRIGHT MILLS

# POWER, POLITICS AND PEOPLE

THE COLLECTED ESSAYS OF C. WRIGHT MILLS

Edited and with an
Introduction by Irving Louis Horowitz

NEW YORK • OXFORD UNIVERSITY PRESS
1963

Grateful acknowledgment is given to the following newspapers, journals and magazines in which the essays in this volume originally appeared.

THE STRUCTURE OF POWER IN AMERICAN SOCIETY. *The British Journal of Sociology,* Vol. IX, No. 1, March 1958. © Routledge & Kegan Paul Ltd. 1958.

THE SOCIAL LIFE OF A MODERN COMMUNITY. *American Sociological Review,* Vol. VII, 1942. Copyright 1942 *American Sociological Review.*

A MARX FOR THE MANAGERS. *Ethics: An International Journal of Legal, Political and Social Thought.* Vol. 52, No. 2, January 1942. Published by the University of Chicago Press.

THE POLITICAL GARGOYLES: BUSINESS AS A SYSTEM OF POWER. *The New Republic,* April 12, 1943. Copyright 1943 by Harrison-Blaine, Inc.

THE TRADE UNION LEADER: A COLLECTIVE PORTRAIT. *Public Opinion Quarterly,* Vol. 9, No. 2, Summer 1945. Copyright 1945 by *Public Opinion Quarterly.*

THE LABOR LEADERS AND THE POLITICAL ELITE. *Industrial Conflict,* edited by Arthur Kornhauser, Robert Dubin, Arthur M. Ross. McGraw-Hill Book Company, Inc., 1954. Copyright 1954 by the McGraw-Hill Book Company, Inc.

THE AMERICAN BUSINESS ELITE: A COLLECTIVE PORTRAIT. *The Journal of Economic History,* Vol. 4, No. 4. Supplement V, December 1945. Copyright New York University Press 1945.

A LOOK AT THE WHITE COLLAR. *Electronics in the Office: Problems and Prospects: Office Management Series,* No. 131, October 1952. Copyright 1952 by American Management Association.

PRAGMATISM, POLITICS AND RELIGION. *The New Leader,* August and September 1942.

THE NAZI BEHEMOTH DISSECTED. *Partisan Review,* September, October 1942. Copyright, 1942, by *Partisan Review.*

COLLECTIVISM AND THE MIXED-UP ECONOMY. *New Leader,* December 19, 1942.

LIBERAL VALUES IN THE MODERN WORLD: THE RELEVANCE OF 19th CENTURY LIBERALISM TODAY. *Anvil and Student Partisan,* Winter, 1952. Copyright 1952 by Bimbo Press.

THE CONSERVATIVE MOOD. *Dissent,* Vol. I, No. 1, Winter 1954. Copyright 1954 by *Dissent.*

THE DECLINE OF THE LEFT. Lecture on the British Broadcasting Company. *Contact.* No. 3, 1959. Copyright © 1959 by the Estate of C. Wright Mills.

CULTURE AND POLITICS: THE FOURTH EPOCH. *The Listener* (published by the British Broadcasting Company), March 12, 1959. Copyright © 1959 by the Estate of C. Wright Mills.

THE NEW LEFT. *New Left Review,* No. 5, September, October 1960. Copyright © 1960 by New Left Review, Ltd.

*To Yara*

# EDITOR'S PREFACE

In preparing the collected papers of C. Wright Mills for publication I have been guided by one central principle: to keep myself from interfering in the two-way communication between author and reader. Thus, except for matters of occasional lapses in punctuation and spelling (very rare I might add), the essays are herein presented as they were originally prepared by Wright Mills.

The outstanding difference from the original, is the replacement of sub-headings (most often put in by periodicals rather than by the author), with a uniform system of Roman numerals—signifying different sections of a particular paper. In large measure, Mills himself used this as a designation, so that the number of places where even sub-headings were deleted was comparatively small. The titles of each essay have been left intact. In a few places it was necessary to subtract or add a word, but the title of each paper can be checked against the title listings in the bibliography for an indication of any changes.

I have chosen to call this the "collected papers" rather than the "selected papers" because POWER, POLITICS, AND PEOPLE covers every major essay done by Wright Mills. Again, the bibliography appended to the back of this volume indicates precisely what has and has not been included. Of those that have not been included a further word is in order. Mills, in his long career, did a number of "topical" pieces which have no clear relevance for the present, and which he himself would have unquestionably excluded from any collection of his essays. Also excluded are summary statements culled from his larger works, which are readily available to the general reading public. Since all of Mills' major statements are herein included, only the literary archaeologist can possibly chafe at the omission of his occasional pieces. And I have tried to satisfy even the most sensitive and careful of readers by supplying this volume with an up-to-date and thorough bibliographical bank.

The one difficult moment came in deciding against prefacing each essay with an editorial abstract. While this is often a useful guide to a reader who wants to know whether or not to read a particular essay, in this case I am making the assumption that the reader is interested in *every* study herein contained, and therefore does not need (and indeed may even resent) a capsule version of each of Mills' pieces. The best "short cut" to an understanding of his writings is through reading them. For this reason, the essays follow each other without editorial commentary.

As for the arrangement of Mills' *corpus*, this matter is dealt with in my introduction. For those who might have preferred an "historical" sequence, instead of the present analytical and topical arrangement, it might be noted that this would have blurred any sound overview of Mills' way of doing social science, and it would have placed an extra burden on those readers unfamiliar with the sociological-linguistic minutiae that characterized the earliest stage of Mills' intellectual production. Nonetheless, since these early essays are no less vital and significant in an appreciation of Mills than his more popular writings (and indeed, form a meaningful intellectual continuum), they appear in part 4 of the book—by which time the reader should be quite ready and able to efficiently cope with the language and structure of sociology.

As a closing word I should simply wish to record my personal and intellectual gratitude to C. Wright Mills. If the reader has as much enjoyment in the reading of his essays as I had in the preparation of them, I shall consider this ample reward for my own small role in Wright's achievement.

ILH

# CONTENTS

## Part Four—KNOWLEDGE

# POWER, POLITICS AND PEOPLE

# AN INTRODUCTION
# TO C. WRIGHT MILLS

"Try to understand men not as an isolated fragment,
not as an intelligible field or system in and of itself.
Try to understand men and women as historical and
social actors, and the ways in which the variety of men
and women are intricately selected and intricately
formed by the variety of human societies. Before you
go through with any piece of work, no matter how
indirectly or occasionally, orient it to the central and
continuing task of understanding the structure and
the drift, the shaping and the meanings, of your own
period, the terrible and magnificent world of human
society in the second half of the twentieth century."—
*The Sociological Imagination*

What was the "magic" which C. Wright Mills possessed?
Why did he become the singular intellectual "hero" of our
age? How did he come to influence a generation of scholars,
students and savants while at the same time suffering the
outrages of ostracism and hostility from many professional
sociologists? Did his reputation finally rest on his contributions to radical politics or to social science—or to both
(and if the last, what was the nature of the "mix")? These
are not simple questions. Nor can any introductory essay
properly claim to exhaust the problems that Mills be-
queathed to us. From my point of view, a realistic evaluation of Mills must begin with how the public and personal
careers of Mills intersect. This in turn may serve as a basis
for settlement of the sort of questions which were asked *by*
Mills and, no less, *about* Mills.

Mills worked out his theory of society carefully, pains-
takingly, and without resort to the familiar crutches which
so often serve as a substitute for fresh insight. His concept

of the "classic" tradition in social science was based on its capacity to satisfy the demands of an age for useful knowledge; for clarification instead of manipulation. Mills was tough-minded enough to face the changing world situation and generous enough to recognize that such changes as are brought about are man made. And what men make can often be unmade. That is why he eschewed the kind of romantic historicism and providential messianism that so often characterizes the truth-seeker. By the same token, his man-sized sociology avoided the opposite empiricist pitfall which converts men into data, and history into autobiography.

The four words: power, politics, people, and knowledge, sum up for me the enterprise of social science as Mills envisioned it. Mills' reputation does not rest upon any single essay or book. Whether he is right or wrong on the causes of World War III, or on the merits of Castro's Cuba may be subject to debate. But what is not open to debate is the *need* for social scientists to address themselves to the great agonies and issues of our age. This Mills did more conscientiously than any of his peers. And as the courage to face the future is the mark of the young, so too, Mills' reputation will increasingly come to rest with those generations still in the process of intellectual formation and fermentation. This is something Mills himself was totally aware of; it was a thought which sustained him on more than one occasion. Mills went into the good fight in the firm belief that truth will out. The response of the public to his "message" and "preachings" (as he called his popular works) did not disappoint him. His victory was both public and private. This study is an attempt to explain at least in part the fruits of this victory.

I

A tough-minded, pragmatic view of sociology as human performance remained characteristic of Mills' writings throughout his career. Mills passed through three distinctive biographical-intellectual phases. First, social philosophy and a full absorption in the classics of social studies; second, an intensive period of empirical research in the middle forties; and third, an effort at combining these interests into a workable style of sociological reflection. The first thorough expression of this last stage was made in the middle 'fifties in his paper on "Two Styles of Social Science Research." *The Sociological Imagination* is largely an elaboration of the ideas first presented in this pivotal paper.

Although technically trained in sociology and philosophy, Mills was indifferent to what he felt to be the specialized trivialities and pretentious rituals toward which so many in these disciplines have drifted. When Mills finally evolved his synthesis of social science and social philosophy his essays took on a distinctive and recognizable "style." If some of his earlier efforts still showed ambivalence between the theoretical and philosophical leanings of classical writings in sociology, and the pragmatic and journalistic tradition characteristic of American social science, by the time of 1945 and his various "collective portraits" of trade-union leadership and the business elite he had performed a methodological breakthrough unique in the annals of contemporary sociology. Mills' feat consisted in combining empiricism and prescriptivism; describing the world of human relations and also presenting solutions (albeit partial solutions) to the worst infections of the American social structure. As Mills once said in a letter to a "white collar wife" published in a weekly mass circulation publication: "It is one thing to talk about general problems on a national level, and quite another to tell an individual what to do. Most 'experts' dodge that question. I do not want to."

Mills' search for answers, no less than for the right questions, meant a conscious abandonment on his part of two established traditions in sociology: empiricism as an ideology limiting discourse to low-level generalities, small group studies, and an ethically unconcerned posture; and rationalism as an ideology committed to abstract solutions of concrete issues, intuitionist appraisals of civilizations and nations, and an ethical involvement having sources independent of and even alien to the findings of the behavioral and historical sciences. To escape the false alternatives proffered by "abstracted empiricism" and "grand theory" meant a confrontation with human relations directly. At first, Mills effected this confrontation in terms of G. H. Mead's observed relations which are also shared relations, and later he augmented this pragmatic account with the findings of Marx, Mannheim and the European tradition of "conflict theory."

What we all observe are men agreeing, men quarreling, men killing. Such atomic facts of observation are the common property of all who care to look. When a factual settlement is made, we can then go forward to an examination of the question *why,* and the more complex question *what for?* To a large degree the "secret" of Mills' extraordinary ability to communicate with professional and popular audiences alike, from readers of *The American Journal of Sociology* to those of *The New York Journal American,* is telescoped in this classic approach to problems of men—an approach Mills felt to be noticeably present in the great figures of nineteenth-century social thought, and no less noticeable by its absence in the proponents of expertise and the prophets of social metaphysics alike. As he said in commenting on Lecky's work: "Those who would think about the nature of society and history in our time have been living off the big men of the nineteenth century." And Mills concluded with a simple reminder: "The trouble is that many of us do not know it."

That Mills did not garner widespread support for his approach is neither a consequence of his admittedly unique personality and temperament, nor a reflection of any particular political viewpoint. His attitude toward problems of war in a thermonuclear age is shared by many; his independent brand of party-less radicalism similarly is shared by many intellectuals; and his critique of American foreign policy is again not uniquely his own. What antagonized many was his singular capacity to transcend the parochialism, the pseudosecularization, and vicious circularity charasteristic of the "peer groups" in American social science. Mills had an instinctive animus for those who would connect scientific methods to national life styles. He was unimpressed by the recitation of differences between sociology in America and elsewhere. What the scientific community has in common far outweighs and overshadows differences.

To emphasize methodological distinctions is furthermore to substitute the search for novelty in place of the search for truth. Mills remained loyal to the latter search. He thus had little trouble communicating with men of knowledge the world over. Indeed, he was in all likelihood the most widely known and best respected American social scientist in Europe, Asia, and especially Latin America. And ironically enough, while the orthodox sociologist wrote of Mills as some sort of intellectual pariah, he was widely appreciated and read by all other sectors of American social science. This fact should not be brushed aside lightly in an age of academic insularity parading under the guise of expertise.

A notable characteristic of the truly great is their unique capacity to fuse the public and private phases of life. Socrates the man and the philosopher are one; Luther the man and the theologian are one; Marx the man and the socialist are one. Without wishing to invite invidious comparison, we must also speak of Wright Mills the man and the sociologist as one. His passion for the biographical form as a necessary part of sound social science research, his profound concern with matters of sociological design and craftsmanship, his vision of man as the essential revolutionizing agent in all social relations—each of these has its counterpart in Mills as a fully developed personality. There are his early efforts at producing an intellectual and intimate autobiography; his lifelong interest in problems of architectural and industrial design which gave substance to his activities in home-building, photography, woodworking, and farming. It isn't simply that Mills took as much joy in building a house or in running a farm (which at one time produced eighty per cent of his necessary foodstuffs) as he did in writing *White Collar* or *The Power Elite*—although this is indeed the case—the essence of the matter is that his sense of craft, design and style was characteristic of his scientific and human activities alike.

As for what Mills called his "vital statistics," they are characteristic enough of many men of social science. He was born in Waco, Texas, of middle-class Irish and English parentage. His boyhood was spent in Sherman, Fort Worth, and Dallas, where he attended a series of Catholic parochial schools and public high schools. His religious impulses were not particularly deep. But he did have an increasingly high respect for those sectors of the clergy who took the Christian mission of social justice and universal peace seriously. He was fond of saying that there were two types of Americans worth talking to: clergymen and students. It is no wonder then that after some early immature efforts at an agnostic critique of supernaturalism, Mills abandoned this as a frame of reference. In mature life he simply lived in terms of the natural world, having no more need for the "hypothesis" of providential design to explain sociological events than Laplace did to explain astronomical events.

After an unpleasant year as an engineering student at Texas A. & M., he went to the University of Texas, where he received his B.A. and M.A. degrees in philosophy and sociology in 1939. With the exception of his election to Phi Beta Kappa, he did not participate in any of the usual extra-curricula college activities. From Texas he went to the University of Wisconsin, where, working under Howard Becker, he received his Ph.D. in sociology and anthropology in 1941. His teaching apprenticeship began at Wisconsin, where he held a teaching fellowship during 1940 and 1941. In 1941 he was appointed assistant professor of sociology at the University of Maryland; in 1945 he was for a brief time special business consultant to the Smaller War Plants Corporation, traveling and preparing a Senate committee report on *Small Business and Civic Welfare*. Immediately after the war end in 1945 Mills was awarded a Guggenheim Fellowship and also received an appointment as assistant professor of sociology at Columbia University. Until 1948 he was director of the Labor Research Division of the Bureau of Applied Social Research, where he worked under the overall supervision of Paul F. Lazarsfeld. After that, he remained at Columbia University in the department of sociology as an associate professor.

During his later years he held visiting lectureships at Brandeis University, the University of Copenhagen, the United States Air War College, and the William A. White Institute of Psychiatry. Mills retained the specifically anthropological capacity for researching people wherever the people were. He studied health needs for the Congress of

Industrial Relations in Detroit, migration patterns of Puerto Ricans to New York, personal influence and mass communication effects on mid-westerners). His later travels to Latin America and Europe assisted him in expanding his vision of the human mission of sociology. Thus he became acutely aware of the threat of thermonuclear warfare during his first visit to Western Europe in the early 'fifties, the dynamics of socialism in his later trips to Russia and Poland, and undertook to study the revolutionary process by going to Cuba at the time of Fidel Castro's emergence. This does not mean that Mills was simply a child of his experiences. It does mean that Mills' strongly pragmatic attitudes conditioned him to observe the social phenomena he was writing about.

In a vital sense, to write of Mills' personal life in a perfunctory and standardized way is a painful violation of everything the man and the scholar stood for. Mills was singularly unimpressed with titles, honors, degrees, positions, and the entire world of inherited feudal values that have been mysteriously grafted on to present-day status conscious America.

Mills had a populist suspicion for any measure of a man that failed to begin and conclude with what he could do in the world and make of the world. He was just as much at home with industrial designers, army officers, business managers and labor leaders, as he was with academic colleagues This was keenly reflected in Mills' peripatetic reading habits. He was as conscientious a reader of *Business Week, U. S. News and World Report,* a raft of student radical and liberal publications, British weeklies, and *The New York Times,* as he was of the professional social science journals. In all truth, Mills grew increasingly suspicious of those who found the groves of academe a retreat and refuge from the cares of the world. In his blazing condemnation of academic pomp and ceremony he carried forward the honorable tradition of American men of letters like Emerson, James, and Veblen. Like them, he never confused the art of intellect with the enterprise of making money or getting promoted. His muscularity of body and mind not infrequently served as an irritant, a reminder of the larger world which exists outside the world of higher

learning. Mills was one of that special breed of men who
could be as comfortable in the Harlem ghetto looking up
at Morningside Heights (where Columbia University is
situated), as in looking down from the Heights at Harlem.
This flexibility of human character was his shield and
buckler. It made him impervious to the outraged cries of
the genteel world of academic *noblesse oblige* and immune
to the hardships of underground life. In his hands sociology
recaptured some of the humane impulse characteristic of
such pioneers as E. A. Ross and Franklin Giddings. Mills
spoke to as well as for, with no less than at, people of all
varieties and strivings. And he did so with a passion that
deteriorated neither into brutality nor sentimentality. This
in turn made Wright Mills an understandable as well as an
understanding person in his own right.

II

The dimension of power which informs Mills' social
science approach represented at its core an incorporation of
the "classic tradition" wherever that tradition was to be
found. From the Franco-Italian school of political sociology he learned of the centrality of the nation-state in regulating the lives of its citizenry; from the German sociology
of Weber he learned both to despise and to recognize the
might of the bureaucratic apparatus in industrial society;
from the American classical economics of Veblen and
Ayres (and later on from Schumpeter) he learned to distinguish between the fetishism of market production characteristic of nineteenth-century social relations, and the
fetishism of market consumption characteristic of what
Galbraith liked to call the "affluent society," but which
Mills more appropriately re-titled the "overdeveloped society."

In effect, Mills arrived at a position which held that
power as the capacity to make and to carry out decisions
even if others resist, functions as an independent social
variable. It is a force found in all sectors of society from
business managers, labor leaders, movie and television
producers and military elites, down to the local organization
of veterans into the American Legion and parents into

Parent-Teacher Associations. For Mills, as for his classical predecessors from Marx to Mannheim, it was a form of metaphysics to ask whether money, rank, status, or occupation represented the *exclusive* foundation of power. The study of the varieties of power was itself a fundamental issue for the social scientist, a problem which could only be obfuscated by asking whether any one form of power or any one kind of social scientist is more "basic" than the next. For Mills, power as the realization of human will remains the critical axis about which the social commonweal spins.

The unsentimental and unromantic image of the social world found in Mills' essays on power stems from this starting point in power as *sui generis*. The forms of power vary, the fact of power remains a constant. Because of this, one can objectively study the industrial power of employers over employees, the political power of a party machine over the rank and file voter, the military power of larger nations over smaller nations. In short, the settlement of the sociological question of how men interact, immediately and directly entails research into questions of superordination and subordination, elites and masses, rulers and ruled, in-groups and out-groups, and members and non-members. This is the fertile ground upon which Mills' sociology proceeds.

Mills' intense sense of commitment only served to sharpen his interest in problems of who gets what, who gives what, the price of victory and the costs of defeat. And if in this emphasis on the power vortex he tended to underestimate the symbolic and juridical limits of force and violence in complex societies (as his liberal critics have held), or refused to acknowledge the extent to which economic domination conditions the character of the struggle for power (as his Marxian critics indicate), the sociological context in which Mills lived and worked must be taken into account. The dominant wings of American sociology during the decades in which Mills was most active (1940-1960), tended to translate all claims of conflicting power into a delicately laced system of "pattern-maintenance" and "tension-management." Both the empiricists and the theorists viewed power with awe, as some sort of divine lever by means of which the social system becomes self-regulating. The *laisser-faire* economic world of Adam Smith became transformed into a *laisser-faire* vision of society as a whole. Power needed no examination in such a scheme, only flatulent praise of its workability disguised behind a heavy veil of meeting its "functional" requirements. Mills as a student of social power and its irreducible demands stood firmly opposed to this "metaphysical pathos" which took for granted the "inevitability" of bureaucracy, or the "structural need" for stratification and class inequality, simply because such phenomena existed.

On the other hand, the only articulate opposition which was expressed to this sociological ideology of consensus during this period was the socialist ideology of class struggle. And while Mills held this to be a superior intellectual posture because it at least squared better with the happenings of the everyday world of power relations, the socialist ideology (at least in its officialist garb) was not yet social science. The socialist approach suffered from its inordinate capacity to translate all patterns of conflict into economic stresses and strains. Not only that, but orthodox socialism had hardened into a Statist ideology, so that the demands not only of science but of socialism as well tended to become submerged into the immediate requirements of Soviet policy. While this last criticism was mitigated considerably by the growth of new forms of socialism in the post-World War II world, Mills continued to discount any effort to reduce the study of power to one type of power only.

If the elimination of private capital entailed human equality, then the aberrations found in the socialist bloc nations during the Stalin era could not have taken place. But they did take place. And Mills was unwilling to seek refuge in euphemistic explanations based on "personality cults" when sound sociological explanations provided by Michels, Simmel, and Weber were ready at hand. According to Mills, doctrines of permanent social revolution based exclusively on economic considerations fare no better than doctrines of permanent social equilibrium based on national considerations. Neither explains the existence of competition and conflict in polity, ideology or morality. The "collective portraits" which Mills painted of selected

"power elites" is an effort to get beyond ideological one-
sidedness, and at the same time achieve a humanly useful
comprehension of the function of power in social life. Just
as the physicist starts with a discussion of the nature of
work and force as the displacement of objects, so too
must the sociologist start with a discussion of the nature
of power as the displacement and reordering of human
objects.

The difficulty with most sociological systems, however,
is that they mistake a starting point for the total framework. The emphasis on sheer power carries with it the
danger of extreme reductionism, of a view of social relations
in which culture has no part and no place. Mills ranged
himself within the classic tradition precisely because he
attempted to account for the force of culture and its products in the human drama. The study of power is the beginning of sociological wisdom—but the essence of that
wisdom is that power resides in men. Hence the existence
of power is a less significant area of study than the human
uses made of power. Men define power; they are not necessarily defined by it. This, at any rate, is the liberating task
of the social sciences.

Power institutionalizes itself in human affairs. We do
not confront one another directly in power relations as do
atoms in physical relations. On the whole, with the exception of certain wartime experiences, we confront each other
symbolically; and more specifically politically. The dating
of revolutions is not in terms of economic or national conditions, but rather in terms of political transformation. We
speak of the French Revolution of 1789, although the
abolition of feudalism took place in the agrarian reforms of
1715; we speak of the Russian Revolution of 1917, although the aristocracy had revealed its economic impotence
long before that time; we speak of the Chinese Revolution
of 1948, even though it occurred in an underdeveloped
economy in which the middle classes had hardly begun to
flourish. In brief, power translates itself into political activity, just as, at a more intimate level, power translates social
interaction into group differentiation and rationalized authority. In line with this, we have to examine Mills' attitudes
toward conservatism, liberalism, and socialism in the

modern period—since politics is never abstract but always politics for and against specific types of organization and concrete forms of rule.

Conservatism was not a position which Mills dealt with too extensively in his papers. In the "Conservative Mood" he explains why this is the case. Conservatism translates the unreflecting reactions of traditionalism into the sphere of conscious reflection. Conservatism is traditionalism become self-conscious and forensic. But lacking in human sources of conservative tradition in America—lacking a noble aristocracy, a wealthy peasantry, or a petty bourgeoisie with a guild inheritance, conservatism can only be a yearning for authority, a mood lurking in the dark corners of the liberal rhetoric. In addition to the absence of an economic gentry with conservative ties, American conservatism is faced with the absence of a cultural aristocracy. But most damaging to the cause of conservatism is a semiconscious realization by the status conscious portion of American society that the liberal rhetoric is a common denominator for social and political climbing.

Although Mills pictured America as a "conservative country without any conservative ideology," the very existence of affluence and prosperity of those most likely to be moved in a right-wing direction curtails the growth of political appetites of post-war America for a total *Weltanschauung*. For these reasons, conservatism represented for Mills, not only an obsolete ideology lacking in material bases of sustenance, but the sort of marginal (and intellectualist) critique of the existing liberal ethos that could not compete for public political support in a climate of life styles that placed greater store by public relations than by public ideologies. Nevertheless, as liberalism in the 1950s tended to wilt into a centrist position in response to the growing dilemmas faced by United States foreign policy, Mills began to recognize that the need for a new wordly posture might indeed enable conservatism to find fertile soil as a functioning alternative to the ills of a contracting world empire.

For the present, liberalism and socialism remain the authentic dialectic of mid-twentieth century politics. As such, Mills devoted a number of his later essays to an assessment of the nature of this dialogue. For upon its outcome depended the shape of politics to come. Mills shared with Mannheim the belief that every age has a political philosophy and ideological credo uniquely its own. Hence, the industrial capitalist era had as its chief political "style," liberalism. With liberalism, the sense of eternal material progress, the formal equalization of men and women under law, and the expansion of a marketplace of ideas corresponding to the marketplace of products, defined the essential content and limits of liberal society as such. Different forms of capitalism—in England, France, Russia, Germany, and the United States—gave rise to different forms of liberal politics and ideology. These very differences were for Mills (who retained from pragmatism the pluralistic faith) a demonstration of the vitality of liberalism in the age of capitalist expansion and optimism.

By the same token, however, the rise of a socialist sector makes Marxian socialism important. It is now in the Soviet Union, China, Poland, and Cuba that differential, pluralistic responses to problems of social development are presented and fought out. Liberalism for its part tends to share with conservatism an obsolescence which is a consequence of the growing homogeneity of capitalism. Mills unashamedly maintained that liberalism is a perishing intellectual commodity to the degree that it becomes identified with an existing social establishment, to the extent that it becomes identified with a monolithic and rigid way of life.

The pluralist, the man receptive to new ideas, the man interested in the social uses of the social sciences, in short the *classic liberal,* must perforce interest himself in Marxisms around the world. Within the dynamism of socialism the liberal canons fulfill themselves. The formal, castrated and official liberalism of new and old frontiers is captive to statist dogma; whether on questions of civil liberties or foreign policy. As such liberalism has lost its capacity to move men. And Mills was behaviorist enough to know that those ideas which have no consequences in public action, have no consequences, period. Mills did not make an appeal to partisan passions (for example, no Marxist could possibly be content with Mills' relativism and his near-total dismissal of dialectical materialist philosophy). He did call for a realistic assessment of contemporary political alignments—and no less, of what the liberal person has to pay attention to in the realm of politics if he wishes to carry forward the classic liberalism of John Stuart Mill and Lionel Hobhouse.

Mills' developing interest in socialist politics was not an effort to ride the waves of doctrine, or a quixotic search for novelty. Neither of these were characteristic of the man in any way. He attempted to fuse a liberal imagination with a sociological leavening—and through such a fusion to revive the sinews of democratic politics in America. Mills sought to explain his own perspective and system of beliefs by entering into an honest dialogue with the socialists. Involved in this dialogue, from Mills' point of view, was a commitment to social science, of which Marxism is a part, and a very important part, both historically and in the present. However, the priority of social science as an empirical and historical whole, made a dogmatic outcome in favor of any one part of this sociological tradition impossible. For taking such a view, Mills earned the animus of those sociologists who refused to acknowledge the centrality of Marxism in its growth; and no less, the opposition of the dogmatic socialists who suspected sociology of being intrinsically a "reformist maneuver."

While the evaluative criteria of Mills are firmly empirical and critical, this is not the exclusive level at which he operated. Mills was too sophisticated a thinker not to appreciate the fact that the political importance of ideas may or may not have anything to do with how scientific or rational a system of beliefs is. Hence, Mills sought to explain the widespread acceptance of Marxism throughout the world on the basis of ideological and moral elements, no less than upon the truth content of the doctrine. Mills personally was a man with deep moral convictions; quite willing to stake his professional reputation on the line in defense of these convictions. The variety of Marxisms are a good thing to have around, because they make possible the dialogue without which life would become trivial and meaningless. The better is the critic of the good. The dialogue is healthy unto itself.

Mills was above all a man of enlightenment, a believer in the practical worth and consequence of ideas. His sympathy for the writings of the Marxians was a belief in the human passions. He had no illusions about the terrorism of Stalinism, but he could ask himself if Stalinism could lead to socialism no less than "reformist socialism." He had no illusions about the cynical uses of Marxism in the Soviet Union, yet he could inquire about the extent to which Marxism even as rhetoric is useful as a policy-making approach. In short, Mills was a contributor to, no less than a commentator upon the dialogue raging within international socialist circles. This paralleled his role in sociology as a contributor to its debates on descriptivism and prescriptivism, consensus and conflict, the meaning of power and authority, etc. In this way, Mills' varied work fulfilled his self-image of the active role of the man of ideas in a world of men.

Nonetheless, the classic tradition is not yet the sociological tradition. Enlightenment liberalism and Victorian Marxism never got beyond the thing, the person, the ideology. Neither adopted an open-ended attitude toward social and political events. And while "biography," Mills' euphemism for the intensive study of personality in its social setting, is an element of sound social science appraisal, it is only when biography is coupled with history, only when a correlation of subjective and objective criteria obtains, that legitimate sociological study is possible. While no science can transcend history as the Marxists taught, it is also true that no history can transcend science. Mills was prepared to accept the fact that sociological inquiry is comparative and relative in nature. What he insisted upon was not an absolute measuring rod of a predeterminist variety, but simply that to compare, to study people in a scientific way, is itself a necessary response to the historical muse.

The uses of historical sociology, and for Mills *all* sociology is historical as it is biographical, guarantees its place in science because it need no longer be assumed that there is an "essential human nature" or a "mysterious core" within men in their social interaction. "Abstractions" of this kind disturbed Mills. He was empiricist enough to understand that sociologists share with novelists a concern for generalizing experience into its broadest types. What they both confront are people—Babbitt, the Children of Sanchez, Sister Carrie. The sociologist does not observe inevitabilities, equilibrium systems, or any parceling of men into neat subspecializations of sociology. This accounts in good measure for his practical need to write on revolution, on thermonuclear war, on minority migrations, on middle-class life in America, and on the growth of an elite in the American labor movement.

The impulse to return sociology to the public from whence it emanated, to deprofessionalize it in fact, had as its basis Mills' recognition that in his natural state, man is essentially irrational, a creature who responds to impulses, political slogans, status symbols, etc. And sociology could provide that means by which man casts off an egoistic, sectarian and mythic pride and grows to maturity. Sociology helps men "know where they stand, where they may be going, and what—if anything—they can do about the present as history and the future as responsibility." Mills boldly employed the "neo-Machiavellians," the great sociologists of the Franco-Italian tradition, as no other American sociologist before him. The work of Mosca, Pareto, Michels and Sorel deeply influenced his thinking on questions, not because they demonstrated that men were oftentimes irrational in their behavioral patterns. This he knew without them. What they did was to offer sociology what Freud and his circle offered psychology—a *rational explanation* for irrational behavior. What made these men important was their development of a scale of measuring irrational behavior which to his mind was unsurpassed and was basically left unaccounted for in the calculations of the "biographers" who wrote the *Chroniques scandaleuses,* and the "historians" who wrote of ideology and *Geisteswissenschaft.* That the "manipulation" of men was possible Mills did not doubt. But that the message of the great sociologists of the past not only dealt with the *mechanisms of persuasion* but also, in this very process, provided a *system of clarification,* proved for Mills that sociology could *cure* human ills as well as explain them. And any science concerned with human beings had to have this prescriptive value—just as medicine and psychology.

People are not simply creatures who have a personal history. Nor are they abstract embodiments of world historical trends. What really distinguishes them is that they have cognition of their historical and biographical processes. The life cycle of animals simply exists but only men can create autobiography. There may exist an abundant variety in the evolution of plant life but only men can comment on the *ethical* worth of this or that given phase of their history. Precisely the stakes which men have in the social order create differential attitudes toward that social order. This grasp of man as a cognitive force preserved Mills from the worst infections of neo-Machiavellian social theory. Knowledge, however tortured that word might be in actual practice, has as its purpose and justification the clarification and not the manipulation of people. This accounts for the nobility of social science as a calling. This is why Mills must be ranged alongside the democratic social theorists of the past as against the elitist tradition which in its cynicism about the capacity of man to know, and to act on the basis of this knowledge, frequently degenerated into apologetics for totalitarian regimes.

The dimension of mind which serves as the social mediator of thought helps to explain a myriad of problems that prior to the evolution of the sociology of knowledge remained shrouded in mystery. This understanding of the social role of ideas accounts for the distortions in knowledge, such as the rural and small town bias of those who forged a social psychology emphasizing adjustment, harmony, self-help, etc. By the same token, this same understanding of the social depth of ideas helps to explicate the rise of experimental science in seventeenth-century Puritan England. Recent studies of this phenomenon have given substance to Mills' claims for the overall existence of independent mental sets which affect the course of scientific development. Mills' early belief in the worth of the study of ideas as an independent social variable, led him to be profoundly affected by Marx's concept of a general theory of ideology, Weber's work on the interconnections between religious movements and industrial values, and Mannheim's programming of the social sources of truth and error in general.

Mills never abandoned the sociology of knowledge as a fruitful area of inquiry. Indeed, in his final coming to grips with Marxism, he worked out a paradigm for the study of political thought which clearly drew upon these earlier formulations, as well as upon his expanded vision of the classical tradition in social science.

In the examination of a political position, Mills insisted on the need to study what seemed to be four central components of any political perspective. The ideology in terms of which institutions and attitudes are justified or criticized; the ethic or worked-out body of ideals and beliefs; the agencies of change, that is the instruments of reform, restoration or revolution; and the theory of a political movement as such, its assumptions about how man in society functions.

Mills appreciated that men are galvanized into action by beliefs and not by abstract forces. The essential task of the social scientist, beyond explaining the beliefs that motivate men, is to urge a course of action based on knowledge rather than opinions. Only in this way could the force of belief be explained without having the social investigator himself become privy to any particular ideology or outlook.

Mills' convictions in sociological theory stemmed from the corrective and clarificatory functions of knowledge. That men can be moved by irrational claims is no proof that they ought to be so moved. That men respond to interests of a decadent or futilitarian variety makes a broad-based social science only more necessary. Indeed, the challenge of society to science, what gave his work a special urgency and appeal, was a recognition that the great struggle of the age was shaping up as a contest between alternative modes of settling human affairs: was settlement to be brought about through knowledge or through force, through science or dogma, through informed technology or mechanical technique?

Mills was so imbued with the rationalist ideal that he perhaps placed too great rather than too little stress upon the curative powers of knowledge. He tended to underestimate the powers of personal and class interest as effective deterrents to change. That he was disappointed and even discouraged by the continued arms race and the politics of deterrence, and no less dismayed by the failure of the United States to respond meaningfully to the revolutions of the underdeveloped peoples for a place in the sun, was matched by his dismay over the "men of knowledge" themselves, their joining in the chorus of rationalization and justification of the least defensible aspects of American society. The antagonism Mills felt at the "secularized" joining of hands between intellectuals and "crackpot" specialists under the cloak of expertise, was the response of a believer in the curative powers of truth and not the cynical or pessimistic observer of life.

Mills' positive commitment to a sociology of knowledge was corrollary to his belief in a greater public need for knowledge of sociology. His critique of the field in *The Sociological Imagination* was aimed precisely at the edifice erected by the professional caste in the name of expertise. Mills shared with Walter Lippman a search for "public philosophy." Only when the public was thoroughly informed could science move beyond the confines of the academy into the world at large. Only then could knowledge as such become morally responsible. Only then could we get a "public sociology."

What Mills meant by the "higher immorality" is that while knowledge is available in abundance, there is a virtual absence of *critical* intellect. "What knowledge does to a man (in clarifying what he is, and setting him free)—that is the personal ideal of knowledge. But today the personal *and* the social ideals of knowledge have coincided in what knowledge does for the smart guy—it gets him ahead; and for the wise nation—it lends cultural prestige, sanctifying power with authority." Mills consecrated his work to returning to a social rather than a private or egoistic conception of knowledge and its relation to power. "Only where publics and leaders are responsive and responsible, are human affairs in democratic order, and only when knowledge has public relevance is this order possible." To reach this critical intelligence, Mills called upon the "classic tradition"—rational and enlightened tradition, in which mind is autonomous and independent of power but, nonetheless, morally related to the mainsprings of social growth.

Nonetheless, this high moral purpose had specific policy-making ramifications. We live in a social science era (in the United States) in which huge funds are put at the disposal of the researcher—without any appreciable net benefits for society (unless the transformation of the sociologist into an administrative functionary is considered a benefit). In Europe, operating with much smaller financial resources. the social scientist has had much greater success in effecting national and regional policies. Why should this be so?

One answer suggested by Mills, and with which I fully concur, is that in the United States, sociological gamesmanship and pseudo-intellectual one-upmanship has produced a boomerang effect. Society has learned not to take the sociologist any the more seriously than he takes himself. This is the dreary and dismal result disguised by the flood of rhetoric maintaining this as the price to be paid for the "secularization" of social science.

In this hoary situation, Mills elicited the fears of the Establishment and the envy of not a few of these "secular" sociologists by demanding to be taken seriously. He could successfully do this because he was, above all else, convinced of the value and high purpose of sociological inquiry. Thus, in answer to our original query: "What was the magic of Mills?"—the reply is ultimately tied to the fact that he succeeded in being taken seriously by friend and foe alike.

The main drift of C. Wright Mills' work is linked to the practical importance of an ethically viable social science. This is so because such a sociology confronts the facts with integrity, and confirms the integrity by doing something about the facts. This then is the "message" of the greatest sociologist the United States has ever produced.

Irving Louis Horowitz

June, 1962
Hobart & William Smith Colleges
Geneva, New York

# PART ONE

PART ONE

# THE STRUCTURE OF
# POWER IN AMERICAN SOCIETY

**I**

Power has to do with whatever decisions men make about the arrangements under which they live, and about the events which make up the history of their times. Events that are beyond human decision do happen; social arrangements do change without benefit of explicit decision. But in so far as such decisions are made, the problem of who is involved in making them is the basic problem of power. In so far as thcy could be made but are not, the problem becomes who fails to make them?

We cannot today merely assume that in the last resort men must always be governed by their own consent. For among the means of power which now prevail is the power to manage and to manipulate the consent of men. That we do not know the limits of such power, and that we hope it does have limits, does not remove the fact that much power today is successfully employed without the sanction of the reason or the conscience of the obedient.

Surely nowadays we need not argue that, in the last resort, coercion is the "final" form of power. But then, we are by no means constantly at the last resort. Authority (power that is justified by the beliefs of the voluntarily obedient) and manipulation (power that is wielded unbeknown to the powerless)—must also be considered, along with coercion. In fact, the three types must be sorted out whenever we think about power.

In the modern world, we must bear in mind, power is often not so authoritative as it seemed to be in the medieval epoch: ideas which justify rulers no longer seem so necessary to their exercise of power. At least for many of the great decisions of our time—especially those of an international sort—mass "persuasion" has not been "necessary;" the fact is simply accomplished. Furthermore, such ideas as are available to the powerful are often neither taken up nor used by them. Such ideologies usually arise as a response to an effective debunking of power; in the United States such opposition has not been effective enough recently to create the felt need for new ideologies of rule.

There has, in fact, come about a situation in which many who have lost faith in prevailing loyalties have not acquired new ones, and so pay no attention to politics of any kind. They are not radical, not liberal, not conservative, not reactionary. They are inactionary. They are out of it. If we accept the Greek's definition of the idiot as an altogether private man, then we must conclude that many American citizens are now idiots. And I should not be surprised, although I do not know, if there were not some such idiots even in Germany. This—and I use the word with care— this spiritual condition seems to me the key to many modern troubles of political intellectuals, as well as the key to much political bewilderment in modern society. Intellectual "conviction" and moral "belief" are not necessary, in either the rulers or the ruled, for a ruling power to persist and even to flourish. So far as the role of ideologies is concerned, their frequent absences and the prevalence of mass indifference are surely two of the major political facts about the western societies today.

How large a role any explicit decisions do play in the making of history is itself an historical problem. For how large that role may be depends very much upon the means of power that are available at any given time in any given society. In some societies, the innumerable actions of innumerable men modify their milieux, and so gradually modify the structure itself. These modifications—the course of history—go on behind the backs of men. History is drift, although in total "men make it." Thus, innumerable entrepreneurs and innumerable consumers by ten-thousand decisions per minute may shape and re-shape the free-market economy. Perhaps this was the chief kind of limitation Marx had in mind when he wrote, in *The 18th Brumaire:* that "Men make their own history, but they do not make it just as they please; they do not make it under circumstances chosen by themselves. . . ."

But in other societies—certainly in the United States and in the Soviet Union today—a few men may be so placed within the structure that by their decisions they modify the milieux of many other men, and in fact nowadays the structural conditions under which most men live. Such elites of power also make history under circumstances not chosen altogether by themselves, yet compared with other men, and compared with other periods of world history, these circumstances do indeed seem less limiting.

I should contend that "men are free to make history," but that some men are indeed much freer than others. For such freedom requires access to the means of decision and of power by which history can now be made. It has not always been so made; but in the later phases of the modern epoch it is. It is with reference to this epoch that I am contending that if men do not make history, they tend increasingly to become the utensils of history-makers as well as the mere objects of history.

The history of modern society may readily be understood as the story of the enlargement and the centralization of the means of power—in economic, in political, and in military institutions. The rise of industrial society has involved these developments in the means of economic production. The rise of the nation-state has involved similar developments in the means of violence and in those of political administration.

In the western societies, such transformations have generally occurred gradually, and many cultural traditions have restrained and shaped them. In most of the Soviet societies, they are happening very rapidly indeed and without the great discourse of western civilization, without the Renaissance and without the Reformation, which so greatly strengthened and gave political focus to the idea of freedom. In those societies, the enlargement and the co-ordination of all the means of power has occurred more brutally, and from the beginning under tightly centralized authority. But in both types, the means of power have now become international in scope and similar in form. To be sure, each of them has its own ups and downs; neither is as yet absolute; how they are run differs quite sharply.

Yet so great is the reach of the means of violence, and so great the economy required to produce and support them, that we have in the immediate past witnessed the consolidation of these two world centers, either of which dwarfs the power of Ancient Rome. As we pay attention to the awesome means of power now available to quite small groups of men we come to realize that Caesar could do less with Rome than Napoleon with France; Napoleon less with France then Lenin with Russia. But what was Caesar's power at its height compared with the power of the changing inner circles of Soviet Russia and the temporary administrations of the United States? We come to realize—indeed they continually remind us—how a few men have access to the means by which in a few days continents can be turned into thermonuclear wastelands. That the facilities of power are so enormously enlarged and so decisively centralized surely means that the powers of quite small groups of men, which we may call elites, are now of literally inhuman consequence.

My concern here is not with the international scene but with the United States in the middle of the twentieth century. I must emphasize "in the middle of the twentieth century" because in our attempt to understand any society we come upon images which have been drawn from its past and which often confuse our attempt to confront its present reality. That is one minor reason why history is the shank of any social science: we must study it if only to rid ourselves of it. In the United States, there are indeed many such images and usually they have to do with the first half of the nineteenth century. At that time the economic facilities of the United States were very widely dispersed and subject to little or to no central authority.

The state watched in the night but was without decisive voice in the day.

One man meant one rifle and the militia were without centralized orders.

Any American, as old-fashioned as I, can only agree with R. H. Tawney that "Whatever the future may contain, the past has shown no more excellent social order than that in which the mass of the people were the masters of the holdings which they ploughed and the tools with which they worked, and could boast . . . 'It is a quietness to a man's mind to live upon his own and to know his heir certain.' "

But then we must immediately add: all that is of the past and of little relevance to our understanding of the United States today. Within this society three broad levels of power may now be distinguished. I shall begin at the top and move downward.

## II

The power to make decisions of national and international consequence is now so clearly seated in political, military, and economic institutions that other areas of society seem off to the side and, on occasion, readily subordinated to these. The scattered institutions of religion, education and family are increasingly shaped by the big three, in which history-making decisions now regularly occur. Behind this fact there is all the push and drive of a fabulous technology; for these three institutional orders have incorporated this technology and now guide it, even as it shapes and paces their development.

As each has assumed its modern shape, its effects upon the other two have become greater, and the traffic between the three has increased. There is no longer, on the one hand, an economy, and, on the other, a political order, containing a military establishment unimportant to politics and to money-making. There is a political economy numerously linked with military order and decision. This triangle of power is now a structural fact, and it is the key to any understanding of the higher circles in America today. For as each of these domains has coincided with the others, as decisions in each have become broader, the leading men of each—the high military, the corporation executives, the political directorate—have tended to come together to form the power elite of America.

The political order, once composed of several dozen states with a weak federal-center, has become an executive apparatus which has taken up into itself many powers previously scattered, legislative as well as administrative, and which now reaches into all parts of the social structure. The long-time tendency of business and government to become more closely connected has since World War II reached a new point of explicitness. Neither can now be seen clearly as a distinct world. The growth of executive government does not mean merely the "enlargement of government" as some kind of autonomous bureaucracy: under American conditions, it has meant the ascendency of the corporation man into political eminence. Already during the New Deal, such men had joined the political directorate; as of World War II they came to dominate it. Long involved with government, now they have moved into quite full direction of the economy of the war effort and of the post-war era.

The economy, once a great scatter of small productive units in somewhat automatic balance, has become internally dominated by a few hundred corporations, administratively and politically interrelated, which together hold the keys to economic decision. This economy is at once a permanent-war economy and a private-corporation economy. The most important relations of the corporation to the state now rest on the coincidence between military and corporate interests, as defined by the military and the corporate rich, and accepted by politicians and public. Within the elite as a whole, this coincidence of military domain and corporate realm strengthens both of them and further subordinates the merely political man. Not the party politician, but the corporation executive, is now more likely to sit with the military to answer the question: what is to be done?

The military order, once a slim establishment in a context of civilian distrust, has become the largest and most expensive feature of government; behind smiling public relations, it has all the grim and clumsy efficiency of a great and sprawling bureaucracy. The high military have gained decisive political and economic relevance. The seemingly permanent military threat places a premium upon them and virtually all political and economic actions are now judged in terms of military definitions of reality: the higher military have ascended to a firm position within the power elite of our time.

In part at least this is a result of an historical fact, pivotal for the years since 1939: the attention of the elite has shifted from domestic problems—centered in the 'thirties around slump—to international problems—centered in the 'forties and 'fifties around war. By long historical usage, the government of the United States has been shaped by domestic clash and balance; it does not have suitable agencies and traditions for the democratic handling of international affairs. In considerable part, it is in this vacuum that the power elite has grown.

(i) To understand the unity of this power elite, we must pay attention to the psychology of its several members in their respective milieux. In so far as the power elite is composed of men of similar origin and education, of similar career and style of life, their unity may be said to rest upon the fact that they are of similar social type, and to lead to the fact of their easy intermingling. This kind of unity reaches its frothier apex in the sharing of that prestige which is to be had in the world of the celebrity. It achieves a more solid culmination in the fact of the interchangeability of positions between the three dominant institutional orders. It is revealed by considerable traffic of personnel within and between these three, as well as by the rise of specialized go-betweens as in the new style high-level lobbying.

(ii) Behind such psychological and social unity are the structure and the mechanics of those institutional hierarchies over which the political directorate, the corporate rich, and the high military now preside. How each of these hierarchies is shaped and what relations it has with the others determine in large part the relations of their rulers. Were these hierarchies scattered and disjointed, then their respective elites might tend to be scattered and disjointed; but if they have many interconnections and points of coinciding interest, then their elites tend to form a coherent kind of grouping. The unity of the elite is not a simple reflection of the unity of institutions, but men and institutions are always related; that is why we must understand the elite today in connection with such institutional trends as the development of a permanent-war establishment, alongside a privately incorporated economy, inside a virtual political vacuum. For the men at the top have been selected and formed by such institutional trends.

(iii) Their unity, however, does not rest solely upon psychological similarity and social intermingling, nor entirely upon the structural blending of commanding positions and common interests. At times it is the unity of a more explicit co-ordination.

To say that these higher circles are increasingly co-ordi-

nated, that this is *one* basis of their unity, and that at times
—as during open war—such co-ordination is quite wilful,
is not to say that the co-ordination is total or continuous,
or even that it is very surefooted. Much less is it to say that
the power elite has emerged as the realization of a plot.
Its rise cannot be adequately explained in any psychological
terms.

Yet we must remember that institutional trends may be
defined as opportunities by those who occupy the command
posts. Once such opportunities are recognized, men may
avail themselves of them. Certain types of men from each
of these three areas, more far-sighted than others, have
actively promoted the liaison even before it took its truly
modern shape. Now more have come to see that their
several interests can more easily be realized if they work
together, in informal as well as in formal ways, and accordingly they have done so.

The idea of the power elite is of course an interpretation.
It rests upon and it enables us to make sense of major
institutional trends, the social similarities and psychological
affinities of the men at the top. But the idea is also based
upon what has been happening on the middle and lower
levels of power, to which I now turn.

### III

There are of course other interpretations of the American system of power. The most usual is that it is a moving
balance of many competing interests. The image of balance,
at least in America, is derived from the idea of the economic market: in the nineteenth century, the balance was
thought to occur between a great scatter of individuals and
enterprises; in the twentieth century, it is thought to occur
between great interest blocs. In both views, the politician is
the key man of power because he is the broker of many
conflicting powers.

I believe that the balance and the compromise in American society—the "countervailing powers" and the "veto
groups," of parties and associations, of strata and unions
—must now be seen as having mainly to do with the middle
levels of power. It is these middle levels that the political
journalist and the scholar of politics are most likely to

understand and to write about—if only because, being mainly middle class themselves, they are closer to them. Moreover these levels provide the noisy content of most "political" news and gossip; the images of these levels are more or less in accord with the folklore of how democracy works; and, if the master-image of balance is accepted, many intellectuals, especially in their current patrioteering, are readily able to satisfy such political optimism as they wish to feel. Accordingly, liberal interpretations of what is happening in the United States are now virtually the only interpretations that are widely distributed.

But to believe that the power system reflects a balancing society is, I think, to confuse the present era with earlier times, and to confuse its top and bottom with its middle levels.

By the top levels, as distinguished from the middle, I intend to refer, first of all, to the scope of the decisions that are made. At the top today, these decisions have to do with all the issues of war and peace. They have also to do with slump and poverty which are now so very much problems of international scope. I intend also to refer to whether or not the groups that struggle politically have a chance to gain the positions from which such top decisions are made, and indeed whether their members do usually hope for such top national command. Most of the competing interests which make up the clang and clash of American politics are strictly concerned with their slice of the existing pie. Labor unions, for example, certainly have no policies of an international sort other than those which given unions adopt for the strict economic protection of their members. Neither do farm organizations. The actions of such middle-level powers may indeed have consequence for top-level policy; certainly at times they hamper these policies. But they are not truly concerned with them, which means of course that their influence tends to be quite irresponsible.

The facts of the middle levels may in part be understood in terms of the rise of the power elite. The expanded and centralized and interlocked hierarchies over which the power elite preside have encroached upon the old balance and relegated it to the middle level. But there are also independent developments of the middle levels. These, it seems to me, are better understood as an affair of entrenched and provincial demands than as a center of national decision. As such, the middle level often seems much more of a stalemate than a moving balance.

(i) The middle level of politics is not a forum in which there are debated the big decisions of national and international life. Such debate is not carried on by nationally responsible parties representing and clarifying alternative policies. There are no such parties in the United States. More and more, fundamental issues never come to any point or decision before the Congress, much less before the electorate in party campaigns. In the case of Formosa, in the spring of 1955 the Congress abdicated all debate concerning events and decisions which surely bordered on war. The same is largely true of the 1957 crisis in the Middle East. Such decisions now regularly by-pass the Congress, and are never clearly focused issues for public decision.

The American political campaign distracts attention from national and international issues, but that is not to say that there are no issues in these campaigns. In each district and state, issues are set up and watched by organized interests of sovereign local importance. The professional politician is of course a party politician, and the two parties are semifeudal organizations: they trade patronage and other favors for votes and for protection. The differences between them, so far as national issues are concerned, are very narrow and very mixed up. Often each seems to be fifty parties, one to each state; and accordingly, the politician as campaigner and as Congressman is not concerned with national party lines, if any are discernible. Often he is not subject to any effective national party discipline. He speaks for the interests of his own constituency, and he is concerned with national issues only in so far as they affect the interests effectively organized there, and hence his chances of re-election. That is why, when he does speak of national matters, the result is so often such an empty rhetoric. Seated in his sovereign locality, the politician is not at the national summit. He is on and of the middle levels of power.

(ii) Politics is not an arena in which free and independent organizations truly connect the lower and middle levels of society with the top levels of decision. Such organizations are not an effective and major part of American life today. As more people are drawn into the political arena, their associations become mass in scale, and the power of the individual becomes dependent upon them; to the extent that they are effective, they have become larger, and to that extent they have become less accessible to the influence of the individual. This is a central fact about associations in any mass society: it is of most consequence for political parties and for trade unions.

In the 'thirties, it often seemed that labor would become an insurgent power independent of corporation and state. Organized labor was then emerging for the first time on an American scale, and the only political sense of direction it needed was the slogan, "organize the unorganized." Now without the mandate of the slump, labor remains without political direction. Instead of economic and political struggles it has become deeply entangled in administrative routines with both corporation and state. One of its major functions, as a vested interest of the new society, is the regulation of such irregular tendencies as may occur among the rank and file.

There is nothing, it seems to me, in the make-up of the current labor leadership to allow us to expect that it can or that it will lead, rather than merely react. In so far as it fights at all it fights over a share of the goods of a single way of life and not over that way of life itself. The typical labor leader in the U.S.A. today is better understood as an adaptive creature of the main business drift than as an independent actor in a truly national context.

(iii) The idea that this society is a balance of powers requires us to assume that the units in balance are of more or less equal power and that they are truly independent of one another. These assumptions have rested, it seems clear, upon the historical importance of a large and independent middle class. In the latter nineteenth century and during the Progressive Era, such a class of farmers and small businessmen fought politically—and lost—their last struggle for a paramount role in national decision. Even then, their aspirations seemed bound to their own imagined past.

This old, independent middle class has of course declined. On the most generous count, it is now 40 per cent of the total middle class (at most 20 per cent of the total labor force). Moreover, it has become politically as well as economically dependent upon the state, most notably in the case of the subsidized farmer.

The *new* middle class of white-collar employees is certainly not the political pivot of any balancing society. It is in no way politically unified. Its unions, such as they are, often serve merely to incorporate it as hanger-on of the labor interest. For a considerable period, the old middle class *was* an independent base of power; the new middle class cannot be. Political freedom and economic security *were* anchored in small and independent properties; they are not anchored in the worlds of the white-collar job. Scattered property holders were economically united by more or less free markets; the jobs of the new middle class are integrated by corporate authority. Economically, the white-collar classes are in the same condition as wage workers; politically, they are in a worse condition, for they are not organized. They are no vanguard of historic change; they are at best a rear-guard of the welfare state.

The agrarian revolt of the 'nineties, the small-business revolt that has been more or less continuous since the 'eighties, the labor revolt of the 'thirties—each of these has failed as an independent movement which could countervail against the powers that be; they have failed as politically autonomous third parties. But they have succeeded, in varying degree, as interests vested in the expanded corporation and state; they have succeeded as parochial interests seated in particular districts, in local divisions of the two parties, and in the Congress. What they would become, in short, are well-established features of the *middle* levels of balancing power, on which we may now observe all those strata and interests which in the course of American history have been defeated in their bids for top power or which have never made such bids.

Fifty years ago many observers thought of the American state as a mask behind which an invisible government operated. But nowadays, much of what was called the old lobby, visible or invisible, is part of the quite visible government. The "governmentalization of the lobby" has proceeded in both the legislative and the executive domain, as well as between them. The executive bureaucracy becomes not only the center of decision but also the arena within which major conflicts of power are resolved or denied resolution. "Administration" replaces electoral politics; the maneuvering of cliques (which include leading Senators as well as civil servants) replaces the open clash of parties.

The shift of corporation men into the political directorate has accelerated the decline of the politicians in the Congress to the middle levels of power; the formation of the power elite rests in part upon this relegation. It rests also upon the semiorganized stalemate of the interests of sovereign localities, into which the legislative function has so largely fallen; upon the virtually complete absence of a civil service that is a politically neutral but politically relevant, depository of brain-power and executive skill; and it rests upon the increased official secrecy behind which great decisions are made without benefit of public or even of Congressional debate.

## IV

There is one last belief upon which liberal observers everywhere base their interpretations and rest their hopes. That is the idea of the public and the associated idea of public opinion. Conservative thinkers, since the French Revolution, have of course Viewed With Alarm the rise of the public, which they have usually called the masses, or something to that effect. "The populace is sovereign," wrote Gustave LeBon, "and the tide of barbarism mounts." But surely those who have supposed the masses to be well on their way to triumph are mistaken. In our time, the influence of publics or of masses within political life is in fact decreasing, and such influence as on occasion they do have tends, to an unknown but increasing degree, to be guided by the means of mass communication.

In a society of publics, discussion is the ascendant means of communication, and the mass media, if they exist, simply enlarge and animate this discussion, linking one face-to-face public with the discussions of another. In a mass society, the dominant type of communication is the formal media, and publics become mere markets for these media: the "public" of a radio program consists of all those exposed to it. When we try to look upon the United

States today as a society of publics, we realize that it has moved a considerable distance along the road to the mass society.

In official circles, the very term, "the public," has come to have a phantom meaning, which dramatically reveals its eclipse. The deciding elite can identify some of those who clamor publicly as "Labor," others as "Business," still others as "Farmer." But these are not the public. "The public" consists of the unidentified and the nonpartisan in a world of defined and partisan interests. In this faint echo of the classic notion, the public is composed of these remnants of the old and new middle classes whose interests are not explicitly defined, organized, or clamorous. In a curious adaptation, "the public" often becomes, in administrative fact, "the disengaged expert," who, although never so well informed, has never taken a clear-cut and public stand on controversial issues. He is the "public" member of the board, the commission, the committee. What "the public" stands for, accordingly, is often a vagueness of policy (called "open-mindedness"), a lack of involvement in public affairs (known as "reasonableness"), and a professional disinterest (known as "tolerance").

All this is indeed far removed from the eighteenth-century idea of the public of public opinion. The idea parallels the economic idea of the magical market. Here is the market composed for freely competing entrepreneurs; there is the public composed of circles of people in discussion. As price is the result of anonymous, equally weighted, bargaining individuals, so public opinion is the result of each man's having thought things out for himself and then contributing his voice to the great chorus. To be sure, some may have more influence on the state of opinion than others, but no one group monopolizes the discussion, or by itself determines the opinions that prevail.

In this classic image, the people are presented with problems. They discuss them. They formulate viewpoints. These viewpoints are organized, and they compete. One viewpoint "wins out." Then the people act on this view, or their representatives are instructed to act it out, and this they promptly do.

Such are the images of democracy which are still used as working justifications of power in America. We must now recognize this description as more a fairy tale than a useful approximation. The issues that now shape man's fate are neither raised nor decided by any public at large. The idea of a society that is at bottom composed of publics is not a matter of fact; it is the proclamation of an ideal, and as well the assertion of a legitimation masquerading as fact.

I cannot here describe the several great forces within American society as well as elsewhere which have been at work in the debilitation of the public. I want only to remind you that publics, like free associations, can be deliberately and suddenly smashed, or they can more slowly wither away. But whether smashed in a week or withered in a generation, the demise of the public must be seen in connection with the rise of centralized organizations, with all their new means of power, including those of the mass media of distraction. These, we now know, often seem to expropriate the rationality and the will of the terrorized or —as the case may be—the voluntarily indifferent society of masses. In the more democratic process of indifference the remnants of such publics as remain may only occasionally be intimidated by fanatics in search of "disloyalty." But regardless of that, they lose their will for decision because they do not possess the instruments for decision; they lose their sense of political belonging because they do not belong; they lose their political will because they see no way to realize it.

The political structure of a modern democratic state requires that such a public as is projected by democratic theorists not only exist but that it be the very forum within which a politics of real issues is enacted.

It requires a civil service that is firmly linked with the world of knowledge and sensibility, and which is composed of skilled men who, in their careers and in their aspirations, are truly independent of any private, which is to say, corporation, interests.

It requires nationally responsible parties which debate openly and clearly the issues which the nation, and indeed the world, now so rigidly confronts.

It requires an intelligentsia, inside as well as outside the universities, who carry on the big discourse of the western

world, and whose work is relevant to and influential among
parties and movements and publics.

And it certainly requires, as a fact of power, that there
be free associations standing between families and smaller
communities and publics, on the one hand, and the state,
the military, the corporation, on the other. For unless these
do exist, there are no vehicles for reasoned opinion, no
instruments for the rational exertion of public will.

Such democratic formations are not now ascendant in
the power structure of the United States, and accordingly
the men of decision are not men selected and formed by
careers within such associations and by their performance
before such publics. The top of modern American society
is increasingly unified, and often seems wilfully co-
ordinated: at the top there has emerged an elite whose
power probably exceeds that of any small group of men
in world history. The middle levels are often a drifting set
of stalemated forces: the middle does not link the bottom
with the top. The bottom of this society is politically fragmented, and even as a passive fact, increasingly powerless: at the bottom there is emerging a mass society.

These developments, I believe, can be correctly understood neither in terms of the liberal nor the Marxian interpretation of politics and history. Both these ways of
thought arose as guidelines to reflection about a type of
society which does not now exist in the United States. We
confront there a new kind of social structure, which embodies elements and tendencies of all modern society, but
in which they have assumed a more naked and flamboyant
prominence.

That does not mean that we must give up the ideals of
these classic political expectations. I believe that both have
been concerned with the problem of rationality and of
freedom: liberalism, with freedom and rationality as supreme facts about the individual; Marxism, as supreme
facts about man's role in the political making of history.
What I have said here, I suppose, may be taken as an attempt to make evident why the ideas of freedom and of
rationality now so often seem so ambiguous in the new
society of the United States of America.

# 2

# THE SOCIAL LIFE
# OF A MODERN COMMUNITY

This is a study of stratification.* It is more painstaking than skillful; it displays more data than imagination of design; its value for social scientists resides more in its "wealth" of "data" than in any theoretical relevance or any "discoveries" made by its authors. No matter how many are on the staff (15 listed), you get out approximately what you put in.

Five other volumes are announced, which perhaps makes examination of this volume precarious. However, Volume I contains "the systematic analysis of the techniques . . . and conceptual framework used . . ." and emphasizes in particular the "class" structure. Therefore, I shall review it in terms of its method and as a study of stratification. Those data and interpretations which are in terms other than "class" are, in this volume, peripheral, and I shall not examine them publicly. Topics of which it is stated that more is to follow in later publications will also be avoided. Mr. Warner is the senior or the sole author of all the volumes, so I shall use his name in the following. The other volumes are to deal with the several "institutions," a "factory system," the "ethnic groups," and the symbolic apparatus of the 17,000 people living in Newberryport, Massachusetts, in the first years of the 1930s.

## I

Science, to Warner, is observation, then classification, then generalization. The "general objective" of this study is "to determine the complete set of social relations" of Yankee City. Under these notions, "huge quantities of data" were "accumulated," and after this collection,

---

\* *The Social Life of a Modern Community*. Volume 1. Yankee City Series. By W. Lloyd Warner and Paul S. Lunt. New Haven: Yale University Press, 1941. Pp. xx-460. $4.00.

Warner, "proceeded to outline the possible ways in which the materials could be treated." It would be easy to become lost in research so conceived. In other contexts such a scheme is verbally belied: "presuppositions" are stated, and it is asserted that an assumption was at first held to the effect that "the fundamental structure of our society, that which ultimately controls and dominates the thinking and actions of our people . . . is economic." P. W. Bridgman is fashionably patted on the back, although his technique is not evidenced when we come to the conceptions used.

"The Conceptual Framework" consists of elaborations of quotations from Durkheim (on the basic sameness of natural and social), and from Simmel (his formalist definition of society), of the idea that all societies are oriented to some "fundamental or integrative structure," that "Yankee City" is a "working whole in which each part had definite functions . . .", of the Parkian separation of individual and social person, of the conventional trichotomous view of society embracing technology, social organization, and "symbolic" systems.

The field techniques used embrace most of the standard ones social scientists have been using, and arguing over, since the twenties. Also a card for each individual in the city was punched with data pertaining to his "participations." The key concept of the study, "class," was not explicitly defined in the chapters on method and concepts.

## II

For "class," it is asserted, was "discovered." Around this "discovery" the remaining 17 chapters are arranged. Since a presupposition of economic determinism was, at first "held," one would think that in order to allow its precise statement and testing this notion would influence the definitions of concepts. But such a notion is not stated nor definitively tested in this book. It is "modified" because in various interviews people said that money isn't everything, referring to wealthy individuals "who didn't set right." In short, it was "found" that "wealth did not guarantee the highest social position" and *therefore* the notion of *economic* classes was abandoned. So: "a class hypothesis" was "developed." It is really a definition: "By class is meant two or more orders of people who are believed to be, and are accordingly ranked by the members of the community, in socially superior and inferior positions." There are several grave inadequacies and confusions displayed in this definition and in the manner in which it was allegedly attained:

(i) "Class" as defined and as used throughout the book indiscriminately absorbs at least three items which, when considering "stratifications," it is very important to separate analytically. (1) The word swallows up the sheerly economic in all its *gradations* (amounts) and in all its *sources* (rentier, salaried, wage-earner, *et al*). For convenience, this dimension will be referred to in this review as *class*. It includes the sheerly economic and *nothing* else. (2) Warner's "class" also points at the distribution of "prestige," "deference," "esteem," "honor:" in general, *status*. This term will be used to point at this prestige dimension, and only at it. On the whole Warner's "class" comes *closest* to status, thus defined. (3) Lastly, Warner's "class" may be taken to mean the distribution of *power, i.e.,* who can be expected to obey whom in what situations.

From the insistence upon merely *one* vertical dimension and the consequent absorbing of these three analytically separable dimensions into the one sponge word "class" flow the chief confusions of interpretation and the empirical inadequacies which characterize this study.

(ii) A further lack of distinction with direct consequences is the equating of "class" with "class-awareness." The gross facts of economic differences—in amount and in source, do not necessarily result in the awareness of these differences on the part of the participants. Yet Warner throws out *economic* class (by absorbing it *indiscriminately* with other dimensions) because of the fact of *status* awareness. It is a double confusion: first, of class with status; and second, of class with *status*-awareness.

The first and direct result of such blurring is that the role of sheerly economic differences cannot be stated hypothetically, much less tested. This (original presupposition) is ruled out because of *status awareness* on the part of some participants in the system. All that the "evidence" in terms of which the sheerly economic factor in stratification was miscellaneously absorbed indicates is that a number of persons did not pronounce *status* judgments on the basis of *mere* wealth. If the distinctions between class and status, between class and class-awareness, and between status and status-awareness had been known and *used,* the observations from interviews would have set interesting problems and hypotheses concerning their precise relations and might have enabled their precise answering by further observation.

These points of inadequacy and confusion, which are implicit in the definition used and which pervade the entire study, spring (1) from an inadequate notion of the functional connections between theory, definition, and method; and (2) more precisely, from a "theory" of stratification that is inadequate even to the data collected.

(i) Little can here be said about methodology. It is simply the art of raising *questions* that are (1) answerable by observation, and (2) whose answers feed back into the theory with which they are *logically* related, indeed, from which they are derived. Operative theory consists in the design of studies which harbor distinctions and concepts enabling such questions. So far as I can see, there is little difference between such questions and what are called hypotheses. This study is barren of theoretical designs from which flow well-articulated questions and plans for their precise and observational answers.

Definitions are important elements in such questions and plans. In this volume there is no set of questions in terms of which the definitions used are framed and which in turn framed the questions. Definitions must be more than (1) logically tight (*i.e.,* defendable in argument) and (2) operationally set (*i.e.,* public and private in their indexical function): they must also be (3) logically significant to a table of questions which are to be answered. This study falls short on all three criteria. I am concerned now with the second: a feature of a good definition is its one dimensionality. If you define a concept along one line, then you can study other items that vary with it. But if you define it so as to make it a sponge word, letting it absorb a number of variables, then you cannot ask questions with it concerning the relations of the analytically isolatable items which it miscellaneously harbors. The central term of this study, "class," falls clearly into this case. And this is the key methodological reason for Warner's theoretical and conceptual inadequacies: *all* the many colored beads are strung upon one vertical string; whereas the data and relevant questions indicate the need for several strings, each for one color of bead.

(ii) The lack of a theory harboring crucial distinctions is sadder than it would perhaps otherwise be in view of the fact that it was not necessary to *work out* such a theory. If Warner had availed himself of post-Marxian discussions in European sociological literature, and I refer especially to Max Weber's, he would have "discovered" in a more exact form such things as he did "discover," as well as several more which would have (1) enlarged his observational sensitivities, (2) enabled him to observe what he did observe more precisely, and (3) which would have helped him to ask and perhaps to answer questions which he was not even able to raise within his own conceptual circle. If he had used an adequate conceptual apparatus, it would have insured nonequivocation as to what he was talking about, and it would have made really valuable and usable the materials gathered. That the literature of stratification was probably not consulted is indicated not only in the index of names but by the concepts that are presented and used. In view of this, it is slightly innervating to read the inaccurately pompous assertions that the study "discovered" that status is ecologically distributed, of the "discovery" of "class" itself and of the "clique." But, for all I know the term "discovery" may still be well used, for it is possible to "discover" only that which one has not known.

There is another unfortunate aspect to Warner's failure to take account of previous literature: the problems which this literature contains and the assertions which it advances (that is, our "knowledge" to date) are not pointed up to be answered and verified by this clump of fact. Facts are expensive, in many ways, and, in so far as is possible, they should be *used* as widely and as crucially as possible. "Many . . . researchers," *writes* Warner on page *six,* "are notoriously guilty of beginning as if no other work had been done. . . ."

The few distinctions indicated above are *not* set forth

here as an *alternative* to anything contained in the study
under review. In any operative sense, Warner has no theory
and gives no crucial distinctions. I will now examine some
empirical and interpretative defaults of these conceptual
inadequacies.

### III

In the "most important . . . aspect of the entire research,
we worked out empirically, by direct observation of a . . .
large sample . . . the existence of six stratified social
classes." What were the criteria used to distinguish one
"class" from another and to locate given individuals in
them? The meaning and the clarity of the entire study
hinges on the answers to this question. Its answer, for a
sample, was first determined by interviews: an individual
belonged where someone in the community placed him. I
take this to be the meaning of "direct observation." Yet
how *direct* is this? We are not uniformly told the "class" of
those who did the ranking. The informants used "economic terms" as designating "superior and inferior positions" (power?) they used "acting right" (style of living),
they referred to membership in "the right families"
(descent), going around with "the right kind of people"
(status circles), and ecological terms. A further criterion
used by Warner was membership in "certain associations
with a well-defined class range." It was noted, although I
do not know if it was used as a *criterion*, that "members of
a class tend to marry within their own order." The ecological areas were apparently used quite exclusively in the
placing of individuals in a rank order. Brief reference in
the grand manner is also made to "type of house, kind of
education, manners, and other symbols of class. In the final
analysis, however, individuals were placed by the evaluations of the members of Yankee City itself. . . ." That is,
the ranking is in terms of status-verbalization. Most, although unfortunately by no means all, of the criteria used
are elements in *status* position, as above defined. But later
it is stated: "It must not be thought that all the people in
Yankee City are aware of all the minute distinctions made
in this book." Such status-awareness as existed tended to be
verbalized by informants ecologically.

When we seek to distinguish the six classes, we immediately run into the fact that different criteria were used at the several levels. Had Warner clearly distinguished class from status, he would have been able to state more directly the differences between the "upper-upper" and the "lower-upper." It seems clear, especially from the "stories" related, that in general the "upper-upper" have status and class, that the "lower-upper" have class without full status by descent, *i.e.,* the "lower-upper" are *nouveau riche*. The status mark of the "upper-upper" is descent, and secondarily, style of life in conjunction with certain status circles. But since Warner tries to work with one dimension, he cannot raise many pertinent questions about these two upper classes, *e.g.:* is it just "the length of time" that the family has participated in status groups that mark off the "upper-upper?" or is it that, plus *some* class at some time, etc? Some of the lower "classes" have family lines in Yankee City as *long* as the "uppers." About how long does it take to move from high class into high status? If there is nothing other than present status itself between the "upper-upper" and "lower-upper," then there is no explanatory basis for the differences between them. Everytime we get a close view of the "upper-uppers" and "lower-uppers" wealth comes in, yet by treating it as one "factor" blurred with other "factors" into the one-dimensional scale, the raising of questions about its precise weight and function in the conference of status is made impossible.

The criteria for distinguishing the "upper-middle," the "lower-middle," the "upper-lower," and the "lower-lower," are not at all clear. One short paragraph deals explicitly with this matter. In the main, the distinctions seem to have run in ecological terms.

It should be remarked that there is no measure of "class" mobility attempted; words like "many" being used in this connection. Perhaps in part this is due to the fact that the study is a-historical. This means, first, that in this study of status, with status-by-descent plainly a very important qualification, there is no *systematic* account of what happens in the succession of generations. Genealogies were apparently taken, but we are not given any systematic results of this. Warner seems to have been more interested in the present "kinship chart." The a-historicity means, secondly, that the study is trendless. It would not have been necessary to follow events chronologically; two base lines could have been set, "then" and "now," and thus at least a rough orientation to changes in time could have been glimpsed. The difficulty of obtaining "historical" material on the Murngin of Australia is no reason why we should not have its obvious advantages in Newberryport, Massachusetts.

### I V

One of the most interesting set of questions which is lost between the confusions of status with class concerns the extent and the precise character of wealth in stratification. There are several types of gross information about "wealth" given: there is an income distribution, and a chapter on "property." Both of these displays are rather isolated from other topics; they are not linked to status, *e.g.* with the subtlety which such an attempt would entail.

In the income distribution we are given the yearly "income" per family by "class," and the extremes in the range of income for each class. The yearly income correlates positively with "class" (status); but the *range* of income for each class is wide. At least one family of the "upper-upper" got only $1,105 (with an average for the "class" of $6,401), whereas at least one "lower-lower" got $2,800 (with an average for the "class" of $883). Without the inclusion of some *measure of dispersion* these figures of averages and ranges are simply not adequate and may well be misleading.

Furthermore, it seems that at least one family in each class *may* have spent more than was earned, (at least one "lower-lower" spent $2,725). But again, without a *sigma,* or a more detailed display of the distribution, one cannot know anything whatever about the *negatively* privileged income classes. Given the credit system (about which *nothing* is said) as a sanction of social controls, this is all the more regrettable. Not violence, but credit may be a rather ultimate seat of control within modern societies. There is no systematic indication of the *sources* of income by "class." Were there banks in Yankee City? Who controls them and whom and what do they control? In the "budgets" presented there is no category for "investment" or "savings."

The chapter on "property" is 5¼ pages long. First "property" is, without any explicit explanation, equated with "real estate," and apparently only domestic real estate at that! Second, there is given the median "ownership" distribution (of real estate) by age, sex, and ethnic group. There is then presented a table on "Real Estate and Class" in which there is no category for "none," the lowest being "Below $3,000," yet only 2,911 of the 17,000 citizens own *any* real estate. There is no display of *property* distributions by "class," of which, in the higher brackets especially, "real estate" is probably a minor factor. Among items of property, real estate is perhaps among the least likely to be an accurate indicator of class *differentials,* if such exist. Not only do we get nothing on property, but in the table on "real estate" there is again no display of the negatively privileged. Despite the set-up of the tallies which these omissions produce, there is, of course, a positive correlation of the "class" (of those who do own any) and the value of real estate owned. It should be noticed that the tallies on real estate are not by families, but by "persons." Statistically and sociologically, relations of wealth and "class" (status) that are imputed in this study are inadequate and unclear.

And again due to the lack of conceptual separation of status and class many pertinent questions were not even asked. For example: is it true that in the succession of generations status flows toward the positively privileged propertied classes? How has status sheerly by descent (if any) conditioned class situations? Have economic chances been hereditarily appropriated? Generically: precisely what are the relations and the mechanisms linking class and status?

**V**

For work of the attempted fineness of this study it is questionable if the six-fold occupational classification used is adequate. Given its resources and assuming a set of precise problems, this study would have seemed an opportunity to construct a better set of occupational categories. For example, a set that would have particular relevance to status phenomena, since this is primarily what the study attempts

to be about. Alba Edwards' census classification had of
necessity to satisfy a very wide set of practical purposes,
which are often irrelevant to research plans and questions.
Three items should illustrate this point and document its
pertinence to the books in hand:

(i) It might be supposed that different styles of living,
characterizing different status levels, might embrace "leisure," or no "occupation." If such had been provided for
in this study, the possibility of displaying the disqualifica-
tion value of any "productive work," as Veblen would have
it, would have been opened. There is nothing decisive on
such questions in this book on status. Veblen's remarks on
this head may not hold true of Yankee City, but one cannot tell in terms of the gross "occupational classification"
used (nor in any other terms here given). We are not told
if "unemployment" includes, say, a rentier, or not. The
meaning of "unemployed" as applied to the "UU" is not
distinguished from the term as applied to the "LL."

(ii) There is one occupational category used, "Professional and Proprietory," into which the UU and LU fall in
about equal percentages. Surely these terms should have
been broken down or at least their range of content detailed.
Since they are not, we are unable to distinguish such differing occupational compositions as may exist between UU
and LU. Again, 17 per cent of the UU are tallied (along
with only 7 per cent of the LU and 29 per cent of the LM)
into "Clerks and Kindred Workers." Have the descendants
of the Yankee sea captains descended to shoe and grocery
clerking? Surely this is interesting enough to warrant a de-
tailing of what the category, "clerk" embraces; certainly
we should be told of the explicit criteria for an individual's
admission into the category. Otherwise we have no control
over, or leads, to interpretations and the possibility of a
comparative use of the materials is zero.

(iii) The undefined term "worker" is used in the discussion of the distribution of "class" members by "industries."
In this distribution the UU "class" is low in contribution
of "workers" to the shoe industry which perhaps overlooks
the number one "worker" of the shoe "workers": the owner
of the plant. Again: sponge words.

## V I

I do not suppose any sociologist has a serious argument with the general "functionalist" assertion that "the parts" of a society are "interrelated" etc. Either the statement is a *tautology* derived from notions with which we begin, or it is a methodological *guide*. What it guides us to is a quest for *specific* mechanisms linking one sector of a given society to another. It is the extent and the *character* of the relationships that should be precisely determined. Warner does not manage to convey "functionalism" in this sense. It remains a statement in an early chapter of a fashionable assumption. Nor is the conventional trichotomy of technology, social organization, and ideology manifestly at *work* within the observation and interpretation of materials. It, too, stands in a prefacing chapter as a leisured item. In particular, the linkage of the social, economic, and political orders are never articulated.

These criticisms are by no means merely theoretical cavil, and they cannot be dodged on the basis of: "one can't do everything." For operating with a far less elaborate theory and set of distinctions (and no doubt without 17,000 cards, the dictaphones and the airplane used by Warner) the R. S. Lynds succeeded in presenting a far superior picture of the composition and mechanics of a modern community. The broad-focused and imaginative eye is the genuine meaning of "functionalism." Are intermarriage chances, the flow of prestige, influenced by what happens in banks? What is the distribution of legal skill by family, by firm? Are there overlaps between the boards of banks, the elders of churches, and the prestige of ministers? Are "social circles" and religious affiliations subtly interwoven with financial interests? How do "clubs" mark one's financial arrival? Are the chances to arrive financially enhanced by affiliation with clubs? It is to be regretted that such mechanics of interaction between the economic, the social, and religious affiliations (not to mention "political" spheres) as may exist were not systematically examined in the case of Yankee City.

Nor is the lack of an eye for interrelations confined in its effects to the lack of discernment of possibly far-flung rela-

tions. Its absence makes uncontrolled many relations that
are alleged, *e.g.*: in "type of house lived in" no economic
distribution operates in the discussion! Again, in presenting
a table of the number of associations to which members of
various denominations belong, we are not given alongside
the numbers of the population in the different denominations. Book and magazine "preference" tallied by "class"
is not controlled nor interpreted in terms of educational
level, income, price of publication, number and ages of
children in family, readiness of access to the sources of
different grades of publications. In the absence of such
items, nothing is really known of the distribution of reading
by "class."

Several lengthy chapters concerned with fascinating
*topics* consist almost entirely of tallies into various categories such as age and sex, ethnic, and "class." These contain a maximum of flat, tallying busy-work with a minimum
of sociological imagination. These tallies are embarrassingly
naked as far as theoretical understanding and explanation
are concerned. This is unfortunately the case in connection
with "associations," "houses," and with others. It is very
conspicuously the case with real estate owned and with
magazines read.

Nor is such explanatory nudity clothed in the summing-
up chapters, which merely repeat in a different arrangement
what was previously presented. These summaries offer
little view of the total community or of each stratum, or
of how they mesh, *e.g.*: "About 50 per cent of its [LM]
members are below 40 years of age." Confronted with such
factual assertions, end on end, which are doubtlessly true,
one is continually asking, "So what?" To answer this, one
must read the reported conversations and brief career lines
which are presented with a minimal attempt to interpret
or to tally into sponge categories raw materials that *are* very
significant.

I am genuinely sorry that the tenor of my review of this
volume has had to be negative in standpoint. For in terms
of what *American* social scientists have done with stratification, the book is a big frog in a very small pond—in size,
if in nothing else. But this is not the ground on which to
judge it as social science. The recent and current interest

of American social scientists in phenomena of stratification is too significant to become afflicted with strabismus now. Stated as precisely and as balanced as I can, the "plusses" and "minuses" of this study are as follows: Plus: in *general* focus (topic) and in accumulated "data." Minus: in theory and in conceptual distinctions. They sum up like this: because the accumulation of "data" is intrinsically related to conceptual distinctions, the "data" accumulated are "plus" only to the extent that they are presented "rawly." Therefore: the chapters of the volume can be ranked in terms of how much reporting there is and how little conceptualizing is attempted. On such a scale Chapter VII is the best in the book. One is inclined to be critical of results roughly to the degree of the fascination of the *topic* and the size of the practical opportunity of the researchers. On the whole, you get out about what you put in, and I don't mean money.

## VII

W. Lloyd Warner attempts in this book* to bring together for the general reader the results of one type of social research. His title might well have been "Some Current Studies of the American Small Town," for his book contains little else, and, in the end, does not form a coherent portrait of American society.

Judging from the points that are most labored, Professor Warner's most important discoveries seem to be that the people of the American town differ from one another as regards the amount of money they make, the occupations they follow, the size and condition of the houses they live in, the color of their skins, how well known their families are, the associations they belong to, and so on. He has also become aware that it is more difficult for us than for our grandfathers to move from rags to riches in half a life time.

There are several criticisms that one ought to make about books of this sort, and it seems worthwhile to make them because they have to do with the habits of many social scientists who would write for the general reader.

(i) There is a great deal of labeling for the sake of

* *American Life: Dream and Reality.* By W. Lloyd Warner. xv plus 268 pp. Chicago: The University of Chicago Press. $3.75.

labeling. For example, to call Lincoln a "collective representation" helps us to understand neither Lincoln nor America. This labeling is part of an academic style of thought which also contains interpretations that do not interpret. For example, the lengthy remarks to the effect that the successful businessman "has very high mobility drives," and "achievement desires" do little else but restate facts with which we began. And to call Memorial Day, "a cult of the dead" scarcely explains its celebration, much less why patriotic organizations get up their demonstrations.

(ii) Social anthropologists are prone to assume that "after all," modern nations are different only in degree from small-scale preliterate cultures and grouplets. This leads to a curious localism which, in turn, severely limits Professor Warner when he writes of the character of American society. The political economy as well as the status system of the nation can neither be deduced nor projected from a series of small town studies.

(iii) Professor Warner sometimes appears to be conservative not through any conviction (I take his convictions to be liberal) but through a simple lack of political imagination. As a result he has come to some opinions more usually encountered in speeches before service clubs than in serious social analysis. "The only possible choice for Americans," he writes, "is . . . between their kind of heirarchy and some other—more likely, one that could not work satisfactorily in a democracy."

Labeling for the sake of labeling, interpretations that do not interpret, local studies stretched to characterize American life, conservatism through lack of political imagination —these seem the essential characteristics of the school of social science represented by Professor Lloyd Warner in this book. Should it not give all contemporary students of man and society pause that so far as ideas of modern society are concerned, the results of this style of research can be put into one small corner of Lord Bryce's *American Commonwealth,* now sixty years old, or of the second volume of de Tocqueville's *Democracy in America,* now one hundred and thirteen years old?

# 3

# A MARX FOR THE MANAGERS*

There is a tendency to interpret modern history, and particularly the twentieth century, in terms of an increasing bureaucratization. In whatever domain of thought the question has arisen there have been able presentations of the facts of the centralization of industrial and administrative organizations. But it is not only in statistical curves that such phenomena receive notice. They make up the stuff of several philosophies of history.

It is no accident that Max Weber is more and more frequently quoted for his thesis that the historical drift may be seen as a bureaucratization of industrial societies, irrespective of their constitutional governments. It is this *form* of organization which is taken to be the substance of history, the more so as it is identified with a growing rationality of modern society.

It is clear that the application of occidental science is an indispensable element in the development of large-scale and planned administrations. For Thorstein Veblen, as well as for Weber, the advent of science is a phenomenon unique and central to Western civilization. Veblen focused more directly upon "the sequence of accumulative technology" and drew inferences directly from the fact of its dominance. Apart from the opaque line of technological rationality, social life is drift and habituation. The irrational institutions, particularly pecuniary ones, are in the main only permissive; all they do is occasionally hinder the spread of a mechanical rationality into all areas of life. It is the men who nurse the big machines, the industrial population, who implement that which makes history.

For Weber, impersonal rationality stands as a polar opposite to personal charisma, the extraordinary gift of lead-

* With Hans H. Gerth.

ers. For Veblen, technology, widely construed, stands opposite irrational institutions. And for both, in whatever
other respects they may differ, the rational, the technical
pole of history will come through; it will increase to dominate the social life of the West.

In this kind of philosophy of history, warfare and revolutions, crises and class struggles, are not the central objects
to be explained. They are part of modern man's destiny, and
as subsidiary processes they further implement the big drift
toward rationality. The irrational is identified with charismatic leaders (Weber) or with "a democracy of emotions"
(Scheler) or "institutionalized masses" (E. Lederer) or
with "pecuniary institutions" (Veblen). Authors who follow Pareto and place emphasis upon revolutionary changes
and historical discontinuities at the price of structures are
likely to see reality under the emblems of oscillating élites.
Occasionally "Youth" serves as the shibboleth of tacit
hopes to escape the inevitable routinized structures of modern societies, and it is also used as an explanation of sudden
crises.

One of the latest formulations which popularize such
interpretations is provided in James Burnham's book.[1] His
thesis is that what is happening in the world will eventuate
neither in socialism nor in capitalism; rather that through
revolutions and wars we move toward "a managerial society." The alternatives of capitalism or socialism, of nationalism or internationalism, are displaced by a formula
which absorbs a number of problems into the explanation
of one phrase. Strangely enough, such apparently diverse
structures as the New Deal, Russian communism, and naziism are taken to be phases on similar roads to this ultimate
ending in "a managerial society."

In common with Spengler, the temper of Burnham's dic-
tion embodies a pervasive cultural pessimism, and from
Marx it borrows the Draconian inevitability of iron necessity. With Lawrence Dennis, Burnham shares a technical
admiration of the efficient machines now prowling out from
Germany and irresistibly attracting half of Russia.

The "managerial world current" is Burnham's demiurge

[1] *The Managerial Revolution: What is Happening in the World*
(New York: John Day Co., Inc., 1941).

of history, for just as a rather petty species of executive manager in the Peloponnesian states became for Plato the World-builder, so Burnham Platonizes and imputes an irresistible movement toward power to the production expert and administrative executive.

This philosophy of history is typically anchored, whether explicitly or not, in two different spheres: (1) in the changing class structure of the corporate capitalism of the twentieth century and (2) in the shifting relationship between the executive and legislative branches of parliamentary governments and administrative growth of the former. Only by understanding what has been happening in these two spheres can we locate Burnham's views. The significance of the trends evidenced in these spheres must be assessed, and their import for the rise to power of various personnel and structures must be drawn. What do they mean for the distribution of political power and the methods of holding it? How do they affect the chances of power of various strata and types of persons in modern societies?

I

There are several facts concerning the shift of class composition and function in twentieth-century capitalism upon which there is agreement. Occupationally, the most striking characteristic is the rise of the "new middle class." Since the first great war of this century it has gained great social weight. It is composed of white-collar groups and of various professions; it makes up the bulk of clerical and technical staffs. It contains the salaried administrator and the expert civil servant, the trained manager and the private engineer. It is the chief repository of those skills necessary to run administrative and industrial machinery, and its members have assumed many of the functions requisite to a capitalist society.

Recognizing the rise to economic and industrial functioning of this class, many writers have set forth lines of social action leading from it. It is precisely around the crucial facts concerning this new middle class that social interpretations have hovered, and in them are anchored disappointed socialist views and not a few prophecies and hopes.

In taking cognizance of the new middle class, G. D. H.
Cole stated in 1937 that it has

> acted politically, as well as economically, as the faithful
> servant of large-scale capitalism. . . . . It has the power to
> organize and carry on industry itself, without the aid of the
> *grande bourgeoisie,* if it can  insure the cooperation or the
> subservience of the proletariat, [and] if the proletariat could
> be reenforced by the adhesion of even a minority of the
> technicians, administrators, and professional men and
> women who form the active section of the new *petite bour-*
> *geoisie,* it could be strong enough. . . . . to build socialism
> against the united hostility of the *grande bourgeoisie* and the
> more reactionary *petite bourgeois* groups.

As over against Continental Socialists, English Socialists
tend to discount the state with its armed forces.

In *The Engineers and the Price System* Veblen set forth
the industrial and economic situation out of which an association and group consciousness of technicians, presumably recruited from this middle class, might arise. For him
the realities of the case lie within the range of industrial
and technological fact. The modern technological system
is indispensable to modern populations, and only the engineers can run it. In the technical planning and execution
of work, "The technicians necessarily take the initiative
and exercise the necessary surveillance and direction."
Given the centralized and intricately connected technological system, "the wholehearted cooperation of the technicians would be . . . indispensable to any effectual movement of overturn." They are essential for any successful
line of revolutionary action. But Veblen does not detail the
means by which an association of engineers might come
about. He does not examine political and class situations,
and the differential chances of power-holding and power-
grabbing do not come within his explicit purview. On this
crucial point he is ambiguous by irony, and behind this
guise he states that, although they are indispensable to any
overthrow, the technicians will not engage in such a line
of action. In so far as workers are organized, it is in organizations "for bargaining, not production," which are "of the
vested interests." Yet, in order to be successful, the engi-

neers' revolution involves "inquiry and publicity" directed at "the underlying population" and the working-out of a "common understanding and a solidarity of sentiment between the technicians and the working force engaged in . . . the greater underlying industries of the system."

There are those among the technocrats who, being less competent than Veblen, were also less cautious. For these the apocalyptic day of seized power follows quickly the night of economic and technical shifts in function.

In 1935 Alfred Bingham stated: "If . . . . the original Marxist concept of a class rising from functional supremacy to political supremacy be followed, it leads today to the conclusion that *the technical and managerial middle classes are slated to be next in the sequence of ruling classes.*" In assessing the chances at power of the new middle class, Cole seeks programmatically to draw their weight into the big rush of the workers. Veblen seeks to draw the workers' support to the engineers among the new class. Bingham fears their support of fascism. But Burnham is not so cautious as all these. It is his thesis that the managers, who, although he does not say so, are drawn from the middle class, *are* increasingly the rulers of modern nations and that we are moving into a society over which they will be absolute lords. The heart of Burnham's thesis and the chief assumption underlying it are contained in the 1935 quotation from Bingham.

One error which pervades this interpretation of the chances at power of managerial elements of the new middle class is the assumption that the technical indispensability of certain functions in a social structure are taken *ipso facto* as a prospective claim for political power. This error is not confined to the view that technical managers and production engineers are going to usher in a society dominated by themselves; it also feeds the widespread notion that in modern Germany the middle class has attained power. If facts are brought to bear upon these points, they will disclose the infeasibility of the basic assumption which underlies them. It is our view that such interpretations unduly short-cut the road from technical indispensability to a grab and hold of power. The short cut establishes too automatic an agreement between the social-economic order and political movements.

It is only by confining the term "capitalism" to production for free markets, to a laissez faire economy under a parliamentary government, that Burnham is able to view imperialist Germany as noncapitalistic. However, there is a type of capitalism that produces for the state rather than for an open market. As a system, such production has always been most profitable. Nineteenth-century capitalism may have preferred peaceful penetration, the open door, and economic pacifism. Imperialist capitalism of the twentieth century increasingly trades at the point of a gun, but it is no less capitalism.

In evaluating the class situation in Germany, we must consider that the group of big industrialists and *Junkers* have not lost power. If occasional members are plucked out for individual discipline, it does not mean that as a stratum they have been deprived of power but merely that what Mr. Thyssen loses becomes Baron von Schroeder's commission. Frequently the inference is made that the governmental regulations of the German war economy, the political allocation of investment capital, raw materials, labor, and the subsidization of chances to export act to the detriment of the capitalist class. To some factions they do. In general, those suffer whose products and establishments are not considered vital for the war economy. The shift from a peacetime to a wartime economy affects this class as does any such crisis. Likewise, the political guidance of investment policies deprives many establishments of profits which under a free market would have been available for reinvestment. However, the funds which are losses to some capitalists are gains for other capitalists. In the political capitalism of Germany the state acts as a co-ordinating and transferring agency. The German army is big business, and to the extent that its acquisitions allow for the incorporation of other nations' businesses, it pays in "plant expansions." Why should munition-makers such as Henschel and Krupp, and airplane manufacturers such as Junker and Messerschmitt, feel thwarted by plant expansions because they are financed from funds that are larger than those that would have been available in an open market and which consist of taxes and governmentally compelled loans? The political control of the total economy secures an investment to the big capitalists and their subcontractors who are considered essential to the war economy. Mr. Funk is no less divorced from the capitalist group than was Mr. Schacht: the latter came out of a bank, while the former emerged from the commercial pages of the Berlin *Boersen-Zeitung*. The war economy makes the estates of the *Junkers* as necessary and safe as under the Kaiser or the Social Democratic regime when they faced the blockade. There is no evidence that the traditional ruling class of big industrialists and *Junkers* in Germany fare worse economically under Hitler than they did under the Kaiser. The *Junkers'* estates have been buttressed by a class of hereditarily entailed peasants. The National Socialist party domesticates labor and the middle class for the owners better than did the Democratic Socialists. Control of prices works primarily for them and only secondarily for the peasant; as part of the consumers and as a labor reserve, the middle class helps carry the load.

The fact that numerous individuals of middle-class extraction have had opportunities and have risen in the social scale does not mean that "the middle class rose to power." On the contrary, the Nazi war economy has violated all material election promises to the middle class. The middle class was politically important in the ascent of the Nazi party to power, but it is a power which they do not share. "Tax-Bolshevism" was not decimated; it was augmented. Wholesale distributions through co-operatives and department stores did not decline under Nazi control. At least half a million independent middle-class retailers closed down. And many independent enterprisers have become factory hands. In the light of such facts, it would be strange to assume that a class gets into power only to curtail its own opportunities and its own interests. Totalitarian regimentation has superseded *Burgfrieden*.

Those individuals of middle-class extraction who have become officers in the army and Gestapo agents, by virtue of their party membership fill occupations which make them part of the state organization. From this state organization and not from their class extraction they derive such power as they have. In monarchial Germany many bureaucrats were recruited from among the *petite bourgeoisie,* but this did not mean that the imperial policy benefited the *petite bourgeoisie.* Nor does the fact that Hitler was a house-painter and Goebbel's father a blacksmith benefit the house-painters and the blacksmiths. The question is: Where is the power? And the answer is: It is the structure of domination, which is the state with its monopoly of physical force, and fused within it the industrialists and their agrarian colleagues. Neither the proclamation nor the social extraction of the political actor is the deciding factor in the use of power. Deeds answer the question *cui bono?* Discrete opportunities for individual jobs is one thing; access to the positions controlling the big business of Europe is quite another. The ascent of certain members of the middle class is more than counterbalanced by the compulsory descent of other members of this class, by the decline of their standard of living, and by the war losses of their youth.

The role of the German lower middle class in the ascent to power of the Nazi party is well known; the meagerness of their political harvest should by now be equally evident. The rise of a few Nazi parvenus into industrial robber barons, booty capitalists of imperialist dimensions, is paid for dearly by the nonowners and by displaced owners. The spoils of the war and levies on Jewry, municipalities, political protectorates, and subjected nations accrue to the propertied class. It is a peculiarity of modern warfare, irrespective of nations and constitutions, that the middle class has nothing material to gain from it. Political capitalism as it now dominates Germany does not benefit middle-class businesses, nor does it lend power to the middle class. Such psychic income of patriotic glory as they receive may compensate for social and economic deterioration. It is, however, *ersatz.*

This middle class contains the managerial professionals with whom Burnham is concerned: he speaks of their grasp of and high chance at further power. The crucial fact in Germany concerning these skilled personnels in their relation to power is that their very indispensability and scarcity value for a war economy insures their loss of income and personal freedom, and provides a decade of overwork. The close supervision over them partakes of army discipline. Not power but subjugation to martial law is their lot. They are as enslaved as any wage-worker. That skill is at a premium does not in itself mean that the skilled have an opportunity for positions entailing power decisions. They are as attached to plants as were serfs to feudal manors— unless their income exceeds 12,000 Reichsmarks (about $4,000) a year. A slight minority of them have salaries above this figure. As experts they give advice, but they receive orders.

*Occupational skill is not identical with class position.* Some engineers are hired men; other engineers do the hiring. A consultant engineer may have his own office, work for his own account, and, economically speaking, be an independent enterpriser. Or an individual with the same type and amount of trained skill may be a production engineer with a fixed salary and fixed stages in his career within an organization. The possession of a skill may well mean quite heterogeneous interests, class positions, and political loyalties. In a democracy, apart from common technical knowledge, technicians may be found on all political sides of many social fences. The technical knowledge of managers and their relation to production is one thing; their class position, political loyalties, and their stake in the current system is quite another. There is no intrinsic connection between the two.

Those who control the experts are not the "political colleagues" of managers but their powerful masters. From a managerial standpoint they may be amateurs, but perhaps it is always the experts in power-grabbing and wielding who, although not specialists in handling implements of production or destruction, master whole nations and purge experts.

Modern industry does require specifically trained staffs. But such occupational roles will be filled irrespective of the type of political system in which this modern industry is situated. The chances at political power for those filling technically indispensable roles is not a function of their technical roles but of their class position and political affiliations, whatever they may be.

Precisely because of their specialization and knowledge

the scientist and technician are among the most easily used
and co-ordinated of groups in modern society. This is
proved in the German experience. The very rigor of their
training typically makes them the easy dupes of men wise
in political ways. In the face of Burnham's depiction of the
sinister motives of dissatisfied managers and in defense of
the trustworthiness, reliability, and loyalty of America's
technical managers to owners and to our society as it is
now duly constituted, it is pertinent to recall the resolution
passed by the representative American Engineering Council. Their stand on the technocracy question was well to the
middle right, and they thought it "appropriate at this time
to record its unqualified admiration of Herbert Hoover . . .
[who is] one of the world's greatest leaders and benefactors
of our time."

All factual reports of the organizations of American scientists and industrial technicians disprove completely spec-
ulations about the singular class position and political stand
of such groups. An American "Soviet" of technically
trained persons would be as politically and socially conservative as any businessmen's service club.

One prop which is used to support belief in the shift of
the managers' *de facto* control of industry to dominance in
the political order is the fact of absentee ownership. Absentee ownership is one of the problems of modern industrial society which certain thinkers, among them Burnham,
solve in favor of the absentee owner's functioning agent.
Where Marx had the coupon-clipping parasites expropiated
by the exploited proletariat, Burnham has them expropriated by their junior partners and social colleagues, the managers. The Marxist class struggle has shifted its stage from
the barricades to the Social Club. The expropriation of
capitalists becomes automatic, intimate, and silent. Despite
Mr. Krassin, an odd engineer whom Burnham cites, the
Russian Revolution does not quite confirm this view.

Burnham notes with satisfaction for his thesis that, while
the absentee owners have been absent, their functioning
managers have been gaining power. But what have the
owners been doing while absent from their businesses?
Veblen did not tell the whole tale in his depiction of the
activities of the leisure class. *Absentee owners have con-*

*tinuously devoted themselves to politics.* Mr. Chamberlain did not lose power because he substituted a premiership for the management of his private steel corporation, and it is said that the contract for the Anderson bomb shelter, instead of a large-scale investment in underground shelters, in London was, among other reasons, not entirely irrelevant to the steel industry. If they are successful, the lords now taking over the guidance of the British Empire's destiny will not lessen the prestige and luster of their class.

Tenants have not become owners because they have had disposition over houses and farms and estates; they have not, during the last three hundred years, automatically dethroned the absentee owning British aristocracy. Nor will the production engineers and administrative experts displace the economic royalists whose confidence they now enjoy.

Burnham's definition of private property significantly omits one aspect of "disposition over goods": the disposition to the next generation. It is pertinent that the sons of the managers do not inherit the managed property but rather the relatives of the absentee owners. It is not usual for managers to sell out the plants which they manage. Socialism begins where a legal order does not provide for succession of property holdings in terms of blood relationship nor for private transfers of property. Hence, in this respect, nazism stands quite remote from communism. In Germany, as far as shifts in property holding are concerned, what has occurred makes for the happiness of owners and their heirs. Only in so far as they may become owners will the managers share in such happiness. It is by overlooking the problem of inheritance of property that naziism and communism appear as two phases of the same movement. Those who hate the Nazi but fear Russian communism know why.

In treating Russian communism and German nazism as basically similar trends, *Burnham confounds the regulatory power of the state with ownership.* The ideal model of thought of economic theory may for certain purposes disregard the regulatory power of the state, but in reality there has never been economic conduct which has not been subject to political and legal regulations. Every tariff and

industrial code, even if totalitarian, distributes differential
opportunities among economic agents, and those who regulate do not thereby own. There is in Russia no private
ownership of the means of production. Nobody owns them.
Burnham's assumption that someone must, even if it be
managers, because someone "controls" them, is a lag from
capitalist way of thinking. His definition of property as
actual disposition means an eternalization of notions of
private property. No commander of a battleship owns it or
transfers it at will. Nor do the heiresses to industrial properties in the United States, Germany, and England lose ownership of machines and offices which their late fathers' production engineers and executives efficiently and faithfully
run for them. The belief in private and hereditary property,
and the maintenance of a society stratified in terms of
property, is not a technical or a "managerial" problem. It
is quite evidently a political and legal problem. And it is
precisely in the sphere of politics that managers do not
significantly differ from owners in their beliefs and loyalties.
Mr. Krassin and Friedrich Engels became communists not
because they were engineers and manufacturers but despite
it.

So far we have considered managers as the members of
the new middle class who are technically and industrially
"concerned directly in production." Burnham, however,
does not restrict the term "manager" to such production and
industrial functions. For him, it apparently includes a type
of government bureaucrat. This duality of meaning, which
pervades his argument, enables him to lend to its cogency
in various contexts by making references to powerful groups
in each of these contexts. Either by violating the principle
of identity or by taking the term "manager" as an emblematic slogan to mean those in power, Burnham exploits the
facts concerning the growth of bureaucratic structures for
his own thesis. Sometimes the "managers" are the "European managerial politican" and frequently they are referred
to as "managers, in and out of government, along with their
bureaucratic and military colleagues," and "the bureaucrats
(for which we may read 'managers')." Yet later it is not
"the bureaucracy but the managing group which is becoming the ruling class." Again, when discussing those who

attain power in the United States, Burnham says, "The bureaucrats in charge of popular mass organizations . . . take their places among the managers." He means the C.I.O. "Who are the managers?" is a real question for those who wish to understand Burnham's argument. They seem to be, as we have said, those in power in whatever context Burnham discusses. They have one trait in common: all the groups mentioned as managers are more or less associated with personnels holding offices in bureaucracies. Thus, much of the cogency that Burnham's thesis has is due to the simple fact that the form of organization all over the world is, perhaps increasingly, bureaucratic. But the ends for which these structures will be used, who will be at their tops, how they might be overthrown, and what movements will grow up into such structures—these are not considered; they are swallowed in the consideration of the *form* of organization, the demiurge of history, the "managerial world current."

## II

Since the late 1920's it has been often observed that the executive branch of parliamentary government has been assuming more weight and functions at the expense of the legislative organs. Wars implement this shift. The legislature may be reduced to an interrogative, occasionally criticizing, and, after executive successes, applauding function. All modern states are bureaucratic. But bureaucracies do not operate without definite social settings.

There are several views of the power relations of a growing bureaucracy. Hegel and his followers, down to Sombart and Burnham, hold that a bureaucracy becomes an autonomous structure with ultimate and supreme power over all classes. Others have not emphasized so much the technical aspect of the machinery of power but its direction and ends. The question *cui bono?* and the question of recruitment of those who dominate in the power decisions of a bureaucracy lead to questions which cannot be answered by confining one's self to the consideration of the *formal* pattern of modern states, whether they be czarist, monarchial, democratic, or totalitarian. It opens the question as to the power relations of the bureaucracy of various classes.

If classes are ultimately defined according to their relations to the means of production, or in terms of property, a bureaucracy is certainly not a class. Typically, the official of a bureaucracy is not allowed to become an economic enterpriser. In so far Hegel is correct; they remain removed from specific economic interests. But if, as in the political capitalism of modern Germany, *a ruling group uses political power for building up private economic power,* for acquiring industrial properties (Göring, for example), it is probable that for once Marx may be correct in calling the state the executive committee of the ruling class. In parliamentary systems the group of owners may find its representation in the ruling party. In Germany the amassing of fortunes by Nazi chieftains does not curb but rather consolidates the power of the owning group. A new composition for an owning group does not destroy it. The robber barons fuse with the older industrialists by sharing their wealth, their interests, and their worries. In some contexts he who hesitates and does not grab is himself an object to be grabbed. Adventurous imperialism under the Nazi aegis has no use for the individual brilliance of a Cecil Rhodes; they organize a disciplined advance comparable only to the older corporate adventures of such companies as the East Indian, but in a world already grabbed they must be even better armed, and they must mobilize an entire nation for their advance.

For Burnham, the import of the growth of executive bureaucracies is the ousting of the capitalist owners. But there is no evidence for this. It is true that in America the corporations have been anti-Roosevelt and that the tension between the owners and the New Deal is due to the increasing of the regulatory power of the state. But this state control has by no means aimed at dislocating ownership. It has, in fact, been security against such dislocation. The New Deal has protected the perpetuation of the system of ownership against the dangers which seem to be inherent in it. It is not property which has been "managed," but the defaults of the property system. And in this respect, naturally, the corporate owners have not resented governmental expansion. They have resented that protection has been extended to small owners, farmers and bank depositors, and to nonowning groups, as trade-unions and the unemployed. The corporate owners have sought to restrict the scope of such protection or "welfare regulation" by the government. The objection is that Roosevelt has "unduly" extended such control to the defaults of the system as it touches propertyless sectors of the population.

What is the role and relation to power decisions of the expert in government? Experts do not make decisions but influence them, and, fortunately for the wielders of power, by virtue of their specialization they are likely to draw different conclusions from the same observations. The turnover of experts within structures of power, military, industrial and governmental, does not conduce to their steady influence upon ultimate decisions. Witness the army purges and the shuffling of "the self-confident, young men" of the New Deal. It is not irrelevant to contrast the insecurity of tenure of the expert with the legally guaranteed inheritance of private owners. In totalitarian regimes the personal insecurity of experts increases proportionately to the influence of their advice. In democracies experts may retire and grumble; in totalitarianism they are liquidated.

But is it true that the state bureaucracies that have grown up are tending to become the repository of power decisions? If not, for what class or social sector are they the instruments?

Harold Laski has pointed out that the assumptions of the British civil servant are "the same as those of the men who own the instruments of production." The general strike of 1926 showed that British bureaucrats will stand socially and politically with the ruling class. Neither their alleged neutrality nor their independence from the class in power has ever been tested by their having to administer policies counter to the loyalties of their class.

It is true that the larger a bureaucracy becomes, the more restricted its head becomes in giving orders. The means built up restrict the ends for which they can be used. But the top knocks off the "managers" before they get to be the depository of *decisional* power. The purges in Germany serve the owners, certainly not the "managers." In Russia the centralization of bureaucratic agencies involved the

purging of any sector of it which was gaining too much
weight and threatening the absolutism of Stalin and his
ruling circle. The history of brain-trusters does not bespeak
the power of the "managers" in the New Deal.

## III

The task of understanding what is happening in the
world today involves a comprehension of such basic issues
as the retention or abolition of private property, the structure of classes, possible political and social movements, and
of war. For it is from such matters and not in the all-
pervasive drift to some *general form* of organization that
one may obtain a view which implements an intelligent and
prepared expectation. To swallow such crucial items and
possibilities into a form of organization is to be engulfed
within the demiurge of history. The questions of events that
require answering which may well be weighty determinants
of the course of history are not merely incidental to some
unilinear tendency toward great organizations. They may
well constitute the pivots of history; they may be points
around which managed structures swing in new and un-
foreseen directions.

Nothing has been more surprising during recent decades
than the disruption of large-scale bureaucratic regimes and
the quick dissolution of armies. And nothing is more astounding than the speed with which new and rival social
machineries may be built up. The czarist police and the
Communist G.P.U. may be equally harsh and brutal in
their techniques of persecution; but this formal sameness
should not obscure the fact that they are directed against
different strata. Nothing is known of wholesale purges of
production executives and army officers under czarism
which would be comparable to the Communist purges of
the middle 1930's. It is such facts as these which make
fruitless a lumping of all executive agencies under one
rubric "the managers."

We must not only consider the formal structures of history; we must also consider the various uses which are
made of them. For the class pivots of such use are also
a part of history—and an important part. Marx believed

that state bureaucracies would remain fairly stable throughout bourgeois revolutionary shifts in power at the top, and Max Weber generalized this view for all revolutions. But this does not seem to be true of twentieth-century bureaucracies. Their very size and complexity make it possible for small alert groups with political loyalties to other machines to become "cells" in them and crucially to snarl and entangle their functioning. Little cells may be formed in bureaucracies which externally carry on their proper work but take commands from political groups on the outside. Such activities do not contribute to continuous bureaucratization.

It is not convincing that a book subtitled "What Is Happening in the World" should be without an explanation of the drive to war. Wars seem to Burnham "natural to society;" they only further the drift toward a form or organization. In seeing capitalism's displacement by a managerial society, Burnham obviates an explanation of war. He vindicates nazism because it succeeded in eliminating unemployment. He has, however, to expand the concept of employment far beyond economic functions. The endowment of unemployed masses not with relief but with barracks and weapons may constitute a "solution," may lead out of unemployment crises, but it is no new precept to solve economic crises by plunging into imperialist warfare. The Nazi drive to war is not nihilism, but imperialism, and old phenomenon in a streamlined form. Factors which are not a part of the hypothetical managerial society but are intrinsic to the structure and power grouping of the real world are needed to explain war. Of particular importance today is the political bolstering and implementation of capitalist crises. "Germany," says Hitler, "must export or die." In shrinking world-markets, German capitalism can conquer outlets for commodities and capital and raw materials only by violence. It is no longer possible by peaceful trade. *Lebensraum* for Central European capitalism means raw materials and chances to export. Socialism in one country may be possible; National Socialism is not.

Burnham suffers from too much Marx: for economic determinism, control over the implements of production

is the only route to power. But as E. A. Ross stated during
the first World War such a view needs to be rounded out
with a doctrine of martial determination. Among wars there
are revolutionary wars which may be capitalized and
guided by self-elected élites but not always. No manager
pushes a button to be immediately and efficiently equipped
with a spontaneous mass-grasp at power. To overlook
the stress of war on loyalty and morale and to count for
naught the deprivations of masses may be helpful contributions to the cogency of a unilinear and formal construction of history, but it does not make for a readiness
to expect the unexpected. To be grounded in history is to
expect of the future that which does not follow mechani-
cally but flows from large decisions not yet made. The
belief in the stability of German totalitarianism and of the
self-split and doom of the Soviet Union is a prognosis of
Burnham's which does not become less a wishful thought
by his dressing it in admiration of the technically efficient.
The loyalties of potential revolutionary strata are not
wholly determined by who has the best parachutes: workers are not necessarily loyal because their employers have
shiny machines; soldiers are not necessarily loyal because
their weapons are the latest.

On the other hand, Dr. Goebbels has correctly remarked
that revolutionary organizations and their animi do not
disappear while underground. They become dangerous in
so far as they succeed by cell techniques in winning the
loyalties of men within the bureaucratic structures. In
France the army was defeated but the generals remained.
The very extension of these bureaucratic structures brings
with it the extension of chaos should they fall during their
supreme test which is defeat in war. It is during such crises
that not the specialist managers but revolutionary leaders
may take over. The Russian and the German revolutions of
1917 and 1918 started in their navies: not with, but against,
officers. We are not so convinced of the stability and
finality of nazism in Europe. American rearmament may
solve the problem of unemployment, and warfare is no
Nazi patent. The military breakdown and the eventual
breakdown of the Nazi war machine may well release
forces which may be primarily apt in engineering revolutions and later in managing staffs of engineers. Their goal

will not be to curb masses but to mobilize them. A prognosis of what is happening in the world today which reduces masses to the mere object of the mythologizing of engineers may well be surprised at the potentialities of the possible opponents of the present managers. If the present ruling owners fall, so may their managers.

Burnham's theory of historical change does not take adequately into account the *de facto* functioning of class structures. For him the constitutents of society are masses and élites. History is now a struggle between managers and weak, because functionally "superfluous," capitalists; later it will be between different managers who will curb the masses with myths. In order to become dominant, all the managers must do is control the functional economy, really run the productive apparatus, silently knock over the remaining capitalists and curb the masses. That is all they have to do!

Modern revolutions are not watched by masses as they occur within the palace of élites. Revolutions are less dependent upon managerial personnel and their myths than upon those who bring to focus and legitimate the revolutionary activity of struggling classes. The Russian revolutionaries may have been slight in number, but the peasants who wanted the land were many, and it is they who make revolutionary leaders successful. The French Revolution was not dissimilar. In Central Europe in 1918 the urban proletariat was the class that pushed the socialist leaders into power. In modern history always behind the élites and parties there are revolutionary masses. Without such masses, parties may shout revolution, but (no matter how expert they may be) they cannot make it.

So far such revolutionary masses, landless peasants, striking workers, and defeated armies have ousted owners and their managers. The productive process is not always and necessarily continuous and ongoing but may well exhibit major breakdowns and discontinuities; from the standpoint of the technologist, it seems to be the dilettantes and amateurs who, coming into power, build up a new staff of expert managers. Such radical shifts in the distribution of power and in the composition of personnel are not illuminated by being covered with the all-over phrase, "the managerial revolution."

# 4

# THE POLITICAL GARGOYLES:
# BUSINESS AS POWER

There are structural trends in the political economy of the United States which parallel those of Germany. They are more important than the fifth-column small-fry and perhaps as important as Nazi armies, for they have an objective chance to shape the societies we are going to live in. "Nothing fundamental in history, program, structure of organization or social outlook divides clearly the policies of the Spitzenverbände [peak trade associations] within the totalitarian countries from those of the liberal-capitalist states." In Germany, Italy and France it was "these bodies who made the critical decisions without which the final destruction of democracy could not have taken place." The unmistakable economic foundations of a corporative system are being formed in this country by monopoly capitalism and its live political gargoyle, the NAM and its affiliates. These are the expertly documented opinions of a political economist who knows Germany and America.

Dr. Brady's book* is a study of the key employers and trade associations of international business: the Reichs-gruppe Industrie and the National Association of Manufacturers, the Zaibatsu and the Federation of British Industries. Because the span and weight of these self-regimented worlds of business is so great, to analyze them is to outline the total political economies of Germany, the United States, Italy, Japan, Britain and Vichy France. Such a comparative study brings out the significance of the "crackpot bureaucrats" and "theorists" of the NAM. For

* *Business as a System of Power*, by Robert A. Brady. New York: Columbia University Press. 340 pages. $3.

here, in brief, are the common structures and associations of the business classes of each major capitalist country and an indication of their logical outcome in the political, economic and ideological spheres. Here, in agreement with Franz Neumann's work, is a theory of the character of fascism which links it with a monopoly capitalism which is interfused with state and implemented by army.

From Dr. Brady's account of Italy we can learn something of the economic and political potentialities of Catholicism; from Japan and Britain we can learn something about the possibilities of our own business cousinhoods and clans; from Vichy France we can learn of the loyalty of business confronted with certain war situations; from Germany we learn about business and foreign policy, about unions whose militancy was absorbed by dependence upon a pluralist state. From all of them, and from the record of our own ruling class, we can learn a lot about business as a system of economic regimentation and a political gargoyle draining from the top gutters the Augean ideology of status capitalism.

The composition of the *status quo* is a major factor in forming the lines of the opposition. Brady has not inferred these lines, but so clearly do they lie in his materials that to discuss them is to display business as a system of power. The character this opposition must assume is indicated by four factors: the extent of "self-regimentation" now existing among business organizations; their pressure upon and interfusion with crucial branches of the government; the decisive role which property plays in the power and ideology of these strata; and the enemies which they, as highly informed and rational bodies, have selected as focal.

As business is more and more bureaucratized under the propertied cliques of the Spitzenverbände, as "outsiders" and small entrepreneurs are mashed out, any interest which comes into conflict with any segment of business has no alternative but to appear to attack all of business and the tenets of the capitalist system for which it stands. The answer to this situation is simple, at least on the ideological front: accept the challenge their organization throws down. Their size and daring leave no choice but for an equal or greater audacity. For the changes which they portend are

much further from the ideal pattern of democracy everyone talks about during wars than any proposal from the
honestly democratic Left.

Given the internal organization and total position of
business, to champion a "genuine" liberal capitalism or a
return to such a system by means of antitrust legislation
or "a mixed economy" is, in effect, to thrust one's face
into a favorite mask of the Spitzenverbände. At the least,
it is to yield to a nostalgia which can never become the
basis of realistic action. The powers and requirements of
the existing economic structure are such that no halfway
economic measure could long retain the political conditions of its being. Trust-busting is not exactly fruitless: it
probably increases economic and political collusion. As
President Roosevelt said in 1938, "The power of a few to
manage the economic life of the nation must be diffused
among the many or be transferred to the public and its
democratically responsible government." An alternative
he mentioned at that time, in recommending the TNEC,
was management by competition; the TNEC has shown
that this is not and, under present technological conditions,
cannot be the case.

The opposition can no longer hide behind the ambiguous formality of "government control of business," for this
mode of attack does not specify who or what government
is. The fact is that a major medium of "control" of business, outside and within the state, is the peak trade association. "Self-government in business" has replaced laissez-
faire; ceasing to be an umpire, the state can carry the
ball. Wars underline this fact. Recent reports of "post-war
planning" by business make it clear. It is not only a question of who can "pressure" the government more strongly;
it is a question of who *is* the operative government. Although the NAM has several attributes of a "government,"
it lacks its own legitimized force. In Germany, Italy and
Japan its counterparts have this essential of truly twentieth-
century business. Therefore, rather than depend so much
upon "government," the opposition must confront that
which gives economic royalists their power, within and
without government: private ownership of the apparatus
of production.

A misunderstanding of Berle's and Mean's earlier remarks on the role of property in the structure of the
business classes has been ridden, not to death, but to the
Right. The error underlying this discussion of the "separation" of ownership and "control" has been to focus upon
business as business and to overlook business as a political
power, an ideology and a system of status.

Although definitive statistics are badly needed, it may
be assumed from such studies as are now available that by
no means is "control" of corporations out of the hands of
their owners. At the top of every country, the executives
are blended by blood and interest, by idea and status with
propertied families and cliques. In Japan the owning business clans formally adopt their executives as members of
the family. The fact that the executive's vision of his own
career-chances lies within the corporate hierarchy is enough
to plant his loyalties in that hierarchy, and this is true
whether he makes one dollar or one hundred thousand
dollars a year. And the trade-association cliques, the supra-managerial level of the business class, are recruited
not only from loyal corporation managers, but also from
the forgotten men of recent discussions: the propertied or
rentier class. It is on the supra-managerial level that members of controlling family dynasties are found. They may
have hired executives to perform the *business* functions of
their ownership; they have by no means turned over the
larger economic and political interests of property to them.
Private ownership of productive property is the crucial
stake defended; around it pivot the hierarchies of power,
and it is central to the attempts to legitimate the undemo-
cratic power of business. It is precisely where this property
is a political, a larger economic and an ideological category
that the Spitzenverbände and the propertied families are
most active. They have increasingly approached economic
matters with a political frame of reference. That is why the
enemy of big business must become politically alive.

The chief social power upon which a genuine democracy can rest today is labor. The political power of business
indicates clearly that it is not enough for labor to struggle
economically with business. Unless trade unions unify into
an independent political movement and take intelligent

action on all important political issues, there is danger that they will be incorporated within a government over which they have little control.

The history of organized business everywhere indicates clearly that it knows its chief enemy to be an independent and political labor movement fructified by pro-labor intellectuals. The history of European labor during the interwar periods shows that its destruction was due, in no small part, to a failure to accept the responsibility and power commensurate with its exercise of economic and political pressure. In the face of the highly organized and politically powerful *status quo,* which Brady has ably portrayed, labor must not merely play at pressure politics and seek a governmental protection which would deprive it of its traditional weapons. Somehow it must become a militant political movement.

Robert Brady has not here been concerned with the form and lines the opposition must take. Placing more weight upon description of the impersonal mechanics of society than upon the schemes of villains or the plans of heroes, he has raised the critical problems. His book will not be a popular one: it is too full of polysyllabic prose. But the facts he has so skillfully gathered necessitate a careful and radical rethinking of what is happening in the capitalist world.

# 5

## THE TRADE UNION LEADER:
## A COLLECTIVE PORTRAIT*

Leftwing intellectuals and business executives have often thumbed the same dictionaries of abuse trying to find suitable language with which to characterize the trade union leader. But nobody has studied him as a social type—at least not in the detail and with the detachment required for finding out what sort of man he is. In order to see the man behind the several conflicting images held of him, we have gathered personal information from 203 trade union leaders representative of the policy-making circles of the American labor movement.

We wanted to know what kinds of men now lead the trade unions and what sorts of careers lie back of them. We wanted to know if a new generation of leaders emerged during the thirties, and, if so, how it differed from previous generations. And we wanted to explore the differences between the leaders of the AFL and the CIO—to find out if these personal differences help us to understand the different public actions and policies of the two organizations. Because of limitations of space, we present this collective portrait with a minimum of interpretation.

The men included in this study are of the top-flight policy-making circles of American trade unions. They are a 50 per cent sample of the presidents and secretaries of national and international unions of both the AFL and the CIO; the presidents and secretaries of the State Federations and of the Departments of the AFL; and the heads of the State Industrial Union Councils of the CIO.

On May 18, 1944, questionnaires were mailed to the men in these positions. By June 10, a 35 per cent sample had been returned. To those who had not replied, a follow-

* (With the assistance of Mildred Atkinson.)

77

up questionnaire was mailed during August and September, 1944. In the accompanying letter, anonymity was guaranteed the individual respondent and our letterheads contained the names of an Advisory Committee of men well known in trade union circles.[1] The usable replies which had come in by October, 1944 are indicated in Table I. The representativeness of our sample is indicated by its large size (50.6 per cent); by the fact that several of our basic tabulations have been run on both the 35 per cent sample and the 50 per cent sample and have been found

TABLE I

AFL & CIO TRADE UNION LEADERS: OFFICIALLY ANNOUNCED PERSONNEL FOR STUDY AND SAMPLE ON WHICH INFORMATION WAS AVAILABLE, 1944

| | A F L | | | | | | C I O | | | T O T A L | | |
| | Unions[3] | | State Fed. | | Deptm. | | Unions | | State Coun-cils[7] | AFL | CIO | AFL & CIO |
| | P[4] | S[5] | P | S | P | S | P | S | | | | |
| Announced Personnel Solicited[2] | 99 | 85 | 50[6] | 48 | 4 | 4 | 39 | 36 | 36 | 290 | 111 | 401 |
| Information Received On | 48 | 38 | 19 | 23 | 2 | 3 | 24 | 21 | 25 | 133 | 70 | 203 |
| Per Cent | 49 | 45 | 38 | 48 | 50 | 75 | 62 | 58 | 69 | 46 | 63 | 51 |

[1] We wish to thank the following individuals for their cooperation in this matter: Boris Shiskin, Economist, AFL; I. M. Ornburn, Secretary-Treasurer, Union Label Trades Department, AFL; James B. Carey, Secretary-Treasurer, CIO; Kermit Eby, Assistant Director, Department of Research and Education, CIO; J. G. Luhrsen, Executive Secretary, Railway Labor Executive Association; Glenn R. Atkinson, Liaison Officer, Railroad Labor Organizations, with Office of Price Administration. We know of only two statistical studies of trade union leaders. Both of them use the data contained in *American Labor Who's Who,* New York, 1925; P. A. Sorokin, "Leaders of Labor and Radical Movements in the United States and Foreign Countries," *American Journal of Sociology* (November, 1927), pp. 382-411; Louis Stanley, "A Cross Section of American Labor Leadership," Appendix III, pp. 412-20, of *American Labor Dynamics,* ed. by H. J. S. Hardman, New York, 1928. The latter study of Stanley provides tabular information on officials of the AFL and of independent unions which we have used to establish trends in various connections. These distributions include 788 persons directly connected with labor unions, 682 of them with the AFL. Unfortunately, we are not told their positions in the unions, but they are separated from the non-union people listed in *American Labor Who's Who,* many of whom are journalists, political party figures, and executives of various labor serving associations. Information on "The 1925 Leaders" is computed from Stanley's tables.

quite similar (according to critical ratios); and by the fact that the proportions of replies from the various types of personnel are rather even. This large response to a mailed questionnaire is, of course, gratifyingly high.

**I**

Approximately 85 per cent of the present officials of the AFL were born in the United States. Fifteen per cent are foreign-born, 10 per cent being of the "old immigration." Seventy-nine per cent of the CIO leaders are American-born—13 per cent of the "old immigration." In 1925, 68 per cent of all the trade union leaders were U.S. born. Today the figure for the combined AFL and CIO leadership is 83 per cent. Thus, the cry of "foreign born agita-

TABLE 2

PLACE OF BIRTH OF LABOR LEADERS[8]

|  | Deceased[9] % AFL & CIO | % AFL | Contemporaries % CIO | % AFL & CIO |
|---|---|---|---|---|
| Foreign Born | 29 | 15 | 21 | 17 |
| Born in US |  |  |  |  |
| Northeast | 24 | 24 | 25 | 24 |
| North Central | 35 | 44 | 31 | 39 |
| South | 7 | 12 | 10 | 11 |
| West | 5 | 5 | 13 | 8 |
| Total Cases | 41 | 130 | 68 | 198 |

[2] According to official mailing lists of AFL (March 7, 1944) and of CIO (February 7, 1944).

[3] If the same man was listed under President and Secretary, he was tallied under President only.

[4] P stands for Presidents.

[5] S stands for Secretaries and Secretary-Treasurers.

[6] Includes Puerto Rico and Alaska.

[7] Some of these men are called "President," some "Chairman," but most are "Secretary-Treasurer." No distinction has been made between such alternative titles.

[8] Two AFL contemporaries are not included in this table. One was born in Alaska, one in the Virgin Islands.

[9] The deceased generation was culled from printed sources. It represents readily available biographical data. The year of birth of the average leader is 1852.

tors," so far as the labor union officials is concerned, has lost whatever relevance it may ever have had. The great bulk of the officials of the two big unions were born citizens of the United States.

The typical regions of birth of the leaders in both union blocs are the Middle Atlantic, the East North Central and the West North Central. Over twice as large a proportion of the AFL leaders come from the West North Central as is the case with the CIO, whereas three times as many CIO leaders are from the Mountain and Pacific regions.

Within the United States there have been several minor shifts in the region of birth between the 1925 and the 1944 groups: (1) for all labor leaders, the 1925 modal regions are the Middle Atlantic and the East North Central. These two divisions contained the place of birth of 58 per cent of the 1925 U.S. born leaders. Of the 1944 U.S. born leaders, 51 per cent are from these two regions; (2) during the last twenty years, the production centers of U.S. labor leaders have moved slightly westward and the modal region of origin has expanded to include the West North Central. The West North Central furnished less than 10 per cent of U.S. born leaders in 1925, while in 1944 almost 20 per cent of the native born leaders came from this region; (3) eleven per cent of the 1925 leaders were born in the South Atlantic, while less than 5 per cent of the 1944 leaders came from that region.

These shifts in places of birth reflect the laws governing immigration, the changing proportion of the foreign-born within the country, and the domestic population shifts. We need not attempt to "correct" for such factors, as we are not here concerned with the relative labor leader productivity of regions, but rather in characterizing the labor leaders as a group in themselves. The current fact and the trend is clear: the typical trade union leader was born in the Northeast section of the United States.

## II

The average trade union leader is 46 years old. This "average," however, does not mean very much, for there are two typical (modal) ages and not one. The differences between the AFL and the CIO leaders are of more interest than the overall average age. The average age of the AFL official is 55; of the CIO official, 42. The AFL leaders are much more spread in age, 19 per cent of them being over 64, a little more than 2 per cent being under 35. The CIO sample contains no official over 64 years of age, and more than 21 per cent of them are under 35. The AFL leaders are, typically, between 45 and 70; the CIO, between 30 and 45.

Available data enable us to compare the ages of certain classes of governmental officials and corporation executives with those of labor leaders. These comparisons must not be taken as conclusive, but they are worth noting. In 1944, the average age of the AFL-CIO leader was 46. The presidents of one hundred large corporations averaged 57 years of age in 1940, the range being 35 to 79 and the modal interval (containing 42 cases) being 50 to 59, strongly skewed toward the sixties (which contains 29 cases).[10] The average age of the executive heads of thirty-of the utility executives, 57; and of the railroad heads, 64.[11] Only one of these men was younger than 45, and

TABLE 3

AFL & CIO TRADE UNION LEADERS:

AGE DISTRIBUTION, SUMMER, 1944

| Age | % of AFL | % of CIO | % of AFL & CIO |
|---|---|---|---|
| 70-85 | 7 | — | 4 |
| 60-69 | 25 | 3 | 18 |
| 50-59 | 38 | 9 | 27 |
| 40-49 | 19 | 40 | 26 |
| 30-39 | 11 | 47 | 24 |
| 25-29 | — | 1 | 1 |
| Total Cases | !29 | 70 | 199 |
| | Me: 55 | Me: 42 | Me: 46 |

five giant corporations was 61 in 1939; the average age for the industrial heads included in this total was also 61;

[10] *Fortune*, February, 1940, p. 51. The average of 57 is computed from 91 of the hundred on whom information was available. The hundred men were heads of the first ten railroad and utilities in respect to assets; the first five companies in oil, steel, chain stores and mining groups; and the first sixty other industrials.

[11] These data are from TNEC Monograph No. ii, by M. E. Dimock and H. K. Hyde, Table X, p. 46. The personnel included

three were under 50, whereas four were 70 or over. Half
of them were 61 (median) or more. The average age of
sixty-two federal administrators (bureau heads) in 1939
was 54. The executive heads of the ten federal departments and of five other large agencies of the federal government in 1939 were an average of 55 years of age.[12]

The average age of these governmental officials is approximately 54; of the corporation executives, 57 to 61;
of the labor leaders, 46. The labor men are thus eight years
younger than the governmental and from eleven to fifteen
years younger than the business men. Even the AFL leaders, who are approximately fourteen years older than the
CIO leaders, are from two to six years younger than the
business leaders and approximately the same age as the
governmental officials.

If we may consider these data as roughly comparable
and crudely representative of the three hierarchies, the
CIO men are almost a new generation within and between
the three houses of power. On the average, they are twenty
years younger than the corporation executives, fourteen
years younger than the AFL leaders, and thirteen years
younger than the governmental officials.[13]

### III

The life circumstances from which the trade union leaders derive are at least in part revealed by the occupations
of their fathers. A collective portrait of the occupational
origins of the leaders of the AFL and the CIO is presented
in Tables 4 and 5. The occupational classification which
we use is by no means satisfactory for general purposes,
but it does catch the results of our study.

---

are executive heads of nineteen of the twenty largest industrials, of
the eight largest utilities, and of the eight largest railroads.

[12] These data are adapted from A. W. MacMahon and J. D. Millet,
*Federal Administrators* (New York, 1939), p. 454 by TNEC No.
II, pp. 48 and 49.

[13] As "governmental" members of the triad, politicians might well
be more comparable than officials, for labor leaders are probably
closer to politicians as types of powerful men than they are to
officials. However, it may be noted that some ten of the bureau
heads were politically recruited.

About 60 per cent of the labor leaders come from laboring families; of these the bulk are skilled labor. There is no significant difference between the proportions of CIO and AFL fathers who followed semi- and unskilled trades. In both, these are negligible sources of recruitment. The next group, 16 per cent, are from farming families—most of them owners of farms. Owners of small businesses are third in rank, making up 14 per cent of the total. The owners of businesses were either independent tradesmen, craftsmen, or had small retail shops. The remainder are rather scattered in origin.

TABLE 4

AFL & CIO TRADE UNION LEADERS: OCCUPATION OF FATHERS

| Occupation | % of AFL | % of CIO | % of AFL & CIO |
|---|---|---|---|
| Professional | 2 | 4 | 3 |
| Business | | | |
|   Business Executive | 1 | 3 | 2 |
|   Owner of Business | 15 | 12 | 14 |
| Clerical | 3 | 9 | 5 |
| Farmer | | | |
|   Owner | 12 | 12 | 11 |
|   Tenant | 2 | — | 1 |
|   Unspecified | 3 | 4 | 4 |
| Labor | | | |
|   Skilled | 53 | 44 | 50 |
|   Semi-Skilled | 6 | 7 | 6 |
|   Unskilled | 3 | 5 | 4 |
| Total Cases | 121 | 68 | 189 |

The differences between the AFL and the CIO leaders are not marked, but it appears that the CIO men are from slightly higher occupational levels; more of them are probably from middle-class homes. Three times as large a proportion of CIO men are from the homes of clerks and salesmen, and twice as many are from professional homes, teachers, preachers, and one medical doctor. Yet slightly more of the fathers of the AFL men were engaged in work which involved the ownership of property than was the case with the fathers of CIO men.

One proposition stands up out of the details: the leaders of labor derive overwhelmingly from the ranks of labor. If the labor leader does not come from a skilled labor home, he comes from a farm family, primarily a farm-owning family, and thirdly from the owners of small business.

Forty-five per cent of the AFL men and 46 per cent of the CIO men claim that their fathers were at some time members of some union. These figures are fairly close to the proportion of leaders who are the sons of workmen. However, men whose fathers were primarily farmers or clerks sometimes claimed unionization for their fathers who were at some time workmen. These percentages are, of course, much larger than the percentage of unionized men among industrial workers at large; until the thirties, with the exception of the small peak of 1919-20, the nonagricultural workers were seldom more than 10 per cent unionized.

TABLE 5

AFL & CIO TRADE UNION LEADERS: OCCUPATION OF GRANDFATHERS

| Occupation | % of AFL | % of CIO | % of AFL & CIO |
|---|---|---|---|
| Professional | 6 | 10 | 8 |
| Business | | | |
|   Business Executive | — | 6 | 2 |
|   Owner of Business | 10 | 6 | 8 |
| Clerical | 1 | — | 1 |
| Farmer | | | |
|   Owner | 18 | 25 | 20 |
|   Tenant | 4 | 4 | 4 |
|   Unspecified | 17 | 14 | 16 |
| Labor | | | |
|   Skilled | 34 | 29 | 32 |
|   Semi-skilled | 2 | 2 | 2 |
|   Unskilled | 8 | 4 | 7 |
| Total Cases | 83 | 51 | 134 |

By comparing the occupations of the fathers with those of the grandfathers, we are able to build up a three-generational pattern. For the labor leaders as a whole, it appears that the great bulk of the grandfathers were farmers and laborers, split about evenly between these two groups (40 per cent of each). Compared with the occupations of the working population as a whole in the middle nineteenth century, however, the laborers are over-represented and the farmers under-represented. The fathers shifted further into labor, around 60 per cent of them becoming workers, while only 16 per cent followed their fathers in farming. Those who did not shift to laboring occupations scattered, primarily, into the petty bourgeois stratum of store owners, a shift which was perhaps experienced as ascent. The difference between grandfathers and fathers in this respect was 8 per cent, as compared with 14 per cent of the fathers. One minor pattern of interest indicates a descent for the fathers; only 3 per cent of them were professional, whereas 8 per cent of the grandfathers were in that bracket. This descent is more marked among fathers of AFL than of CIO leaders.

Comparing the leaders of the two union blocs for these trends in family background, it seems that fewer of the CIO grandfathers were laborers and more were farmers; that perhaps slightly more of these farmers were owners, and fewer of them tenants. The CIO fathers scattered out from this grandfather base in a slightly wider area than did the AFL fathers. The same proportion followed farming, but fewer went in for laboring jobs and for petty bourgeois ownership, and slightly more into white-collar occupations. The age differences between the two groups of leaders and the changing occupational compositions might well explain these latter differences. But regardless of explanation, the family background of the present CIO leaders is slightly higher than that of the AFL men, although both are dominantly from laboring families.

The only figures which we have for the occupational origins of business men which might be comparable with these data on labor leaders is of the year 1928. There is reason to believe that the pictures these data present are comparable because, in so far as they have changed over the sixteen year interval, they have probably changed in the direction of the inference we shall make involving them. These data, even if they contain substantial errors, clearly point to the wide differences in occupational origins of labor leaders and business leaders. Approximately 56 per cent of the business leaders came from the "business executives and owners" level, 13 per cent were sons of professionals, while only 11 per cent were from labor. But only

[11] Adapted from Taussig and Joslyn, *American Business Leaders,* Table 20, p. 88. *Fortune* (February, 1940), although not giving "occupation of father," states that thirty-two of the one hundred executives "can be called self-made men"; twelve in the industrials group clearly inherited their jobs; so far as available records show, fifty went to college. See above for the selection of these one hundred men.

16 per cent of the labor leaders were from the business executives and owners level, 3 per cent from professional, while 60 per cent were from laboring homes.[14]

### IV

Given the relatively low occupational origins of the trade union officials, their educational attainments are surprisingly high: twenty-two per cent of the total group went to college. The rest are rather evenly split between high school and grammar school (41 per cent, high school; 36 per cent, grammar school).

TABLE 6

AFL & CIO TRADE UNION LEADERS: HIGHEST EDUCATIONAL LEVEL ATTAINED

| Educational Level | % of AFL | % of CIO | % of AFL & CIO |
|---|---|---|---|
| Post Graduate | 3 | 3 | 3 |
| College | 13 | 29 | 19 |
| College Graduate | 4 | 9 | 6 |
| Some College | 9 | 20 | 13 |
| High School | 39 | 46 | 41 |
| HS Graduate | 18 | 24 | 20 |
| Some HS | 21 | 22 | 21 |
| Grade School | 45 | 20 | 36 |
| GS Graduate | 27 | 13 | 22 |
| Some GS | 18 | 7 | 14 |
| No Formal Educ. | — | 2 | 1 |
| Total Cases | 125 | 68 | 193 |

The difference between the formal education of AFL and CIO leaders is clear cut: the CIO men are better educated. Thirty-two per cent of the CIO leaders are college men, although not this many finished college; only 16 per cent of the AFL men went to college. Slightly more than 3 per cent in both union blocs have had post-graduate training. Forty-six per cent of the CIO and 39 per cent of the AFL are of the high school level of education. On the grammar school level, the difference is even clearer. Only around 22 per cent of the CIO failed to rise above the grammar schools, whereas 45 per cent of the AFL men are in this category.

Do these differences between the educations of the AFL and CIO men result from differences in age? A cross-tabulation of age and level of schooling reveals the following patterns. Of the men in their thirties, 31 per cent in the AFL are college men, whereas 42 per cent in the CIO are college men. But of the AFL and CIO men in their forties and fifties, there are no significant differences in the proportions who went to college. The modal decade of age of the AFL leaders is the fifties; the modal educational rank (of the three school units) is grammar school. The modal age decade for the CIO leaders is the thirties, and their modal educational rank is high school. Thus there have been differences between the AFL and the CIO in the selection of younger leaders. The young men who have risen in the CIO are better-educated.

A cross-tabulation of the occupations of fathers and the education of labor leaders confirms this pattern. Of the sons of all three grades of workmen, 29 per cent of those in the CIO went to college, whereas only 8 per cent of the sons of laborers in the AFL went to college. This cross-tabulation also reveals that a smaller proportion of the sons of laborers got above grammar school than the sons of other occupational levels; that the sons of business-owning fathers had a much better chance to go to college; and that the farmers' sons were more likely to go to college than the workers' sons.

In Table 6 we have translated all educational experiences into the standard school hierarchy. But 21 per cent of the labor leaders have also experienced another type of "formal" education. These 21 per cent appear to have struggled for an education, i.e., they attended night schools, took correspondence courses, or went to "business colleges." Fifty-five per cent of these educational strugglers are high school men, the rest having attended grammar schools. Over one-half of the men having this kind of educational experience took correspondence courses, most of them in some white-collar field. The great bulk of the remainder attended business college.

Only 0.5 per cent of the labor leaders failed to experience any formal education, whereas 4 per cent of the population has. Only 10 per cent of the adult population went to college, whereas 22 per cent of the labor leaders have. Twenty-six per cent of the population are of high school and 58 per cent are of the grammar school level;

42 per cent of the labor leaders are high school and 36 per cent are grammar school men. The labor leaders are definitely better educated than the adult male population at large, but are probably not so well-educated as business executives. And neither labor nor business leaders are as highly educated as governmental officials of comparable rank.[15]

## V

Slightly more than half of the trade union leaders are Protestant, 35 per cent are Catholics, 10 per cent state no religious affiliation, slightly more than 4 per cent are Jews. The difference between AFL and CIO leaders' religious affiliations are not marked. There are slightly more of Jewish and of Protestant faith and slightly fewer Catholics among the CIO men. There are, however, more a-religious men in the AFL.

TABLE 7

AFL & CIO TRADE UNION LEADERS: MEMBERSHIP IN RELIGIOUS ORGANIZATIONS

| Religion | % of AFL | % of CIO | % of AFL & CIO |
|---|---|---|---|
| Catholic | 36 | 33 | 35 |
| Jewish | 3 | 7 | 4 |
| Protestant | 49 | 54 | 51 |
| None | 12 | 6 | 10 |
| Total Cases | 117 | 63 | 180 |

When these figures are compared with the church affiliations of the total population, the extent of affiliation *claimed* by the labor leaders far exceeds that of the population at large. About 55 per cent of the population thirteen years of age and over are affiliated with no church, whereas only 10 per cent of the labor leaders admit to this condition.[16]

[15] These figures should be used cautiously, for if the sample is biased by self-selecting factors, it would directly affect the educational distributions. The figures on the male population over 25 years of age are as of 1940 (*U.S. Census, Summary 1940, Second Series*, p. 5). The percentages for the adult male population are figured from a base including 1.6 per cent "not reported." The labor leaders base does not include those not reported. In the T & J sample of 1928 business leaders, 45 per cent had experienced college, 32 per cent graduating. *Op. cit.*, p. 181.

[16] Figures for the religious composition of the U.S. population 13 years of age and over are from the *Religious Census*.

This difference is all the sharper in view of the fact that generally women belong to churches in higher percentages than do men. About three in every ten church members in the population over thirteen years of age are Catholic, whereas almost four out of every ten of those trade union leaders who are church members are Catholic. About 5 per cent of church members at large are Jewish—about the same as the proportion of Jews among those labor leaders who belong to any religious organization. About 62 per cent of the church-going population over thirteen years of age belong to Protestant denominations; only 56 per cent of the church organized labor leaders belong to these churches.

## VI

Well over half of the contemporary trade union leaders are Democrats, but as a group the labor leaders do not take the Republican Party as a very serious alternative. Apart from the Democratic majority, their affiliations are rather scattered. There are about as many "independents" as Republicans among them, and a handful belong to various third parties.

The AFL circle of leaders are five times as Republican as the CIO, and twice as many of the AFL leaders are "independent." There are about the same proportion of Socialists in the two union blocs. The AFL has no ALP members listed in this sample, and there are slightly more than twice as great a proportion of men in the CIO who are in

TABLE 8

AFL & CIO TRADE UNION LEADERS: POLITICAL PARTY AFFILIATION, SUMMER, 1944

|  | % of AFL | % of CIO | % of AFL & CIO |
|---|---|---|---|
| Democratic | 54 | 58 | 56 |
| Republican | 22 | 5 | 15 |
| "Independent"[17] | 18 | 9 | 15 |
| American Labor Party | — | 19 | 7 |
| Socialist | 3 | 3 | 3 |
| "Some Other Third Party" | 3 | 6 | 4 |
| Total Cases | 115 | 65 | 180 |

[17] Includes "Gomper's policy," "no party," and "nonpartisan."

"some third party" than in the AFL. Of the AFL leaders, only 5 per cent fall outside the standard brands of Democrats, Republicans, and "independents," whereas 28 per cent of the CIO leaders are outside this circle. The reason for this is the ALP, which has enrolled 19 per cent of our sample of CIO men.

The CIO men appear to be actively interested in some specific political party. From the pattern which the CIO affiliation assumes, we might infer that, were there a third party similar to the American Labor Party on a national scale, the CIO leaders would support it. However, at the present time, about 72 per cent of all the trade union leaders belong to one or the other of the two dominant parties (77 per cent of the AFL men, 63 per cent of the CIO). The AFL men are overwhelmingly Democratic; then they are Republican; and then "independent." The CIO leaders are even more overwhelmingly Democratic, but rather than the second choice being Republican or "independent," they are ALP or "some other third party."

Several of the individuals who named Republican as their party affiliation, particularly the two or three in the CIO, qualified their answers with such statements as "but never vote straight ticket." This probably means that they are "local Republicans" because of the local requirements of their union activities, but in national matters lean toward the Democratic Party. This would explain the difference between the officials of the national unions as compared with state organizations, the officials of the latter usually being more politically active in local and state machines.[18]

Do the differences between the AFL and the CIO party affiliations result from the simple fact of the younger ages of the CIO men? A cross-tabulation reveals that the few

[18] A cross-tabulation of religious and political affiliation reveals nothing significant. Thus, the ALP members of the CIO are quite evenly distributed among the three major religions and "no religion." The Jews in both unions tend to be either Democrats or third party. In the AFL there are almost three times as many Catholic Democrats as there are Catholic Republicans or Catholic "independents," whereas there are only one-third more Protestant Democrats than Protestant Republicans. In both union blocs those claiming religious membership tend to be Democratic, independent, or Socialist, there being no a-religious Republicans or Communists.

Republicans in the CIO are young men, whereas the Democrats in the AFL are quite evenly scattered among the age groups (35 per cent of the AFL Democrats, for instance, are over 60 years of age). However, the "independents" in the AFL do definitely tend to be younger men, even if the "independents" of the CIO are quite evenly distributed in age. The small number of cases which emerge from this cross-tabulation do not enable us to say anything else that would be statistically reliable.

The differing amounts and types of energy which leaders of union blocs have given to political action does not show up in party affiliations. The age differences may have something to do with these differences in political energy, if we may assume its existence. Young men who are *already* at or near the top of the trade union hierarchy may search more readily than older men for *other* channels for initiative and ambition. They will not only be more energetic in organizing new unions, but may be more ready to take to political outlets. Older men who are at the top of some hierarchy, especially during a dynamic period such as unions have gone through in the last fifteen years, are much less likely to reach out than to use their time and energy in measures of personal and union security. The *young man already at the top* of one pyramid, may very well hold images of his success which involve other power hierarchies. And being young, he is less likely to be integrated at a suitable height in existing political organizations.

In addition to age, social origin may be involved in the differences in amount and type of political action between leaders of the two union blocs. A cross-tabulation of political party affiliation and father's occupation reveals the following. In the AFL, 13 per cent of sons of business owners are third party members, whereas 8 per cent of the sons of working men are third party members. In the CIO, 41 per cent of the sons of professional men, business executives, business owners, and clerks and salesmen are third party members.[19] These figures are quite small, and should be taken merely as suggestions. Nevertheless, it may well be that, once they have identified themselves with the purposes

[19] In the AFL sample, when cross-tabulated, there were no sons from professional, business executive, clerk, or salesmen groups.

of labor unions, men coming from higher occupational, social, and educational levels are inclined to be more "assertive" than the sons of laboring men. In so far as this initiative is politically channeled, we might expect more third-party action from men of such extraction. Our data suggests, although it does not prove, that there is something in this hunch.

TABLE 9

PARTY AFFILIATION OF AMERICAN LABOR LEADERS, 1925 AND 1944

|  | % of AFL LEADERS | | % of ALL LEADERS[22] | |
|---|---|---|---|---|
|  | 1925 | 1944 | 1925 | 1944 |
| Democratic | 21 | 55 | 19 | 56 |
| Republican | 16 | 22 | 15 | 16 |
| "Independent"[20] | 26 | 18 | 24 | 15 |
| Third Parties[21] | 37 | 5 | 42 | 13 |
| Total Cases | 320 | 115 | 363 | 180 |

Table 9 reveals what might be called the effect of the "New Deal" upon the political party affiliation of labor leaders. Between 1925 and 1944, more trade union leaders became members of some specific party (24 per cent of them were "independent" in 1925, but only 15 per cent were in this Gomperian category in 1944). For trade union leaders as a whole, third party affiliations have declined from 42 per cent to 13 per cent, despite the CIO affiliations with the ALP. These general differences between 1925 and 1944 also hold for the AFL leaders alone, except that the decline of third party affiliations is even more drastic. The Republicans have gained very slightly; the Democratic party has jumped from 19 per cent to 56 per cent during these last two decades.

[20] In the 1944 data "independent" includes "Gomper's party," "no party," and "nonpartisan." Its meaning for the 1925 data is not specified.

[21] The composition of this group has changed. For all leaders in 1925, it consisted of 16.8 per cent progressives, 24.8 per cent "labor parties." In 1944 it consisted of 6.7 per cent ALP, 2.8 per cent Socialist, 3.8 per cent "some other third party."

[22] The 1925 data included AFL and "independent unions;" the 1944, AFL and CIO.

## VII

The pre-union careers of the labor leaders fall into two distinct occupational patterns. The great bulk of these men simply took jobs in the trade or industry with which they were later to deal as officials of a union. They do not appear to have taken these jobs merely to become members and thus labor officials. They were located on the worker level.

There is, however, another career pattern which is of great interest. Before they became union officials, 20 per cent of the labor leaders have held jobs "higher" than the jobs organized by their respective unions. Most of these jobs are in the white-collar brackets—accounting, clerical work, and salesmanship predominating, but they also include real estate men, teachers, social workers, ministers, one acrobat, and one professional ball player.

Eighteen per cent of the AFL leaders have followed this white-collar pattern, while 23 per cent of the CIO men have done so.[23] In both organizations the white-collar pattern is slightly more frequent among the state officials than among the officers of the Internationals, and in both union blocs more of the secretaries have held white-collar jobs than have the presidents. Only 10 per cent of the AFL and 13 per cent of the CIO International presidents have gone through the white-collar link, whereas 24 per cent of the secretaries of the AFL unions and 33 per cent of the secretaries of the CIO unions have done so.

The white-collar experience overlaps somewhat with the experiences of night and correspondence schools and business colleges (25 per cent of the men who have held white-collar jobs prior to becoming union officials were such educational strugglers). But the experience is even more closely associated with a college education; forty-six per cent of the labor leaders who have been white-collar workers are college men.

The pre-union career involving white-collar jobs and/or educational struggle may take two forms:

(1) A man already located in an occupation above the level of jobs organized by his future union may take a job

---

[23] These figures exclude the few officials of white collar and professional unions (all of these fall into the first major pattern).

in some trade union, usually a local. Because of union rules, he will usually go through the ritual of briefly taking a job in the shop in order to become a member of the union. There is thus a ritual link in his white-collar career. There is a slight tendency, although not enough perhaps to be called a trend, among some of the younger men which indicates that white-collar workers who became unemployed during the thirties took jobs of a laboring character out of need, and then went into labor union work. Our information on this point is not conclusive enough to permit a statistical statement.

(2) A man who is working as a skilled laborer and has never held any other type of job may struggle to rise from the ranks of labor into a white-collar position. The years during which he struggled for education and for better jobs, as well as the character of these experiences and of his occupational origin, indicate that he was not particularly bent on a union career. But this struggle upward was eventually channeled into a trade union hierarchy.

The climbing patterns within the trade union heirarchies are rather well defined. The typical labor leader began his trade union work in some local. The very few exceptions to this rule are men with better educations (college or business school) and some technical capacity (newspaper work and accounting seem to be the chief talents involved). Not counting "delegates," who cannot be called holders of "positions," it appears that 16 per cent of the heads of AFL Internationals have held posts in state organizations and 21 per cent of the heads of state organizations have at some point in their careers held positions in Internationals. Only 11 per cent of the CIO officials of Internationals have held state positions, whereas 24 per cent of the state heads have at some time during their careers held positions in Internationals. The dominant pattern, however, is rather clearly forked just above the local level: one way leads to the headship of an International and the other leads to the top of a state organization. Virtually all routes to trade union leadership begin in the locals.

Regardless of the particular career pattern which he has followed, the typical trade union leader is a man who has climbed a long way. Considering his occupational origin and the character and extent of his education, the top flight trade union post is definitely a perch of "success." We have figures on the salaries of forty-nine presidents and thirty-eight secretaries of Internationals affiliated with the AFL. Salaries for the presidents range from $4,000 to $30,000 a year, the mean average being $9,641. The salary range for the secretary-treasurers is from $3,600 to $30,000, the average being $8,098.[24] Our statistical information on the "expense accounts" of labor leaders does not warrant any generalization, nor comparison with various types of business and governmental personnel. It is, however, worth noting that, ten years after graduating, the class of 1929 at Yale was making an average salary of $4,350. Only 4 per cent of the 367 men who reported were making $10,000 or more. Harvard Business School graduates of 1920 averaged $8,500 after ten years.

Five facts stand out from these details of the trade union career: (1) the majority of these leaders have worked as laborers in the industries with which they later dealt as union officials; (2) the majority took their first union jobs with a local; (3) from this local there are two rather segregated routes upward, one leads to the top of a national or international union, the other leads to the top of a state federation. There is about a 20 per cent criss-cross between these two hierarchies; (4) after he has arrived, the trade union leader attains a salary which is definitely in the top brackets. Thus, he may typically display at least some of the psychological trends associated with "self-made" men; (5) there is a tendency for another type of career pattern to emerge. It involves only a short stop at the local and more crossing back and forth between the local-to-international and the local-to-state-federation hierarchies. More crucially, it involves a white-collar link in the pre-union occupational career. The men whose careers embody this pattern tend to be better educated. If the needs for a more rationalized trade union administration, a more centralized management, and for more formally specialized personnel are effectively felt in the policy-making circles of American trade unions, we may expect this career-pattern to become

[24] These figures are computed from the itemized list in the *Postal Record*, December, 1943, pp. 440-41.

an explicit trend. This tendency is, and will continue to be, reinforced by a master trend in the economic structure at large, which all available data bear out. The occupational structure is becoming more rigid and, statistically speaking, it is becoming more difficult for the bright young man born into relatively low circumstances to climb above the position occupied by his father.

Ascent for the bright working class boy, as well as for the educated middle-class youngster, has perhaps of late been more likely within trade union channels than within the heirarchies of business. This is suggested by the greater proportion of men of lower occupational origin who are at the top in trade unions as compared with business (and probably governmental) positions of comparable income and power; by the younger age at which the trade union leader attains these positions; and by the lesser amount of formal education apparently required for the union career. Previously, and even today in many unions, a higher education was not seen as an asset for a trade union career. If present trends continue, however, we may expect that the climb to success in unions will require a better education, and we may expect more able young men to follow the trade union route to positions of income in the three big places of power. At the present time, labor's leadership contains a greater proportion of the sons of laborers than any other group of comparable income on which statistical information is available. Although existing information is meager, statistically speaking the CIO has offered young men of working class parents a faster road to a position of power than any other organization, except the Armed Forces, during the past decade.

# 6

# THE LABOR LEADERS
# AND THE POWER ELITE

Viewed from one special angle, the labor unions have become organizations that select and form leaders who, upon becoming successful, take their places alongside businessmen in and out of government and politicans in both major parties among the national power elite; for one function of labor unions—like social movements and political parties—is to contribute to the formation of this national power elite.

As new men of power, the labor leaders have come only lately to the national arena. Samuel Gompers was perhaps the first labor man to join, even though temporarily and quite uneasily, the national power elite. His self-conscious attempt to establish his place within this elite and, thus, to secure the labor interest as integral to national interests has made him a prototype and model for the national labor career. Sidney Hillman was not, of course, the only labor man to take up this course during the forties, but his lead during the early war years, his awareness of himself as a member of the national elite, and the real and imagined recognition he achieved as a member ("Clear it with Sidney") signaled the larger entrance, after the great expansion of the unions and after the New Deal, of labor leaders into the power elite.

## I

We need not now become too fancy or too precise with the term "national power elite." By using it, I only mean to refer to the circles and individuals who as a collectivity share decisions having national consequences. In so far as events are decided, the power elite as a collectivity makes the decisions. No one, I believe, wants to argue that the chief of a roadside fruit stand has as much, or more, power in various social areas of life as the head of a multimillion-dollar corporation or that a lieutenant on the line in Korea is as powerful as the Chief of Staff in the Pentagon or that a deputy sheriff carries as much authority as the President of the United States. Well then, the power elite is a relative term; it refers to those who have the most say-so about those events that are decided. The definitive problem is at what level you wish to draw the line—you could by enlargement define the elite out of existence—and this varies with what you are interested in studying.

No one has made a systematic study of the most powerful actors in the political, economic, and military spheres of the United States social structure. We have partial studies, dating mainly from the muckraker era and from the thirties, which, by the way, are often more imaginative than systematic and more ideological than empirical. None of them includes labor leaders. Certainly today, however, no such study could be adequate, must less complete, if it did not include the top leaders of the major unions. There is, of course much disagreement over how much power and what kind of power the men of labor now have; but this very fact points to them as a factor that must be reckoned with by those who would understand the main drift and the ostensibly powerful actors within it.

In this essay I will not be able to answer the very complicated question of "how much power" labor leaders now have, for no one could do so without also answering the same question for business executives, government officials, admirals and generals, major politicans, and other top national types. To state the question in answerable terms requires that we compare labor leaders with other members of the power elite as a total bracket, for the power of one can only be measured against the power of another.

There is, in addition, the question of just what role this entire elite plays in the shaping of our historic era. It may be best to conceive of history as not in any way the realization of the will of social actors. History may "just move along by itself," even though powerful actors attempt to move and shape it, and so things go on behind men's backs.

There is an extreme view that by their schemes a relatively small group make history. And, of course, there are many intermediate views, some of them quite intricate. I shall not examine this range of issues here except toward the end of these remarks, and then only casually.

What I will attempt to do in this preliminary statement,[1] is to discuss in general terms the national roles of the key men of American labor and raise several questions about the functions of labor unions and of their top personnel.

## II

For a long time now it has been traditional to contrast business or market unionism with ideological or political unionism, as if these were types of unions or, at least, of ideologies. But it is probably more useful to think of these terms as simply indicators of two *contexts* in which unions operate. Unions may shift their attention to one or the other and may employ different tactics in one or the other at the same time, as well as at different times. This shifting is one meaning of such assertions as that the market is political and the politics has relevance for the market and that labor must now operate in a political economy. Yet we always have to remember that "labor" also operates in more local contexts and serves more local interests.

In fact, as we all know, there have been three major areas in which labor leaders have traditionally sought to share power with businessmen in economic roles and, now, with businessmen in political roles. *First,* in the plant or the local labor market, which at present does not seem to me to be the center of attention or struggle. *Second,* in the enterprise and in industry-wide sets of enterprises. Since the later thirties it is in this area that the sharpest disagreements have been raised, for this is the territory par excellence of managerial prerogative, upon which labor leaders have, of course, encroached. The notions of guaranteed annual wages, of profit sharing, of stabilized production schedules, of a controlled ratio of prices, profits, and wages, of indus-

---

[1] Preliminary, that is, to *The American Elite: A Study of the High and Mighty* (to be published by the Oxford University Press), on which I am now at work.

trial councils, or of "codetermination"—all lie here, although they, of course, may spill over into the third area. *Third,* in the national political economy, where big power blocs jockey with one another for a share in national decisions. For the sake of analysis this area should include, I believe, the international functions labor people have recently assumed in ECA and the Department of State.

I have reminded the reader of these contexts in which unions and their leaders operate in order to make this simple but often overlooked point: much controversy over the "nature" and function of labor organizations and of their leaders could be avoided if the disputants would continually specify to which context they have reference.

For example, in the first context a union may very well have as its major function the control of a job empire, yet, at the same time, in the third context it can be operating as a pressure group for power accumulation, a power to be used for broad as well as narrow purposes. It seems to me metaphysical, in the bad (*i.e.,* the uncontrolled) sense, to argue that the first function is the "real" one and the other not, or vice versa.

I shall return to this contextual principle of locating and interpreting union functions. Here I need only remark that in this general essay I am mainly concerned with labor leaders as members of the power elite in the national context of the political economy.

### I I I

Not all national labor leaders—although certainly more of them now than 25 years ago—have taken up the posture of the elite before themselves and before the nation. Much of the often curious behavior and maneuvering of labor chieftains over the last decade is explainable by their search for status within the national power elite, for in this context they have displayed extreme sensitivity to prestige slights. They feel that they have arrived, and so they want in. They want, "just like other big shots," to share the key decisions. The accoutrements they have gained are on local, national, and international levels. In middle- and small-sized cities labor leaders now sit with Chamber of Commerce officials on civic enterprises. They receive honorary academic de-grees. On the national level they expect and they get seats on production boards and desks in price-control agencies. On the international scene labor men have served with ECA missions, and as labor attachés they are now in American embassies all over the globe.

Their claim for status and power rests on their already increased power, not on property, income, or birth; and power in such situations as theirs is a source of uneasiness as well as a base of operations. It is not yet a solid and continuous base having the force of use and law. Their touchiness about prestige matters, especially on the national scene, is due (1) to their self-made character; [2] it is also due (2) to the well-known fact that their self-making was helped no end by government and the atmosphere it created in the decade after 1935; they are government-made men, fearing that they can be unmade by government. Their un-easy status is also a reflection (3) of the fact that they are simply new to the power elite and its ways. Finally, is it too much to suggest that (4) they feel a tension between their publics: their union members, before whom they can-not be too big a shot or too closely associated with inherited enemies, and their newly found companions and routines of life?

In the meantime in Washington, as well as in Europe, these men feel themselves to be members of a national elite, and they act that way and talk that way. They jockey for better positions and more say-so, which some of them understand now often entails greater prestige recognition, within this elite in which group they seldom or never acknowledge membership before the members of their union.

Many observers mistake the newer status accoutrements of labor leaders for *evidence* of labor's power. In a way they are, but in a way they are not. They *are* when they are bottomed on and lead to power. They *are not* when they become status traps for leaders, without resulting power. In such matters it is well to remember that this is no

[2] See facts and figures in C. Wright Mills, *The New Men of Power*, New York, Harcourt Brace, 1948, esp. Chap. 5, "The Self-Made Men."

chicken-and-egg issue. The chicken is power and comes first, the egg is status and comes out of this chicken.

## I V

Like business executives and large owners, labor leaders as a group are not wholly unified. Yet the often noted tendency of "the other side" to regard any move by any unit of one side as having significance in terms of the whole indicates clearly that, in the views, expectations, and demands of these men, they do form blocs, even if unwillingly. They see one another as members of blocs, and in fact they are interknit in various and quite intricate ways. But labor's men do not seem to have any continuous general staff, just as business does not center in Morgan's office. It is more complicated than that.

Individual unions may lobby for particularistic interests, which is the key to such lack of unity as labor as a bracket displays. But increasingly the issues they face and the contexts in which they must face them are national in scope and in effect; and so they must coordinate labor's line with reference to a national context, on pain of loss of power.

It is known informally and has been demonstrated statistically that the personal characteristics of these leaders, as well as their view of their organizational interests, differ according to the organizational bloc to which their unions belong. Both are self-made men of power running—if the reader will forgive me—patrimonial bureaucracies.

The leaders of the AFL and of the CIO operate in two different kinds of hierarchies. And the differences are not merely organizational; the two houses of labor are inhabited by different types of men, related within each organization in different ways. At the top of the AFL's gerontocracy are older, relatively uneducated men who have authority over much younger, better-educated men. Age and education cause some tension within the AFL. At the top of the more professional bureaucracy of the CIO are slightly older men who are quite well educated, and these better-educated leaders exercise authority over slightly younger and less well-educated men. Age and education are graded according to organizational structure. The facts of age, education, and types of hierarchy make for further differences in character, as well as outlook, between AFL and CIO leaders, which I shall not here examine.

**V**

The corporate executive, like the labor leader, is a practical man and an opportunist, but for him enduring means, developed for other purposes, are available for the conduct of his political as well as his business-labor affairs. The corporation is now a very stable basis of operation; in fact, I believe that it is more stable and more important for the continuance of the American arrangement than the lifetime family. The big corporations as a group give the executives a stable base for durable expectations; so the business member of the power elite can rely upon them in the pursuit of his short-term goals and opportunistic maneuvering.

But the union, unlike the corporation, is often in a state of protest; it is on the defensive in a sometimes actually, and always potentially, hostile society. It does not provide such enduring means, which are ready-made and at the labor elite's disposal. If the labor leader wants such means, even for his little goals, he must himself build and maintain them.

In the context of his union the labor leader is an elected official, dependent ("in the last analysis," which is not always made by history) upon the loyalty of fellow leaders and upon the rank and file of his organization. The great organizing upsurge of the thirties showed that officers who were not sufficiently responsive to the demands of industrial workers could lose power. The corporation manager, on the other hand, in the context of his corporation is not an elected official in the same sense. His power does not depend upon the loyalty of the men who work for him, and he does not usually lose his job if a union successfully invades his plants. The upsurges of the thirties did not oust the managers, whose responsibilities are not to the workers whom they employ but to themselves and to their scattered stockholders.

This difference in power situation means that the power of the business leader is likely to be more continuous and more assured than that of the labor leader; the labor leader is more likely to be insecure in his job if he fails to "deliver the goods."

Adventure, or what Max Weber called "booty," capitalism produces robber barons; in a somewhat delayed fashion and on a much smaller scale, labor unionism produces its labor racketeers. There is a Commodore Vanderbilt, and there is a Robert Brindell. At one point in its career industrial capitalism produces the sober, bourgeois entrepreneur, afraid of the encroachments of government upon his liberty. Correspondingly, labor unionism produces its sober labor leader, believing in voluntarism, afraid of government encroachments, not interested in labor solidarity, but working for independent and sovereign craft unions. There is the early Henry Ford, and there is Samuel Gompers.

Many American unions are still in the Gompers or Ford stage, and there are still spotty areas in the local union world which call to mind Brindell and Vanderbilt. Yet if the old unionists have at times become *condottieri* leading roughneck bands for local robber barons, the new unionists may in time become administrators of disciplined and contented workers for large bureaucratized corporations, for now there is a new type of correspondence between business and labor and new types of leaders on each side within the power elite. It is not a mechanical or an exact corresponding, but it is coming about. The mass industries have produced in the world of giant corporations the engineering, managerial type of leader, and the unionization of these mass industries by the new business unionism is slowly beginning to produce an engineering, managerial type of labor leader. In a similar way both corporations and unions have come increasingly to operate in the context of the political economy; and so in a similar way the types of leaders they select and form become shaped for survival and efficiency in this larger context.

## V I

However it may be with the business and political elite, there's nothing, it seems to me, in the make-up of the *current* labor leaders, as individuals and as a group, to lead us to believe that they can or will transcend the strategy of maximum adaptation. By this I mean that they react more than they lead and that they do so to retain and to expand their position in the constellation of power and advantage. Certain things could happen that would cause the downfall of the present labor leadership or sections of it, and other types of leaders might then rise to union power; but the current crop of labor leaders is pretty well set up as a dependent variable in the main drift.

Everyone seems agreed that United States unions, with minor exceptions, have eschewed "ideologies" and "programs" and have been "pragmatic" to an extreme degree.[3] This, however, is not saying as much as those who keep reiterating it seem to feel. One could substitute "corporations" or "political parties" for unions in the same sentence and have just as true a proposition. The problem of analysis for all these practical social creatures is not the earnest search for their outlook and programs and certainly not the search for new ways of moaning when no program is found other than the classic aim of "more." To analyze the national role of unions we should ignore what their leaders say, except strictly as strategical rhetoric, and examine two other problems:

First, just what major functions do these organizations fulfill (for whom and how) in the main drift?

Second, what is the main drift, the most likely outcome of the interplay between these power blocs for the changing shape of the political economy as a whole?

By the main drift, or master trend, I mean the general direction, if any, of the jockeying and compromises and struggles of organizations and of elites under present-day conditions. If they are strictly pragmatic and out to maximize their security of power and gain greater pay-offs, then what happens to them depends as much upon the whole context and their strength in it as upon any intentions they might have. So, given the several contexts in which these organizations and leaders *are* expedient, what main line, what direction are these organizations assuming?

If these are our questions, then, it seems to me, "the

[3] See *ibid.,* Chap. 9, "Programs and Expediencies," esp. pp. 239-240.

field of labor" as it is now instituted is not entirely an
intelligible unit of study. It is clear that we cannot understand labor leaders without understanding labor unions; it
should also be clear that we cannot understand these unions
without understanding the business corporation and the
modern state; and we cannot understand any of these
structures today except as they interact with one another
to form the going concern of the political economy.

This is not merely an affirmation of the important, although often mushy, principle that phenomena must be
understood contextually. I mean more than that. I mean
that I have come to the assumption that neither labor leaders nor labor unions are at the present juncture likely to
be "independent variables" in the national context and that
therefore most of their aspects and responses in which we
are interested are more easily and more adequately explained as functions of other factors and contexts than of
scholarly or gossipy details about their nature and doings.

Of course, this *is* in part a matter of the perspective which
we assume. If we were interested in some administrative
detail of unionism or some narrowed sequence of the history
of a given union or were writing to inform businessmen
what "labor" may do, then we might confine ourselves. But
the perspective we choose to take up is set by the type of
question of which I have given two examples.

## VII

There cannot very well be an interpretation of the labor
leader without a theory of the labor organization and of
such "movement" as it displays. The labor leader is a social
actor, playing one of his major roles within a labor union
and using that role as the base for all other public roles. The
leader must adapt to whatever this union becomes; only
within the limits it sets can he lead. Although these limits
sometimes seem quite broad, he is, in the first instance, a
union-made product.

If the labor union is an army, the labor leader is a generalissimo.

If the union is a democratic town meeting, the leader is
a parliamentary debater.

If the union is a political machine, the leader is a political boss.

If the union is a business enterprise, supplying and withholding for a price a labor force, the labor leader is an entrepreneur, a contractor of labor.

If the union is a pressure group, the leader is busily at the hub of national pressure, in the halls of the invisible government.

If the union is a regulator of the workingman's industrial animosity, the labor leader is a salaried technician of animosity, gearing men at work into this organization and then easing the organization through the fluctuations of American society.

There is little question but that, at some point in the history of one or another union, we can find each of these functions predominating and the leaders spending most of their time, attention, and energy in fulfilling the role indicated. Even in cross section today one can find solid examples of each of them. These several functions vary in their mixture according to the economic and political times, according to the phase and position of particular unions, and according to the context in reference to which we raise our question. Two questions, in fact, are presented.

First, under what conditions does one or another function come to predominate so as to be typical of, and central to, "the unions" at a given time?

Second, is there any tendency, because of the structural drift and the phases of contemporary unions, for unions as a whole to be more readily understood primarily in terms of one of these functions?

In this essay I have to skip consideration of the first question. If our answer to the second question is yes, then we must elaborate the function, especially in terms of further-running consequences when they interplay with the tendencies of corporations and of the state. Today, when all the major unions are in rather well-consolidated phases, no large organizational move is under foot, and all unions are the beneficiaries of a perilous boom based on war preparation; today, the unions operate as pressure groups in a manner quite like the Farm Bureau and the Trade Associations. My answer to the second question, then, is Yes,

the central function of labor organizations in the national
political economy today is that of a mass-organization
pressure group. And what this means is, that it is in terms
of this image that most of what labor leaders do and fail
to do can most readily be understood.

But the labor leader is a union-made product, I've said,
*in the first instance.* For successful, top leaders there is a
second instance. For such a leader is also made (selected
and formed) by his membership in the national power
elite and by what happens to him there. All that I have
suggested here and briefly illustrated is that we must see
and try to understand the leader as a man moving in the
overlap of these contexts, the union world and the world
of the national power elite. He is a man acting and thinking
at the point of their intersection and the social mechanics
as well as the context of his thinking and acting involve the
coincidences and collisions of both spheres.

### VIII

As members of the national power elite, labor leaders, by
means of machines, run national pressure groups of mass
organizations recruited from intermediate skill and income
levels in urban areas. As procapitalist, hardheaded, pressure-group captains and as members or would-be members of the national elite, in so far as labor men talk
seriously of programs, they will invariably conceive of
them as realizable alongside the present corporations and
within the present state framework. The leadership should
gain more decision within the power elite; the organizations should accumulate more power and be integrated
more firmly within the corporation; the membership should
get a heavier, steadier cut within the present framework of
the political economy.

These unions are less levers for change of that general
framework than they are instruments for more advanta-
geous integration with it. The drift their actions implement,
in terms of the largest projections, is a kind of "procapitalist
syndicalism from the top." They seek, in the first instance,
greater integration at the upper levels of the corporate

economy rather than greater power at the lower levels of the work hierarchy, for, in brief, it is the unexpressed desire of American labor leaders to join with owners and managers in running the corporate enterprise system and influencing decisively the political economy as a whole.

Their basis of operation is the mass organization, whereas that of business managers is the massed property they control or manage, and that of the politicians, the electorate, encased as well as may be in the political machine. Those who think of labor in political terms should not overlook the fact that pressure groups may be as powerful as political parties (or more so). Moreover their power tends to be less responsible. They are "private"; and so their leaders need not make any pretense at doctrinal justification or public accountability. All of which, in a situation like ours, no doubt increases their effectiveness. For the businessman, the politician, and the labor leader— each in curiously different ways—the more apathetic the members of their mass organizations (as long as they don't get restless and as long as they back up their leaders in "crises"), the more operating power the leaders have as members of the national power elite.

# 7

# THE AMERICAN BUSINESS ELITE:
# A COLLECTIVE PORTRAIT

I

The *Dictionary of American Biography* contains 1,464 biographies of eminent American businessmen. Among them are most of the well-known financial and business figures, as well as many others never widely known or else long forgotten. The announced criterion for inclusion in the D.A.B. is that the person "did something notable in some field of American life." Over 100 "consulting specialists" handled the various lists of candidates for inclusion; these specialists included economic and business historians.

The businessmen in the D.A.B. were not necessarily "rich," although on the average they were well above the middle ranges of income and property for their respective generations. Some were "founders" of companies which became huge enterprises only after their deaths. Their specific occupations ranged from fur trader to international banker; 14.8 per cent of them were in finance; 27.9 per cent, trade; 39.5 per cent, manufacturing; 4.0 per cent, extractive; and 13.8 per cent, transport and communication.

In a certain sense the persons who appear in the *Dictionary of American Biography* may be considered the historical elite of the United States. The businessmen born between 1570 and 1879 who make up 11 per cent of that total will here be called "the American business elite."[1] Admittedly the term as applied to the D.A.B. data is open to some objection. The D.A.B. omits some persons who were outstandingly wealthy in their day and were in that sense part of the business elite. Many persons who are in-

[1] Briefly, the D.A.B. includes persons who died before 1927-1935, the exact date depending upon the alphabetical position of the name in question. The present study includes the original twenty volumes of the D.A.B. It does not include the one supplementary volume, which was issued too late for inclusion in these tabulations.

cluded in the D.A.B. and indexed as "businessmen" were probably selected because of their political importance rather than *primarily* because of their success in business. Yet, this list does form a convenient point of departure for an over-all view of the social characteristics of eminent American businessmen.

In the absence of any other convenient basis for historical statistical treatment, we have codified certain biographical information in the D.A.B that bears upon commonly held opinions concerning the careers of eminent businessmen.[2] Biographical information about each member of the business elite was placed on a thirty-five-item schedule. Most of the items were rather standard indicators of class status, career and character, but for most of them our information from the D.A.B. was not deemed sufficient to permit reliable statistical presentation.[3] The information obtained bears mainly upon four questions: (1) What has been the relevance of regional migrations, especially westward migration, for upward movement among the American business elite? (2) What have been the class levels of the parents of the business elite of each generation? (3) What have been the education and (4) the participation in politics of the members of this elite?

[2] Members of the author's seminars at the University of Maryland, A. B. Conner, C. R. Ecker, R. Kolodner, A. B. Levin, Freya Mills, C. C. Packman, M. O. Shumate, L. C. Stein, P. S. Ward, M. K. White, R. Wolfson, A. I. Biggs, B. M. Biron, M. P. Conklin, S. Feldman, J. K. Freeze, N. F. Garman, L. M. Glenn, M. L. Isaacs, F. M. Kohout, P. Kolodner, R. S. Lamond, B. Margolis, E. M. Medwedeff, H. N. Miller, F. Pfeiffer, E. C. Reid, B. A. Richards, C. J. E. Servin, M. D. S. Shea, R. D. Shur, V. P. Stortz, M. Whitlow, coded and tabulated the data to be presented. We wish to thank Dumas Malone and Harris Starr, who supplied requested information about the editing of the D.A.B., and Richard Hofstadter, Frank Freidel, and Kenneth Stampp for their generosity during frequent consultations. For any deficiencies or errors in the design or presentation of the study, I am responsible.

[3] This does not necessarily imply criticism of the D.A.B. as a source for sociological work on collective biographies. It is not known how many of these deficiencies are due to the schedulers' lack of persistence and how much relevant information was actually not in the D.A.B. On many items which we have run, the schedules were rechecked against the biographies for that one item. In several cases this slightly increased our usable returns.

In order to answer these questions for various periods, we have divided the men studied into seven generations.[4] The first generation, born between 1570 and 1699, was Colonial. In the second generation many members outlived the Revolution, but as a group the generation was mainly pre-Revolutionary. During the Revolutionary years they ranged from their forties to their seventies. The third generation, born 1730–1759, was the younger Revolutionary generation. At the time of the Revolution, they ranged from pre-adolescence to their forties. The men of the fourth generation, born 1760–1789, were from twelve to forty-one years of age when Jefferson took office. This generation apparently profited from American neutrality during the Napoleonic wars. The men of the fifth generation, born 1790–1819, were among those who began the first large migrations beyond the Alleghenies; this group also includes the first "industrial" generation of American businessmen. The sixth generation, born 1820–1849, fought the Civil War and earned such fortunes as it provided. Among its members were many of the so-called robber barons. The seventh generation, born 1850–1879, largely escaped the Civil War but rose to eminence during its economic aftermath. This last generation was somewhat between the ages of forty and seventy during the First World War.

[4] These generations were determined in conference with three professional historians, each of whom was requested to set up a periodization for the American social structure. Approximately thirty to thirty-five years were then subtracted from the middle years of these pivotal eras and treated as the middle year of birth for each of our generations. These units were checked for each of the tables: all data were tabulated by decades, and each three decades making up a single generation were inspected. The decade structure of each generation appeared to be satisfactorily homogeneous in each of the tabulations. The first period, 1570-1699, was rather arbitrarily determined by the distribution of our data and the range of the earlier generations. The births occurring during this period are evenly distributed over the 120 years. The seventh generation is somewhat biased in favor of short-lived persons and anything associated with this fact: it contains more persons born in the fifties than in the sixties and more born in the sixties than in the seventies.

## TABLE I

## THE AMERICAN BUSINESS ELITE: PLACE OF ORIGIN (O) AND OF SUCCESS (S) BY TIME OF BIRTH, 1570-1879

### Generations by Time of Birth

| Place | 1570-1699 O | 1570-1699 S | 1700-1729 O | 1700-1729 S | 1730-1759 O | 1730-1759 S | 1760-1789 O | 1760-1789 S | 1790-1819 O | 1790-1819 S | 1820-1849 O | 1820-1849 S | 1850-1879 O | 1850-1879 S | Total O | Total S |
|---|---|---|---|---|---|---|---|---|---|---|---|---|---|---|---|---|
| New England | 15.7% | 52.9% | 32.6% | 39.1% | 35.9% | 33.1% | 43.3% | 30.6% | 43.0% | 23.6% | 25.2% | 15.5% | 17.0% | 9.1% | 32.0% | 22.2% |
| Mid. Atlantic | 3.9 | 29.4 | 32.6 | 47.8 | 26.5 | 45.2 | 17.8 | 31.2 | 28.4 | 38.4 | 37.1 | 39.5 | 26.1 | 39.4 | 29.2 | 38.7 |
| East N. Central | — | — | — | — | — | 1.6 | 1.3 | 4.5 | 2.9 | 12.1 | 8.9 | 15.6 | 19.4 | 24.3 | 6.2 | 12.2 |
| West N. Central | — | 2.0 | — | 2.2 | — | 2.4 | 2.6 | 5.1 | 1.5 | 6.8 | 1.0 | 5.1 | 7.3 | 3.0 | 1.9 | 4.9 |
| South Atlantic | 2.0 | 11.8 | 6.5 | 10.9 | 8.7 | 12.1 | 10.9 | 12.7 | 9.7 | 9.7 | 5.5 | 6.7 | 10.9 | 9.1 | 8.1 | 9.2 |
| East S. Central | — | — | — | — | — | — | 0.6 | 3.8 | 4.1 | 1.7 | 4.7 | 4.3 | 3.0 | 0.6 | 3.2 | 2.4 |
| West S. Central | — | — | — | — | 0.8 | 0.8 | 0.6 | 2.5 | — | 2.2 | 0.1 | 0.9 | 3.0 | 4.2 | 0.5 | 1.8 |
| Mountain | — | — | — | — | — | — | — | 1.3 | 0.2 | 1.0 | — | 3.9 | 2.4 | 6.1 | 0.3 | 2.5 |
| Pacific | — | — | — | — | — | — | 0.6 | 2.6 | — | 3.6 | — | 7.9 | — | 3.0 | 0.0 | 4.3 |
| Foreign | 78.4 | 3.9 | 28.3 | — | 28.1 | 4.8 | 22.3 | 5.7 | 10.2 | 0.9 | 17.5 | 0.6 | 10.9 | 1.2 | 18.6 | 1.8 |
| Total | 100.0 | 100.0 | 100.0 | 100.0 | 100.0 | 100.0 | 100.0 | 100.0 | 100.0 | 100.0 | 100.0 | 100.0 | 100.0 | 100.0 | 100.0 | 100.0 |
| Total Careers | 51 | | 46 | | 124 | | 157 | | 412 | | 509 | | 165 | | 1,464 | |

Note: For this table, as well as Tables 2 and 4, the standard errors of proportion are larger for the first two columns than for the remaining five. Critical ratios, however, indicate that the differences between the first and second columns are significant.

**II**

Regional movement was studied by comparing in the careers of the elite their place of origin[5] and the place of their success. "Success" has been defined as the first upward move from the level of the first regular jobs.[6] This rather broad conception was used in order to give full play to the migrations, in order not to cut down our usable sample, and because a good many of those extracted from the upper class took rather low first "regular" jobs.

Table 1 gives an over-all picture of the places of origin and success by regional divisions. Thirty-two per cent of the business elite originated in New England, whereas 22.2 per cent succeeded there. A great many of the New Englanders migrated to the Middle Atlantic states, where a total of 38.7 per cent succeeded but where only 29.2 per cent orginated. In the Middle Atlantic area there were always more successes than origins.[7] It is the modal locality of success for the American business elite.

When regional movement is examined for each of the seven generations, changes in the pattern of migration become apparent. See Tables 2, 3, 4. In Tables 2 and 3, East includes New England, the Middle Atlantic, and South Atlantic states; all others of the ten census divisions are defined as West.

The only two patterns of migration and upward mobility that show a continual rise in the proportions of origins are

[5] "Place or origin" means the place of birth unless (a) the family of the subject moved before the subject was ten years of age, or (b) before the subject's dependence upon the family was terminated; occasionally, (c) locality of elementary schooling was taken as the indicator of place of origin. The decisive idea which guided us in all doubtful cases of origin was where the subject "grew up." "Place of origin" thus means the locality of the major preoccupational biography.

[6] This does not preclude the possibility that these first jobs were already high. Ascent or success does not necessarily mean "from poor to rich," but is relative to the beginning levels. See Table 3, however, for cross tabulations of class origin, migrations, and upward mobility.

[7] The data on Table 1, like the other tables in this report, are broken down by generations, as defined in footnote 4 above.

West-West and West-East (Table 2). Were we able to correct our figures for general population growth, these

TABLE 2

THE AMERICAN BUSINESS ELITE: PLACE OF ORIGIN AND OF SUCCESS,

BY TIME OF BIRTH, 1570–1879

MOVEMENTS EAST AND WEST*

| Place of Origin and Success | | Generations by Time of Birth | | | | | | | Total |
|---|---|---|---|---|---|---|---|---|---|
| O | S | 1570-1699 | 1700-1729 | 1730-1759 | 1760-1789 | 1790-1819 | 1820-1849 | 1850-1879 | |
| East | East | 20.4% | 71.7% | 70.3% | 65.6% | 64.1% | 50.6% | 43.6% | 56.5% |
| East | West | — | — | 1.7 | 8.8 | 17.0 | 17.0 | 10.4 | 13.0 |
| West | West | — | — | 0.8 | 4.7 | 7.6 | 11.6 | 25.8 | 9.7 |
| West | East | — | — | — | 0.7 | 1.0 | 3.2 | 9.2 | 2.5 |
| Foreign | East | 77.6 | 26.1 | 23.1 | 12.8 | 7.4 | 8.3 | 6.1 | 12.4 |
| Foreign | West | 2.0 | 2.2 | 4.1 | 7.4 | 2.9 | 9.3 | 4.9 | 5.9 |
| Total | | 100.0 | 100.0 | 100.0 | 100.0 | 100.0 | 100.0 | 100.0 | 100.0 |

* *East* includes New England, the Middle Atlantic, and the South Atlantic. All others of the ten census divisions are defined as *West*. The totals in this table are less than those in Table I because the few "foreign successes" are not here included. The table comprises 98.4 per cent of the total elite from the D.A.B.

two patterns would, in part, be explained by the rising proportion of population in the West.[8]

Inspection of the first two generations reveals a rather sudden drop in the proportion of foreign origin and a quick monopoly of elite chances for eastern-originated American

[8] The population and the economic character of the divisions and regions used in the tables changed greatly during the time span with which we are concerned. Ideally, these difficulties of changing and heterogenous categories might be overcome by progressive redefinitions of the regions in terms of such factors as population density. Such a refinement would lower the proportions of origins and successes in "the West." In view of the small numbers in our sample and the chaotic and unreliable conditions of population statistics for the earlier periods, such precision is not entirely possible, and the attempt would seem mislocated. But we have compared the percentage of total successes in the West with the percentage of total population in the West. The resulting figures show that the former exceeded the latter only from around 1780 to 1810 (for the generation, that is, born 1760-1789); thereafter the latter exceeded the former.

businessmen (Table 2). This might have been due to the fact that the time span for the first "generation" is 120 years, whereas the second generation covers only 29 years. But on examining the distribution of cases by decades in these two time units, we find that they are very evenly distributed in this respect. The very large proportion of foreign-originated businessmen which the D.A.B. includes for our first generation lowers the probability of a bias in favor of American-originated men for our second generation, since we have no reason to suppose a sudden shift in the criteria for inclusion. Nor is there evidence of any uneven bias in the availability of domestic and foreign records. Therefore, the quick development of such large differences is probably not due to the bias of our categories, to the bias of the D.A.B. selection, or to sampling errors.[9] They appear to be characteristics of historical reality.

In Table 3 we present the fragmentary results which our

TABLE 3

THE AMERICAN BUSINESS ELITE: PLACE OF ORIGIN AND OF SUCCESS,

AND EXTRACTION BY SOCIAL CLASS, 1570–1879

Extraction by Social Class

| Place of Origin and Success | | 1760-1849 | | 1850-1879 | |
| O | S | Upper Class | Lower Class | Upper Class | Lower Class |
|---|---|---|---|---|---|
| East | East | 65.2% | 52.3% | 50.5% | 41.9% |
| East | West | 13.3 | 18.6 | 10.3 | 9.3 |
| West | West | 8.7 | 8.7 | 23.7 | 25.6 |
| West | East | 2.2 | 1.2 | 8.3 | 4.7 |
| Foreign | East | 6.2 | 10.2 | 3.1 | 11.6 |
| Foreign | West | 4.4 | 9.0 | 4.1 | 6.9 |
| Total* | | 100.00 | 100.0 | 100.0 | 100.0 |

* This table comprises 78.9 per cent of the elite born in the periods involved.

data allow us of a cross tabulation of class of origin[10] and migration pattern of success. For the period from 1570 to 1759, our sample is so cut down by this cross tabulation that we can furnish no statistically reliable information.

[9] The critical ratio, C.R., $= \dfrac{D_{p1 \cdot p2}}{O_{p1 \cdot p2}}$ , of 20.4% and 71.7% is 18.4.

[10] For a more adequate conception of class of origin, see Table 5.

If we combine the next three generations, which altogether cover the period from 1760 to 1849,[11] we see that 18.6 per cent of these men originated in the eastern lower class and migrated West to success; whereas only 13.3 per cent of eastern upper-class extraction migrated to western success.[12] For this middle period, 9.0 per cent originated outside the United States in lower classes and went to the West for their success; whereas only 4.4 per cent originated outside the United States in the upper classes and migrated to western areas. If these proportions are compared with those for the last generation, the members of which came to the approximate age of thirty-five around the year 1900, we see that the eastern lower-class subjects did not migrate to the West in quite so high a proportion (9.3 per cent) as did the eastern upper-class subjects (10.3 per cent); and, furthermore, that the West was no longer so much a cradle of lower-class foreign-born successes as it appears to have been during the middle period. Six and nine-tenths per cent of the generation was lower-class foreign born who succeeded in the West, whereas 4.1 per cent was upper-class foreign born who migrated to western areas and there achieved success.

Tables 2 and 3 suggest that for only a relatively small proportion of the business elite was migration to the West relevant for success. In this small group, more of those who were born in the eastern lower classes during the years 1760–1849 took the journey than did those who were born in the eastern upper classes. At all times for which we have information, these latter show more of a tendency to remain in the East, clustered around the established centers of economic power and manipulation.

Table 4 displays a pattern in the movements of those who originated and those who succeeded in the South as well as in the movements of those who originated and those who succeeded in the North. Those originating in the South and succeeding in the North form a similar propor-

<hr>

[11] The three generations composing this time period are homogeneous with regard to the items considered here.

[12] The critical ratio of these two proportions indicates that the chances are 98 in 100 that this difference is statistically significant.

tion of the total as do those originating in the North and succeeding in the South. However, since the total number originating in the South, regardless of place of success, is much smaller than the number originating in the North, the migrations out of the South and to success in the North form, for the entire historical period, a much higher ratio of migration to origin base. Half as many originating in the South migrated to northern success as originated in the South and succeeded there; whereas only one in every eighteen of those who originated in the North migrated to southern success. Contrary to the general trend, both the

TABLE 4

THE AMERICAN BUSINESS ELITE: PLACE OF ORIGIN AND SUCCESS,

BY TIME OF BIRTH, 1570–1879

MOVEMENTS NORTH AND SOUTH*

| Place of Origin and Success | | Generations by Time of Birth | | | | | | | Total |
|---|---|---|---|---|---|---|---|---|---|
| O | S | 1570-1699 | 1700-1729 | 1730-1759 | 1760-1789 | 1790-1819 | 1820-1849 | 1850-1879 | |
| North | North | 18.4% | 65.2% | 64.7% | 64.5% | 71.5% | 70.4% | 64.4% | 66.8% |
| North | South | — | — | — | 3.6 | 4.6 | 3.8 | 6.7 | 3.7 |
| South | South | — | 6.5 | 6.7 | 9.2 | 8.8 | 7.9 | 8.7 | 7.9 |
| South | North | 2.0 | — | 2.6 | 2.8 | 4.6 | 2.2 | 8.7 | 3.7 |
| Foreign | North | 67.4 | 23.9 | 19.3 | 12.1 | 9.5 | 13.7 | 10.7 | 14.8 |
| Foreign | South | 12.2 | 4.4 | 6.7 | 7.8 | 1.0 | 2.0 | 0.8 | 3.1 |
| Total | | 100.0 | 100.0 | 100.0 | 100.0 | 100.0 | 100.0 | 100.0 | 100.0 |

* *North* includes New England and the Middle Atlantic, East North Central, and West North Central states. *South* includes the South Atlantic, East South Central, and West South Central states. Cases involving the remaining divisions are omitted in this tabulation. The table comprises 91.5 per cent of the total elite from the D.A.B.

North-South and the South-North patterns of upward mobility decline for the sixth generation, 1820–1849. This is apparently due to the Civil War, as the members of this generation were approximately twenty-five to thirty years of age during the war. Contrary to expectations of the time, these figures indicate that very few of the northern-originated business elite made the first major step up by going south during reconstruction.

Although we have plotted the movements, the information which has been presented does not enable us to satisfy our interest in the causal relevance of westward migration for upward mobility among the business elite. Certainly we are not entitled to answer the even more general question of the relevance of the "frontier" for success patterns in the United States. There are three general reasons for this:

(i) Our sample includes only "elite" businessmen. From it we cannot learn anything directly about other fields of success, such as farming, nor about the middle and lower ranges of success in any field, including business. Nor do we know how much more successful, or how much quicker, if at all, the successes of those who went west would have been had they remained in the East.

(ii) We cannot present the total demographic picture with which to "correct" our portrait of the migrations of businessmen. By relating the proportion of the total population in the West at the approximate year of each generation's success with the proportion of East to West migrants among the business elite, we can obtain a comparison of total western successes with total western population. Such a procedure does not, however, differentiate the sources of the total western population, whether migrants from the East or abroad, or whether of western origin. Only the total western successes, regardless of origins, may be very crudely compared with the proportion of the general population in the West at the times of their successes.

(iii) Our data permit us to determine only something of the direct effects of westward migration upon the careers of members of the business elite. They do not enable us to say anything about the indirect effects of "the West" upon their upward mobilities. These indirect effects—the influence on business prosperity of an expanding market open for domestic exploitation, of governmentally cheap natural resources, of the unorganized generosity of immigrant labor—these may very well have been more crucial than any personal migration in the upward reach of the business elite. These tables focus upon businessmen. We are not studying business, nor are the data thus far presented neces-

sarily adequate indices of the economic mechanics of the
upper-class situation. For such matters, analyses of mass
economic data are more appropriate than analyses of the
careers of the elite.

We cannot, for example, infer from the very small number of successes made outside the United States (see Table
2) that this small a proportion of business successes has
been due to economic activities and conditions abroad.
Rather, the figures indicate that the business elite as persons did not travel abroad and there experience their first
major upward mobility. The same caution applies to the
domestic patterns of migration. As Thomas Jefferson wrote,
"Merchants have no country. The mere spot they stand on
does not constitute so strong an attachment as that from
which they draw their gains." [13]

## III

From what class and occupational levels did the business
elite originate? Were there higher proportions of "self-
elevating" men in some generations than in others? Did the
"self-elevating" men employ education as a vehicle for their
ascent, or were educational advantages monopolized by
those born in the upper classes? What were the types and
levels of education attained by various generations of American businessmen? What were the political connections of
the business elite? Are class of origin, education attained,
occupation of father, and political office held interrelated?
Are the different generations characterized by significantly
different constellations of these attributes? Tentative answers to these questions may be discerned from Tables
5-10.

The class of origin of the American business elite is consistently upper, both absolutely and in proportion to the
number of fathers in the various class levels of the population. Table 5 suggests that *of the total elite only 10.4 per
cent came from the lower class,* while an additional 25.9
per cent were born in families of the lower-middle class.

[13] Quoted by A. J. Nock, *Jefferson* (New York: Harcourt, Brace
and Company, 1926), p. 108.

These figures, and all those presented here which involve class origins, drastically understate the fact of the overwhelmingly upper-class production of upper-class businessmen; for at all times in the history of the United States there have been, of course, vastly more lower- than upper-class families. We cannot compute the relative contributions to the business elite of the several economic levels, for no adequate occupational statistics are available before the latter nineteenth century. When we consider, however, that probably over 90 per cent of the eighteenth-century population consisted of quite small farmers, laborers, indentured servants, and slaves,[14] that probably the nineteenth-century population contained a similar proportion consisting of small farmers, native and immigrant laborers, and slaves, the meaning of these figures on the class extraction of elite businessmen stands out quite clearly. The best statistical chance of becoming a member of the business elite is to be born into it.

Although this general result contradicts various myths and propaganda, it further confirms data previously gathered on various elite groups and is quite in line with expectations derived from competent economic analyses.[15]

A pilot study of 328 D.A.B. capitalists, financiers, and bankers indicates that only during one period of birth, 1800-1839, did the chances of lower-class boys to enter the business elite approach those of boys born in the upper classes.[16] During this middle period, about one third of the business elite were from the lower class, whereas about one third were from each of the two remaining classes used. Before and after this early nineteenth-century period of birth, well over half of the elite businessmen were from the upper of the three classes.

---

[14] In 1763, probably about one third of the people of North America were "legally unfree." Evarts B. Greene, *The Revolutionary Generation, 1763-1790* (New York: The Macmillan Company, 1943), p. 75.

[15] See P. Sorokin, *Social Mobility* (New York and London: Harper and Brothers, 1927), for various references to this literature.

[16] Prepared by Miss M. G. Stavropoulos and Miss K. M. Wood in "The Sociology of Professions" at the University of Maryland, 1943; unpublished.

## TABLE 5

### THE AMERICAN BUSINESS ELITE: EDUCATIONAL LEVEL AND EXTRACTION BY SOCIAL CLASS, 1570–1879

#### Generations by Time of Birth

| Class of Extraction | 1570-1699 | 1700-1729 | 1730-1759 | 1760-1789 | 1790-1819 | 1820-1849 | 1850-1879 | Total |
|---|---|---|---|---|---|---|---|---|
| Upper | 38.9% ⎫ 80.6% | 69.0% ⎫ 85.7% | 42.9% ⎫ 77.9% | 23.6% ⎫ 60.2% | 25.6% ⎫ 62.8% | 19.8% ⎫ 57.0% | 41.3% ⎫ 70.7% | 28.3% ⎫ 63.7% |
| Upper Middle | 41.7 ⎭ | 16.7 ⎭ | 35.0 ⎭ | 36.6 ⎭ | 37.2 ⎭ | 37.2 ⎭ | 29.4 ⎭ | 35.4 ⎭ |
| Lower Middle | 16.7 ⎫ 19.4 | 9.5 ⎫ 14.3% | 14.3 ⎫ 22.1 | 28.4 ⎫ 39.8 | 29.4 ⎫ 37.2 | 29.6 ⎫ 43.0 | 18.1 ⎫ 29.3% | 25.9 ⎫ 36.3 |
| Lower | 2.7 ⎭ | 4.8 ⎭ | 7.8 ⎭ | 11.4 ⎭ | 7.8 ⎭ | 13.4 ⎭ | 11.2 ⎭ | 10.4 ⎭ |
| Total* | 100.0 | 100.0 | 100.0 | 100.0 | 100.0 | 100.0 | 100.0 | 100.0 |

* This table comprises 78.8 per cent of the total elite from the D.A.B.

*A more sweeping picture of the trends suggested by Table 5 may be obtained by combining the two upper classes into "upper;" the two lower classes into "lower;"* combining generations one, two, and three; generations four, five, and six; and comparing these two periods with the last generation. Of the men born between 1570 and 1759, 80.6 per cent were from upper-class homes. Of the men born between 1760 and 1849, only 59.5 per cent were from the upper classes; whereas of those born between 1850 and 1879, 70.7 per cent originated in the upper economic levels of the American social structure.

The primary indicator of "class of origin," if more definite information was not available, was the "occupation of father." This was not, however, the only basis of classification. Other subsidiary indicators included: inheritances of property, class level of mother if it involved business holdings later used by the future elite, and the financial aid of other relatives. Education was taken as an indicator only if private schools known to be expensive were attended or if private tutors were employed for considerable lengths of time. Cases of the dead father and the struggling mother were tallied lower class. If a member of the textile elite was the son of a poor father but went to work with an uncle who owned several large textile factories, we tallied upper class. The first position held by the subject was sometimes used as a subsidiary indicator but only if it was taken during youth and involved the ownership of large property. For each of the 1,155 cases for which sufficient information was available, the class of origin was discerned by the pattern of the primary and the several secondary indicators.[17] The schedules were edited twice—each time independently—for this item.

Table 6 shows the occupations of the fathers of members of the business elite. We are able to add information on an eighth generation, 1879-1907, which practically completes these materials for the total span of United States history. Most of the qualifications made in connection with class ex-

[17] For the technique of "discernment," see Mirra Komarovsky, *The Unemployed Man and His Family* (New York: The Dryden Press, 1940), Appendix 1.

traction are also relevant for this table on the occupations of fathers. We must emphasize that figures on the occupational composition of the total population at the varying times of birth of members of the elite are not available for the first six generations. This table undoubtedly overstates the relative productivity of the laboring and farming occupations and understates the proportions from business and

TABLE 6

THE AMERICAN BUSINESS ELITE: OCCUPATIONS OF THE FATHERS, 1570–1879

Generations by Time of Birth

| Occupation of Father | 1570-1699 | 1700-1729 | 1730-1759 | 1760-1789 | 1790-1819 | 1820-1849 | 1850-1879 | 1879-1907* | TOTAL† |
|---|---|---|---|---|---|---|---|---|---|
| Profession | 29.2% | 14.8% | 6.5% | 14.1% | 18.1% | 22.6% | 18.7% | 12.6% | 18.7% |
| Business | 33.3 | 63.0 | 67.7 | 53.3 | 29.3 | 35.5 | 47.7 | 63.1 | 40.0 |
| Public Official | 12.5 | 18.5 | 9.7 | 6.5 | 7.6 | 3.9 | 4.7 | — | 6.4 |
| Farming | 4.2 | 3.7 | 12.9 | 18.5 | 34.9 | 23.2 | 21.5 | 7.6 | 23.8 |
| Skilled Craft | 20.8 | — | 3.2 | 7.6 | 5.5 | 10.6 | 2.8 | 7.9 | 7.3 |
| Unskilled and Semiskilled | — | — | — | — | 3.8 | 2.6 | 3.7 | 2.7 | 2.5 |
| Clerical and Salesmen | — | — | — | — | 0.8 | 1.6 | 0.9 | 6.1 | 0.9 |
| Total | 100.0 | 100.0 | 100.0 | 100.0 | 100.0 | 100.0 | 100.0 | 100.0 | 100.0 |

\* Recomputed from Taussig and Joslyn, *American Business Leaders*, p. 312, Table A-4. Our category, "public official," was not used by Taussig and Joslyn. We have computed "business" from their "minor executive," "major executive," "owner of large business," and "owner of small business." Carl Joslyn has kindly examined these operations made on his data. It will be noticed that only in the cases of "farming" and "clerical" do the Taussig and Joslyn data perhaps violate the trends in our own figures, and these cases are certainly the ones most likely to be drastically influenced by shifts in the total occupied population. This table comprises 58.6 per cent of the total elite from the D.A.B.

† This total column does not include the Taussig and Joslyn data in the eighth generation.

the professions. We may, however, inspect the internal composition of the occupational origins of the business elite by the various generations.

These figures tend generally to confirm our findings on class of origin. In each of the generations, except one, 1790-1819, business and the professions produced the majority of the business elite.

*For all generations, 40.4 per cent of the elite are derived from businessmen alone.* For those born between *1790 and 1819, however, only 47.5 per cent* were derived from business *and* the professions. This generation attained the

## TABLE 7

## THE AMERICAN BUSINESS ELITE: TYPE OF HIGHEST LEVEL OF EDUCATION, 1570–1879

### Generations by Time of Birth

| Highest Level of Education | 1570–1699 | 1700–1729 | 1730–1759 | 1760–1789 | 1790–1819 | 1820–1849 | 1850–1879 | TOTAL |
|---|---|---|---|---|---|---|---|---|
| College Degree | 27.8% | 28.6% | 12.0% | 10.9% | 13.8% | 20.0% | 27.4% | 18.2% |
| 1–3 Years College | 33.3 | 9.5 | 18.7 | 8.7 | 10.0 | 17.9 | 25.3 | 15.4 |
| "Private School" or Tutor | 33.3 | 23.8 | 8.0 | 6.5 | 3.0 | 3.6 | 5.5 | 5.0 |
| Business School or Law Office | 5.5 | | 4.0 | 2.2 | 2.7 | 2.2 | 4.2 | 2.7 |
| "Good" but Unspecified | 16.7 | 4.8 | 12.0 | 3.3 | 5.9 | 5.3 | 0.7 | 5.3 |
| *(subtotal)* | 83.3% | 66.7% | 54.7% | 31.6% | 35.4% | 49.0% | 63.1% | 46.6% |
| High School or Academy | 16.7 | 9.5 | 6.7 | 14.1 | 19.4 | 23.0 | 16.4 | 18.7 |
| Grammar School | | 9.5 | 8.0 | 17.4 | 22.3 | 14.3 | 15.1 | 16.3 |
| Apprentice Only | | 4.8 | 21.3 | 20.7 | 8.2 | 5.3 | | 7.9 |
| "Negligible" | | 9.5 | 9.3 | 16.2 | 14.7 | 8.4 | 5.4 | 10.5 |
| *(subtotal)* | 16.7 | 33.3 | 45.3 | 68.4 | 64.6 | 51.0 | 36.9 | 53.4 |
| Total* | 100.0 | 100.0 | 100.0 | 100.0 | 100.0 | 100.0 | 100.0 | 100.0 |

* This table comprises 78.2 per cent of the total elite from the D.A.B.

*average age of thirty-five at the approximate year 1840.*
This and the preceding and the following generations (comprising the total span 1760-1849) contain the modal proportions of the sons of farmers and skilled laborers. This span of years also contains the highest proportion of men of lower-class origin to enter the elite.

The drop in the proportions of farmers and laborers after the 1840's is apparently absorbed, directly or intermediately, by the business strata. Of those business elite born between 1879 and 1907, only 18.2 per cent originated in farming *and* laboring families.

In Table 7 it may be seen that 18.2 per cent of all members of the American business elite have been graduates of colleges and that a total of 33.3 per cent have been enrolled for some period of time in some college. When we consider that in 1940, when the proportion of persons over twenty-five years of age who had been enrolled in college was at its historical peak, only 10.0 per cent of these adults had been enrolled in college,[18] it is clear that the business elite has been educated well above the level of the general adult population. If the top five educational categories in Table 7 are summed and called "high" and the total of the last four categories are summed up to "low," it appears that *46.6 per cent of the total business elite* was "highly educated." [19]

Table 7 shows that the *least well-educated members* of the business elite *were of the two generations which cover the birth years 1760-1819.* These individuals came to the approximate age of *thirty-five from around 1810 to 1840.* A higher proportion of the members of these "middle

[18] Sixteenth Census, "United States Summary" (Washington, 1943), Table 6.

[19] That the D.A.B. sample is not biased toward including businessmen of higher education is perhaps suggested by the Taussig and Joslyn educational figures. In their sample, big businessmen actually in the higher offices of business organizations in 1928 were educated as follows: 31.9 per cent, college graduates; 13.4 percent, college nongraduates; 28.0 per cent, high school or equivalent; 25.7 per cent, grammar school; and 1.0 per cent, none. F. W. Taussig and C. S. Joslyn, *American Business Leaders* (New York: The Macmillan Company, 1932), p. 162, Table 37.

period" generations received only a "negligible" education, were apprentices only, attended only grammar school, high school, or academy.

The categories used in these tables are certainly not of the best; they were more or less determined by the condition of the biographical accounts. The categories are geared closely enough to these data to permit reliable tallying and yet are abstracted enough to permit comparisons and allow a general picture of the changing educational situation of the American business elite.

If we cross-tabulate the class of origin with the education attained (Table 8), we are able to find out the extent to which the lower-class subjects were able to use education as a vehicle for their upward climb.

Of those business elite who originated in upper-class homes 65.7 per cent obtained a "higher education." The range across the various generations is from 50.0 per cent to 79.2 per cent. Only 19.8 per cent of lower-class extraction were during their youth educated to the same high level, the range of the various generations being from none to 37.5 per cent. This highest proportion of the lowly born who received a higher education occurred in the generation which came to the approximate age of thirty-five in 1780.[20] Table 8 suggests that about one fifth of the lower-class men used higher education in their upward climb, that those from the upper class were better educated during the Colonial period and the latter nineteenth century than during the middle years of United States history, and that there is a trend in the later generations for a greater proportion of those originating in the lower or the upper classes to obtain a higher education. Those of upper-class extraction have had better educational chances, whereas at all times the majority of those born poor who became business elite rose without benefit of higher education.

[20] The total number of cases from which this 37.5 per cent was computed is rather small; the figure is quite unstable.

## TABLE 8

### THE AMERICAN BUSINESS ELITE: EDUCATIONAL LEVEL AND EXTRACTION BY SOCIAL CLASS, 1570-1879

Extraction by Social Class and Generations

| Education Attained* | 1570-1699 | | 1700-1729 | | 1730-1759 | | 1760-1789 | | 1790-1819 | | 1820-1849 | | 1850-1879 | | Total | |
|---|---|---|---|---|---|---|---|---|---|---|---|---|---|---|---|---|
| | Upper | Lower | Upper | Lower | Upper | Lower | Upper | Lower | Upper | Lower | Upper | Lower | Upper | Lower | Upper | Lower |
| Higher | 73.3% | | 6.9% | | 74.4% | 37.5% | 50.0% | 18.4% | 55.3% | 13.4% | 69.6% | 20.7% | 79.2% | 23.2% | 65.7% | 19.8% |
| High School or Below | 26.7 | 100.0 | 38.1 | 100.0 | 25.6 | 62.5 | 50.0 | 81.6 | 44.7 | 86.6 | 30.4 | 79.3 | 20.8 | 71.8 | 34.3 | 80.2 |
| Total | 100.0 | 100.0 | 100.0 | 100.0 | 100.0 | 100.0 | 100.0 | 100.0 | 100.0 | 100.0 | 100.0 | 100.0 | 100.0 | 100.0 | 100.0 | 100.0 |

* "Higher" means the sum of the first five categories in Table 7. "High school or below" comprises the last four categories in Table 7. This table comprises 67.5 per cent of the 1,464 total cases.

**I V**

Eminent American businessmen have participated quite heavily in the political life of the United States. They have held public offices in local, state, and federal administrations. These offices range from sheriff of a small county to Secretary of State. Two facts stand out in Table 9: first, that *45.7 per cent of the eminent businessmen in the* Dictionary of American Biography *held political offices during the course of United States history;* second, *that after around 1780 the proportion of business elite holding office dropped very sharply and remained on a lower level.*

The number of offices held is not, of course, an adequate measure of political influence or participation. We included in "office" party posts of consequence, but no distinction was made in our tabulations between elected and appointed positions. Most of the offices appear to have been of rather high importance. Because these tabulations omit entirely pressure-group activity, lobbying, the hiring and financial backing of political agents, and other less obvious forms of political activity, our figures underestimate the extent of "political participation" of the business elite. This fact makes all the more impressive the high proportion of business elite who actually held offices.

The political elite and the business elite have apparently overlapped to a large degree, and "laissez faire" has not at any time worked in reverse. Elite businessmen have intervened in the political process in decisively high proportions.[21]

An explanation of the trends in office holding across the various generations has to account for the sharp drop between the third and fourth generations (birth date 1760) and the lower plateau for the latter three or four generations (since around 1790). This drop seems to occur about the time of the Revolution, when the composition of the politi-

[21] Our schedules on "The American Political Elite" are not yet complete enough to permit a cross check on this. We are particularly interested in the type and number of governmental officials whose departments have to do with the regulations of business and who are mobile between public and private structures.

## TABLE 9

### THE AMERICAN BUSINESS ELITE: NUMBER OF POLITICAL OFFICES HELD, 1570-1879

#### Generations by Time of Birth

| Number of Offices Held | 1570-1699 | 1700-1729 | 1730-1759 | 1760-1789 | 1790-1819 | 1820-1849 | 1850-1879 | TOTAL |
|---|---|---|---|---|---|---|---|---|
| Three or more | 45.09% } 68.6% | 51.11% } 68.9% | 50.40% } 71.2% | 20.26% } 46.4% | 18.67% } 44.2% | 17.8% } 38.3% | 11.45% } 39.2% | 22.36% } 45.7% |
| One or two | 23.53 | 17.77 | 20.80 | 26.14 | 25.55 | 20.5 | 27.71 | 23.39 |
| None at all | 31.37 | 31.11 | 28.80 | 53.59 | 55.77 | 61.7 | 60.84 | 54.25 |
| Total* | 100.0 | 100.0 | 100.0 | 100.0 | 100.0 | 100.0 | 100.0 | 100.0 |

* This table comprises 99.6 per cent of the total elite from the D.A.B.

## TABLE 10

### THE AMERICAN BUSINESS ELITE: OFFICE HOLDING AND EXTRACTION BY SOCIAL CLASS, 1570-1879

#### Extraction by Class and Generations

| Office Holding | 1570-1699 | | 1700-1729 | | 1730-1759 | | 1760-1789 | | 1790-1819 | | 1820-1849 | | 1850-1879 | | Total | |
|---|---|---|---|---|---|---|---|---|---|---|---|---|---|---|---|---|
| | Upper | Lower | Upper | Lower | Upper | Lower | Upper | Lower | Upper | Lower | Upper | Lower | Upper | Lower | Upper | Lower |
| Held office | 75.9% | 28.6% | 72.2% | 66.7% | 81.1% | 58.8% | 52.2% | 45.8% | 45.0% | 42.1% | 35.9% | 37.6% | 43.6% | 31.1% | 48.1% | 40.3% |
| Held none | 24.1 | 71.4 | 27.8 | 33.3 | 18.9 | 41.2 | 47.3 | 54.2 | 55.0 | 57.9 | 64.1 | 62.4 | 56.4 | 68.9 | 51.9 | 59.7 |
| Total* | 100.0 | 100.0 | 100.0 | 100.0 | 100.0 | 100.0 | 100.0 | 100.0 | 100.0 | 100.0 | 100.0 | 100.0 | 100.0 | 100.0 | 100.0 | 100.0 |

* This table comprises 77.2 per cent of the total elite from the D.A.B.

cal elite probably shifted from foreign born to native born. Since businessmen are reported to have played a large role in setting up the new political institutions, the drop in the proportion of office-holding businessmen seems difficult to understand—if, indeed, our sample is adequate on this point. It may be suggested that during the Colonial period a considerable proportion of the governors' councils were members of the business elite.[22] These councils ignored territorial representation. The new state upper houses, which were based on territorial representation, tended to include fewer of the business elite, who were clustered in the urban centers. Our data do not allow us to verify this.

If the agents of political institutions intervened in business contexts more frequently during the lifetime of the last generation, 1859-1879, we might expect more counterintervention in political institutions by the business elite. We do not have career data with which to verify this, but on the basis of other analyses for the latter periods we suppose that such data would indicate an upward trend in political participation.[23] Our figures fail to catch this because they do not include a good sample of businessmen active in the twentieth century and because the mode of relation between business and politics has changed from old-fashioned office holding to less explicit arrangements.

We do not know how many of these political offices held were occupied after the business career was more or less terminated or whether they occurred between business

[22] Cf. C. P. Nettels, *The Roots of American Civilization* (New York: F. S. Crofts and Company, 1938), pp. 311-12. In connection with our data on political office holding among the business elite, there is the possibility that the D.A.B. is biased toward including those eminent businessmen who were also eminent in other contexts, including the political. We have no way of checking this for certain. If, however, such a bias does exist, it would distort only the figures on the proportions at any given time; if we may assume that it operated constantly across the generations, the trends we have indicated might still be correct.

[23] Donald C. Blaisdell, *Economic Power and Political Pressures* (Temporary National Economic Committee, Monograph No. 26. Washington: Government Printing Office, 1941), is the latest factual account of the matter.

jumps. Therefore, we cannot definitely say whether this office holding indicates "honors" or an instrumental use of political offices within the careers of members of the business elite.

In all generations, except one, 1820-1849, members of the business elite originating in the upper class have held political offices in greater proportions than those who sprang from the lower class. Table 10 suggests that before 1780 and after 1900 the proportions from the upper class who held offices definitely exceeded those from the lower class. During the middle periods from about 1810 to 1870, the proportions of businessmen from the lower class who held offices are almost as high as those from the upper class. For the entire historical elite, it appears that members of lower-class extraction did not gain whatever advantages or honors were available through personally holding political offices to the same extent as did those from the upper class. Regardless of class extraction, however, the American business elite have held offices in considerable proportions.

### V

The problem of social mobility among businessmen is so complex that no solution could be offered without data on credit institutions, on marriages into the upper classes, on the relevance of wars and tariffs for given lines of business, and so on.[24] We have not been able to gather these data for a sufficient proportion of our 1,464 members of the business elite to handle them statistically.

If further investigation could round out the picture of opportunities for success in business, we might be able to give new meanings to "mercantilism," "laissez faire," and "monopoly capitalism." Assuming that these words refer to social structures, one might view them in terms of the careers of successful businessmen.

---

[24] Our schedule contained detailed requests for these items as well as for religious affiliations, indications on status, membership in voluntary associations, etc. The information obtained is not adequate for statistically reliable use.

For the mercantilist elite, the pattern of success might include political influence (indicated by offices, charters, and associates) *via* social status (by descent or intermarriage), and business success *via* political influence. For laissez faire, the pattern of success might involve a larger proportion of upwardly mobile persons, less (direct) political connections, and less emphasis upon social status or ancestry. Laissez faire might also mean that there is a split between the economic and the political elite, that they are no longer identical persons, that the economic elite rises somewhat at the expense of the political elite, and that connections between the two become attenuated and surreptitious.

In monopoly capitalism the pattern of success might indicate decreased chances for members of the lower classes and a return to political influence (perhaps indirect). At the top, the political and economic elite might come closer together with the common purpose of buttressing existing bureaucratic structures. However, for men trained for several generations in laissez faire ideology, this coming together might be less obvious than the structural result might lead us to expect. During crises the power connections might become stronger and more obvious; they may be legitimated in terms of the alleged "know-how" of the business elite, their lack of compensation ("dollar-a-year"), and their patriotism.

These and other items in the careers of the elite which may be hypothetically inferred from the changing political economy are supported only in a tenuous manner by the data we have available; more thorough verification cannot be made with the data we have been able to gather from the D.A.B. None of our findings, however, seems to contradict this general picture.

## VI

If we disregard the methodological qualifications which have been advanced, we may derive the following assertions about the American business elite during the several stages of its history:

The business elite of the earlier Colonial period came from abroad (78.8 per cent) and from the upper classes (80.6 per cent). Their fathers were in business (33.3 per cent), the professions (29.2 per cent), or held public office (12.5 per cent). Remaining clustered in the young cities of the northeastern coast, they also held political office (68.6 per cent) and were typically (83.3 per cent) well educated. The minority among them which came from the skilled-craft stratum (20.8 per cent) were less well educated and did not hold political office so frequently as did those from the upper classes.

The generation coming to maturity during the second third of the eighteenth century was predominantly of American origin; quite abruptly American businessmen monopolized the elite positions in this country, and the first native generation of top businessmen, along with their sons, were among the Revolutionists. They continued to originate in New England, but many of them began the pattern of migrating to the Middle Atlantic states. These first Americans were of upper-class origin (85.7 per cent), and 63.0 per cent of them were born of fathers in business, whereas 18.5 per cent had fathers who held public office. They were not quite so well educated (66.7 per cent) as their foreign-originated predecessors (83.3 per cent), but they were, of course, far above the average American in this respect. They held political office in the same proportion as the earlier men, and the minority among them from the lower classes (14.5 per cent) were less well educated and were slightly less likely to hold political office (66.7 per cent) than were the upper-class majority (72.2 per cent).

The younger Revolutionary generation, men whose ages ranged from their teens to around forty when the Revolution occurred, was similar to the preceding generation in locality and in pattern of migrations. From one fourth to one third of them were foreign born; the vast majority were from New England and the Middle Atlantic area, but almost twice as many succeeded in the Middle Atlantic states as originated there. A few of the native Americans trickled westward, and there were proportionately twice as many businessmen of foreign origin who went beyond the Alleghenies for their success as in the preceding generation.

Compared with our preceding generation, a slightly smaller proportion of the younger Revolutionary men were from the upper classes (77.9 per cent) but a higher proportion were from the homes of businessmen (67.7 per cent). There were also a larger proportion from farming families (12.9 per cent) and fewer from professional families (6.5 per cent) and from the families of public officials (9.7 per cent). It may be that a few of the sons of yeoman farmers of New England now began to succeed as businessmen in the Middle Atlantic states. This Revolutionary generation was definitely less well educated than were their predecessors; 54.7 per cent of them were "highly educated." As in all generations, those from the upper classes were definitely better educated than those of lower-class extraction. However, for almost the last time in the history of the United States, over one half (58.8 per cent) of the lower-class boys who entered the business elite came to hold political offices, although the upper-class boys still were much more likely to attain political position (81.1 per cent). As a group, the members of this generation reached the peak of all generations of American business elite in the proportion who held political office (71.2 per cent).

The members of the next three generations came to maturity during the first three quarters of the nineteenth century. They reached the age of thirty-five around 1810, 1840, and 1870. During the first two of these three generations, about 43.0 per cent originated in New England, but a high proportion of these migrated from that region; they went in large numbers to the Middle Atlantic area, and they also began to follow the population movements westward: from 8.0 per cent to 17.0 per cent of them went west to their success. The peak years in the history of the elite for success in the West of eastern migrants are 1840 and 1870. Naturally, more of the nineteenth-century elite were born in the West (11.6 per cent) in the last three generations, yet even so the proportion of western population is larger than the proportion of western successes, regardless of their origins. More of those from lower-class homes went west to success (18.6 per cent) than did those of upper-class extraction (13.3 per cent). Also, proportionately more of the relatively few originating abroad and in the lower classes went west to business success (9.0 per cent) than did those who were from foreign upper classes (4.4 per cent). Very few of the business elite of northern origin achieved their success by going south during reconstruction.

In the nineteenth century the business elite was composed of significantly more men from the lower class than was the case previously or than has been the case since. The peak year in the history of the United States in this respect was 1870. Not only were 43.0 per cent of the elite who then came to approximately thirty-five years of age born in the two lower classes, but there were also more from the upper-middle class than from the upper. This had not been the tendency in previous generations. These three nineteenth-century generations were the first and, so far, the last generations of business elite in the history of the United States to contain more than 25 or 30 per cent from the lower classes. Charles Beard has examined a "super-elite" of eleven men who performed immense business operations from 1865 to 1900; he finds that only two of the eleven built their fortunes on family inheritances and that only one obtained a higher education.[25] But this was not the proportion among the broad elite we are studying. Our tabulations fully confirm the general view that the early nineteenth century was the historical cradle of business success for those of lower-class origin. It is perhaps a comment on how much can be made from a small taste of such experience to realize that even during this peak of upward mobility, only about one third of the business elite came from the lowest of three classes, whereas this class probably contained nine tenths of the employed population.

More of the fathers of the generation coming to success around 1840 were farmers (34.9 per cent) than previously.

[25] Charles A. and Mary R. Beard, *Rise of American Civilization* (New York: The Macmillan Company, 1936), II, 173 ff.

The historical peak for the proportion whose fathers followed skilled laboring jobs (10.6 per cent) occurs around 1870.

Definitely fewer of these nineteenth-century elite were "highly educated." The low point for the businessmen's entire history is the 31.6 per cent who were highly educated: this group came to the approximate age of thirty-five in 1810. Even during this period, however, about three times as many of these from upper-class homes were highly educated than were those of lower-class extraction.

The nineteenth-century elite did not hold political office in the same high proportion as did the business elite of the eighteenth century. Yet the percentages who did hold political office range from 38.3 to 46.4 per cent. The differences between the office holding of those from the upper classes and those from the lower classes are not very great: in the early nineteenth century slightly more from the upper classes held office; in the latter part of that century, however, those from the lower classes began to hold office in higher proportions and in 1870 those from the lower classes (37.6 per cent) had a slight lead over these from the upper classes (35.9 per cent). It is generally held that the southern planters were more prone to enter Congress personally; whereas members of the business elite relied on lawyers to speak for them.[26] This may be true, but if one includes party and state offices, appointive as well as elective, it is clear that quite a high proportion of the business elite personally held office in the various phases of the governing of America.

Between the times of Jackson and Lincoln, the social status of the business elite was considerably improved. Although it is true that no class pattern of national consequence was deeply entrenched, there was a competition for status between the planter of good family and the rising merchant. *Hunt's Merchants' Magazine*, published during the middle years, glorified the "self-made merchant" as equally respectable with "the luxurious planter, the time serving politician, or the cringing office seeker."[27] A rough analysis of the content of such publications as *Hunt's* indicates that the nineteenth century was a period in which the status of the business elite rose. This competition for status, among other perhaps more material questions, was settled practically and in blood by the Civil War.

The last generation for which we have presented data came to the approximate age of success around 1900. Only 10.4 per cent of this generation migrated from the East to western success, although, naturally, more of them originated in the West and succeeded there than was previously the case. Proportionately more originated in the West and went east to success than originated in the East and succeeded in the West. A slightly higher proportion from the upper classes went west from the East (10.3 per cent) than was the case for those from the lower classes who made the trip (9.3 per cent); this reverses the nineteenth-century trend of upward mobility and migration westward.

This last generation is, in many respects, more comparable to the seventeenth- and eighteenth-century patterns than to those of the nineteenth century. A similarly high proportion came from the upper classes (70.7 per cent), and a member of the lower class had diminished chances of rising to the business heights. The fathers of this generation were overwhelmingly businessmen (47.7 per cent) or professional men (18.7 per cent) or farmers (21.5 per cent). Only 6.5 per cent of them were from homes of laborers.

They were a good deal better educated than the nineteenth-century elite, 63.1 per cent of them having obtained "higher education." Only 28.2 per cent of those from the lower classes, however, went above the high-school level, whereas 79.2 per cent of the upper classes did.

In one respect they followed the long trend of United States history: 39.2 per cent held political office. This proportion is quite in line with the gradual dropping of this trait by the nineteenth-century business elite. Those who did hold office, however, were more likely to be from the

[27] *Hunt's Merchants' Magazine,* I (September 1839), 201. Quoted by Jerome Thomases, in *Mississippi Valley Historical Review,* XXX (December 1943), 398.

upper classes (43.6 per cent) than from the lower (31.1 per cent).

The best time during the history of the United States for the poor boy ambitious for high business success to have been born was around the year 1835. Since then the proportion of those in his position who realized their hopes has definitely declined, despite the steady growth in the total numbers of the elite. The best time for a boy not able to attend college, but wishing big business success, to have been born was around 1775. Since then the proportion of his type in the business elite has declined. The eastern boy wishing business success of the higher type and going west to find it should not have been born after around 1835 if he was to have the best statistical chances.

For the whole of the United States history: the typical member of the American business elite is of northeastern origin (61.2 per cent). He did not migrate westward to success. He was definitely of the upper classes by birth (63.7 per cent) and was educated well above the level of the general population (46.6 per cent being in the "higher" category). The father of the business elite has typically (40.4 per cent) been a businessman. And 45.7 per cent of the business elite of America have held office in its various political structures.

# A LOOK AT THE WHITE COLLAR

In the 1952 political campaign, no major candidate encountered the white-collar problem. This was so despite the alleged importance of the independent vote, which is very much—although not entirely—a white-collar vote. Yet the absence of political noise does not eliminate the insistence of the issue. Alongside the farm problem and the labor problem, there is in the United States today a white-collar problem.

I do not need to stress this because we all know it. Those who are concerned with office management know it because, first—being white-collar people themselves—they are personally a part of the problem; and second—being employers or advisers to employers—they are professionally involved with the white-collar problem.

They are, in short, members of white-collar strata, and at the same time they deal with the personnel issues of the white-collar employee. Of course, these two problems overlap; in fact, they are merely different ways of looking at the white-collar people. Yet they *are* different problems.

## I

What is the personnel problem? Obviously the specific problems of different companies differ quite markedly; therefore, advice and counsel about them must be based on individual measurement and so be custom-tailored. For example, a large corporation in New York has different sorts of problems from a small partnership in Decatur, Illinois. Moreover, personnel problems will differ depending on whether a company employs mainly routine clerical workers or prima donna salesmen or, again, salaried professionals.

Nevertheless, there is a general tension and there is a general range of problems. Before I state these problems generally, however, let me put them in quite specific terms. The office manager's difficulty would be solved completely if his employees came to him as a body and said: "We think too much time is wasted in these coffee breaks in the morning. It's getting so we can't work well with these breaks. We just get started, and then there's the coffee break, and it drags along, and then it's lunch time. Now, we really come here to work for you, and that's what we want to do—work. So why not eliminate these coffee breaks?"

Well, now, if that should happen, wouldn't he feel, "By God, they really *do* want to work!" And wouldn't his major problem be solved? Let me say right away that, on the basis of extensive scientific investigation, I have found out that this is not going to happen in any office tomorrow. Why isn't it? To answer that, we have seriously to understand the problem of incentive, as well as certain big factors beyond management's control that affect the work motives in the office.

From the personnel standpoint, the problem of human incentive is threefold: how to get people (1) to work hard and strive well, (2) to be happy and contented in their work, and (3) to do these things for as low a money cost to the organization as possible.

Professors these days, especially when addressing business men, are not supposed to talk about money. Some professors, however, say that money is not enough to secure incentives to work—and I happen to agree with that. But we should not kid ourselves: A thousand dollars a year covers a multitude of grievances. And to say that money isn't enough is not to say that it is not necessary. There are very few outfits that would not get out more work if they doubled the salaries of their employees. Let us review this problem of money as a motive for work.

## II

During much of the nineteenth century, fear of hunger was a major incentive to work, and the economic whip was the major instrument of business discipline. Let us not be squeamish: It is a fact that a good dose of unemployment among office workers would go a long way toward solving the problem of work incentive. The whole nineteenth century proved that fear of poverty and plain want is a powerful stimulus to work and that unemployment does promote discipline in the factory and in the office.

But two things make those methods impossible, or at least ineffective, today: first, the organization of labor unions and, second, the shift in the whole political mood of our time. The great depression and the resulting change in the political tone of American life, among other things, represented a revolt against that incentive and that discipline. And, regardless of which party wins a particular election, that is a permanent, popular shift. The sanctions of want and unemployment are just not politically acceptable today in America, and the fight that the unions would put up if they were introduced would tear the whole American setup apart.

In boom times, the positive incentive of a higher share of the proceeds of work replaces the negative incentive of fearful unemployment. But, once a conventional standard of living is reached, some people will not respond to higher income as an incentive; they will take the increase in more leisure rather than in more money. Moreover, in a tight employment market, regardless of any reasonable income, they will take some of that leisure on the job.

So, in a capitalist society such as this one, the economic incentive tends to break down, negatively and positively. *Negatively,* lack of money and fear of unemployment cannot be used publicly and widely as an incentive with any degree of success. *Positively,* more money as such—even granted that it is feasible in view of standards of profit— will not promote the kind of zealous and cheerful efficiency that I suspect management really wants in its offices.

By no means is this the situation in all firms, but I am trying to look ahead, and I believe that it is the model of the future—for wage workers and for white-collar employees too, especially of the more routine sort.

What next? Here, as in England and Germany, when this state is reached, there is a resort to noneconomic incentives. Attempts are made to raise the "social status" of the employee by giving him a more humane treatment within the operations of the firm. Now, there is a lot of make-believe about much of this "human relations in industry" and good-fellow stuff. Sometimes it is done merely to keep salaries low by psychological nonsense. Sometimes it is done to freeze out a threatening union drive. But sometimes, I believe, it is done out of the single desire to solve personnel problems, to make a business get along with the work. Yet, even if the economic motives of the company management are definitely subordinated—as they are more likely to be in good times with tight employment markets— still there is one point at which the attempt bogs down.

Let me put it like this: When you're up in the corner, private enterprise can make only an economic appeal to the employee. For, in the view of the white-collar employee, the aim of the business is to make profit, and it is using the employee to enable it to do so. Material gain therefore tends to be the only effective stimulus of private enterprise as such.

On the other hand, when the worker is part of an industry or firm which he feels is partly his, the appeal can be made to his sense of obligation. In wartime, for example, work incentives operate which seem to the employee to transcend the private economic goal of the company. Then, too, on cost-plus contracts, many firms can well afford to subordinate the economic quarrel with their employees. But, when the nationalist incentive flags, there is a search for some other, some larger identification. This sort of question is much debated, and well debated too, in England today.

IV

But suppose there is no war incentive. What then? One answer, as in England, centers around "nationalization." Such an answer is no longer only a move toward economic equality. It is also part of an attempt to stiffen the flagging incentive to work. How is nationalization expected to do this? By providing an employee identification—the nation —that is larger and, if you will, more noble than the material profits of a private firm. For, if it is true that money incentives are negatively no longer possible, and positively not sufficient to insure cheerful and willing efficiency, then, from the standpoint of a nation in an era of war, some real incentive that goes beyond money must be provided.

The attitude toward the meaning of work and its proper incentives are among the most important questions Americans have now to face. For the key factor in any economy is the character of the motives evoked to induce its people to work. I believe we are reaching a point in this country where the old incentives to labor—the economic whip and the increased gain—are running down and where there are no new incentives to take their place.

The work incentives of our employees and our own work expectations are inherited from a time when most of the people at work were on their own. But today less than one-fifth of the people of America work for themselves, and most of these are farmers.

America is a nation of dependent employees trying to operate on a work psychology appropriate to a nation of independent, free enterprisers.

**V**

Now, that is the general problem faced by the personnel man or office manager. But he is also attempting to handle the people of the white-collar world. He is likely to forget that, for as a managerial employee he sees them mainly in only one milieu: their place of work. That workplace is, in their minds, a major key to all the other worlds in which they live. But the office manager tends to see the work role as complete in itself—and, from the angle of his immediate interest, it is. He is trying to organize that office so that work will be turned out efficiently and cheaply per unit. They are so often trying to do as little as they can in their office role, because their interests, what they really live for, are usually elsewhere. What management considers an end, they think of strictly as a means.

That is why the personnel problems of white-collar people cannot be solved at the point of production. These problems are deeply entangled with the problems of the white-collar group as a stratum, or rather as a new white-collar pyramid within the old nineteenth-century pyramid of entrepreneur and wage worker. These white-collar people have undergone some quite drastic changes since 1900. Among the major trends that have made for a decline in their general position are the following:

(i) *The white-collar employees can no longer borrow prestige* from the old-type Entrepreneurial Boss as they could 40 years ago. For their work is no longer similar to that of the independent middle class. Given the increased size of the workplace, they cannot borrow prestige from the new Executive Boss as easily as they could 30 years ago. Nor, given the increased impersonality of much of their work routine, can they borrow it so easily from The Management or The Firm, or The Esteemed Customer.

There is no longer the sharp split which existed 30—and even 20—years ago between the foreign-born, foreign-languaged, immigrant wage worker and the more "prestige-ful" native-born office employee. For, with the cutting off of immigration in the last generation, the whole population, including wage workers, is rapidly rising into the category of "native white of native parentage." The white-collar people are a new, unlocated stratum, not an appendage of the old middle classes, and they are insecure in prestige, often to the point of a virtual status panic.

(ii) In the meantime—as they have lost this prestige— *the average white-collar income has dropped* until it is only slightly above, and in several important cases lower than, the average income of various wage-working groups. This is in contrast to the 1890 situation, when, on the average, the white-collar people made about double. And today it is also true, income apart, that many of the side benefits of white-collar employment—sick leave, paid vacations, more pleasant working conditions—have now been conquered by many wage workers. In fact, wage workers in some cases have obtained more of that sort of benefit than have many white-collar employees.

(iii) As the mechanization of the office proceeds—and it has only begun—*many white-collar jobs will become more routine, and they will be subject to the same unemployment threat as wage work.* And the white-collar people know this.

There is a lot of debate about unemployment due to technological changes. I think it adds up to this: If the economy is expanding, and if the total hours of work decline in proportion to the total increased efficiency of the machines, then displacement by machines will be short-term; people will get new jobs although many of them will have to change jobs. But, if the economy does not expand, and if hours are not shortened in proportion to increased productivity, then there will be technological unemployment on a permanent basis.

Right now, of course, there is a shortage of office workers, and the proportionate demand for office workers has been increasing much more than the demand for shop people. But, on any long-term view, this immediate situation is due to the increased productivity of the mechanized shop and the lack of machines in the office. How the balance of shop and office will turn out, say in 1975, no one can predict—but it is obvious that, with the new machines, if there is not an enormous expansion of the entire economy, with drastically decreased hours, people in offices *will* be displaced by machines.

In the meantime, many white-collar people do fear unemployment due to the machine revolution in the office— and, in so far as their loss of security and their flagging work incentive are concerned, that is what counts now.

(iv) *The skills which the individual white-collar employee practices are often not as various as they used to be* and often do not permit the degree of autonomy they once did. And, in many cases, these skills do not take as long to learn. Moreover, *the virtual monopoly of high-school education which white-collar employees once held is no longer theirs, and frequently their jobs do not require much formal education.* Naturally that has decreased the security and prestige of the white-collar mass.

But that is not the whole story. These new office machines have a double-barreled effect; on the one hand, they degrade masses of semiskilled workers. On the other hand, they lead to a professional elite of salaried employees. Does this mean an upgrading of some office workers? An enlargement of their jobs, rather than a routinization? Not necessarily, and obviously not for many people. The centralization of planful reflection and of top skills parallels the routinization of the white-collar hierarchy. We do not know where the line between job enlargement and job routinization will be drawn. But we can be fairly certain that many executive functions will be broken down and routinized in the course of the machine revolution in the office. On top, and just below the top, there will be more intellectualized skills needed and, down the line, fewer skilled operations.

But again the question: Will the mass of office workers be upgraded to these new, near-the-top levels of skill? Probably not many. People to fill these jobs will be recruited from new generations of college graduates, who will probably also be trained in the firm specifically for these newer, more skilled jobs.

The average white-collar employee today does not, I believe, have much reason to look forward to more intriguing work because of the industrialization of the office.

### V I

All these trends—the lowered chance to borrow prestige, the relative decrease in real income, the threat of unemployment, the routinization of many skills—in one way or another affect the white-collar people with whom management must deal. When you add them up, one big fact emerges:

Slowly the white-collar employee is coming up against a situation very similar to that of the shop worker. And note this: It is not so much because the white-collar worker has been mashed down but rather because the wage worker has been lifted up.

That fact is back of much of the tension and uneasiness of many white-collar employees today. And all these tensions have a way of being specified by a drive for unions. Ask yourself: "Why haven't the white-collar man and the black-shirted woman managed to do something about their relative social and economic position, while wage workers have?" One answer seems immediate and clear: In an age of organization, the white-collar people have had no organizations while the many wage workers are effectively unionized.

So there is a struggle going on in the white-collar mind. It is a contest between those interests and techniques loosely referred to as "organized business" and those referred to as "organized labor." I believe that business managers will lose many of the white-collar people, just as, over the past 20 years, they have lost many of the shop people. In my opinion, it is mainly a question of time before offices are significantly unionized.

I know that office unionization has ebbed and flowed— and mainly ebbed. But business men ought to ask themselves, in view of all the facts, "Why *aren't* more offices unionized?" The answer, for offices of any size, seems quite clear to me: It is not because of anything management does or doesn't do. And it is not primarily because of any peculiar, union-proof "psychology" of white-collar people. It is simply because the existing unions have not felt it worth their while to go all-out for white-collar unionism.

We must remember that big unionization is only 15 years old and that the unions have been pretty busy in the shops. The cost per head of unionizing shop workers is usually less than for office workers. The technique is better worked out, and the unions have had more organizing experience in that area. But all that is needed is a real decision to unionize the white-collar employees and the gaining of appropriate organizational experience.

When the time comes, management may think it can stave off unions by giving its employees what the unions are out to win for them. My hunch is that it will not succeed. Besides, if management really does succeed, then the aim of the unions will in a sense have been realized anyway.

One great question which business men, along with other Americans, are going to be facing in the next 10 or

15 years is whether or not unionization, as we know it, will solve the problems of work incentive and of work gratification for white-collar people, as well as for wage workers. Frankly I have my doubts. But that, of course, is another set of problems, mainly political and psychological, up the line. In the meantime, the unionization of white-collar workers *will* solve many of their income and security problems, in the same sense that unions have solved such problems for many wage workers.

**9**

# THE PROBLEM
# OF INDUSTRIAL DEVELOPMENT

**I**

When we think about "the underdeveloped society,"
we must also think about "the overdeveloped society."
There are two reasons for this: first, if we do not do so, we
tend to think of everything as moving towards The Developed—it is the old notion of nineteenth-century evolutionism. And this is no longer a very fruitful idea. Second, to
think of the polar types leads us to think about a third type
—an ideal which we should always keep in mind: the properly developing society. We need all three types—not just
the two.

In an underdeveloped society, the means of production
are not sufficient, judged by historical standards, to permit
a decent life. Life is dominated by a struggle for existence
or, to put it more technically: *the standard of living severely
limits the style of life.*

In an overdeveloped society, the means of livelihood are
so great that life is dominated by the struggle for status,
based on the acquisition and maintenance of commodities.
Here, *the style of life is dominated by the standard of living.* In such a society, there is conspicuous production and
much waste; the principle of fashion is built into almost
everything, and planned obsolescence becomes a central
feature of the economic and social system. Change is very
rapid, intensively promoted—and quite irrational.

In a properly developing society, I should think that men
would have a choice among various styles of life, and that
no one would be dominated by a struggle for mere standards
of minimum living.

The theme of our seminar is change and resistance to it—and this morning the psychological aspects of these. But these—"change" and "resistance"—are both abstractions. No one is for total change of just any sort, and no one is altogether against all change. So at once several questions occur. We must ask: what changes? at what tempo? in what direction? and what are the required conditions?

The answer of this seminar, put very generally, is that we are talking about (1) a planned and structural change (2) of a total society (3) at a very fast tempo and (4) in the direction of the overdeveloped society.

It is obvious, I take it, that the psychological requirements of such a change are nothing less than new types of men and women, for human beings of one sort or another are selected and formed by societies, and in the undeveloped societies today there are not yet enough men and women of an industrially relevant sort. That is why we are talking not only about economic levels, but about what kinds of men and women are going to prevail, to become ascendant, in our epoch, all over the world.

The hard economic core of our problem has been put very clearly. It is this: Leaving aside aid from already developed countries, in order to industrialize as we know industrialization requires: (1) an increase in agricultural productivity; (2) an investment of the surplus thus achieved in capital goods for industry; while (3) holding consumption levels down. I do not think you can get away from these simple hard facts, and I do not think that you can believe that the amount of aid that is going to be given by already developed countries will enable you to get away from them.

After all, is it not a fact, that the amount of aid—of credits and grants—which the United States has given to other countries of the world, large as it may seem, has not gone very much to Latin American countries? The principle of that aid has seemed to be whether or not the country receiving it is militarily relevant to the United States.

If then we leave aside the question of aid of the massive sort that would be needed, we are always referred back to these three hard economic facts. The psychological inference from them is that a type of industrial man is required and built by the economic processes that are demanded.

### III

We know of only two general models of industrialization. Each has its own institutional and psychological requirements. Psychological factors are pre-conditions, and also results, of each of these economic models.

The first is the classic way of capitalism. Historically, it was not planned; it just grew. It is crescive. Its major institutional conditions are private ownership of the means of production, each of which are rather small in scale; it also requires a rational bureaucracy, along with a calculatable law, as a kind of framework. Its psychological condition and consequence is a man who has material gain uppermost; who is individuated—no guilt or anxiety is experienced if he "gets ahead"; in fact, he feels guilty if he does not. He is disciplined for work, which means that he spends the most alert hours of the best days of his life working. He is sober and calculating, and in that sense rational. In short: the classic capitalist entrepreneur. After the accumulation of capital is done, then you do not need this type of man so much. Historically, a thick stratum of such small enterpreneurs is the historically specific condition of North American industrialization.

The second model of industrialization is communist. The world historical significance of the Soviet revolution is that for the first time in history, successful industrialization is put through without a class of capitalists. Communism, most briefly described, is "forced industrialization." Karl Marx was quite mistaken, in that communism has not come about *after* capitalism nor does it grow very well *within* it. Industrially speaking, and historically, it is a kind of "substitute capitalism." The world default of capitalism, in failing to industrialize the world, is one of communism's conditions of success. Only in underdeveloped or very little developed countries has the Communist Party made great advances and won power. Communism, like capitalism, requires certain types of men; not the private entrepreneur, the economic man, but a political man who is dedicated and willful and whose superego, whose conscience, is restricted to the disciplined party. His reference group—the circle of significant others to whom he responds—is restricted in the final analysis to this party. He too has a puritanical strain; he too glorifies work, in his case of a collective sort. A party composed of such men is the agency of history-making in the communist way of industrialization.

## IV

There is one difference between these two models of great significance. Let me put it in terms of two models of historical change. First, the model which Engels made clear: history is made up of innumerable decisions of innumerable men, canceling out and reinforcing one another —as for example, in the movement of prices on a free market. Each individual is confined to his milieu and no man's decision means very much in the total process. This of course is the sociological meaning of history as fate.

History can be made only in this way, until two conditions occur: (1) the means of power—economic, political and military—must be enormously enlarged in scale, and (2) these means must be decisively centralized and controlled. When this occurs, certain groups may then become history-makers: those who have access to these enlarged and centralized means of history-making. They are limited, of course, by the structure of their established means of action, but they have much more freedom to decide and to exercise their will in the making of history than do people who do not have access to such means of power. This is the position of both the Soviet communists and the U. S. capitalists directing elite today.

But it is not the condition in which the underdeveloped world finds itself. Here change is still *mainly* history as fate, and the major resistance to change—such as industrialization—is the semiorganized stalemate of wills that prevails within these societies.

Now, I do not think it is true that the entire population

of all underdeveloped countries *want* to become industrialized. No population is going spontaneously to industrialize itself. We must determine the *agencies* of industrialization, for anonymous economic forces in the world today,
both internal and external to the underdeveloped world,
are now rather set against rapid structural industrialization.
In brief, I believe that the agency today can only be political. Our problem is basically a political problem. Even to
state the sociological issues requires that we think in terms
of the political agencies we intend to use, for unless there
is first built the means of power sufficient to do the job,
and unless these means are centralized enough for human
decisions to make a difference, we cannot speak of a structural change of the sort we have in mind when we speak
of industrial development.

## V

Accordingly, it seems to me, two problems confront us.
One has to do with the political apparatus of many underdeveloped countries. The second has to do with the problem
of democratic values. The two problems are interrelated.

The governing cliques, classes and institutions in the
underdeveloped world often have it very good. Why *should*
they want to change? Given unequal development of the
sort which Professor Lambert has made so clear to us,
they, the developed sections inside the underdeveloped
world—in the capitol and on the coast—are a curious sort
of imperialist power, having internal colonies, as it were.
They are sometimes states but not really nations, and the
states they dominate are often parasites on the economy
rather than instruments to create a new economy. Often
the political apparatus of the underdeveloped country is
full of *political capitalists;* sometimes, in fact, the governing
apparatus is a network of rackets: men get ahead and stay
ahead on the expectation that things cannot be done legitimately. As sociologists, we had better study this sort of
thing as an "obstacle." I think it is more important often
than the "traditionalism" of indigenous populations, and
many other such problems.

Of course, the overdeveloped society is also often a network of rackets, but "the take" is bigger and it is spread around more. More people tend to be in on it. (By the way, I am of course not speaking of Latin America, but of Southeast Asia, the Near East, and all those sorts of places).

It is under some such conditions as these that we must ask about democratic values. The question may be put very simply: can you get a fast accumulation of capital, with all that this involves for the level of consumption, within a democratic system? I am rather doubtful of this, but I am less concerned here with the mechanism and forms of democracy than with its content. There is a distinction, which is one of the greatest moral dilemmas that men face today: the distinction between "what men are interested in" and "what is to the interests of men."

This, of course, brings us back to the types of human being that will become ascendant models in the kinds of industrial societies we may wish to work for. We must ask the question in an ultimate form: is freedom *inherent* in man as man? I am rather inclined to believe that it may not be. In the case of the Chinese, perhaps—speaking technically—there is no superego; they are not individuated enough; they are group-integrated and group-responsible to such an extent that they do not really know the conception of freedom. It is not "in their grain," as it is in the case of those peoples that have experienced the great bourgeois revolutions of the last two centuries.

This whole issue of freedom may be called the problem of the cheerful robot. We know that men can be turned by coercion into robots. We did not know before our own times that they could cheerfully and willingly turn themselves into robots.

I do not believe that either the USSR or the USA is altogether a substantive democracy. That is to say, I do not believe that either is a properly developing society. Moreover, these two giant states are becoming more and more alike. I wish that we had time to go into this, for the problem of the parallelism of the USA and the USSR is one of the most important in contemporary world history. In both of these states work is alienated; men sacrifice themselves to work in order to acquire things of which they dream, and what they dream of is very similar. It is a kind of consumer's paradise, a kind of department store where everything is free.

The problem of the underdeveloped society is to achieve a higher material development of a sort that avoids the sad features of the overdeveloped society, and hence makes possible a variety of human beings, of styles of life, perhaps never before seen in human history.

In the short time—and it is the first time—that I have been in South America, my own conviction has been strengthened that you may very well have part of the answer. You really are on your own: the answer for you is not available in historical Europe or in contemporary North America or in Soviet Russia. Whether it is available among you, I do not know. Perhaps it is good that you encounter *obstacles* to those kinds of development. My own hope is that you would liberate your cultural imaginations from all these other models, especially that of North America, and think freely upon what you really want. In this case "utopian thinking" means merely that you imagine all the range of alternatives that might exist, and then consider the conditions of each of them, and the psychological and human consequences of each. Until you do this, I do not really understand how you can properly consider the obstacles to achieving industrial development of a humane sort.

# PART TWO

PART TWO

I

# PRAGMATISM, POLITICS AND RELIGION

These are times in which men feel about their feelings. Charles Morris has wrought what he has felt into an articulate work and he has felt susceptibly.* That many may believe that feeling has engulfed his thought need not detract from the sensitiveness of the feeling. Nor need it diminish the wise things we can learn from his book. Detailed appreciation of his literary renderings of six philosophies of life will here be foregone; it can only be noted that he considers the Buddhist path of detachment from desire; the Dionysian's abandonment to elemental impulses; the Promethean path of unceasing reconstruction; the Apollonian way of rational moderation; the Christian path of love in the grand manner; the Mohammedan route of the holy war. These six orientations are rejected in favor of a seventh: the Maitreyan, which is composed of just an equal slice of the Dionysian, the Promethean, and the Buddhist stuff in man, although I think it is closest to a Buddhism with concessions. What Morris offers is a personal and accommodative celebration of the modern fact of self-estrangement.

In the process he has set forth a view of human nature and a philosophy of history; he has responded to an intellectual crisis which many have felt within themselves; he has assumed a theory of human agony; and he has rejected (in principle) American pragmatism, especially a particular development of which it may be capable. These are important matters which must be examined. Morris as prophet must withstand criticism of Morris as intellect, for we have

* *Paths of Life: Preface to a World Religion.* By Charles Morris. New York: Harper and Bros. 1942. pp. 257. $3.00.

no new counterprophecy to offer. Appreciative of his bringing of his self forward for public scrutiny, we have the
responsibility of making that scrutiny as penetrating as
we can.

I

Morris works with "paths of life" and "types of personality" and his aim is to seat the former in the latter. To
do this he must lean strongly toward a biological determination of personality and see personality as something super-
historical. His classification of men rests upon a quite debatable psychology of interests and of literary "traits."
However qualified these views may be in their explicit
statements, they work underneath the argument and at
crucial points. Types of personality, each a varying mixture of three generalized elements, are seen to give rise
to "types of society!" Rivalry between nations and classes
are seen to exhibit conflicts between types of personality,
preference for which characterizes the nations and classes
in question. The world crisis is seen in these terms. For
Spengler's "soul" view of culture and history, Morris sub-
stitutes a more sophisticated conception, but one which,
after all, is quite like elite theories of history, though without their usual pose of toughness. Thus, the theory of
human nature leads into a personalist philosophy of history,
and this is the weakest link in the Buddhist chain which
Morris would weave for Prometheus.

In reality, "paths of life" are less expressions of "types
of personality" than vice versa. And both must be tied to a
third feature which in its genuine import is quite lacking
in Morris' scheme: *the positions and careers set by particular social structures.* In their interactions with wide biological possibilities, these conditions form and select types
of personality, and in terms of such conditions "paths of
life" are evolved and accepted. Due to historical circumstances some of these ideologies may be abstracted and
generalized. Then, in a competition of ideologies, they may
be taken up by men in certain social positions and strata.
Understanding of "ways of life" is gained by their precise
social imputation to these positions and strata; nothing,

except obscurist poeticizing, seems to be gained by juggling their most abstracted statements above one's personal moods. To be very concrete: Who can seriously imagine a Dionysian scrub woman? Or, a Buddhist money-driven supersalesman? Or, from another slant, probably all save one or two of Morris' types would not willingly go to war. Compare selective service, ostracism, and jail. How can one speak seriously of Maitreyan's "going his own way without apology?" Because they lack such crude sociological bases, Morris' statements of paths of life are more floating symbols than firmly anchored and specifically understood historical types. And because of this they are guides that do not know the actual paths that are possible.

The interest in forms of individuality, pursued by Morris, can only be realized by an interest in forms of society. And this holds for an interest in doctoring up individual paths of life. The basic problem of Morris is that of estrangement, of self-alienation. That is why he is so interested in Buddhism's attitude of detachment, why he says he writes for people "who cannot go home again," and that is why the god and the salvation he accepts is derived from Buddhist literatures: the signal characteristic of Maitreyanism is the "attitude of generalized detached-attachment." It is generalized in order that it may not be attached to particular elements in the self or in the world which may pass away. It is the wary orientation of a man who has been hurt, who fears he will be hurt again and who is frustrated. It is an island *of* the self-alienated and *for* personal safety in an impersonal world that is big, tough, and inescapable. But is an island within.

Maitreyanism, in which everything is "only one element," is not a solution; it is a precarious balance of that which precipitates the problem of self-estrangement. Had Morris taken seriously a social theory of the self, and implemented it with an adequate view of social structures, he would have seen that the problem of estrangement arises from an urbanized, pecuniary, and minutely divisioned society and that the ground problem cannot be solved by moral consideration of personal ways of life. Yet when he gives up Prometheus as central, he can only put the matter in such terms as he has. And these terms are a personalist, naively idealistic view of historical change underpinned by a thoroughly inadequate view of human nature.

To escape a condition means and material must be grasped as well as ideal ends envisioned. That self-estrangement arises from a social-historical condition has been adequately demonstrated by such men as Marx, Simmel, Fromm. In order to transform the conditions of estrangement (*or* granting, for argument's sake the personalist view of history, to remake the self), we must be dominantly Promethean or perhaps Mohammedan, if we must use these loose symbols. Only the Promethean can build a society which will intentionally form *any* type personality. What is meant by "man" I do not know, but men live in history and are formed thereby; Morris does not like contemporary history; yet the Maitreyan is not a history-making entity. And Prometheus cannot build a society as a Promethean and then turn into a Maitreyan or a Buddhist or any other self. Each day he destroys and builds the materials of his self he becomes a more confirmed Promethean, especially if he is winning. But he has steadily been losing, and that is one way of the crisis. Two directions lead out from this crisis: the one is religious, in Morris' general sense; the other is political and it is to be left to Dewey. Instead of rigorously examining why Prometheus falters, which would entail a social and political study, Morris has written the apologetics for the Maitreyan religion.

## II

To the several thousand churches, cults, and sects existing in America today, Charles Morris would add another. Rude statistical facts do not adequately dispose of his work, but they are indicative of the fact that not many citizens will take to what he offers. Certainly, those with their collars on backward may be intrigued. But sociologically, as a door to a church, this one is not on any street level. However, the coming of "the future Enlightened One, the Friend," Maitreya, has been foretold by no less a guy than Buddha. Honestly, if Morris had been less an academic philosopher and a little more of the philosophical clown, which every serious thinker ought to harbor, he would not have been so damned agonized and perhaps he would not have proclaimed an academic cult.

We must grasp his book as an indicator of what is happening in parts of our intellectual world. For books, too, are parts of the crises, although I am not sure how important a part. This one manifests the crisis of American pragmatism: Promethean man falters, turns softly inward, and feels in quest of salvation. One who remembers the thirties must ask how this has happened; for until recently it would not have been expected. In the thirties, those academic philosophers who attended to social happenings were bravely fussing with mouse-like reforms. And even Morris, whose main interests have been technical philosophy, wrote a pamphlet in which he linked pragmatism with the New Deal. Perhaps here in this political linkage we find a clue to the understanding of his latest book; for it must be seen in political as well as in personal and intellectual terms.

After their flirtations with the left, many withdrew with feelings of guilt, and then attained anchorage and safety in strongly nationalist affirmations. This was one major pattern among a lot of things that happened. Morris follows it only in its very beginning; for he is entirely without the nationalist frenzy. More subtly and entirely honestly, perhaps more deeply torn and frustrated by historical events and by their nimbus, he withdraws to peer out at history and at nations very personally. The one way is to leap out of yourself into an hysteric conformism with one form of loutish agony; the other is to withdraw into your own self to search therein for a "path of life." But both are ways of giving in.

In an age of mass discipline and armies few indeed are the civilized men who can "select" "what interest is to be given dominance in the self." Nor with the high commands on the loose is it permissible seriously to speak of "knowledge alone" not being enough and of its paralyzing the capacity for decision. In armies and in social movements which make history, and hence the types and paths of persons, it is lack of knowledge that is to be deplored. For now ignorance becomes irresponsibility.

It is understandable but it is to be denounced as unreal and ungeared that in such a time thinkers should begin delicately to consider "individual differences" and personal forms as primary. It is precisely upon this retreat inward to contemplate "the individual as a center" that Morris' major inadequacy, his philosophy of history, rests; and from this inadequacy his failure to see what may still be workable as a new center in the Promethean derives.

## III

"The agony of man," begins Morris, "is inherent in his life and inescapable." Not for all men. And is "agony" "in" "his" "life" or is it that there are agonies planted in certain conditions of certain lives? If it is the former, then perhaps agony is inescapable; if it is the latter, certainly "agonies" may be open to modification, if there is the intelligence and the power. But if we take the first view, we will speak of personalist world religions.

Men are agonized all right, if they have the opportunity to feel about it, but they are not agonized because they have lost their souls. There is nothing "inherent" about agonies. To say that "enormous wars, drastic economic chaos" etc. are "outward signs that the human agony has become acute" is a mode of statement amounting to glossing and nonsense. The things that are agony may be put bluntly: one of them is the fact that men are facing chance and death without feeling any deep social anger in the process.[1] There isn't anything behind agonies except the steel produced by other men and used by other men under orders of a given social, political and economic system. And when I read of "the trap of existence" I cannot but reflect that it is often of such a character that some can buy their way out of it. Indeed there is a whole business made of it by those technicians of personal agony, the psychiatrists. In this world, those traps that nobody can buy his way out of have to be thought and fought out of.

To talk about "human agony" and "salvation" and "traps of existence" is merely to hide the operative causes of painfully concrete agonies behind the mask of "sensitivity"

---

[1] This is one of the meanings of such facts as are reported by Hanson Baldwin, "The Need for Toughness," *N. Y. Times,* July 27, 1942.

which men build for themselves when confronted with
agonizing conditions. However, much it may serve as personal legitimation for wholesale death, there are times when
display of personal sensitivities are fancy ways of avoiding
the intellectual responsibility of explaining what is happening in the world so that men may understand and act. Men
are much more than political animals, but there are times
when they must be this above all, or else they lose all their
other beings. If this is such a time, then reveling in other
features of the self may be irresponsibility.

If we are seriously to talk of "paths of life," we have to
talk of wars and political movements for they are concerned, whether their actors know it or not, with manipulating the conditions of possible paths for individuals. Even
the technicians of personal agonies are more and more
realizing that many internal horrors will only be eradicated
by social-political action. Just as wars are required for the
traumatic neurosis of war, so must there be a type of competition in order to implant competitive neurosis. And if I
am correct in thinking Morris' problem to be that of self-
estrangement, then it will never be solved in the terms and
mood which he is using.

## IV

The currents of events that now mash in upon men are
obviously not religious, unless religion is so *defined* as to
embrace everything that happens that is of steady consequence for men. Morris writes: "The most general mode
for the conduct of life of an individual is that individual's
way of salvation; the beliefs and techniques which underlie
and implement that way constitute the religion of that individual." Such definitions might well mean that any man's
occupation was his salvation and the ground of his religion.
For by economic necessity and in virtue of their dominance
of his alert hours, "occupations" are, for the most of men,
"the most general mode for the conduct of life" and they
set major conditions for personality types and for personal
out-looks and in-looks. Such definitions as Morris' are not
conducive to understanding the world or one's self
or what is happening in either. They are better fitted for

evocation of mood than for brisk understanding. It is as if Morris had relaxed and let a swarm of words out of the disciplined domain of the *Theory of Signs*.[2] What sort of priorities have deprived a mind of the fine-edged steel it has exhibited in technical matters?

Those who already feel that way, will say that with his latest book, Morris has enlarged his range of interests. Others will perhaps say, in a phrase of Weber's, that he has made the sacrifice of the intellect. Twenty years ago, Weber indicated that many modern intellectuals felt the need of outfitting their souls with "guaranteed, genuine antiques." The matter is now beyond personal curiosities. It is very well, indeed, that world happenings have *not* been refracted for the American population in a religious way, for if this should ever happen, the religion involved would not be as subtle nor as harmless as Morris' secularized definitions make religion out to be.

## V

Much of the cogency of Morris' work derives from the genuine inadequacies of Dewey's Promethean outlook. *Paths of Life* may be viewed as a "reaction" to pragmatism because until now Morris has been among the most diligent of pragmatists; because he conceives the Promethean (pragmatic) way as dominant at least in America, and yet rejects it as adequate, setting forth the apologetics for a new religion.

Although there is nothing very subtle nor even "personal" about the bulk of human agonies, there may be ignorance of their full conditions. Dewey's tendency to impute agonies merely to ignorance has been one of the defects of his Promethean view. In his basic categories, Prometheus has been too technological and not deeply enough political. The reasons for this perspective have to do with the social path of pragmatism as an academic movement.

The course of pragmatism may be tied down socially by

[2] *Foundation of the Theory of Signs* ("International Encyclopedia for Unified Science," Vol. 1, No. 2 [Chicago, 1938]) By Charles Morris.

attention to the careers of pragmatists or by attention to the positions of their publics. Pragmatists have typically been sons of the middle class rising within these strata into rather comfortable academic professions. The publics of pragmatism have varied from Charles Peirce's minute circle, to James' large throngs of ladies and ministers, to G. H. Mead's graduate students and colleagues. The publics of Dewey have been typically professional, ranging from school teachers to the subscribers of the *New Republic* whose average income in 1931 was officially estimated as $5700. In contrast to self-pronouncements, and in spite of valiant stands on particular issues, articulate pragmatism has in social fact never been the ideology of lower income groups and occupations. The one exception, and it works for the argument I am about to present, is the public school teachers. At the most, pragmatism has been the ideology of the liberal professional man, however much he may have thought about the disadvantaged.

Now maybe the faltering of the pragmatic type of Promethean is due less to his alleged "religious" inadequacies than to what has arisen from his social position. Maybe because of this position he never attained an adequately anchored political orientation. But this would not be as much "Prometheus' " fault as the result of the academic position of most of those who have lived by being liberal Protheans.

Because he has deposited so very many of his values in a statement of method, it is often difficult for Dewey, or for us, to have a clear-eyed view of his social content. As method, pragmatism is overstuffed with imprecise social value; as a social-political orientation, it undoubtedly has a tendency toward opportunism. It is really *not* opportunist, because in the very statement of method there lies the assumptions of the Jeffersonian social world. It is quite firmly anchored. But in lesser hands than Dewey's, many things may happen. And the assumptions of Jeffersonian rural democracy tend now to mask the character and shape of political power.

The political experience of most pragmatists has been limited to the university. Perhaps this is a disheartening milieu for sensitive men in a time when history has spiraled itself into the hard knot of dilemma. In insisting upon treading its way through many particular problems, Dewey's pragmatism has relaxed its hold on men unwillingly lost in the interstices of gigantic trends. Dewey has said that patience is something he has learned to treasure. But patience may mean defeat and this must be faced.

In Morris' hands pragmatism does not grow impatient and political; it is shattered upon religious deficiencies personally imputed to it. Politically and in effect, Deweyan patience has swallowed what live content there was in Dewey's view. Dewey himself leaves Prometheus formally tied to a continual reconstruction of the world in which he moves but slowly and has no "final end." Realizing this and intimidated by cold, swift history, a pragmatist can be disheartened about "the moral crisis" in which there is no final end to sustain his little self. He can then search for one, whatever this may mean. Or he can use his technologic mind to grasp the means which might transform the objective conditions of such concrete agonies as men know. The demands of such agonies cannot be finally legitimated. But only the professor will worry over this. Dewey has not "solved the problem of value," but sociologically, one must ask: For whom does such a problem really exist? If men in the large were as snarled as the ethicists and religionists make themselves out to be, there would not be any human action and we should probably all starve. Also, as philosophy and politics show, there comes a point when any solution of any "value problem" becomes: Who can kill whom? Or in peaceful civilized countries: Who can have whom put in jail? That's tough for the philosopher, but that's the way things really are. The rest seems a mixture of often weird conventions and sham. You may dress up the killing as you will but in the individual's real path of life there it has been and there it is.

Just what the goals, the course, and the means of the Promethean today should be I cannot say in full. But *this* is our general condition. It ought not to compel us to make the surrender and dish up, in our own minds, messianic world religions. Rather it should lead us to remain frustrated and attendant until we are in a position to see how to have the knowledge and the power to remake the social orders which trap us. He who can bear frustration may be able to use it at least intellectually; he who cannot stand it and yet has not the grace of silence, will only clutter up the work at hand.

And he who cannot withstand the world collapse of all his hopes will never enter the kingdom of his own self. For he has lost the management of this self and alien beings can press upon it. Once there were some men living in a valley and they had so much to do they couldn't even agree what it was. One of them detached himself and went a little way up the side of a hill, where the air was rarer and the valley looked blurred. And an old Promethean, who for some eighty years had known how it was, said, only goats climb the highest mountains.

# 2

## THE NAZI BEHEMOTH*

### I

Franz Neumann's book is at once a definitive analysis of the German Reich and a basic contribution to the social sciences. No book could be both these things and not contain political directives. In looking closely at one complex object, Neumann reveals in sensitive outline many features of all modern social structure. He has that knack of generalized description that describes more than its immediate object; and he sees many things in that object, Germany since 1918, as "the specific working out of a general trend." To lift his style of analysis above the mere depictive and into understanding he pauses in a concrete portrayal to present a typology of possibilities. For example, of the relations of a state to a party in any one-party system, of kinds of imperialism, of the relations between banking and industrial capital, or of political patterns *vis-à-vis* the Reich and the various sections of her empire. Almost a third of Neumann's sentences are comparatively informed, and when he uses history, as in the reweaving of the rope of charismatic legitimations, he always comes up to face the day before yesterday now more clearly understood.

When events move very fast and possible worlds swing around them, something happens to the quality of thinking. Some men repeat formulae; some men become reporters. To time observation with thought so as to mate a decent level of abstraction with crucial happenings is a difficult problem. Its solution lies in the *using* of intellectual residues of social-history, not jettisoning them except in precise confrontation with events.

Franz Neumann's book represents the best tradition of the social sciences in Germany, which came to full stature during the twenties. He looks down a neo-Marxist slant

* Behemoth: The Structure and Practice of National Socialism. By Franz Neumann. Oxford Press. $4.00.

further subtilized by Max Weber's distinctions and deepened by a sociologically oriented psychiatry. His thinking is thus sensitively geared to great structural shifts and to happenings in the human mind.

Such reporting as his book accomplishes is of central facts tied down by the best documentation available. And there is no repeating of formulae in it: Marx may bear a nineteenth-century trademark in some matters, but, as Neumann again makes clear by a fresh intellectual act, the technique, the elements, and the drive of his thinking is more than ever relevant, and right now. There are so many who have "forgotten" what they once half understood and who take the easy ways out that it is downright refreshing to experience a book which displays a really analytic heritage with perception and with craftsmanship.

## II

Neumann's Germany is a type of capitalism; he calls it "totalitarian monopolistic capitalism." Those who would deny this characterization are forced by Neumann's study (a) to do some tall (and narrow) defining of "capitalism" which can be justified against his careful usage of the term, and/or (b) to deny the thoroughly documented and, it seems to me, determining facts which Neumann has drawn together concerning the operation of the basic institutions of capitalism in Germany.

One of the generic errors of those who do not see the German economy as capitalistic is Marx's view that capitalism is an anarchy of production. Of course, as Max Weber contended, modern Western capitalism is nothing of the sort. It is rationalized and planned. The more monopolization continues, the more capitalism is controlled and planned. "States" have interfered less in the mechanisms of *laissez-faire* than have monopoly capitalists. Many of those who would deny the advantages of capitalism to Germany do so within a definition of pre-twentieth century capitalism. However much this may help along the pleasant attitudes held of capitalism in other countries, it is not fair to the capitalists of Germany. They are not so old-fashioned as those who talk about their demise. And they are not so unhistorical.

To define "capitalism" as consisting of the "free competition" of a large number of independent entrepreneurs with freedom of contract and trade is, of course, to speak of the past. A more enduring trait, and therefore one better fitted to be seized upon in a definition, is the major institution of modern society: private property in the means of production. Now rapid technological change, requiring heavy investments, further augments the gobbling up of the little by the big and this monopolization eventuates in an extremely rigid economic structure. Powerful corporations demand guarantees and subsidies from the state. Thus, in an era of monopolization "the administrative act" and not "the contract" becomes "the auxiliary guarantee of property." Intervention becomes central, and: "who is to interfere and on whose behalf becomes the most important question for modern society." In Germany, as seen by Neumann, National Socialism has tied the economic organization into the web of "industrial combinations run by the industrial magnates." By means of the newer implementation of property, the administrative command, the cartellization of German business has proceeded rapidly. The Nazis saved the cartel system, whose rigidities were sorely beset by the depression. Since then their policies have consistently resulted in a further monopolization into the orbit of the big corporations. The cartels and the political authority have been welded together in such a way that private hands perform such crucial politico-economic tasks as the allocation of raw materials.

But who runs the giant cartels? Behind cartellization there has occurred a centralizing trend which has left power decisions and profits in the lap of the industrial magnates, realized many an old dream not shared by the now regimented workers or the small business men now virtually eliminated. The dreams come true in Germany may well be those of the industrial *condottiere* everywhere. Among specific Nazi politics which have implemented this oligarchification of capitalism is Aryanization: Jewish property expropriated has not gone to the "State," but to industrialists such as Otto Wolff and Mannesmann. (Apart from the Jewish case, there is a definite trend away from any thought of genuine nationalization.) The power of such industrial combines has also been augmented by the "Germanization" of business in conquered territories. The "Continental Oil Corporation" of Berlin is predominantly composed of the most important German banks and oil corporations. Heavy industry in Lorraine was equitably distributed—among five German combines. More important than these processes has been the industrial revolution in chemistry, subsidized by the State, but deriving its dynamic from capitalism, and rendering power to giant combines in the same way that all property in the means of production confers power, but more brutally. The hard outlines of the cartel powers are further confirmed by the near assimilation of finance capital by the monopolists of industrial capital.

Neumann has shown that profit motives hold the economic machinery of the Reich together. But given its present monopoly form, capitalism demands the stabilizing support of a total political power. Having full access to and grip upon such power is the distinctive advantage of German capitalism. Profits in a situation of great demand and with plant expansion improving the competitive position and thereby profits—this is the motivating force of the set-up. Gottfried Feder is quite dead. Those who, in the face of Neumann's documentation, would accept Feder's "anticapitalist" mumbling as a true characterization of Germany have many facts to deny.

And they must give an explanation of her belated imperialist war: Any thesis about Germany which does not explain her adventurous role in the war is inadequate. Such explanation cannot be performed by modern curse words (outmoded psychiatry), nor by the finger smugly pointed at bad gangs out for "power," nor by reference to merely formal growth of "bureaucracies." It requires attention to the economic structure and its political apparatus that lead dynamically into war. Neumann has not resolved this problem with the subtlety which he undoubtedly commands, but the type of characterization he offers of Germany seems to me the only one so far available which not only allows an explanation but which already has the job three-quarters done. Germany's expansion is the result of the dynamics of a younger monopolized capitalism in a situation where trade and investments can only be conquered by political means. Neumann has established in detail that this imperialism is primarily the policy of industrial leadership and the outcome of the internal antagonisms of the German capitalist economy. "It is the aggressive, imperialist, expansionist spirit of German big business unhampered by consideration for small competitors, for the middle classes, free from control by the banks, delivered from the pressure of trade unions, which is the motivating force of the economic system." This does not mean, however, that every element in Germany is a "tool" of industrial magnates.

### III

For the problem of elites is not identical with that of the socio-economic structure, however much the two are linked in a going concern. There are four elite elements dominating Germany today. Monopoly of the means of production and of the means of violence sustain them. And each of them has its bureaucracy. Power lies within and between these four groups. All influential decisions must be understood with primary reference to them; all propaganda is to be understood in terms of their needs to control, conjure, and mask the attentions of the ruled classes from the consequences of their decisions. Power in Germany is deposited with monopoly capitalists, especially in the heavily industrial sectors; the Nazi Party; the state bureaucracy; and the armed forces.

These are the rulers and the rest are the ruled, but these form at times an uneasy front, and the ruled may well be watching carefully. From these four angles, interests, anchored in the entire social structure but especially in violence and production, coalesce into the central aim: continual preparation and maintenance of imperialist war. To grasp this clearly is to see the structure of the regime as a total thing, called Behemoth.

War gives National Socialism not only glory but a stabilization of its power; to industry it gives profits, conquers foreign markets and accumulates booty capital. Neumann sees the bureaucracy, relatively unchanged by the Nazi conquest of power, marching with the victorious. This may be doubtful, but certainly the army has gotten "everything it wanted." In the trade policy, as well as in war, if we may so distinguish, the political and economic elites see eye to eye. Here there is an identity of interests and aims among the divisions of the ruling class. The Nazi elite have further consolidated themselves, as have managers, by climbing *via* political power into the ownership of heavy industry. The Herman Goering Works, which might well make capitalists everywhere envious, is the grandiose example of this process. "Political power without . . . a solid place in industrial production is precarious." Thus do economic men die. The Nazis used the knowledge and ruthlessness possessed by big industry; big industry used the antidemocracy, antiunionism, and violence of the Nazis. They are not too unhappy together.

In contrast with the profits and the self-manned organizations of business, labor's wages are near-stabilized, and it has no organizations of its own. From 1932-1938 wages and salaries rose 66 per cent, whereas "other income" rose 146 per cent; at the same time production nearly doubled. Neumann's experience with labor organizations in Germany make his detailed statement of the conditions of labor and of labor policy definitive. The labor market is authoritatively controlled to the limit of human recalcitrance. The working class is regimented and fragmented in order to prevent any common basis for movements, and the individual workman is isolated and terrorized. The "interference" of the party and the "State" in "economics" has again helped old dreams to come true. Not only has the prevailing class structure been accepted; in the process of the ruling elites' consolidation, it has been riveted and clinched from the upper side.

The army with its close ties to industrial and agrarian capital would seem to be a further bulwark against any attempt of the party or state to move against capitalism. Profits for capitalists, prestiged positions in the army for their sons; power and prestige for the army—these elements coincide as the system runs into war. Himmler, the party in general, has by no means succeeded in gaining jurisdiction over the army. The uneasy and often indefinite balance of power between the four elites is counterbalanced by the antagonisms which beset the system and lend to the elites a total fear of the working class. Again the analysis is pointed to explain war.

# IV

Just as the basic outline of the political and economic structure is teased out from the legal and doctrinal verbiage, so are the ideologies of the regime explained in terms of the composition and developmental trends of the social structure and its various strata. Ideologies and social structure are seen conjointly, which is the only way to see either in accurate and telling focus. For in some situations nothing that is said can be taken at its face value, and it is more important to know meanings than to test for truth. Indeed, the way to political reality is *through* ideological analysis. This is the way that Neumann has taken, and this is why his account of Nazi ideology is at times definitive and always interesting. His account of the blending of geopolitics and international law to form a "Germanic Monroe Doctrine" is a model for such analysis. If this particular style of imputation is intellectually too brutal, it stands in fortunate contrast to Rauschnigg, de Sales, Vierick, and others who have not controlled their understanding of Nazi proclamations, ideas, and policies by careful reference to their anchorage in the evolving features of the political-economic structure.

Ideas are political cloaks. The ideology of *Gemeinschaft, e.g.,* masks the impersonality of a rationalized society. Those academic sociologists who in American silos learn from a "primary-group" society, take note: Jefferson died in 1826. As human relations become impersonal by virtue of bureaucratic intervention, the ideologies of "community" and of "leadership" have been imposed. In a similar contradiction Neumann shows that as the political power of the state has increased, the doctrine of the totalitarian state has been rejected by Nazi intellectuals.

Anti-Semitism has its economic functions which work conjointly with propagandistic uses: it aids monopolization by distributing spoils to industrial capitalists whose support is vital, it diverts the discontent of small Aryan businessmen, and attempts to satisfy the anti-capitalist feeling of those areas of the masses who want wholesale expropriation. Thus, anti-Semitism operates as a surrogate for class struggle by heaping hatred upon one "enemy"; in the same act it seeks to "unify" the Aryan community.

The manner in which Nazi doctrine is shaped by the need to ensnare various strata is neatly illustrated by its inclusion of perverted Marxist elements. "Proletarian racism" stands as a strategical surrogate for "proletariat;" nationalist war against capitalism, for "class struggle;" "people's community," for "classless society," and so on. Thus has the Marxist May Day become a national holiday.

Neumann's style of imputation systematically accomplishes two objectives: it makes possible a controlled understanding of doctrinal formulations by referring them to political crises and social structure; and it enables an ingenious *use* of *changes* in ideology in detecting which strata of the population was not ensnared by the previous line. The Nazi line has changed frequently.


# V

The analysis of Behemoth casts light upon capitalism in democracies. To the most important task of political analysis Neumann has contributed: if you read his book thoroughly, you see the harsh outlines of possible futures close around you. With leftwing thought confused and split and dribbling trivialities, he locates the enemy with a 500 watt glare. And Nazi is only one of his names.

Not only does acceptance or rejection of Neumann's analysis set the type of understanding we have of Germany, it sets our attitude toward given elements in other countries, sights the act of our allegiance, places limits upon our political aspirations: helps us locate the enemy all over the world. That is why Franz Neumann's book is not only the most important to appear about Germany; it is a live contribution to all leftwing thinking today. His book will move all of us into deeper levels of analysis and strategy. It had better. Behemoth is everywhere united.

# 3

# COLLECTIVISM
# AND THE 'MIXED-UP' ECONOMY

The relations between freedom and security cannot be stated until these terms are broken up and connected to given conditions. They cannot be fruitfully stated as blanket abstractions.

The spheres and strata of which we are asking and answering questions about freedom and security must be precisely determined. For such explicit delimitations must always accompany the terms if they are to be realistically used. Thus, we would speak of *economic* freedom *for* laborers, *political* freedom *for* small Persian retailers, *economic* security *for* English bankers, or *for* Negro sharecroppers, *religious* freedom *for* Hebrews or *for* Irish Catholics, and so on. Then these delimited and specific kinds of freedom and security would be related to one another in quite various ways. For example, we would speak of security in an equal education for every youth as safeguarding security in the equality of occupational and inter-marriage chances. That is what would be involved in a thorough analysis of the problems of freedoms and securities. Here I shall only analyse an imputed relation between one kind of economic freedom for a restricted number and other types of freedom for the bulk of the American population.

John Chamberlain's argument is that the only, or at least a major, guarantee of political freedom and personal independence for the bulk of men is the existence of private economic enterprise, or more specifically, private ownership of the means of production.

This argument represents a *petty bourgeois* conception of liberty and freedom. It might hold where free enterprise and private property were closely linked and made up the dominant and widely diffused conditions of labor. Under modern conditions, this view is unrealistic and inapplicable. More importantly, it has dangerous consequences not set forth by Chamberlain. Masked in the guise of "little entrepreneurs," its functional outcome would most likely be the further rule of bureaucratically managed corporations.

The "freedom" which private enterprise today safeguards is, in the first place, freedom for . . . private enterprisers, to sell and buy and make profit. *Only* if the bulk of men lived by such operations, that is, were independent entrepreneurs, or could become such, might this economic arrangement safeguard freedom *for* the bulk of men *in* other spheres (such as the political). But in modern industrial society the mass of men are, and must be, dependent workers. This paramount fact of *dependent, collective* work is firmly anchored in large scale technology; it finds a parallel and a further anchorage in an extremely narrow distribution of property.

The condition under which private economic enterprise led to independence and freedom in other spheres for the bulk of men was the dominance of an economic system of small proprietorships each based upon self-owned and operated property. These conditions formed the cradle for classic democracy. Under them it is possible to speak of private property and independent work as a basis for political freedom, and for at least a chance at equality. Now these conditions are gone and no nostalgic wish nor reference to Jefferson by John Chamberlain will ever make shopkeepers out of employees unless we throw away the efficiency of our productive forces.

The issue of freedom and security is, of course, an alternative statement of the problem of democracy and socialism. And I do not see why the aims of socialism need not be quite identical with the aims of classic democracy. It is the means of attaining these ends which now must differ. The new means, the democratically planned utilization of collectivized means of production, are urged upon us by the new conditions which separate us from the early nineteenth century. The most important of these, the large scale industrial bases, results in the decrease of "self-employed," or independent, workers.

Here are the latest figures: In December, 1940, the

self-employed numbered 6 million out of a total labor force of 54.5 million. The pattern of the War, including the distribution of war contracts, is estimated to decrease this minority to 4.7 million self-employed by December, 1943—and this despite an estimated total labor force of around 62.3 million, which includes the decrease of the "independent" unemployed down to 2 million. It is under these conditions that we must speak of freedom, that "we" must plan the conditions of such freedoms as we may enjoy. For no longer can training in "independent" work gear men into freedom in their work as in other spheres. The economic conditions of historical democracy cannot be the economic conditions of any future democracy. It seems to me that he who believes that political and personal freedom can only be anchored in an independent economic life had better give up the ideal of freedom.

"Free enterprise" today may mean freedom *for* a handful *in* the economic sphere of action. But it means dependence upon this handful for the mass of working men, and constant fear of being engulfed by them for the smaller business men. It is not a question of having political freedom and economic insecurity under a regime of business *or* lack of political freedom and economic security under a collectivized ownership and operation of the means of production. That is an unreal statement of alternatives! It is unreal because it is not informed by the existing reality of collective, dependent work nor by the consequence of this economic reality for political power, as will be indicated below. Men are not much less *dependent* in their economic lives, under corporate capitalism than perhaps they would be under collectivist planning. It is a question of *who* or *what men* are dependent *upon,* and of the institutional means they have available for *control* of this dependency. For security and freedom may live together under conditions where both of them mean a chance to *control* what you are dependent upon.

Within the enlarging areas controlled by large scale business, there are fewer and fewer institutional channels open for such control. John Chamberlain half admits this when he tries to locate freedom in the *"interstices"* of private and collective economics. When he speaks of "state-

chained jobs" vs. the freedom to *shift* jobs he is merely
restating the *employer's* point of view of freedom: "If you
don't like working for me under these terms, then you are
free to go work somewhere else." Such a smooth mobility
of labor can only be assumed in the abstractions of the classical economists. It is not freedom to "shift" jobs as much
as guarantee of a job and collective *control* over the already
collective conditions and results of any job that seems important in safeguarding both security and freedom in all
spheres for all working men.

A. P. Lerner's argument for a Mixed Economy rests
directly upon the theory of freedom I have just examined.
He justifies the existence of a section of private enterprise
because he believes that this would be an anchorage for
freedom for all men in all spheres. Only this assumption
makes intelligible his second question and answer: He
wants to know what is to be left private (for freedom) and
what is to be collective (for security).

He asks: Can a political economy be mixed and yet
efficient? And he answers: Surely, because "we'll" decide
what is to be collectivized and what is to be left private
in terms of which is the more efficient! This is, of course,
not an argument at all, but a circle which by-passes the
question by setting up a formal criterion which simply
swallows the point to be proved. There are several auxiliary
remarks of Lerner's which it is fruitful to disassemble:
(1) Why should the mere erection of the norm of "efficiency" "automatically" provide "substantial guarantees such as
a minimum inalienable income for everybody"? Sheer, economic *efficiency* might well call for killing-off the old
and lame and troublesome, rather than guaranteeing them
an income. Efficiency cannot be socially pointed or educated by the norm of . . . efficiency. Perhaps it is merely a
more cogent name for the nonexistent dominance of a free-
market. (2) Why should he assume that the failure of a
mixed economy fully to use its resources "would inevitably
result" in its replacement by collectivism? This would only
be the case if the people in charge of the collectivist side of
the mixture had power of life and death over the private
enterprisers' side. And if this were so, how could private
enterprisers be free enough to live by *our* risks in order to

safeguard *their* "freedom"? (3) Why is it "arrogant pessimism" and "irresponsible" to hold that the "human race"
is incapable of learning that governmental spending in
peacetime, as in war, could keep up employment? Who
knows that those in power will inevitably know John Mayn-
ard Keynes so well and want to practice him? It isn't a
question for the "human race," nor a matter for the "nineteenth-century economists" to learn. It is less a question
of *the diffusion of knowledge* than of power relations and
economic stakes. Moreover, (4) Why *should* government
"guarantee an adequate money demand for the products
of private enterprise"? That is, subsidize the defaults of
private enterprise as an element of an economy or as an
economic system? To insure "freedom"? But if private enterprise needs this governmental guarantee it is too weak
an economic anchorage for anybody's "freedom,"—even
the freedom for the little private enterprisers who are being
gobbled daily by the freedom of the big enterprisers in the
W.P.B. (5) Lerner speaks of the norm of efficiency governing whether something is to be collectivized or private. But
who or what decides about this? Unless this private enterprise is to be equal in power with government, I presume
that the government is. Having a monopoly on the legitimate use of force, government can control and set conditions of differential "efficiency." So, again, the problem of
freedom lies less directly in the economic sphere than in the
political sphere and "its" control of the economic.

Two issues are left over after A. L. Lerner finished mix-
ing up the economy: a more precise and realistic, a less
formal criterion of what is to be left in private hands and
what is to be collectivized. And a statement of the respective
weights of the state and the private entrepreneurs in the
distribution of power; or, in other words, the *political* conditions and consequences of a mixed economy. The edi-
tors of *Fortune* face both these problems in no uncertain
terms. (Supplement to *Fortune,* December, 1942: *"The
Domestic Economy."*) They unmix the mixed-up economy
of Lerner and Chamberlain, and point out in effect the realistic implications of ideal, abstract systems.

The sophisticated Tories, who wrote *Fortune's* plan

know: that total freedom (laissez-faire) for business men would wreck even business as a system; that "laissez-faire" is no longer a guarantee of economic security [nor] a guarantee of freedom." More crucially, they think that "only the state can stop the drift to collectivism. Economic power," they write, "is in Washington and will probably stay there. The only realistic question is: to what use will that power be put?" They, too, therefore propose a "mixed economy," but unlike Lerner and Chamberlain, they give a concrete answer to just who is to have what parts of this mixture.

"The counter-revolution" (when was the revolution? the New Deal!) they propose "is a return to the higher values of individualism." They "propose to restore the creative, risk-taking, profit-seeking competitive individual to the legitimate throne of a sovereign market." The "condition of private industry must be one of (the state's) primary concerns." This "daring individual, the risk-taking entrepreneur, should . . . become the darling of America's future economy." But it seems he is not so very daring. For (a) government must *place* him upon his trapeze and (b) government must spread a soft net under his antics. "The industrialist must enlist the aid of . . . the power of government."

To this "uncommon individual," rather than Wallace's vagaries of the "common man," they would give America and the world: "We aim to make him feel that this country and century are peculiarly his." The common man will be taken care of by governmental spending, social security, and public works judiciously chosen so as not to challenge private competition. The government is to "underwrite the whole economy," that is, the doom-laden consequences of the daring entrepreneur whom government has placed upon the throne. The pattern begins to emerge. Here is a real plan about a mixture of economics with some politics thrown in.

A mixed economy would not be a mixed economy for long, nor would it lead to a mixed and competitive political regime. Given the size and power of business today, a mixed economy would most probably result in the governmental side subsidizing the rise and the defaults of the private enterprise side, running around with a net to catch the daring young risk-taker's enterprises everytime he is about to fall, break his neck and mash the whole damned audience. For as *Fortune* knows (Chamberlain and Lerner pay no real attention to it) the only way to secure *economic* "Freedom" for the enterpriser is for the state to subsidize him!

The *political* condition and consequence of this would probably be a corporate-business State. Economic power may be in Washington to stay, but Washington is full of business men who aim to stay. I will not call this arrangement "fascism," for the word has become a loose label for anything somebody doesn't like. But if this is the probable mixture of a mixed economy and its political condition and consequences, then it is obvious that the argument that freedom rests upon a mixed economy is false and dangerous.

A governmental "monopoly" of jobs would not make less secure my chance to yelp than would a set of corporation's monopoly of jobs, especially if the latter's monopoly were guaranteed by their corporate business state. Given its scale and concentration, private forms of business enterprise possess the power and "freedom" that rests on "free" enterprise. Given the parallel distribution of property and income, this means not only that a narrow business oligarchy is in a strategic place for influencing bureaucratic government decision. It means that they may infiltrate into the bureaucratic cells of the government. And that is precisely what they have been and are doing.

We are no longer faced with the problem of stating the political results of types of economic arrangements. For by now everybody, definitely including Big Business, knows that we must speak of the political and the economic in one breath, of a *political economy*. This means, in another set of terms, that "business" and "government" are more and more becoming one. That their "conflict" has been institutionalized within "government" and that it increasingly goes on without benefit of Congress. And that when Congress does enter the power fights it is in terms of these inter-bureaucratic battles. It means that "business" can and well may become "government." Only as this is approached can the "entrepreneur" become the "darling of the economy" and be given America and the century. *Fortune* has accepted a bastard version of the Marxian theory of the state: it *should* become the political committee for the ruling stratum of big business. I am not here concerned with imputing motives; these are the consequences and conditions which *Fortune's* plan seem to me to mask.

As government and business become increasingly interlocked, economic questions will more and more become: who is to staff the points of political decision in the governmental hierarchies and pinnacles? The new questions of freedoms and securities must be put in the fore of these decisions. And not in abstractions nor the nostalgic wish for the dominance of petty bourgeoisie, for today "the political freedom of free enterprise" means the power of Corporations over and within the State.

# 4

## LIBERAL VALUES
## IN THE MODERN WORLD

Most of us now live as spectators in a world without political interlude: fear of total permanent war stops our kind of morally oriented politics. Our spectatorship means that personal, active experience often seems politically useless and even unreal. This is a time when frustration seems to be in direct ratio to understanding, a time of cultural mediocrity when the levels of public sensibility have sunk below sight. It is a time of irresponsibility, organized and unorganized; when common sense, anchored in fast-outmoded experience has become myopic and irrelevant. Nobody feels secure in a simple place; nobody feels secure and there is no simple place.

It is a time when no terms of acceptance are available, but also no terms of rejection: those on top seem stunned, distracted, and bewildered, and don't know what to do. But what is much more damaging to us: those on the bottom are also without leaders, without counter-ideas, don't know what to do, do not have real demands to make of those in key positions of power.

Whatever the political promises of labor and leftward forces 15 years ago, they have not been fulfilled; whatever leadership they have developed has hidden itself for illusory safety, or been buried by events it neither understands nor wishes to control. Organized labor in the forties and early fifties has been mainly another adaptive and adapting element. What goes on domestically may briefly be described in terms of the main drift toward a permanent war economy in a garrison state.

Internationally, of course, the world of nations has been polarized into two dead-locked powers, with no prospects of a structured peace, with a penumbra of variously graded and variously dependent satellites, puppets, and vacuums. For the first time in its easy history, the United States finds itself a nation in a military neighborhood, having common frontiers with a big rival. The United States is a sea and air power from an external position; wherever it turns, it faces a vast land-power with an internal position. In the meantime, Europe has become a virtual colony, held by military force and economic dependence, And neither in the West nor in the East do U.S. spokesmen seem to have ideas and policies that have genuine appeal to the people residing there.

Internationally and domestically, the death of political ideas in the United States coincides with the general intellectual vacuum to underpin our malaise. Insofar as ideas are involved in our political impasse, these ideas center in the nature and present day situation of liberalism. For liberalism is at once the main line of our intellectual heritage and our official political philosophy. I shall not here attempt a full analysis of liberalism's connection with the modern malaise. I only want to lay out some key themes, which I believe must be taken into account in any examination of liberalism today.

I

Like any social philosophy, liberalism can conveniently be understood and discussed: (1) as an articulation of *ideals* which, no matter what its level of generality, operates as a sort of moral optic and set of guidelines for judgments of men, movements and events; (2) as a *theory,* explicit or implied, of how a society works, of its important elements and how they are related, of its key conflicts and how they are resolved; (3) as a social phenomenon, that is, as an *ideology* or political rhetoric—justifying certain institutions and practices, demanding and expecting others. In these terms, what is the situation of liberalism today?

As a set of articulated *ideals,* liberalism has been and is a major part of "the secular tradition of the west." As a political *rhetoric,* liberalism has been the ideology of the rising middle class. As a *theory* of society, liberalism is confined in relevance to the heroic epoch of the middle class. These points are connected, for as a carrier of ideals, liberalism has been detached from any tenable theory of modern society, and however engaging in its received condition, it is no longer a useful guide-line to the future. For the eighteenth and part of the nineteenth centuries, liberal theory did clarify and offer insight; for the twentieth century, it just as often confuses.

## II

Liberalism, as a set of ideals, is still viable, and even compelling to Western men. That is one reason why it has become a common denominator of American political rhetoric; but there is another reason. The ideals of liberalism have been divorced from any realities of modern social structure that might serve as the means of their realization. Everybody can easily agree on general ends; it is more difficult to agree on means and the relevance of various means to the ends articulated. The detachment of liberalism from the facts of a going society make it an excellent mask for those who do not, cannot, or will not do what would have to be done to realize its ideals.

As a kind of political rhetoric, liberalism has been banalized: now it is commonly used by everyone who talks in public for every divergent and contradictory purpose. Today we hear liberals say that one liberal can be "for," and another liberal "against," a vast range of contradictory political propositions. What this means is that liberalism as a common denominator of American political rhetoric, is without coherent content; that, in the process of its banalization, its goals have been so formalized as to provide no clear moral optic. The crisis of liberalism (and of American political reflection) is due to liberalism's success in becoming the official language for all public statement. To this fact was added its use in the New Deal Era when, in close contact with power, liberalism became administrative. Its crisis in lack of clarity is underpinned by its use by all interests, classes, and parties.

It is in this situation that professional liberals sometimes make a fetish of indecision, which they would call open-mindedness, as against inflexibility; of the absence

of criteria, which they would call tolerance, as against dog-
matism; of the formality and hence political irrelevance of
criteria, which they would call "speaking broadly," as
against "details."

We may not, of course, dismiss liberalism merely because it is a common denominator of political rhetoric.
Its wide use as justification limits the choices and, to some
extent, guides the decisions of those in authority. For if it
is the common denominator, all powerful decisions made
in the open must be justified in its terms, and this may
restrain the deciders even if they do not "believe in it."
For men are influenced in their use of authority by the
rhetoric they feel they must employ. The leaders as well
as the led, and even the mythmakers, are influenced by
prevailing rhetorics of justification.

Liberals have repeatedly articulated a secular humanism, stressing the priceless value of the individual personality, and the right of each individual to be dealt with
in accordance with rational and understandable laws, to
which all power is also subject. They have been humanist
in the sense that they see man as the measure of all things:
policies and events are good or bad in terms of their effect
on men; institutions and societies are to be judged in terms
of what they mean to and for the individual human being.
Liberals have assumed that men should control their own
life-fates. It is in terms of this value that the entire concern with consent to authority and the opposition to violence should be understood. All loyalties to specific movements and organizations tend, for the liberal, to be conditional upon his own principles, rather than blindly to
an organization. Liberals have assumed that there are
rational ways to acquire knowledge, and that substantive
reason, anchored in the individual, provides the way out.

As a set of such ideals, liberalism has very heavily
contributed to the big tradition of the West, but it is not
the sole carrier of this tradition; it is not to be identified
with it. And it is a real question whether today it is the
most whole-hearted carrier of it, for it is to be greatly
doubted that, as a theory of society, liberalism is in a
position to lead or help men carry these ideals into
realization.

So, if as ideal, liberalism is the secular tradition of the West, as a theory of society, which enables these ideals, it is the ideology of one class inside one epoch. If the moral force of liberalism is still stimulating, its sociological content is weak; it has no theory of society adequate to its moral aims.

## III

The assumptions of liberal theories about society, have to do with how liberal values could be anchored, with how they could operate as guide to policy. The liberal ideals of the eighteenth and nineteenth centuries were anchored in several basic assumptions about the condition of modern society that are no longer simple or clear:

(i) Liberalism has assumed that both freedom and security, its key values, flourish in a world of small entrepreneurs. But it is quite clear that one of the most decisive changes over the last hundred years is the enormous increase in the scale of property units. This has meant that the ideals of liberty and of security have changed: absolute liberty to control property has become tyranny. The meaning of freedom, positively put, has to be restated now, not as independence, but as control over that upon which the individual is dependent. Security, once resting on the small holding, has become, in the world of large property, anxiety —anxiety produced by the concentration of process and by the manner of living without expectation of owning. Positively, security must be group-guaranteed; individual men can no longer provide for their own futures.

If a particular ideal of freedom assumes for its realization the dominance of a scatter of small property, then, the social meaning of this ideal is quite different from a statement of freedom that assumes a situation of concentrated property. It is in its theory of society, tacit or explicit, that we find the political content of a social philosophy. If men assume the dominance of huge-scale property, and yet state eighteenth-century ideals, they are off base. In the kindergarten of political philosophy one learns that the idea of freedom *in general* is more serviceable as politically irrelevant rhetoric than ideal. Twentieth-century problems cannot be solved by eighteenth-century phrases. Liberty is not an a-priori individual fact, and it has been a social achievement only when liberal ideals have fortunately coincided with social realities.

Order can be reconciled with liberty by an underlying common sentiment, or by a balance of harmoniously competing groups. Common sentiment can grow from slow-paced tradition or be imposed from a powerful center. Competitive balance can be maintained only if each faction remains small enough and equal enough to compete freely. But now there is no common sentiment, and there is no balance, but a lop-sided competition between and among dominant factions and midget interests.

Liberalism, in the nineteenth-century epoch of its triumph, never really took into account the changing economic foundations of the political ideals and forms it espoused. That simple fact goes far to explain the decline of liberalism in authoritative cogency. This is the fact upon which Marxism has been correctly focused and upon which it has capitalized.

(ii) Many classic liberals, perhaps especially of the Rousseauian and Jeffersonian persuasion, have assumed the predominance of rural or "small city states," in brief, of a small-scale community. Liberal discussion of the general will, and liberal notions of "public opinion" usually rest on such assumptions. We no longer live in this sort of small-scale world.

(iii) A third assumption about society, characteristic of classic liberalism, has been the stress upon the autonomy of different institutional orders. In the beginning, as with Locke, it would split off religious institutions from the political, so that the political justifications, whatever they may be, had to be secular. Later on, the economic order was split from the political order, in the classic case of laissez-faire, perhaps coming to a head in the early philosophical radicals in England. But that was not the end of making different institutional orders autonomous. The kinship order was also to be split from the other orders so that there was a free marriage market, just as there was a free commodity market.

Moreover, in each of these orders a similar principle

was upheld: that of individual freedom of choice—as an economic agent; as a presumptuous political man, who had to be shown before he would obey; as a man on the marriage market making a free contract with his partner; and so on.

But what has happened is the fusion of several institutional orders; the co-ordination of the major orders has become the contemporary reality. We see in the United States today an increased coincidence and fusion of the economic, political, and military orders.

(iv) A fourth underlying sociological assumption, probably the most subtle and far-reaching, certainly the most philosophically relevant, is that the individual is the seat of rationality. When liberals speak of rationality and "the increase of enlightenment," they have assumed that the individual will be increased in stature and dignity because *his* power to reason and *his* knowledge will be increased. But the decisive fact here, as signified quite well by such writers as Max Weber and Karl Mannheim, is that the seat of rationality has shifted from the individual and is now in the big institution. The increase of enlightenment does not necessarily wise up the individual. This has to do with the distinction of substantative from formal rationality, in short, the growth of a bureaucratic organization of knowledge. The prevailing character as well as the distribution of rationality now leads to a whole set of questions to which we have no contemporary liberal answers. This modern weakness and irrationality of the individual, and especially his political apathy, is crucial for liberalism; for liberalism has classically relied on the reasoning individual as its lever for progressive change.

(v) Tied in with the belief in the growth of the individual's substantive rationality is the belief in the explicitness of authority. Men, as individuals or as groups of individuals, could learn to know who exercised power and so could debate it or obey. But today, one of the crucial political problems "for experts," as for laymen, is to locate exactly who has the power.

It is fashionable now, especially among those who have left what radical circles remain, to suppose that "there is no ruling class," just as it was fashionable in the thirties to suppose a set of class villains to be the source of all social injustice and public malaise. I should be as far from supposing that some enemy could be firmly located, that some one or two set of men were responsible, as I should be from supposing that it is all merely impersonal, tragic drift. The view that all is blind drift is largely a fatalist projection of one's own feeling of impotence and perhaps a salve of guilt about it. The view that all is due to the conspiracy of an easily locatable enemy is also a hurried projection from the difficult effort to understand how structural shifts open opportunities to various elites and how various elites take advantage or fail to take advantage of them. To accept either view is to relax the effort rationally to understand in detail how it is.

There are obviously gradations of power and opportunities among modern populations, which is not to say that all ruling powers are united, or that they fully know what they do, or that they are consciously joined in conspiracy. One can, however, be more concerned with their structural position and the consequences of their decisive actions than with the extent of their awareness or the impurity of their motives. But such analysis has not been part of the liberal tradition, nor does this tradition provide decisive help in undertaking it.

### IV

The root problem of any "democratic" or "liberal"— or even humanist—ideals is that they are in fact statements of hope or demands or preferences of an intellectual elite psychologically capable of individually fulfilling them, but they are projected for a population which in the twentieth century is not at present capable of fulfilling them.

What is inferred from this depends, in part, upon what is seen to be the causes of this mass incapability, and, in part, simply upon the degree of sanguinity. In nineteenth-century liberalism, the causes were seen largely as ignorance; so the answer was education. This was true of classic liberalism and, in part, of classic socialism, although the meaning and the further reasons for ignorance were more sophisticatedly worked out by socialist than by liberal writers. In the twentieth century, serious thinkers have further developed this socialist view, whether or not they know it as socialist, and have come to see that the whole structure of modern society, in particular its bureaucratic and communication systems virtually expropriate from all but a small intellectual elite the capacity for individual freedom in any adequate psychological meaning of the term.

The intellectual question for liberals, then, rests on the confrontation of the old individual ideals with new social and psychological facts. The old social anchors of individual freedom and individual security of small scattered properties and small-scale communities are gone; the roots of these values in autonomously operating institutions are dried up; the seat of rationality is no longer unambiguously the individual; the centers of power are as often hidden as explicit. And so the question becomes whether the ideals themselves must be given up or drastically revised, or whether there are ways of re-articulating them that retain their old moral force in a world that moral liberals never made.

**5**

# THE AMERICAN
# POLITICAL ELITE:
# A COLLECTIVE PORTRAIT*

Abraham Lincoln was born in a log cabin but William Henry Harrison was born in a plantation mansion. Once Harry Truman ran a small haberdashery, but Franklin D. Roosevelt's family might as well have been in the silver spoon business. John Jay, the first U. S. Supreme Court Justice, was a member of a top aristocratic family of New York; Justice Louis D. Brandeis was the son of a Jewish immigrant to Massachusetts.

Teddy Roosevelt and Averill Harriman began with gilt-heavy, family-made advantages. But William N. Doak, a former wage worker, became, after trade union leadership, Secretary of Labor; and President Andrew Johnson was once a runaway boy from a tailor's shop.

Before becoming President, Woodrow Wilson was a college professor; Zachary Taylor, a professional soldier. Tom Clark was a professional lobbyist before becoming Truman's Attorney General. But George B. Cortelyou, one-time civil service clerk, held three cabinet posts under T. R. Roosevelt.

In the U. S. political world, there have been statesmen of high personal ability; there have also been men who arrived politically only because of the abilities of their relatives. Some top politicians have done well in offices for which they were excellently equipped; others have done well in positions for which they were in no way prepared. And still others, prepared or not, have not done so well, being remembered if at all, for their inept use of high political office for low ulterior purposes.

* (With the assistance of Ruth Mills.)

They have come from New York and Virginia, from farms and huge cities, from Maine and Kentucky, even some from foreign lands as well as Florida and California. There was even one woman, Frances Perkins. And so it goes. Among the hundreds of top American politicians one can find at least two or three who represent almost anything one looks for. So one can go on endlessly collecting anecdotes and little images—but they will not add up to any conclusions about the types and the usual careers of the men who as a group have manned the topside of U. S. politics.

If we would understand the American politician we must collect information about, not one or two, or even fifty, but the hundreds who—since the Constitution was set up in 1789 through Truman's second administration—have represented the political elite. For the important questions about American politicians have to do with the *types* of men who have gotten into high political position, and with how these types have changed during the course of American history.

To call any selection of men the "American Political Elite" is to invite disagreement about the selection, the men, and the term "elite." Nevertheless, we have studied the biographies of 495 men who have held the most prominent positions in America. For the executive branch, we selected all the presidents and their cabinets; for the legislative, the vice-presidents—who head the Senate—and the Speakers of the House; and for the judicial branch, we have included all the justices of the Supreme Court. Undoubtedly, this selection misses some top men, and perhaps some of those selected do not deserve to be included. Yet these 495 men are certainly among those who must be called top politicos.

We call them "The American Political Elite" because during the course of American history they have had the most of what there has been to have of formal political authority and prestige. As we have examined the facts and figures of their origins and careers, we have found that they form a gallery of types, a sort of collective portrait of the American political elite.

**I**

The first big fact about elite American politicians as a whole is that they have never been representative of a cross-section of the American people. Almost six out of ten of them came to political eminence from quite prosperous family circumstances. They were comfortable boys whose fathers were usually prosperous and often wealthy men. Insofar as the chance to achieve political eminence rests upon family background, these politicians have had much better chances than the average American: their families could afford to give them distinct advantages in the selection and pursuit of their careers. Moreover, six times as many come from the very top as from the very bottom of American society.

(i) Some 58 per cent are from the upper bracket—the upper 5 or 10 per cent of the American population. In this figure, 30 per cent are from the upper class of landed aristocracy, big merchants, industrialists, financiers of nationwide prominence or professional families of great wealth and national standing. And 28 per cent are from the prosperous upper-middle class of businessmen, farmers, and professionals, who, although not of national stature, nevertheless were economically successful and locally prominent.

(ii) Another 24 per cent are from the middle class which is neither rich nor poor; although their fathers were generally respected businessmen or farmers, or were in the professions of law and medicine—or were dead at the time the future politicians left school leaving their otherwise prosperous families in less comfortable, but manageable, circumstances.

(iii) About 18 per cent come from what may be called lower class—although only 5 per cent came from the lowest class of poor wage workers or destitute, although undoubtedly honest, small businessmen and farmers. The remaining 13 per cent came from small-business or small-farming families that were not doing so well, but could hold their heads above dire poverty, or had fathers who were craftsmen.

Over the long pull of American history the fact of relatively high origin and of the extremely low chances for men of lower class origin to reach the political top hold true. Upper-class recruitment was most frequent in the period of the Founding Fathers—among those reaching elite positions between 1789 and 1801, 71 per cent came from the upper classes, 20 per cent from the middle, and 6 per cent from the lower. Yet, with several ups and downs, there has been a slight tendency for more middle and lower class sons to enter the political elite: in the latest political generation, 1933-1952, this plebian tendency reaches its historical climax: 30 per cent were from upper classes, 26 per cent from the middle, 37 per cent from the lower. This tendency is probably supported by the spread of educational advantages to middle and lower classes during the twentieth century.

The men who have held the different positions in the political elite are not so different in their classes of origin. The Supreme Court Justices and the Secretaries of State, however, are most frequently of the upper classes (75 and 72 per cent respectively). A seat on the Court probably requires the most advanced education and learning, which is most easily had by men from upper classes. Secretaries of State must contact the upper levels of other governments; the need for social aplomb and of the strange ways of diplomacy is more easily met by upper-class men. Even Ulysses S. Grant, paying off his friends with cabinet posts, appointed Hamilton Fish as Secretary of State, in order, it has been said, to give an air of refinement to his cabinet.

Over half the Vice-presidents, Secretaries of the Interior, Navy and War, Attorney Generals and Postmaster Generals have also been recruited from the upper classes, with more of the remainder coming from the middle classes than the lower.

Exceptions to the general rule of upper-class men are found in the case of the presidents (for Upper, Middle and Lower, their origins are 50, 22 and 28 per cent), and the Speakers of the House, and the Secretaries of the Treasury. In all these positions there are of course more upper-class men than from any other class, but there are nearly as many men of lower as of middle-class origin. The comparatively low origin of the Secretaries of the Treasury is perhaps due to the fact that this position, especially in the

Civil War era, has often been filled by self-made business-men.

In the newer cabinet positions of Secretaries of Agriculture, Commerce and Labor, upper-class recruitment is not general. The Secretaries of Agriculture most frequently (58 per cent) have come from the middle classes, while the Secretaries of Commerce and/or Labor most frequently (60 per cent) come from the lower class.

Another way to look at the origins of the Political Elite is to examine the occupations of their fathers at the time their sons left school. In every generation of U. S. history the political elite have come from business and professional families in much greater proportions than the proportions of such types of families in the American population at large warrant.

The proportions of *professional* men in the U. S. occupied population has never exceeded 7 per cent, and has averaged at about 2 per cent;[1] but 25 per cent of the political elite come from such father's homes. *Businessmen* have never exceeded 10 per cent of the total American labor force, but 18 per cent of the political elite were sons of businessmen. *Farmers* have never dropped below 18 per cent and have averaged over 50 per cent of the American working force, but only 20 per cent of the elite come from old homesteads. Moreover, the "farmers" whose sons have entered the political elite have much more likely been prosperous than not.


## II

It is never a disadvantage for a man bent on entering politics to have a father who is the governor of the state or a senator in Washington. Even an uncle or a father-in-law in such positions can be very helpful. Some 18 per cent of the political elite have had fathers who were in some kind of political office about the time their sons left school, and when the political connections of all relatives are considered, we find that 35 per cent of the American political

[1] By "average" we mean the proportions for 1870—the mid-point between 1789 and 1952.

elite *are known* to have had such political connections at the time they were setting out on their careers.[1] In this there is some decrease: before the end of the Civil War about 4 out of 10, after the Civil War about 3 out of 10, had political connections among relatives.

There *are* of course political dynasties in elite American politics—the Adams family being only the outstanding and best known. Yet, it can be safely said that throughout U. S. history well over half of the American political elite have come from families *not* previously connected with political affairs. They come more frequently from families highly placed in terms of money and position than political influence.

The social position of the top politicians is further emphasized by the fact that at least 51 per cent of the 495 men came from "old families," most of whom settled in the United States in the seventeenth century. Moreover, this figure is not loaded historically.

### III

Since so many of the political elite come from families able to offer them distinct advantages, it is not surprising that no less than 64 per cent of them have graduated from college. That figure is all the more striking when we bear in mind that even today—the historical peak of American education—only 6 or 7 per cent of all the people in the U. S. old enough to have gone have, in fact, gone to college. Even in the first quarter of the nineteenth century, when very few people indeed were college educated, 51 per cent of the men then holding elite political positions had graduated. Generally, each generation of the political elite has included larger proportions of college graduates, thus paralleling on a much higher level, the educational history of Americans at large. Moreover, over 40 per cent of the men

[1] This may be an underestimation, because, in the case of not-so-well-known men, if the biographer does not mention connections one way or another, and we could not check the relatives involved in the *Dictionary of American Biography* or another such source, we did not assume any connections.

reaching elite positions after 1901 have received a law degree after their four years of regular college and attendance at a law school.

Startling as these figures are, when compared with the average education of the American people, they nevertheless may well underestimate the educational standing of these political men, especially in the early years of the Republic. For, when colleges were not wide-spread many people received as good, if not better educations by being tutored or by attending a good "academy," but, in the absence of specific information, we classified such people with the high school graduates.

Of course, men who started out on higher class levels had better chances to be educated. Seventy-six per cent of the upper, 58 per cent of the middle, and 32 per cent of the lower class boys graduated from college. On the other end of the scale, only 3 per cent of the upper class boys, but 29 per cent of the lower class, failed to finish high school.

Moreover, the colleges attended by the political elite are much more likely to be Ivy League schools than is the case for the ordinary college graduate. Harvard and Princeton lead with about 8 per cent of all the elite among their alumni; Yale is third with about 5 per cent. A full quarter of all the political elite attended Ivy League schools, and well over one-third of those who went to any college went to Ivy League schools. And if one lowers one's standards to include such famous schools as Dartmouth and Amherst, Rutgers and Lafayette, and so on, then a third of all the elite, and 45 per cent of those who ever spent any time in college, went to top-notch eastern schools.

### I V

Since about 1825 there have always been fewer men entering high politics from the eastern regions of the country than grew up there. The tendency of these men was to leave the Eastern seaboard, and, like the population at large, their westward trek was pronounced from 1825 to 1901.

Who are these men who left their regions of boyhood? We have already seen how many of them come from upper-class families and had family political connections. Now we find that the political elite who originated in such families—where they already had good entré to politics and to economic livelihood—were most likely to remain in the region where they grew up. We also find that men from the lower classes did not move from their boyhood homes. In fact, statistically, men of the lowest origin have been almost as likely to remain where they were as those on the upper levels. One might suppose that the very rich did not need to move away and the very poor could not afford to do so. At any rate, it is a fact that movement westward was most characteristic of men coming from the middle classes. Twice as many middle-class men as upper-class men moved west[1] after growing up but before entering politics. One rather minor way up for such middle-class men has involved the journey to under-developed areas of the American continent, where they could rise *with* the region to which they went.

## V

Top American politicians have not only been politicians. In fact, only five of our 495 political elite followed no career other than politics—and most of these were civil servants. The single biggest fact about the occupations of our political elite is that more than 75 per cent of them have been lawyers. Twenty-one per cent have been businessmen, 10 per cent journalists or writers; the rest are scattered, and only 3 per cent have been professionally military.

Before the Civil War it was usually enough to have been a lawyer; after then fewer of the political elite have been lawyers and those who were lawyers more often carried out their practice in connection with business or even academic life. That historical flare, the Civil War, signalizing the industrialization of the American economy, is directly reflected in the pre-political careers of political men. Over three times as many of them had business careers immedi-

---

[1] Since most of the men who moved "south" were leaving the New England area, one might also be tempted to include them with those going West and say that almost three times as many middle-class men as upper-class went to less developed areas.

ately after the Civil War than just before it; and since then that fact has remained more or less constant: about one third of our recent (1921-1952) political elite have been businessmen.

The legends of the spoilsmen—of the influence of businessmen in politics in the post-Civil War period—are not merely legends, and the myth of the self-made captain of industry rising to an elite political position is no myth. But in thus characterizing one phase of American politics one must not forget that there were businessmen in politics before the Civil War, and there have been many more since then. The lawyers, by the way, have tended to be upper-class men; the businessmen, lower class. There have been usually more businessmen in all elite positions after the Civil War, but especially in the Departments of the Treasury, and War (including Defense) and among Postmaster Generals.

Besides carrying on business activities or legal practices or both, considerable proportions of the political elite have engaged in military service although not as a major profession: their war-time services were interruptions of their regular careers. Over one third of all the political elite— and about half of the presidents—have performed military service in some capacity. Nine out of ten of the members of the elite who have been in military service simply responded to emergencies. Only 7 per cent of all those in military service, and 3 per cent of the entire elite, were professional soldiers.

Over-all, fewer top politicians after 1865 than before then have seen military service in any form. Sixty-three per cent of the presidents before the Civil War, but 44 per cent afterward, have been in uniform.

Those politicians who have seen military service were on rather high military levels: three fourths of them were commissioned officers—in fact 25 per cent were generals and admirals, and 56 per cent were above the rank of Army captain and Navy lieutenant. On the bottom: only 9 per cent were noncommissioned or petty officers or less. Moreover, the great majority were directly commissioned, or—as in the early days—had the means to recruit their own troops. Only about one fourth of those ever in military service rose from the ranks.

## VI

The advantages of working up from the political bottom —from local offices—are made dubious by the fact that about as many elite politicians—about one fourth—began their careers on the national level as on the local. As a matter of fact, if you want to reach the political top, it seems better to start on the state level rather than on the local or the national. At least, over half of those who eventually made it started out in state politics.

From the formation of the government right up to 1921, generation after generation, the proportions of elite who have *ever* held local and/or state offices decreased from 93 to 69 per cent. The *time* spent in such offices also decreased, although not so consistently. Since 1921, however, the importance of state and local offices in the elite career has made a comeback. On the average, 74 per cent have held local or state offices or both before entering the elite.

Even though relatively few of the political elite *began* their political careers on the national level, 84 per cent held national positions before entering the elite. In fact, most men have been working on the national level of politics at the time they are chosen or elected for elite office.

Since about 1881, there has been a steady rise in the proportions serving apprenticeships on the national level; during the New and Fair Deals, 93 per cent of all the elite had national positions before entering their first elite position. Moreover, the time spent in these national offices has, in general, risen much more than the numbers of men holding them. In 1789-1801 the median number of years spent in national office before entering elite office was 2.8 years; in 1881-1901 it was 6.5; but from 1933-1952, it was 8.1 years.

Since membership in the U. S. House of Representatives is a prerequisite for one of the elite positions under study— the Speaker—it is not surprising to find that many of the elite have been in the House. Yet Speakers of the House represent only 8 per cent of all our political elite, whereas

40 per cent have at one time been in the House of Representatives, usually before entering elite positions. Like
membership in state legislatures, however, membership in
the House of Representatives has, since the Civil War,
become less frequent.

The decline in state and local apprenticeships, and the
increase in national positions before entering the elite, tie
in with another characteristic of the more recent political
career. Since there are so many more elected positions on
the lower levels and relatively few on the national, more
recent members of the elite are likely to have reached their
position through appointments rather than elections. Once
most of the men who could be considered elite in politics
got there because people elected them up the hierarchy of
offices—72 per cent of the elite in office during the first
three quarters of the nineteenth century had been elected to
all or most of their positions before reaching their highest
elite office; only 29 per cent rose through appointments.
But of late, men become big politically because small
groups of men, themselves elected, appoint them—58 per
cent of the elite in 1933-52 rose from all or mostly
appointed offices, 24 per cent through election.

## VII

Since, on the average, men enter the political elite when
they are about 52 years old, remain there on the average
of 3 years, yet live to be about 75 years, it is obvious that
they have post-elite careers. For nearly one third, their
highest office has climaxed their life work: 19 per cent
(mostly Supreme Court Justices) died in or shortly after
retiring from elite positions and 12 per cent retired from
active life of any sort, after leaving highest elite positions.

Most of the remaining two thirds who continued in active
life after their high posts did not leave politics. Twenty-
three per cent had further political careers mainly on the
national level, and 18 per cent more combined political
with nonpolitical careers. Only 18 per cent of all the
political elite have carried on nonpolitical careers and
for a little over half of these their high position served as an
intermediate juncture between two different types of non-

political careers. Thus, a lawyer works politically until he reaches the top, then, after occupying elite position becomes an executive of a bank or manufacturing firm. Or, as did Jim Farley—a former Postmaster General who after years of political activity capped by this post, becomes president of the Coca Cola Corporation.

Thus, unless a member of the political elite dies or retires after his highest elite position—which is not the most frequent occurrence for any but Supreme Court Justices—he will usually continue to be active politically on the national level of politics.

## VIII

Some politicians hold elite positions much longer than others; some enter high position at later periods in their careers than others. For a crude gauge of the role of politics in the lives of these men, we may compare the total length of time spent in any kind of political office with the total length of time spent in any kind of nonpolitical activities.

For the entire political elite, the median number of years spent in politics was 22.4; in nonpolitical activities, 22.3!

Thus, these top politicians have spent about the same time working at politics as at other professions. (For some of these years, of course, they were working at both at the same time.)

This *over-all* fact, however, is somewhat misleading; there is a definite historical trend. Until the Civil War, top politicians spent more time in politics than in nonpolitical pursuits. But since the Civil War, the typical member of the political elite has spent more years working outside of politics than in it. Strictly political careers reached a peak in the generation of 1801-1825, with 65 per cent of the total life work spent in politics. Outside activities reach their peak in the Progressive Era, 1901-1921; at that time, professionals and reformers seem briefly to have entered elite positions, seventy-two per cent of this generation's active working time was taken up by nonpolitical activities.

# 6

## THE CONSERVATIVE MOOD

In the material prosperity of post-war America, as crackpot realism has triumphed in practical affairs, all sorts of writers, from a rather confused variety of viewpoints, have been groping for a conservative ideology.

They have not found it, and they have not managed to create it. What they have found is an absence of mind in politics, and what they have managed to create is a mood.

The psychological heart of this mood is a feeling of powerlessness—but with the old edge taken off, for it is a mood of acceptance and of a relaxation of the political will.

The intellectual core of the groping for conservatism is a giving up of the central goal of the secular impulse in the West: the control through reason of man's fate. It is this goal that has lent continuity to the humanist tradition, re-discovered in the Renaissance, and so strong in nineteenth century American experience. It is this goal that has been the major impulse of classic liberalism and of classic socialism.

The groping for conservative ideas, which signifies the weakening of this impulse, involves the search for tradition rather than reason as guide; the search for some natural aristocracy as an anchor point of tradition and a model of character. Sooner or later, those who would give up this impulse must take up the neo-Burkeian defense of irrationality, for that is, in fact, the only possible core of a genuinely conservative ideology. And it is not possible, I believe, to establish such an ideology in the United States.

# I

Russell Kirk's "prolonged essay in definition" (*The Conservative Mind*) is the most explicit attempt to translate the conservative mood into conservative ideas. His work, however, does not succeed in the translation it attempts. When we examine it carefully we find that it is largely assertion, without arguable support, and that it seems rather irrelevant to modern realities, and not very useful as a guideline of political conduct and policy.

(i) The conservative, we are told, believes that "divine intent rules society," man being incapable of grasping by his reason the great forces that prevail. Along with this, he believes that change must be slow and that "providence is the proper instrument for change," the test of a statesman being his "cognizance of the real tendency of Providential social forces."

(ii) The conservative has an affection for "the variety and mystery of traditional life" perhaps most of all because he believes that "tradition and sound prejudices" check man's presumptuous will and archaic impulse.

(iii) "Society," the conservative holds, "longs for leadership," and there are "natural distinctions" among men which form a natural order of classes and powers.

When we hold these points close together, we can understand each of them more clearly: they seem to mean that tradition is sacred, that it is through tradition that the real social tendencies of Providence are displayed, and that therefore tradition must be our guide-line. For whatever is traditional not only represents the accumulated wisdom of the ages but exists by "divine intent."

Naturally we must ask how we are to know which traditions are instruments of Providence? Which prejudices are "sound?" Which of the events and changes all around us are by divine intent? But the third point is an attempted answer: If we do not destroy the natural order of classes and the hierarchy of powers, we shall have superiors and leaders to tell us. If we uphold these natural distinctions, and in fact resuscitate older ones, the leaders for whom we long will decide.

It is pertinent to ask Mr. Kirk at what moment the highly conscious contrivances of the founding fathers became traditional and thus sanctified? And does he believe that society in the U. S.—before the progressive movement and before the New Deal reforms—represented anything akin to what he would call orders and classes based on "natural distinctions?" If not, then what and where is the model he would have us cherish? And does he believe that the campaign conservatives—to use the phrase of John Crowe Ransom—who now man the political institutions of the U. S., do or do not represent the Providential intent which he seeks? How are we to know if they do or do not, or to what extent which of these do?

Insofar as the conservative consistently defends the irrationality of tradition against the powers of human reason, insofar as he denies the legitimacy of man's attempt collectively to build his own world and individually to control his own fate, then he cannot bring in reason again as a means of choosing among traditions, of deciding which changes are providential and which are evil forces. He cannot provide any rational guide in our choice of which leaders grasp Providence and act it out and which are reformers and levelers. In the end, the conservative is left with one single principle: the principle of gratefully accepting the leadership of some set of men whom he considers a received and sanctified elite. If such men were *there* for all to recognize, the conservative could at least be socially clear. But as it is, there is no guide-line within this view to help us decide which contenders for the natural distinction are genuine and which are not.

Conservatism, as Karl Mannheim makes clear, translates the unreflecting reactions of traditionalism into the sphere of conscious reflection. Conservatism is traditionalism become self-conscious and elaborated and forensic. A noble aristocracy, a peasantry, a petty-bourgeoisie with guild in-

heritance—that is what has been needed for a conservative
ideology and that is what Prussia in the early nineteenth
century had. It was to the spell of tradition among these
surviving elements of a pre-industrial society that conservatism could appeal. The Prussian upper classes lacked
the elasticity of the English, and their country lacked an
important middle class. Accordingly, they could avoid the
English gradualism and the blurring of clear-cut ideologies
in parliamentary compromises. In addition, caught between
military neighbors, their military set could become a key
element in Prussian society. Burke was the stimulus, but it
was the German elaboration of his response to the French
Revolution that resulted in a fully developed conservatism,
sharply polarized against liberalism.*

If England already softened conservative thought with
liberal elements, in America, liberalism—and the middle
classes that bore it as a deep-seated style of thought—has
been so paramount as to preclude any flowering of genuinely conservative ideology.

Here, from their beginnings the middle classes have been
predominant—in class and in status and in power.** There
is one consequence of this simple fact that goes far to explain why there can be no genuinely conservative ideology
in the United States.

There is simply no stratum or group in the population
that is of any political consequence to whose traditions
conservatism could appeal. All major sections and strata
have taken on, in various degrees and ways, the coloration
of a middle-class liberal ethos.

### I V

The greatest problem of those American writers who
would think out a conservative ideology of any political
relevance is simply the need to locate the set of people and

---

* Cf. Mannheim, " Conservative Thought," *Essays in Sociology
and Social Psychology* (Ed. and Trans. by Paul Kecskemeti. New
York: Oxford, 1953).

** For an elaboration of the factors in the triumph of liberalism
in the U. S., see Gerth and Mills, *Character and Social Structure*
(New York: Harcourt Brace, 1953, pp. 464-472).

to make clear the interests that their ideology would serve. There are those, of course, who deny that politics has to do with a struggle for power, but they are of no direct concern to politics as we know it or can imagine it. There are also those who deny that political philosophies are most readily understood as symbols of legitimation, that they have to do with the defense and the attack of powers-that-be or of would-be powers; but by this denial a writer makes himself rather irrelevant to the intellectual features of the public decisions and debates that confront us.

The yearning for conservative tradition, when taken seriously, is bound to be a yearning for the authority of an aristocracy. For without such a more or less fixed and visible social anchor for tradition and for hierarchy, for models of conduct in private and in public life, that are tangible to the senses, there can be no conservatism worthy of the name. And it is just here—at the central demand of conservatism—that most American publicists of the conservative yen become embarrassed. This embarrassment is in part due to a fear of confronting and going against the all-pervading liberal rhetoric; but it is also due to four facts about the American upper class:

*First,* American writers have no pre-capitalist elite to draw upon, even in fond remembrance. Mr. Kirk, for example, cannot, as European writers have been able to do, contrast such hold-overs from feudalism, however modified, with the vulgarity of capitalist upper elements. The South, when it displayed an "aristocracy" was a region not a nation, and its "aristocrats," however rural, were as much a part of capitalist society as were the New England upper strata.

*Second,* the very rich in America are culturally among the very poor, and are probably growing even more so. The only dimension of experience for which they have been models to which serious conservatives might point is the material one of money-making and money-keeping. Material success is their sole basis of authority.

*Third,* alongside the very rich, and supplanting them as popular models, are the synthetic celebrities of national glamor who often make a virtue out of cultural poverty and political illiteracy. By their very nature they are transient figures of the mass means of distraction rather than sources of authority and anchors of traditional continuity.

*Fourth,* it is virtually a condition of coming to the top in the American political economy that one learns to use and use frequently a liberal rhetoric, for that is the common denominator of all proper and successful spokesmen.

There are, accordingly, no social strata which serious minds with a conservative yen might celebrate as models of excellence and which stand in contrast to the American confusion the conservatives would deplore.

**V**

The American alternative for those interested in a conservative ideology seems to be (1) to go ahead—as Mallock, for example, in his 1898 argument with Spencer did—and defend the capitalist upper classes, or (2) to become socially vague and speak generally of a "natural aristocracy" or a "self-selected elite" which has nothing to do with existing social orders, classes and powers.

The first is no longer so popular among free writers, although every little tendency or chance to do it is promptly seized upon by conservative publicists and translated into such pages as those of *Fortune* magazine. But, more importantly, if it is useful ideologically it must be a dynamic notion and hence no fit anchor for tradition. On the contrary, the capitalist elite is always, in the folklore and sometimes in the reality of capitalism, composed of self-making men who smash tradition to rise to the top by strictly personal accomplishments.

The second alternative is now the more popular. In their need for an aristocracy, the conservative thinkers become grandly vague and very general. They are slippery about the aristocrat; generalizing the idea, they make it moral rather than socially firm and specific. In the name of "genuine democracy" or "liberal conservatism" they stretch the idea of aristocracy in a quite meaningless way, and so, in the end, all truly democratic citizens become aristocrats. Aristocracy becomes a scatter of morally superior persons rather than a strategically located class. So it is with Ortega y Gasset and so it is with Peter Viereck, who writes that it is not "the Aristocratic class" that is valuable but "the aristocratic spirit"—which, with its decorum and *noblesse oblige,* is "open to all, regardless of class."

This is not satisfactory because it provides no widely accepted criteria for judging who is elite and who is not. Moreover, it does not have to do with the existing facts of power and hence is politically irrelevant. And it involves a mobile situation; the self-selecting elite can be no fixed anchor. Some have tried to find a way to hold onto such a view, as it were secretly, not stating it directly, but holding it as a latest assumption while talking about, not the elite, but "the mass." That, however, is dangerous, for again, it goes so squarely against the liberal rhetoric which requires a continual flattery of the citizens.

Both these alternatives, in fact, end up not with an elite that is anchored in a tradition and hierarchy but with dynamic and ever-changing elite continually struggling to the top in an expanding society. There is simply no socially, much less politically, recognized traditional elite and there is no tradition. Moreover, whatever else it may be, tradition is something you cannot create. You can only uphold it when it exists. And now there is no spell of unbroken tradition upon which modern society is or can be steadily based. Accordingly, the conservative cannot confuse greatness with mere duration, cannot decide the competition of values by a mere endurance contest.

## V I

In one of its two major forms, as instanced by Mr. Kirk, the defense of irrationality rests upon pre-capitalist, in fact pre-industrial, bases: it is simply the image of a society in which authority is legitimated by traditionalism and interpreted by a recognized aristocracy.

In its other major form the defense rests upon what is perhaps the key point in classic liberal capitalism: it is the image of a society in which authority is at a minimum because it is guided by the autonomous forces of the magic market. In this view, providence becomes the unseen hand of the market; for in secular guise Providence refers to a faith that the unintended consequences of many wills form a pattern, and that this pattern ought to be allowed to work itself out.

In contrast to classic conservatism, this conservative liberalism, as a call to relax the urge to rational planning, is very deep in the American grain. Not wishing to be disturbed over moral issues of the political economy, Americans cling all the more to the idea that the government is an automatic machine, regulated by a balancing out of competing interests. This image of government is simply carried over from the image of the economy: in both we arrive at equilibrium by the pulling and hauling of each individual or group for their own interests, restrained only by legalistic and amoral intepretation of what the law allows.

George Graham has noted that although Americans think representative government a wonderful thing, they hold that representatives are merely "politicians" who as a class are of a fairly low order; that although they willingly honor the dead statesmen of the past, they dishonor the politicians of the present. Professor Graham infers from this, as well as other facts, that "perhaps what Americans yearn for is a complete mechanization of politics. Not a dictator but a political automat is the subconscious ideal," something that will measure up "to the modern standards of being fully automatic and completely impersonal."*

In the United States the economic order has been predominant among institutions, and therefore the types of men and their characteristic traits are best interpreted in terms of the evolving economic system. In turn, the top men, almost regardless of how top is defined, have always included in one way or another those who are at the top of the economic system.

Insofar as one can find a clue to the basic impulse of the Eisenhower administration, it is the attempt to carry out this sacrifice of politics to the free dominance of economic institutions and their key personnel. It is a difficult task, perhaps even one that only crackpot realists would attempt,

* *Morals in American Politics.* (New York: Random House, 1953, p. 4).

for now depression and wars, as well as other perils and complications of modern life, have greatly enlarged the federal government and made it an unwieldy instrument.

At the center of their ideology, the capitalist upper circles and their outlying publicists have had and do have only one political idea: it is the idea of an automatic political economy. This is best known to us as simply the practical conservatism of the anti-New Dealers during the Thirties of which the late Senator Robert Taft was perhaps the prime exemplar. It has been given new life by the frightening spectacle of the enlarged, totalitarian states of Germany yesterday and Russia today. And now it has become the only socially anchored conservative rhetoric in the American managerial elite, who now blend with the formal political directorate.

## VII

And yet on the practical political level the conservative groping has not been much more than a set of negative reactions to any signs of "liberal" or "progressive" policies or men. Conservatives have protested their individual rights rather than any common duties. Such duties as they have set forth—the trusteeship of big corporations, for example —have been all too transparently cloaks for harder and narrower interests. For a dozen years, the New and Fair Deals carried forth a series of specific personalities and policies and agencies that have been the shifting targets of conservative bile. Yet, for electoral purposes, that bile had to be ejected into the *"progressive"* atmosphere carried forth and sustained by the New Deal.

American conservatives have not set forth any conservative ideology. They are conservative in mood and conservative in practice but they have no conservative ideology. They have no connection with the fountainheads of modern conservative thought. In becoming aware of their power they have not elaborated that awareness into a conscious ideology. Perhaps it is easiest for people to be conservative when they have no sense of what conservatism means, no sense of the conservative present as being only one alternative to what the future might be. For if one cannot say that

conservatism is unconsciousness, certainly conservatives
are often happily unconscious.

## VIII

The poverty of mind in U. S. politics is evidenced in practice by the fact that the campaign liberals have no aim
other than to hold to the general course of the New and
Fair Deals, and no real ideas about extending these administrative programs. The campaign conservatives, holding
firmly to utopian capitalism (with its small, passive government and its automatic economy), have come up against
the same facts as the liberals and in facing them have be-
haved very similarly. They have no real ideas about how to
jettison the welfare state and the managed war economy.

In the meantime both use the same liberal rhetoric,
largely completed before Lincoln's death, to hold matters
in stalemate. Neither party has a political vocabulary—
much less political policies—that are up-to-date with the
events, problems and structure of modern life. Neither
party challenges the other in the realm of ideas, nor offers
clear-cut alternatives to the electorate. Neither can learn
nor will learn anything from classic conservatism of Mr.
Kirk's variety. They are both liberal in rhetoric, traditional
in intention, expedient in practice.

You can no more build a coherent conservative outlook
and policy on a coalition of big, medium and small business,
higher white collar employees and professional people,
farmers and a divided South than you could build a radical
outlook and policy on a coalition of big city machines,
small business men, lower white collar people, a split and
timid labor world, farmers and a divided South.

Within each party and between them there is political
stalemate. Out of two such melanges, you cannot even sort
out consistent sets of interests and issues, much less develop
coherent policies, much less organize ideological guidelines
for public debate and private reflection.

This means, for one thing, that "politics" goes on only
within and between a sort of administrative fumbling. The
fumbles are expedient. And the drift that they add up to

leads practically all sensitive observers to construct images
of the future that are images of horror.

## IX

One thinks of the attempt to create a conservative
ideology in the United States as a little playful luxury a
few writers will toy with for a while, rather than a serious
effort to work out a coherent view of the world they live
in and the demands they would make of it as political men.

More interesting than the ideas of these would-be conservative writers is the very high ratio of publicity to ideas.
This is of course a characteristic of fashions and fads, and
there is no doubt that the conservative moods are now
fashionable. But I do not think we can explain intellectual
fashions, in particular this one, by the dialectic that runs
through intellectual discourse, nor by the ready seizure by
vested interests of ideas and moods that promise to justify
their power and their policies.

For one thing, policy makers often do not usually feel the
need for even reading, much less using in public, much less
thinking about, the conservative philosophies. When Robert
Taft, before his death, was asked if he had read Russell
Kirk's book, he replied that he did not have much time
for books. Like the radical writers of the previous decade,
conservative writers of the forties and fifties are not in firm
touch with power elites or policy makers.

Another reason America has no conservative ideology
is that it has no radical opposition. Since there is no radical
party, those who benefit most from such goods and powers
of life as are available have felt no need to elaborate a
conservative defense of their positions. For conservatism is
not the mere carrying on of traditions or defense of existing
interests: it is a becoming aware of tradition and interests
and elaborating them into an outlook, tall with principle.
And this happens usually only when the tradition and the
top position which benefit from it are really attacked.

Neither a radical ideology nor a conservative ideology
but a liberal rhetoric has provided the terms of all issues
and conflicts. In its generic ambiguities and generality of
term this rhetoric has obfuscated hard issues and made

possible a historical development without benefit of hard conflict of idea. The prevalence of this liberal rhetoric has also meant that thought in any wide meaning of the term has been largely irrelevant to such politics as have been visible.

Underneath the immediate groping for conservatism there is, of course, the prosperity that has dulled any deeper political appetite in America's post-war period. It is true that this prosperity does not rest upon an economy solidly on its own feet, and that for many citizens it is not so pleasant as they had probably imagined. For it is a prosperity that is underpinned politically by a seemingly permanent war economy, and socially by combined incomes. Still, no matter how partial, or how phoney by old fashioned standards, the atmosphere is one of prosperity.

It is true, of course, that the radicalism of western humanism did not and does not depend for its nerve or its muscle upon fluctuations of material well-being. For those who are of this persuasion are as interested in the level of public sensibility and the quality of everyday life as in the material volume and distribution of commodities. Still, for many, this prosperity, no matter how vulgar, has been an obstacle to any cultural, much less political, protest.

More specific than this general climate of prosperity has been the tiredness of the liberal, living off the worn-out rubble of his rhetoric; and, along with this, the disappointment of the radical, from the turns of Soviet institutions away from their early promise to all the defeats that have followed in the thirty years of crisis and the deflation of radicalism.

The tiredness of the liberal and the deflation of radicalism are in themselves causes of the search for some kind of a more conservative point of view. It is good, many seem to feel, to relax and to accept. To undo the bow and to fondle the bowstring. It is good also, perhaps, because of the generally flush state of the writers and thinkers, for we should not forget that American intellectuals, however we may define them, are also personally involved in the general level of prosperity. To this we must also add the plain and fancy fright of many who once spoke boldly; the attacks upon civil liberties have touched deeply their anxieties and have prodded them to search for new modes of acceptance.

These are sources of the conservative impulse from the standpoint of the old left and liberal centers—to which most of the intellectuals have felt themselves to belong. From the right of center, there have also been impulses—impulses that were always there, perhaps, but which have come out into large print and ample publicity only in the post-war epoch. First of all there are interests which, no matter what their prosperity, require defending, primarily large business interests, and along with this, there is the need, which is felt by many spokesmen and scholars as great, for cultural prestige abroad. One prime result of the increased travel abroad by scholars, stemming from the anti-American rebuffs they have experienced, is the need to defend in some terms the goodness of American life. And these little episodes have occurred in a larger context of power: a context in which the economic and military and political power of the U. S. greatly exceeds her cultural prestige, and is so felt by the more acute politicians and statesmen at home and abroad.

The campaign conservatives will continue to go in for public relations more than for ideology. Just now they do not really feel the need for any ideology; later a conservative ideology of the kinds we have been discussing will appeal to no one. The radical humanist will continue to believe that men collectively can and ought to be their own history-makers and that men individually can to some extent and should try fully to create their own biographies. For those who still retain this minimum definition, the current attempts to create a conservative ideology do not constitute any real problem.

In the meantime, political decisions are occurring, as it were, without benefit of political ideas; mind and reality are two separate realms; America—a conservative country without any conservative ideology—appears before the world a naked and arbitrary power.

# 7

## THE DECLINE OF THE LEFT

Opposition to established culture and politics often consists of scattered little groups working in small circulation magazines, dealing in unsold cultural products. Outsiders, however, may also be members of an opposition of their very own. Sometimes such "Left" establishments have been as confining in their values, as snobbish in their assignment of prestige as any national establishment. In fact, they may seem *more* restrictive because of their usual pretensions not to be; and because dogmatic gospel is frequently needed more by minority circles than by those who are secure in major institutions and who readily borrow prestige from indubitable authority.

So it is naive to assume that the major division among the cultural workmen of a western nation is between those who are "established" and, somehow, unfree and those who are of an advanced guard—creative in culture and radical in politics. People who call themselves "Left," or "advanced guard," or "high-brow" are often as fully routinized—although usually not as durable—as those in a national establishment. The Left establishment also creates and sustains a cultural and political climate, sets the key tasks, the suitable themes, and establishes the proper canons of value, taste, and reality.

In our time, there is no Left establishment anywhere that is truly international and insurgent—and at the same time, consequential.

Today in the Soviet Union there is no real legal basis for opposition: opposition (or "revisionism") is disloyalty; political and cultural activities are embraced by the establishment of the Communist Party, which is nationalistic, official, and—on due occasion—coercive.

221

Today in the United States there is no Left: practical political activities are monopolized by an irresponsible two-party system; cultural activities—although formally quite free—tend to become nationalist or commercial or merely private.

Today in Western Europe what remains of the older Left is weak; its remnants have become inconsequential as a cultural and political center of insurgent opposition. "The Left" has indeed become "established." Even if the Left wins state power, as in Britain, it often seems to its members to have little room for maneuver—in the world or in the nation.

There are two major explanations of this condition in Western Europe and in the United States: first, the nationalization of Communism, which was the seat of the old Left; and second, more generally, the expropriation from cultural workmen of their means of distribution, and, increasingly, of cultural production.

During the thirties, people on the Left in Western society had to define their position with reference, primarily, to the doctrines of the Communist Party whether they were in it or not. The history of cultural and political opposition within most nations was closely linked with the history of the Soviet Union which is, in brief, the story of the nationalization of the international Left and the translation of Marxism itself into a rhetoric of rigid cultural defense and political abuse.

Up to the end of the Second World War, all this could be overlooked by many intellectuals. Cultural and political struggles still seemed to be within and between nations as the encounter in Spain made evident. Right and Left could be defined as Fascism and anti-Fascism. But for many people, the nationalization of Communism soon became obvious—and unbearable. Although still worldwide in its efforts, Communism had become the instrument of one national elite, and its political force within various nations was often as reactionary as that of any other great power. No longer could socialism, in all its viable meanings, be identified with the Soviet Union, nor the Soviet Union acknowledged as *the* carrier of the values of the Left. Communism—or Stalinism—in fact, was no longer unambiguously "Left" and in some countries—Poland and Yugoslavia, for example—it became, on occasion, conservatism.

In the West, many Leftward circles were so closely identified with Communism that when Communism was reduced to Stalinism, those Leftward circles declined or collapsed. They had become too dependent on this one orientation to survive intact, much less to flourish.

The case of America in these respects is of special significance because of the enormity of this nation's means of power, because of the *formal* freedom that political and cultural activities enjoy, and because inside the United States Communism has never been a real political force.

In the thirties many American intellectuals made believe that they were revolutionaries. Came World War II, and rather suddenly they became patriots. To be sure, at this decisive turn in the history of American life and thought, they did grumble a bit, in a literary way, but, it was a grumbling about a society with which in actual practice they were well satisfied. Now, after the War, they have come to celebrate this society, but in reality they know very little about it, and they are not trying very hard to find out.

Often, the remnants of the Left circles of the thirties— the ex-Communists—have become what I like to call "The Old Futilitarians." In their U. S. version, these ex-fighters are often quite shrill: They have stood up in another fashion in another era, but now they are done with fighting. This is the simple fact underlining the rich assortment of their guilt. Out of that guilt, many of them have become dogmatic and, often, professional anti-Communists. They have not carried forth into the fifties any traditions of the Left. Rejecting these altogether, they have come to embody and to display a kind of weariness with any politics of moral concern, for which they have substituted the nationalist celebration.

What is interesting about the ex-Communists turned professional is the fact that their anti-Communism is quite similar in psychological form to anti-Semitism. At least I find it difficult to tell the difference between the anti-Communism of some of my ex-friends and the anti-Semitism of those who have always been my enemies. Both assume the

immutability of Communists (or of Jews): once a Communist or a Jew always a Communist or a Jew. Both assume
that any contact is polluting; that in any attempted coöpera-
tion with "them," the Communists or the Jews will exploit
the chances offered and clannishly win out; that anyone
who may doubt this is simply naive, or perhaps secretly, or
unconsciously, a Communist or a Jew. There is the same
choked-up exasperation with detached reasoning about
Communists; about new beginnings in the Soviet bloc after
the death of Stalin. There is the same interpretation of texts
to reveal "Stalinist Mentality." In brief, any detachment
from unconditional nationalism is identified as treason.

In the United States today, the ex-Communist turned
professional is not as shrill as he was several years ago;
but he has certainly played an important part in creating
the sour and disillusioned atmosphere that younger cultural
workmen have grown up in since the end of World War II.

The complacency of the young is a counterpart of the
futility of the old. It is difficult to find pure types or examples of The Young Complacents. They represent more an
underlying mood than a stable type of man, and they are
very much subject to fashion. For a British case, consider
one Englishman with many American connections. Writing
about himself in a curious and, surely, un-American magazine called—of all things—*Encounter,* he asserts that he
feels "like a contented lackey of the Welfare State, a flattered traveler on gravy trains. . . . Her Majesty's Government fed, housed and clothed me (in khaki) for four years,
then civilly obliged me to jump the demob queue and return to Oxford. By way of bonus it give me an interest in
soldiers that I still retain. The Commonwealth Fund nur-
tured me on two long visits to the United States . . . the
Social Science Research Council wished on me money to
prepare a study of American military attitudes: I hope to
complete this in the next year while basking in California
at the expense of the Ford Foundation. A philanthropic
publisher advanced some dollars for a book on George
Washington which I have just about finished."

Perhaps the clue to this mood is The Young Complacent's feeling that, after all, he has been treated rather well;
behind that, of course, is the glorious and vulgar fact of

economic prosperity. Political passions and moral convictions "leave him cold." Perhaps his posture results from
the strain to be bright and interesting—and fashionable.
Perhaps it results from the fact that he tends to judge the
society in which he lives on the basis of his personal career
within it, thus confusing his own modest personal success
with the quality and conditions of social justice. He does
not examine the criterion of success itself, and the effects of
meeting it upon those selected and formed by it. To base
one's political mood and moral judgment upon modest
success is—and it is still a good phrase—the Philistine
mood of the petty bourgeoisie.

In the West, especially in the United States, apart from
the postures of sophisticated weariness and the curious
complacency of the literary young, there are many further
attitudes that stop political reflections as an active force—
for example, "The Scientific Posture" of Social Investigators. So many intelligent academic people won't talk
seriously about the politics of war and peace, slump and
boom, democracy and tyranny. They won't, or they can't,
go beneath the official stereotypes. They favor such terms
as "specialty" as used in "not my specialty," thus treating
themselves, in a sense, as minor divisions of a big department store. Many of them are ever so bright and clever, but
they seem unable, or they refuse, to relate their skills to
their sensibilities. They are fully rational, but they refuse
to reason. Anything outside their particular methods they
call speculation or scholarship—which they define as "writing books out of other books," and which they think a low
form of activity. They are often dogmatic, less about any set
of beliefs than about the limits of reason itself. Many of
them are administrative intellectuals—head-deep in war-
relevant "social research." Some of these types, who now
head up semiofficial research-cartels, published marvelous
stuff during the thirties. But now they are so committed to
the cultural and military apparatus, and to their own affluent role in it, that they cannot afford, psychologically, to
confront their own position and the political meaning of
their work. Too sophisticated to attempt argument for their
politically subservient practices, they simply refuse explicit
comment.

The collapse of the Left and the more general attempt to divorce intellectual activities from politics of any sort is based, then, upon the dogmatic and sour anti-Communism of The Old Futilitarians; upon The Young Complacents' uninformed boredom with politics and their ignorance of its human meanings today; upon the merely literary fads and personal prosperity of The Philistine as Thinker; and upon the unexamined conservatism and scientific pretentions of The Behavioral Scientists. As a loosely knit coalition, largely unconscious, these types are attempting to establish a nationalist mood to which conformity is demanded, and in terms of which reputations and careers are made and unmade.

Behind the rise of these intellectuals and behind the fatal nationalization of Left establishments, there is a structural trend in the cultural apparatus of America. Today, the real treason of Western intellectuals is based on the bureaucratic establishment of their cultural existence. It is not—as Julian Benda would have it—that they are "useful," but that they, themselves, do not control the uses made of them and their work. What now confronts them in the Overdeveloped Society is the expropriation of their cultural apparatus itself.

In capitalistic societies over the last two centuries, all that has happened to work in general—in a word, alienation—is now rapidly happening to cultural, scientific, and artistic endeavor. In different nations this alienation occurs in different ways: but whether it occurs by political or commercial co-ordination from above or by voluntary withdrawal of cultural workmen themselves, the results are comparable. We, the cultural workmen, do not have access to the means of effectively communicating images and ideas; others who own and operate the mass media stand between us and our potential publics. But more than that, we are losing control of the very means of cultural production itself. The condition of intellectual work, as well as of the distribution of its products, is increasingly bureaucratic. More and more culture becomes an adjunct of marketing, or of the bureaucratic ethos, or of both. The demands for intellectual and technical personnel and for new kinds of what Lionel Trilling calls "consciousness by formulation" are being eagerly met by intellectuals in research-cartels and busy teams of semi-intellectuals. Is not the deplorable situation of the serious movie-maker the prototype for most cultural workmen? We are cut off from possible publics, and such publics as remain are being turned into masses by those businessmen or commissars who control the means of communication. In their hands, these are often less means of communication than means of mass distraction.

In several basic trends and official actions, the United States and the Soviet Union are becoming increasingly alike.

Both are supersocieties, geographically and ethnically. Unlike the nations of Europe, each has amalgamated on a continental domain great varieties of peoples and cultures. Each has expanded mightily in territory as well as in power.

The power of both is based on technological development which has been made into a cultural and social fetish, rather than an instrument under continual public appraisal and control; and to this military and economic fetish, the organization of all life is increasingly adapted. The means of production are so arranged that in the name of efficiency, work is alienated; the means of consumption are culturally exploitative.

In both the U. S. and the U. S. S. R., as the political order is enlarged and centralized, it becomes less political and more bureaucratic; less the locale of a struggle than an object to be managed. Within both, most men are the objects of history, adapting to structural changes with which they have little or nothing to do.

In neither the U. S. nor the U. S. S. R. are there nationally responsible parties which debate openly and clearly the issues which the world now so rigidly confronts. The two-party state is without programmatic focus and without organizational basis for it. We must recognize that, under some conditions, the two-party state can be as irresponsible as the one-party state.

In neither nation is there a senior civil service firmly linked to the world of knowledge and sensibility and composed of skilled men who, in their careers and aspirations, are truly independent of corporation interest (in the U. S.) and of party dictation (in the U. S. S. R.).

In neither are there voluntary associations, as central facts of power, that link individuals, smaller communities, and publics with the state, the military establishment, and the economic apparatus. Accordingly, there are no readily available vehicles for reasoned opinions, no instruments for the rational exertion of public will.

The kind of public that democratic theorists imagined does not prevail in either the U. S. or the U. S. S. R., nor is it the forum within which a politics of real issue is regularly enacted.

The classic conditions of democracy and democratic institutions do not flourish in the power structure of the United States or the Soviet Union. Publics, voluntary associations, and responsible parties have, at most, a restraining role in the making of their history. Accordingly, most men of decision in these countries are not men selected and formed by careers within such associations and parties, and by their performances before such publics. History-making decisions and lack of decisions are virtually monopolized by elites who have access to the means—both material and cultural—by which history is now being made.

In cultural affairs, as well as in basic structure, similarities are becoming apparent. In the United States there is no long-standing traditional establishment of culture on the European model; in Russia, such an establishment was more or less destroyed by the revolution.

The "Materialism" of the Soviet Union, for example, is no more important a religious and spiritual fact than the "Christianity" of the West—especially of the United States, where religion itself is now a quite secular activity. Neither the official atheism of the Russians, nor the official Christianity of the Americans means very much today for national policy, cultural endeavor, or the quality of everyday life. In our time, religious—as well as educational—institutions tend to become other mass media, tend to be shaped by major economic, military, and political forces. They do not originate; they adapt. What real moral issue in our time has any sizable religious community discovered, defined, or witnessed?

In their classic period, liberal observers expected and assumed that universal education would, no doubt, replace ignorance with knowledge, and so indifference with public alertness. But educational matters have not turned out this way. Nowadays, precisely the most "liberal" educators feel that something has gone wrong.

Like religion, education in the United States competes with, and takes its place alongside, the other mass means of distraction, entertainment, and communication, These fabulous media do not often truly communicate; they do not connect public issues with private troubles; they seldom make clear the human meaning of impersonal, atrocious events and historical decisions. They trivialize issues; they convert publics into mere "media markets."

In both United States and U. S. S. R., education becomes a part of the economic and military machines. Men and women who are trained to fulfill technical functions in bureaucracies have little to do with the ends and meanings.

In underdeveloped countries, of course, we witness a movement from mass illiteracy to formal education; in the overdeveloped nations the movement is from mass education to educated illiteracy.

Although cryptic, does not this formula indicate in one sentence "the natural history of mass education?"

Everywhere, the image of the self-cultivating man as the goal of the human being has declined. It is the *specialist* who is ascendant in both Russia and America. The man whose field is most specialized is considered most advanced. Many cultural workmen, especially social investigators, try to imitate the supposed form of physical science. As a result they abdicate the intellectual and political autonomy of the classic traditions of their disciplines. Much social science nowadays is pretentious triviality; it is a set of bureaucratic techniques that inhibits social inquiry by methodological pretentions; that congests the work at hand by the obscurity of grand theory and trivializes itself by concern with minor problems that have no connnection with issues of public relevance or troubles of individuals.

In both the U. S. and the U. S. S. R. the specialist's ascendancy is underlaid, of course, by the ascendancy of physical science in the form of military and economic facts. In America, today, man's very relation to nature is being taken over by science machines, which are, at once, part of the privately incorporated economy and military ascendancy. Now, "science" is regularly identified with its more lethal or its more commercially-relevant products; it is less a part of the broad cultural traditions than of a closed-up and secret set of internationalist enterprises; less a realm in which the creative individual is free to innovate than a bureaucracy in which its cultural legacy is exploited by crash-techniques. The secrets of nature are made secrets of state, as science itself becomes a managed part of the machinery of World War III, and in the United States a part, also, of the wasteful absurdities of capitalism.

There is no set of free influential intellectuals in either country—in or out of the universities—that carries on the big discourse of the Western world. There are no truly independent minds that are directly relevant to powerful decisions.

I do not wish to minimize the important differences between the establishment of culture in the Soviet Union and in the United States. I wish neither to excuse the brutal facts of Soviet cultural tyranny, nor to celebrate the formal freedom of cultural workmen in the West. Surely there is enough such celebration of self and denunciation of a supposed enemy.

The formal freedom of the West rests upon cultural traditions of great force; this freedom is very real; it has been, and *is* immensely valuable. But, now, we must ask to what extent the continuation of this freedom is due to the fact that it is *not* being exercised. Certainly, in America today, there is much more celebration and defense of civil liberties than insurgent and effective use of them. Are not the cultural workmen of the West, by their intellectual and moral defaults, throwing away the legacy of their freedom?

We should bear in mind, however, that the ideals that we Westerners associate with the classic, liberal, bourgeois period of modern culture may well be rooted in this one historical stage of this one type of society. Such ideals as personal freedom and cultural autonomy may not be inherent, necessary features of cultural life as such. Our general belief that they will arise everywhere as insurgent ideals whenever occasion permits may be merely a provincial generalization of one historically specific place and epoch. The conditions of freedom that were characteristic of much of the eighteenth and nineteenth century West, are as well known as the fact that these same conditions have never prevailed in most of the world and, now, do not *flourish* in the West.

Also, we must understand that bureaucratization of culture may be brought about not only by co-ordination from above—by total persuasion—and by coercion; but also may result from the dominance of a completely commercial use of culture, with the voluntary self-co-ordination of cultural workmen.

Often, in totalitarian societies, intellectuals are locked up; in formal democracies, often, they lock themselves up, they withdraw from politics. This, I think, is what has been happening in the Western societies, and especially in the United States of America.

The withdrawal of intellectuals from political concerns is, in itself, a political act, but it is a pseudo withdrawal. To withdraw from politics today can only mean "in intent;" it cannot mean "in effect." In reality, its effect is to serve whatever powers prevail if only by distracting public attention from them. Such attempts may be the result of fear or fashion, or of sincere conviction—induced by success. Regardless of the motive, to attempt withdrawal is to become subservient to existing authorities and to allow other men to determine the meaning of one's own work. In 1790 John Adams wrote: "Bad men increase in knowledge as fast as good men, and science, art, taste, sense and letters are employed for the purposes of injustice and tyranny, as well as those of law and liberty; for corruption as well as for virtue."

In our present situation of the impoverished mind and lack of political will, United States intellectuals, it seems to me, have a unique opportunity to make a new beginning. If we want to, we can be independent craftsmen. To suggest programs for men who work culturally is not the same as for any other group. In the West it is precisely the character and position of many intellectuals and artists—and to some extent, still, of many scientists—that they are free to decide what they will or will not do in their working life. They are still free to consider the political decisions that they *are* making by their work. No other group of men is as free in just these ways; no other group, just now, is as strategically placed for possible innovation as those whose work joins them to the cultural apparatus; to the means of information and knowledge; to the means by which realities are defined, by which programs and politics are elaborated and presented to publics.

But what kinds of "politics" *can* intellectuals now pursue?

Today, a direct party struggle is not open to intellectuals either in America or in a Soviet bloc. (Whether it is open to intellectuals of Western Europe they would know better than I.) There is no movement or party or organization in America today that has a real chance to influence decisions of consequence and, at the same time, is open to the work of intellectuals. Given this, I think it is a waste of time and talent for American intellectuals to busy themselves with merely local and ineffective "politics" in the *name* of independent political action.

Yet we know that we cannot expect to maintain, much less to use, cultural freedom without waging a political as well as a cultural struggle, without realizing that these two struggles must be joined; and, I think, this joint political-cultural struggle must be waged in intellectual and moral ways rather than in a more direct political way. I do not believe that American intellectuals should attempt, merely, to guide or relate themselves to one class or organization. I do not believe, for example, that it is only "Labor" or "The Working Class" that can transform American society and change its role in world affairs. In brief, we can no longer say what ought to be done without saying, specifically, who ought to do it; and I, for one, do not believe in abstract social forces—such as The Working Class—as *the* universal historical agent.

Intellectuals have created standards and pointed out goals. Then, always, they have looked around for other groups, other circles, other strata to realize them. It is time, now, for us in America to try to realize them ourselves— in our own lives, in our own direct action, in the immediate context of our own work.

Now, we ought to repossess *our* cultural apparatus and use it for our own purposes.

This should be done personally and literally. It is a mistake for us to swallow ourselves in some great, vague, abstract, political "We." Of course, as creators and upholders of standards, we *do* want to generalize for other men the ideals for which, as public men, we stand; but we ought not to do so in a merely optative mood. We ought to do so, first of all, by acting in our own immediate *milieux*.

We are free men. Now we must take our heritage seriously. We must make clear the perils that threaten it. We must stop defending civil liberties long enough to use them. We must attempt to give content to our formal democracy by acting within it. We must stop whining about our own alienation long enough to use it to form radical critiques, audacious programs, commanding views of the future. If *we* do not do these things, who will?

National establishments and official lines have always benefited by denying the close connection between culture and politics. Left thinking has always assumed these connections and tried to make them explicit. Now, we must make clear the absurdity of the definitions of reality and the pretentions to truth of established culture by debunking it and revealing its political meanings. As intellectuals, we should conduct a continuing, uncompromising criticism of this established culture from the standpoint of—what so-called practical men of affairs call—utopian ideals.

Unless we do this we have no chance to offer alternative definitions of reality. And, of course, that is our major business. If we, as intellectuals, do not define and re-define reality, who will?

The writers among us bemoan the triviality of the mass media, but why—for the money and the prestige—do they allow themselves to be used in its silly routines by its silly managers? These media are part of *our* means of work which have been expropriated from us and are being used, now, by others for corrupting purposes. We should write and speak for these media on our own terms or not at all. We should ostracize the ghosts and the hacks who accept the terms of the expropriators, and attack them as men who prostitute their free talents and who disgrace us as an intellectual community.

Professors in America complain, yet they allow themselves to be exploited, turned into tired and routine people,

or into ineffectual entertainers. Why do they not demand
that staffs be sufficiently enlarged to enable men and women
to be properly educated, and to enable educators to control
the serious work they have to do?

It is easy for anyone to see that the two political parties
—and Congress—have often defaulted, that they neither
represent nor clarify alternatives to policies or lack of policies. But why must their obfuscations be elaborated, their
confusions echoed by writers and newsmen who make a
routine of the journalistic lie?

It is easy to see that officials of the United States Department of State now operate a censorship that is as arbitrary, rigid, and stupid as any in the Soviet Zone; but why
do American publishers and newsmen *accept,* for instance,
the ban on news of China, on what is happening among one
fourth of mankind? Why don't they fight for the right—in
both the U. S. and China—to know and to tell? Why don't
they really attempt to send one hundred newsmen to China
tomorrow morning?

It is easy to see that military metaphysicians are making
science into a Science Machine. But why must scientists and
technicians be so eager to develop the new weaponry; to
turn themselves into such political servants?

It is easy to see that religion has publicly become a mere
blessing of the thrust toward World War III. But why must
preachers and rabbis and priests support the moral irresponsibility of the elite that is serving this thrust?

It is easy to see that official definitions of world reality
are often absurd and, sometimes, even paranoid lies. But
why must scholars and publicists disseminate these absurd,
inadequate definitions of reality? Why must they study the
trivial subjects they do, rather than confront the insistent
and significant problems of our time?

We cannot expect to create a Left with mere slogans—
much less with the tired old slogans that bore us so.

We cannot create a Left by abdicating our roles as intellectuals to become working-class agitators or machine-
politicians, or by play-acting at any other direct political
action.

We *can* begin to create a Left by confronting issues as

intellectuals in our own work, and is it not obvious that *the* issue is now World War III?

In our studies of Man and Society, we must become fully comparative on a worldwide scale and in particular, we must re-examine with all the technical resources at our command our views concerning the Soviet Union, China, and the United States; and we must do so from viewpoints that are genuinely detached from *any* enclosure of mind or nationalist celebration.

We must become internationalists again. For us, today, this means that we, personally, must refuse to fight the Cold War; that we, personally, must attempt to get in touch with our opposite numbers in all countries of the world—above all, those in the Sino-Soviet Zone of nations.

With them we should make our own separate peace. Then, as intellectuals—and so as public men—we should act and work as if this peace—and the exchange of values, ideas, and programs of which it consists—is everybody's peace, or surely ought to be.

In summary, what we must do is to define the reality of the human condition and to make our definitions public; to confront the new facts of history-making in our time, and their meanings for the problem of political responsibility; to release the human imagination by transcending the mere exhortation of grand principle and opportunist reaction in order to explore all the alternatives now open to the human community.

If this—the politics of truth—is merely a holding action, so be it. If it is also a politics of desperation, so be it. But in this time and in America, it is the only realistic politics of possible consequence that is readily open to intellectuals. It is the guide line and the next step. It is an affirmation of one's self as a moral and intellectual center of responsible decision; the act of a free man who rejects "fate;" for it reveals his resolution to take his *own* fate, at least, into his own hands.

# 8

## CULTURE AND POLITICS

We are at the ending of what is called The Modern Age. Just as Antiquity was followed by several centuries of Oriental ascendancy which Westerners provincially call The Dark Ages, so now The Modern Age is being succeeded by a post-modern period. Perhaps we may call it: The Fourth Epoch.

The ending of one epoch and the beginning of another is, to be sure, a matter of definition. But definitions, like everything social, are historically specific. And now our basic definitions of society and of self are being overtaken by new realities. I do not mean merely that we *feel* we are in an epochal kind of transition. I mean that too many of our explanations are derived from the great historical transition from the Medieval to the Modern Age; and that when they are generalized for use today, they become unwieldy, irrelevant, not convincing. And I mean also that our major orientations—liberalism and socialism—have virtually collapsed as adequate explanations of the world and of ourselves.

### I

These two ideologies came out of The Enlightenment, and they have had in common many assumptions and two major values: in both, freedom and reason are supposed to coincide: increased rationality is held to be the prime condition of increased freedom. Those thinkers who have done the most to shape our ways of thinking have proceeded under this assumption; these values lie under every movement and nuance of the work of Freud: to be free, the individual must become more rationally aware; therapy is an aid to giving reason its chance to work freely in the course of an individual's life. These values underpin the main line of Marxist work: men, caught in the irrational anarchy of production, must become rationally aware of their position in society; they must become "class conscious"—the Marxian meaning of which is as rationalistic as any term set forth by Bentham.

Liberalism has been concerned with freedom and reason as supreme facts about the individual; Marxism as supreme facts about man's role in the political making of history. But what has been happening in the world makes evident, I believe, why the ideas of freedom and of reason now so often seem so ambiguous in both the capitalist and the communist societies of our time: why Marxism has so often become a dreary rhetoric of bureaucratic defense and political abuse; and liberalism, a trivial and irrelevant way of masking social reality. The major developments of our time can be adequately understood in terms of neither the liberal nor the Marxian interpretation of politics and culture. These ways of thought, after all, arose as guide-lines to reflection about types of society which do not now exist. John Stuart Mill never examined the kinds of political economy now arising in the capitalist world. Karl Marx never analyzed the kinds of society now arising in the Communist bloc. And neither of them ever thought through the problems of the so-called underdeveloped countries in which seven out of ten men are trying to exist today.

The ideological mark of The Fourth Epoch—that which sets it off from The Modern Age—is that the ideas of freedom and of reason have become moot; that increased rationality may not be assumed to make for increased freedom.

## II

The underlying trends are well known. Great and rational organizations—in brief, bureaucracies—have indeed increased, but the substantive reason of the individual at large has not. Caught in the limited milieux of their everyday lives, ordinary men often cannot reason about the great structures—rational and irrational—of which their *milieux* are subordinate parts. Accordingly, they often carry out series of apparently rational actions without any ideas of the ends they serve, and there is the increasing suspicion that those at the top as well—like Tolstoy's generals— only pretend they know. That the techniques and the rationality of science are given a central place in a society does not mean that men live reasonably and without myth, fraud and superstition. Science, it turns out, is not a technological Second Coming. Universal education may lead to technological idiocy and nationalist provinciality, rather than to the informed and independent intelligence. Rationally organized social arrangements are not necessarily a means of increased freedom—for the individual or for the society. In fact, often they are a means of tyranny and manipulation, a means of expropriating the very chance to reason, the very capacity to act as a free man.

The atrocities of The Fourth Epoch are committed by men as "functions" of a rational social machinery—men possessed by an abstracted view that hides from them the humanity of their victims and as well their own humanity. The moral insensibility of our times was made dramatic by the Nazis, but is not the same lack of human morality revealed by the atomic bombing of the peoples of Hiroshima and Nagasaki? And did it not prevail, too, among fighter pilots in Korea, with their petroleum-jelly broiling of children and women and men? Auschwitz and Hiroshima—are they not equally features of the highly rational moral-insensibility of The Fourth Epoch? And is not this lack of moral sensibility raised to a higher and technically more adequate level among the brisk generals and gentle scientists who are now rationally—and absurdly—planning the weapons and the strategy of the third world war? These actions are not necessarily sadistic; they are merely businesslike; they are not emotional at all; they are efficient, rational, technically clean-cut. They are inhuman acts because they are impersonal.

### III

In the meantime, ideology and sensibility quite apart, the compromises and exploitations by which the nineteenth-century world was balanced have collapsed. In this sixth decade of the twentieth century the structure of a new world is indeed coming into view.

The ascendancy of the USA, along with that of the USSR, has relegated the scatter of European nations to subsidiary status. The world of The Fourth Epoch is divided. On either side, a superpower now spends its most massive and co-ordinated effort in the highly scientific preparation of a third world war.

Yet, for the first time in history, the very idea of victory in war has become idiotic. As war becomes total, it becomes absurd. Yet in both the superstates, virtually all policies and actions fall within the perspective of war; in both, elites and spokesmen—in particular, I must say, those of the United States—are possessed by the military metaphysic, according to which all world reality is defined in military terms. By both, the most decisive features of reality are held to be the state of violence and the balance of fright.

Back of this struggle there is the world-encounter of two types of political economy, and in this encounter capitalism is losing. Some higher capitalists of the USA are becoming aware of this, and they are very much frightened. They fear, with good justification, that they are going to become an isolated and a second-rate power. They represent utopian capitalism in a world largely composed of people whose experiences with real capitalism, if any, have been mostly brutal. They profess "democracy" in a nation where it is more a formal outline than an actuality, and in a world in which the great majority of people have never experienced the bourgeois revolutions, in a world in which the values deposited by the Renaissance and the Reformation do not restrain the often brutal thrust to industrialize.

United States foreign policy and lack of foreign policy is firmly a part of the absurdity of this world scene, and it is foremost among the many defaults of the Western societies. During the last few years, confronting the brinks, I have often suspected that the world is not at the third world war largely because of the calculation and the forbearance of the Soviet elite.

What kind of a society is the USA turning out to be in the middle of the twentieth century? Perhaps it is possible to characterize it as a prototype of at least "The West." To locate it within its world context in The Fourth Epoch, perhaps we may call it The Overdeveloped Society.

The *Underdeveloped Country* as you know, is one in which the focus of life is necessarily upon economic subsistence; its industrial equipment is not sufficient to meet Western standards of minimum comfort. Its style of life and its system of power are dominated by the struggle to accumulate the primary means of industrial production.

In a *Properly Developing Society,* one might suppose that deliberately cultivated styles of life would be central; decisions about standards of living would be made in terms of debated choices among such styles; the industrial equipment of such a society would be maintained as an instrument to increase the range of choice among styles of life.

But in *The Overdeveloped Nation,* the standard of living dominates the style of life; its inhabitants are possessed, as it were, by its industrial and commercial apparatus: collectively, by the maintenance of conspicuous production; individually, by the frenzied pursuit and maintenance of commodities. Around these fetishes, life, labor and leisure are increasingly organized. Focused upon these, the struggle for status supplements the struggle for survival; a panic for status replaces the proddings of poverty.

In underdeveloped countries, industrialization, however harsh, may be seen as man conquering nature and so freeing himself from want. But in the overdeveloped nation, as industrialization proceeds, the economic emphasis moves from production to merchandizing, and the economic system which makes a fetish of efficiency becomes highly inefficient and systematically wasteful. The pivotal decade for this shift in the United States was the twenties, but it is since the ending of the second world war that the overdeveloped economy has truly come to flourish.

Surely there is no need to elaborate this theme in detail; since Thorstein Veblen formulated it, it has been several times "affluently" rediscovered. Society in brief has become a great sales-room—and a network of rackets: the gimmick of success becomes the yearly change of model, as in the mass-society fashion becomes universal. The marketing apparatus transforms the human being into the ultimately-saturated man—the cheerful robot—and makes "anxious obsolescence" the American way of life.

## V

But all this—although enormously important to the quality of life—is, I suppose, merely the obvious surface. Beneath it there are institutions which in the United States today are as far removed from the images of Tocqueville as is Russia today from the classic expectations of Marx.

The power structure of this society is based upon a privately incorporated economy that is also a permanent war economy. Its most important relations with the state now rest upon the coincidence of military and corporate interests—as defined by generals and businessmen, and accepted by politicians and publics. It is an economy dominated by a few hundred corporations, economically and politically interrelated, which together hold the keys to economic decision. These dominating corporation-hierarchies probably represent the highest concentration of the greatest economic power in human history, including that of the Soviet Union. They are firmly knit to political and military institutions, but they are dogmatic—even maniacal—in their fetish of the "freedom" of their private and irresponsible power.

I should like to put this matter in terms of certain parallel developments in the USA and the USSR. The very terms of their world antagonism are furthering their similarities. Geographically and ethnically both are supersocieties; unlike the nations of Europe, each has amalgamated on a continental domain great varieties of peoples and cultures. The power of both is based upon technological development. In both, this development is made into a cultural and a social fetish, rather than an instrument under continual public appraisal and control. In neither is there significant craftsmanship in work or significant leisure in the non-working life. In both, men at leisure and at work are subjected to impersonal bureaucracies. In neither do workers control the process of production or consumers truly shape the process of consumption. Workers' control is as far removed from both as is consumers' sovereignty.

In both the United States and the Soviet Union, as the political order is enlarged and centralized, it becomes less political and more bureaucratic; less the locale of a struggle than an object to be managed. In neither are there nationally responsible parties which debate openly and clearly the issues which these nations, and indeed the world, now so rigidly confront. Under some conditions, must we not recognize that the two-party state can be as irresponsible as is a one-party state?

In neither the USA nor the USSR is there a senior civil service firmly linked to the world of knowledge and sensibility and composed of skilled men who, in their careers and in their aspirations, are truly independent—in the USA of corporation interests, in the USSR of party dictation.

In neither of these superpowers are there, as central facts of power, voluntary associations linking individuals, smaller communities and publics, on the one hand, with the state, the military establishment, the economic apparatus on the other. Accordingly, in neither are there readily available vehicles for reasoned opinions and instruments for the national exertion of public will. Such voluntary associations are no longer a dominant feature of the political structure of the overdeveloped society.

The classic conditions of democracy, in summary, do not exactly flourish in the overdeveloped society; democratic formations are not now ascendant in the power structure of the United States or of the Soviet Union. Within both, history-making decisions and lack of decisions are virtually monopolized by elites who have access to the material and cultural means by which history is now powerfully being made.

## V I

I stress these parallels, and perhaps exaggerate them, because of the great nationalist emphasis upon the differences between the two world antagonists. The parallels are, of course, due in each case to entirely different sources; and so are the great differences. In the capitalist societies the development of the means of power has occurred gradually, and many cultural traditions have restrained and shaped them. In most of the Communist societies they have happened rapidly and brutally and from the beginning under tightly centralized authority; and without the cultural revolutions which in the West so greatly strengthened and gave political focus to the idea of human freedom.

You may say that all this is an immoderate and biased view of America, that America also contains many good features. Indeed that is so. But you must not expect me to provide A Balanced View. I am not a sociological book-keeper. Moreover, "balanced views" are now usually surface views which rest upon the homogeneous absence of imagination and the passive avoidance of reflection. A balanced view is usually, in the phrase of Royden Harrison, merely a vague point of equilibrium between platitudes.

I feel no need for, and perhaps am incapable of arranging for you, a lyric upsurge, a cheerful little pat on the moral back. Yet perhaps, by returning to my point of beginning, I can remind you of the kinds of problems you might want to confront. I must make two points only: one about fate and the making of history; the other about the roles many intellectuals are now enacting.

Fate has to do with events in history that arc the summary and unintended results of innumerable decisions of innumerable men. Each of their decisions is minute in consequence and subject to cancellation or reinforcement by other such decisions. There is no link between any one man's intention and the summary result of the innumerable decisions. Events are beyond human decisions: history is made behind men's backs.

So conceived, fate is not a universal fact; it is not inherent in the nature of history or in the nature of man. In a society in which the ultimate weapon is the rifle; in which the typical economic unit is the family farm and shop; in which the national-state does not yet exist or is merely a distant framework; and in which communication is by

word of mouth, handbill, pulpit—in *such* a society, history
is indeed fate.

But consider now the major clue to our condition, to the
shape of the overdeveloped society in The Fourth Epoch.
In modern industrial society the means of economic production are developed and centralized, as peasants and arti-
sans are replaced by private corporations and government
industries. In the modern nation-state the means of violence and of administration undergo similar developments,
as kings control nobles and self-equipped knights are replaced by standing armies and now by fearful military
machines. The *post-modern* climax of all three developments—in economics, in politics, and in violence—is now
occurring most dramatically in the USA and the USSR. In
the polarized world of our time, international as well as
national means of history-making are being centralized. Is
it not thus clear that the scope and the chance for conscious
human agency in history-making are just now uniquely
available? Elites of power in charge of these means do now
make history—to be sure, "under circumstances not of
their own choosing"—but compared to other men and
other epochs, these circumstances themselves certainly do
not appear to be overwhelming.

And surely here is the paradox of our immediate situation: the facts about the newer means of history-making
are a signal that men are not necessarily in the grip of fate,
that men *can* now make history. But this fact stands ironically alongside the further fact that just now those ideologies which offer men the hope of making history have declined and are collapsing in the overdeveloped nation of
the United States. That collapse is also the collapse of the
expectations of the Enlightment, that reason and freedom
would come to prevail as paramount forces in human history. It also involves the abdication of many Western intellectuals.

## VII

In the overdeveloped society, where is the intelligentsia
that is carrying on the big discourse of the Western world
*and* whose work as intellectuals is influential among parties

and publics and relevant to the great decisions of our time? Where are the mass media open to such men? Who among those in charge of the two-party state and its ferocious military machines are alert to what goes on in the world of knowledge and reason and sensibility? Why is the free intellect so divorced from decisions of power? Why does there now prevail among men of power such a higher and irresponsible ignorance?

In The Fourth Epoch, must we not face the possibility that the human mind as a social fact might be deteriorating in quality and cultural level, and yet not many would notice it because of the overwhelming accumulation of technological gadgets? Is not that the meaning of rationality without reason? Of human alienation? Of the absence of any role for reason in human affairs? The accumulation of gadgets hides these meanings: those who use them do not understand them; those who invent and maintain them do not understand much else. That is why we may not, without great ambiguity, use technological abundance as the index of human quality and cultural progress.

## VIII

To formulate any problem requires that we state the values involved and the threat to these values. For it is the felt threat to cherished values—such as those of freedom and reason—that is the necessary moral substance of all significant problems of social inquiry, and as well of all public issues and private troubles.

The values involved in the cultural problem of freedom and individuality are conveniently embodied in all that is suggested by the ideal of The Renaissance Man. The threat to that ideal is the ascendancy among us of The Cheerful Robot, of the man with rationality but without reason. The values involved in the political problem of history-making are embodied in the Promethean ideal of its human making. The threat to that ideal is twofold: On the one hand, history-making may well go by default, men may continue to abdicate its willful making, and so merely drift. On the other hand, history may indeed be made—but by narrow elite circles without effective responsibility to those who must try to survive the consequences of their decisions and of their defaults.

I do not know the answer to the question of political irresponsibility in our time or to the cultural and political question of The Cheerful Robot; but is it not clear that no answers will be found unless these problems are at least confronted? Is it not obvious that the ones to confront them, above all others, are the intellectuals, the scholars, the ministers, the scientists of the rich societies? That many of them do not now do so, with moral passion, with intellectual energy, is surely the greatest human default being committed by privileged men in our times.

# 9

## THE NEW LEFT

It is no exaggeration to say that since the end of World War II in Britain and the United States smug conservatives, tired liberals and disillusioned radicals have carried on a weary discourse in which issues are blurred and potential debate muted; the sickness of complacency has prevailed, the bi-partisan banality flourished. There is no need—after your book—to explain again why all this has come about among "people in general" in the NATO countries; but it may be worthwhile to examine one style of cultural work that is in effect an intellectual celebration of apathy.

Many intellectual fashions, of course, do just that; they stand in the way of a release of the imagination—about the cold war, the Soviet bloc, the politics of peace, about any new beginnings at home and abroad. But the fashion I have in mind is the weariness of many NATO intellectuals with what they call "ideology," and their proclamation of "the end of ideology." So far as I know, this began in the mid-fifties, mainly in intellectual circles more or less associated with the Congress for Cultural Freedom and the magazine *Encounter*. Reports on the Milan Conference of 1955 heralded it; since then, many cultural gossips have taken it up as a posture and an unexamined slogan. Does it amount to anything?

Its common denominator is not liberalism as a political philosophy, but the liberal rhetoric, become formal and sophisticated and used as an uncriticised weapon with which to attack Marxism. In the approved style, various of the elements of this rhetoric appear simply as snobbish assumptions. Its sophistication is one of tone rather than of ideas: in it, the *New Yorker* style of reportage has become politically triumphant. The disclosure of fact—set forth in a bright-faced or in a dead-pan manner—is the rule. The facts are duly weighed, carefully balanced, always hedged. Their power to outrage, their power truly to enlighten in a political way, their power to aid decision, even their power to clarify some situation—all that is blunted or destroyed.

So reasoning collapses into reasonableness. By the more naive and snobbish celebrants of complacency, arguments and facts of a displeasing kind are simply ignored; by the more knowing they are duly recognized, but they are neither connected with one another nor related to any general view. Acknowledged in a scattered way, they are never put together: to do so is to risk being called, curiously enough, "one-sided."

This refusal to relate isolated facts and fragmentary comment with the changing institutions of society makes it impossible to understand the structural realities which these facts might reveal; the longer-run trends of which they might be tokens. In brief, fact and idea are isolated, so the real questions are not even raised, analysis of the meanings of fact not even begun.

Practitioners of the no-more-ideology school do of course smuggle in general ideas under the guise of reportage, by intellectual gossip, and by their selection of the notions they handle. Ultimately, the-end-of-ideology is based upon a disillusionment with any real commitment to socialism in any recognizable form. *That* is the only "ideology" that has really ended for these writers. But with its ending, *all* ideology, they think, has ended. *That* ideology they talk about; their own ideological assumptions, they do not.

Underneath this style of observation and comment there is the assumption that in the West there are no more real issues or even problems of great seriousness. The mixed economy plus the welfare state plus prosperity—that is the formula. US capitalism will continue to be workable; the welfare state will continue along the road to ever greater justice. In the meantime, things everywhere are very complex, let us not be careless, there are great risks . . .

This posture—one of "false consciousness" if there ever was one—stands in the way, I think, of considering with any chances of success what may be happening in the world.

First and above all, it does rest upon a simple provincialism. If the phrase "the end of ideology" has any meaning at all, it pertains to self-selected circles of intellectuals in the richer countries. It is in fact merely their own self-image. The total population of these countries is a fraction of mankind; the period during which such a posture has been assumed is very short indeed. To speak in such terms of much of Latin-America, Africa, Asia, the Soviet bloc is merely ludicrous. Anyone who stands in front of audiences—intellectual or mass—in any of these places and talks in such terms will merely be shrugged off (if the audience is polite) or laughed at out loud (if the audience is more candid and knowledgeable). The end-of-ideology is a slogan of complacency, circulating among the prematurely middle-aged, centred in the present, and in the rich Western societies. In the final analysis, it also rests upon a disbelief in the shaping by men of their own futures—as history and as biography. It is a consensus of a few provincials about their own immediate and provincial position.

Second, the end-of-ideology is of course itself an ideology —a fragmentary one, to be sure, and perhaps more a mood. The end-of-ideology is in reality the ideology of an ending: the ending of political reflection itself as a public fact. It is a weary know-it-all justification—by tone of voice rather than by explicit argument—of the cultural and political default of the NATO intellectuals.

All this is just the sort of thing that I at least have always objected to, and do object to, in the "socialist realism" of the Soviet Union.

There too, criticism of *milieux* are of course permitted —but they are not to be connected with criticism of the structure itself: one may not question "the system." There are no "antagonistic contradictions."

There too, in novels and plays, criticisms of characters, even of party members, are permitted—but they must be displayed as "shocking exceptions": they must be seen as survivals from the old order, not as systematic products of the new.

There too, pessimism is permitted—but only episodically and only within the context of the big optimism: the tend-

ency is to confuse any systematic or structural criticism
with pessimism itself. So they admit criticisms, first of this
and then of that: but engulf them all by the long-run historical optimism about the system as a whole and the goals
proclaimed by its leaders.

I neither want nor need to overstress the parallel, yet in
a recent series of interviews in the Soviet Union concerning socialist realism I was very much struck by it. In Uz-
bekistan and Georgia as well as in Russia, I kept writing
notes to myself, at the end of recorded interviews: "This
man talks in a style just like Arthur Schlesinger Jr." "Surely
this fellow's the counterpart of Daniel Bell, except not so
—what shall I say?—so gossipy: and certainly neither so
petty nor so vulgar as the more envious status-climbers.
Perhaps this is because here they are not thrown into such
a competitive status-panic about the ancient and obfuscat-
ing British models of prestige." The would-be enders of
ideology, I kept thinking, "Are they not the self-coordi-
nated, or better the fashion-coordinated, socialist realists
of the NATO world?" And: "Check this carefully with the
files of *Encounter* and *The Reporter.*" I have now done
so; it's the same kind of . . . thing.

Certainly there are many differences—above all, the fact
that socialist realism is part of an official line; the end of
ideology is self-managed. But the differences one knows. It
is more useful to stress the parallels—and the generic fact
that both of these postures stand opposed to radical criticisms of their respective societies.

In the Soviet Union, only political authorities at the top
—or securely on their way up there—can seriously tamper
with structural questions and ideological lines. These authorities, of course, are much more likely to be intellectuals
(in one or another sense of the word—say a man who
actually writes his own speeches) than are American politicians (about the British, you would know better than I).
Moreover, such Soviet authorities, since the death of
Stalin, *have* begun to tamper quite seriously with structural
questions and basic ideology—although for reasons peculiar to the tight and official joining of culture and politics
in their set-up, they must try to disguise this fact.

The end-of-ideology is very largely a mechanical reaction

—not a creative response—to the ideology of Stalinism. As such it takes from its opponent something of its inner quality. What does it all mean? That these people have become aware of the uselessness of Vulgar Marxism, but not yet aware of the uselessness of the liberal rhetoric.

But the most immediately important thing about the "end of ideology" is that it *is* merely a fashion, and fashions change. Already this one is on its way out. Even a few Diehard Anti-Stalinists are showing signs of a reappraisal of their own past views; some are even beginning to recognise publicly that Stalin himself no longer runs the Soviet party and state. They begin to see the poverty of their comfortable ideas as they come to confront Khrushchev's Russia.

We who have been consistently radical in the moral terms of our work throughout the postwar period are often amused nowadays that various writers—sensing another shift in fashion—begin to call upon intellectuals to work once more in ways that are politically explicit. But we shouldn't be merely amused—we ought to try to make their shift more than a fashion change.

The end-of-ideology is on the way out because it stands for the refusal to work out an explicit political philosophy. And alert men everywhere today do feel the need of such a philosophy. What we should do is to continue directly to confront this need. In doing so, it may be useful to keep in mind that to have a working political philosophy means to have a philosophy that enables you to work. And for that, at least four kinds of work are needed, each of them at once intellectual and political.

In these terms, think—for a moment longer—of the end-of-ideology:

(1) It is a kindergarten fact that any political reflection that is of possible public significance is *ideological*: in its terms, policies, institutions, men of power are criticized or approved. In this respect, the end-of-ideology stands, negatively, for the attempt to withdraw oneself and one's work from political relevance; positively, it is an ideology of political complacency which seems the only way now open for many writers to acquiesce in or to justify the *status quo*.

(2) So far as orienting *theories* of society and of history

are concerned, the end-of-ideology stands for, and presumably stands upon, a fetishism of empiricism: more
academically, upon a pretentious methodology used to state
trivialities about unimportant social areas; more essayisti-
cally, upon a naive journalistic empiricism—which I have
already characterized above—and upon a cultural gossip
in which "answers" to the vital and pivotal issues are
merely assumed. Thus political bias masquerades as epistemological excellence, and there are no orienting theories.
(3) So far as the *historic agency of change* is concerned,
the end-of-ideology stands upon the identification of such
agencies with going institutions; perhaps upon their piece-
meal reform, but never upon the search for agencies that
might be used or that might themselves make for a structural change of society. The problem of agency is never
posed as a problem to solve, as our problem. Instead there
is talk of the need to be pragmatic, flexible, open. Surely
all this has already been adequately dealt with: such a
view makes sense politically only if the blind drift of human
affairs is in general beneficent.

(4) So far as political and human *ideals* are concerned, the
end-of-ideology stands for a denial of their relevance—except as abstract ikons. Merely to hold such ideals seriously
is in this view "utopian."

But enough. Where do *we* stand on each of these four
aspects of political philosophy? Various of us are of course
at work on each of them, and all of us are generally aware
of our needs in regard to each. As for the articulation of
ideals: there I think your magazines have done their best
work so far. That is *your* meaning—is it not?—of the emphasis upon cultural affairs. As for ideological analysis,
and the rhetoric with which to carry it out: I don't think
any of us are nearly good enough, but that will come with
further advance on the two fronts where we are weakest:
theories of society, history, human nature; and the major
problem—ideas about the historical agencies of structural
change.

We have frequently been told by an assorted variety of
dead-end people that the meanings of Left and of Right
are now liquidated, by history and by reason. I think we
should answer them in some such way as this:

The Right, among other things, means—what you are doing, celebrating society as it is, a going concern. Left means, or ought to mean, just the opposite. It means: structural criticism and reportage and theories of society, which at some point or another are focussed politically as demands and programmes. These criticisms, demands, theories, programmes are guided morally by the humanist and secular ideals of Western civilization—above all, reason and freedom and justice. To be "Left" means to connect up cultural with political criticism, and both with demands and programmes. And it means all this inside *every* country of the world.

Only one more point of definition: absence of public issues there may well be, but this is not due to any absence of problems or of contradictions, antagonistic and otherwise. Impersonal and structural changes have not eliminated problems or issues. Their absence from many discussions—that *is* an ideological condition, regulated in the first place by whether or not intellectuals detect and state problems as potential *issues* for probable publics, and as *troubles* for a variety of individuals. One indispensable means of such work on these central tasks is what can only be described as ideological analysis. To be actively Left, among other things, is to carry on just such analysis.

To take seriously the problem of the need for a political orientation is not of course to seek for A Fanatical and Apocalyptic Vision, for An Infallible and Monolithic Lever of Change, for Dogmatic Ideology, for A Startling New Rhetoric, for Treacherous Abstractions—and all the other bogeymen of the dead-enders. These are of course "the extremes," the straw men, the red herrings, used by our political enemies as the polar opposite of where they think they stand.

They tell us, for example, that ordinary men can't always be political "heroes." Who said they could? But keep looking around you; and why not search out the conditions of such heroism as men do and might display? They tell us we are too "impatient," that our "pretentious" theories are not well enough grounded. That is true, but neither are they trivial; why don't they get to work, refuting or grounding them? They tell us we "don't really understand" Rus-

sia—and China—today. That is true; we don't; neither do
they; we are studying it. They tell us we are "ominous" in
our formulations. That is true: we do have enough imagination to be frightened—and we don't have to hide it: we
are not afraid we'll panic. They tell us we "are grinding
axes." Of course we are: we do have, among other points
of view, morally grounded ones; and we are aware of them.
They tell us, in their wisdom, we don't understand that The
Struggle is Without End. True: we want to change its form,
its focus, its object.

We are frequently accused of being "utopian"—in our
criticisms and in our proposals; and along with this, of
basing our hopes for a New Left *politics* "merely on reason," or more concretely, upon the intelligentsia in its
broadest sense.

There is truth in these charges. But must we not ask:
what now is really meant by utopian? And: Is not our
utopianism a major source of our strength? "Utopian"
nowadays I think refers to any criticism or proposal that
transcends the up-close *milieux* of a scatter of individuals:
the *milieux* which men and women can understand directly
and which they can reasonably hope directly to change. In
this exact sense, our theoretical work is indeed utopian—
in my own case, at least, deliberately so. What needs to be
understood, and what needs to be changed, is not merely
first this and then that detail of some institution or policy.
If there is to be a politics of a New Left, what needs to be
analysed is the *structure* of institutions, the *foundation* of
policies. In this sense, both in its criticisms and in its proposals, our work is necessarily structural—and so, *for us,*
just now—utopian.

Which brings us face to face with the most important
issue of political reflection—and of political action—in
our time: the problem of the historical agency of change,
of the social and institutional means of structural change.
There are several points about this problem I would like
to put to you.

First, the historic agencies of change for liberals of the
capitalist societies have been an array of voluntary associations, coming to a political climax in a parliamentary
or congressional system. For socialists of almost all varie-

ties, the historic agency has been the working class—and
later the peasantry; also parties and unions variously composed of members of the working class or (to blur, for now,
a great problem) of political parties acting in its name—
"representing its interests."

I cannot avoid the view that in both cases, the historic
agency (in the advanced capitalist countries) has either
collapsed or become most ambiguous: so far as structural
change is concerned, *these* don't seem to be at once available and effective as *our* agency any more. I know this is
a debatable point among us, and among many others as
well; I am by no means certain about it. But surely the fact
of it—if it be that—ought not to be taken as an excuse for
moaning and withdrawal (as it is by some of those who
have become involved with the end-of-ideology); it ought
not to be bypassed (as it is by many Soviet scholars and
publicists, who in their reflections upon the course of advanced capitalist societies simply refuse to admit the political condition and attitudes of the working class).

Is anything more certain than that in 1970—indeed this
time next year—our situation will be quite different, and—
the chances are high—decisively so? But of course, that
isn't saying much. The seeming collapse of our historic
agencies of change ought to be taken as a problem, an
issue, a trouble—in fact, as *the* political problem which *we*
must turn into issue and trouble.

Second, is it not obvious that when we talk about the
collapse of agencies of change, we cannot seriously mean
that such agencies do not exist. On the contrary, the means
of history-making—of decision and of the enforcement of
decision—have never in world history been so enlarged
and so available to such small circles of men on both sides
of The Curtains as they now are. My own conception of the
shape of power—the theory of the power elite—I feel no
need to argue here. This theory has been fortunate in its
critics, from the most diverse points of political view, and
I have learned from several of these critics. But I have not
seen, as of this date, any analysis of the idea that causes me
to modify any of its essential features.

The point that is immediately relevant does seem obvious: what is utopian for us is not at all utopian for the

presidium of the Central Committee in Moscow, or the higher circles of the Presidency in Washington, or—recent events make evident—for the men of SAC and CIA. The historic agencies of change that have collapsed are those which were at least thought to be open to *the left* inside the advanced Western nations: those who have wished for structural changes of these societies. Many things follow from this obvious fact; of many of them, I am sure, we are not yet adequately aware.

Third, what I do not quite understand about some New-Left writers is why they cling so mightily to "the working class" of the advanced capitalist societies as *the* historic agency, or even as the most important agency, in the face of the really impressive historical evidence that now stands against this expectation.

Such a labor metaphysic, I think, is a legacy from Victorian Marxism that is now quite unrealistic.

It is an historically specific idea that has been turned into an a-historical and unspecific hope.

The social and historical conditions under which industrial workers tend to become a-class-for-themselves, and a decisive political force, must be fully and precisely elaborated. There have been, there are, there will be such conditions; of course these conditions vary according to national social structure and the exact phase of their economic and political development. Of course we can't "write off the working class." But we must *study* all that, and freshly. Where labor exists as an agency, of course we must work with it, but we must not retreat it as The Necessary Lever—as nice old Labor Gentlemen in your country and elsewhere tend to do.

Although I have not yet completed my own comparative studies of working classes, generally it would seem that only at certain (earlier) stages of industrialization, and in a political context of autocracy, etc., do wage-workers tend to become a class-for-themselves, etc. The "etcs." mean that I can here merely raise the question.

It is with this problem of agency in mind that I have been studying, for several years now, the cultural apparatus, the intellectuals—as a possible, immediate, radical agency of change. For a long time, I was not much happier with this idea than were many of you; but it turns out now, in the spring of 1960, that it may be a very relevant idea indeed.

In the first place, is it not clear that if we try to be realistic in our utopianism—and that is no fruitless contradiction—a writer in our countries on the Left today *must* begin there? For that is what we are, that is where we stand.

In the second place, the problem of the intelligentsia is an extremely complicated set of problems on which rather little factual work has been done. In doing this work, we must—above all—not confuse the problems of the intellectuals of West Europe and North America with those of the Soviet Bloc or with those of the underdeveloped worlds. In each of the three major components of the world's social structure today, the character and the role of the intelligentsia is distinct and historically specific. Only by detailed comparative studies of them in all their human variety can we hope to understand any one of them.

In the third place, who is it that is getting fed up? Who is it that is getting disgusted with what Marx called "all the old crap"? Who is it that is thinking and acting in radical ways? All over the world—in the bloc, outside the bloc and in between—the answer's the same: it is the young intelligentsia.

I cannot resist copying out for you, with a few changes, some materials I've just prepared for a 1960 paperback edition of a book of mine on war:

"In the spring and early summer of 1960—more of the returns from the American decision and default are coming in. In Turkey, after student riots, a military junta takes over the state, of late run by Communist-Container Menderes. In South Korea too, students and others knock over the corrupt American-puppet regime of Syngman Rhee. In Cuba, a genuinely left-wing revolution begins full-scale economic reorganization—without the domination of US corporations. Average age of its leaders: about 30—and certainly a revolution without any Labor As Agency. On Taiwan, the eight million Taiwanese under the American-imposed dictatorship of Chiang Kai-shek, with his two million Chinese grow increasingly restive. On Okinawa—a

US military base—the people get their first chance since
World War II ended to demonstrate against US seizure
of their island: and some students take that chance, snake-
dancing and chanting angrily to the visiting President: "Go
home, go home—take away your missiles." (Don't worry,
12,000 US troops easily handled the generally grateful
crowds; also the President was "spirited out the rear end
of the United States compound"—and so by helicopter to
the airport). In Great Britain, from Aldermaston to London, young—but you were there. In Japan, weeks of student rioting succeed in rejecting the President's visit,
jeopardize a new treaty with the USA, displace the big-
business, pro-American Prime Minister, Kishi. And even
in our own pleasant Southland, Negro and white students
are—but let us keep that quiet: it really *is* disgraceful.

"That is by no means the complete list; that was yesterday; see today's newspaper. Tomorrow, in varying degree,
the returns will be more evident. Will they be evident
enough? They will have to be very obvious to attract real
American attention: sweet complaints and the voice of
reason—these are not enough. In the slum countries of
the world today, what are they saying? The rich Americans,
they pay attention only to violence—and to money. You
don't care what they say, American? Good for you. Still,
they may insist; things are no longer under the old control;
you're not getting it straight, American: your country—it
would seem—may well become the target of a world hatred
of the like of which the easy-going Americans have never
dreamed. Neutralists and Pacifists and Unilateralists and
that confusing variety of Leftists around the world—all
those tens of millions of people, of course they are mis-
guided, absolutely controlled by small conspiratorial groups
of trouble-makers, under direct orders straight from Moscow and Peking. Diabolically omnipotent, it is *they* who
create all this messy unrest. It is *they* who have given the
tens of millions the absurd idea that they shouldn't want
to remain, or to become, the seat of American nuclear
bases—those gay little outposts of American civilization.
So now they don't want U-2's on their territory; so now
they want to contract out of the American military machine; they want to be neutral among the crazy big an-

tagonists. And they don't want their own societies to be
militarized.

"But take heart, American: you won't have time to get
really bored with your friends abroad: they won't be your
friends much longer. You don't need *them*; it will all go
away; don't let them confuse you."

Add to that: In the Soviet bloc, who is it that has been
breaking out of apathy? It has been students and young
professors and writers; it has been the young intelligentsia
of Poland and Hungary, and of Russia too. Never mind that
they've not won; never mind that there are other social
and moral types among them. First of all, it has been these
types. But the point is clear—isn't it?

That's why we've got to study these new generations of
intellectuals around the world as real live agencies of historic change. Forget Victorian Marxism except whenever
you need it; and read Lenin again (be careful)—Rosa
Luxemburg, too.

"But it's just some kind of moral upsurge, isn't it?"
Correct. But under it: no apathy. Much of it is direct non-
violent action, and it seems to be working, here and there.
Now we must learn from their practice and work out with
them new forms of action.

"But it's all so ambiguous. Turkey, for instance. Cuba,
for instance." Of course it is; history-making is always ambiguous; wait a bit; in the meantime, *help* them to focus
their moral upsurge in less ambiguous political ways; work
out with them the ideologies, the strategies, the theories that
will help them consolidate their efforts: new theories of
structural changes of and by human societies in our epoch.

"But it's utopian, after all, isn't it?" No—not in the sense
you mean. Whatever else it may be, it's not that: tell it to
the students of Japan.

Isn't all this, isn't it something of what we are trying to
mean by the phrase, "The New Left?" Let the old men
ask sourly, "Out of Apathy—into what?" The Age of Complacency is ending. Let the old women complain wisely
about "the end of ideology." We are beginning to move
again.

# PART THREE

# I

## THE COMPETITIVE PERSONALITY

### I

For liberals, competition has never been merely an impersonal mechanism regulating the economy of capitalism. It has been a guarantee of political freedom, a system for producing free individuals, and a testing field for heroes. These have been the alibis of the liberals for the hurt that competition has caused the people ground between the big sharp edges of its workings.

In every area of life, liberals have imagined independent individuals freely competing so that merit might win and character develop: in the free contractual marriage, the Protestant church, the voluntary association, the democratic state, as well as on the economic market. Competition is the way liberalism would integrate its historic era; it is also the central feature of liberalism's style of life.

The hero of liberalism has exemplified the ways of competition in every sphere of life, but it was in the economic sphere that his merit came out most clearly, and it was by virtue of his business career that he attained power and glory and even the legendary purity of which heroes are made.

As the worlds of monopoly spread out their grasp, the classic exemplar of liberalism, the old captain of industry, took on, at least in his cruder images, a somewhat bloated and overbearing shape. By the twentieth century he had been replaced in the business world by other types of economic men, among them the industrial rentier and the corporation executive, the little business and white-collar men, as well as a type we shall presently describe as the new entrepreneur. None of these have successfully filled the heroic place of the old, undivided captain of industry.

The public image of the rentier is not that of a productively competitive man; he is either the stealthy miser or the lavish consumer. He doesn't live the business-wise life of competition, and even the liberal economists dislike his economic role. The corporation executive has never been a popular middle-class idol; he is too cold and high with impersonal power. On the engineering side, he is part of inexorable science, and no economic hero; and on the business side, he is correctly seen as part of the big finance.

It was the little man of business, with all his engaging human characteristics, who became the hero of liberalism in the early twentieth century. He has been seen as the somewhat woebegone inheritor of the old captain's tradition, even if only by default. The harder his struggle has become, the more sympathetic and the more heroized his image has been drawn; yet his plight has been a sad one, for he cannot live up to the heritage by which he is burdened.

The laws and planning of the Progressive Era, the muckraking, the square deals and new freedoms were, at least verbally, attempts to buck up the little businessman, that he might better live up to the carefully presented image of him. Much of the New Deal was dealt in his honor, lest he become a forgotten man. And in the decade after 1933, he became even more officially the hero of the liberal system; no less than 390 bills in his behalf were introduced for consideration by the Congress.

The Monographs and Hearings of the Temporary National Economic Committee are the last great scholarly and official monument to liberalism's little hero. Like other large attempts on behalf of things as they are imagined or hoped to be, the TNEC fetishizes competition and heroizes little business. But it does so under an enormous burden of fact. Only the necessary screen of political rhetoric, the peculiar structure of political representation, and the myopia induced by small-town life has kept this senatorial fetish and this heroic image alive. Now that the TNEC is well buried by war, we may treat it as a symbol,* having

* An excellent case study and partial summary of the Hearings has recently been written by David Lynch: *The Concentration of Economic Power,* Columbia University Press (New York, 1946). Some of the TNEC series have been brought up through the war in a publication of the Smaller War Plants: "Economic Concentration and World War II," U. S. Senate, 79th Congress, 2nd Session, Document No. 206 (Washington, 1946).

positive as well as negative references. For underneath its rhetoric and resting on its facts, we may discern the present role of competition as well as some new types of economic men and women, who are living a new competitive life in the age of corporate bureaucracy.

What the million dollars' worth of TNEC facts demonstrate, no matter how they are arranged, is the detailed accuracy of Veblen's remark that competition is by no means dead, only now it is chiefly "competition between the businessman who controls production, on the one side, and the consuming public, on the other side; the chief expedient in this business-like competition being salesmanship and sabotage." What the TNEC documents was already well supposed, but now the documentation is directly from the mouths of the men who run things. In telling of the manner in which competition has been hedged in by giant corporations, and by groups of smaller corporations acting collectively, they have made clear the locus of the big competition and the masklike character of liberalism's rhetoric.

Yet for the benefit of their imaginary hero, the senators, and their experts, have persisted in fetishizing this mask of big business. They have proposed that the good old captains of industry be given a rebirth with the full benefit of governmental midwifery.

Charles Beard has remarked that this proposal resembles not a mouse creeping out of a mountain of fact but a mere squeak. Yet it remains the best that the official liberal has to say about the economic facts of life. In continuing to see competition as salvation from complicated trouble, the priestlike senators in charge of the ceremony naturally fall into the old petty-bourgeois complaints; and the experts, perhaps for the record, fall in with the senators. Now they are together in the big volumes with their thin little wisdom. But their wisdom is nostalgic, and their offerings are dwarfed by the great facts of the modern economy. Their mood ought to be the mood of plight, but they have succeeded in setting up a bright image of the little businessman, who could be rehabilitated as the hero of their system, if only competition were once more to prevail.

## II

This liberal hero, the little businessman, has a tendency to forget the senatorial rhetoric put out in his behalf; he doesn't seem to want to develop his character by free and open competition. Last year in six middle-sized cities, arbitrarily selected samples of little businessmen were asked if they thought "free competition was by and large a good thing." With authority and vehemence they all answered, Yes, of course, what do you mean? Then they were asked, "Here in this, your town?" Yes, they said, but now hesitating a little. Finally: How about here in this town in furniture, or groceries—or whatever the man's specific line was. Their answers were of two sorts: Yes, if it's fair competition, which turned out to mean something very simple and understandable: If it doesn't make me compete. The second type of answer also adds up to the brotherliness of the little businessmen, and their competitive opposition to the public: Well, you see, in certain lines, it's no good if there are too many businesses. You ought to kinda keep the other fellow's business in mind. The little businessman wants to become big, not by directly eating up the other fellow's business in competition, but by the indirect ways and means practiced by his own particular heroes—those already big. In the dream life of the little businessman, the sure fix is replacing the open market.

But if the little businessman is going back on his liberal spokesmen, he cannot really be blamed, for the liberal spokesmen, without knowing it, have also been going back on their little business hero. Only government, these spokesmen say, can save little business; they would *guarantee* by law the chances of the small business stratum. And if you guarantee a chance, it is no longer a chance; it is a sinecure. What this means is that all the private and public virtues that self-help, manly competition, and cupidity are supposed to foster would be denied the little businessman. The government would expropriate the very basis of political freedom and the flourishing of the free personality. If, as the chairman of the Smaller War Plants Corporation has said, "Democracy can only exist in a capitalistic system in which the life of the individual is controlled by supply and demand," then it is all over with democracy. However, the chairman adds, that to save capitalism, the government "must prevent small business from being shattered and destroyed." In the new way of salvation, inherited from the Progressive Era, the old faith in supply and demand is replaced by the hope of governmental aid and legalized comfort.

Big business doesn't have to compete and doesn't; little business sometimes has to and always hates it; and all the while, liberal government is trying to ration out the main chance, thus helping to destroy the old meaning of competition as a style of life.

### III

In the old style of life, the way up, according to the classic pattern of liberalism, was to establish a small business enterprise and to expand it by competition with other such enterprises. That was the economic cradle of the free personality and, given the equality of opportunity and of power that it assumed, the guarantee of political democracy. The new way up is the white-collar way: to get a job within a governmental or a business bureaucracy and to rise, according to the rules that prevail, from one prearranged step to another. For some 75 per cent of the urban middle class, the salaried employee component, this fate replaces heroic tactics on the open market.

Before each rung of the fixed ladders, the salaried employees may compete with one another, being in training for the next step; but their field of competition is too hedged in by bureaucratic regulation to give issue to the results expected from open competition across a free market. It is more likely to be seen as grubbing and backbiting: a bureaucracy is no testing field for heroes. The great, main chance of old becomes a series of small calculations, stretched out over the working lifetime of the individual. And these new middle classes are slowly beginning to give up their independence, in favor of a declaration of collective dependence: some 14 per cent of them are now in trade unions. They are beginning to dream of going up together, as members of modern businesslike unions.

This shift from business enterpriser to white-collar employee, along with the decline of the free farmer, is the master occupational change of twentieth-century social structure. It is a terrible blow at the old competitive life and at the personal and political consequences that the old pattern was supposed to have.

The white-collar man *enters* the public view as a tragic figure. He takes up where the little businessman ended; the powerless, little-man aspect engulfs whatever heroic features might be thought up for him. The white-collar people, it would seem, are not being heroized by the old middle class; indeed, they can only be heroized collectively, as they join unions or fight inflations or patiently live out their slow misery. As individuals, they are only insecure and tortured creatures, being pushed by forces or swallowed by movements that they do not understand, and that senators do not have to face. At the center of the picture is business bureaucracy with its trained managerial staff and its tamed white-collar mass. And it is within these structures of monopoly that the bulk of the middle-class men and women must make their prearranged ways.

## IV

Yet, all this does not mean that the spirit of the old competition is entirely dead. There still remains an area where a type of go-gettem has found nourishment. If the agents of this new competition are not exactly the stuff of old-fashioned heroes, that is only because the conditions that prevail are so different; their initiative is being put to a harder test.

Against the unheroic backdrop of big business and the white-collar mass, within and between the bureaucratic patterns of success, a new type of entrepreneur has arisen. In contrast to the classic little businessman, who operated in a world opening up like a row of oysters under steam, the new entrepreneur must operate in a world in which all the pearls have already been grabbed up and are carefully guarded.

The only manner by which the new entrepreneur can express his initiative is by servicing the powers that be, in the hope of getting his cut. And he serves them by "fixing things," between one big business and another, between big business and government, and between business as a whole and the public. He gets ahead because men in power do not expect that things can be done legitimately, because these men know fear, because their spheres of operation are broader than their capacities to observe, and because they are personally not very bright.

As a competitor, the new entrepreneur is an agent of the bureaucracies he serves, and what he competes for is the good will and favor of those who run the business system. His chance exists because there are several of these bureaucracies, private and public, having complicated entanglements with one another and with the public. Unlike the little white-collar man, he does not often stay within any one corporate bureaucracy; his path zig-zags within and between bureaucracies, and he has made a well-worn path between big business and the regulatory agencies of the federal government.

He is a live wire, full of American know-how, and if he does not invest capital, his success is all the greater measure of his inherent worth, for this means that he is genuinely creative. Like the more heroic businessmen of old, he manages to get something for very little or nothing.

The new entrepreneur is very much at home in the "business services," in which bracket fall the commercial researcher and the public relations man, the advertising agencies, the labor relations expert, and the mass communication and entertainment industries. For the bright, young, educated man, these fields offer limitless opportunities, if he only has the initiative and the know-how, and if only the anxieties of the bureaucratic chieftains hold up.

The power of the old captain of industry rested, it is said, upon his engineering ability and upon his financial sharp dealing. The power of the present-day chieftain rests upon his control of the wealth piled up by the old captain and increased by a rational system of guaranteed tributes. The power of the new entrepreneur rests upon his personality and upon his skill in using it to manipulate the anxieties of the chieftain.

Now the concentration of power has modified the character and the larger meaning of competition. The competition in which these new entrepreneurs engage is not so much a competition for markets of commodities or services: it is a bright, anxious competition for the good will of the chieftain by means of personality. The "supply and demand" of the impersonal market does not decide the success or failure of the new entrepreneur; his success is decided by the personal decisions of intimately known chieftains of monopoly.

The new entrepreneur has this in common with the ordinary white-collar worker: the careers of both are administered by powerful others. The difference is that the toadying of the white-collar employee is small scale and unimaginative; he makes up the stable corps of the bureaucracy, and initiative is regimented out of his life. The new ulcered entrepreneur, running like Sammy, operates on the twin-faced edges of the several bureaucracies. He comes to the immediate attention of the men who make the big decisions as he services their fears and eagerly encourages their anxious whims.

Part of the frenzy of the new entrepreneur is due to the fact that in his life there are no objective criteria of success. For such types, the last criteria are the indefinite good will of the chieftains and the shifting symbols of status. Part of his frenzy may also be due to his apprehension that his function may disappear. For many of the jobs he has been doing for the chieftains are now a standardized part of business enterprise and no longer require the entrepreneurial flair, but can be performed by the cheaper and more dependable white-collar man. Besides, the new entrepreneur, with his lavish expense account, sometimes gets into the public eye as a fixer—along with the respectable businessman whose work he does—and even as an upstart and a crook. The same publics that idolize initiative become incensed when they find a grand model of success based, quite purely, upon it.

We may view the true scene of the new entrepreneur's operation as the personality market. Like the commodity market before it, the top levels of this market may well become an object to be administered rather than a play of free forces driven by crafty wile and unexampled initiative. Indeed, the new shape competition may take in this last remaining competitive market can already be seen. Its human meaning is displayed lower down the hierarchy, where bureaucratized business meets the public.

## V

At this intersection, personality markets of a more stabilized sort have arisen. Three immediate conditions are needed: First, an employee must be part of a bureaucratic enterprise, in which his work is supervised by an authority over him. Second, it must be his regular business to contact a public from within this bureaucracy; he is thus the bearer of the firm's good name before anyone who cares to show up. Third, the public which he contacts must be anonymous, a mass of urban strangers.

One of the biggest of the several personality markets that may be isolated for study involves the salesperson in the metropolitan department store. Unlike the small independent merchant, the salesperson cannot haggle over prices. Prices are fixed by other employees of the bureaucracy. She cannot form her character by buying cheaply and selling wisely. Experts fix the market price; specialists buy the commodities which she is to sell. She cannot form her character by the promotional calculations and self-management of the classic heroes of liberalism or of the new entrepreneurs. There is only one area of her occupational life in which she is "free to act." That is the area of her own personality. She must make of her personality an alert, obsequious instrument whereby goods are distributed.

The white-collar worker, like the wage worker in a modern factory, is alienated from the tools and products of her labor; indeed, she does not even mix labor with raw stuff to produce things. The white-collar worker on a personality market must not only sell her time and energy; she must also "sell herself." In the normal course of her work, she becomes self-alienated. For, in the personality market, the personality itself, along with advertising, becomes the instrument of an alien purpose.

If there are not too many plant psychologists or personnel experts around, the factory worker is free to frown as he works. But not so the white-collar employee. She must put her personality into it. She must smile when it is the time to smile. An interviewer, working in the biggest store in the world, recently observed of one of her experienced sales colleagues: "I have been watching her for three days now. She wears a fixed smile on her made-up face, and it never varies, no matter to whom she speaks. I never heard her laugh spontaneously or naturally. Either she is frowning or her face is devoid of any expression. When a customer approaches she immediately assumes her hard, forced smile. It amazes me because although I know that the smiles of most salesgirls are unreal, I've never seen such calculation given to the timing of a smile. I myself tried to copy such an expression, but I am unable to keep such a smile on my face if it is not sincerely and genuinely motivated."

In this market the human expressions are no longer expressions of private aspirations. For all the features of the character, especially the familial ones—the kindly gesture, tact, courtesy, the smile—now become expressions of the company's aspirations. They are the salaried mask of the individual, available by the week, designed to advance the competitive position of the store with the public. Year after year they are enforced by the store's bureaucratic discipline, including the "professional shopper" who reports to the personnel department. In due course, this life of alienation sets up its own traits in the personality, selected, constructed, and used as instruments in the competitive struggle of the employees within the store, and between the store and the consuming public. Such is the creative function of the new competition.

Yet the personality market, in one sense, is still subject to the old laws of supply and demand. When a "seller's market" exists and labor is hard to buy, the well-earned aggressions of the salespeople come out and jeopardize the good will of the buying public. When there is a "buyer's market" and jobs are hard to get, the salespeople must repress again and practice politeness. Thus the laws of supply and demand, as in an older epoch of capitalism, continue to regulate the intimate life-fate of the individual and the kind of personality that may be developed and displayed.

The old competition is dead, even if the old liberal alibis for it are now incarnate as fetishes. But new kinds of competition, making new kinds of people, have arisen. Near the top of the new hierarchy are the new entrepreneurs, the bureaucratic fixers and the business experts; and at the bottom are the people on the personality markets. Somewhere in between, the little businessman struggles to gain the stable security of big business by having his tribute also guaranteed, and yet, in the *name* of competition, hoping somehow for the main chance.

Both of the newer types serve the bureaucracies, and both, in their own way, practice the creative art of selling. In a restricted market economy, salesmanship is truly praised as a creative act, but it is entirely too serious a matter to be trusted to mere creativity. The more alert chieftains are becoming aware of this. The really great opportunities for expropriation are in the field of the human personality itself. The fate of competition, and the character it will assume, depends upon the success or failure of the adventures of monopolists in this field.

# 2

## THE MIDDLE CLASSES
## IN MIDDLE-SIZED CITIES

The problems which the middle classes pose for the social scientist are typically metropolitan in character and nation-wide in scope. White-collar workers in particular, are thought of in connection with big cities, and most recent discussions of the middle classes as a whole focus either upon the nation or upon the metropolis. The sociology and politics of these strata in middle-sized[1] cities may nevertheless be worthy of study.

Such cities are convenient units for empirical analyses; they offer a point of contrast for information and theory dealing with nations or with big cities, and despite the fact that many large problems may be more sharply posed in national and metropolitan areas, some of the issues of politics and social structure take on fresh meaning and reality when translated into the concrete terms of smaller and more readily understood units.

[1] Middle-sized cities include those between 25,000 and 100,000 population. Middle classes include the smaller business and the white-collar people. The small business stratum includes retail, service, wholesale, and industrial proprietors employing less than 100 workers. (In the present data from Central City, the small business men employ far fewer, on the average 2 to 4.) The white-collar strata include families in the salaried professions and minor managerial positions, clerks and stenographers and bookkeepers, salesmen in and out of stores, and foremen in industry.

Materials used in this paper were gathered, in connection with studies having quite other purposes, for the Office of Reports, Smaller War Plants Corporation (6 cities extensively covered), and the Bureau of Applied Social Research, Columbia University (one city intensively covered). This is publication number A-70 of the latter institution. My colleague, Miss Helen Schneider, has been most helpful in her criticism of this manuscript.

If one keeps in mind the "place" of the middle-sized city in the nation and in relation to various city-size groups, it is a convenient point of anchorage for more extensive analysis of stratification, politics, and ideology. The position of the U. S. middle classes cannot be fully determined without attention to those living among the 15 million people who in 1940 resided in the 320 middle-sized cities.

I

A city's population may be stratified (a) objectively in terms of such bases as property or occupation or the amount of income received from either or both sources. Information about these bases may be confined to the present, or may include (b) the extractions, intermarriages, and job histories of members of given strata. Such "depth stratification" adds a time dimension to the contemporary objective bases of stratification. Subjectively, strata may be constructed according to who does the rating: (c) each individual may be asked to assign himself a position, (d) the interviewer may "intuitively" rate each individual, or (e) each individual may be asked to stratify the population and then to give his image of the people on each level.[2]

Properly designed studies in stratifiction will use both objective and subjective criteria: indeed, one of the key problems of stratification theory is to account for such discrepancies as may thus appear.

The general problem of stratification and political mentality has to do with the extent to which the members of an objectively defined stratum are homogeneous in their political alertness, outlook and allegiances, and with the degree to which their political mentalities and actions are in line with the interests demanded by the juxtaposition of their objective position and their accepted values.

Irrational discrepancies between the objectively defined bases of a stratum, the subjectively held policies of its members and their commonly accepted values do not necessarily point to problems of method. They may indicate the "false

[2] In the present paper, we are not concerned with the intuitive ratings of interviewers, and space will not permit us to utilize fully the quantitative data available.

consciousness" of the stratum we are examining.[3] Lack of structural unity and of political direction are symptoms of the many problems covered by this term that have as yet only been touched by modern empirical research.

Political mentalities may or may not be closely in line with objectively defined strata, but a lack of correspondence is a problem to be explained—in terms of the homogeneity of the situation of the stratum, the social relations between its members, the reach and content of the mass media and of the informal networks of communication that lie along each stratum, etc.

In examining the stratification and politics of the white collar and small business strata in middle-sized cities, we are concerned with whether or not each of them is a homogeneous stratum, with the degree and the content of political consciousness that they display, and with whether they reveal any independence of policy, or are politically dependent upon the initiative and ideologies of other strata.

The objective stratification of the U. S. middle-sized city has fallen into a rather standardized pattern. It will naturally vary from one city to another in accordance with the degree and type of industrialization and the extent to which one or two very large firms dominate the city's labor market. But the over-all pattern is now fairly set:

When the occupations of a cross section of married men in Central City[4] are coded in 24 groups and ranked according to average family income, five strata are crystallized out: between each of them there is a "natural" break in average income whereas the average income of the occupations making up each income stratum are relatively ho-

_____

[3] "False consciousness," the lack of awareness of and identification with one's objective interests, may be statistically defined as the deviant cases, that is, those which run counter to the main correlations in a table: for example, the rich who vote Socialist, the poor who vote Republican. "Objective interests" refer to those *allegiances and actions* which would have to be followed if the *accepted values* and desires of the people *involved in given strata situations* are to be realized.

[4] A mid-western city of 60,000 population selected as "the most typical" on the basis of 36 statistical indicators gathered on all mid-western cities of 50-80,000 population. On the over-all index for all cities of 100, Central City was 99.

mogeneous. These strata, with their average weekly income (August, 1945), are as follows:

(1) Big Business and Executives..................$137.00
(2) Small Business and Free Professionals......... 102.00
(3) Higher White-collar⁵....................... 83.00
(4) Lower White-collar⁶....................... 72.00
(5) Wage Workers⁷............................ 59.00

These strata fall objectively into the "old" (1 and 2) and the "new" middle classes (3 and 4). Both these classes, however, are definitely split by income, and this split, as we shall see, is also true of other variables.

There is one point on which both objective and subjective methods of strata construction give similar results. Of all the strata in the middle-sized city, the small businessmen and the white-collar workers occupy the most ambiguous and least clearly defined social position: (a) The images which observers on other objective levels of the city ascribe to these occupational groups seem to vary the most widely and to be the least precise; (b) Correspondingly, in terms of a great many attributes and opinions, the white-collar people and, to a lesser degree, the smaller businessmen are the least homogeneous strata. Both in the subjective images held of various strata and in their objective attributes, the city is polarized; the small businessmen and the white-collar workers make up the vaguer and "somewhere in-between" strata.

## I I

When we ask people in the several objectively defined strata to discuss the position and rank of the small business-man, a fundamental difference occurs between the ranking

⁵ Salaried professional and semiprofessional, salesmen, government officials, minor managerial employees; income range: $80.00 to $87.00.
⁶ Government protection and service, clerks, stenographers and bookkeepers, foremen; income range: $71.00 to $76.00.
⁷ Due to wartime "up-grading" there are in this sample very few "manual laborers"; these make about $14.00 less than the skilled and semiskilled average.

given him by upper class and that given him by lower-class observers.[8]

To the lower-class observer, little businessmen are very often the most apparent element among "the higher-ups" and no distinctions are readily made between them and the "business" or "upper class" in general. Upper-class observers, on the other hand, place the little businessmen—especially the retailers—much lower in the scale than they place the larger businessmen—especially the industrialists. Both the size and the type of business influences their judgment.

In fact, two general images are held of small businessmen by upper-class people. They correspond to two elements of the upper class: (a) The socially new, larger, industrial entrepreneurs rank small business rather low because of the *local* nature of these little businessmen's activities. Such upper-class people gauge prestige to a great extent by the scope of a business and the social and business "connections" with members of nationally known firms. These criteria are opposite to the status-by-old-family-residence frequently used by the second upper-class element: (b) The old family rentier ranks the smaller businessmen low because of his feeling about their background and education, "the way he lives." And, as we shall see, the smaller businessmen cannot often qualify with these standards.

Both upper-class elements tend to stress a Jewish element among the smaller business stratum (although there are very few Jewish families among the smaller businessmen in Central City) and both more or less agree with the blend of "ethical" and "economic" sentiment expressed by an old-family banker: "The independent ones are local operators; they do a nice business, but not nationally. Business ethics are higher, more broadminded, more stable among industrialists, as over against retailers. We all know that."

But wage-worker families do not know all that. They ascribe power and prestige to the small businessman without really seeing the position he holds within the upper strata. "Shopkeepers," says a lower-class woman, "they go in the

[8] These remarks are based on 45 open-ended interviews in Central City, a baby sample within the parent sample; and some 60 random interviews in 6 other middle-sized cities.

higher brackets. Because they are on the higher level. They don't humble themselves to the poor."

(a) The social composition and (b) the actual power position of the small business stratum help us to understand these ambiguous images.

(a) Since they earn about the same average income as the free professionals, the small businessmen are in the Number Two income bracket of the city. But they are not at all similar to the other high income groups in occupational, intermarriage and job histories. In these respects, the free professionals are similar to the big business owners and executives, whereas the smaller businessmen crystallize out as a distinct stratum different from any other in the population.[9]

Almost three fourths of the small businessmen are derived from the upper half of the occupational-income hierarchy. Yet this relative lack of mobility is not the only, nor necessarily the most relevant point at hand: when we compare small business with other occupations of similar income level, we notice that they contain the greatest proportion of ascending individuals now in the higher income brackets: 18 per cent of those who are urban-derived had wage-worker fathers and 9 per cent had low-income white-collar fathers. Thus 27 per cent come from the lower groups. The free professional and big businessmen, on the other hand, do not include any individuals who derive from wage-worker or low income white-collar.

Slightly more than half of these small businessmen have married girls whose fathers were in the upper-half of the income-occupation ranks. About 40 per cent of them married daughters of wage workers; the remaining married into the lower income white-collar stratum. This 40 per cent cross with wage workers is well over three times greater than for any other of the occupational groups in the higher income brackets.

[9] The figures on small businessmen which are given below are quite small: in an area sample of 882 homes we caught 37 small businessmen. No per cents from such a small base are given unless they are significant according to critical ratios. Nevertheless, the results should be taken with a grain of salt, and caution exercised in any further use made of them: in reality, we are here dealing with qualitative materials.

The job histories of these little businessmen reveal the same basic pattern. Only one out of five of them were in a job as high as small business at the time of their marriage (their average age is now around 48) whereas almost half of them were working for wages at that time. Well over half (57 per cent) did wage work for their first full-time job.

In contrast, all the free professionals were professionals by the time they married, and three fourths of the salaried professionals—who make on the average $13.00 a month less than the small businessmen—were in their present jobs when married. At the bottom of the society we find the same type of rigidity: 9 out of 10 of all grades of labor were wage-worker or low income white-collar.

There is rigidity at the bottom and at the top—except among small businessmen who, relative to comparable income groups, have done a great deal of moving up the line.

Almost twice as high a proportion of the big business and free professional men have graduated from high school as is the case for small businessmen, despite the fact that the small businessmen are slightly younger. Moreover, the wives of small businessmen rank fourth in education, just above laborer's wives, in our five-fold occupation-income strata; over half of their wives never finished high school, as compared with only one-fourth of the wives of men in comparable income groups.

The small businessmen are of the generally upper ranks only in income; in terms of occupational origin, intermarriage, job history, and education, more of them than of any other occupational group of such high income are "lower class." A good proportion of them have rather close biographical connections with the wage worker strata. These findings help us explain the difference between the images held of them by members of the upper and of the lower strata. The upper class judges more on status and "background;" the lower more by income and the appearances to which it readily leads.

(b) The ambiguous prestige of small business people has to do with power as well as with "background": the small businessmen, especially in cities dominated by a few large industrial firms, are quite often "fronts" for the larger business powers. They are, civically, out in front busily accomplishing all sorts of minor projects and taking a lot of praise and blame from the rank and file citizenry. Among those in the lower classes who, for one reason or another, are "anti-business," the small business front is often the target of aggression and blame; but for the lower-class individual who is "pro-business" or "neutral," the small businessmen get top esteem because "they are doing a lot for this city."

The prestige often imputed to small business by lower-class members is based largely on ascribed power, but neither this prestige nor this ascribed power is always claimed, and certainly it is not often cashed in among the upper classes by small businessmen. The upper-class businessman knows the actual power setup; if he and his clique are using small businessmen for some project, he may shower public prestige on them, but he does not "accept" them and he allows them only such "power" as he can retain in his control.

### III

The centers of organizational life for the top are the Chamber of Commerce and the service clubs, and for the bottom, the several trade unions. There are vast differences in their scope, energy and alertness to chances to play the larger civic role. The Chamber of Commerce is more compact and disciplined in its supporting strata and more widely influential in its infiltration and attempted manipulations of other voluntary associations. It is, in many towns, a common denominator of other voluntary organizations. Its hands, either openly *via* "committees" or covertly *via* "contacts," are in all "community" affairs of any political consequence. But the trade unions do not typically reach out beyond themselves, except when their leaders are included in projects sponsored by the Chamber of Commerce.

If both CIO and AFL unions operate in a city, the Chamber of Commerce can very often play them off against one another; usually the old AFL men are quite flattered by being included in Chamber of Commerce committees which thus build them up before the citizenry as representing "labor" in this town. The younger CIO men are confronted with the choice of following this older route of compromised inclusion or of playing the lone wolf, in which case they rest their civic chances entirely upon their strictly union success.

The organization of the Small Business Front is quite often in the hands of the Chamber of Commerce; and many of the hidden wires behind the scene are manipulated by the local bank setup, which is usually able to keep The Front in line whenever this is considered necessary by large industrial firms. The political and economic composition of a well-run Chamber of Commerce enables the organization to borrow the prestige and power of the top strata; its committee includes the "leaders" of practically every voluntary association, including labor unions; within its organizations and through its contacts, it is able virtually to monopolize the organizing and publicity talent of the city. It can thus identify its program with the unifying myth of "the community interest."

This well-known constellation of power underpins the ambiguity of prestige enjoyed by small businessmen, and provides the content of their ideology and political efforts.

### I V

The ideology of small businessmen rests upon their identification with business as such. They are well organized, but "their" organizations are pretty well under the thumb of larger businesses and the banks. The power of big business is exercised by means of threats "to leave town," by simply refraining from participation in various organizations, by control of credit sources, and by the setting up and using of small businessmen as fronts. The small businessmen, nevertheless, cling to the identity: "business is business." They do not typically see, nor try to act upon, such differences as may exist between the interests of big and little business. The benefits derived from "good relations" with the higher-ups of the local business world, and the prestige striving, oriented toward the big men, tend to strengthen this identification, which is organized and promoted by their associations.

One of the best contemporary sources of information on

small business ideology is provided by the field hearings of the SWPC.[10] These are "gripe sessions" usually held in local hotels in the presence of a congressman or his delegate. A rough content analysis of these discussions, occurring during the late war, reveals that the bull's-eyes of the small businessman's aggression are labor and government. The attitude toward "labor" magnifies its power: "We know that labor, at the present time, has the upper hand. They tell us what to do." And the resentment is quite personalized: "Think of the tremendous wages being paid to laboring men . . . all out of proportion to what they should be paid . . . a number of them have spoken to me, saying they are ashamed to be taking the wages." And another one says: "I had a young man cash a check at the store on Monday evening for $95.00 . . . Another case . . . made a total of $200.00 for 30 days . . . We would not class him as half as good as our clerks in our store . . . Naturally to hire men today to do this common labor we are going to have to compete with (war factories)." "A man has to run shorthanded or do the work himself."

Toward government, the attitude is resentment at its regulations and at the same time many pleas for economic aid and political comfort. The only noticeable talk against big business is in such governmental statements, by staff members of Senate committees, as: the definition of a small businessman is one who "hasn't got an office or representative in Washington." The independent little businessman believes: "We are victims of circumstances. My only hope is in Senator Murray, who, I feel sure, will do all in his power to keep the little businessman who, he knows, has been the foundation of the country [etc.] . . . We all know no business can survive selling . . . at a loss, which is my case today, on the new cost of green coffee."

"Small business . . . what is it?" asks the manager of a small business trade association. "It is American Business . . . it is the reason we have an American Way." Such phrases as "the little businessman who has built up, by sweat, tears and smiles, a business . . ." underline the im-

---

[10] See, e.g., Hearings, Senate Small Business Committee, S. Res. 298 (76th Congress) Part 6.

portance placed by this stratum on its own virtue. The ideology of and for small business thus carries self-idealization to the point of making it the content of nationalism.

The attitude toward "government" is blended with a self-estimate of virtue: the criterion of man is success on Main Street: "Another thing that I resent very much is the fact that most of these organizations are headed by men who are not able to make a success in private life and have squeezed into WPA [sic] and gotten over us and are telling us what to do, and it is to me very resentful. And all these men here know of people who head these organizations, who were not able to make a living on Main Street before (the war)."

This ideology apparently rests to some extent upon a sense of insecurity. For example, in Central City, the wives of low income businessmen worry about "how the postwar situation will affect you and your family" more than any other strata, although they are followed closely by the lower white-collar people. Sixty per cent of the low income business people worry a great deal, as against 45 per cent of those of higher income. The small business families are apparently aware that they make up the margin of free private enterprise. And—in view of their ascent—perhaps they remember that everything that goes up can come down.

It is also of interest to notice that the wives of smaller businessmen are not nearly so sure as one might expect that "any young man with thrift, ability and ambition has the opportunity to rise in the world, own his own home, and earn $5,000 a year." In Central City[11] only 40 per cent of them believe it, as against 68 per cent of the higher income business people. They are still, however, a good deal more optimistic than the low income white-collar people (26 per cent) who are the most pessimistic stratum in the city. About 37 per cent of the wage workers' wives, regardless of income, are optimistic of the climb.

[11] We first asked this ascent question in general; then we followed it up with: "Could he do it in (Central City)?" The optimism of all strata dropped greatly when the question was brought closer home to them.

## V

The lower classes sometimes use the term, "white-collar," to refer to everybody above themselves. Their attitude varies from the power-class criterion: they are "pencil pushers" who "sit around and don't work and figure out ways of keeping wages cheap," to the social-pragmatic criterion: "The clerks are very essential. They are the ones who keep the ball rolling for the other guy. We would be lost if we didn't have the clerks." This latter attitude may be slightly more frequent among those workers whose children have become clerks.

The upper classes, on the other hand, never acknowledge the white-collar people as of the top and sometimes place them with laborers. An old upper-class man, for instance, says: "Next after retailers, I would put the policemen, firemen, the average factory worker and the white-collar clerks." Interviewer: "You would put the white-collar people in with the workers?" "Well, I think so. I've lived in this town all my life and come to the bank every day but Sunday, and I can't name five clerks downtown I know."

The white-collar people are split down the middle by income, extraction, intermarriage, job history, and education. Of the men in the higher of the two white-collar income classes, 61 per cent are derived from the upper-half of the extraction-income hierarchy, as compared with 49 per cent of the lower white-collar men who are from the upper half by extraction.[12]

The *urban* origins of the several occupations of the higher white-collar stratum are homogeneous as regards extraction; but the lower white-collar stratum of urban origin contains occupations of quite different extraction which cancel out into a misleading average: The clerks are closer in origin to the higher white-collar as a whole, about 50 per cent being from the upper half, whereas the foreman are quite like labor,[13] only 25 per cent being from the upper half.

[12] There are 117 families in our higher white-collar group, and 92 in the lower. In the general origin table, farm owners are put with upper half, farm tenants and laborers with the lower half.

[13] The cases of government protection and service were too few to permit a reliable calculation.

In intermarriage, job mobility and education similar situations exist: members of the higher white-collar bracket are homogeneous in intermarriage: about half of them have married women whose fathers were in the upper half of the hierarchy. The lower white-collar stratum is split: the women whom clerks marry are similar in background to the wives of the upper white-collar. Foremen, on the other hand, show a tendency to marry more along the lines that the labor strata follow; yet they marry small businessmen's daughters in about the same proportion (27 per cent) as clerks, minor managerials and salaried professionals, thus forging another link between small businessmen and the laboring class.

The salesmen and the salaried professionals have not experienced much job mobility: 6 out of 10 of them were in higher white-collar at the time of their marriage. In the lower white-collar, again foremen stand out as exceptions: 67 per cent of them were wage workers at their time of marriage and 75 per cent worked for wages in their first full-time job.

Whereas the formal education of the clerks is similar to that of higher white-collar (only 5 to 11 per cent of high white-collar and clerks never going beyond grade school), 40 per cent of the foremen have never gone beyond grade school; this places them educationally only a little above skilled workers.

The lower white-collar is thus not a homogeneous stratum by extraction, intermarriage or job history. Some of the occupations in it are sociologically affiliated with labor and some with the occupations we have ranked by income as higher white-collar.

The white-collar people are, as we have seen, split by income. But the images held of them as a whole seem to be drawn from the occupations belonging to the lower half of the white-collar income level. The upper white-collar people, especially the salesmen, tend to merge with the sponge term, "business," and are thought of as "businessmen" by many members of the upper class. Most upper-class people derive their images of the white-collar people largely from stereotypes of "the clerk."

The ambiguous rank of the small businessman is explained by his social origin and by the "power" which is ascribed to him by the lower but denied to him by the upper. The ambiguous position of the white-collar worker, on the other hand, rests less upon *complications* in, and pressures on his power position than upon his absence of power. They have no leaders active in civic efforts; they are not, as a stratum, represented in the councils; they have no autonomous organizations through which to strive for such political and civic ends as they may envision; they are seldom, if ever, in the publicity spotlight as a group. No articulate leaders in these cities appeal directly and mainly to white-collar people or draw their strength from white-collar support.

The few organizations in which white-collar employees predominate—the Business and Professional Women's Clubs, the Junior Chamber of Commerce, and the YWCA —are so tied in with business groups as such, that they have little or no autonomy. Socially, the lower white-collar is largely on "the Elk level" and the higher white-collar usually is in the No. 2 or 3 social clubs; in both these situations they form part of a "middle-class mingling" pattern. They are "led," if at all, by salesmen and other such "contact people" who are themselves identified with "business."

The organized power of the middle-sized city does not include any autonomous white-collar unit. Which way the unorganized white-collar people will swing politically and which of the two civic fronts they will support seems to depend almost entirely upon the strength and prestige of autonomous labor organizations within the city, a point to which we shall return.

### VI

The ideology of the white-collar people rises rather directly out of their occupations and the requirements for them. They are not a well defined group in any other readily apparent sense. This ideology is not overtly political, yet by political default, it is generally "conservative" and by virtue of the aspects of occupation which it stresses, it sets up "social" distinctions between white-collar and labor and makes the most of them.

Those white-collar people in middle-sized cities, for example, who "contact the public" exhibit the psychology of people working a small and personally known market from within small and moderate-sized firms. In this respect, they are the typological opposites of salesgirls in metropolitan department stores who work a mass public of strangers. Fifty-three small merchants and salespeople in Central City,[14] almost unanimously knew personally the people they served and were very "happy" about their work. Their attitude towards this work is seldom material. It rests upon a communalization between buyer and seller: 63 per cent spontaneously mentioned enjoyment at contacting their public, which is twice as high as for any other single reason for liking their work.

This general ideology has four discernible contents: (a) the idea that they are *learning about human nature,* which is mentioned by about one-fourth of them; (b) the feeling that they *borrow prestige* from their customers; sometimes the prestige source includes the merchandise itself or the store, but its center is normally the customer; (c) the opposite of prestige borrowing: the feeling of *power in manipulating the customer's appearance and home;* this is more apparent, of course, among cosmetic and clothing sellers; (d) The idea of *rendering service:* about one-fourth speak explicitly in terms of an ideology of service, which is interwoven in various ways with the other contents.

These key elements in the occupational ideology of salespeople in medium-sized cities, (1) rest upon the facts of a small and personally known market; (2) in emphasizing just this contact aspect of their work, the white-collar people seize upon precisely an occupational experience which wage workers do not and cannot have; they make a fetish of "contacts"; and (3) the ideology, as a whole and in its parts, is either neutral or pro-business in orientation.

Similar ideological analysis of other occupations making

[14] Twelve were small business operators; two-thirds are women; about one-half of the total have finished high school. The implicit contrast with metropolitan salesgirls is anchored on quotational materials gathered over several years by Mr. James Gale, "Types of Macy Salesgirls," seminar paper, University of Maryland, Graduate School.

up our two white-collar strata reveal similar tendencies. Nothing in the direct occupational experience of the white-collar in middle-sized cities propels them towards an autonomous organization for political or civic power purposes. The social springs for such movements, should they occur, will be elsewhere.

The direct appeal to higher wages, through collective action, which the trade unions hold out, is in tension with these occupational ideologies.

"I can't understand why they don't organize," says a business agent for an old-line union. "They got a high school education or more. Looks to me like they'd be the ones to organize, not the man in the ditch with fourth grade education. But it seems to work out just the other way . . . The solution is to come down to earth and realize that the prestige of this would-be manager and assistant manager is camouflage for cheap wages. The glory of the idea of the name takes the place of wages . . . that's all I can figure out." [15]

Such a contrast between status and class interest, which is rather typically known by alert trade union men, leads us to expect that only if labor gets civic power and prestige will the white-collar people in these cities string along. So long as their occupational ideology and status claims remain as they are, they will not make a "class fight," although they will try to share in the results, if those who make it for them win out.

### VII

In the general polarization of the middle-sized city's stratification, the top and the bottom are becoming more rigid: 73 per cent of the upper half of the income-occupation scale is descended from the upper half. There is also a rather distinct polarization in organization life, in ideological loyalty, and in political tendency.

[15] There are of course other reasons, besides status claims and occupational ideologies for the difficulties of unionizing white-collar workers; see C. Wright Mills, "The White Collar Unions: A Statistical Portrait and an Outline of Their Social Psychology" (forthcoming).

There are no available symbols which are in any way distinctly of the white-collar strata. Contrary to many expectations, these middle groups show no signs of developing a policy of their own. Neither in income nor mentality are they unified. The high white-collar are 40 per cent more Republican than their lower white-collar colleagues.

They do not feel any sharp crisis specific to their stratum. They drift into acceptance of and integration with a business-run society punctuated by "labor troubles." In these cities, it may be pretentious to speak of "political tendencies" among white-collar workers. And such problems as the relations of party, trade union, and class cannot even be posed. The white-collar people are not a homogeneous class; they are not in trade unions; neither major party caters specifically to them, and there is no thought of their forming an independent party.

Insofar as political and civic strength rests upon organized economic power, the white-collar workers can only derive such strength from "business" or from "labor." Within the whole structure of power, they are dependent variables. They have no self-starting motor moving them to form organizations with which to increase their power in the civic constellation. Estimates of their political tendencies in the middle-sized cities, therefore, must rest upon larger predictions of the manner and outcome of the civic struggles of business and labor.

Only when "labor" has rather obviously "won out" in a city, if then, will the lower white-collar people go in for unions. If the leaders of labor are included in compromise committees, stemming from Chamber of Commerce circles, then such white-collar groups as exist will be even more so.

Lenin's remark that the political consciousness of a stratum cannot be aroused within "the sphere of relations between workers and employers" holds doubly true for white-collar employees in these cities. Their occupational ideology is politically passive. They are not engaged in any economic struggle, except in the most scattered and fragmentary way. It is, therefore, not odd that they lack even a rudimentary awareness of their economic and political interests. Insofar as they are at all politically available, they form the rear guard either of "business" or of "labor"; but in either case, they are very much rear guard.

Theories of the rise to power of white-collar people are generally inferred from the facts of their numerical growth and their indispensability in the bureaucratic and distributive operations of mass society. But only if one assumes a pure and automatic democracy of numbers does the mere growth of a stratum mean increased power for it. And only if one assumes a magic leap from occupational function to political power does technical indispensability mean power for a stratum.

When one translates such larger questions into the terms of the middle-sized American city, one sees very clearly that the steps from growth and function to increased political power include, at a minimum, political awareness and political organization. The white-collar workers in these cities do not have either to any appreciable extent.

# THE SOCIAL ROLE
# OF THE INTELLECTUAL

I

American intellectuals are suffering the tremors of men who face overwhelming defeat. They are worried and distraught, some only half aware of their condition, others so painfully aware of it that they must obscure it by busy work and self-deception.

Pragmatism was the nerve of progressive American thinking for the first several decades of this century. It took a rather severe beating from the fashionable left-wing of the thirties and since the latter years of that decade it has obviously been losing out in competition with more religious and tragic views of political and personal life. Many who not long ago read John Dewey with apparent satisfaction have become vitally interested in such analysts of personal tragedy as Soren Kierkegaard. Attempts to reinstate pragmatism's emphasis upon the power of man's intelligence to control his destiny have not been taken to heart by American intellectuals. They are obviously spurred by new worries and are after new gods.

Rather than give in to the self-pity and political lament which the collapse of hope invites, Arthur Koestler proposes, in the *New York Times,* a Fraternity of Pessimists who are to live together in "an oasis." Melvin Lasky, writing in the *New Leader,* responds to Koestler by urging intellectuals, in Spinoza's phrase, "neither to cry nor to laugh but to understand." The president of the American Sociological Society, George Lundberg, ascribes contemporary disasters and disasters apparently yet to come, to the fact that the social sciences have not developed as rapidly nor along the same lines as physical science. Malcolm Cowley, of the *New Republic*, wonders why the war years have produced so little that may be considered great American literature. As for live political writing, intellectuals from right of center to revolutionary left seem to believe that there just isn't any. In a feeble attempt to fill the gap, Walter Lippmann's *The Good Society,* originally published in 1937, is reprinted and even acclaimed by at least one anxious reviewer. Many writers who are turning out post-war plans to suit every purse and taste busily divert the attentions of their readers from current political decisions and bolster their hopes by dreams of the future. Stuart Chase and other proponents of a brave new postwar economic world achieve a confident note at the expense of a political realism which worries even John Chamberlain.

Dwight Macdonald has correctly indicated that the failure of nerve is no simple retreat from reason. The ideas current are not merely fads sweeping over insecure intellectuals in a nation at war. Their invention and distribution must be understood as historical phenomena. Yet what is happening is not adequately explained by the political defeat of liberal, labor, and radical parties—from the decision in Spain to the present.

To understand what is happening in American intellectual life we have to consider the social position of its creators, the intellectuals. We have to realize the effect upon them of certain deep-lying trends of modern social organization.

## II

We continue to know more and more about modern society, but we find the centers of political initiative less and less accessible. This generates a personal malady that is particularly acute in the intellectual who has labored under the illusion that his thinking makes a difference. In the world of today the more his knowledge of affairs grows, the less effective the impact of his thinking seems to become. Since he grows more frustrated as his knowledge increases, it seems that knowledge leads to powerlessness. He feels helpless in the fundamental sense that he cannot control what he is able to foresee. This is not only true of the consequences of his own attempts to act; it is true of the acts of powerful men whom he observes.

Such frustration arises, of course, only in the man who feels compelled to act. The "detached spectator" does not know his helplessness because he never tries to surmount it. But the political man is always aware that while events are not in his hands he must bear their consequences. He finds it increasingly difficult even to express himself. If he states public issues as he sees them, he cannot take seriously the slogans and confusions used by parties with a chance to win power. He therefore feels politically irrelevant. Yet if he approaches public issues "realistically," that is, in terms of the major parties, he has already so compromised their very statement that he is not able to sustain an enthusiasm for political action and thought.

The political failure of nerve has a personal counterpart in the development of a tragic sense of life. This sense of tragedy may be experienced as a personal discovery and a personal burden, but it is also a reflex of objective circumstances. It arises from the fact that at the centers of public decision there are powerful men who do not themselves suffer the violent results of their own decisions. In a world of big organizations the lines between powerful decisions and grass-root democratic controls become blurred and tenuous, and seemingly irresponsible actions by individuals at the top are encouraged. The need for action prompts them to take decisions into their own hands, while the fact that they act as parts of large corporations or other organizations blurs the identification of personal responsibility. Their public views and political actions are, in this objective meaning of the word, irresponsible: the social corollary of their irresponsibility is the fact that others are dependent upon them and must suffer the consequences of their ignorance and mistakes, their self-deceptions, and their biased motives. The sense of tragedy in the intellectual who watches this scene is a personal reaction to the politics and economics of irresponsibility.

Never before have so few men made such fateful decisions for so many people who themselves are so helpless. Dictatorships are but one manifestation of this fact. Mass armies all over the world are its living embodiment, and the Cairo and Teheran and Yalta conferences are its most impressive symbols. The soldier may face death, yet have no voice in the network of decisions which leads him to recapture Burma or garrison India. Power is an impersonal monster; those who do the taking understand only its technique and not its end.

The networks of military decision may be traced further up the line to the centers of political power. There, plans are made by the older men who do not face the chance of violent death. This contrast between the elder statesman and the young soldier is not a popular topic to stress during war, but it is nevertheless one foundation for the modern man's urgently tragic sense of life. When the man who fights and dies can also make the decision to fight in the light of his own ideals, wars can be heroic. When this is not the case, they are only tragic.

Contemporary irresponsibility may be collective; no one circle of men may make the most fateful decision; there may, indeed, be no single fateful decision, only a series of steps in a seemingly inevitable chain, but these considerations do not relieve the resulting tragedy. On the contrary, they deepen it.

The centralization of decision and the related growth of dependence are not, however, confined to armies; although that is where they may be seen in their most immediate form. Organized irresponsibility is a leading feature of modern industrial societies everywhere. On every hand, the individual is confronted with seemingly remote organizations and he feels dwarfed and helpless. If the small business man escapes being turned into an employee of a chain or a corporation, one has only to listen to his pleas for help before small business committees to realize his dependence. More and more people are becoming dependent salaried workers who spend the most alert hours of their lives being told what to do. In climactic times like the present, dominated by the need for swift action, the individual feels dangerously lost. As the London *Economist* recently remarked, "The British citizen *should be* an ardent participant in his public affairs; he *is* little more than a consenting spectator who draws a distinction between 'we' who sit and watch and 'they' who run the state."

Such are the general frustrations of contemporary life. For the intellectual who seeks a public for his thinking—

and he must support himself somehow—these general frustrations are made acute by the fact that in a world of organized irresponsibility the difficulty of speaking one's mind has increased for those who do not speak popular pieces.

If the writer is the hired man of an "information industry," his general aims are, of course, set by the decisions of others and not by his own integrity. But the freedom of the so-called free-lance is also minimized when he goes to the market; if he does not go, his freedom is without public value. Between the intellectual and his potential public stand technical, economic, and social structures which are owned and operated by others. The world of pamphleteering offered to a Tom Paine a direct channel to readers that the world of mass circulations supported by advertising cannot usually afford to provide one who does not say already popular things. The craftsmanship which is central to all intellectual and artistic gratification is thwarted for an increasing number of intellectual workers. They find themselves in the predicament of the Hollywood writer: the sense of independent craftsmanship they would put into their work is bent to the ends of a mass appeal to a mass market.

Even the editor of the mass circulation magazine has not escaped the depersonalization of publishing, for he becomes an employee of a business enterprise rather than a personality in his own right. Mass magazines are not so much edited by a personality as regulated by an adroit formula.

Writers have always been more or less hampered by the pleasure and mentality of their readers, but the variations and the level to which the publishing industry has been geared made possible a large amount of freedom. The recent tendency towards mass distribution of books—the 25 cent "pocket books"—may very well require, as do the production and distribution of films, a more cautious and standardized product. It is likely that fewer and fewer publishers will pass on more and more of those manuscripts which reach mass publics through drug stores and other large-scale channels of distribution.

Although, in general, the larger universities are still the

freest of places in which to work, the trends which limit the independence of the scholar are not absent there. The professor, after all, is legally an employee, subject to all that this fact involves. Institutional factors naturally select men for these universities and influence how, when, and upon what they will work and write. Yet the deepest problem of freedom for teachers is not the occasional ousting of a professor, but a vague general fear—sometimes politely known as "discretion," "good taste," or "balanced judgment." It is a fear which leads to self-intimidation and finally becomes so habitual that the scholar is unaware of it. The real restraints are not so much external prohibitions as control of the insurgent by the agreements of academic gentlemen. Such control is naturally furthered by Hatch Acts, by political and business attacks upon "professors," by the restraints necessarily involved in the Army's program for the colleges, and by the setting up of committees by trade associations of subjects, like history, which attempt to standardize the content and effects of teaching. Research in social science is increasingly dependent upon funds from foundations, and foundations are notably averse to scholars who develop unpopular theses, that is, those placed in the category of "unconstructive."

The United States' growing international entanglements have subtle effects upon some American intellectuals: to the young man who teaches and writes on Latin America, Asia, or Europe and who refrains from deviating from acceptable facts and policies, these entanglements lead to a voluntary censorship. He hopes for opportunities of research, travel, and foundation subsidies.

*The means of effective communication are being expropriated from the intellectual worker. The material basis of his initiative and intellectual freedom is no longer in his hands. Some intellectuals feel these processes in their work. They know more than they say and they are powerless and afraid.*

In modern society both freedom and security depend upon organized responsibilty. By "freedom" and "security," I do not mean independence for each individual; I mean merely that men have effective control over what they are dependent upon. The ethics and politics of democracy center on decisions which vitally affect people who have no voice in them. Today, everywhere, such decisions are central to the lives of more and more people. A politics of organized irresponsibility prevails, and because of it, men in high places must hide the facts of life in order to retain their power.

When irresponsible decisions prevail and values are not proportionately distributed, you will find universal deception practiced by and for those who make the decisions and who have the most of what values there are to have. An increasing number of intellectually equipped men and women work *within* powerful bureaucracies and *for* the relatively few who do the deciding. And if the intellectual is not directly hired by such organizations, then by little steps and in many self-deceptive ways he seeks to have his published opinions conform to the limits set by them and by those whom they do directly hire.

### III

Any philosophy which is sensitive to the meaning of various societies for personal ways of life gives the idea of responsibility a central place. That is why it is central in the ethics and politics of John Dewey and of the late German sociologist, Max Weber. The intellectual's response to the tragic fact of irresponsibility has a wide range but we can understand it in terms of where the problem is faced. The tragedy of irresponsibility may be confronted introspectively, as a moral or intellectual problem. It may be confronted publicly, as a problem of the political economy.

Along this scale there are (1) simple evaluations of our selves; (2) objective considerations of events; (3) estimates of our personal position in relation to the objective distribution of power and decision. An adequate philosophy uses each of these three styles of reflection in thinking through any position that is taken.

(i.) If ethical and political problems are defined solely in terms of the way they affect the individual, he may enrich his experience, expand his sensitivities, and perhaps adjust to his own suffering. But he will not solve the problems he is up against. He is not confronting them at their deeper sources.

(ii.) If only the objective trends of society are considered, personal biases and passions, inevitably involved in observation and thought of any consequence, are overlooked. Objectivity need not be an academic cult of the narrowed attention; it may be more ample and include meaning as well as "fact." What many consider to be "objective" is only an unimaginative use of already plotted routines of research. This may satisfy those who are not interested in politics; it is inadequate as a full orientation. It is more like a specialized form of retreat than the intellectual orientation of a man.

(iii.) The shaping of the society we shall live in and the manner in which we shall live in it are increasingly political. And this society includes the realms of intellect and of personal morals. If we demand that these realms be geared to our activities which make a public difference, then personal morals and political interests become closely related; any philosophy that is not a personal escape involves taking a political stand. If this is true, it places great responsibility upon our political thinking. Because of the expanded reach of politics, it is our own personal style of life and reflection we are thinking about when we think about politics.

The independent artist and intellectual are among the few remaining personalities equipped to resist and to fight the stereotyping and consequent death of genuinely lively things. Fresh perception now involves the capacity continually to unmask and to smash the stereotypes of vision and intellect with which modern communications swamp us. These worlds of mass-art and mass-thought are increasingly geared to the demands of politics. That is why it is in politics that intellectual solidarity and effort must be centered. If the thinker does not relate himself to the value of truth in political struggle, he cannot responsibly cope with the whole of live experience.

## I V

If he is to think politically in a realistic way, the intellectual must constantly know his own social position.

This is necessary in order that he may be aware of the sphere of strategy that is really open to his influence. If he forgets this, his thinking may exceed his sphere of strategy so far as to make impossible any translation of his thought into action, his own or that of others. His thought may thus become fantastic. If he remembers his powerlessness too well, assumes that his sphere of strategy is restricted to the point of impotence, then his thought may easily become politically trivial. In either case, fantasy and powerlessness may well be the lot of his mind. One apparent way to escape both of these fates is to make one's goal simply that of understanding.

Simply to understand is an inadequate alternative to giving in to a personal sense of tragedy. It is not even a true alternative; increased understanding may only deepen the sense of tragedy. Simply to understand is perhaps an ideal of those who are alienated but by no means disinherited—*i.e.,* those who have jobs but don't believe in the work they are doing. Since "the job" is a pervasive political sanction and censorship of most middle class intellectuals, the political psychology of the scared employee becomes relevant. Simply understanding is an ideal of the man who has a capacity to know truth but not the chance, the skill, or the guts, as the case may be, to communicate them with political effectiveness.

Knowledge that is not communicated has a way of turning the mind sour, of being obscured, and finally of being forgotten. For the sake of the integrity of the discoverer, his discovery must be effectively communicated. Such communication is also a necessary element in the very search for clear understanding, including the understanding of one's self. For only through the social confirmation of others whom we believe adequately equipped do we earn the right of feeling secure in our knowledge. The basis of our integrity can be gained or renewed only by activity, including communication, in which we may give ourselves with a minimum of repression. It cannot be gained nor retained by selling what we believe to be our selves. When you sell the lies of others you are also selling yourself. To sell your self is to turn your self into a commodity. A commodity does not control the market; its nominal worth is determined by what the market will offer. And it isn't enough.

We insist upon clarity and understanding in order to govern our decisions by their consequences. Clear understanding of the political world and of our place within it is also indispensable if we are to keep an appropriate distance from ourselves. Without this distance men collapse into self-pity and political lament. We must constantly shuttle between the understanding which is made possible by detachment and the longing and working for a politics of truth in a society that is responsible. The problems which make a difference, both personally and politically, arise in the active search for these goals. The solutions which may be truthful and adequate require episodes of detachment from political morality and from considerations of self.

The phase of detachment may be isolated from its political context and in the division of labor become an end in itself. Those who restrict themselves to work only such segments of intellectual endeavor may attempt to generalize them, making them the basis for political and personal orientation. Then the key problem is held to rise from the fact that social science lags behind physical science and technology, and political and social problems are a result of this deficiency and lag. Such a position is inadequate.

Alienation must be used in the pursuit of truths, but there is no reason to make a political fetish out of it. Much less may it serve as a personal excuse. Certainly more secure knowledge is needed, but we already have a great deal of knowledge that is politically and economically relevant. Big businessmen prove this by their readiness to pay out cash to social scientists who will use their knowledge for the ends of business. Many top economic brains are now hired by big business committees; and a good social scientist is often fired from government, under business pressure, only to be hired by business or by one of its front organizations.

The political man does not need to wait upon more knowledge in order to act responsibly now. To blame his inaction upon insufficient knowledge serves as a cheap escape from the taking of a political stand and acting upon it as best he can. If one half of the relevant knowledge which we now possess were really put into the service of the ideals which leaders mouth, these ideals could be realized in short order. The view that all that is needed is knowledge ignores the nub of the problem as the social scientist confronts it: he has little or no power to act politically and his chance to communicate in a politically effective manner is very limited.

There are many illusions which uphold authority and which are known to be illusions by many social scientists. Tacitly by their affiliations and silence, or explicitly in their work, the social scientist often sanctions these, rather than speak out the truth against them. They censor themselves either by carefully selecting safe problems in the name of pure science, or by selling such prestige as their scholarship may have for ends other than their own.

## V

The above acceptances of the *status quo* proceed directly. The present may also be accepted—and made spuriously palatable—by unanchored expectations of the future. This method is now being used in the production and publicity of hundreds of "postwar plans."

The big businessman sets the technological trap by dangling his baubles before the public without telling precisely how they may be widely distributed. In a similar manner, the political writer may focus attention away from the present and into the several models of the future. The more the antagonisms of the actual present must be suffered, the more the future is drawn upon as a source of pseudo-unity and synthetic morale. Intellectuals and publicists have produced such a range of "plans" that there is now one to satisfy every one. Most of these commodities are not plans with any real chance to be realized. They are baits for various strata, and sometimes for quite vested groups, to support contemporary irresponsibilities. Postwar "planning" is the "new propaganda."

Discussions of the future which accept the present basis for it serve either as diversions from immediate realities or as tacit intellectual sanctions of future disasters. The postwar world is already rather clearly scheduled by authoritative decisions. Apparently, it is to be a balance of power within the collective domination of three great powers. We move from individual to collective domination, as the nations which have shown themselves mightiest in organizing world violence take on the leadership of the peaceful world. Such collective dominance may lead either to counter-alliances and bigger wars, or to decisions not effectively responsible to the man who is born in India or on an island of the Caribbean.

There is very little serious public discussion of these facts and prospects, or of the causes of the current war. Yet the way to avoid war is to recognize its causes within each nation and then remove them. Writers simply accept war as given, refer to December 7 when it all began, and then talk of the warless future. Nobody goes further in the scholarly directions of the inter-war investigations of the causes of modern wars. All that is forgotten, hidden beneath the rather meaningless shield, "Isolationist." It is easier to discuss an anchorless future, where there are as yet no facts, than to face up to the troublesome questions of the present and recent past.

In the covenants of power the future is being planned, even if later it must be laid down in blood with a sword. The powerless intellectual as planner may set up contrary expectations; he will later see the actual function of his "planning." He is leading a prayer and such prayer is a mass indirection.

Discussion of world affairs that does not proceed in terms of the struggle for power within each nation is interesting only in the political uses now made of it by those in power. Internal power struggles are the only determinants of international affairs which we may influence. The effective way to plan the world's future is to criticize the decisions of the present. Unless it is at every point so anchored, "planning" disguises the world that is actually in the works; it is therefore a dangerous disguise which permits a spurious escape from the anxieties surrounding the decisions and happenings of the present.

## VI

The writer tends to believe that problems are *really* going to be solved in *his* medium, that of the word. Thus he often underplays the threat of violence, the coercive power always present in decisive political questions. This keeps the writer's mind and energies in general channels, where he can talk safely of justice and freedom. Since the model of his type of controversy is rational argumentation, rather than skilled violence or stupid rhetoric, it keeps him from seeing these other and historically more decisive types of controversy. These results of the writer's position, his work and its effects, are quite convenient for the working politician, for they generally serve to cover the nature of his struggles and decisions with ethically elaborated disguises. As the channels of communication become more and more monopolized and party machines and economic pressures, based on vested shams, continue to monopolize the chances of effective political organization, his opportunities to act and to communicate politically are minimized. The political intellectual is, increasingly, an employee living off the communicational machineries which are based on the very opposite of what he would like to stand for. He would like to stand for a politics of truth in a democratically responsible society. But such efforts as he has made on behalf of freedom for his function have been defeated.

The defeat is not at the hands of an enemy that is clearly defined. Even given the power, no one could easily work his will with our situation, nor succeed in destroying its effects with one blow. It is always easier to locate an external enemy than grapple with an internal condition. Our impersonal defeat has spun a tragic plot and many are betrayed by what is false within them.

# 4

# THE SOCIOLOGY OF STRATIFICATION

In New York City, some people taxi home at night from Madison Avenue offices to Sutton Place; others leave a factory loft in Brooklyn and subway home to East Harlem. In Detroit there is Grosse Pointe, with environs, and there is Hamtramck, without environs; in a thousand small towns the people live on either side of the railroad track. In Moscow, high party members ride cautiously in black cars to well-policed suburbs; other people walk home from factories to cramped apartments. And in the shadow of swank Washington, D. C., apartment houses, there are the dark alley dwellings.

In almost any community in every nation there is a high and a low, and in many societies, a big in-between.

If we go behind what we can thus casually observe while standing on street corners, and begin seriously to observe in detail the 24-hour cycle of behavior and experience, the 12-month cycle, the life-long biography of people in various cities and nations, we will soon be forced to classify. We might well decide to make our classification of people in terms of the social distribution of valued things and experiences; to find out just which people regularly expect to and do receive how many of the available valued things and experiences, and, on every level, why. Such a classification is the basis of all work in stratification.

In any society of which we know some people seem to get most of such values, some least, others being in between. The student of stratification is bent on understanding such ranking of people, and in finding out exactly in what respects these ranks differ and why. Each ranking or stratum in a society may be viewed as a stratum by virtue of the fact that all of its members have similar chances to gain the things and experiences that are generally valued, whatever they may be: things like cars, money, toys, houses, etc.; experiences, like being given respect, being educated to certain levels, being treated kindly, etc. To belong to one stratum or to another is to share with the other people in this stratum similar chances to receive such values.

If, again, we go behind these strata of people having similar life-chances, and begin to analyze each stratum and the reasons for its formation and persistence, sooner or later we will come upon at least four factors that seem to be quite important keys to the general phenomena. We call these "dimensions of stratification." Each is a way of ranking people with respect to their different chances to obtain values, and together, if properly understood, they enable us to explain these differing chances. These four dimensions are occupation, class, status and power.

## I

By an occupation we understand a set of activities pursued more or less regularly as a major source of income.

From the individual's standpoint, occupational activities refer to types of skill that are marketable. These skills range from arranging mathematical symbols for $1000 a day to arranging dirt with a shovel for $1000 a year.

From the standpoint of society, occupations as activities are functions: they result in certain end products—various goods and services—and are accordingly classified into industrial groups.

As specific activities, occupations thus (1) entail various types and levels of skill, and (2) their exercise fulfills certain functions within an industrial division of labor.

In the United States today the most publicly obvious strata consist of members of similar occupations. However it has been and may now be in other kinds of societies, in contemporary U.S.A. occupations are the most ostensible and the most available "way into" an understanding of stratification. For, most people spend the most alert hours of most of their days in occupational work. What kind of work they do not only monopolizes their wakeful hours of adult life but sets what they can afford to buy: most people who receive any direct income at all do so by virtue of some occupation.

As sources of income, occupations are thus connected with *class* position. Since occupations also normally carry an expected quota of prestige, on and off the job, they are relevant to *status* position. They also involve certain degrees of *power* over other people, directly in terms of the job, and indirectly in other social areas. Occupations are thus tied to class, status, and power as well as to skill and function; to understand the occupations composing any social stratum, we must consider them in terms of each of these interrelated dimensions.

The most decisive occupational shift in the twentieth century has been the decline of the independent entrepreneurs ("the old middle class" of businessmen, farmers, and fee professionals) and the rise of the salaried employees ("the new middle class" of managers and salaried professionals, of office people and sales employees). During the last two generations the old middle class has bounded from 6 to 25 per cent, while the wage workers as a whole have levelled off, in fact declining from 61 to 55 per cent. In the course of the following remarks we will pay brief attention by way of illustration to these three occupational levels in the cities of the United States.

## II

"Class situation" in its simplest, objective sense has to do with the amount and source of income. A class is a set of people who share similar life choices because of their similar class situations.

Today, occupation rather than property is the source of income for most of those who receive any direct income: the possibilities of selling their services in the labor market, rather than of profitably buying and selling their property and its yields, now determine the class-chances of over four fifths of the American people. All the things money can buy and many that men dream about are theirs by virtue of occupational level. In these occupations men work for someone else on someone else's property. This is the clue to many differences between the older, nineteenth century world of the small propertied entrepreneur and the occupational structure of the new society. If the old middle class of free enterprisers once fought big property structures in the name of small, free properties, the new middle class of white-collar employees, like the wage-workers in latter-day capitalism, has been, from the beginning, dependent upon large properties for job security.

Wage-workers in the factory and on the farm are on the propertyless bottom of the occupational structure, depending upon the equipment owned by others, earning wages for the time they spend at work. In terms of property, the white-collar people are *not* "in between Capital and Labor;" they are in exactly the same property-class position as the wage-workers. They have no direct fiscal tie to the means of production, no prime claim upon the proceeds from property. Like factory workers—and day laborers for that matter—they work for those who do own such means of livelihood.

Yet if bookkeepers and coal miners, insurance agents and farm laborers, doctors in a clinic and crane operators in an open pit have this condition in common, certainly their class situations are not the same. To understand the variety of modern class positions, we must go beyond the common fact of source of income and consider as well the amount of income.

In the middle thirties the three urban strata, entrepreneurs, white-collar, and wage-workers, formed a distinct scale with respect to median family income: white-collar employees had a median income of $2,008; entrepreneurs, $1,665; urban wage-workers, $1,175. Although the median income of white-collar workers was higher than that of the entrepreneurs, larger proportions of the entrepreneurs received both high-level and low-level incomes. The distribution of their income was spread more than that of the white collar.

The wartime boom in incomes, in fact, spread the incomes of all occupational groups, but not evenly. The spread occurred mainly among urban entrepreneurs. As an income level, the old middle class in the city is becoming less an evenly graded income group, and more a collection of different strata, with a large proportion of lumpen-bourgeoisie who receive very low incomes, and a small, prosperous bourgeoisie with very high incomes.

In the late forties (1948, median family income) the income of all white-collar workers was $4,058, that of all urban wage-workers, $3,317. These averages, however, should not obscure the overlap of specific groups within each stratum: the lower white-collar people—sales-employees and office workers—earned almost the same as skilled workers and foremen,* but more than semiskilled urban wage-workers.

In terms of property, white-collar people are in the same position as wage-workers; in terms of occupational income, they are "somewhere in the middle." Once they were considerably above the wage-workers; they have become less so; in the middle of the century they still have an edge but, rather than adding new income distinctions within the new middle-class group, the over-all rise in incomes is making the new middle class a more homogeneous income group.

Distributions of property and income are important economically because if they are not wide enough, purchasing power may not be sufficient to take the production that is possible or desirable. Such distributions are also important because they underpin the class structure and thus the chances of the various ranks of the people to obtain desired values. Everything from the chance to stay alive during the first year after birth to the chance to view fine art; the chance to remain healthy and if sick to get well again quickly; the chance to avoid becoming a juvenile delinquent; and very crucially, the chance to complete an intermediary or higher educational grade—these are among the chances that are crucially influenced by one's position in the class structure of a modern society.

These varying, unequal chances are factual probabilities of the class structure. It does not follow from such facts that people in similar class situations will necessarily become conscious of themselves as a class or come to feel

* It is impossible to isolate the salaried foremen from the skilled urban wage-workers in these figures. If we could do so, the income of lower white-collar workers would be closer to that of semi-skilled workers.

that they belong together. Nor does it follow that they will necessarily become aware of any common interests they may objectively share, or that they will become organized in some way, in a movement or in a party, in an attempt to realize such interests. Nor does it follow that they will necessarily become antagonistic to people in other class situations and struggle with them. All these—class-consciousness and awareness of common interests, organizations and class-struggle—have existed in various times and places and, in various forms, do now exist as mental and political fact. But they do not follow logically or historically from the objective fact of class structure. In any given case, whether or not they arise from objective class situations is a matter for fresh empirical study.

## III

Prestige involves at least two persons: one to *claim* it and another to *honor* the claim. The bases on which various people raise prestige claims, and the reasons others honor these claims, include property and birth, occupation and education, income and power—in fact almost anything that may invidiously distinguish one person from another. In the status system of a society these claims are organized as rules and expectations which regulate who successfully claims prestige, from whom, in what ways, and on what basis. The level of self-esteem enjoyed by given individuals is more or less set by this status system.

There are, thus, six items to which we must pay attention: From the claimant's side: (1) the status claim, (2) the way in which this claim is raised or expressed, (3) the basis on which the claim is raised. And correspondingly—from the bestower's side: (4) the status bestowal or deferences given, (5) the way in which these deferences are given, (6) the basis of the bestowal, which may or may not be the same as the basis on which the claim is raised. An extraordinary range of social phenomena are pointed to by these terms.

Claims for prestige are expressed in all those mannerisms, conventions and ways of consumption that make up the styles of life characterizing people on various status levels. The "things that are done" and the "things that just aren't done" are the status conventions of different strata. Members of higher status groups may dress in distinct ways, follow "fashions" with varying degrees of regularity, eat at certain times and places with certain people. In varying degrees, they maintain an elegance of person and specific modes of address, have dinners together, and are glad to see their sons and daughters intermarry. "Society" in American cities, debutante systems, the management of welfare activities—these often regiment the status activities of upper circles, where exclusiveness, distance, coldness, and condescending benevolence toward outsiders are characteristic.

Claims for prestige and the bestowal of prestige are often based on birth. The Negro child, irrespective of individual "achievement," will not receive the deference which the white child may successfully claim. The immigrant, especially a member of a recent mass immigration, will not be as likely to receive the deference given the Old American, immigrant groups being generally stratified according to how long they, and their forebears, have been in America. Within "the native-born white of native parentage," certain "Old Families" receive more deference than do other families. In each case—race, nationality and family— prestige is based on, or at least limited by, descent, which is perhaps most obviously a basis of prestige at the top and at the bottom of the social ladder. European nobilities and rigidly excluded racial minorities represent the acme of status by descent, the one high, the other low.

Upper-class position typically carries great prestige, all the more so if the source of the money is property. Yet if the possession of wealth in modern industrial societies leads to increased prestige, rich men who are too fresh from lower class levels may experience great difficulty in "buying their ways" into upper-status circles. Often, in fact, impoverished descendants of once high level Old Families receive more deference from more people than do wealthy men without appropriate grandparents. The facts of the *nouveau riche* (high class without high prestige) and the broken-down aristocrat (high prestige without high class) refute the complete identification of upper-prestige and upper-class position, even though, in due course, the broken-down aristocrat often becomes simply broken-down, and the son of the *nouveau riche,* a man of "clean, old wealth." The possession of wealth also allows the purchase of an environment which in time often leads to the development of those "intrinsic" qualities of individuals and families that are required for higher prestige. When we say that American prestige has been fluid, one thing we mean is that high economic class position has led rather quickly to high prestige. A feudal aristocracy, based on old property and long descent, has not existed here. Veblen's *The Theory of the Leisure Class* was focused primarily upon the U. S. post-civil war period and the expressions of prestige claims raised in lavish economic ways by the *nouveau riche* of meat, railroads, and steel.

The prestige of the middle strata in America is based on many principles other than descent and property. The shift to a society of employees has made *occupation* and *education* crucially important. Insofar as occupation determines the level of income, and different styles of life require different income levels, occupation limits the style of life. In a more direct way, different occupations require different levels and types of education, and education also limits the style of life and thus the status successfully claimed.

Some occupations are reserved for members of upper-status levels, others are "beneath their honor." In some societies, in fact, having no work to do brings the highest prestige, prestige being an aspect of property class, the female dependents of high-class husbands becoming specialists in the display of expensive idleness. But only those who do not need to work, yet have more income than those who must, are likely to obtain prestige from idleness. For those for whom work is necessary but not available, "leisure" brings disgrace. And income from property does not always bring more prestige than income from work; the amount and the ways the income is used are more important than its source. A small rentier may not enjoy esteem equal to that of a moderately paid doctor.

Among the employed, those occupations which pay more, involve more mental activities, and some power to supervise others seems to place people on higher prestige levels. But sheer power does not always lend prestige: the political boss gives up prestige, except among his machine members, for power; constitutional monarchs, on the other hand, may gain ceremonial prestige but give up political power. In offices and factories, skilled foremen and office supervisors expect and typically receive an esteem which lifts them above unskilled workers and typists. But the policeman's power to direct street masses does not bring prestige, except among little boys.

The type of education, as well as the amount, is an important basis for prestige: "Finishing schools" and "Prep schools" turn out women and men accomplished in a style of life which guarantees deference in some circles. In others, the amount of intellectual skill acquired through education is a key point for estimation. Yet skill alone is not as uniform a basis for prestige as is skill connected with highly esteemed occupations.

The extent to which claims for prestige are honored and by whom they are honored, may vary widely. Some of those from whom an individual claims prestige may honor his claims, others may not; some deferences that are given may express genuine feelings of esteem; others may be expedient strategies for ulterior ends. A society may, in fact, contain many hierarchies of prestige, each with its own typical bases and areas of bestowal, or one hierarchy in which everyone uniformly "knows his place" and is always in it. It is in the latter that prestige groups are most likely to be uniform and continuous.

Imagine a society in which everyone's prestige is absolutely set and unambivalent; every man's claims for prestige are balanced by the prestige he receives, and both his expression of claims and the ways these claims are honored by others are set forth in understood stereotypes. Moreover, the bases of the claims coincide with the reasons they are honored; those who claim prestige on the specific basis of property or birth are honored because of their property or birth. So the exact volume and types of deference expected between any two individuals are always known, expected, and given; and each individual's level and type of self-esteem are steady features of his inner life.

Now imagine the opposite society, in which prestige is

highly unstable and ambivalent: the individual's claims are
not usually honored by others. The way claims are expressed are not understood or acknowledged by those from
whom deference is expected, and when others do bestow
prestige, they do so unclearly. One man claims prestige on
the basis of his income, but even if he is given prestige, it is
not because of his income but rather, for example, because
of his education or appearance. All the controlling devices
by which the volume and type of deference might be directed are out of joint or simply do not exist. So the prestige system is no system, but a maze of misunderstanding,
of sudden frustration and sudden indulgence, and the individual, as his self-esteem fluctuates, is under strain and full
of anxiety.

American society in the middle of the twentieth century
does not fit either of these projections absolutely, but it
seems fairly clear that it is closer to the unstable and ambivalent model. This is not to say that there is no prestige
system in the United States; given occupational groupings,
even though caught in status ambivalence, do enjoy typical
levels of prestige. It is to say, however, that the enjoyment
of prestige is often disturbed and uneasy, that the basis of
prestige, the expressions of prestige claims, and the ways
these claims are honored, are now subject to great strain,
a strain which often throws men and women into a virtual
status panic.

As with income, so with prestige: U. S. white-collar
groups are differentiated socially, perhaps more decisively
than wage-workers and entrepreneurs. Wage earners certainly do form an income pyramid and a prestige gradation,
as do entrepreneurs and rentiers; but the new middle class,
in terms of income and prestige, is a superimposed pyramid, reaching from almost the bottom of the first to almost
the top of the second.

People in white-collar occupations claim higher prestige
than wage-workers, and, as a general rule, can cash in their
claims with wage-workers as well as with the anonymous
public. This fact has been seized upon, with much justification, as the defining characteristic of the white-collar strata,
and although there are definite indications in the United
States of a decline in their prestige, still, on a nation-wide

basis, the majority of even the lower white-collar employees —office workers and salespeople—enjoy a middle prestige place.

The historic bases of the white-collar employees' prestige, apart from superior income, have included (1) the similarity of their place and type of work to those of the old middle-classes which has permitted them to borrow prestige. (2) As their relations with entrepreneur and with esteemed customer have become more impersonal, they have borrowed prestige from the firm itself. (3) The stylization of their appearance, in particular the fact that most white-collar jobs have permitted the wearing of street clothes on the job, has figured in their prestige claims, as have (4) the skills required in most white-collar jobs, and in many of them the variety of operations performed and the degree of autonomy exercised in deciding work procedures. Furthermore, (5) the time taken to learn these skills and (6) the way in which they have been acquired by formal education and by close contact with the higher-ups in charge has been important. (7) White-collar employees have monopolized high school education—even in 1940 they had completed 12 grades to the 8 grades for wage-workers and entrepreneurs. They have also (8) enjoyed status by descent: in terms of race, Negro white-collar employees exist only in isolated instances—and, more importantly, in terms of nativity, in 1930 only about 9 per cent of white-collar workers, but 16 per cent of free enterprisers and 21 per cent of wage-workers, were foreign born. Finally, as an underlying fact, (9) the limited size of the white-collar group, compared to wage-workers, has led to successful claims to greater prestige.

## IV

To be powerful is to be able to realize one's will, even against the resistance of others. The power position of groups and of individuals typically depends upon factors of class, status, and occupation, often in intricate inter-relations.

Given occupations involve specific powers over other people in the actual course of work; but also outside the job area, by virtue of their relations to institutions of property as well as the typical income they afford, occupations lend power. Some occupations require the direct exercise of supervision over other employees and workers, and many white-collar employees are closely attached to this managerial cadre. They are the assistants of authority: the power they exercise is a derived power, but they do exercise it.

Property classes may involve power over job markets and commodity markets, directly and indirectly; they may also support power, because of their property, over the state. As Franz Neumann has neatly indicated, each of these powers may be organized for execution, in employers association, cartel, and pressure group. From the underside of the property situation, propertyless wage workers may have trade unions and consumers co-ops which may be in a struggle with the organized powers of property on each of these three fronts.

When we speak of the power of classes, occupations and status groups, however, we usually refer more or less specifically to political power. This means the power of such groups to influence or to determine the policies and activities of the state. The most direct means of exercising such power and the sign of its existence are organizations, either composed of members of certain strata, or acting in behalf of their interests, or both. The power of various strata often implies a political willfulness, a "class-consciousness" on the part of members of these strata. But not always: there can be, as in the case of "un-organized, grumbling workers," a common mentality among those in common strata without organizations. And there can be, as in the case of some "pressure groups," an organization representing the interests of those in similar strata without any common mentality being notable among them.

The accumulation of political power by any stratum is generally dependent upon a triangle of factors: willful mentality, objective opportunity, and the state of organization. The opportunity is limited by the group's structural positions within the stratification of the society; the will is dependent upon the group's awareness of its interests and ways of realizing them. And both structural position and awareness interplay with organizations, which strengthen awareness, and are made politically relevant by structural position.

## V

What is at issue in theories of stratification and political power is (1) the objective position of various strata with reference to other strata of modern society, and (2) the political content and direction of their mentalities. Questions concerning either of these issues can be stated in such a way as to allow, and in fact demand, observational answers only if adequate conceptions of stratification and political mentality are clearly set forth.

Often the "mentality" of strata is allowed to take predominance over the objective position.

It is, for example, frequently asserted that "there are no classes in the United States" because "psychology is of the essence of classes" or, as Alfred Bingham has put it, that "class groupings are always nebulous, and in the last analysis only the vague thing called class-consciousness counts." It is said that people in the United States are not aware of themselves as members of classes, do not identify themselves with their appropriate economic level, do not often organize in terms of these brackets or vote along the lines they provide. America, in this reasoning, is a sandheap of "middle-class individuals."

But this is to confuse psychological feelings with other kinds of social and economic reality. The fact that men are not "class conscious" at all times and in all places does not mean that "there are no classes" or that "in America everybody is middle class." The economic and social facts are one thing. Psychological feelings may or may not be associated with them in rationally expected ways. Both are important, and if psychological feelings and political outlooks do not correspond to economic or occupational class, we must try to find out why, rather than throw out the economic baby with the psychological bath, and so fail to understand how either fits into the national tub. No matter what people believe, class structure as an economic arrangement influences their life chances according to their positions in it. If they do not grasp the causes of their conduct this does not mean that the social analyst must ignore or deny them.

If political mentalities are not in line with objectively defined strata, that lack of correspondence is a problem to be explained; in fact, it is the grand problem of the psychology of social strata. The general problem of stratification and political mentality thus has to do with the extent to which the members of objectively defined strata are homogeneous in their political alertness, outlook, and allegiances, and with the degree to which their political mentality and actions are in line with the interests demanded by the juxtaposition of their objective position and their accepted values.

To understand the occupation, class, and status positions of a set of people is not necessarily to know whether or not they (1) will become class-conscious, feeling that they belong together or that they can best realize their rational interests by combining; (2) will have "collective attitudes" of any sort, including those toward themselves, their common situation; (3) will organize themselves, or be open to organization by others, into associations, movements, or political parties; or (4) will become hostile toward other strata and struggle against them. These social, political, and psychological characteristics may or may not occur on the basis of similar objective situations. In any given case, such possibilities must be explored, and "subjective" attributes must *not be used as criteria* for class inclusion, but rather, as Max Weber has made clear, stated as probabilities on the basis of objectively defined situations.

Implicit in this way of stating the issues of stratification lies a model of social movements and political dynamics. The important differences among people are differences that shape their biographies and ideas; within any given stratum, of course, individuals differ, but if their stratum has been adequately understood, we ought to be able to expect certain psychological traits to recur. Our principles of stratification enable us to do this. The probability that people will have a similar mentality and ideology, and that they will join together for action, is increased the more homogeneous they are with respect to class, occupation, and prestige. Other factors do, of course, affect the probability that ideology, organization, and consciousness will occur among those in objectively similar strata. But psychological factors are likely to be associated with *strata,* which consist of people who are characterized by an intersection of the *several* dimensions we have been using: class, occupation, status, and power. The task is to sort out these dimensions of stratification in a systematic way, paying attention to each separately and then to its relation to each of the other dimensions.

## VI

The meaning of the term "proletarianized," around which major theories of changes in stratification have revolved, is by no means clear. In the definitions set forth here, however, proletarianization might refer to shifts of "middle-class occupation" toward wage-workers in terms of income, property, skill, prestige or power, irrespective of whether or not the people involved are aware of these changes. Or, the meaning may be in terms of changes in consciousness, outlook, or organized activity. It would be possible, for example, for a segment of people higher in all respects to become virtually identical with wage-workers in income, property, and skill, but to resist becoming like them in prestige claims and to anchor their whole consciousness upon illusory prestige factors. Only by keeping objective position and ideological consciousness separate in analysis can the problem be stated with precision and without unjustifiable assumptions about wage-workers, white-collar workers, and the general psychology of social classes.

When the Marxist, Anton Pannekoek, for example, refuses to include propertyless people of lower income rather than skilled workers in the proletariat, he refers to ideological and prestige factors. He does not go on to refer to the same factors as they operate among the "proletariat," because he holds to what can only be called a metaphysical belief that the proletariat is *destined* to win through to a certain consciousness. Those who see white-collar groups as composing an independent "class," *sui generis,* often use prestige or status as their defining criterion rather than economic level. The Marxian assertion, —for example, L. B. Boudin's, —that salaried employees "are in reality just as much a part of the proletariat as the merest day laborer," obviously rests on economic criteria, as is generally recognized when his statement is countered by the assertion that he ignores "important psychological factors."

The Marxist in his expectation assumes *first* that wage-workers, or at least large sections of them, do in fact, or will at any moment, have a socialist consciousness of their revolutionary role in modern history. It assumes, *second,* that the middle classes, or large sections of them, are acquiring this consciousness, and in this respect are becoming like the wage-workers or like what wage-workers are assumed to be. *Third,* it rests this contention primarily upon the assumption that the economic dimension, especially property, of stratification is the key one, and that it is in this dimension that the middle classes are becoming like wage-workers.

But the fact that propertyless employees (both wage-workers and salaried employees) have not automatically assumed any unified political posture clearly means that propertylessness is not the only factor, or even the crucial one, determining inner-consciousness or political will.

Neither white-collar people nor wage-workers in the United States have been or are preoccupied with questions of property. The concentration of property during the last century has been a slow process rather than a sharp break inside the life span of one generation; even the sons and daughters of farmers—among whom the most obvious "expropriation" has gone on—have had their attentions focused on the urban lure rather than on urban propertylessness. As jobholders, moreover, salaried employees have generally, with the rest of the population, experienced a rise in standards of living: propertylessness has certainly not necessarily coincided with pauperization. So the centralization or property, with consequent expropriation, has not been widely experienced as "agony" or reacted to by proletarianization, in any psychological sense that may be given these terms.

Objectively, the structural position of the white-collar mass is becoming more and more similar to that of the wage-workers. Both are, of course, propertyless, and their incomes draw closer and closer together. All the factors of their status position, which have enabled white-collar workers to set themselves apart from wage-workers, are now subject to definite decline. Increased rationalization is lowering the skill levels and making their work more and more factory-like. As high-school education becomes more universal among wage-workers, and the skills required for many white-collar tasks become simpler, it is clear that the white-collar job market will include more wage-worker children.

So, in the course of the next generation, a "social class" between lower white-collar and wage-workers will probably be formed, which means, in Weber's terms, that between the two positions there will be a typical job mobility. This will not, of course, involve the professional strata or the higher-managerial employees, but it will include the bulk of the workers in salesroom and office. These shifts in the occupational worlds of the propertyless are more important to them than the existing fact of their propertylessness.

The assumption that political supremacy follows from functional, economic indispensability often underlies theories of the rise to power of one or the other strata in modern society. It is assumed that the class that is indispensable in fulfilling the major functions of the social order will be the next in the sequence of ruling classes. Max Weber in his essay on bureaucracy has made short shrift of this idea: "The ever-increasing 'indispensability' of the officialdom, swollen to millions, is no more decisive for this question [of power] than is the view of some representatives of the proletarian movement that the economic indispensability of the proletarians is decisive for the measure of their social and political power position. If 'indispensability' were decisive, then where slave labor prevailed and where freemen usually abhor work as a dishonor, the 'indispensable' slaves ought to have held the positions of power, for they were at least as indispensable as officials and proletarians are today. Whether the power . . . as such increases cannot be decided a priori from such reasons."

Yet the assumption that it can runs all through most

literature on stratification. Just as Marx, seeing the para-
sitical nature of the capitalist's endeavor, and the real function of work performed by the workers, predicted the
workers' rise to power; so James Burnham (and before him
Harold Lasswell and John Corbin) assumed that since the
new middle class is the carrier of those skills upon which
modern society more and more depends, it will inevitably,
in the course of time, assume political power. Technical and
managerial indispensability is thus confused with the facts
of power struggle, and overrides all other sources of power.
The deficiency of such arguments must be realized positively: we need to develop and to use a more open and
flexible model of the relations of political power and stratification.

Increasingly, class and status situations have been removed from free market forces and the persistence of tradition, and been subject to more formal rules. A government management of the class structure has become a
major means of alleviating inequalities and insuring the
risks of those in lower-income classes. Not so much free
labor markets as the powers of pressure groups now shape
the class positions and privileges of various strata in the
United States. Hours and wages, vacations, income security
through periods of sickness, accidents, unemployment, and
old age—these are now subject to many intentional pressures, and, along with tax policies, transfer payments,
tariffs, subsidies, price ceilings, wage freezes, et cetera,
make up the content of "class fights" in the objective meaning of the phrase.

The "Welfare State" attempts to manage class chances
without modifying basic class structure; in its several
meanings and types, it favors economic policies designed to
redistribute life-risks and life-chances in favor of those in
the more exposed class situations, who have the power, or
threaten to accumulate the power, to do something about
their case.

Labor union, farm bloc, and trade association dominate
the political scene of the Welfare State, and contests within
and between them increasingly determine the position of
various groups. The state, as a descriptive fact, is at the
balanced intersection of such pressures, and increasingly

the privileges and securities of various occupational strata depend upon the bold means of organized power. Pensions, for example, especially since World War II, have been a major idea in labor union bargaining, and it has been the wage-worker that has had bargaining power. Social insurance to cover work injuries and occupational diseases has gradually been replacing the common law of a century ago, which held the employee at personal fault for work injury and the employer's liability had to be proved in court by a damage suit.

In so far as such laws exist, they legally shape the class chances of the manual worker up to a par with or above other strata. Privileges of status and occupation, as well as income level, have been increasingly subject to the power pressures of union, trade association, and government, and there is every reason to believe that in the future this will be even more the case.

# 5

## PLAIN TALK ON FANCY SEX

Two kinds of prostitution have for a long time been standard in America:

*The Old-Line Prostitute.*—There is the five to fifteen dollar woman who makes no bones about what she is: on the street, or in a house, or provided by bell boy or taxi driver. Waitresses, beauty-parlor operators, salesgirls, and the like, have traditionally been more likely than women in other jobs to succumb to such lowly temptation; and—as the Vice Commission of Chicago revealed in 1911—they have usually yielded out of dire want, and because of a series of adroit traps laid for their innocence. The image is of a salesman, a soldier, a frightened college boy who calls a bell boy to get him a girl and turns off the light in the hotel room as soon as she comes, the whole transaction being mean and scared, and involving in all ten or fifteen dollars. Such old-line prostitution still exists, but it is only one type.

*Upper-Class Prostitution.*—There is also the prostitution and the semiprostitution indulged in by rich men and moneyed youth, by busy millionnaires as well as playboys and men of executive standing. The plutocratic classes in fact have always included types of men who have been able to buy attractive girl companions. Back Street is still inhabited, and during inflation the same apartment and girl may even be shared—known or unknown—by several men having different travel schedules. In Greece and in Rome, in eighteenth-century England and in twentieth-century America—upper-class men have had their pick of the most erotically talented and beautiful women available. Apart from sexual eccentricities and perversions which have always been found among idle elements of upper classes, the standard upper-class pattern is the series of kept women, of mistresses—rather than the casual party girl.

*The Expense-Account Girl.*—What the recent disclosures of high-priced sex and deluxe vice—centering in the upholstered sewers of New York Cafe Society—have brought to light is that another type of prostitution has been flourishing. Really getting under way during the cost-plus days of World War II, in some ways, it represents a democratizing of night-ways previously available only to upper classes.

Along with the established upper-class prostitutes and mistresses of American plutocracy—with which it overlaps —this newer girl system involves elegant women with light morals and respectable businessmen with heavy expense accounts. The part-time prostitute involved in it does not slink into a hotel to be used in the dark by a half-frightened salesman, or wait in a hidden Back-Street apartment for an upper-class man. Her customer is proud to show her off expensively to his business and night club associates. In one evening, she makes what it takes the "poor but honest working girl" a week or a month to make. She lives better and she dresses better and she has more excitement than most white-collar girls and in fact most wives.

Like many other people today, the expense-account girl lives on the hope that things will be different next week, next month, next year. For she is not so likely to be a success as a would-be model or an aspiring bit-player. Unlike the old-line prostitute, but like the upper-class mistress, the expense-account girl succumbs more from hope than from want. What she hopes for is a career in one of the glamour industries—stage, screen, TV, fashion—and in the meantime, the gilded good time. She does not believe that her good time activities as a party girl stand in the way of her aspirations. On the contrary, she believes, often correctly, that by bringing her to the attention of the right people, her partying may well help her career.

*Public Vices and Private Morality* —Expense-account vice does not rest merely upon the passions of men and the weaknesses of women. Back of it are certain long-run trends in the quality of public and private life in America.

To understand how radically public idols of womanhood have changed, one need only compare the innocent Sweet-

heart of America, Mary Pickford of 1920, with that newest
idol of hip-swinging, breast-dangling eroticism, Marilyn
Monroe of 1952.

In the fashion, advertising and entertainment industries,
girls are carefully selected and trained for the display of
erotic promise. What else is much of what makes up these
industries?

What makes this important is not the recent disclosure
that the promises so lavishly given are frequently fulfilled.
What makes it nationally important is that the women in
and around these industries—along with the cafe society
habitues with whom they are in contact—set the models
of appearance and conduct which are imitated all down the
national hierarchy of glamour. And that hierarchy includes
the good housewife in the Chicago suburb, as well as the
salesgirl in the Decatur five and ten with her style of walk-
ing carefully and unsuccessfully modeled after the latest
movie queen.

All this public eroticism which floods the mass media in
America is at once a reflection and a contributing cause of
drastic changes in private morality: there is no doubt but
that the value of chastity in the unmarried female has
declined, and that the respectability of the experienced
woman has gone up. This change has occurred all over
America. And all over America it has affected the marriage
market: it is no longer the case that the girl with experience
is the girl who has fallen below marriage. In fact, often
quite the contrary. The devaluation of premarital chastity is
the larger reason why some of the freshest, most beautiful
women in America, when properly approached can now be
had for $500.00.

The idea that vice in big American cities involves only
idle rich boys and poor country girls is ridiculously innocent. The men involved are by no means boys, they are
not idle, they need not personally be rich, and they are not
interested in poor or innocent or country girls. The women
involved are not exactly girls, they may have come from
smaller cities, but they are not very much big city, they are
not innocent, and they are not exactly poor.

Vice, first of all, is one of the service trades that make up

the night life of business. Those engaged in vice—the pro-
curers, the prostitutes, the customers—simply buy and sell
assorted varieties of erotical service, and many of them are
known to their associates as quite respectable.

But there is a deeper sense in which vice is business: the
high-priced party girl is now a helpmate of the great American salesman. It is now widely known that the American
salesman of a certain type and position is quite ready to
provide women for his would-be customer and to pay for
them out of the expense account provided by the firm.

Sex is involved in American business with firms and
between firms. Inside the firm it is likely to be petty, mean,
and directly exploitive. There is the boss who uses a
girl employee on threat—direct or indirect—of losing her
job, or not getting a pay increase, or not getting a promo-
tion. That sort of thing—which is more likely in smaller
than in larger businesses—is directly related to the employment market: when jobs are hard to come by and harder
to hold, when wages and salaries are low, then bosses, office
managers, foremen, and junior executives have the best
chance to demand erotical services along with typing and
dressmaking and other skills. But when, as now, jobs go
crying, there is not much such exploitation inside the firm.

Between firms, girls are used as pawns of the great
American game of salesmanship. Erotical services are
provided as part of the build up and entertainment which
speeds along the big order. The night-life of New York is
very largely run on the expense account, and many of the
customers are out-of-towners with wives not present. New
York at night, in short, is a town full of salesmen who en-
tertain buyers from out of town. These simple facts set the
stage for the high-priced looking, tasting, and feeling that
goes by the name of entertainment. They provide the opportunity for high-priced vice. But why do the girls go
wrong?

*Why Girls Go Wrong.*—The expense-account girl wants
a glamorous *career,* and since men largely control the
success or failure of such careers, she wants to be seen by
men who hold such positions, or who she thinks hold
such positions. And she feels, quite understandably that
it is easier to meet them in an intimately crowded night club

than in the impersonally crowded waiting room of an outer office.

She wants, in due course, a successful *marriage,* which means either a marriage to a moneyed man or to a man who can help her career, or both. In her mind, her position as a party girl by no means marks her off as a woman who has fallen below the marriage level. On the contrary, among other things, Cafe Society is of course a marriage market. For she is seen there by precisely the men who she feels are essential to career as well as to marriage.

She wants a *good time,* and in the big city this means an expensive time, which, in turn, means that men of her own age and of her old circles cannot provide her with the kind of time she wants. That is why she becomes the associate of older men.

Wanting the expensive good time also means that she needs *money,* chiefly for clothes, and presents, primarily clothes. The expensive account girl is not simply out for money. She does not expect to get rich and retire from her night-time activities. Money, for now, is simply a means for the easy life and the continuous good time, and in the future there is always the lucky chance of a zooming career, or the great hope of a deluxe marriage into the upper circles of American wealth and glamour.

All these positive motives—career, marriage, good time, money—would not work unless the girl had been released from certain inhibitions deeply felt by her grandmother. The key inhibition is of course the value of pre-marital chastity.

What used to uphold this value was (1) fear of shameful social disgrace, (2) fear of unwed pregnancy, and (3) fear of being barred forever from respectable marriage.

All three of these fears have been largely removed from the life of many American girls.

The would-be model or actress can hardly be expected to feel herself disgraced when she is acting out precisely the kind of high life which those whom she would imitate have made the acme of national glamour.

No intelligent girl in New York has any difficulty in being fitted with a birth control device by a competent doctor for the sum of 10 dollars.

And it is now an established fact among sexologists that in most circles of American life, virginity is not required in a marriage partner. In fact, in many circles, the contrary is the case.

The devaluation of pre-marital chastity is the larger reason why respectable girls, in their own eyes and in the eyes of their associates, remain respectable while providing erotical display and service at a price. Together with the inflated hopes, which in some girls become a virtual panic for success, they explain the psychology of the expense-account girl. American salesmanship and plutocratic demand provide the opportunity. Wherever such motive and opportunity meet, you get the expense-account girl. In fact, wherever attractive, ambitious girls meet men with the money or power to realize their ambitions, sex will be available at a price.

# 6

# DIAGNOSIS OF
# OUR MORAL UNEASINESS

Moral distrust of men in public life is an old American convention. In the current campaign, however, it has reached unprecedented heights: each of the leading candidates has felt it necessary to make public an accounting of his personal income.

One must of course discount heavily the wonderful make-believe and wild accusation of campaign oratory. And yet there is an anxious insistence about this term, "corruption," which signifies a wide-spread concern with public morality and personal integrity. This concern has been sharpened by the election, along with other commanding issues, but, like those issues, it has been an underlying worry in most areas of American life over the past decade.

Many disclosures have spurred the moral worry. At West Point, some of our most carefully selected boys have cheated to get by. In other schools all over the country, college men have played dishonest basketball at the request of crooked gamblers. In New York City there have been girls from quite respectable homes who could be bought by holidaying businessmen for a few hundred dollars from playboys in the business. In Washington, as well as in state capitals, there have been men in high places who have accepted bribes and yielded to pull. During the late war, anyone with smart money and the right connections could have all the black-market meat and gasoline he cared for. American gangsters, we now know, are the specialized personnel of nation-wide businesses having syndicated connections with one another and with local public authorities. Those who read business manuals in addition to newspapers can learn that there are men whose consciences have been replaced by expert accountants and high-priced lawyers. And all over the country, upper-middle and upper-class tax-dodgers personally treat March 15th as an invitation to a game of ingenious lying and skillful deceptions.

## I

Immorality being very much in the public eye, both presidential candidates have addressed themselves to it. Both have narrowed it to an issue of the political sphere, and both have asserted that "corruption in government" is primarily a matter of corrupt men. I think that both candidates are mistaken, that corruption in government is one aspect of a more general immorality, and that our moral level is now primarily a matter of a corrupting society.

Of course there can be corrupt men in sound institutions, but when institutions are corrupting, many of the men who live and work in them are necessarily corrupted. From this point of view, the most important question about the Nixon affair is not whether Senator Nixon was or is morally insensitive, but whether or not any young man in American politics who has come as far and as fast as Senator Nixon could very well have done so today without possessing or acquiring a somewhat blunted moral sensitivity.

Think of it this way. When a handful of men do not have jobs, and do not seek work, we may look for the causes in their immediate situation and character. But when 12 million men are unemployed, then we cannot believe that all of them suddenly "got lazy" and turned out to be "no good." Economists call this "structural unemployment"—meaning, for one thing, that the men involved cannot themselves control their job chances. I think many of the problems of white-collar crime and relaxed public morality, of high-priced vice and fading personal integrity, are problems of structural immorality.

Many people are at least vaguely aware that this is so. As news of higher immoralities breaks, they often say, "Well, another one got caught today," thereby implying that the cases disclosed are symptoms of a much more widespread condition. And there is good probative evidence that they are right. But what is the underlying condition of which all these instances are symptoms?

## II

The moral uneasiness of our time—in politics and economics, in family life, educational institutions, and even in our churches—is due to this key fact: the older values and codes of uprightness no longer grip us, nor have they been replaced by new values and codes which would lend moral meaning and sanction to the life-routines we must now follow.

It is not that we have explicitly rejected our received codes; it is rather that to many of us they have become hollow. No moral terms of acceptance are any longer available, but neither are any moral terms of rejection. As individuals, many of us are morally defenseless; as groups, politically indifferent. It is this generalized lack of commitment that accounts for the one half of us who do not vote in presidential elections. And this is what is meant when it is said that we are morally confused.

The American literature of practical inspiration reveals a significant shift in "what it takes to succeed." The sober personal virtues of will power and honesty, of high-mindedness and the constitutional inability to say Yes to The Easy Road—this latter nineteenth century image has given way to "the most important single factor, the effective personality," which "commands attention by charm," and "radiates self-confidence." In this "new way of life," one must smile often and be a good listener, talk in terms of the other man's interest and make the other feel important—and, regardless of integrity, one must do all this sincerely. Many personal relations, in short, have become part of "public relations," a sacrifice of selfhood on a personality market, to the sole end of individual success.

The value of work, once a gospel value in a largely rural America, is now typically understood to be a mere means to ends that lie wholly in the sphere of "leisure." At the same time, leisure itself has largely become merely a part of consumption, no longer part of a full life, but a substitute for it. For to this sphere also, the means of mass production—the machineries of amusement—have been applied. Rather than allow and encourage men to develop their sensibilities and unfold their creativities, their leisure merely wears them out. Our characters are largely formed by our leisure, and our leisure now carries no self-discipline and makes little appeal to our higher capacities. Much work is merely a way to make money; much leisure is merely a way to spend it. And when the two compete, leisure wins hands down.

Of course, such trends do not affect all Americans, in fact, statistically speaking, probably only a few. But they do affect enough people who are socially visible to be themselves socially felt. And the people typically affected tend to be people who influence the level of public, and eventually of private, sensibility.

In our economic and political institutions there are now men who wield enormous power, but have never had to win the moral consent of those over whom they hold this power. Every such naked interest, every new, unsanctioned power of corporation, farm bloc, labor union, and governmental agency, that has risen in the past two generations, has been clothed with morally loaded slogans. For what is *not* done in the name of the public interest? As these slogans wear out, new ones are industriously made up, also to be banalized in due course. And all the while, recurrent economic and military crises spread fears, hesitations and anxieties, which give new urgency to the busy search for moral justifications and decorous excuses.

There are many reasons for this banalization of old values and the failure to create new and viable ones. There is the recent growth of big cities, where men live without local roots and relations are impersonal, individualistic and blasé. There is the residential and business movement from state to state and city to city which further weakens the close, informal controls of personal relations and deeply-felt communities of interest. There is the shrinkage of family life, especially among the urban upper classes, and the consequent decline of interest in family position and reputation across the generations. There is, in short, the great unsettling of many people without personal ties, family continuity, or communal relations.

But regardless of the reasons, the absence of any moral order of belief exposes us to the influences of a commercial culture, the mass media manipulations of frenzied entertainment and distraction. In due course, such a "turn-over" of appeals and codes and values as we are subjected to leads to distrust and cynicism, to a sort of Machiavel-lianism-for-the-little-man.

### III

But there is one old value which has not markedly de-clined: the value of money and of the things money can buy—these, even in inflated times, seem as solid and en-during as stainless steel. As many other values are weak-ened, the question for Americans becomes not "Is there anything that money, used with intelligence, will not buy?" but, "How many of the things that money will *not* buy are valued and desired more than what money *will* buy?"

Whenever the standards of the moneyed life prevail, the man with money, no matter how he got it, will eventually be respected. A million dollars, as Peter Odegard once re-marked, covers a multitude of sins. It is not only that men want money; it is that their very standards are pecuniary. In a society in which the money-makers have had no seri-ous rival for repute and honor, the word "practical" comes to mean useful for private gain, and "common sense," the sense to get ahead financially. The pursuit of the moneyed life is the commanding value, in relation to which the influ-ence of other values has declined, so men easily become morally ruthless in the pursuit of easy money and fast estate-building.

A great deal of American corruption—although not all of it—is simply a part of the old effort to get rich. Today, however, the context in which the old drive must operate has changed. When both economic and political institu-tions were small and scattered—as in the simpler models of classical economics and Jeffersonian democracy—no man had it in his power to bestow or to receive great favors. But when political institutions and economic opportunities are at once concentrated and linked, then public office can be used for private gain.

Governmental agencies, I believe, contain no more of the higher immorality than do business corporations. Po-litical men can grant financial favors only when there are economic men ready and willing to take them. And economic men can seek political favors only when there are political agents who can bestow such favors. The publicity spotlight, of course, shines brighter upon the transactions of the men in government, for which there is good reason. Our expectations being higher, we are more easily disappointed by public officials. Businessmen are *supposed* to be out for themselves, and if they successfully skate on legally-thin ice, we honor them for having gotten away with it. In a business civilization, the rules of businesses are carried over into government—especially when so many businessmen have gone into government.

We should not forget that during the forties, and before that during the twenties, and before that in the railroading nineteenth century, political corruption was a major public issue. During each of these periods—regardless of the party in power—businessmen have exerted their greatest political influence.

Businessmen as such are thus in no position to express their indignation at the disclosure of political corruption, for not only are they directly involved in it, but the organizations of many businesses are by no means above it. How many executives would really fight for a law requiring a careful and public accounting of all executive contracts and "expense accounts?" High income taxes have resulted in a whole series of collusion between big firm and higher employee. There are many ingenious ways to cheat the spirit of the tax laws, and the standards of consumption of many high-priced men are determined more by complicated expense accounts than by simple take-home pay.

#### IV

The immediate cause of much white-collar crime is simply that there are now many laws on the books that are not in the heart. People obey these laws, when they do, not because they feel that it is morally right, but because they are afraid of being caught. Like prohibition, income taxes, war-time regulations and price controls exist without the support of firm moral convention. It is merely illegal to cheat them, but it is often considered smart to get away with it.

Laws without supporting moral conventions invite crime, but much more importantly, they spur the growth of an expedient, amoral attitude. In our kind of society—with its absence of pre-capitalist traditions—the only way to do away with such training devices is to change the laws and their enforcement so that, unlike the current income tax, they do not depend upon individual integrity. Another way is to pass only laws that result from great social movements with concomitant changes in moral codes, but there is no such movement underway in any area of American society today.

Honesty may be the "best" policy, but honesty is not enough. If public officials are to be morally responsible, there must also be a sense of morally political purpose. For in politics those who have no moral beliefs are likely to become the tools of those who do. And today, "those who do" include morally committed Communists, as well as the corrupted, who are amorally committed to practical gain.

A furious emphasis upon "practicality" and "administrative efficiency" is often due to an absence of moral sin. The question is, "Practical for what, efficient for whom?" If there *is* a genuine moral aim, it will continuously be made relevant to practical policies and operations. Mere *profession* of "ultimate moral aims" is simply cant, the repetition of which, in an immoral context, increases the amoral cynicism of half-intelligent people.

## V

Increasingly we feel that there is something synthetic about our big men. Their style, and the conditions under which they become "big," opens them to the charge of the build-up and the front. One feels, even when it is not there, the slickness of the pre-fabricated. And in fact, the advertising and public relations technique has been extended from the peddling of brand-name tooth paste and movie stars to the "development" of national politicians.

The immediate political meaning of the higher immorality, and of our own moral uneasiness, is that there is in

America today no set of Representative Men whose conduct and character are above the taint of the pecuniary morality, and who constitute models for American imitation and aspiration. There is no set of men with whom we can identify in the untroubled feeling that we should rightfully model our character upon theirs. Perhaps that is why we have of late become so interested in exemplary images of historical figures. At any rate, in this fundamental and psychological sense, we are today a leaderless democracy.

To call for such Representative Men is by no means merely to ask that one set of rascals be thrown out, and good men put in. Nor is it merely to call for "administrative re-organization." For such men cannot be synthetically created; by definition, they carry and sustain a moral culture and they cannot do so if our adherence to them is of the order of our preference for a particular movie star.

It is sometimes held, and more frequently felt, that moral men cannot be developed in an immoral society, but that a moral society cannot be developed without moral men. Such a chicken-and-egg quandary is a verbal snag for the dull-witted, and a verbal trick of those who do not really want moral improvement. In fact there is no chicken-and-egg *problem*. There is simply a sequence of chickens who lay eggs and of eggs from which chickens are hatched. In like manner, there is a social sequence in which men are selected and formed by institutions, and in which men willfully modify and create their institutions.

Where there are moral men in immoral institutions, you seek to improve the institutions. When there are immoral men in moral institutions, you kick the rascals out. When you are confronted by immoral men in immoral institutions, you follow Jefferson's advice and revolt. If you are fortunate enough to encounter moral men in moral institutions, you seek to maintain them as a standard for other areas of your public life.

There is thus in a democracy no dilemma on this score, but a dialectic, in which the moral quality of both men and institutions can be progressively improved. Yet it is the moral man—and especially the set of socially visible or Representative Men—who by demanding moral change can best dramatize moral issues. And, at any rate, our criteria for judging institutions should always include the quality of the men and women they develop and select.

"Crisis" is a bankrupted term because so many men in high places have evoked it in order to cover up their extraordinary policies and deeds. As a matter of fact, it is precisely the absence of genuine crises that has beset our morality. For such crises involve situations in which men at large are presented with genuine alternatives, the moral meanings of which are clearly opened to public debate. Our higher immorality and the general weakening of older values have not involved such crises, but on the contrary, have been matters of creeping indifference and a silent hollowing out.

It is to create, to force, to make articulate such crises that Representative Men would find one major role in a democracy. Being men of conscience, they would stand up to corrupting institutions and thus become the pivots around which these institutions could be redirected. But they could not do that if they were not sustained by a morally oriented movement. That is why the current furor over morals in public life will be mere "campaign rhetoric" if it is not focused upon the institutions and values of American society as well as upon current leaders. No matter what types of men are available, they cannot change moral values unless people find themselves in practical positions to uphold the values espoused. The moral quality of both men and institutions must be progressively improved.

Frankly, I do not believe that such a set of Representative Men will emerge in the United States of our time. The character-forming influences required are feeble, and the opportunities for such men, should they arise, to replace our current national idols, are scarce. But I do believe that the creation of such Representative Men should be a major aspiration of our collective political life. For only the presence of such men, and the moving conditions for their maximum influence, could change the sourness of the higher immorality into the everyday sweetness of a morally free society.

# 7

# WOMEN:
# THE DARLING LITTLE SLAVES

Mlle. Simone de Beauvoir would pass judgment on institutions according to whether or not they offer concrete opportunities to individuals, and the opportunities in which she is interested are summed up in the liberty of the individual "to transcend himself, to engage in freely chosen projects." * It is just this humanistic liberty, she believes, that women do not have. Like many Negroes and Jews, they are judged not as individuals but as members of a stereotyped bracket. This not only discourages their womanly efforts to become productive individuals, but more grievously, leads to their not making the effort. Accordingly, the central question to which Mlle. de Beauvoir's book is addressed is "How can a human being in woman's situation attain fulfillment?"

The difficulty in reviewing her book is that it contains so much that is interesting that one wants to summarize it at length, but it is so stimulating that one wishes to comment upon it in detail. For, by pulling out from under most of the standard arguments their assumptions of fact, Mlle. de Beauvoir has opened up the whole topic for a fresh and uninhibited argument.

## I

Much of her own analysis follows vigorously upon acceptance of a radically sociological interpretation of personality and character. I will first try to summarize her point of view in five points:

* Simone de Beauvoir, *The Second Sex* (Translated and edited by H. M. Parshley) New York: Alfred A. Knopf, 1953. 732 pp. $10.00.

(i) To the biologist, a woman is simply a female of the species. But no fact about the female fixes the meaning or sets the destiny of woman. For the body is but a limiting factor for our projects, and our projects are set not by our biology but by our values. We cannot know the nature of women apart from her situation, upon which her nature so largely depends.

The female's inferiority to the male varies according to the level of material and social technique that prevails. If her muscles are not so strong, still she is quite as capable of operating modern semiautomatic machines. And her enslavement to the species, the burdens of maternity, are crushing only if she undergoes frequent pregnancies and if custom and economic conditions force her to constant attendance upon the young. The facts of biology themselves take on the values that we give them, and woman is a female only "to the extent that she is defined as such in her experienced situation. Anatomy is *not* destiny. And even her consciousness of her femininity does not define woman, for this consciousness is itself acquired under specific historical conditions. Like man, woman is not only a member of a species, she is an historical creation.

(ii). The little girl feels herself to be "an autonomous individual," even though she lives in the Kafka-like world of childhood. But at adolescence, when the boy "makes his way actively towards adulthood" the girl begins to wait for the man who will shape her adulthood. (328) What she becomes will not depend upon her own efforts; (335) she can only become an adult by modeling herself upon men's dreams (335), and to please men she must abdicate the attempt to become an independent being (335). That is why her adolescence is so difficult. She becomes an adult only by becoming a woman, but she can become a woman only by giving up an independent existence.

(iii). "Most women are married, or have been, or plan to be, or suffer from not being." (425) For man, marriage does not prohibit real and productive activity, but woman's interests are almost necessarily divided between marriage and personal aspiration of profession; and for her these are often irreconcilable. When she finds a husband, she gives up her independent aspirations and life projects. Daily intimacy, in or out of marriage, does not necessarily lead to fellowship or understanding or sympathy. In fact, marriage is in principle "obscene . . . in so far as it transforms into rights and duties those mutual relations which should be founded on a spontaneous urge."

(iv). Love, whatever it may be, is not to be had "forever after" in marriage. The truth is that eroticism is in profound tension with marital and family life. The aim of marriage is to institute the economic and reproductive functions, but love cannot be instituted; routine cannot be adventure; fidelity is not passion. "In principle marriage and love have nothing in common," (437) and the attempt to reconcile them is a *tour de force.* (439) In a well-regulated yet spontaneous life, physical love is a series of happy episodes with no external duties attached; to be authentic, love must be free: dependent upon no external constraint. (447-8) The idea of "conjugal love" is to say the least equivocal, and to say the most, merely a "tender and respectful sentiment." (448)

(v). Nor does giving birth to children and rearing them provide a satisfactory solution: ". . . the mother enjoys the comforting illusion of feeling that she is a human being in herself, a value. But this is only an illusion." The meaning of pregnancy is ambiguous, woman's attitude towards it ambivalent. (497) "Mother love," which is by no means a "natural" feeling, does not imply reciprocity. "Maternity," in short, "is usually a strange mixture of narcissism, altruism, idle daydreaming, sincerity, bad faith, devotion and cynicism." (513) And, with all that, maternity is not enough: To restrict women to maternity would only perpetuate her situation of dependency and meaningless routine. Besides, after her menopause, woman still has about one-half of her adult life to live.

## II

So: What should be done?

(i). Although there are genuine exceptions, women fail to gain human dignity, Mlle. de Beauvoir believes, because such dignity can only be the result of a free and independent existence, and "only independent work of her own can assure woman's genuine independence." As long as man is economically responsible for the couple, its members cannot be equal. (480) By this Mlle. de Beauvoir apparently does not mean merely that more women should go to work, but she knows that many unmarried women at work really want to escape from work by marriage, and that many unmarried women who work regard their work as a temporary burden. What she presumably means is that women, after being given identical educations as men, should become "highly trained professional women" or "highly placed women in business" with profound, permanent interests in their work.

(ii). Marriage as a "career" for women must, Mlle. de Beauvoir thinks, be "prohibited." (482) It cannot be a mutual completion if it is based, as it now generally is, upon an original mutilation. Each of the marriage partners should, as men now are, be "integrated as such in society at large." (479) And "since marriage does not generally involve physical love, it should seem reasonable to separate them quite candidly." Sexual episodes do not prevent either marriage partner from leading a joint life of amity with the other; adultery would lose its ugly character when based on liberty and sincerity rather than, as at present, on caution and hyprocrisy.

(iii.) Narcissism, great loves and mystical religions—there is a chapter on each—are simply womanly ways of trying to make her prison habitable, rather than ways of escaping from it. Even love, if authentic, would require woman's economic independence: her capacity to work toward ends of her own without using man as an agent.

(iv). In the end, realization of her ideal involves not only a revolution in the relations of men and women, but in the world in which they both are to live as human beings. "Only in a socialist world would woman" by work attain liberty. What Mlle. de Beauvoir wants, in short, is "what the Soviet Revolution *promised:* "women raised and trained exactly like men, working under exactly the same conditions; erotic liberty recognized by custom; the obligation of women to earn their own living; marriage a free agreement broken at will; maternity completely voluntary, with authorized birth control and abortion; married and unmar-

ried women to have identical rights; the state to provide
pregnancy leaves and to assume charge of the children,"
signifying not that they would be *taken away* from their
parents, but that they would not be *abandoned* to them."
(725)

There is no attempt to discuss the consequences of these
proposals in detail as a packaged program. Yet she knows
that one could not raise in our world a female human being
who would be a homologue of the male human being: it
would be an oddity, and she quotes Stendhal: "The forest
must be planted all at once." (726) But then she falls back
into a faith in social evolution which will "arrive at complete economic and social equality, which [in turn] will
bring about an inner metamorphosis." (729)

### III

(i.) Simone de Beauvoir is well aware that when an individual is kept in a situation of inferiority, the fact is that
he does become inferior. Woman, in Mlle. de Beauvoir's
view, is at the center of conflicting expectations: she is a
glossy little animal but also a dishwasher, an attentive
mother, but also a steadfast companion. The result is
slightly nervous. Under present conditions, many women
*are* quite dreadful creatures. So are many men. Many wom-
en do not attain the dignity of the independent human being. Neither do many men. But it is about women, and the
conditions that make them dreadful, that Simone de Beauvoir cries out. I agree both with her cry and with its humanistic basis. But I cannot help but feel that she often confuses
the conditions of woman with the generic human condition.

In writing about the second sex she really ought to have
thought more systematically about the first sex and about
human beings in general. For she tends to impute to all
men what is in fact true of only very few of them: a transcendent flight, a life of accomplishment. It is true that she
at time recognizes that this is not so, but she does not take
it into systematic account as she compares "the" situation
of men with "the" situation of women. She complains that
women are not free "to shape the concept of femininity."
But then neither are men free to shape the concept of mas-

culinity. Both concepts are stereotypes and both limit the human being.

(ii.) "Throughout history they have always been subordinated to men," writes Mlle. de Beauvoir, to which her translator adds: "With rare exceptions, perhaps, like certain matriarchial rulers, queens, and the like," to which we must add, as a handy example: including the American suburban queens on the $10,000 to $50,000 level.

The suburban queen clings to her "dependency" because to lose them would mean to lose her privileges; and her privileges are many. The fact that she has a child or two does not to my mind eliminate the fact that she is often simply a parasite, and as a parasite an exploiter. One does not blame these privileged women. It is not their "fault" that they are incapable of making anything of their freedom.

Although she does comment on it, I do not think she takes into sufficiently systematic account the intricacy, and the various outcomes, of the power struggle between many men and women. She knows that woman, who in our epoch is losing her femininity, often wishes to retain its privileges while man wants her to retain its limitations, (719) and they are victims of each other and of the stalemate between them. But she does not stress enough the real power that many women have and use: if man is transcendent and authoritarian, woman is often manipulative: the form of power for the immanent. (393) If men command, women seduce. Resentment often causes a frigidity, real or feigned, which is often used as a feminine tool of power.

(iii.) There is of course no such thing as Woman, or no such thing as The Condition of Woman. It is all the more sad that this is not concretely recognized, in an attempt to make some sort of classification of women according to their condition, because if one is not born a woman, but rather becomes one, then the woman she becomes depends quite largely on her experienced situation. Woman stands in these pages all too often as one generalized type, and the condition that makes her this type is presumed to be more or less universal in the West. The historical sketch could have provided clues to such a classification of condition and character, but it stands more or less isolated from the more general analysis. Somewhere in her book she admits about everything anyone might say, but she does not take many of them into *systematic* account—this she could only do if she worked with adequate *classifications*. In their absence she is often general in the worst sociological sense, in the sense of being unconnected with specific types of circumstances. In the end, I believe, this fault rests on a further deficiency: she does not provide appropriate classifications. Such classifications are the first and necessary step toward simplifying and hence understanding complicated subjects, and it is the only way to do justice to a complete topic without becoming vague.

Her explanations are all too often exasperatingly vague. For example, over and over again she says that the development of femininity does not depend entirely upon the physiological unfolding,—which is certainly true—but "upon the subject's total attitude toward existence" (405)—which is certainly vague to the point of obscurity. Or, again, in her sympathetic account of feminine homosexuality she states that it is neither deliberate nor fated, but rather "an attitude chosen in a certain situation." (424) But what, of any human complexity, is not? And exactly what situations are most conducive to this choice on the part of exactly which types of women? We are given no systematic answers. The female is not born a woman, but becomes one; but that does not mean, as Mlle. de Beauvoir asserts, that it is "civilization as a whole" that produces her. Civilization as a whole does not produce anything. (267) After one has eliminated the explanations of woman according to biological and psychological fate—and this Mlle. de Beauvoir does well—one must *specify* the necessary and sufficient social causes which produce the various *types* of women available to our observation in different societies.

Mlle. de Beauvoir's solution to the man-woman problem, put in its briefest form, is the elimination of woman as we know her—with which one might agree, but to which one must add: and the elimination of man as we know him. There would then be male and female and each would be equally free to become an independent human being.

No one can know what new types of human beings would be developed in this historically unique situation, but perhaps in sharing Mlle. de Beauvoir's passion for liberty we would all gladly forego femininity and masculinity to achieve it; and perhaps the best types would follow Coleridge's adage and become androgynous characters in an androgynous world.

In the meantime, Mlle. de Beauvoir is an idealist without being a romantic: she does not merely assert the values of some other world, but tries, quite desperately it seems to me, to develop ideas that will aid women to reshape their situation. She does not believe that people are capable of all things if they only have the will, for she knows that the will too is conditioned and sometimes determined by overwhelming conditions.

Is her book, as has been claimed, a classic?

When we call a book a "classic" we may be merely expressing approval of its excellence, or we may be saying that even after the assertions it makes are superseded, its form will remain a quite splendid cultural product. But the excellence and the readaibility of this book are marred by wordy portrayals of often simple and readily agreed upon points. The style is not classic, and by style I mean style of reflection as fused with style of expression. I know the easy danger of such comment, but I must say, simply, that the book is verbose, even padded; that the historical account, although at times insightful, is more often at once abstract and skimpy; and that the philosophical comments and vocabulary are more like plugs for existentialism than propositions and definitions essential to the argument. All this is the more unfortunate because the book is nevertheless indispensable reading for any woman who wishes to become more alert to her own possibilities, and for any man who wishes to understand what these possibilities might be. She has written one of those books that remind us how little we really *think* about our own personal lives and problems, and she invites us and helps us to do so.

# THE UNITY
# OF WORK AND LEISURE

During the course of a recent study, I came upon a man who was doing three things at once, or rather who was having three things done to him at once. With one eye and an ear, he looked at and listened to a baseball game on TV. With his other ear he listened to jump music on the radio beside his chair. With his other eye and both hands he thumbed a brightly colored magazine.

He was not drunk, although he was somewhat out of health by several years of overeating. He was not sick, although he did complain of worrying a good deal and, now that he had reached forty, of a vague bodily discomfort. He said that he was not tired, but still, on week ends, he was pretty much beat. He only worked eight hours a day, five days a week, but with the traffic and all it took him about an hour each way to and from work, which, after all, made 10 hours a day.

Then, too, his work was too petty to be interesting but too complex to be routine, and, although he had rather a good job, it had no personal significance to him whatsoever.

The year before he had bought a garden machine that did everything—and a truly huge amount of seed. But after the first season, the thing was hard to start and he had found out that it would not weed between the rows. Yes, he had a camera—didn't everyone?—but he had taken about everything there was to take around him, and when they had not come out like those in the picture magazines, even though his was a very expensive camera, he had become discouraged. His wife, he said, was playing bridge with the girls, in order, he said, smilingly, to get some relief from his being in the house all week end. Yes, she had tried to paint for a while, but she couldn't learn to draw and did not actually enjoy doing those abstractions.

Talking with this man, one could see that he was not unintelligent but that he was rather in a muddle about public affairs, snatching impatiently and haphazardly at the easy, emphatic conclusions. And as for his private life, one could see that although he was not aware of being unhappy, still the ground tone of his life experience was the state of sluggish distraction in which I had found him that Sunday afternoon.

I

I do not know if this man represents the Average Middle Class American, but I do suppose that his condition is less exceptional than that of the fortunate and talented people whom we have heard this afternoon describing what they and other Americans at leisure do. For most of our speakers—in fact or as ideal—have two things in common which set them off as a tiny minority in the United States population: their leisure and their work form a unity. And they are capable of genuine individuality.

For such people, leisure does not exist as a special problem in separate realm. Their life-work is an independent sphere of self-cultivating action which requires and contains what others call leisure.

Apart from mere animal rest, the problem of leisure does not arise in a society or for an individual until work has been split from life. For if our work allows us to express our true interests and to facilitate their more skillful expression, then our leisure is not escape, or recuperation, or that tired frenzy by which we strive for the animated glee we call fun.

Today many people have to trivialize their true interests into "hobbies," which are socially considered as unserious pastimes rather than the center of their real existence. But only by a craftsmanlike style of life can the split domains of work and leisure become unified; and only by such self-cultivation can the everyday life become a medium for genuine culture. The deeper problems of leisure, and of the cultural content of leisure time, can be solved only when leisure and work are easy companions rather than tense opposites.

## II

The most significant fact about work and play in modern times is that as the hours organized by work have decreased, the remaining hours have been intensively organized for commercial purposes. As the machinery of production has destroyed work as independent, meaningful action, it has given many people more free time. But now the machinery of amusement is destroying the freedom of this time.

The mere chronological fact of more time on our hands is a necessary condition for the cultivation of individuality, but by no means guarantees it. As people have more time on their hands, most of it is taken away from them by the debilitating quality of their work, by the pace of their everyday routine, and by the ever-present media of mass distraction.

The mass production of distraction is now as much a part of the American way of life as the mass production of automobiles. In fact, the values that make up this way of life are more and more the values of an ethic of leisure. For, as work declines in meaning and gives no inner direction or center, leisure becomes the end of life itself, and the leisure ethic swallows up all values, including those of work.

## III

The most important questions to ask of any sphere of society are: What kinds of men and women does it tend to create? What personal styles of life does it inculcate and reinforce?

When we ask these questions seriously we have to answer: Of course there is a minority that uses leisure for self-cultivation. I do not know whether that minority getting smaller, standing still, or becoming larger. But deeper point perhaps is that genuine self-cultivation—genuine art—tends to be cut off from the major r of American life. It is not a part of the average texture of everyday life in America.

When it does occur it is among a fortunate minority or it is an episode. And this minority is not counted among those whom we celebrate.

Those we celebrate are the jabbering, aimless, light-witted heroes of popular culture. Here are the cheerful illiterates at whose easy, empty chatter we chuckle. Here are the taut, mammary girls we so loudly admire as images of the female. Here are the athletes who have broken really important statistical records.

These personnel of the machinery of amusement are character-forming influences of the first order. By their pervasive distribution among the young, and by the absence of alternatives, such homey clowns, erotic ladies and statistical athletes become the models of the adolescent's world of leisure. Where in America today can those who are coming into new leisure-time look for models of self-cultivation rather than of distraction and mere pastime?

## I V

All the ugly clamor of the radio, which has now been visualized on television, has become so much a part of the texture of our daily life that we do not truly experience it any more. It is good that we do not, else we should all become blathering idiots. But for this protection we pay a price: we become blasé. Our eyes and ears and feelings and imaginations withdraw in panic lest they be shattered. And this happens to us so early that we do not know that it is happening. By our trained inattention, we thus blunt our capacity for liberating experience as we block off those experiences that would stultify us.

But what leisure—genuine leisure—ought to do is relax our attention so that we come to know better our true selves and our capacities for creative experience. Beyond animal rest, which is both necessary and for many today quite difficult to get, genuine leisure allows and encourages our development of greater and truer individuality. Leisure ought to be what work ought to be, and what neither of them usually is: a sphere of independent action.

But more than that: genuine leisure, especially today, requires periods of genuine privacy. For without privacy, there is no chance to discover, to create, and to reinforce our individuality. And it is the lack of privacy—one must say, the fear of privacy—which places most of our non-working time at the disposal of these forces of modern society that would stereotype our tastes and lower the level of our enjoyment.

## V

We ought to judge the quality and level of our personal culture by the best that has been achieved anywhere and any time, and we ought to go further than that: with our material equipment, and the more ample time it might make available, we ought to project our ideals even higher than the best mankind has ever achieved. Were we to do this, seriously and imaginatively, we would see that our choice is between genuine leisure, which enlarges the feeling and reason, and spurious leisure, which blunts the very capacity for truly personal experience.

The first thing to be said about this choice is that most Americans never get to make it. They have grown up in a leisure pattern of distraction and sloth, and they do not really know the world of self-cultivation.

The second thing to be said is that this is not due to any inherent mediocrity of taste and capacity on their part.

There is, of course, a widespread idea, often and carefully repeated, that on the market for leisure, the consumers determine the products, that people get childish fare because that is what they really want. We should not be misled by this naive and mistaken "democracy of taste," in the name of which merchants of amusement reinforce the prevailing low levels of experience in America. What a man does with his leisure is determined by the leisure experiences that are most readily available to him, and by his sensibilities and tastes. But what has happened is this:

As the hours of nonwork have increased, the mass means of communication and entertainment have trained the sensibilities and tastes of a generation or more of Americans. For levels of sensibility are, in fact, largely acquired, by atmosphere and by training.

Moreover, these means of entertainment have become so continuously and so unavoidably available that the effort involved to cultivate and to gratify individual tastes is simply too great to be widely expected. In order really to allow a choice between genuine leisure and the spurious leisure that now prevails, the commercial producers who now hold the field would at least temporarily have to be put out of business.

## VI

It has not been my purpose this afternoon to give angry, confident answers to the so-called problems of leisure in America. For surely, in our situation, it is more fruitful to ask the right questions than to provide the half answers now available to us.

What I have asked is whether, properly conceived, there is any special problem of leisure?

For is not any life worth living as life in which both work and leisure are but phases of one meaningful whole, a life which is largely composed of truly independent domains of experience, a life in which the mass means of distraction are not felt to be necessary?

The so-called problem of leisure, in short, is the problem of how we can heighten the qualities of experience in all areas of American life to such an extent that there will be no problem of leisure.

# 9

## MASS SOCIETY
## AND LIBERAL EDUCATION

The transformation of a community of publics into a mass society is one of the keys to the meaning of modern life. It is a structural trend that leads directly to many of the psychological and political problems that Americans, especially those concerned with liberal education, now confront. In every industrial society, these problems are of national relevance, and in each of them the trend is rooted in the nation as a set of metropolitan areas. For it is from such metropolitan centers that there has spread those forces that are destroying or minimizing the classic liberal public and making for the ascendency of the mass society.

### I

The United States today is not altogether a mass society, and it has never been altogether a community of publics. These phrases are names for extreme types. Although they point to certain features of reality, they are themselves constructions. Social reality is always, or so it seems to me, some sort of mixture. But the point is that one can most readily understand just how much of what is mixed into it, if one first states, in terms of explicit dimensions, the clear-cut and extreme types.

At least four dimensions must be attended to if we are to understand the differences between public and mass: (a) There is first, the ratio of the givers of opinion to its receivers, which is, I think, the simplest way to state the key meaning of the formal media of communication. More than anything else, it is the shift in this ratio which is central to the problems of the public and of public opinion in latter-day phases of democracy.[1] (b) There is second, the organization of communication, of which the most decisive aspect is the possibility of answering back an opinion without internal or external reprisals being taken.[2] (c) Third, there is the ease with which opinion is effective in the shaping of decisions of powerful consequence. This opportunity for people to act out their opinions collectively is of course limited by their positions in the structure of power.[3] (d) Fourth, there is the degree to which instituted authorities, with their sanctions and controls, infiltrate the public. Here, the key problem becomes the degree of genuine autonomy from instituted authority which the public has.[4]

By combining these dimensions, it is possible to construct

[1] At one extreme on the scale of communication two people talk personally with one another; at the other extreme, one spokesman talks impersonally through a communications net to millions of hearers and viewers. In between these two extremes, there are assemblages and political rallies, parliamentary sessions, law court debates, small discussion circles dominated by one man, open discussion circles with talk moving freely back and forth among fifty people, and so on.

[2] Three conditions set the organization of communication: first, technical conditions of the means of communication, in imposing a lower ratio of speakers to listeners, may obviate the possibility of freely answering back. Second, informal rules, resting upon conventional sanction and upon the informal structure of opinion leadership, may govern who can speak, when, and for how long. Such rules may or may not be in congruence with, third, formal rules, with institutional sanction, which govern the communication process. In the extreme case, we may conceive of an absolute monopoly of communication to pacified media groups whose members cannot answer back even "in private." At the opposite extreme, the conditions may allow and the rules may uphold the wide and symmetrical formation of opinion.

[3] This structure may be such as to limit decisively this capacity, or it may allow or even invite it. The structure may confine it to local areas or enlarge its area of opportunity; may make it intermittent or more or less continuous.

[4] At one extreme, no agent of the formal system of authority moves among the autonomous public. At the other extreme, the public becomes a mass terrorized into uniformity by the infiltration of informers and the universalization of suspicion. One thinks of the late Nazi street and block system, the eighteenth century Japanese kumi, the Soviet cell structure. In the end, the formal structure of power coincides, as it were, with the informal ebb and flow of influence by discussion, which is thus killed off.

models of publics and diagrams of the societies with which they seem congruent. Since "the problem of public opinion" is now set by the eclipse of the classic bourgeois public," we are here concerned with only two types: [5]

In a *public* as I understand the term, virtually as many people express opinions as receive them; public communications are so organized that there is a chance immediately and effectively to answer back to any opinion expressed in public. Opinion formed by such discussion readily finds an outlet in effective action against, if necessary, prevailing systems and agents of authority, and authoritative institutions do not interpenetrate the public, which is thus more or less autonomous in its operations. When these conditions prevail, we have the working model of a community of publics, and this model, as we shall presently see, fits pretty closely the several assumptions of classic democratic theory.

At the opposite extreme, in a *mass,* far fewer people express opinions than receive them; for the community of publics becomes an abstracted collectivity of individuals who receive impressions from the mass media. The communications that prevail are so organized that it is difficult or impossible for the individual to answer back immediately or with any effect. The realization of opinion in action is controlled by authorities who organize channels for such action. The mass has no autonomy from institutions; on the contrary, agents of authorized institutions interpenetrate this mass, reducing any autonomy it may have in the formation of opinion by discussion.

The public and the mass may be most readily distinguished by their dominant modes of communications: in a community of publics, discussion is the ascendant mode of communication, and the mass media, if they exist, simply enlarge and animate discussion, linking one *primary public* with the discussions of another. In a mass society, the dominant type of communication is by the formal media and the publics become *media markets,* by which I mean all those exposed to the contents of given mass media.

[5] I shall not here consider a type of "public" which might be called *conventional consensus,* and which is a feature of traditional societies in which there is no idea of public opinion as it has arisen in the modern, western world.

Let us pause for a moment and consider generously the classic public of democratic theory, in the spirit in which Rousseau once cried: "Opinion, Queen of the World, is not subject to the power of kings; they are themselves its first slaves."

The key feature of public opinion which the rise of the democratic middle classes initiates is the free ebb and flow of discussion. In this community of publics anyone who would speak, can and anyone who is interested, does. The possibilities of answering back, of organizing autonomous organs of public opinion, of realizing opinion in action, are automatically established by democratic institutions. For the public opinion that results from discussion is understood to be a resolution that is to be carried out by public action; it is, in one version, the "general will" of the people, which parliament or Congress enacts into law, thus lending to it institutional force. Parliament, as an institution, crowns all the primary publics; it is the archetype for each of the scattered little circles of face-to-face citizens discussing their public business.

This eighteenth-century idea of public opinion parallels the economic idea of the free market economy. Here is the public, composed of discussing circles of opinion, peers crowned by parliament; there is the market composed of freely competing entrepreneurs. As price is the result of anonymous, equally-weighted, bargaining individuals, so is the public of public opinion the result of each man having thought things out for himself and contributing his weight to the great formation. To be sure, some might have more influence on the state of opinion than others, but no one man or group monopolizes the discussion, or by himself determines the state of opinion that prevails.

Innumerable discussion circles are knit together by mobile people who carry opinions, and struggle for the power of larger command. The public is thus organized into associations and parties, each representing a viewpoint, each trying to acquire a place in parliament or Congress, where the discussion continues. The autonomy of these discussion circles is a key element in the idea of "public opinion" as a democratic legitimation. The opinions formed are actively realized within the prevailing institutions of power; and all authoritative agents are made or broken by the prevailing opinions of primary publics.

Insofar as the public is frustrated in realizing its demands upon its agents, it may come to question the symbols of authority to which it has been devoted. Such questioning is of course of a deeper order than criticism of specific policies, but new political parties, of left or right, may attempt in their agitation to use the discussion of specific policies in order to bring the legitimations themselves into question. So, out of the little circles of people talking with one another, the large forces of social movements and political parties develop; and the discussion of opinion is the phase in a total act by which public affairs are conducted.

So conceived, the public is the loom of classic, eighteenth-century democracy; discussion is at once the thread and the shuttle tying the discussion circles together. It lies at the basis of the conception of authority by discussion, based on the hope that truth and justice will somehow carve out of society a great apparatus of free discussion. The people are presented with problems. They discuss them. They decide on them. They formulate viewpoints. These viewpoints are organized, and they compete. One viewpoint "wins out." Then the people act out this view, or their representatives are instructed to act it out, and this they promptly do.

Such are the images of classic democracy which are still used as the working legitimations of power in American society. You will recognize this description as a set of images out of a fairy tale; they are not adequate even as an approximate model of how this society works.

In our situation of half-mass and half-public, the term public, in fact, has come to have a specialized meaning, which dramatically reveals its eclipse. From the standpoint of the public actor—the democratic politician, for example —some people who clamor publicly can be identified as "Labor" and others as "Business," and still others as "Farm." Those who cannot readily be so identified make up the "Public." In this usage, "the public" is composed of the unidentified and nonpartisan in the world of defined and partisan interests. It is socially composed of well-educated salaried professionals, especially college professors, of nonunionized employees, especially white-collar people, along with non-employing, self-employed professionals and small businessmen.

In this faint echo of the classic notion, the public consists of those remnants of the middle classes, old and new, whose interests are not explicitly defined, organized, or clamorous. In a curious adaptation, "the public" often becomes, in fact, "the unattached expert," who, although well informed, has never taken a clear-cut, public stand on those controversial issues which are brought to a focus by organized interests. What the public stands for, accordingly, is often a vagueness of policy (called open-mindedness), a lack of involvement in public affairs (known as reasonableness), and a professional disinterest (often known as tolerance).

Some members of such official publics, as in the field of labor-management mediation, start out very young and make a career out of being careful to be informed but never to take a strong position; and there are many others, quite unofficial, who take such professionals as a sort of model. The only trouble is that they are acting as if they were disinterested judges but they do not have the power of judges. Hence their reasonableness, tolerance and openmindedness do not often count for much in the shaping of human affairs.

From almost any angle of vision that we might assume, when we look upon the community of publics, we realize that we have moved a considerable distance along the road to the mass society. At the end of that road there is totalitarianism, as in Nazi Germany or in Communist Russia. We are not yet at that end; in the United States today, media markets are not entirely ascendant over primary publics. But surely we can see that the success of the demagogue in exploiting these media, and the decreased chance to answer back, is certainly more a feature of a mass society than of a community of publics. And there are many other signs.

What is happening might again be stated in terms of the historical parallel between the commodity market in the economic order and in the public of public opinion. In brief, there is a movement from widely scattered little powers to concentrated powers and the attempt at monopoly control from powerful centers. And in the centers of economics, of politics, and of opinion, power is partially hidden; they are centers of manipulation as well as of authority. The small shop serving a small neighborhood is replaced by the anonymity of the national corporation; mass advertisement replaces the personal influence of opinion between merchant and customer. The political leader hooks up his speech to a national network and speaks, with appropriate personal touches, to a million people he never saw and never will see.

Entire brackets of professions and industries are in the "opinion business," impersonally manipulating the public for hire. *In the primary public,* the competition of opinions goes on between people holding views in the service of their interests and their reasoning. *But in the mass society* of media markets, competition, if any, goes on between the crowd of manipulators with their mass media on the one hand, and the people receiving their propaganda on the other.

Under such conditions, it is not surprising that a conception of public opinion as a mere impression or as a reaction—we cannot say "response"—to the content of the mass media should arise. In this view, the public is merely the collectivity of individuals each rather passively exposed to the mass media and rather helplessly opened up to the suggestions and manipulations that flow from these media. The fact of manipulation from centralized points of control constitutes, as it were, an expropriation of the information and change of opinion participated in by the old multitude of little opinion producers and consumers operating in a free and balanced market.

### III

In attempting to explain the ascendancy of mass over public, there are four major trends to which we should pay attention; for if we do not we shall not be able to speculate fruitfully about the task of the college for adults in the metropolitan society of masses. These four structural trends of our epoch seem to me to coincide in their effects; they transform public into mass.

(i). The rise of bureaucratic structures of executive power, in the economic, the military, and the political orders, has lowered the effective use of all these smaller voluntary associations operating between the state and the economy on the one hand, and the family on the other. It is not only that the institutions of power have become large-scale and inaccessibly centralized; they have at the same time become less political and more administrative. It is within this great change of framework that the organized public has waned.

In terms of *scale,* the transformation of public into mass has been underpinned by the shift from a political public decisively restricted in size (by property and education, as well as by sex and age) to a greatly enlarged mass having only the qualifications of citizenship and age. In terms of *organization,* the transformation has been underpinned by the shift from the individual and his primary community to the voluntary association and the mass party as the major units of organized power.

Voluntary associations have become larger to the extent that they have become effective; and to the extent that they have become effective, they have become inaccessible to the individual who would participate by discussion in their policies. Accordingly, along with older institutions, these voluntary associations have lost their grip on the individual. As greater numbers of people are drawn into the political arena, these associations become mass in scale, and because of the increased scale of the power structure, the power of the individual becomes more dependent upon these mass associations, and yet these are less accessible to his influence.[6]

Elections become first (1) contests between two giant and unwieldy parties, neither of which the individual can

---

[6] At the same time—and also because of the metropolitan segregation and distraction, which I shall discuss in a moment—the individual becomes more dependent upon the means of mass communication for his view of the structure as a whole.

truly feel that he influences, and neither of which is capable of winning psychologically impressive majorities. Second (2), more and more, elections are decided in the irrational terms of silly appeals; less and less on clear and simple statements of genuine issue. Certainly the techniques of advertisement, and their use in the mass persuasion of an electorate, becomes more important than rational argument over real issues in public. And, in all this, the parties are of the same general form as other mass associations.[7]

What is not available is the association which has three characteristics: the association that is at once (1) a context in which reasonable opinions may be reached, (2) an agency by which reasonable activities may be undertaken and (3) a powerful enough unit, in comparison with other organizations of power, to make a difference. Now the primary publics are either so small as to be swamped, and hence give up; or so large as to be merely another unit of the general distant structure of power, and hence inaccessible. And in either case they are the more readily subjected to distorted images of the world by the mass media.

(ii). As the scale of institutions has become larger and more centralized, so have the range and intensity of the opinion makers' efforts. For the means of opinion-making —and this is the second master trend—have paralleled in range and efficiency the other institutions of greater scale that make up the modern society of masses. There is universal compulsory education—the seed-bed of nationalist propaganda and white-collar skills—and there are the media of mass communication. These mass media have apparently great variety and competition, but each of them often seems to be competing in terms of variations of a few standardized themes; and freedom of effective opinion seems

[7] Well might E. H. Carr conclude: "To speak today of the defense of democracy as if we were defending something which we knew and had possessed for many decades or many centuries is self-deception and sham—mass democracy is a new phenomenon—a creation of the last helf-century—which it is inappropriate and misleading to consider in terms of the philosophy of Locke or of the liberal democracy of the nineteenth century. We should be nearer the mark, and should have a far more convincing slogan, if we spoke of the need, not to defend democracy, but to create it." *The New Society,* pp. 75-76.

more and more to operate within and between vested interests, organized and unorganized, that have ready and continual access to the media.

Early observers such as Charles Horton Cooley believed that the increase of the range and volume of the mass media would, as I have said, enlarge and animate the public,[8] but what it has done has helped kill it off. I do not refer merely to the higher ratio of deliverers of opinion to receivers and to the decreased chance to answer back. Nor do I mean merely the violent banalization and stereotyping of our very sense organs which these media make almost necessary. I have in mind a sort of technological illiteracy, which is expressed in three ways:

a. these media, especially television, have encroached upon the small-scale discussion, upon the leisurely human interchange of opinion.

b. these media do not connect the information on issues that they do provide with the troubles felt by the individual. They do not increase rational insight into tensions, neither those in the individual nor those of the society which are reflected in the individual. On the contrary, they distract attention from such tension. They carry a general tone of animated distraction, a suspended agitation, but it is going nowhere and has nowhere to go: the chief distracting tension of the media is between the wanting and the not having of commodities or of women held to be good looking. As they now generally prevail, the media not only fail as an educational force, they are a malign force—in that they do not reveal to the viewer the sources of his tension and anxiety, his inarticulate resentments and half-formed hopes.

[8] In Cooley's optimistic view, written before radio and movies, the formal media are understood as simply multiplying the scope and pace of popular discussion. Modern conditions, he writes, "enlarge indefinitely the competition of ideas, and whatever has owed its persistence merely to lack of comparison is likely to go, for that which is really congenial to the choosing mind will be all the more cherished and increased." Still excited by the breakup of local, conventional consensus, he sees the means of communication as furthering the conversational dynamic of classic democracy and with it the growth of rational and free individuality. *Social Organization,* p. 93; see Chapter IX.

c. these media do not enable the individual to transcend the narrow *milieux* in which he lives, or truly connect them with the larger realities of what is happening in the world. On the contrary, they obscure these connections by distracting his attention and fastening it upon artificial frenzies that are resolved within the program framework, usually by violent action, or by what is called humor. In short, for the viewer, not really resolved at all. I shall later return to this point.

(iii). A third explanation for the ascendancy of masses has to do with the class, status and occupational structure of modern society, of which the most important shift in the twentieth century has been the numerical decline of the old middle class of independent entrepreneurs and practitioners, and the rise of the new middle class of dependent white-collar workers.[9] This change in the economic and social make-up of the middle classes carries two meanings for the transformation of public into mass:

(a) Up until the later nineteenth century, in fact into the Progressive Era, the old middle class acted as an independent base of power, for the individual and for the class. Political freedom and economic security were both anchored in the fact of small-scale independent properties, and these scattered properties, and their holders, were integrated economically by free and autonomous markets, and politically by the process of representative democracy. The white-collar groups are not such an independent base of power: economically, they are in the same situation as propertyless wage workers; politically they are in a worse condition, for they are not organized.

(b) The second meaning of this shift has to do with what is called civic spirit as well as what is called nationalism. Civic spirit is nationalism on a local basis; nationalism is civic spirit written large. At least, the psychological scheme for each is much the same:

[9] *Cf.* Mills, *White Collar* (New York: Oxford University Press, 1951). Roughly, in the last two generations, as proportions of the middle classes as a whole, the old middle class has declined from 85 to 44 per cent; the new middle class has risen from 15 to 56 per cent. See pp. 63 ff.

People in the top levels of the nation or the city voluntarily run various enterprises and push various interests. The underlying population, identifying themselves with these top people, believe these enterprises to be in their interest also, and indeed accept the *identification of these interests with the welfare of the nation or the city as a whole.* Sometimes they are right; sometimes they are wrong; but in either case energetic management by the leaders and cheerful acquiescence of the population are indispensable requirements for the kind of morale known as civic spirit or nationalism.

In any well-run American city, the men and women of the independent middle class have been the traditional chieftains of civic drives and enterprise. For one thing, they usually have the time and money that is needed; at least some of them are fairly well educated. Their work in conducting a small business is said to train them for initiative and responsibility, and does put them in touch with the administrative and political figures of the city, who, in fact, are usually drawn from their circles. In addition, the small businessman often stands to benefit personally as a result of civic improvement: better roads and streets, for example, lead to greater sales for the retail merchant. Mere self-interest often dictates that the businessman should be someone civically. By participating actively in civic affairs, he widens his circle of contacts and customers.

There is no need to stress the point that as the old public rested upon such entrepreneurs, so the decline of the public rests upon the transformation of the middle class into salaried employees, often employees of a local branch of a national corporation.[10] In fact, one thing that is happening in America today is that the structure of such loyalty as was once centered in the city is shifting to the massive corporation.[11] In terms of power, this is realistic; in terms of notions of the classic public, it is disastrous.

(iv). A fourth master trend making for a mass society is

[10] C. Wright Mills, "Small Business and Civic Welfare," Senate Document No. 135, 79th Congress, 2nd Session, Washington, 1946.
[11] See, *e.g.,* W. H. Whyte, Jr., Is Anybody Listening? (Simon & Schuster, 1952).

the rise of the metropolis, and the only point I want to make about it is that the growth of this metropolitan society has segregated men and women into narrowed routines and *milieux,* and it has done so with the constant loss of community structure.

The members of a community of publics know each other more or less fully, because they meet in the several aspects of the total life routine. The members of a metropolitan society of masses know one another only fractionally: as the man who fixes the car, or as that girl who serves your lunch, or as the woman who takes care of your child at school during the day. Pre-judgment and stereotype flourish when people meet people only in this segmental manner. The humanist reality of others does not, cannot, come through.

There are two implications of this I would mention: (a) Just as people tend to select those mass media that confirm what they already believe and enjoy, so do they tend, by the mere fact of segregated *milieux* and routines, to come into touch with those whose opinions are similar to theirs. Others they tend to treat flippantly. In such a situation as the metropolitan society, they develop, in their defense, a blasé manner that reaches deeper than a manner. They do not, accordingly, experience genuine clash of viewpoint or issue. And when they do, they tend to consider it an unpleasantry. (b) They are so sunk in the routines of their *milieux* that they do not transcend, even in discussion, much less by action, these more or less narrow *milieux.* They do not gain a view of the structure of their society and of their role within it. The city is a structure composed of *milieux;* the people in the *milieux* tend to be rather detached from one another; being more or less confined to their own rather narrow ranges, they do not understand the structure of their society. As they reach for each other, they do so by stereotype and through prejudiced images of the creatures of other *milieux.* Each is trapped by his confining circle; each is split from easily identifiable groups. It is for people in such narrow *milieux* that the mass media can create a pseudoworld beyond, and a pseudoworld within, themseves as well.

Publics live in *milieux,* but they can transcend them—individually, by intellect and education; socially, by discussion and by public action. By reflection and debate, and by organized action, a community of publics comes to feel itself, and comes in fact to be active at points of structural relevance. But members of a mass exist in *milieux* and they cannot get out of them, either by mind or by activity, except—in the extreme case—under "the organized spontaneity" of the bureaucrat on a motorcycle. We have not yet reached the extreme case, but observing metropolitan man in the mass we can surely see the psychological preparations for it.

The man in the mass is sunk into stereotyped experience, or even sunk by it; he cannot detach himself in order to observe it, much less to evaluate it. Rather than the internal discussion of reflection, he is often accompanied through his life with only a half conscious monologue. He has no projects of his own; he fulfills the routines that exist. He does not transcend whatever he is at any moment, he does not, he cannot, transcend even his daily *milieux.*

He takes things for granted and makes the best of them. He tries to look ahead, a year or two perhaps, or even longer if he has children or a mortgage, but he does not seriously ask, What do I want? How can I get it? A vague optimism sustains him, broken occasionally by little miseries and disappointments that are soon buried. He is smug, from the standpoint of those who think something might be the matter with the mass style of life in the metropolitan frenzy where self-making is an externally busy branch of industry. By what standards does he judge himself and his efforts? Where are the models of excellence for this man? In the mass, he tends to lose such self-confidence as he ever had, for life in such a society of masses both implants and implements insecurity and impotence.

The political structure of a democratic state assumes the public, and in its rhetoric asserts that this public is the very seat of sovereignty. But given all those forces that have centralized and enlarged and made less political and more administrative the American political life; given all the metropolitan segregation that is no community; given the transformation of the old middle class into something which perhaps should not even be called middle class; and given all the mass communications that do not truly communicate —what is happening is the decline of a set of publics that is sovereign, except in the most formal and in the most rhetorical sense. And moreover the remnants of such publics as remain in the interstices of the mass society are now being frightened out of existence. They lose their strength; they lose their will for rationality, and for rationally considered decision and action. They are alone and they are afraid.

## I V

If even half of what I have said is true, you may well ask: what is the task of the liberal college for adults? Insofar as it is—in ideal at least—truly liberal, the first answer is: *to keep us from being overwhelmed.* Its first and continuing task to to help produce the disciplined and informed *mind* that cannot be overwhelmed. Its first and continuing task is to help develop the bold and sensible individual who cannot be overwhelmed by the burdens of modern life. The aim is nothing more and can be nothing less. And in this, the aim of the liberal school for adults is no different from that of any liberal education; but there are other answers, more specific answers.

The school for adults, after all, does start from a different juncture in the biography of the person and accordingly must deal with a different set of expectations. Knowledge and intellectual practice must be made directly relevant to the human need of the troubled person of the twentieth century, and to the social practices of the citizen. For he must see the roots of his own biases and frustrations if he is to think clearly about himself, or about anything else. And he must see the frustration of idea. of intellect, by the present organization of society, if he is to meet the tasks now confronting the intelligent citizen.

Given our interest in liberal, that is to say in liberating, education, there are two things that the college for adults can do and ought to do: (1) What the college ought to do for the individual is to turn personal troubles and concerns into social issues and rationally open problems. The aim of the college, for the individual student, is to eliminate the need in his life for the college; the task is to help him to become a self-educating man. For only that will set him free. (2) What the evening college ought to do for the community is to fight all those forces which are destroying genuine publics and creating an urban mass; or stated positively: to help build and to strengthen the self-cultivating liberal public. For only that will set them free.

These two concerns ,if we take them seriously, come together in the three areas which are the focal concerns of the Center for the Study of Liberal Education for Adults: I. the content and methods of teaching; II. the development of leadership; and III. the coordination of the school with other organizations, which I shall discuss in terms of the political relevance of the college for adults.[12]

## V

The college of the metropolitan area is usually concerned with the training of skills that are of more or less direct use in the vocational life. This is an important task to perform, but I shall not discuss it here, for (1) it is a matter that hinges in great part for each school upon the local labor market and upon the vocational interests of students; moreover (2) job advancement is not the same as self-development although the two are systematically confused.[13]

Very broadly speaking the function of education as it was first set up in this country was political: to make citizens more knowledgeable and better thinkers. In time, the function of education shifted from the political to the economic; to train people for better paying jobs. This was especially so with reference to the high school movement, which met the demands of the business economy for white-collar skills, at public expense. So far as the political task is concerned, in many schools, that has been reduced to the firm inculcation of nationalist loyalties and the trivialization of life known as "life-adjustment."

[12] Brochure, from the Center, undated.
[13] *Cf.* C. Wright Mills, "Work Milieu and Social Structure," *Proceedings,* 1954, of Mental Health Society of Northern California.

A liberal education, especially for adults, cannot be merely vocational,[14] but among "skills," some are more, and some are less, relevant to the liberal arts aim. I do not believe that skills and values can so easily be separated as in our search for the supposed neutrality of skills we sometimes assume. And especially not when we speak seriously of liberal education. Of course, there is a scale, with skills at one end and values at the other, but it is the middle range of this scale, which I would call *sensibilities,* that should interest us most.

To train someone to operate a lathe or to read and write is pretty much an education of skill; to evoke from someone an understanding of what they really want out of their life or to debate with them stoic, Christian and humanist ways of living, is pretty much a clear-cut education of values. But to assist in the birth among a group of people of those cultural and social and political and technical sensibilities which would make them genuine members of a genuinely liberal public—this is at once a training in skills and an education of values.

Alongside skill and value we ought to put sensibility, which includes them both and more besides: it includes a sort of therapy in the ancient sense of clarifying one's knowledge of one's self, it includes the imparting of all those skills of controversy with oneself which we call thinking, and with others which we call debate.

We must begin with what concerns the student most deeply. We must proceed in such a way and with such materials as to enable him to gain increasingly rational insight into these concerns. We must try to end with a man or a woman who can and will by themselves continue what we have begun: the end product of the liberal education, as

[14] I agree with A. E. Bestor, who writes that "if the schools are doing their job, we should expect educators to point to the significant and indisputable achievement in raising the intellectual level of the nation—measured perhaps by larger per capita circulation of books and serious magazines, by definitely improved taste in movies and radio programs, by higher standards of political debate, by increased respect for freedom of speech and of thought, by marked decline in such evidences of mental retardation as the incessant reading of comic books by adults." *Educational Wastelands* (Univ. of Ill., 1953), p. 7.

I have said, is simply the self-cultivating man and woman.

Not the epistemology of, but the therapy resulting from, the Socratic maxim is perfectly sound, and especially so for the liberal education in the adult school. There should be much small group discussion, and at least some of the skills of the group therapist ought to be part of the equipment of the teacher.[15]

Whether he knows it or not, the man in the mass is gripped by personal troubles, and he is not able to turn them into social issues, or to see their relevance for his community nor his community's relevance for them.

The knowledgeable man in the genuine public is able to do just that; he understands that what he thinks and feels to be personal troubles are very often not only that but problems shared by others and indeed not subject to solution by any one individual but only by modifications of the structure of the groups in which he lives and sometimes the structure of the entire society.

Men in masses have troubles although they are not always aware of their true meaning and source. Men in publics confront issues, and they are aware of their terms. It is the task of the liberal institution, as of the liberally educated man, continually to translate troubles into issues and issues into the terms of their human meaning for the individual.

In the absence of deep and wide political debate that is really open and free within the framework of a metropolitan community, the adult school could and should become a hospitable framework for just such debate. Only if such procedures are built into the college for adults will that college be liberal, that is liberating, and at the same time real; encouraging people to get in touch with the realities of themselves and of their world.

### VI

The network of informal communication in the primary public may select and refract, it may debunk or it may

---

[15] I do not believe in discussion for its own sake, or for its therapeutic effect alone, at least not in school. If people have not yet earned the intellectual right to an opinion they ought in a school to be made to shut up long enough to start earning the right.

sanction what is said in the formal media, or by the authorities. Everyone who talks with others is part of this network, and the ideal public is composed of people who are opinion peers in a community of such publics. But there are gradations of social and intellectual skills: it is reasonable to suppose that certain types of people may be more important than others in channeling the flow of talk and in mediating the impact of the formal media, the authoritarian assertion, the demagogic shout. Some people will be more readily and more frequently articulate. Some will carry greater weight than others. I will not call these "opinion leaders" for that term has been used in a quite different sense than I intend here.[16] I shall call them simply informal leaders. They are the people who are willing to stand up and be counted, and who, while standing up, can say something that is listened to.

The existence of these informal leaders is one major reason why opinion is not subject to the overweening dominance of the structure of power and its mass media. For they rally those who by their informal discussions manufacture opinion. They are the radiant points, the foci of the primary public. This primary public is at times a resistor of media and of their pressure upon the individual. If there is any socially organized intelligence that is free to answer back, and to give support to those who might answer back, it must somehow be this primary public. Now insofar as such circles exist, the effective strength of any formal medium lies in its acceptance by these informal circles and their unofficial leaders. And the same is true of liberal education.

The job of the college for adults, I should think, would be to try to get into touch with such informal leaders. For it is around them that real publics could develop. If they could be encouraged to look upon the adult college as a place in which to experience an expansion of their own social skills and public sensibilities they would, I am sure, become prime referral agencies; they could become your liaison with the various publics of your community. With them and through them you could strengthen and help

[16] Paul Lazarsfeld, *et al., The People's Choice.*

animate such publics, and then you could set free in many of its members the process of self-education.

To bring such people out, to help develop them into a community, you must surround your students with models of straightforward conduct, clarified character, and open reasonableness, for I believe it is in the hope of seeing such models that many serious people go to lectures rather than more conveniently reading books. If there are not such men and women on your faculties, you will not attract those who are potential rallying points for the genuine liberal public. In the end, all talk of liberal education, of personnel and curriculum and programming and the rest of it, is nonsense if you do not have such men and women on your faculties. For in the end, liberal education is the result of the liberating and self-sustaining touch of such people.

And their existence in a community as a creative minority is, in the end, the only force that might prevail against the ascendancy of the mass society, and all the men and apparatus that make for it. For in the end, it is around them and through them that liberated and liberating publics come to articulate form and democratic action.

### VII

I have not yet discussed the relation of the school with other organizations in the metropolitan community, the third point of importance to the Center. It is a complicated issue that I cannot adequately cover in the time available. Let me say only that I doubt that education, for adults or for adolescents, is the strategic factor in the building of a democratic polity. I think it is in the picture and must be, but given its present personnel and administration, and its generally powerless position among other politically relevant organizations, it cannot and will not get the job done. Only if it were to become the framework within which more general movements that were under way— movements with more direct political relevance—were going on, only then would it have the chance to take the place in American political life that it ought to. Only then could it in fact do fully what I have suggested it ought nevertheless to try now to do. For men and women cannot develop and use their highest potentiality in and through educational institutions: they can do that only within and through all of their institutions. And educational work cannot be the sole preparation for such a humane and political life; it can only be part of it, helping it, to be sure, once it is part of the general movement of American civilization.

In the meantime, in the absence of such movements, we cannot dodge the fact that to the extent that the adult college is effective, it is going to be political; its students are going to try to influence decisions of power.

If there were parties or movements that were related to ideas and within which ideas of social life were truly debated and connected with real personal troubles; and if these movements had a chance to win or to influence power—then there might be less public need of colleges for adults. Or if they did exist, it would be within these movements.

But in the absence of such moving publics, these schools ought to become the framework within which such publics exist, at least in their inchoate beginnings, and by which their discussions are fed and sustained. But to do so, they are going to have to get into trouble. For publics that really want to know the realities of their community and nation and world are, by that determining fact, politically radical. Politics as we know it today often rests upon myths and lies and crackpot notions; and many policies, debated and undebated, assume inadequate and misleading definitions of reality. When such myth and hokum prevail, those who are out to find the truth are bound to be upsetting. This is the role of mind, of intellect, of reason, of ideas: to define reality adequately and in a publicly relevant way. The role of education, especially of education for adults, is to build and sustain publics that will "go for," and develop, and live with, and act upon, adequate definitions of reality.

# 10

## MAN IN THE MIDDLE: THE DESIGNER

The American designer is at once a central figure in what I am going to call the cultural apparatus and an important adjunct of a very peculiar kind of economy. His art is a business, but his business is art and curious things have been happening both to the art and to the business—and so to him. He is caught up in two great developments of twentieth-century America. One is the shift in economic emphasis from production to distribution, and along with it, the joining of the struggle for existence with the panic for status. The other is the bringing of art, science and learning into subordinate relation with the dominant institutions of the capitalist economy and the nationalist state.

Designers work at the intersection of these trends; their problems are among the key problems of the overdeveloped society. It is their dual investment in them that explains the big split among designers and their frequent guilt; the enriched muddle of ideals they variously profess and the insecurity they often feel about the practice of their craft; their often great disgust and their crippling frustration. They cannot consider well their position or formulate their credo without considering both cultural and economic trends, and the shaping of the total society in which these are occurring.

I want briefly (1) to define certain meanings and functions of the cultural apparatus, and (2) to indicate the economic context in which the designer now does his work. It may then be useful (3) to invite you to reconsider certain ideals for which the designer might stand in the kind of world in which Americans are coming to live.

I

Our images of this world and of ourselves are given to us by crowds of witnesses we have never met and never shall meet. Yet for each of us these images—provided by strangers and dead men—are the very basis of our life as a human being. None of us stands alone directly confronting a world of solid fact. No such world is available: the closest we come to it is when we are infants or when we become insane: then, in a terrifying scene of meaningless events and senseless confusion, we are often seized with the panic of near-total insecurity. But in our everyday life we experience not solid and immediate facts but stereotypes of meaning. We are aware of much more than what we have ourselves experienced, and our experience itself is always indirect and always guided. The first rule for understanding the human condition is that men live in a second-hand world.

The consciousness of men does not determine their existence; nor does their existence determine their consciousness. Between the human consciousness and material existence stand communications and designs, patterns and values which influence decisively such consciousness as as they have.

The mass arts, the public arts, the design arts are major vehicles of this consciousness. Between these arts and the everyday life, between their symbols and the level of human sensibility, there is now continual and persistent interplay. So closely do they reflect one another that it is often impossible to distinguish the image from its source. Visions whispered long before the age of consent, images received in the relaxation of darkness, slogans reiterated in home and in classroom, determine the perspective in which we see and fail to see the worlds in which we live; meanings about which we have never thought explicitly determine our judgments of how well and of how badly we are living in these worlds. So decisive to experience itself are the results of these communications that often men do not really believe what they "see before their very eyes" until they have been "informed" about it by the official announcement, the radio, the camera, the hand-out. Communications not only limit experience; often they expropriate the chances to have experience that can rightly be called "our own." For our standards of credibility, and of reality itself, as well as our judgments and discernments, are determined much less by any pristine experience we may have than by our exposure to the output of the cultural apparatus.

For most of what we call solid fact, sound interpretation, suitable presentation, we are increasingly dependent upon the observation posts, the interpretation centers, the presentation depots of the cultural apparatus. In this apparatus, standing between men and events, the meanings and images, the values and slogans that define all the worlds men know are organized and compared, maintained and revised, lost and found, celebrated and debunked.

By the cultural apparatus I mean all those organizations and *milieux* in which artistic, intellectual and scientific work goes on. I also mean all the means by which such work is made available to small circles, wider publics, and to great masses.

The most embracive and the most specialized domain of modern society, the cultural apparatus of art, science and learning fulfills the most functions: it conquers nature and remakes the environment; it defines the changing nature of man, and grasps the drift of world affairs; it revivifies old aspirations and shapes new ones. It creates models of character and styles of feeling, nuances of mood and vocabularies of motive. It serves decision-makers, revealing and obscuring the consequences of their decisions. It turns power into authority and debunks authority as mere coercion. It modifies the work men do and provides the tools with which they do it; it fills up their leisure, with nonsense and with pleasure. It changes the nature of war; it amuses and persuades and manipulates; it orders and forbids; it frightens and reassures; it makes men weep and it makes men laugh, go numb all over, then become altogether alive. It prolongs the life-span and provides the violent means to end it suddenly. It predicts what is going to happen and it explains what has occurred; it helps to shape and to pace an epoch, and without it there would be no consciousness of any epoch.

The world men are going to believe they understand is now, in this cultural apparatus, being defined and built, made into a slogan, a story, a diagram, a release, a dream, a fact, a blue-print, a tune, a sketch, a formula; and presented to them. Such part as reason may have in human affairs, this apparatus, this put-together contraption, fulfills; such role as sensibility may play in the human drama, it enacts; such use as technique may have in history and in biography, it provides. It is the sect of civilization, which—in Matthew Arnold's phrase—is "the humanization of man in society." The only truths are the truths defined by the cultural apparatus. The only beauty is experiences and objects created and indicated by cultural workmen. The only goods are the cultural values with which men are made morally comfortable or morally uneasy.

## II

As an institutional fact, the cultural apparatus has assumed many forms. In some societies—notably that of Russia—it is established by an authority that post-dates capitalism: it is thus part of an official apparatus of psychic domination. In some—notably the nations of Western Europe—it is established out of a tradition that pre-dates capitalism; it is thus part of an Establishment in which social authority and cultural prestige overlap. Both cultural tradition and political authority are involved in any cultural Establishment, but in the USA the cultural apparatus is established commercially: it is part of an ascendent capitalist economy. This fact is the major key to understanding both the quality of everyday life and the situation of culture in America today.

The virtual dominance of commercial culture is the key to America's cultural scope, confusion, banalization, excitement, sterility. To understand the case of America today, one must understand the economic trends and the selling mechanics of a capitalist world in which the mass production and the mass sale of goods has become The Fetish of human life, the pivot both of work and of leisure. One must understand how the pervasive mechanisms of the market have penetrated every feature of life—including art, science and learning—and made them subject to the pecuniary evaluation. One must understand that what has happened to work in general in the last two centuries has in the twentieth century been happening to the sphere of artistic and intellectual endeavor; these too have now become part of society as a salesroom. To understand the ambiguous position of the cultural workman in America one must see how he stands in the overlap of these two worlds: the world of such an overdeveloped society with its ethos of advertisement, and the world of culture as men have known it and as they might know it.

However harsh its effects upon the nature of work, the industrialization of underdeveloped countries must be seen as an enormous blessing: it is man conquering nature, and so freeing himself from dire want. But as the social and physical machineries of industrialization develop, new purposes and interests come into play. The economic emphasis moves from production to distribution and, in the overdeveloped society, to what is called "merchandising." The pivotal decade for this shift in the USA was the twenties, but it is in the era since the ending of World War II that the new economy has flowered like a noxious weed. In this phase of capitalism, the distributor becomes ascendant over both the consumer and the producer.

As the capacity to produce goes far beyond existing demand, as monopoly replaces competition, as surpluses accumulate, the need is for the creation and maintenance of the national market and for its monopolistic closure. Then the salesman becomes paramount. Instead of cultivating and servicing a variety of publics, the distributor's aim is to create a mass volume of continuing sales. Continuous and expanding production requires continuous and expanding consumption, so consumption must be speeded up by all the techniques and frauds of marketing. Moreover, existing commodities must be worn out more quickly for as the market is saturated, the economy becomes increasingly dependent upon what is called replacement. It is then that obsolescence comes to be planned and the economic cycle deliberately shortened.

There are, I suppose, three kinds of obsolescence: (1) technological, as when something wears out or something better is produced; (2) artificial, as when something is deliberately designed so that it *will* wear out; and (3) status obsolescence, as when fashions are created in such ways that consumption brings disgrace or prestige in accordance with last year's or with this year's model, and alongside the old struggle for existence, there is added the panic for status.

It is in this economic situation that the designer gets his Main Chance. Whatever his esthetic pretension and his engineering ability, his economic task is to sell. In this he joins the advertising fraternity, the public relations counsel, and the market researcher. These types have developed their skills and pretensions in order to serve men whose God is the Big Sell. And now the designer joins them.

To the firm and to its products he adds the magical gloss and dazzle of prestige. He plans the appearance of things and their often fraudulent packaging. He lays out the interiors and decorates the exteriors of corporate businesses as monuments to advertising. And then, along with his colleagues, he takes the history of commercial fraud one step further. With him, advertising is not one specialized activity, however central; with his capitalist advent, the arts and skills and crafts of the cultural apparatus itself become not only adjuncts of advertising but in due course themselves advertisements. He designs the product itself as if it were an advertisement, for his aim and his task—acknowledged by the more forthright—is less to make better products than to make products sell better. By brand and trademark, by slogan and package, by color and form, he gives the commodity a fictitious individuality, turning a little lanolin and water into an emulsified way to become erotically blessed; concealing the weight and quality of what is for sale; confusing the consumer's choice and banalizing her sensibilities.

The silly needs of salesmanship are thus met by the silly designing and redesigning of things. The waste of human labor and material become irrationally central to the per-

formance of the capitalist mechanism. Society itself becomes a great sales room, a network of public rackets, and
a continuous fashion show. The gimmick of success becomes the yearly change of model as fashion is made universal. And in the mass society, the image of beauty itself
becomes identified with the designer's speed-up and de-
basement of imagination, taste and sensibility.

## I V

The cultural workman himself, in particular the designer,
tends to become part of the means of distribution, over
which he tends to lose control. Having "established a market," and monopolized access to it, the distributor—along
with his market researcher—claims to "know what they
want." So his orders—even to the free-lance—become
more explicit and detailed. The price he offers may be
quite high; perhaps too high, he comes to think, and perhaps he is right. So he begins to hire and to manage in
varying degree a stable of cultural workmen. Those who
allow themselves to be managed by the mass distributor
are selected and in time formed in such a way as to be altogether proficient, but perhaps not quite first-rate. So the
search goes on for "fresh ideas," for exciting notions, for
more alluding models; in brief, for the innovator. But in the
meantime, back at the studio, the laboratory, the research
bureau, the writers' factory—the distributor is ascendant
over many producers who become the rank-and-file workmen of the commercially established cultural apparatus.

In this situation of increasing bureaucratization and yet
of the continual need for innovation, the cultural workman
tends to become a commercial hack or a commercial star.
By a star, I mean a producer whose productions are so
much in demand that he is able, to some extent at least,
to make distributors serve as *his* adjuncts. This role has its
own conditions and its own perils. The star tends to be
trapped by his own success. He has painted this sort of
thing and he gets $20,000 a throw for it. This man, how-
ever affluent, may become culturally bored by this style
and wants to explore another. But often he cannot: he is
used to the $20,000 a throw and there is demand for it. As

a leader of fashions, accordingly, he is himself subject to
fashion. Moreover, his success as a star depends upon his
playing the market: he is not in educative interplay with a
public that supports him as he develops and which he in
turn develops. He too, by virtue of his success, becomes a
marketeer.

The star system of American culture—along with the
commercial hacks—tend to kill off the chance of the cultural workman to be a worthy craftsman. One is a smash
hit *or* one is among the failures who are not produced; one
is a best seller *or* one is among the hacks and failures; one
is either absolutely tops *or* one is just nothing at all.

As an entrepreneur, you may value as you wish these
several developments; but as a member of the cultural apparatus, you surely must realize that whatever else you may
be doing, you are also creating and shaping the cultural
sensibilities of men and women, and indeed the very quality
of their everyday lives.

## V

The mere prevalence of the advertiser's skills and the
designer's craft makes evident the falseness of the major
dogma of the distributor's culture. That dogma is that "we
only give them what they want." This is the Big Lie of mass
culture and of debased art, and also it is the weak excuse
for the cultural default of many designers.

The determination of "consumer wants and tastes" is
one characterizing mark of the current phase of capitalism
in America—and as well as what is called mass culture.
And it is precisely in the areas in which wants *are* determined and changed that designers tend to do their work.

The merchandising apparatus, of which many designers
are now members, operates more to create wants than to
satisfy wants that are already active. Consumers are trained
to "want" that to which they are most continually exposed.
Wants do not originate in some vague realms of the consumer's personality; they are formed by an elaborate apparatus of jingle and fashion, of persuasion and fraud.
They are shaped by the cultural apparatus and the society
of which it is a part. They do not grow and change as the

consumer's sensibilities are enlarged; they are created and they are changed by the process by which they are satisfied and by which old satisfactions are made unsatisfactory. Moreover, the very canons of taste and judgment are also managed by status obsolescence and by contrived fashion. The formula is: to make people ashamed of last year's model; to hook up self-esteem itself with the purchasing of this year's; to create a panic for status, and hence a panic of self-evalution, and to connect its relief with the consumption of specified commodities.

In this vast merchandising mechanism of advertisement and design, there is no inherent social purpose to balance its great social power; there is no built-in responsibility to anybody except to the man who makes the profit. Yet there is little doubt that this mechanism is now a leading fixer of the values and standards of American society, the foremost carrier of cultural sensibility, and quite comparable in influence to school, to church, to home.

This apparatus is now an adjunct of commercial establishments which use "culture" for their own noncultural—indeed anticultural—ends, and so debase its very meaning. These uses of culture are being shaped by men who would turn all objects and qualities, indeed human sensibility itself, into a flow of transient commodities, and these types have now gotten the designer to help them; they have gotten him to turn himself into the ultimate advertising man. When you think about it—if you do—it really is amazing: the old helpmate of the salesman, the Air Brush Boy, the corporal of retailing—hase become the generalissimo of anxious obsolescence as the American way of life.

## VI

I have of course been describing the role of the designer at what I hope is its worst. And I am aware that it is not only in the field of design that the American ambiguity of cultural endeavor is revealed, that it is not only the designer who commits the cultural default. In varying degrees all cultural workmen are part of a world dominated by the pecuniary ethos of the crackpot business man and also of a world unified only vaguely by the ideals of cultural sensibility and human reason. The autonomy of all types of cultural workmen has in our time been declining. I also want to make it clear that I am aware of the great diversity among designers and the enormous difficulty any designer now faces in trying to escape the trap of the maniacs of production and distribution.

The problem of the designer can be solved only by radical consideration of fundamental values. But like most fundamental considerations his can begin very simply.

The idea of the cultural apparatus is an attempt to understand human affairs from the standpoint of the role within them of reason, technique and sensibility. As members of this cultural apparatus, it is important that designers realize fully what their membership means. It means, in brief, that you represent the sensibilities of man as a maker of material objects, of man as a creature related to nature itself and to changing it by a humanly considered plan. The designer is a creator and a critic of the physical frame of private and public life. He represents man as a maker of his own *milieu*. He stands for the kind of sensibility which enables men to contrive a world of objects before which they stand delighted and which they are delighted to use. The designer is part of the unity of art, science and learning. That, in turn, means that he shares one cardinal value, that is the common denominator of art, science and learning and also the very root of human development. That value, I believe, is craftsmanship.

From craftsmanship, as ideal and as practice, it is possible to derive all that the designer ought to represent as an individual and all that he ought to stand for socially and politically and economically. As ideal, craftsmanship stands for the creative nature of work, and for the central place of such work in human development as a whole. As practice, craftsmanship stands for the classic role of the independent artisan who does his work in close interplay with the public, which in turn participates in it.

The most fundamental splits in contemporary life occur because of the break-up of the old unity of design, production and enjoyment. Between the image and the object, between the design and the work, between production and consumption, between work and leisure, there is a great cultural vacuum, and it is this vacuum that the mass distributor, and his artistic and intellectual satrap, have filled up with frenzy and trash and fraud. In one sentence, what has been lost is the fact and the ethos of man as craftsman.

By craftsmanship I refer to a style of work and a way of life having the following characteristics:

(i) In craftsmanship there is no ulterior motive for work other than the product being made and the processes of its creation. The craftsman imagines the completed product, often even as he creates it; and, even if he does not make it, he sees and understands the meaning of his own exertion in terms of the total process of its production. Accordingly, the details of the craftsman's daily work are meaningful because they are not detached in his mind from the product of the work. The satisfaction he has in the results infuses the means of achieving it.

This is the root connection between work and art: as esthetic experiences, both involve the power "to catch the enjoyment that belongs to the consummation, the outcome, of an undertaking and to give to the implements, the objects that are instrumental in the undertaking, and to the acts that compose it something of the joy and satisfaction that suffuse its successful accomplishment."*

To quite small circles the appeal of modern art—notably painting and sculpture, but also of the crafts—lies in the fact that in an impersonal, a scheduled, a machined world, they represent the personal and the spontaneous. They are the opposite of the stereotyped and the banalized.

(ii) In craftsmanship, plan and performance are unified, and in both, the craftsman is master of the activity and of himself in the process. The craftsman is free to begin his working according to his own plan, and during the work he is free to modify its shape and the manner of its shaping. The continual joining of plan and performance brings even more firmly together the consummation of work and its instrumental activities, infusing the latter with the joy of the former. Work is a rational sphere of independent action.

* G. H. Mead, *The Philosophy of the Act,* (Chicago, '38) p. 454.

(iii) Since he works freely, the craftsman is able to learn from his work, to develop as well as use his capacities. His work is thus a means of developing himself as a man as well as developing his skill. This self-development is not an ulterior goal, but a cumulative result of devotion to and practice of his craft. As he gives to work the quality of his own mind and skill, he is also further developing his own nature; in this simple sense, he lives in and through his work, which confesses and reveals him to world.

(iv) The craftsman's way of livelihood determines and infuses his entire mode of living. For him there is no split of work and play, of work and culture. His work is the mainspring of his life; he does not flee from work into a separate sphere of leisure; he brings to his non-working hours the values and qualities developed and employed in his working time. He expresses himself in the very act of creating economic value; he is at work and at play in the same act; his work is a poem in action. In order to give his work the freshness of creativity, he must at times open himself to those influences that only affect us when our attentions are relaxed. Thus for the craftsman, apart from mere animal rest, leisure may occur in such intermittent periods as are necessary for individuality in his work.

(v) Such an independent stratum of craftsmen cannot flourish unless there are publics who support individuals who may not turn out to be first-rate. Craftsmanship requires that such cultural workmen and such publics define what is first-rate. In the Communist bloc because of official bureaucracies, and in the capitalist because of the commercial ethos, standards are now not in the hands of such cultural producers and cultural publics. In both the mere distributor is the key to both consumption and production.

Some cultural workmen in America do of course remain independent. Perhaps three or four men actually earn a living here just by composing serious music; perhaps fifty or so by the writing of serious novels. But I am concerned now less with economic than with cultural requirements. The role of the serious craftsman requires that the cultural workman remain a cultural workman, and that he produce for other cultural producers and for circles and

publics composed of people who have some grasp of what
is involved in his production. For you cannot "possess"
art merely by buying it; you cannot support art merely by
feeding artists—although that does help. To possess it you
must earn it by participating to some extent in what it
takes to design it and to create it. To support it you must
catch in your consumption of it something of what is involved in the production of it.

It is, I think, the absence of such a stratum of cultural
workmen, in close interplay with such a participating public, that is the signal fault of the American cultural scene
today. So long as it does not develop, the position of the
designer will contain all the ambiguities and invite all the
defaults I have indicated. Designers will tend to be commercial stars or commercial hacks. And human development will continue to be trivialized, human sensibilities
blunted, and the quality of life distorted and impoverished.

As practice, craftsmanship in America has largely been
trivialized into pitiful hobbies: it is part of leisure, not of
work. As ethic, it is largely confined to small groups of
privileged professionals and intellectuals. What I am suggesting to you is that designers ought to take the value of
craftsmanship as the central value for which they stand;
that in accordance with it they ought to do their work; and
that they ought to use its norms in their social and economic and political visions of what society ought to become.

Craftsmanship cannot prevail without a properly developing society; such a society I believe would be one in
which the fact and the ethos of craftsmanship would be
pervasive. In terms of its norms, men and women ought
to be formed and selected as ascendant models of character. In terms of its ethos, institutions ought to be constructed and judged. Human society, in brief, ought to be
built around craftsmanship as the central experience of
the unalienated human being and the very root of free
human development. The most fruitful way to define the
social problem is to ask how such a society can be built.
For the highest human ideal is: to become a good craftsman.

# THE COMPLACENT YOUNG MEN

In Great Britain and the United States there is much generalized anguish about there having been Causes in the thirties, but not anymore. A good deal of all this, I think, is less social pain than intellectual malarky. What it means is that in the thirties the Causes were all set up and little moral or intellectual effort was required to get with them. At present, the social energy to develop such Causes is not accessible.

As a result of this there is the often complained of dreariness of the recent cultural scene and the obvious international fact of the political default of cultural workmen. This complaint and this default rest upon the unmet need: (1) to formulate private troubles out of the vague uneasiness of individuals; (2) to make public issues out of indifference and malaise; and (3) to pick up both the uneasiness and indifference—formulated as troubles and issues—in problems open to inquiry.

Private uneasiness and public indifference, intellectually speaking, rest upon an unawareness of both value and peril. We are consequently required to recognize imperiled values and to make a statement about what might be imperiling them. The unfulfilled promise of political thinking that is also culturally sensible stems from the failure to assert the values as well as the perils, and the relationship between them.

That is easy to say and is easy to do, if we've got the brains and the imagination. What is difficult about it is to keep doing it without falling into one or another of the old dead-ends of established slogans—left, right, and center— that lie about in such profusion. Thinking that is at once political and cultural nowadays requires the thinker to establish and re-establish his own little slogans, and with

them continually to state troubles and values and the relations between them.

The young men of Great Britain represented by John
Osborne's angry young man in *Look Back In Anger* have
not yet begun to make explicit these troubles and values.
They have not made plain—and I don't think they know—
the reasons for their anger. What they have done, and with
great skill, is to specify the mood of personal uneasiness and
the quality of public indifference. They have done so mainly
in the direction of private troubles. But even in that direction they have not succeeded in converting uneasiness into
explicit troubles; I don't think they can without also translating the public malaise and indifference into political
issues. And certainly they have not connected private
troubles and public images inside a line-up of their own
problems.

Conservatives have often explained political radicalism
in terms of personal frustration, but the point, I think,
might now better be shifted about: personal radicalism
ought to be imputed to political frustration. The frustrations
which now cause a few young Britons to become angry, it
seems to me, are basically political. But the young men
have no political focus within which to express them, so
their anger turns inward. Anger becomes a trouble of
character, an embitterment of private *milieux*—not a shove
toward the formulation of "good, brave causes."

That, is seems to me, is the key to the ambiguity of
Jimmy Porter's character and the reason for the limited
locale of his wonderful desperation. It is what makes his
anger border on hysteria and it is the reason he can find
no way out. *Look Back in Anger* is about the inchoate
personal troubles that may occur when the political issues
that lie behind them are left unformulated. The society
by which this character is caged he believes to be in grievous decline, and since he is a passionate political man without any political role, he has taken the miseries of the
decline upon himself and they are ruining his personal life.
No more causes—and no more coziness. The next question
would seem to be: which way will he look—personal
coziness or "good, brave, causes?" But in this play there is
no answer.

# I

I do not mean that such writers are concerned merely with "personal relations" and ought to be concerned with great, "burning issues." I mean that just the kind of personal relations which do concern them cannot be understood unless they are recognized as closely connected with burning issues which are as yet not formulated. And because they do not recognize this there are no burning issues for the characters they invent.

Having no political focus for their grievances, they are possessed by too many reasons for anger. Their anger is blind in the simple sense that it has no suitable target. Jimmy Porter's main target, for example, is his wife, and although he plays about with the class distinctions between them, he knows she's not really fair game, and certainly not an adequate cause for his discontents. He has the feeling that what's wrong, what's phoney is "the whole damned thing," and so he is wildly abusive. So many targets—poverty, church, religion-in-general, decorum, the noisiness of women, homosexuals, in-laws—and none of them connected, none of them set up politically inside a real idea of what is happening in the great society. He has nowhere to catch hold, his is a total anger which dominates him hysterically. There is desperation in this drama all right, but the cause and the meaning of this desperation have not gotten into it. It is a truncated drama. It is a partial drama of not altogether understood symptoms.

The alienation of personal from political life has been generally characteristic of most people in the formal democracies for a long time; now it is true as well of many people engaged in intellectual and cultural work. That divorce is the source of their creation, although I hope not of their creativity. If we suppose, for example, one difference in the situation of Jimmy Porter, Jimmy Porter as a character would no longer exist: a political movement which in its outlook and activities was alive to both the private troubles and the public issues in which he is involved. This obvious point I raise in order to make clear that what is intellectually deficient about the angry young men, the general culture failure upon which their work rests, is a lack of the sociological imagination.

This lack is much more apparent in the work of Kingsley Amis than in that of John Osborne. Had Amis' *Lucky Jim* been written by some young instructor from Ohio, I doubt that it would have attracted much attention. It is another echo, a generation afterwards, of Sinclair Lewis' little set-to with provinciality and hypocrisy, with boredom and stupidity, against all-around pettiness, in which only the image of The Big City is the escape from it all.

## II

Provinces are, even in England, provincial; sometimes the provinciality involves cultural pretense, and sometimes this pretense is mistakenly identified with all cultural work. I don't see much else in the character of Amis' *Lucky Jim,* James Dixon. He is a part written for one of those roles James Stewart used to play: you know, where he's a nicely clownish, bumbling and helpless male, altogether loveable by the masculine Jean Arthur. Add to that the grimaces of a TV-comic, and what else is there? His kind of yearning is merely one of the standard cultural accompaniments of urbanization—which at this date, and in Britain, does seem the mood of a curiously ambitious and curiously maladroit hick. Unlike Jimmy Porter, James Dixon is not in the middle of any big try. Presumably he just wants to get away from it all—to London, and if he can get the girl too, then he's got his happy ending. In the truncated but less unreal world of Jimmy Porter, no happy ending is in sight.

I think Mr. Amis is quite right when he declares that he is no angry young man. He is a young complacent. Although by no means twins, the two types are very much around just now, and both, I think, are symptoms of the same set of conditions. And that is the point: they are more symptoms of a condition than symbols of any political or cultural orientation.

On the surface they are symptoms of the divorce of political reflection from cultural work, and of the default in the West generally of the classic political task of cultural workmen. But beneath that, and especially in Britain, they are symptoms of the collapse of the established pattern and of gentlemanly cultural aspiration, *and* also of such "proletarian" patterns and aspirations as have prevailed. They are symptoms of the rise to cultural articulation of the new middle classes and their white-collar worlds, *and* also of the inadequacy of these worlds as a point of new beginnings.

The cries of pain and the clownish grimaces are cultural expressions of the new white-collar formations. The Young Complacents are not only spokesmen for this class, they are quite successful members of it, or they are trying to be. The Angry Young Men are spokesmen for it too, but they are against the kind of situation it has placed them in, and they do not take as their own the aspirations it provides.

## III

As everyone must now know, this white-collar pyramid of technicians, managers, teachers, accountants, salesmen —discovered by Marxist revisionists in the decade before World War I—is the major change in the social and class structure of all industrial countries in the second quarter of the twentieth century. It is not only their enormous increase in numbers, along with the leveling off or decline of wage workers and of the old middle class of people of business and the free professions. It is that the ethos, the style of life, they embody also tends to become quite generally ascendent.* The theme of the "provincial universities" and its use as a symbol, as well as the talk about "using culture in order to get one" and much else—all that must be understood in connection with the place of the expanded universities as the cradles of the white-collar worlds.

In the United States, this change in the social topography has not made the general cultural impact it has recently been making in Britain. For one thing, white-collar education is much more widely established in America; for

* For a statement of the cultural and political meanings of these strata, see *White Collar: The New Middle Classes* (New York: Oxford University Press, 1951); and further up the line, *The Power Elite* (New York: Oxford University Press, 1956).

another, in the United States there is such a clutter of styles and postures, aspirations and fashions. Omnivorous America can seemingly gobble up everything and celebrate it all. Any established pattern is harder to find—and certainly harder to disturb.

In Britain, however, there has been one ascendent pattern of aspiration, quite widely respected and certainly fully expressed in cultural activity and production: the model of the gentleman in his established order. This was the model which Max Weber, in an echo of German national liberalism before World War I, enviously held up against the "lacquered plebians" of Prussia who were not up to playing such a national role. And it is an order and a character that the United States has never known. America does not now have an establishment—the overlap of authority and culture to form a semi-official realm of prestige which transforms power into authority, and makes of proper cultural work the authoritative point of national reference.

It is this political and cultural formation, of course, that some younger writers have rejected; that is why they are "vulgar." Theirs is a near total rejection, but it is a rejection that does not stand on any alternative social basis in which they can really believe. Certainly not "labor," despite the groping "to believe in it."

In a quite literal, although complicated sense, the fuss about Osborne, Amis, and their colleagues is a fuss about a class conflict. The clash is between white-collar culture and the culture of the established order; "labor" is culturally quite off to the side. That the young writers do not truly believe in any of these cultures is both the cause and the expression of their central confusion: the confusion of the very terms of human and of cultural success. It is this confusion that the angry young men and the young complacents of Great Britain represent and express. And it is this confusion, and the ambiguous conflict lying back of it, in which they seem to be parochially entrapped.

I am of course deliberately exaggerating the case, but isn't the line something like this. No upper class, no labor class, no middle class makes them feel cozy and/or politically alive. Just now the higher circles are indeed presiding over the etcetera but with no real prospects; the labor party seems to be in the process of the self-liquidation of one of the last (non-Communist) socialist parties in the western world; the new middle classes are getting the hell out, to Canada, Australia—it would be more fun in America—or clawing and biting their way to the top of the old society. And the young complacents and the angry young men? In one sentence, are they not the internal emigrants of Great Britain?

I cannot help but think that all of this represents another instance, in the west, of the ascendency of the international hayseed. There's a showdown on socialism, on its very meaning as well as on its chances, going on in Eastern Europe. But there is a more important showdown than that one. For those concerned with the politics of culture and the culture of politics, the problems now lie in the international encounter of those models of characters which are being formed and selected as ascendent models of the human being in the United States and in Russia. In both there is a showdown on all the modern expectations about what man can *want* to become.

In the American white-collar hierarchies and in the middle levels of the Soviet "intelligentsia"—in quite differing ways but with often frightening convergence—there is coming about the rise of the cheerful robot, of the technological idiot, of the crackpot realist. All these types embody a common ethos: rationality without reason. The fate of these types and this ethos, what is done about them and what they do—that is the real, even the ultimate, showdown on "socialism" in our time. For it is a showdown on what kinds of human beings and what kinds of culture are going to become the models of the immediate future, the commanding models of human aspiration. And it is an epochal showdown, separating the contemporary from the modern age. To make that showdown clear, as it affects every region of the world and every intimate recess of the self, requires a union of political reflection and cultural sensibility of a sort not really known before. It is a union now scarcely available in the western cultural community. Perhaps the attempt to achieve it, and to use it well, is the showdown on human culture itself.

The withdrawal of cultural workmen from politics, in

America as well as in Britain, is of course part of the international default, which is both cultural and political, of the western world today. In both countries, the young complacents and the angry young men are quite free. Nobody locks them up. Nobody has to. They are locking themselves up. The angry ones in the totality of their own parochial anger; the complacent ones in their own unimaginative ambitions. Isn't that among the main points our friends in Poland and Hungary and Yugoslavia ought to grasp, about the United States and Great Britain in the middle of the twentieth century? And shouldn't the young men of Great Britain re-examine their reasons for anger?

## 12

# THE BIG CITY:
# PRIVATE TROUBLES AND PUBLIC ISSUES

Consider the metropolis—the horrible, beautiful, ugly, magnificent sprawl of the great city. For many upper-class people, the personal solution to "the problem of the city" is to have an apartment (with private garage under it) in the heart of the city, and one hundred miles out, a house and garden by notable architects, on a hundred acres of private land. In these two controlled environments—with a small staff at each end an a private helicopter connection —most people could solve many of the personal problems caused them by the facts of the city. But all this, however splendid, does not solve the public issues that the structural fact of the city poses. What should be done with this wonderful monstrosity? Break it all up into scattered units, combining residence and work? Refurbish it as it stands? Or, after evacuation, dynamite it and build new cities according to new plans in new places? What would those plans be? And who is to decide and to accomplish whatever choice is made? These are structural issues; to confront them and to solve them requires us to consider political, economic and esthetic issues that affect innumerable *milieux*.

## I

Perhaps the most fruitful distinction with which the sociological imagination works is this distinction—between personal troubles and public issues.

*Troubles* have to do with an individual's character and with those limited areas of social life of which he is directly and personally aware. Accordingly, to state and to resolve troubles we must look at the individual as a biographical entity and examine the scope of his immediate *milieux*— the social setting that is directly open to his personal experience and to some extent to his willful activity. A trouble is a private matter: values cherished by an individual are felt by him to be threatened.

*Issues* have to do with matters that transcend these local environments of the individual and the limited range of his life. They have to do with the organization of many such *milieux* into the institutions of society as a whole, with the ways, for example, in which various neighborhoods overlap to form the larger structures of a great metropolitan area. An issue is a public matter: values cherished by publics are felt to be threatened. Often there is debate about what these values really are, and about what it is that really threatens them. It is the very nature of an issue, unlike even widespread trouble, that it cannot very well be defined in terms of the everyday environments of ordinary men. An issue, in fact, often involves a crisis in institutional arrangements.

Such a crisis now exists in connection with the big cities of the Western societies.

In terms of troubles and issues—to illustrate the distinction further—consider briefly unemployment. When, in a city of 100,000, only *one* man is unemployed, that is his personal trouble, and for its relief we properly look to the character of this man, his skills, and his immediate opportunities. But when in a nation of 50 million employees, 15 million are unemployed, that is an issue, and we may not hope to find its solution within the range of opportunities open to any one individual. The very structure of opportunities has collapsed.

Consider war. The personal problem of war, when it occurs, may be how to survive it or how to die in it with honor; how to make money out of it; or how to climb into the higher safety of the military apparatus. In short, according to one's values, to find a set of *milieux* and within it to survive the war or to make one's death in it effective. But the structural issues of war have to do with its causes; with what types of men it throws up into command; with its effects upon economic and political and religious institutions; with the unorganized irresponsibility of a world of nation-states.

Consider marriage. Inside a marriage a man and a

woman may experience personal troubles, but when the
divorce rate during the first four years of marriage is 250
out of every 1,000 attempts, that indicates a structural
issue having to do with the institutions of marriage and the
family and other institutions that bear upon these.

Insofar as the elements of an economy are so arranged
that slumps occur, the problem of unemployment becomes
incapable of personal solution. Insofar as war is inherent
in the nation-state system and in the uneven industrialization of the world, the ordinary individual, in his restricted
*milieux,* will be powerless—with or without psychiatric
aid—to solve the troubles this lack of system imposes upon
him. Insofar as the family as an institution turns women
into darling little slaves and men into their chief providers
and unweaned dependents, the problem of a satisfactory
marriage remains incapable of purely private solution.

*And* insofar as the overdeveloped megalopolis and the
overdeveloped automobile are built-in features of the overdeveloped society, the problems of urban living will not be
solved by personal ingenuity and private wealth.

What we experience in the specific, everyday *milieux* of
the city is often caused by structural changes in the society
as a whole. Accordingly, to understand the changes of
many personal *milieux,* we are required to look beyond
them. And the number and variety of such structural
changes increase as the institutions within which we live
become more embracing and more intricately connected
with one another.

## II

The forces that are shaping the big city are structural
forces.

But the awareness and the effective action of "the citizens" are limited to a scatter of local *milieux.*

That, I think, is a good definition of what is meant by
a mass society, and of the city as its major locale. As we
become more aware of our condition we come to feel that
we are living in a world in which we are merely spectators.
We are acted upon, but we do not act. We feel that our

personal experience is civically irrelevant, and our political will a minor illusion. Although we do not panic, we are often distracted and we are usually slightly bewildered. The more we come to understand our condition as a mass, the more frustrated we are likely to become—for we feel that our very knowledge leads to powerlessness. We live in metropolitan areas that are not communities in any real sense of the word, but rather unplanned monstrosities in which we, as men and women, are segregated into narrowed routines and limited *milieux*. In this metropolitan society, we develop, in our defense, a blasé manner that reaches deeper than a manner. We do not, accordingly, experience genuine clash of viewpoint. And when we do, we tend to consider it merely rude. We are sunk in our routines, and by them. We do not gain a view of the structure of our society as a whole and of our role within it. Our cities are composed of narrow slots, and we, as the people in these slots, are more and more confined to our own rather narrow ranges. Each is trapped in his confining circle; each is split from easily identifiable groups.

Given all those forces that have made our cities less political and more administrative; all the mass communications that do not truly communicate; all the metropolitan segregation that is no community—what is happening is the decline of a set of *publics* that is sovereign, except in the most formal and in the most rhetorical sense.

### I I I

All this—and more—is what we mean when we speak of a mass society. The big city, I believe, is the focus for the human problems of this kind of society, if only because it is a convenient way to present what I am afraid seem utopian solutions. I would call your attention to that fact: virtually all truly sensible plans to re-shape the big city into some kind of reasonably human envioronment do seem utopian. The great point is always to ask *why* this is so. For then we come upon those forces over which we seem to have little or no control, but which in fact are determining how we must try to live. Reasonable and human plans seem utopian, from the standpoint of the practical and irrational, the often stupid and selfish interests that are now shaping our big cities.

Historically, these cities have come about without design, indeed without any reasoning about their meaning for the way men live in them. They are the results of many small decisions of innumerable people; but also, increasingly, of the deliberate—although always partial—plans of larger interests. These larger and more powerful interests are now often quite explicit and quite wide in their consequence.

The main forces that *consciously* shape the structure of the city today are private commercial interests, along with the presumably public interests that are more or less beholden to them. What has happened to Toronto (and to St. Louis) first of all, is the private expropriation and the profitable misuse of the very landscape in which the men, the women, the children of these cities are now trying to live.

These conscious interests, however, are allowed to operate in their chaotic and often disastrous manner because of *the civic vacuum* into which the people of a mass society have now fallen. What has happened to Toronto (and to St. Louis) is planless drift, civic incompetence, and civic apathy.

Such cities as these are the focal points of a society full of private people in a state of public lethargy, alternating on occasion with a state of animated distraction. Many people live in ugly wastelands, but in the absence of imaginative standards, most of them do not even know it. Their cities and suburbs are filled with built-in inconvenience, with nagging frustrations of the everyday life; but being habituated to these, many people often take them to be part of some natural order.

(i) In part, I have noted, the city is the result of blind drift. Accordingly, the problem of the city is how to transcend local *milieux* in order to consider publicly, imaginatively, planfully the city as a structure: to see it, in brief, as a public issue, and to see ourselves as a public—rather than as men in a mass trapped by merely personal troubles. We must realize, in a word, that we *need* not drift blindly; that we can take matters into our own hands.

(ii) In part, I have noted the city is the result of the partial planning of deliberate interests. Accordingly, the problem of the city is the problem of political or civic irresponsibility. Intellectually, this means that we must locate the blame for decisions being made and lack of decisions being committed about our cities. How else can we speak of responsibility? Politically, it means that we must organize and agitate against these sources of decision and lack of decision that fail to consider properly the human landscape in which we must live.

(iii) The city is necessarily a collective product and one that is never finished. In this it is unlike the variety of paintings and sculptures which we possess; at the same time it is the major locale of man's art; the visual scene in which he lives. But increasingly it is an inhuman landscape. Accordingly, the city is *the* esthetic problem—but more than that, it is the problem of the politics of esthetics. And to solve this problem there must come about a truly wide and deep discussion of the esthetics of the urban area —which is to say, a discussion of the quality and meaning of human life itself in our time.

## IV

I cannot answer for you the political and esthetic problems of your cities. You must answer them, first of all by confronting them boldly. In an effort to make more concrete what I have been trying to say here, I should like to address myself, in conclusion, to members of those rather inchoate professions that are directly concerned with the city.

Most city planners and designers work mainly on *milieux;* most architects beautify the *milieux* of the rich and polish up the face of the corporation. They patch up bits and pieces of already partial structures. But now at least the best among them have reached a point where they are uneasy about the work they do. They are coming up against structural problems, and up against those who by their decisions and defaults determine many *milieux*. Men are not equal in power. The private in an army has no chance to view the whole structure of the army, much less to direct it. But the general does. *His* means of information, of vision, of decision are much greater. In like manner with the owner of a development tract, as against an individual householder. In short, are we not coming to see that the chaos of our cities is first of all part of an irresponsible economic and political system? And second, that, after all, the city planners themselves are in something of an esthetic chaos?

Let me put all this in terms of some questions to the city planners, and to those interested in the city as a place for human living.

(i) Is the ugly, frustrating and irrational structure of the city *now* due so much to fate, to haphazard forces, or can you now identify circles of men who are responsible for decisions that affect the innumerable *milieux* that make up the city? Historically, the answer is obviously fate. But the bulldozer fleet and the real estate interests are now putting an end to fate of this kind. And city governments too—surely you will agree that often they seem most readily understandable as committees for a complex of real estate interests?

(ii) Is the architect merely to work on beautifying the isolated *milieux* of wealthy persons—or is he to be concerned with the planning of the human landscape for all people? Is he content to be the subordinate of the irrational and greedy powers that now shape the structure of our environment—or is he to be a member of an autonomous profession that demands a voice in decisions of structural consequence being debated by publics?

(iii) There has been much talk about the lack of any discernible *order* in our present environment. I think this largely nonsense. Is not the common denominator capital gain and material accumulation? Is not the pattern of our environment very largely that of real estate interests and advertising maniacs? To such types our cities are not at all disorderly; on the contrary, they are as orderly as the files to title deeds.

(iv) The sensibility of the designer, the architect, the artists, the city planner—is it not in conflict with this ethos of the capitalist? Are they content to be the subordinates of men who, seeing a forest, immediately think only of board feet? Of men who, seeing a new color, think immediately of how it might make obsolete last year's fashion in ladies' dresses, automobiles and soon, private houses? Are they in short willing to be part and parcel of the commercial frenzy, the banalization of sensibility and the deliberate planning of obsolescence?

(v) The people really concerned with the problems of the city are now confronting questions, I believe, that the intellectuals of the thirties confronted. For example, is there a contradiction between corporate capitalism and publicly responsible planning? What are the proper relations of reform and revolution? What *is* "practical" and what *is* "utopian?" Does not utopian mean merely: whatever acknowledges other values as relevant and possibly even as sovereign? But in truth, are not those who in the name of realism act like crackpots, are they not the utopians? Are we not now in a situation in which the only practical, realistic down-to-earth thinking and acting is just what these crackpot realists call "utopian?"

Our professions and crafts that have to do with the city are now in chaos, and without agreed-upon standards. Our task—as professional people and as citizens—is to formulate standards; to set forth as a conference ten or twelve propositions on which we are willing to stand up. Let us begin this, here and now.

# PART IV

# I

# THE CULTURAL APPARATUS

The first rule for understanding the human condition is that men live in second-hand worlds. They are aware of much more than they have personally experienced; and their own experience is always indirect. The quality of their lives is determined by meanings they have received from others. Everyone lives in a world of such meanings. No man stands alone directly confronting a world of solid fact. No such world is available. The closest men come to it is when they are infants or when they become insane: then, in a terrifying scene of meaningless events and senseless confusion, they are often seized with the panic of near-total insecurity. But in their everyday life they do not experience a world of solid fact; their experience itself is selected by stereotyped meanings and shaped by ready-made interpretations. Their images of the world, and of themselves, are given to them by crowds of witnesses they have never met and never shall meet. Yet for every man these images—provided by strangers and dead men—are the very basis of his life as a human being.

The consciousness of men does not determine their material existence; nor does their material existence determine their consciousness. Between consciousness and existence stand meanings and designs and communications which other men have passed on—first, in human speech itself, and later, by the management of symbols. These received and manipulated interpretations decisively influence such consciousness as men have of their existence. They provide the clues to what men see, to how they respond to it, to how they feel about it, and to how they respond to these feelings. Symbols focus experience; meanings organize knowledge, guiding the surface perceptions of an instant no less than the aspirations of a lifetime.

Every man, to be sure, *observes* nature, social events, and his own self: but he does not, he has never, observed most of what he takes to be fact, about nature, society, or self. Every man *interprets* what he observes—as well as much that he has not observed: but his terms of interpretation are not his own; he has not personally formulated or even tested them. Every man talks about observations and interpretations to others: but the terms of his *reports* are much more likely than not the phrases and images of other people which he has taken over as his own. For most of what he calls solid fact, sound interpretation, suitable presentations, every man is increasingly dependent upon the observation posts, the interpretation centers, the presentation depots, which in contemporary society are established by means of what I am going to call the cultural apparatus.

## I

This apparatus is composed of all the organizations and *milieux* in which artistic, intellectual and scientific work goes on, and of the means by which such work is made available to circles, publics, and masses. In the cultural apparatus art, science, and learning, entertainment, malarkey, and information are produced and distributed. In terms of it, these products are distributed and consumed. It contains an elaborate set of institutions: of schools and theaters, newspapers and census bureaus, studios, laboratories, museums, little magazines, radio networks. It contains truly fabulous agencies of exact information and of trivial distraction, exciting objects, lazy escapes, strident advice. Inside this apparatus, standing between men and events, the images, meanings, slogans that define the worlds in which men live are organized and compared, maintained and revised, lost and cherished, hidden, debunked, celebrated. Taken as a whole, the cultural apparatus is the lens of mankind through which men see; the medium by which they interpret and report what they see. It is the semiorganized source of their very identities and of their aspirations. It is the source of The Human Variety—of styles of living and of ways to die.

Nowadays in the overdeveloped society, everyday life and the mass arts; private lives and public entertainment; public affairs and the stereotypes put out about it—they reflect one another so closely that it is often impossible to distinguish image from source. So decisive to experience itself are the results of these communications that often men do not really believe what "they see before their very eyes" until they have been "informed" about it by the national broadcast, the definitive book, the close-up photograph, the official announcement. With such means, each nation tends to offer a selected, closed-up, and official version of world reality. The cultural apparatus not only guides experience; often as well it expropriates the very chance to have experience that can rightly be called "our own." For our standards of credibility, our definitions of reality, our modes of sensibility—as well as our immediate opinions and images—are determined much less by any pristine experience than by our exposure to the output of the cultural apparatus.

The most embracive and the most specialized domain of modern society, this apparatus fulfills the most functions: such role as *reason* may have in human affairs, this apparatus, this put-together contraption, fulfills. Such part as *sensibility* may play in the human drama, it carries out. Such use as scientific *technique* may have in history and in geography, it provides. It is the seat of civilization, which —in Matthew Arnold's phrase—is: "the humanization of man in society." The only truths are those defined by some cultural apparatus. The only *beauty* is the objects created or indicated by some set of cultural workmen. The only *good* is the variety of cultural values with which men are made morally comfortable or morally uneasy.

## II

It is in terms of some such conception as this apparatus that the politics of culture may be understood. Around the world today some *intellectuals* play leading roles in the politics of their nation; other are altogether withdrawn

from political concerns; seemingly without political orientation, they are political inactionaries. Some *artists* happily
smash national and party idols; others, equally happy no
doubt, busily invent new images of them. Some *scientists*
seem glad to become leading fixtures of their nation's
equipment for war; others are traitors and some no doubt
are spies. The range of the cultural workmen's politics is
coextensive with the range of politics; at any given time in
projection, in hope, in fantasy—it goes well beyond the
working range of the politicians.

To carry out a political role explicitly is to try to influence decisions of consequence and so to engage in a
struggle for power. It is to justify prevailing powers and
the decisions of the powerful, or—as the case may be—to
debunk the powerful and oppose authoritative decisions.
Such politics is a conscious work: it is a book, a drawing,
a pamphlet, addressed to questions of policy to agents of
authority, to political publics.

But the politics of cultural work is not to be identified
with the explicit political views or activities of cultural
workmen. There is a great difference between enacting a
political role and being, by virtue of one's work, politically
relevant. The political choices of individuals must be distinguished from the political functions, uses and consequences of the cultural work they do.

That a scientist working in a laboratory may honestly
conceive of himself as a disembodied spirit does not make
any the less real the objective consequences of his discovery for the ultimate ends of bombing the population of
a city of which he has never heard. Surely it is now evident that nothing happens in modern science, in "research"
or in "development," that is not of probable military, economic, and political relevance.

And not only in science. That an artist simply may not
care about anything but the way a certain shade of blue
explodes in the eye does not make any the less real the
function of his picture when it is seized upon by men of
nationalist purpose. And nowadays any artistic product
may well be seized upon in the building of cultural prestige
for national authority.

That a sociologist cares only about the mathematical

properties of "a new scaling device for attitude studies" does not detract from the objective function of his work in helping generals to prod farm boys to kill off more Japanese, or corporation executives to manipulate all the more brightly their sounds and images going out endlessly to 50 million homes in order to increase the sales-volume of a new shade of lipstick of a new presidential face.

Although not all cultural workmen are concerned with politics, their work is increasingly of central relevance to the great issues of war or peace, to the nationalist celebration and competition, and to the very quality of everyday life. We cannot examine merely the individual workman and his choices: The cultural apparatus as a whole is established and used by dominant institutional orders. Growing up and working within it, educated by it, many cultural workmen today never feel the need to make political choices simply because they are in fact committed before the age of political consent.

## III

As an institutional fact, the cultural apparatus assumes many forms, but everywhere today it tends to be part of some national establishment. This term, "establishment," is of course your (a British) term. The ambiguity with which you (they) use it is at once too lovely and too useful for a mere sociologist to avoid stealing it. I now serve notice that I do intend to steal it, although I promise that I shall try not to make of it a Concept. In general, the term points to the overlap of culture and authority. This overlap may involve the ideological use of cultural products and of cultural workmen for the legitimation of power, and the justification of decisions and policies. It may involve the bureaucratic use of culture by the personnel of authoritative institutions. But the essential feature of any establishment is a traffic between culture and authority, a tacit co-operation of cultural workmen and authorities of ruling institutions. This means of exchange between them includes money, career, privilege; but above all, it includes *prestige*. A zone of at least semiofficial prestige which is at once of culture and of authority is the zone of any establishment.

(i) To the powerful, cultural prestige lends "weight." Ideologies may justify explicitly, but it is prestige that truly celebrates, that transforms more power into spellbinding authority. The prestige of culture is among the major means by which powers of decision are made to seem part of an unchallengeable authority. That is why the cultural apparatus, no matter how internally free, tends in every nation to become a close adjunct of national authority and a leading agency of nationalist propaganda.

(ii) To the cultural workman, the prestige borrowed from association with authority lends increased importance and "dignity" to his work—and to himself. It makes of him a national point of reference for the rank-order of cultural work and of cultural workmen. What is so loosely called "the climate of opinion" refers to just such points of national reference for the producers, the consumers, and the products of cultural work; it refers, in brief, to those who are fashion-leaders in matters of cultural and political opinion; and who privately, as well as formally, certify others, their work, their taste.

National establishments tend to set the relations of culture and politics the important tasks, the suitable themes, the major uses of the cultural apparatus. In the end, what is "established" are definitions of reality, judgments of value, canons of taste and of beauty.

## IV

Cultural activities require financial support. Even the most advanced-guard writer must eat. Of course, as a part-time writer, he may be independently wealthy; he may earn his money by noncultural activities; he may be supported by his wife or wives. But in any economy, without a capital investment or some continuing material support —in brief without money—cultural activities cannot very well go on, much less can they be established.

A set of publics are also required. These may consist of small circles of producers who form their own publics or of one hundred million inexpert consumers of culture.

The size of the cultural public—as well as the prestige, class, and power of its members—are major clues to cultural orientation. A John Stuart Mill writing with a receptive Parliament in mind clearly occupies a different position than a Soviet novelist oriented to party officials or an American professor writing for other professors.

The money and the public for culture are of course related. The source and amount of the money, and the extent and nature of the public go far to determine the character of a cultural apparatus and the position of cultural workmen. These are also the terms in which the specific national histories of culture are most conveniently understood. It is useful to remind you of the three stages into which a "natural history of modern culture" tends generally to fall:

(i) In Europe, including Russia, the modern cultural apparatus begins as a patronage system: patrons personally support culture and also form the public for which it is produced. The cultural apparatus is established upon a pre-capitalist basis, in close relation to princely house, to church, to monarch, and later to bourgeois patrician. By his work, the cultural workman brings prestige to such higher circles and to the institutions over which they rule. Part of the coterie of these authorities, his status is often ambiguous and insecure: he is usually dependent upon the whims of The Great Ones, whom he advises, amuses, instructs.

(ii) Then emerges the bourgeois public: the cultural workman becomes an entrepreneur. He earns money by the sale of cultural commodities to anonymous publics. For a brief liberal period in Western history, he stands on common ground with the bourgeois entrepreneur. Both fight against the remnants of feudal control—the businessman to break the bonds of the chartered enterprise, the writer to free himself from the insecurities of patronage. Both fight for new kinds of freedom, for an unbounded market for wool and shoes, for an anonymous public for novels and portraits.

The decline of patronage and the dependence of culture upon publics is a decisive turn in culture and in politics. A great deal of the modern history of culture, until well into the twentieth century, has to do with the transition from Stage One to Stage Two. In fact, most of our inherited images of "the intellectual" and of "the artist" are based upon experience of this second stage. It has provided the models of the cultural creator that still prevail among us: the inherently and necessarily free man, and the cherished and heroic notion of the advance-guard. This notion, one might say, is "the myth" of the intellectual, the artist, the lone inventor, and even of the scientist. It is still clung to mightily, being identified with freedom itself by those whose ideal is *not* to become established, not to become connected with authority, and who, in brief, have sought to be autonomous members of some autonomous cultural apparatus.

(iii) In the Third Stage, which we now enter, several tendencies evident in the Second, are carried to their logical outcome: the cultural apparatus is established politically or commercially; the cultural workman becomes a man who is qualified, politically or commercially. Both money and public are "provided," and in due course so are cultural products themselves: cultural work is not only guided: culture is produced and distributed—and even consumed—to order. Commercial agencies or political authorities support culture, but unlike older patrons, they do not form its sole public. The public for culture is enormously enlarged and intensively cultivated into the condition of a receptive mass.

In the extreme, as in modern totalitarianism, all "observation posts" from which realities can be observed are available only to the duly qualified; all "interpretation centers" are subject to doctrinal or pecuniary review; all "presentation depots" are carefully-guarded points of access to masses or the markets. The competition of ideas and of images is confined to a narrowed range, the exact limits of which are seldom known. By trial and error they must be found out, and the attempt to do so is judged officially, sometimes bloodily; or judged comercially, often ruthlessly.

Any establishment of culture means the establishment of definitions of reality, values, taste. But in the third stage these definitions are subject to official management and, if need be, backed up by coercion. Debate is limited. Only certain views are allowed But more than that, the terms of debate, the terms in which the world may be seen, the standards and lack of standards by which men judge of their accomplishments, of themselves, and of other men—these terms are officially or commercially determined, inculcated, enforced.

Today, of course, all three stages of establishment exist side by side, in one nation or another, in one division of culture or another. Accordingly, the politics of culture and the culture of politics around the world are quite various.

## V

In underdeveloped countries, the cultural apparatus is usually confined to very small circles and to rudimentary middle classes. Often it consists of only a few distributors and consumers, linked by education to the cultural machineries of more developed nations. These unhappy few often form the only public available for cultural products and services. Their countries are often filled with masses of people whose lives are dominated by the historical round of subsistence in family, village and tribe, and by mass illiteracy and the pre-industrial grind of poverty. Such facts limit and often make impossible any larger public and any larger support for cultural activities.

In many such countries the main task of the indigenous intelligentsia is often understood by its members to be the political creation of a national economy and a national state. For them the cultural task and the political struggle are clearly one. From its beginnings, their cultural apparatus is filled with political vision and demand. That is the most striking and important fact about the paramount role of "the intellectuals" of the underdeveloped areas.

Brought into being by the schools of Western nations, they are often condemned to a declassé kind of existence. Although of course there is great variation, they tend to be an intellectual proletariat which can find no suitable place among the illiterate masses, among the beginnings of the middle classes, or in such alien organizations of Western business or government agencies as may exist. In these

governing institutions, "the best places" are usually reserved for men from the governing nation. Yet they too
have argued the political alternatives argued in Europe,
and they have taken quite seriously the political ideals and
economic aspirations provided by their Western experience.

Given their situation, and the condition of their countries, they have tended to reject the capitalism of the West.
In their minds, as in their societies, capitalism is linked
with an imperial rule that has excluded them from coveted
positions and subjected their countries to domination in all
spheres of life. They feel that so long as they are merely
capitalist, their countries will not become modern industrial nations. Their rejection of capitalism may or may not
be accompanied by acceptance of Communism. But usually their insurgent nationalism is intimately linked with
the desire to build industry, suddenly and on a great scale.
Accordingly, the Soviet way to industrialize is quite appealing to them.[1]

## VI

What is characteristic of the cultural establishment of
leading West-European nations is their historic duration
as semiofficial formations of prestige which are somewhat
independent from national authority but which have great

[1] We must, of course, keep in mind the great variety of societies
and of cultural situations covered by the term "underdeveloped
country." India and China, for example, are "underdeveloped countries," but they have had great, ancient, and elaborate cultural organizations and products, quite distinct from those of the West.
At first, as from the seventh to the eleventh centuries, they have in
many cultural respects surpassed the Western world. Yet: their cultures have never included science in the Western sense. Moreover,
the culture of India has been part of a crippling caste system; that
of China, of a crippling bureaucracy of Mandarins. In the modern
period, neither has been able successfully to cope with the results
of the scientific divisions of Western cultural apparatuses. China's
cultural apparatus is now being thoroughly revolutionized on the
Soviet model, and the Mandarin, as well as the "old hand" of the
West, are replaced by new types of men. India's cultural legacy is
seen by the world at large, and by many Indians educated to Western
aspirations, as something to be overcome rather than a means of the
new and rapid development that is desired.

relevance to it. Although decisively modified, they often retain something of the flavor of patronage. Pre-capitalist in origin, in varying degree, they have resisted merely economic forces; in varying degree, they have seemed autonomous.

In France, it is said, Men of Letters have formed a sort of tribune that is in part a political, in part a literary, and altogether a nationalist matter. The writer is "the public conscience." Speaking as a moralist, often he has been "a supreme oracle of public affairs."[2] althought by no means always an effective one. The center of the French establishment is The Academy, and The Ministry of Education which embrace virtually all features of cultural endeavor. Even the most "radical" members of this apparatus tend somehow still to feel themselves inside representatives of French culture.

In Germany, the professoriate, historically seated in state universities, has been the bearer of German science and scholarship, its members the national insiders of the German establishment. Near the top of the general hierarchy of prestige, they have also been among the higher servants of the state, and yet once seated, rather autonomous within it.

In England, what is called "The Establishment" at any given time seems a vague formation and rather closed-up. Yet viewed historically, it appears to have been generously assimilative. At its center are the older universities, the higher civil service, the monarchy; these have been firmly connected with county families and their gentry culture. From the points of this triangle of university, government, and social class, The Establishment has radiated wondrously in the attempted embrace of the politics and the culture of nation, empire, and commonwealth.

In all these European countries, established cultural workmen have often been held in high esteem. During Stage Two, they remained somewhat in tension with the commercial ethos of capitalism, and with the expanded authority of the modern state. They have been based upon pre-capitalist (often anticapitalist) traditions and institu-

[2] Herbert Luthy, "The French Intellectual," *Encounter,* August 1955, p. 5.

tions, and they have themselves constituted one such basis. As formations of prestige, they long resisted the naked force of money; closely related to political authorities, at the same time they have been autonomous from them. In both these respects, of course, the European cultural agencies and cultural workmen are undergoing decisive change.

## VII

In the Soviet Union, Stage One is now at best a vague memory of scattered old men. The features of Stage Two are absent or perilously underground. Despite "revisionism," the Soviet Union now represents one rather pure type of Stage Three. The source of money is the one-party state; masses of people are the managed public for culture; cultural activities are official activities. Opposition is traitorous, and exists mainly as a more or less hidden literary mood. In the absence of opposition parties, cultural activities become the only available form of opposition.

The physical terror and psychic coercion of The Purge seem necessary to an official establishment of this type. For its very basis is a fusion of the special skills of cultural workmen and special tests of political loyalty, and it is dominated by a political management of status, reputation, and public shaming. Suddenly the official line changes; then the only innocent man is the man who has accomplished nothing—because he is too young or because he has quietly withdrawn from work. Since any mature and active cultural workman has a quotable past, the very history of the intelligensia leaves in its wake a cumulative guilt. The disgraced man's past is publicly turned against him: His one opportunity is to out-compete those who vilify him—he must vilify his own past and his own work. Such self-accusation and recanting may be an expedient adjustment to authority, or a genuine reversal of values. To understand which it is in any given case one must realize the totality of allegiance to The Party, and one must think in terms of traumas, and of activities well known in the religious sphere as penance and conversion.

In the Soviet bloc, the cultural apparatus is established by an authority that *post-dates* capitalism: An official apparatus of psychic domination, it is quite fully a part of political authority.

In the leading nations of Western Europe, the cultural apparatus is established out of a tradition that *pre-dates* capitalism: In it the authority of tradition and the prestige of culture have been intricately joined.

Both cultural tradition and political authority are involved in any establishment of culture, but in the United States the cultural apparatus is established in a third way. Above all, culture is part of an ascendant capitalist economy, and this economy is now in a condition of seemingly permanent war. Insofar as cultural activities are established, they are established commercially or militarily.

This, I believe, is the signal fact about the culture and politics of the United States today. Cultural activities, on the one hand, tend to become a commercial part of an overdeveloped capitalist economy, or, on the other, an official part of the Science Machine of the Garrison State. If cultural activities are not felt to be relevant to these points of concern, they carry little or no public consequence.

Everywhere today, the Science Machine and the Mass Culture Industry are intricate and fascinating developments; in twentieth-century America, they are indispensable to the understanding of the cultural apparatus. Science—historically seated in universities and connected rather informally with private industry—has now become officially established, in, of, for, and by the military order. Private corporations and military agencies together support and guide the major scientific activities that go on in America.

Many an American intellectual, artist, scientist is becoming an important adjunct of a very peculiar kind of economy. His work is a business, but his business is with idea, image, technique. He is caught up, first, in the shift in economic emphasis from production to distribution, and along with this, the joining of the struggle for exist-

ence with the merchandised panic for status. Mass culture
in all its ramifications for cultural life, and for the nature
of the overdeveloped seciety itself, rests upon the ascendancy of the commercial distributor. Mass culture in the
United States is essentially commercial culture.

Many cultural workmen are also caught up in the general shift by which art, science and learning are brought
into subordinate relation to the dominant institutions of
capitalist economy and nationalist state.

They are at the intersection of these two developments,
and their dual involvement in them explains the major divisions among them and the enriched muddle of ideals they
variously profess; the insecurity they often feel about the
practice of their crafts, their generally low social prestige
and relative income, and their emulation of the style of the
businessman.

The virtual dominance of commercial culture is the immediate ground of America's cultural scope, confusion,
banality, excitement, sterility. In this overdeveloped society, the mass production, the mass sale, the mass consumption of goods has became The Fetish of both work
and leisure. The pervasive mechanisms of the market have
indeed penetrated every feature of life—including art, science and learning—and made them subject to the pecuniary evaluation. In a word, what has happened in the last
two centuries to work in general is now rapidly happening
to artistic, scientific and intellectual endeavor: now these
too become part of society as a set of bureaucracies and
as a great salesroom.

The cultural workman has little control over the means
of distribution of which he becomes a part. The distributor—along with his market researcher—"establishes a
market" and monopolizes access to it. Then he claims to
"know what they want." The orders he gives, even to the
free-lance, become more explicit and detailed. The price
he offers may be quite high—perhaps too high, he comes
to think, and perhaps he is right. So he begins to hire and
in varying degree to manage a stable of cultural workmen.
Those who thus allow themselves to be managed by the
mass distributor are selected, and in time formed, in such
ways as to be altogether proficient, but not quite compelling

in their attractions. Accordingly, the search goes on for "fresh ideas," for exciting notions, for more luring models; in brief: for the innovator. But in the meantime, back at the studio, the laboratory, the research bureau, the writer's factory—the distributor manages many producers who become rank-and-file workmen of the commercially established cultural apparatus.

There is increasing bureaucracy but also there is the frenzy for new fashions. In this situation, the cultural workman tends to become either a commercial hack or a commercial star. By The Star, I refer to a person whose productions are so much in demand that, to some extent at least, he is able to use distributors as his adjuncts. This role has its own conditions and its own perils: The Star tends to be culturally trapped by his own success. He has painted this sort of thing and he gets $5000 a throw for it. However affluent, he often becomes culturally bored by this style and wants to explore another. But often he cannot: he is used to the $5000 a throw and there is demand for "his style." As a leader of fashions he is himself subject to fashion. Moreover, his success as a star depends upon his "playing the market:" he is not in any educative interplay with publics that support his development. By virtue of his success, The Star too becomes a marketeer.

Some cultural workmen of course do remain independent. Perhaps three or four men actually earn a living in the wealthy United States merely by composing serious music; perhaps twenty-five or so, merely by writing serious novels. But generally the star system tends to kill off the chance of the cultural workman to be a worthy and independent craftsman. One is a smash-hit or one is among the failures; one is a best-seller or one is among the hacks and the failures; one is either absolutely tops or one is just nothing at all.

## IX

Behind these developments, there is the signal fact that between the Jeffersonian era and World War II the United States has not contained any enduring and nationally respected establishment, academy, professoriate. Any such zone of semiofficial cultural prestige that has existed has been publicly unimportant and transient. There have been no recognized centers of cultural certification and judgment. No continuous upholders of standards of taste and cultivation have held publicly recognized positions. Certainly the cultural producer as such has not been regularly among The Representative Men of the Nation. No cultural establishments of the European type have existed in the United States.

(i) Underlying these facts is the unopposed ascendency of capitalism and liberalism. The bourgeoisie from its national beginnings has been unhampered by feudal power and prestige—by any pre-capitalist strata or powers or institutions. Accordingly, its members have easily monopolized both social prestige and political power as they have created and occupied the top positions of the class structure.

(ii) The very rich in America have not been notable as a self-cultivating elite. There have been no strata to which this bourgeoisie might have been assimilated or with which it might trade class for status, and with status, "culture." In the status medley which the very rich of America have created, prestige has not been gained in the self-disciplined ways of cultural production and expert consumption. No nationally significant class of rentier gentlemen or county gentry sat in the nineteenth century countryside writing books, plays, histories, or painting pictures; nor, after the early days of the Republic, have American politicians been prone—as the French are said to be—to literary production. Even their own utterances are typically shaped by hired ghosts. Neither the very rich nor the politically powerful have generally been a durable and central public for live artists and intellectuals. Their sons have become lawyers, not sculptors; graduates of business schools, not writers; and these sons, the daughters of the very rich have married.

(iii) All this stands in contrast to the rise of the European bourgeoisie. In Europe, to gain mere economic position has not been also to gain prestige and power. In Europe, the pomp of state, the dignity of church, the honor of violence—*and* the halo of cultural sensibility—have

rested upon feudal powers, which have monopolized strategic positions of authority—*and* of culture. Only slowly
and after much struggle have the sons of the bourgeoisie
come to rise alongside these strata, and in the course of
generations to displace them. In its struggle, the bourgeosie
was itself transformed; to some extent it was made over
in the honorific ways of pre-capitalistic kinds of cultural
sensibilities and political opinion.

Upon the American bourgeoisie—continuously predominant in wealth, power, and prestige—upon this bourgeoisie, as patron and as public, cultural workmen have
been conspicuously dependent. It is the businessman who
has established and run colleges and universities, the libraries and museums. And cultural workmen themselves
have often felt considerable gratitude towards the "men
who have produced" the "men who have met payrolls."
The prestige of the businessman has been aided by his cultural philanthropy—although perhaps only in a rather minor way: He has not needed any such prop. He has gained
prestige and honor on the basis of his claimed merit of
function; and functional merit has had to do with the
building of businesses, which have not needed any cultural halo.

The capitalist producer has been felt to possess and even
to create the ascendant American values: usefulness and
efficiency. Even the most independent cultural critics have
honored these same values. America's foremost critic in
the period of America's most deep-going criticism—Thorstein Veblen in the Progressive Era—assumed these values
as indubitable. He was opposed to the power of business
precisely because he felt that businessmen did not truly
serve these values, but rather those of waste and idleness.
In short, Joseph Schumpeter's notion that under capitalism intellectuals generally tend to erode its foundations—
that they inevitably become critics of consequence—does
not generally hold true of the United States.

## X

In the short time at our disposal, I cannot qualify as I
should like to do these charcoal sketches of the relations

of culture and politics. Yet in concluding the present lecture, I should like to suggest to you that it is just the sort of establishment that Europe *has* known that many American intellectuals (as well as sophisticated circles of the ruling elite) want very much to bring about in the United States. I do not believe that they will make it—any more than I believe that these kinds of establishments prevail in Europe. For Europe too is increasingly subject to those tendencies which now affect all cultural establishments as they enter The Fourth Epoch. The form toward which they now drift is more pronounced, even flamboyant, on the one hand, in the USSR, and on the other, in the USA.

The world polarity of cultural establishments is now between the USA and the USSR—the one commercial, the other political, both military and both moving away from the ideals of Stage Two. These two now seem the cultural models of the future. In the meantime, between them lies Western Europe—whose types of establishment are grievously declining and the underdeveloped countries—whose cultural apparatus, being inchoate, is not yet established in any of the three major historical types.

# 2

# LANGUAGE, LOGIC AND CULTURE

Problems of a sociology of knowledge arise when certain conceptions and findings of the cultural sciences are confronted by theories of knowing and methodology. Awareness of the social and economic factors operative in the reflective process has arisen within American sociology as peripheral notations on specific researches and as implicit in psychology when sociologically approached.[1] However, the relevant sociological materials, particularly as they bear on the nature of mind and language, are as yet unexploited by those interested in sociological theories of knowledge and in the cultural careers of ideas.

Sociologies of knowledge have found elaborate statement in other contexts,[2] but American social scientists have not assimilated or developed theories adequate to carry on historical reconstructions of thought from a cultural standpoint, nor have they attempted systematically to state the implications of such an attempt for methodology and theories of reflection.[3] Despite this lack of postulational framework and empirical hypotheses, assumed and unanalyzed "answers" to certain theoretical questions are operative in the minds of many sociologists. It is the

[1] Cf. L. Wirth's preface to Karl Mannheim's *Ideology and Utopia*, xxi, New York, 1936.

[2] The German *Wissenssoziologie* and the French sociological theories of knowledge. For a reasonably adequate bibliography of the German materials, see Wirth-Shils' translation of Mannheim, *op. cit.*, 281 ff. For French, see reviews and monographs in *L'Année Sociologique*, vols. I-XII.

[3] Cf. however, H. Becker's brief, substantive presentations scattered through his and H. E. Barnes' *Social Thought from Lore to Science*, New York, 1938.

business of the theorist to articulate such assumptions as precise hypotheses and to examine them critically.

There are two viewpoints from which the social determination of mentality and ideas may be regarded. These are *historical* and *socio-psychological*. Without a formulation of mind which permits social determinants a role in reflection, assertions on the larger historical level carry less intellectual weight. A theory of mind is needed which conceives social factors as intrinsic to mentality. We may view the problems of a sociology of knowledge on a historical level; but we must also view our generic hypothesis on the socio-psychological level.

One chief defect of extant sociologies of knowledge is that they lack understanding and clear-cut formulations of the *terms* with which they would connect mind and other societal factors. This deficiency is, in turn, rooted in a failure to recognize the psychological problems arising from the acceptance of the generic hypothesis.

Sidney Hook has recently contended that it is not difficult to point out "historical relations" of "rationalism" with "conservatism;" "empiricism" with "liberalistic" political orientations.[4] It is not difficult to impute historical relations, but what exactly is a historical relation? Although doctrines, like other complexes in culture, have a sort of existence apart from any one or two biological organisms, we must admit that ultimately reflection (a process whereby beliefs come to be doubted, discarded, or reformulated) has its seat in a minded organism and is a symbolic performance by it. Perhaps any one individual does not seriously dent a given system of belief. Perhaps in the long historical trends of belief, the drift of thought is, as Lecky believed,[5] determined more by minute changes effected by hundreds of thinkers than by a dozen "great" ones. Nevertheless, we must ask for the *modus operandi* of these rejections, reformulations, and acceptances. The rounding out of a systematic sociological theory of knowledge involves our handling that question in socio-psychological categories. Granted that changes in culture influence trends

[4] *Social Frontier,* vol. VI, no. 32, Feb. 1938.
[5] *History of the Rise and Influence of Rationalism in Europe* (1919 edition), vol. I, 15-16; vol. II, 100-101.

in intellectual work and belief we must ask *how* such influences are exerted. That is a question to be answered by a social psychology, a psychology which studies the impact of social structures and objects, of class biases, and technological changes upon the mind of an organism.

Strictly speaking, the psychological is not "the personal." The individual is not the point of departure for contemporary social psychology; the "mental" is not understood apart from definitely social items. At present, the sociology of knowledge needs a more adequate psychological base than has been given it. Many sociologists of knowledge disregard psychological considerations as "irrelevant to a sociological setting" of intellectual patterns. The sociopsychological "aspect of the problem is either altogether disregarded or is disguised in terms which baffle empirical investigation."[6] We find this deficiency exhibited by Marxists. From psychological and epistemological standpoints, such general terms as are used by Marxists to relate "ideas" and societal factors (*e.g.,* "reflect," "mold," "determine," "penetrate") are not incisive; question-begging, they hide inadequate analysis. Marxists have not translated their connective terms into sound and unambiguous psychological categories.[7] Much criticism of their numerous attempts at ideological analysis are ground in the implicit assumption, on the part of both Marxists and their critics, of traditional, individualistic theories of mind. What is needed is a concept of mind which incorporates social processes as intrinsic to mental operations.

This lack of psychological formulation is by no means confined to Marxism. More sophisticated sociologies of knowledge contain the same deficiency. Mannheim, *e.g.,*

[6] Hans Speier, "The Social Determination of Ideas," gives a brief indication of the need for handling the problems of a sociology of knowledge on a psychological level. *Social Research,* May 1938.

[7] K. Marx, *Capital,* vol. I, 25, 84-85, and Introduction to *Critique of Political Economy.* V. Lenin, *Materialism and Empirio-Criticism,* p. 300. Engels, *Feuerbach,* pp. 73, 96, 177. Also, M. M. Bober, *Marx's Interpretation of History,* 298. More recently, see Pannecoek's psychologically feeble attempt to relate "thought" and social factors in *Science and Society,* vol. I, Summer 1937, 445. For positive contributions of Marxism to the sociology of knowledge, cf. Mannheim, *op. cit.,* 51, 66-67, 69, 110, 112, 248, 278.

covers up his psychological inadequacy with a vague and unanalyzed "collective unconsciousness."[8] The psychological difficulties attendant upon such a conception are evidently not recognized.

Even if we grant that "thought" in some manner involves social processes, the thought is, nevertheless, a lingual performance of an individual thinker. We cannot "functionalize" reflection in social terms by postulating a "collective subject;"[9] nor can we avoid the fact that there is no "group mind" by conveniently using implicit conceptions of "collective subjects." We can socially functionalize a given thinker's production only when we have made explicit, and systematically applied, a sound hypothesis of the specific socio-psychic mechanisms by which cultural determinants are operative. Without a thorough-going social theory of mind, there is real danger that research in the sociology of knowledge may become a set of mere historical enumerations and a calling of names. Only with such construction can we gain a clear and dynamic conception of the relations imputed between a thinker and his social context. Until we build a set of theoretically substantial hypotheses of socio-psychological nature, our research is likely to remain frustrated and our larger theoretical claims feeble. I wish to advance two such hypotheses.

The first is derived from the social statement of mind presented by G. H. Mead.[10] It is his concept of the "generalized other" which, with certain modification and extension, we may employ to show how societal processes enter as determinants into reflection.[11] The generalized other is the internalized audience with which the thinker converses: a focalized and abstracted organization of attitudes of those implicated in the social field of behavior and experience. The structure and contents of selected and subsequently selective social experiences imported into mind

[8] *Op. cit.*, 28, 30-48.

[9] Cf. von Schelting's review of Mannheim's *Ideology and Utopia*, *Amer. Sociol. Rev.*, Feb. 1936, 665.

[10] *Mind, Self, and Society*. Chicago, 1934. Also see bibliography of Mead's articles.

[11] *Op. cit.*, 155 ff.

constitute the generalized other with which the thinker converses and which is socially limited and limiting.[12]

Thinking follows the pattern of conversation. It is a give and take. It is an interplay of meanings. The audience conditions the talker; the other conditions the thinker and the outcome of their interaction is a function of both interactants. From the standpoint of the thinker, the socialization of his thought is coincidental with its revision. The social and intellectual habits and character of the audience, as elements in this interaction, condition the statement of the thinker and the fixation of beliefs evolving from that interplay. Thought is not an interaction as between two impenetrable atoms; it is conversational and dynamic; *i.e.,* the elements involved interpenetrate and modify the existence and status of one another. Imported into mind, this symbolic interplay constitutes the structure of mentality.

It is conversing with this internalized organization of collective attitudes that ideas are logically, *i.e.,* implicitly, "tested." Here they meet recalcitrance and rejection, reformulation and acceptance. Reasoning, as C. S. Peirce has indicated,[13] involves deliberate approval of one's reasoning. One operates logically (applies standardized critiques) upon propositions and arguments (his own included) from the standpoint of a generalized other. It is from this socially constituted viewpoint that one approves or disapproves of given arguments as logical or illogical, valid or invalid.

No individual can be logical unless there be agreement among the members of his universe of discourse as to the validity of some general conception of good reasoning. Deliberate logical approval is based upon comparison of the argument approved with some common idea of how

[12] My conception of the generalized other differs from Mead's in one respect crucial to its usage in the sociology of knowledge: I do not believe (as Mead does, *op. cit.,* 154) that the generalized other incorporates "the whole society," but rather that it stands for selected societal segments. Mead's statements regarding this point are, I believe, functions of an inadequate theory of society and of certain democratic persuasions. These are not, however, logically necessary to the general outline of his social theory of mind.

[13] *Collected Papers of Charles Peirce,* vol. II, 108, Cambridge, Mass., 1934.

good argument should appear. The "laws of logic" impose a restriction upon assertion and argument. They are the rules we must follow if we would socialize our thought.[14] They are not arrived at intuitively, nor are they *given,* "innate within the mind." They are not to be "taken as formulating generic characters of existences outside of inquiry or the traits of all possible being." Rather, the principles of logic are "the rules by means of which the meanings of our terms are explicated . . . the principles of logic are . . . conventional without being arbitrary . . . they are shaped and selected by the instrumental character of discourse, by the goals of inquiry and discourse."[15]

There is evidence that the so-called laws of proof may be merely the conventional abstract rules governing what are accepted as valid conversational extensions. What we call illogicality is similar to immorality in that both are deviations from norms. We know that such thought-ways change.[16] Arguments which in the discourse of one group

[14] Jean Piaget's experiments on children substantiate such a viewpoint. Cf. *Language and Thought of the Child,* New York, 1926; *Judgment and Reasoning in the Child,* New York, 1928. For Durkheim's view of the rise of logical categories from social forms, see his and Mauss' monograph in *L'Année Sociologique,* vol. VI, Paris, 1903, 1-72; also M. Granet's Durkheimian analysis of non-Aristotelian Chinese categories, in *La Pensée Chinoise.* Paris, 1934.

[15] Ernest Nagel, "Some Theses in the Philosophy of Logic," *Phil. of Sci.,* Jan. 1938; 49-50. Nagel notes "a marked tendency" in pure logic towards the view "that the subject matter of logic is discourse." The linguistic view of logic I believe eminently sound, but with a growing recognition of the social and behaviorial character of language, it needs to be set within a social context. From another angle, I should ask of Nagel that some order be found among these "shifts" in the "goals of inquiry and discourse" which shape and select the principles of logic. Such an attempt would require a sociological implementation. An attempt to isolate the social determinants of "goals of inquiry and discourse" would not only be in line with the program of the sociology of knowledge but, if successful, would strengthen Nagel's thesis that the principles of logic are "conventional without being arbitrary."

[16] Bogoslovsky in his *Technique of Controversy,* New York, 1928, has shown that, *e.g.,* John Dewey's writings reveal grave logical fallacies if judged by the rules of classical logic. He attempts to delineate a new set of logical principles based on an analysis of Dewey's actual modes of thought. Bogoslovsky is tabulating new rules that have come into being. No logician can "make up" a system of logic. Like coins, they are genuine by virtue of their dominant currency.

or epoch are accepted as valid, in other times and conversations are not so received.[17] That which was long meditated upon is now brushed aside as illogical. Problems set by one logic are, with a change in interests, outgrown, not solved.[18] The rules of the game change with a shift in interests, and we must accept the dominant rules if we would make an impress upon the profile of thought. Our logical apparatus is formulated by the rebuffs and approvals received from the audiences of our thought. When we converse with ourselves in thought, a generalized other as the carrier of a socially derived logical apparatus restricts and governs the directions of that thought. Although not always the ultimate critique, logical rules serve as an ultimatum for most ideas. Often on this basis are selected out those ideas which will not be spoken, but forgotten; those that will not be experimentally applied, but discarded as incipient hypotheses. In general, conformity to current principles of logic is a necessary condition for the acceptance and diffusion of ideas. This is true because principles of logic are the abstracted statements of social rules derived from the dominant diffusion patterns of ideas. In attempting to implement the socialization of our interests and thought, we acquire and utilize a socially derived logical apparatus. Within the inner forum of reflection, the generalized other functions as a socially derived mechanism through which logical evaluation operates.

Social habits are not only overt and social actions which recur,—they leave residues, "apperceptive masses," which conform to dominant and recurring activities and are built by them. In human communities, such dominant fields of behavior have implications in terms of systems of value. The interest-evaluative implication of a social structure has been termed its ethos.[19] Dominant activities (*e.g.*, occupations) determine and sustain modes of satisfaction, mark definitions of value preference; embodied in language, they make perception discriminatory. The stuff of

[17] Cf. Lecky, *op. cit.*, vol. II, 100-101, etc. Also Sumner's *Folkways*, 33, 174-175, 193-195, 225.
[18] Cf. Dewey's article in *Creative Intelligence*, 3. New York, 1917.
[19] Cf. H. Speier's usage of ethos, *op. cit.*, 196.

ideas is not merely sensory experiences, but meanings which have back of them collective habits.

When a system of social actions actually "breaks down" in "social conflict," *some* thinkers call this a "social problem," but not all "conflicts" of all groups are termed problematic by all thinkers. "Social problems" are not universally recognized as problematic, as occasions for thought: there is no *"the* economic problem." The "direction" of organized social action which sustains specific values conditions what constitutes a problem. The value-interest implications of a social structure are the guiding threads along which problems emerge. Problems are relative to an ethos.[20]

The thinker does not often play an immediate active role in large social strata or institutional frames, and hence, does not build through direct action a generic pattern of habit and value which would constitute a selective detector of "problems," a background of mind. Nevertheless, there are two other modes by which he may come to be influenced by such residues. He may intentionally identify himself with an ethos[21] rooted in a structure of social habits, thus vicariously participating in and articulating a particular social segment's interests; or, if his thought is appreciatively diffused, members of his audience will possess mental characteristics built by direct social action. It is often through such audiences that a thinker is culturally claimed, because, when his doctrine and his *further* thought gravitate toward a responsive audience it means that he has

[20] Cf. T. Parson's presentation of Max Weber's notion of *Wertbeziehung,* ("relevance to value"), as a methodological concern, *i.e.,* as an organizing principle within empirical research, *The Structure of Social Action,* 593, 601 ff., New York, 1938.

[21] This "special pleading" is the most usual "connection" imputed —often it is considered exhaustive. (*E.g.,* S. Hook: *Marxist Quarterly,* vol. I, 454). Undoubtedly many social doctrines are definitively affected by their originator's or publicist's interest in intentionally aiding or hindering the perpetuation of a social movement or institution; but I would not confine the connection between thought and other cultural items to a thinker's conscious "interest" or the conscious utilization of a doctrine as a "social forensic" by any professional talker. If this were the only connection to be ascertained, then our generic hypothesis would be seriously weakened. We should have to impute to the thinker the attributes of the "eco-

responded (whether he is at first aware of it or not) to
"problems" defined by the activities and values of his audience. A reflective response to a social environment, assimilated by its members, is always related to the "needs"
of that particular environment. Defined operationally (externally and behaviorially), that environment is the largely
unreflective behavior patterns of a specific set of groups,
*e.g.,* a class, or a set of institutions. Viewed internally, as
a function or field of mind, we have contended for this environment's influence on thought, because such specific
fields of social behavior develop and sustain organized sets
of attitudes; when internalized, these constitute a thinker's
generalized other which functions as that with and against
which he carries on his internal conversation. It is by virtue of this essentially social structure of mind that sociological factors influence the fixation not only of the evaluative but also of the intellectual. On the one hand, the generalized other is an element involved in the functioning and
conditioning of the outcome of the reflective processes; it
is the seat of a logical apparatus; on the other hand, it is
constituted by the organized attitudinal implicates of cultural forms, by institutional ethos, and by the behavior
of economic classes.

When confronted with a system of thought, or the reasoned assertions of a thinker, our sociological perspective
toward knowledge attempts to "locate" a set of determinants within contemporaneous fields of societal values. We
try to locate the thinker with reference to his assimilated
portion of culture, to delineate the cultural influences in
his thought and the influences (if any) of his thought upon
cultural changes.

---

nomic man," *i.e.,* knowing what are his social interests and thinking
accordingly. Moreover, the connection stated merely in terms of
"interest" begs the major question; it tells us nothing as to exactly
*how* such "social interests" climb into thinking, and this is what we
must explain. Without such an explanation, the imputation of interest connotes that the relationship occurs "rationally," within the
mind of the thinker, within his conscious intellectual and social
intentions. If the sociology of knowledge is to be psychologically
limited to this economic man theory of the thinker, we had all better reduce our expectations of it, both as theory and as an integrating viewpoint for cultural reconstruction of intellectual history.

In an attempt to outline approaches to this problem, we now take another angle of departure from which we cast a hypothesis and a methodology. We might conceive the following set of remarks as a formulation of another socio-psychological "mechanism" connecting thinking with societal patterns. We construct it from a conjunction of the social dimensions of language with the fundamental role of language in thought. By approaching the interrelatedness of sociality and reflection, our perspective enables us to view as a "unit" matters which have traditionally been handled on three levels of theory. Between them are two "gaps" which we "fill." First, we consider the nature of language and meaning in terms of social behavior. Second, we consider the nature of reflection in terms of meaning and language.

From a concept of language as an "expression of antecedent ideas," the psychologists have gravitated toward a functional conception of language as a mediator of human behavior. From the isolated grammatical and philological field ethnologists have moved to the social-behavioral setting of linguistic materials.[22] Given additional cogency by their convergence, both these movements proceed toward the notion that the meanings of symbols are defined and redefined by socially co-ordinated actions. The function of words is the mediation of social behavior, and their meanings are dependent upon this social and behavioral function. Semantical changes are surrogates and foci of cultural conflicts and group behavior. Because language functions in the organization and control of behavior patterns, these patterns are determinants of the meanings in a language. Words carry meanings by virtue of dominant interpretations placed upon them by social behavior. Interpretations or meanings spring from the habitual modes of behavior which pivot upon symbols. Such social patterns of behavior constitute the meanings of the symbols. Non-linguistic behaviors are guided or manipulated by linguistic

[22] For an excellent summary of these movements' literature, see E. Esper's article "Language" in *Handbook for Social Psychology,* ed. Carl Murchison. Worcester, Mass. 1934. See his comments on Grace DeLaguna and B. Malinowski.

materials, and language is the ubiquitous string in the web of patterned human behavior.

We can view language functionally as a system of social control. A symbol, a recurrent language form, gains its status as a symbol, an event with meaning, because it produces a similar response from both the utterer and the hearer.[23] Communication must set up common modes of response in order to be communication; the meaning of language is the common social behavior evoked by it. Symbols are the "directing pivots" of social behaviors. They are also the indispensable condition of human mentality. The meanings of words are formed and sustained by the interactions of human collectivities, and thought is the manipulation of such meanings. Mind is the interplay of the organism with social situations mediated by symbols. The patterns of social behavior with their "cultural drifts," values, and political orientations extend a control over thought by means of language. It is only by utilizing the symbols common to his group that a thinker can think and communicate. Language, socially built and maintained, embodies implicit exhortations and social evaluations.[24] By acquiring the categories of a language, we acquire the structured "ways" of a group, and along with the language, the value-implicates of those "ways." Our behavior and perception, our logic and thought, come within the control of a system of language. Along with language, we acquire a set of social norms and values. A vocabulary is not merely a string of words; immanent within it are societal textures—institutional and political coordinates. Back of a vocabulary lie sets of collective action.

No thinker utilizes the total vocabulary afforded by his

[23] Cf. Mead, *op. cit.,* sec. II.

[24] K. Burke puts it thus: "Speech takes its shape from the fact that it is used by people acting together. It is an adjunct of action—and thus naturally contains the elements of exhortation and threat which stimulate action and give it direction. It thus tends naturally towards the use of implicit moral weightings: the names for things and operations smuggle in connotations of good and bad—a noun tends to carry with it a kind of invisible adjective, and a verb an invisible adverb." *Permanence and Change,* 243-244. Cf. also Marcel Granet, *op. cit.,* for discussion of the heavy value-dimension in Chinese vocabularies and syntax.

societal context nor is he limited to it. We acquire the systematic vocabularies of intellectual traditions built by other thinkers from diverse cultures. We build an intellectual orientation by gathering for ourselves a dictionary of interrelated terms. As we "grow" intellectually, we selectively build new linguistic habits. Like other habits, linguistic or conceptual ones are built on previous residues. Prior linguistic and conceptual accomplishments are conditions for the acquisition of new habits of thought, new meanings. Thinking is the selection and manipulation of available symbolic material.

We may "locate" a thinker among political and social coordinates by ascertaining what words his functioning vocabulary contains and what nuances of meaning and value they embody. In studying vocabularies, we detect implicit evaluations and the collective patterns behind them,— "cues" for social behavior. A thinker's social and political "rationale" is exhibited in his choice and use of words. Vocabularies socially canalize thought.

We must recognize the priority of a system of meanings to a thinker. Thinking influences language very little, but thought, as Malinowski has indicated, "having to borrow from (social) action its tool, is largely influenced thereby."[25] No thinker can assign arbitrary meanings to his terms and be understood. Meaning is antecedently *given;* it is a collective "creation." In manipulating a set of socially given symbols, thought is itself manipulated. Symbols are impersonal and imperative determinants of thought because they manifest collective purposes and evaluations. New nuances of meaning which a thinker may give to words are, of course, socially significant in themselves;[26] but such "new" meanings must in their definition draw upon the meanings and organization of collectively established words in order that they may be understood, and they are conditioned thereby; and so is the acceptance and/or rejection of them by others.

Here, again, the thinker is "circumscribed" by his audience, because, in order to communicate, to be understood, he must "give" symbols such meanings that they

[25] "The Problem of Meaning in Primitive Languages," *op. cit.,* 498.
[26] Cf. Karl Mannheim, *op. cit.,* 74.

call out the same responses in his audience as they do in himself. The process of "externalizing" his thought in language is thus, by virtue of the commonness essential to meaning, under the control of the audience. Socialization is accompanied by revision of meaning. Seldom do identical interpretations obtain. Writings get reinterpreted as they are diffused across audiences with different nuances of meanings. We call the tendency to telescope (by variations of interpretation) the meaning of concepts into a given set of social habits, ethnocentricism of meaning.[27] Functionally, *i.e.,* as far as communication obtains, the reader is a factor determining what the thinker writes.

A symbol has a different meaning when interpreted by persons actualizing different cultures or strata within a culture. In facing problems incident to a translation from Chinese to English, I. A. Richards got "the impression that an unwritten and unelucidatable *tradition* accompanies and directs their interpretation," and that "this tradition is *by no means uniform.*"[28] We hold that this *tradition* which is *by no means uniform* is the linguistic reflex of the socially controlled behaviors from which a scholar is derived, which he "lives" (behaviorally and/or vicariously), or which constitutes the audience of his thought, or all three. These "esoteric determinants of meaning" are the logical interpretants,"[29] residues derived from the meaningful behavior of such constellations:

A block in social actions, *e.g.,* a class conflict, carries a reflex back into our communicative medium and hence into our thought. We then talk past one another. We interpret the "same symbol differently. Because the co-

---

[27] *E.g.,* approached with this "lead" in mind, the "diffusion pattern" of the Bible exhibits one reason for its continuance: its language is capable of being "strained" (reinterpreted) through the purposes and orientations implicitly contained in the languages of a great variety of cultural segments and milieux.

[28] *Mencius on the Mind,* 33. New York, 1932.

[29] The incipient theory of meaning found in C. S. Peirce is compatible with the sociological slant on meaning. I find in his work an added support for a belief in an intrinsic, controlling relation of social habits to reflection through meaning. For Peirce, "the ultimate meaning (logical interpretant) of a concept is a habit change." (*Collected Papers,* vol. V, paragraph 476.) Habits are, of course, socially acquired and transmitted.

ordinated social actions sustaining the meaning of a given symbol have broken down, the symbol does not call out the same response in members of one group that it does in another, and there is no genuine communication.

Richards detects in the Chinese thinking of Mencius' period a strong *dependence of conception upon social purpose*. Mencius' thought on man was governed by a social purpose, the "enforcement of a schema of conduct." The concepts which he utilized were good servants of the accepted moral and social order. The success of Richards' study leads us to consider tenable the hypothesis that *conceptions* and distinctions, including those of our philosophic and social jargon, are such as to "hide" factors from us in the interests of social purposes woven through various cultural patterns.

Different traditions of thinking have different distinctions in their vocabularies, and these differences are related to differences in other spheres of their respective cultural setting. The distinctions in Chinese thinking are quite different from those in Western thought. The Chinese, for example, did not set the subject over against the object, and hence had no "problem of knowledge." Nor did Chinese thought of this period separate psychology and physics into two separate studies. Richards suggests:

> The problems which for any one tradition are obtrusive—especially the more insoluble of them, and thus, it may seem, the more "important"—may often have arisen as a result of accident—grammatical or social. *(Op. cit., 3–5)*

The manner in which "lack" of distinctions in a language limits thought and the formulation of problems is aptly illustrated by Richards' analysis of the Chinese word for "aged." There is no distinction between age in the chronological sense and the sense of an ethical pattern toward those who are old. Consequently, Mencius cannot separate in his thinking a man's age and the reverence that is due him because of it. Here is a direct connection of a *mos,* embodied in language, with a limitation of thinking. Thinkers of Mencius' period do not "discuss or treat as open to discussion the rightness of paying respect to age as age."[30] Their language would not allow a definition of the

---

[30] I. A. Richards, *op. cit.,* 55-56.

problem. The employment of one word for both chronological age and the honorable pattern of behavior toward
old persons reflects and preserves the unquestioned appro-
priateness of the reverential conduct better than any separate terms could. Agreement with the *mos* or institution was
evoked by the very mentioning of the symbol around which
it was organized and which defined it in behavior. Chinese
thinking on this head is thus seen to operate within an unquestioned limit set by the language itself.

What if this *mos,* reverence to old age, were to change
radically? What if shortage of young men for warriors in
a long series of wars force the group to shift its respect to
"young warrior" roles? What would then happen to the
old concept now carrying dual meaning? It would become
ambiguous and eventually, split. Newly sanctioned social
habits force new meanings and changes in old meanings.
A distinction would be drawn which was not existent in
Mencius' thinking. Problems would result from the competing meanings where before an unquestioned belief had
reigned. Thus is reflection related in terms of meanings to
areas of conflicts and drifts within social orders.[31]

It is a necessary consequence of any unaccustomed perspective that matters traditionally, viewed disjunctively, be
considered conjunctively. I have presented certain coordinates for a sociological approach to reflection and knowledge, viewing conjointly sociality and mind, language and
social habit, the noetic and the cultural. Such contexts may
be said to operate as determinants in thought in the sense
that given social textures there will be present certain various and limited materials for assimilation; or, in the sense

[31] I am indebted to C. E. Ayres for indicating the similar instance
involved in the rise of the concept "capital." Since Aristotle, it was
agreed that money is obviously sterile. Hence, for "money" and
"wealth," the substitution of the equivocal "capital" *as a factor in
production.* The "capitalist fallacy" may be regarded as a continuation of the "mercantilist fallacy" which pivoted around the fluid
concept "wealth." It is significant that "capital" emerged in the
period and milieu in which bookkeeping underwent its great development. The ambivalence of "capital" represents in a business
culture a confusion of bookkeeping entries with things, machines.
As in Mencius' period, no one debated the differences between
*pecuniary* and *physical* capital. I am not implying that the classi-
cists' dual usage was deliberately cultivated as special pleading.

that thinkers programmatically identify themselves with an order of interests. I have analyzed the matter more deeply (1) by instituting the socio-psychological problem of the *modus operandi* of such determinations, and (2) by advancing and partially elaborating as hypotheses two connective mechanisms. It should be apparent that these formulations also provide research leads equipping attempts at concrete reconstructions of intellectual patterns from a cultural standpoint.

# 3

## SITUATED ACTIONS AND
## VOCABULARIES OF MOTIVE

The major reorientation of recent theory and observation in sociology of language emerged with the overthrow of the Wundtian notion that language has as its function the "expression" of prior elements within the individual. The postulate underlying modern study of language is the simple one that we must approach linguistic behavior, not by referring it to private states in individuals, but by observing its social function of coordinating diverse actions. Rather than expressing something which is prior and in the person, language is taken by other persons as an indicator of future actions.[1]

Within this perspective there are suggestions concerning problems of motivation. It is the purpose of this paper to outline an analytic model for the explanation of motives which is based on a sociological theory of language and a sociological psychology.[2]

As over against the inferential conception of motives as subjective "springs" of action, motives may be considered as typical vocabularies having ascertainable functions in delimited societal situations. Human actors do vocalize and impute motives to themselves and to others. To explain behavior by referring it to an inferred and abstract "motive" is one thing. To analyze the observable lingual mechanisms of motive imputation and avowal, as they function in conduct is quite another. Rather than fixed elements "in" an

[1] See C. Wright Mills, "Bibliographical Appendices," Section I, 4: "Sociology of Language" in *Contemporary Social Theory,* Ed. by Barnes, Becker & Becker, New York, 1940.
[2] See G. H. Mead, "Social Psychology as Counterpart of Physiological Psychology," *Psychol. Bul.,* VI: 401-408, 1909; Karl Mannheim, *Man and Society in an Age of Reconstruction,* New York, 1940; L. V. Wiese-Howard Becker, *Systematic Sociology,* part I, New York, 1932; J. Dewey, "All psychology is either biological or social psychology," *Psychol. Rev.,* vol. 24:276.

individual, motives are the terms with which interpretation of conduct *by social actors* proceeds. This imputation and avowal of motives by actors are social phenomena to be explained. The differing reasons men give for their actions are not themselves without reasons.

First, we must demarcate the general conditions under which such motive imputation and avowal seem to occur.[3] Next, we must give a characterization of motive in denotable terms and an explanatory paradigm of why certain motives are verbalized rather than others. Then, we must indicate mechanisms of the linkage of vocabularies of motive to systems of action. What we want is an analysis of the integrating, controlling, and specifying function a certain type of speech fulfills in socially situated actions.

The generic situation in which imputation and avowal of motives arise, involves, first, the *social* conduct of the (stated) programs of languaged creatures, *i.e.*, programs and actions oriented with reference to the actions and talk of others; second, the avowal and imputation of motives is concomitant with the speech form known as the "question." Situations back of questions typically involve *alternative* or *unexpected* programs or actions of which phases analytically denote "crises."[4] The question is distinguished in that it usually elicits another *verbal* action, not a motor response. The question is an element in *conversation*. Conversation may be concerned with the factual features of a situation as they are seen or believed to be or it may seek to integrate and promote a set of diverse social actions with reference to the situation and its normative pattern of expectations. It is in this latter assent and dissent phase of conversation that persuasive and dissuasive speech and vocabulary arise. For men live in immediate acts of ex-

[3] The importance of this initial task for research is clear. Most researches on the verbal level merely ask abstract questions of individuals, but if we can tentatively delimit the situations in which certain motives *may* be verbalized, we can use that delimitation in the construction of *situational* questions, and we shall be *testing* deductions from our theory.

[4] On the "question" and "conversation," see G. A. DeLaguna, *Speech: Its Function and Development,* 37 (and index), New Haven, 1927. For motives in crises, see J. M. Williams, *The Foundations of Social Science,* 435 ff, New York, 1920.

perience and their attentions are directed outside themselves until acts are in some way frustrated. It is then that awareness of self and of motive occur. The "question" is a lingual index of such conditions. The avowal and imputation of motives are features of such conversations as arise in "question" situations.

Motives are imputed or avowed as answers to questions interrupting acts or programs. Motives are words. Generically, to what do they refer? They do not denote any elements "in" individuals. They stand for anticipated situational consequences of questioned conduct. Intention or purpose (stated as a "program") *is* awareness of anticipated consequence; motives are names for consequential situations, and surrogates for actions leading to them. Behind questions are possible alternative actions with their terminal consequences. "Our introspective words for motives are rough, shorthand descriptions for certain typical patterns of discrepant and conflicting stimuli."[5]

The model of purposive conduct associated with Dewey's name may briefly be stated. Individuals confronted with "alternative acts" perform one or the other of them on the basis of the differential consequences which they anticipate. This nakedly utilitarian schema is inadequate because: (a) the "alternative acts" of *social* conduct "appear" most often in lingual form, as a question, stated by one's self or by another; (b) it is more adequate to say that individuals act in terms of anticipation of *named* consequences.

Among such names and in some technologically oriented lines of action there may appear such terms as "useful," "practical," "serviceable," etc., terms so "ultimate" to the pragmatists, and also to certain sectors of the American population in these delimited situations. However, there are other areas of population with different vocabularies of motives. The choice of lines of action is accompanied by representations, and selection among them, of their situational termini. Men discern situations with particular

[5] K. Burke, *Permanence and Change*, 45, New York, 1936. I am indebted to this book for several leads which are systematized into the present statement.

vocabularies, and it is in terms of some delimited vocabulary that they anticipate consequences of conduct.[6] Stable vocabularies of motives link anticipated consequences and specific actions. There is no need to invoke "psychological" terms like "desire" or "wish" as explanatory, since they themselves must be explained socially.[7] Anticipation is a subvocal or overt naming of terminal phases and/or social consequences of conduct. When an individual names consequences, he elicits the behaviors for which the name is an integrative cue. In a *social* situation, implicit in the names for consequences is the social dimension of motives. Through such vocabularies, types of societal controls operate. Also, the terms in which the question is asked often will contain both alternatives: "Love or Duty?", "Business or Pleasure?" Institutionally different situations have different *vocabularies of motive* appropriate to their respective behaviors.

This sociological conception of motives as relatively stable lingual phases of delimited situations is quite consistent with Mead's program to approach conduct socially and from the outside. It keeps clearly in mind that "both motives and actions very often originate not from within but from the situation in which individuals find themselves. . . ."[8] It translates the question of "why"[9] into a "how" that is answerable in terms of a situation and its typical vocabulary of motives, *i.e.,* those which conventionally accompany that type situation and function as cues and justifications for normative actions in it.

It has been indicated that the question is usually an index to the avowal and imputation of motives. Max Weber defines motive as a complex of meaning, which appears to the actor himself or to the observer to be an adequate

[6] See such experiments as C. N. Rexroad's "Verbalization in Multiple Choice Reactions," *Psychol. Rev.,* Vol. 33:458, 1926.

[7] Cf. J. Dewey, "Theory of Valuation," *Int. Ency. of Unified Science,* New York, 1939.

[8] K. Mannheim, *Man and Society,* 249, London, 1940.

[9] Conventionally answerable by reference to "subjective factors" within individuals. R. M. MacIver, "The Modes of the Question Why," *J. of Soc. Phil.,* April, 1940. Cf. also his "The Imputation of Motives," *Amer. J. of Sociol.,* July 1940.

ground for his conduct.[10] The aspect of motive which this conception grasps is its intrinsically social character. A satisfactory or adequate motive is one that satisfies the questioners of an act or program, whether it be the other's or the actor's. As a word, *a motive tends to be one which is to the actor and to the other members of a situation an unquestioned answer to questions concerning social and lingual conduct.* A stable motive is an ultimate in justificatory conversation. The words which in a type situation will fulfill this function are circumscribed by the vocabulary of motives acceptable for such situations. Motives are accepted justifications for present, future, or past programs or acts.

To term them justification is *not* to deny their efficacy. Often anticipations of acceptable justifications will control conduct. ("If I did this, what could I say? What would they say?") Decisions may be, wholly or in part, delimited by answers to such queries.

A man may begin an act for one motive. In the course of it, he may adopt an ancillary motive. This does not mean that the second apologetic motive is inefficacious. The vocalized expectation of an act, its "reason," is not only a mediating condition of the act but it is a proximate and controlling condition for which the term "cause" is not inappropriate. It may strengthen the act of the actor. It may win new allies for his act.

When they appeal to others involved in one's act, motives are strategies of action. In many social actions, others must agree, tacitly or explicitly. Thus, acts often will be abandoned if no reason can be found that others will accept. Diplomacy in choice of motive often controls the diplomat. Diplomatic choice of motive is part of the attempt to motivate acts for other members in a situation. Such pronounced motives undo snarls and integrate social actions. Such diplomacy does not necessarily imply intentional lies.

[10] *Wirtschaft und Gesellschaft,* 5, Tubingen, 1922, " 'Motiv' heisst ein Sinnzusammenhang, Welcher dem Handlenden selbst oder dem Beobachtenden als sinnhafter 'Grund' eines Verhaltens in dem Grade heissen, als die Beziehung seiner Bestandteile von uns nach den durchschnittlichen Denk- und Gefühlsgewohnheiten als typischer (wir pflegen in sagen: 'richtiger') Sinzusammenhang bejaht Wird."

It merely indicates that an appropriate vocabulary of motives will be utilized—that they are conditions for certain lines of conduct.[11]

When an agent vocalizes or imputes motives, he is not trying to *describe* his experienced social action. He is not merely stating "reasons." He is influencing others—and himself. Often he is finding new "reasons" which will mediate action. Thus, we need not treat an action as discrepant from "its" verbalization, for in many cases, the verbalization is a new act. In such cases, there is not a discrepancy between an act and "its" verbalization, but a difference between two disparate actions, motor-social and verbal.[12] This additional (or *"ex post facto"*) lingualization may involve appeal to a vocabulary of motives associated with a norm with which both members of the situation are in agreement. As such, it is an integrative factor in *future* phases of the original social action or in other acts. By resolving conflicts, motives are efficacious. Often, if "reasons" were not given, an act would not occur, nor would diverse actions be integrated. Motives are common grounds for mediated behaviors.

Perry summarily states the Freudian view of motives "as the view that the real motives of conduct are those which we are ashamed to admit either to ourselves or to others."[13] One can cover the facts by merely saying that scruples (*i.e., moral* vocabularies of motive) are often efficacious and that men will alter and deter their acts in terms of such motives. One of the components of a "generalized other," as a mechanism of societal control, is vocabularies of acceptable motives. For example, a business man joins the Rotary Club and proclaims its public-spirited vocabulary.[14] If this man cannot act out business conduct without so doing, it follows that this vocabulary of motives is an im-

---

[11] Of course, since motives are communicated, they may be lies; but, this must be proved. Verbalizations are not lies merely because they are socially efficacious. I am here concerned more with the social function of pronounced motives than with the sincerity of those pronouncing them.

[12] See F. Znaniecki, *Social Actions,* 30, New York, 1936.

[13] *General Theory of Value,* 292-293, New York, 1936.

[14] *Ibid.,* 392

portant factor in his behavior.[15] The long acting out of a role, with its appropriate motives, will often induce a man to become what at first he merely sought to appear. Shifts in the vocabularies of motive that are utilized later by an individual disclose an important aspect of various integrations of his actions with concomitantly various groups.

The motives actually used in justifying or criticizing an act definitely link it to situations, integrate one man's action with another's, and line up conduct with norms. The societally sustained motive-surrogates of situations are both constraints and inducements. It is a hypothesis worthy and capable of test that typal vocabularies of motives for different situations are significant determinants of conduct. As lingual segments of social action, motives orient actions by enabling discrimination between their objects. Adjectives such as "good," "pleasant," and "bad" promote action or deter it. When they constiute components of a vocabulary of motives, *i.e.,* are typical and relatively unquestioned accompaniments of typal situations, such words often function as directives and incentives by virtue of their being the judgments of others as anticipated by the actor. In this sense will be able to influence [himself or others]."[16] The "control" of others is not usually direct but rather through manipulations of a field of objects. We influence a man by naming his acts or imputing motives to them—or to "him." The motives accompanying institutions of war, *e.g.,* are not "the causes" of war, but they do promote continued integrated participation, and they vary from one war to the next. Working vocabularies of motive have careers that are woven through changing institutional fabrics.

Genetically, motives are imputed by others before they are avowed by self. The mother controls the child: "Do not do that, it is greedy." Not only does the child learn what to do, what not to do, but he is given standardized motives

---

[15] The "profits motive" of classical economics may be treated as an ideal-typical vocabulary of motives for delimited economic situations and behaviors. For late phases of monopolistic and regulated capitalism, this type requires modification; the profit and commercial vocabularies have acquired other ingredients. See N. R. Danielian's *AT & T,* New York, 1940, for a suggestive account of the *noneconomic* behavior and motives of business bureaucrats.

[16] *Social Actions,* 73.

which promote prescribed actions and dissuade those pro-
scribed. Along with rules and norms of action for various
situations, we learn vocabularies of motives appropriate to
them. These are the motives we shall use, since they are a
part of our language and components of our behavior.

The quest for "real motives" set over against "mere
rationalization" is often informed by a metaphysical view
that the "real" motives are in some way biological. Accompanying such quests for something more real and back of
rationalization is the view held by many sociologists that
language is an external manifestation or concomitant of
something prior, more genuine, and "deep" in the individual. "Real attitudes" versus "mere verbalization" or
"opinion" implies that at best we only infer from his language what "really" is the individual's attitude or motive.

Now what *could we possibly* so infer? Of precisely *what*
is verbalization symptomatic? We cannot *infer* physiological processes from lingual phenomena. All we can infer
and empirically check[17] is another verbalization of the
agent's which we believe was orienting and controlling
behavior at the time the act was performed. The only social
items that can "lie deeper" are other lingual forms.[18] The
"Real Attitude or Motive" is not something different in
kind from the verbalization of the "opinion." They turn
out to be only relatively and temporally different.

The phrase "unconscious motive" is also unfortunate.
All it can mean is that a motive is not explicitly vocalized,
but there is no need to infer unconscious motives from such
situations and then posit them in individuals as elements.
The phrase is informed by persistence of the unnecessary
and unsubstantiated notion that "all action has a motive,"
and it is promoted by the observation of gaps in the relatively frequent verbalization in everyday situations. The
facts to which this phrase is supposedly addressed are
covered by the statements that men do not always ex-

[17] Of course, we could infer or interpret constructs posited in
the individual, but these are not easily checked and they are not
explanatory.
[18] Which is not to say that, physiologically, there may not be
cramps in the stomach wall or adrenalin in the blood, etc., but the
character of the "relation" of such items to social action is quite
moot.

plicitly articulate motives, and that *all* actions do not pivot around language. I have already indicated the conditions under which motives are typically avowed and imputed.

Within the perspective under consideration, the verbalized motive is not used as an index of something in the individual but *as a basis of inference for a typal vocabulary of motives of a situated action.* When we ask for the "real attitude" rather than the "opinion," for the "real motive" rather than the "rationalization," all we can meaningfully be asking for is the controlling speech form which was incipiently or overtly presented in the performed act or series of acts. There is no way to plumb behind verbalization into an individual and directly check our motive-mongering, but there is an empirical way in which we can guide and limit, in given historical situations, investigations of motives. That is by the construction of typical vocabularies of motives that are extant in types of situations and actions. Imputation of motives may be controlled by reference to the typical constellation of motives which are observed to be societally linked with classes of situated actions. Some of the "real" motives that have been imputed to actors were not even known to them. As I see it, motives are circumscribed by the vocabulary of the actor. The only source for a terminology of motives is the vocabularies of motives actually and usually verbalized by actors in specific situations.

Individualistic, sexual, hedonistic, and pecuniary vocabularies of motives are apparently now dominant in many sections of twentieth-century urban America. Under such an ethos, verbalization of alternative conduct in these terms is least likely to be challenged among dominant groups. In this milieu, individuals are skeptical of Rockefeller's avowed religious motives for his business conduct because such motives are not *now* terms of the vocabulary conventionally and prominently accompanying situations of business enterprise. A medieval monk writes that he gave food to a poor but pretty woman because it was "for the glory of God and the eternal salvation of his soul." Why do we tend to question him and impute sexual motives? Because sex is an influential and widespread motive in our society and time. Religious vocabularies of explanation and of motives are now on the wane. In a society in which religious motives have been debunked on a rather wide scale, certain thinkers are skeptical of those who ubiquitously proclaim them. Religious motives have lapsed from selected portions of modern populations and other motives have become "ultimate" and operative. But from the monasteries of medieval Europe we have no evidence that religious vocabularies were not operative in many situations.

A labor leader says he performs a certain act because he wants to get higher standards of living for the workers. A business man says that this is rationalization, or a lie; that it is really because he wants more money for himself from the workers. A radical says a college professor will not engage in radical movements because he is afraid for his job, and besides, is a "reactionary." The college professor says it is because he just likes to find out how things work. What is reason for one man is rationalization for another. The variable is the accepted vocabulary of motives, the ultimates of discourse, of each man's dominant group about whose opinion he cares. *Determination of such groups, their location and character, would enable delimitation and methodological control of assignment of motives for specific acts.*

Stress on this idea will lead us to investigations of the compartmentalization of operative motives in personalities according to situation and the general types and conditions of vocabularies of motives in various types of societies. The motivational structures of individuals and the patterns of their purposes are relative to societal frames. We might, *e.g.*, study motives along stratified or occupational lines. Max Weber has observed:

> . . . that in a free society the motives which induce people to work vary with . . . different social classes. . . . There is normally a graduated scale of motives by which men from different social classes are driven to work. When a man changes ranks, he switches from one set of motives to another.[19]

The lingual ties which hold them together react on persons to constitute frameworks of disposition and motive. Re-

[19] Paraphrased by K. Mannheim, *op. cit.,* 316-317.

cently, Talcott Parsons has indicated, by reference to differences in actions in the professions and in business, that one cannot leap from "economic analysis to ultimate motivations; the institutional patterns *always* constitute one crucial element of the problem."[20] It is my suggestion that we may analyze, index, and guage this element by focusing upon those specific verbal appendages of variant institutionalized actions which have been referred to as vocabularies of motive.

In folk societies, the constellations of motives connected with various sectors of behavior would tend to be typically stable and remain associated only with their sector. In typically primary, sacred, and rural societies, the motives of persons would be regularly compartmentalized. Vocabularies of motives ordered to different situations stabilize and guide behavior and expectation of the reactions of others. In their appropriate situations, verbalized motives are not typically questioned.[21] In secondary, secular, and urban structures, varying and competing vocabularies of motives operate co-terminally and the situations to which they are appropriate are not clearly demarcated. Motives once unquestioned for defined situations are now questioned. Various motives can release similar acts in a given situation. Hence, variously situated persons are confused and guess which motive "activated" the person. Such questioning has resulted intellectually in such movements as

[20] "The Motivation of Economic Activities," 67, in C. W. M. Hart, *Essays in Sociology,* Toronto, 1940.

[21] Among the ethnologists, Ruth Benedict has come up to the edge of a genuinely sociological view of motivation. Her view remains vague because she has not seen clearly the identity of differing "motivations" in differing cultures with the varied extant and approved vocabularies of motive. "The intelligent understanding of the relation of the individual to his society . . . involves always the understanding of the types of human motivations and capacities capitalized in his society . . ." "Configurations of Culture in North America," *Amer. Anthrop.,* 25, Jan.-Mar. 1932; see also: *Patterns of Culture,* 242-243, Boston, 1935. She turns this observation into a quest for the unique "genius" of each culture and stops her research by words like "Apollonian." If she would attempt constructively to observe the vocabularies of motives which precipitate acts to perform, implement programs, and furnish approved motives for them in circumscribed situations, she would be better able to state precise problems and to answer them by further observation.

psychoanalysis with its dogma of rationalization and its systematic motive-mongering. Such intellectual phenomena are underlaid by split and conflicting sections of an individuated society which is characterized by the existence of competing vocabularies of motive. Intricate constellations of motives, for example, are components of business enterprise in America. Such patterns have encroached on the old style vocabulary of the virtuous relation of men and women: duty, love, kindness. Among certain classes, the romantic, virtuous, and pecuniary motives are confused. The asking of the question: "Marriage for love or money?" is significant, for the pecuniary is now a constant and almost ubiquitous motive, a common denominator of many others.[22]

Back of "mixed motives" and "motivational conflicts" are competing or discrepant situational patterns and their respective vocabularies of motive. With shifting and interstitial situations, each of several alternatives may belong to disparate systems of action which have differing vocabularies of motives appropriate to them. Such conflicts manifest vocabulary patterns that have overlapped in a marginal individual and are not easily compartmentalized in clearcut situations.

Besides giving promise of explaining an area of lingual and societal fact, a further advantage of this view of motives is that with it we should be able to give sociological accounts of other theories (terminologies) of motivation. This is a task for the sociology of knowledge. Here I can refer only to a few theories. I have already referred to the Freudian terminology of motives. It is apparent that these motives are those of an upper bourgeois patriarchal group with strong sexual and individualistic orientation. When introspecting on the couches of Freud, patients used the only vocabulary of motives they knew; Freud got his hunch and guided further talk. Mittenzwey has dealt with similar

[22] Also motives acceptably imputed and avowed for one system of action may be diffused into other domains and gradually come to be accepted by some as a comprehensive portrait of *the* motive of men. This happened in the case of the economic man and his motives.

points at length.[23] Widely diffused in a postwar epoch, psychoanalysis was never popular in France where control of sexual behavior is not puritanical.[24] To converted individuals who have become accustomed to the psychoanalytic terminology of motives, all others seem self-deceptive.[25]

In like manner, to many believers in Marxism's terminology of power, struggle, and economic motives, all others, including Freud's, are due to hypocrisy or ignorance. An individual who has assimilated thoroughly only business congeries of motives will attempt to apply these motives to all situations, home and wife included. It should be noted that the business terminology of motives has its intellectual articulation, even as psychoanalysis and Marxism have.

It is significant that since the Socratic period many "theories of motivation" have been linked with ethical and religious terminologies. Motive is that in man which leads him to do good or evil. Under the aegis of religious institutions, men use vocabularies of moral motives: they call acts and programs "good" and "bad," and impute these qualities to the soul. Such lingual behavior is part of the process of social control. Institutional practices and their vocabularies of motive exercise control over delimited ranges of possible situations. One could make a typal catalog of religious motives from widely read religious texts, and test its explanatory power in various denominations and sects.[26]

In many situations of contemporary America, conduct is controlled and integrated by *hedonistic* language. For large population sectors in certain situations, pleasure and pain are now unquestioned motives. For given periods and

[23] Kuno Mittenzwey, "Zur Sociologie der psychoanalystischer Erkenntnis," in Max Scheler, ed. *Versuche zu einer Sociologie des Wissens,* 365-375, Munich, 1924.

[24] This fact is interpreted by some as supporting Freudian theories. Nevertheless, it can be just as adequately grasped in the scheme here outlined.

[25] See K. Burke's acute discussion of Freud, *op. cit.,* Part I.

[26] Moral vocabularies deserve a special statement. Within the viewpoint herein outlined many snarls concerning "value-judgments," etc., can be cleared up.

societies, these situations should be empirically determined. Pleasure and pain should not be reified and imputed to human nature as underlying principles of all action. Note that hedonism as a psychological and an ethical doctrine gained impetus in the modern world at about the time when older moral-religious motives were being debunked and simply discarded by "middle-class" thinkers. Back of the hedonistic terminology lay an emergent social pattern and a new vocabulary of motives. The shift of unchallenged motives which gripped the communities of Europe was climaxed when, in reconciliation, the older religious and the hedonistic terminologies were identified: the "good" is the "pleasant." The conditioning situation was similar in the Hellenistic world with the hedonism of the Cyrenaics and Epicureans.

What is needed is to take all these *terminologies* of motive and locate them as *vocabularies* of motive in historic epochs and specified situations. Motives are of no value apart from the delimited societal situations for which they are the appropriate vocabularies. They must be situated. At best, socially unlocated *terminologies* of motives represent unfinished attempts to block out social areas of motive imputation and avowal. Motives vary in content and character with historical epochs and societal structures.

Rather than interpreting actions and language as external manifestations of subjective and deeper lying elements in individuals, the research task is the locating of particular types of action within typal frames of normative actions and socially situated clusters of motive. There is no explanatory value in subsuming various vocabularies of motives under some terminology or list. Such procedure merely confuses the task of explaining specific cases. The languages of situations as given must be considered a valuable portion of the data to be interpreted and related to their conditions. To simplify these vocabularies of motive into a socially abstracted terminology is to destroy the legitimate use of motive in the explanation of social actions.

# 4

# METHODOLOGICAL CONSEQUENCES
# OF THE SOCIOLOGY OF KNOWLEDGE

Many thinkers who have addressed themselves to the problem hold that the sociology of knowledge has no relevance for epistemology; that sociological investigations of inquiries have no consequences for norms of "truth and validity."[1] It is possible that the problem has been instituted in too narrow and yet in too gross a fashion. It is true that from knowledge of the "social position" of a

[1] Von Schelting's review of Mannheim's *Ideologie und Utopie* concludes: "The nonsense first begins when one believes that factual origin and social factors . . . in any way affect the value of ideas and conceptions thus originated, and especially the theoretic achievements" (*American Sociological Review*, I, No. 4, 634). Thus the relating of modes of thought to social-historical situations is conceived to carry with it no legitimate criticism or reformulation of "traditional" criteria of validity and truth (cf. T. Parsons' review of von Schelting's *Max Weber's Wissenschaftslehre* [*American Sociological Review*, I, No. 4 675 f]). Hans Speier, in recording a similar belief, speaks of the "encroachment of sociology upon a philosophic domain" and distinguishes between "promotive" and "theoretical" thought; the latter, conceived to have "truth" alone as its aim, apparently is not to be analyzed sociologically. With Grünwald, Speier says: "The validity of a judgment does not depend upon its genesis" (*American Sociological Review*, I, No. 4, 682, in reviewing E. Grünwald's *Das Problem einer Soziologie des Wissens;* cf. also Speier, "The Social Determination of Ideas," *Social Research*, V, 2). Thus, on epistemological grounds, von Schelting and Speier would limit the subject matter and implications of sociology of knowledge. R. K. Merton apparently accepts this negative position in "The Sociology of Knowledge," *Isis*, XXVII, No. 3 (75), 502-3. R. Bain and R. M. McIver, in papers read at Atlantic City, 1937, also indicate that they see no epistemological consequences of sociology of knowledge. G. H. Sabine takes this position in "Logic and Social Studies," *Philosophical Review*, XLVIII (1930), 173-74.

thinker one cannot deduce that his statements are true or false. In this crude sense sociology of knowledge is epistemologically inconsequential. But the matter is more complicated; the consequences are less direct.

An analytic examination of the negative positions concerning the epistemological consequences of sociology of knowledge and a resolution of the generic issue to which it is presumably addressed will advance obliquely and will include answers to the questions: (1) What is the generic character, derivation, and function of epistemologic forms, criteria of truth, or verificatory models? (2) Exactly wherein, at what junctures, and in what types of inquiry may social factors enter as determinants of knowledge?

It is apparent that "truth" and "objectivity" have application and meaning only in terms of some accepted model or system of verification. He who asserts the irrelevance of social conditions to the truthfulness of propositions ought to state the conditions upon which he conceives truthfulness actually to depend; he ought to specify exactly what it is in thinking that sociological factors cannot explain and upon which truth and validity do rest. Those who take the negative position must state what sort of things these criteria of truth and validity are, how they are derived, and how they function. There have been and are many ways of determining "truth" and "validity." Which specific criteria do they have in mind? The canons of Aristotelian logic?

Fritz Mauthner conducted a vigorous, if brief, sociological examination of these canons, suggesting that the diffusion of Indian grammatic studies and traditional cultural factors influenced their formulation and persistence.[2] Dewey has offered an empiraclly based theory which views this logic culturally as formulatory of the categories of speech prevalent in Greek society. He has also shown the operation of class and consequent social-esthetic factors in these criteria of validity, and the conditions under which they arose.[3]

[2] *Aristotle,* trans. C. D. Gordon (New York, 1907).
[3] *Experience and Nature* (New York, 1929), pp. 48-50, 87, 91-92. For references to and a statement of a sociological theory of the character and shifts in logics cf. my "Language, Logic, and Culture," *American Sociological Review,* IV (1939), 5.

The official and monopolistic paradigm of validation and truth accepted by medieval scholasticism was most certainly influenced by such factors as "the hierarchically centralized position of the intellectual elite with its political as well as intellectual power and its strict memory, faith, and dialectical norms of recruitment. Also by the fact that by virtue of this social organization for several centuries, the *logica utens* and the perception schema of each individual thinker were common to major sectors of the elite."[4]

Does the position under question invoke some more modern epistemological formulations, say those of the seventeenth and eighteenth centuries? Mannheim has soundly suggested that these were conditioned by the revolutionary status of the middle class, particularly by its "individualistic" character.[5] E. Conze has capably suggested the "Bourgeois Origins of Nominalism."[6] Certainly Descarte's protestant epistemology is open to sociological investigation. And the "utilitarian" and "experimental" canons of verification were certainly given impetus by the social ethos of seventeenth-century Puritanism.[7]

There have been and are diverse canons and criteria of validity and truth, and these criteria, upon which determinations of the truthfulness of propositions at any time depend, are themselves, in their persistence and change, legitimately open to social-historical relativization.[8] Moreover, we have at hand sociological theories concerning the character and emergence of certain of them. Criteria, or observational and verificatory models, are not transcendental. They are not drawn theoretically pure from a Greek heaven, although "choice" and usage of one set of them may be so justified. Nor are they part of an a priori, or in-

[4] C. Wright Mills, "Types of Rationality" (unpublished MS).

[5] K. Mannheim, *Ideology and Utopia,* trans. L. Wirth and E. Shils (New York, 1936); Part I, esp. pp. 24-28.

[6] *Marxist Quarterly,* I, 1; Nos. 2 and 3 contain discussions; see also P. P. Wiener, "Notes on Leibnitz's Conception of Logic and Its Historical Context," *Philosophical Review,* November, 1939.

[7] See R. K. Merton, *Science, Society, and Technology in Seventeenth-Century England* (Bruges, Belgium, 1938), and references therein.

[8] In addition to studies cited above, see Sorokin, who isolates and utilizes several different forms of validation as key items for study (*Social and Cultural Dynamics* [New York, 1937], Vol. II).

nate, equipment of "the mind" conceived to be intrinsically logical.[9]

On the contrary: the historical diversity of such models supports Dewey's view that they are generated by and are drawn from inquiries proceeding in given times and societies. Dewey's thesis concerning the character and historical occasion of logical and epistemological formulations[10] empirically accounts for the historical data. For forty years he has contended that the verificatory models upon which imputations of truthfulness rest are forms drawn from existent inquiries and have no meaning apart from inquiries: "Inquiry (logic *e.g.*) is the *causa cognoscendi* of logical forms, primary inquiry is itself *causa essendi* of the forms which inquiry into inquiry discloses."[11] Careful examination reveals no fundamental disagreement between Dewey's and Mannheim's conceptions of the generic character and derivation of epistemological forms.[12] "The indirect approach to truth," states Mannheim, "though social history will in the end be more fruitful than a direct logical approach." Mannheim's view overlaps the program that Dewey has pursued since 1903, when he turned from traditional concerns and squabbles over the ubiquitous relation of thought in general to reality at large, to a specific examination of the context, office, and outcome of a type of inquiry.[13]

In terms of the norms upon which ideas were accepted and rejected, C. S. Peirce analyzed four segments from

    [9] *E.g.,* Hans Speier speaks of "a property of human nature which enables man to search for truth" ("The Social Determination of Ideas," *op. cit.,* pp. 186, 193). For a contrary view see below; also A. Goldenweiser's *Robots or Gods?* (New York, 1931), p. 53.

    [10] *Logic; The Theory of Inquiry* (New York, 1938), chap. i; "Philosophy," *Research in Social Science,* ed. W. Gee, pp. 251 ff. See also H. Reichenbach, *Experience and Prediction* (Chicago, 1938), chap. i.

    [11] Dewey, *Logic,* p. 4.

    [12] *E.g.,* ". . . the representative modes of thought and their structure, from which a conception is built up as to the nature of truth in general . . . the concept of truth itself is dependent upon the already existing types of knowledge" (Mannheim, *op. cit.,* p. 262).

    [13] *Studies in Logical Theory* (Chicago, 1909), chaps. i-iv.

Western intellectual history.[14] His comparative and quasi-sociological work was preliminary to his own acceptance of an observational and verificatory model which he himself analyzed out and generalized from laboratory science. But not all thinkers, even philosophers, have gone about the "choice" of what verificatory model was to guide their thinking so consciously and thoroughly as Peirce. The "acceptance" (usage) and "rejection" of verificatory models by individual thinkers and by elites is another juncture at which extralogical, possibly sociological, factors may enter and be of consequence to the validity of an elite's thinking.

Mannheim's "total, absolute, and universal" type of "ideology" in which social position bears upon "the structure of consciousness in its totality," including form as well as content, may be interpreted to mean this social-historical relativization of a model of truth, or the influence of a "social position" upon "choice" of one model as over against another. Mannheim's remarks do not contradict this more explicit and analytic statement.

Those who contend that sociological investigations of thinking have no consequences for the truth or validity of that thinking misunderstand the source and character of the criteria upon which truth and validity are at any time dependent. They also overlook the fact that these criteria themselves and the selective acceptances and rejections of one or another of them by various elites are open to cultural influence and sociological investigation. Apparently they assume, without surveying the possibilities, that whatever validity depends upon, it cannot be examined empirically and sociologically. This view is underpinned by a blurred theory of knowledge and mind that prohibits analysis of those aspects or junctures in knowledge processes at which extra-logical factors may enter and be relevant to the truthfulness of results. For their attack is often against the view that the validity of a judgment depends upon its genesis,

[14] "Methods of Fixing Belief," *Collected Papers* (Cambridge, Mass., 1934), Vol. V, Book II, chap. iv, sec. v. Peirce's pragmatic papers contain very suggestive leads for the sociologist of knowledge (see esp. secs. ii and v).

and they are inclined to interpret "genesis" in terms of an individual's motivation for thought.[15]

It is true that the current "scientific" thought-model, drawn in the main from post-Renaissance physical inquiry, distinguishes between the truth of the results and the motives and social conditions of an inquiry. For this paradigm demands that assertions be verified by certain operations which do not depend upon the motives or social position of the assertor. Social position does not directly affect the truthfulness of propositions tested by this verificatory model. But social positions may well affect whether or not it or some other model is used by types of thinkers today and in other periods. By no means have all thinkers in all times employed this particular verificatory model. Indeed, many do not now accept it. Many contemporary social scientists only know this physical-science model by name, and their "usage" is limited to the sprinkling of a few terms through their writings. This particular model did not and could not have existed prior to the wholesale rise of physical science in western Europe, for it was drawn from this type of inquiry.

But even in inquiries satisfying this paradigm the motives or social positions of the thinker do not exhaust the aspects of inquiries which may be relative to social factors. Any observational and verificatory pattern may itself be socially relativized, and the "selection" and use of any model (as well as its specific diffusion pattern across variegated elites) is open to sociological explanation. Two other aspects of inquiries that are open to possible social-historical influences and that may bear on criteria, and hence on truthfulness and validity of results, may be mentioned:

(i) The categories upon which all discourse and inquiry depend are related to social situations, to cultural determinants. Numerous investigators[16] have indicated how con-

---

[15] *E.g.,* Speier distinguishes the type of thinking that in his view is not open to sociological investigation from the "promotive" type which is on the basis of the individual thinker's epistemological motivation and intention (see below).

[16] Dewey, *Logic: The Theory of Inquiry,* chap. i; E. Vivas, "A Note on the Question of Class Science," *Marxist Quarterly,* I, No. 3, 437 ff.; see Mills, "Language, Logic, and Culture," *op. cit.,* pp.

cepts, as surrogates of societal contexts, may shape inquiries that apparently are foot loose and socially free. Detection of the societally conditioned meanings of the terms upon which an inquiry depends may be viewed as a critique of the warrantability of this inquiry's results. In C. W. Morris' terms the "pragmatic" (which includes the sociological) dimension of the language process is basically related to the semantical and syntactical.[17] What is taken as problematic and what concepts are available and used may be interlinked in certain inquiries.[18] It should be noted that within the sociological perspective, the problems which occasion reflection may be viewed from numerous angles as connective of intellect and culture. Viewing the selection of problems in terms of motivating values is only one, the grossest, mode of connection.

(ii) Closely linked with such a view of categories is the social theory of perception. In acquiring a technical vocabulary with its terms and classifications, the thinker is acquiring, as it were, a set of colored spectacles. He sees a world of objects that are technically tinted and patternized. A specialized language constitutes a veritable a priori form of perception and cognition,[19] which are certainly relevant to the results of inquiry. Epistemologies have differed widely as to the manners in which empirical elements enter into knowledge. But however variously they have incorporated empirical elements, in looking at the world for verification their concepts have conditioned what they have seen. Different technical elites possess different perceptual capa-

---

676-80, for a statement and references; and particularly M. Granet's application of Durkheim's sociological theory of categories, *La Pensée chinoise* (Paris, 1938) also C. Wright Mills, "M. Granet's Contribution to Sociology of Knowledge" (mimeographed material, Department of Sociology, University of Wisconsin [1940])—available upon request.

[17] *Foundations of the Theory of Signs* ("International Encyclopedia of Unified Sciences," Vol. I, No. 2 [Chicago, 1938]). This book and the movements it represents are very suggestive American sources for sociology of knowledge.

[18] Mills, "Language, Logic, and Culture," *op. cit.,* pp. 675 ff.

[19] See G. A. DeLaguna, *Speech* (New Haven, 1927), p. 344 and Index: "Perception"; also M. Sherif, *The Psychology of Social Norms* (New York, 1936) (see references).

cities. Empirical verification cannot be a simple and positivistic mirror-like operation. Thus the observational dimensions of any verificatory model are influenced by the selective language of its users. And this language is not without social-historical imprint. The implications of this social view of perception for simple correspondence theories of truth, e.g., are obvious. Failure to recognize such junctures in inquiry that are relevant to the "truthfulness," "objectivity," and "impartiality" of the results of inquiry issues in an arbitrary limitation of the legitimate subject matter of an empirical sociology of knowledge.

An argument long used against all forms of relativism frequently appears in discussions[20] of the present problem: either the relativist's own assertion and argument are themselves relative, in which case he has no grounds for denying or imputing truth to the thought of others, or his argument and assertion are unconditionally true, and hence relativism is self-contradictory.[21] This argument may be put in strict logical form: (a) Thinking is functional of cultural factors. (Hence, its "objective," "impartial validity," is destroyed.) (b) The sociology of knowledge is a type of thinking. (c) Therefore, the sociology of knowledge is functional of cultural factors. (Hence, it cannot be "objective," "valid.") Now Mannheim himself has empirically documented abc-linkage.[22] He has indicated the cultural and political conditions of the sociology of knowledge. It is the premises hung after the "hences" and their assumptions that we need to examine.

These anti-relationistic arguments apparently ignore the character and status of epistemological forms (see secs. (i) and (ii) above). They assume the existence of an absolute truth having no connection to inquiry; and they are signifi-

[20] E.g., von Schelting, American Sociological Review, p. 667. I am leaving open whether or not von Schelting's is an adequate statement of Mannheim's position. I am concerned not with defense or appraisal of Mannheim's work, nor of von Shelting's in toto, but only with the one point. In general, however, I find Mannheim's "relationism" (Ideology and Utopia, esp, pp. 253 ff., 269-70) quite tenable. The position is logically imperfect and unsatisfactory only from an absolutist viewpoint.

[21] Cf. E. Vivas' statement and able dissection of this argument (op. cit., p. 443).

[22] Ideology and Utopia, chap. i.

cant only from an absolutist viewpoint. The imputations of the sociologist of knowledge may be tested with reference to the verificatory model generalized, *e.g.,* by Peirce and Dewey. Their truthfulness is then in terms of this model. Granted that this model is no *absolute* guaranty, it seems the most probable we have at present. (As a practical fact, if we would socialize our thought among professional thinkers today, we must cast it in such terms.) Criteria are themselves developing things. A precondition for "correcting" the model for future use is self-consciously to use it now. "Inquiry into inquiry [logic] is . . . a circular process, it does not depend on anything extraneous to inquiry."[23]

The assertions of the sociologist of knowledge escape the "absolutist's dilemma" because they can refer to a degree of truth and because they may include the *conditions* under which they are true. Only conditional assertions are translatable from one perspective to another. Assertions can properly be stated as probabilities, as more or less true. And only in this way can we account for the fact that scientific inquiry is self-correcting. The sociologist may without contradiction also point out social factors conditioning failure to use this particular model. Mannheim quite correctly claims that new criteria for social science may emerge from the inquiries of the sociology of knowledge. It is entirely possible. I shall elaborate the point below. It is enough here to realize that "traditional criteria" emerge from logical analysis of "traditional" types of inquiry. The attempt to restrict the object matter and implications of the sociology of knowledge in order to save its assertions is mislocated and not consonant with modern theories of knowledge.[24]

[23] Dewey, *Logic: The Theory of Inquiry,* chap. i.

[24] Moreover, in his criticism of Mannheim, von Schelting does not appear to take into account the fact that the existence of *purpose* and *perspective* does not necessarily mean that the results of inquiry must be false; it merely means that its truth is always conditional, not absolute. Since the turn of the century many logicians and social psychologists have contended that all inquiry has a purposive element and is within a particular perspective. Mannheim's epistemological work, fragmentary as it is, does not deny the fact of purpose and perspective in an effort to save some "traditional conception of truth" framed on a spectator, godlike theory of mind.

Another such attempt is advanced by those who would limit the sociology of knowledge to investigation of the conscious attempts of a promoter to find a public; the social conditions of types of promoters; means of diffusing ideas persuasive of values, etc.[25] From this point of view the sociology of knowledge can have no epistemological relevance or object matter because it can study thoroughly only a "promotive" type of thought. In so far as it examines "theoretical thinking" ("the aim of [which] is . . . simply truth"), it is apparently limited to examination of "the selection of certain problems." In addition to individual motivation, there is a second differentiation of the two types of thinking: the public of the philosopher (theoretic) is "the timeless ranks of those who seek the truth." Neither of these differentiations is analytic enough. It does not help any to say that they are different "qualities of thinking." I take this public of the "theoretical" thinker to be the members of a technical elite, generically delimited as (a) those who read his work or who he thinks will; that is, those participating, more or less meaningfully, in his universe of discourse. (b) They are persons engaged in doubting, criticizing, and fixing their beliefs, *i.e.*, in thinking,[26] (c) in a way that satisfies the conditions of some thought-model, the forms of which they are more or less aware of and which they strive to follow. This is what "seeking truth" means. Thus analyzed sociologically, "philosophers" and "theoretic" thinking certainly constitute data for the sociologist of knowledge. The very existence of such a group is sociologically significant. The origins and consequences of such groups in various contexts have received little explicit attention. I have already indicated how the "selection" of criteria, and criteria themselves, are open to sociological investigation, how the categories of technical discourse, the problems addressed, and perceptual schemata may influence the direction and validating forms of thinking.[27]

[25] *E.g.*, Speier, "Social Determination of Ideas," *op. cit.*, pp. 199 and 200.

[26] See Peirce, *op. cit.* Also E. Freeman, *The Categories of Peirce* ("Chicago Series" [Chicago, 1937]), pp. 39-40.

[27] Speier's failure to recognize these points as open to social influence is probably conditioned by exclusive concern with one type

Furthermore, for a thinker merely to wish, or to be motivated, to attain truth does not guarantee or imply whether or not his assertions are true. Much less, whether he or they are open to social relativization. "True" is an adjective applied to propositions that satisfy the forms of an accepted model of verification. In the model now dominant among secular, professional thinkers, verification is independent of the individual's motive for thinking, whether it be "truth" or "persuasion." I do not see that we are justified at this stage of research in differentiating types of thinking in terms of epistemological motivation. Such are not the kind of types we need and can use in dissection. For it would take a social-psychological analysis of a thinker to determine whether or not he really was, or believed he was, aiming at truth, *i.e.,* following or attempting to follow a verificatory model. One could properly identify "theoretic" thinking only in terms of a given verificatory model. In research we cannot fruitfully impose "ours" upon past thinkers. There have been several models in Western thought, and I have already indicated that they are themselves open to social-historical relativization.[28]

There is in our time no common form of validation to which all will submit their assertions. This epistemological condition presents an opportunity to study comparatively the diverse norms themselves, their function, and genesis. In the face of epistemologic diversity and confusion it seems foolish to call our work irrelevant to some one arbitrarily selected set of norms which were derived from a particular gamut of inquiry or concocted from miscellaneous beliefs.

---

of socio-psychologic mechanism connecting ideation and culture. In his article he accepts only "need," "problem," and "interests" of the thinker. "The relations between ideas and social reality is . . . constituted in the medium of needs" ("Social Determination of Ideas," *op. cit.,* p. 183). See my "Language, Logic, and Culture," *op cit.,* in which this view is criticized and other modes of relation advanced.

[28] Speier's paper ("Social Determination of Ideas," *op. cit.*), is valuable in its acute remarks on "social actions" and the ambiguity of the term "need" as it appears in many sociologies of knowledge; but he has failed to analyze what he terms "theoretic" thinking. The limitations he would exact of sociology of knowledge are without adequate justification.

But the tasks for sociologists of knowledge implied by such statements are not too clear. They need to be indicated more precisely. Of course, as Wirth has indicated, we aspire to contribute to "the social-psychological elaboration of the theory of knowledge itself." I am here concerned with pointing up the usefulness of such work to sociologists, *i.e.,* the methodological function of sociology of knowledge.

The sociologist of knowledge need not rest with factual examination and relativization of aspects of knowledge processes. For such experience places him strategically, on a comparative and contextual basis, for positive methodological construction. We need here to realize Dewey's identification of epistemology with methodology. This realization carries the belief that the deriving of norms from some one type of inquiry (even though it have wide prestige, *e.g.,* "physical science") is not the end of epistemology. In its "epistemologic function" the sociology of knowledge is specifically propaedeutic to the construction of sound methodology for the social sciences.[29] Had Mannheim consistently recognized this, he would have avoided ambiguities and mislocations in his work. But, on the whole, Mannheim as epistemologist is concerned with the detection and correction of limitations of social-political inquiries.[30] In his review of Rice's *Methods*[31] he abstracts some notions and forms which control inquiries of American and German sociologists, criticizes each style of study by the other in supplementary fashion, and briefly links the two in a general research model which he submits social inquiry should follow if it would issue into firm knowledge.

[29] L. Wirth has correctly indicated that an incipient sociology of knowledge has often been an unexploited by-product of methodological discussions (Preface to Mannheim, *op. cit.,* pp. xvii-xxiii).

[30] As was Spencer, *Study of Sociology* (1873) and J. S. Mill, *A System of Logic,* Book VI. Notice the manner in which Spencer moves from discovery of procedural fallacies having social sources, from "the many modes in which evidence may be vitiated," to the construction of methodological techniques designed to obviate such fallacies and vitiations. The idea that detection of social sources of error may lead to sounder methodology is clearly evidenced. In this connection cf. E. Durkheim, *Règles de la méthode sociologique* (Paris, 1895), chap. ii.

[31] *American Journal of Sociology,* Vol. XXXVIII, No. 2 (1932).

Von Schelting is incorrect in implying that Mannheim does not "postulate the possibility of objective validity for cognitive achievements."[32] In fact, Mannheim does not stop with the mere assumption. He goes on as a sound methodologist to attempt formulations of criteria for social inquiry in terms of existent modes of social thought as empirically ascertained by logic and a contextual sociology of knowledge. If Mannheim has fallen short in his attempts to enunciate sound criteria for social inquiries, it is not due to misconceptions of the character of epistemological forms nor to "epistemological inconsistency."

> The desire to treat politically important problems without being a victim to bias was responsible for the development in Germany of . . . . *Wissenssoziologie.* This new branch of research, intended to be an organ of critical self-control has already succeeded in detecting and subjecting to control important sources of error.[33]

This certainly is indicative of one generic meaning of the epistemological relevance of sociology of knowledge. The sociologist of knowledge joins the live logician and social methodologist in the critical building of sounder methods for social research.

Among the specific issues he may fruitfully problematize are those concerning the respective methods of physical and social inquiry. There are those who, in the name of science, would impose the procedural forms of the former on the latter in wholesale fashion; and there are social students who will have nothing to do with physical science. The sociologist of knowledge grounded in comparative understanding may not only establish social sources for the two extreme positions, but, constructively, he may implement the planned alteration of certain physical forms that are found advisable to achieve fruitfully the transfer.

"Experiment" as a verificatory form is an instance in

[32] *Op. cit.,* p. 667.
[33] Mannheim, *op. cit.,* p. 281; also see Mannheim, *Man and Society in an Age of Reconstruction* (New York, 1940), in which methodological problems of "social planning," as a type of thought, are constructively presented.

point. Dewey, *e.g.*, has abstracted this form from physical inquiry and has attempted to generalize it for all "inquiry *qua* inquiry." His writings are informed by failure to see fully and clearly the difficulties and the ambiguities associated with the physical paradigm of inquiry and particularly, "experiment," when applied to social data. Experiment in a societal situation does have characteristics and problems which experiment in a laboratory does not possess. For instance, the "control" and manipulation necessary to "experimental" work as it occurs in physical science often assume political and evaluative dimensions that experiment in laboratory contexts does not.[34] And the "reconstitution" of an object, which according to Dewey is necessary before it can function as an object of knowledge, involves many issues. To say the least, the attempt to carry this laboratory technique over into social data precipitates methodological and political problems to which Dewey and his disciples have not squarely addressed themselves.

Inadequacy at this point, and others, suggests that there is need to analyze social researches in their cultural and intellectual contexts and attempt to articulate the inchoate rules implicit within them. In this manner we may empirically supplant the a priori assumptions that there is or is not, that there should or should not, be any essential difference between social inquiry and physical science. Such analysis would also enable explicit and sophisticated formulation of problems peculiar to social inquiry.

Problems of "value" arise within and frustrate social inquiry. To state one aspect of the problem: how do the research problems actually addressed by social scientists involve evaluations and how, if at all, do such involvements condition the truthfulness of results?[35] Questions of value should not be taken *überhaupt*. Located as snarls in social inquiry, questions of value become specific and genuine. They need to be answered by sociological analyses of spe-

---

[34] See L. H. Lanier's recent presentation of the point (*Southern Review*, Vol. V, No. 1, 1939). For comprehensive documentation and partial ramification cf. my "Reflection, Behavior, and Culture," pp. 91-102, available at the University of Texas library.

[35] Cf. T. Parsons' (*Structure of Social Action* [New York, 1937], pp. 593, 601 ff.) references to and discussion of Max Weber's "*Wertbeziehung*."

cific disciplines and problems arising in them. Not only the content of values in social inquiries should be detected, but how values creep in, and how, if at all, they condition the direction, completeness, and warrantability of the results of research. In this way we may gain a position from which to formulate rules of evidence that will prevent exhortation from informing our results. Such contextual examinations will permit precise definition of issues that are now vague.

Perhaps the central methodological problem of the social sciences springs from recognition that often there is a disparity betwen lingual and social-motor types of behavior. Now the sociologist of knowledge is explicitly concerned with factual investigations of the verbal components of action, with the "common sense," *e.g.,* articulations of various cultures. In this field one of his problems is the ascertaining of differential disparities obtaining between overt systems of behavior and what is said by the actors in different cultural contexts. Such systematic investigations would have consequences for the construction of techniques of investigation.[36] They should enable the methodologist to build into his methods standard margins of error, different rates of discount for different *milieux.* They would show (for various cultural actions, types of subjects, and various modes of verbalization) *how much* and *in what direction* disparities between talk and action will probably go. In this way factual investigations should provide a basis for rules for the control and guidance of evidence and inference.[37]

Because of its dominantly academic position in American sociology, systematic theorizing has proceeded in textbooks for students, not for research. What effect has this

[36] Since the writing of this paper, R. K. Merton has indicated the point with reference to a specific study ("Fact and Factitiousness in Ethnic Opinionnaires," *American Sociological Review,* February, 1940, pp. 21-22).

[37] Here sociologists can garner suggestions from critical historiography which attempts to locate (culturally and biographically) observers (*e.g.,* Roman popes) of social events in order properly to discount their recorded observations. This method is aware of the differences of societal occurrences as seen and written of by variously situated reporters. See A. W. Small, *Origins of Sociology,* esp. pp. 48, 84, 85, 98; H. E. Barnes, *A History of Historical Writings* (Norman, Okla., 1937), chap. x.

had on the research model to which sociologists have looked for verification of their work, and hence on its validity?

The ideal of intimacy of contact to which Cooley practically assimilated the conception of society, with consequent distortion and partiality, has its roots in certain American cultural traditions[38] and in compensation for the actual depersonalization and secondary character of life in an urban-industrial order.

The emphasis upon continuous process as a central category in American sociology has perhaps aided the overlooking of revolutionary dislocations in "social change." Safe multiple-factor views as to historical causation are very convenient to a "liberal democratic" view of politically implemented social change. Pluralistic causes are easily carried to a point at which no action is possible; revolutionary manipulation calls for belief in a monistic cause.

These are fragmentary items close at hand which the sociologist of knowledge is in a position to examine. The detailed self-location of social science, if systematically and sensitively performed, not only will lead to detection of errors in methods under way but constructively will result in presentation of sounder paradigms for future research.

[38] T. V. Smith, *Beyond Conscience* (New York, 1934), *e.g.:* "Social distance is [considered] a dire fate . . . immoral in our Christian tradition" (p. 111).

# THE LANGUAGE
# AND IDEAS OF ANCIENT CHINA

## I

A few of the younger men in American sociology are becoming tired of the paste-pot eclecticism and text-book tolerance which have characterized much of their tradition. They are learning that an open mind is all too often merely an empty head, and tolerance a substitution of politeness and politics for analytic rigor. Instead of the jumble of speculation and busy work which goes to make up large portions of social psychology, they feel the need of a sociological psychology that would be socially and historically relevant, and a strict counterpart and parallel endeavor to physiological science.[1]

The sources of this view are many and farraginous, but back of it lies the French tradition. This lineage is related to De Bonald and De Maistre, and receives an initial crystallization in Comte's classification of the sciences, is recast and deepened by Espinas, DeRoberty and Durkheim.[2] With the latter, the view became formally wedded to the structure of French academic life. Out of the theories of Durkheim have flowed concrete and systematic monographs: five by Levy-Bruhl on the sociology of morality and preliterate mentality; Abel Rey, Francis Cornford, on Greek mentality and myth; Jane Harrison, Pierre-Maxime Schuhl on the Greeks; by Durkheim himself on Australian religion and mind; Alexandre Moret on Egypt; Halbwachs on the social frames of memory. There are others.

These works are known to the rank and file of Ameri-

---

[1] Such a general view informs the theory and hypotheses contained in the writer's "Situated Actions and Vocabularies of Motive," *American Sociological Review,* Dec. 1940.

[2] See E. Benot-Smullyan's Harvard thesis; microfilm No. 18, Dept. of Sociology, University of Wisconsin.

can sociologists only at second hand, or more often at third. The unfortunate thing about this is that no secondary writings can adequately convey this tradition's fortunate balance of brilliant analysis with firm empiricism. Because they are methodologically sophisticated the members of the "Durkheim school" have educated eyes and if at times their theories are a little floating, careful formulation will render them *vera causa*. It is a bracing thing to come to direct grips with such a monographic tradition, one that is carefully and consistently analytical.

Besides this methodological awareness, French sociologists have made two related contributions: a sociologistic psychology and the suggestive beginnings of a sociological theory of knowledge, mind, and language. Implicit within sociologistic psychology is the view now becoming known as sociology of knowledge. French sociology is an extremely important source for this emerging discipline. For latent within the sociologistic psychology is its application to intellectual phenomena; and more to the point: that application has been, in France, through language: Society exercises an influence on our intellectual functions in a particularly powerful manner through language, a social creation which exists before these functions and survives them. Also, through logical operations and scientific techniques which it subtilizes and, in fact, through all acquisitions of scientific results which so rapidly enrich our conceptology from the time that we begin to reflect.[3]

In the monographs already mentioned this latent tendency has become articulated and it has been put to work on various bodies of data.

Sociology of knowledge is at present many things to a lot of men. It is not yet wise to attempt rigid systematization of its outlines. More portions drawn from past theories must be picked out, torn apart, and tentatively welded to empirical monographs. But in one aspect, sociology of knowledge may be said to be working toward a theory of mind and knowledge which takes as its data not an individual's performances or tests, but the entirety of intellectual history. A theory is an explanation of some phenom-

---

[3] G. Dumas (ed.), *Traité de Psychologie,* Vol. 2, 1924, page 1126.

ena. Drawing upon the theories and findings of all social science, sociology of knowledge is an attempted explanation of the phenomena of intellectual history. In its explanations of these materials it appeals to the data of social history. And in order to trace the mechanisms connective of mentality and society, the sociology of knowledge must be informed by a "psychology" that is socially, ethnologically, and historically relevant.[4]

Besides much of the French tradition, such a sociologistic statement of sociology of knowledge will be able to draw from (a) the German "folk-psychology" and (b) those American traditions that have received sophisticated articulation in the theories of G. H. Mead.

(a) Folk-psychology undertook to approach the materials of "social psychology" through a study of cultural history. As it focused on mental operations, obviously intellectual history was adduced. The generation after Lazarus and Steinthal made the two currents of folk and physiological psychology major and generic channels of research. Within the cradle of Hegel's objective idealism the attempt was made to concretize and illuminate the movement of mental development with anthropological, historical, and linguistic data. Despite "individualistic" taints confusedly carried over into his sociological view, Wundt followed Lazarus and Steinthal in the effort to get at the operations of mind not through direct study of individuals, but in terms of the intellectual and social residues of mental processes. On the basis of the external facts of culture, Wundt approached psychological phenomena; on the basis of intellectual history and in terms of culture, he explored the operations of mind.[5]

(b). It seems strange that no one has explicitly raised the question of the *data* drawn upon by Mead in the construction and elaboration of his social theory of mind. Mead mentions dog fights in connection with the conversation of

[4] Mills, C. Wright, "Language, Logic, and Culture," *American Sociological Review,* Oct. 1939. This article is addressed to this problem of the *modus operandi.*
[5] See discussion of folk-psychology and references in Fay Karpf's *American Social Psychology,* pp. 42-54; Goldenweiser, Alexander, *History, Psychology and Culture.*

gestures and the rise of the self. And he did have a dog that followed him about and fought other dogs so that Mead would be stimulated to thought. But after the days at Leipzig, Mead did not prosecute "research" in the laboratory manner. He was trained, or rather, had trained himself, in the history of general ideas. He knew the history of Western philosophy and of physical science thoroughly, intimately.

I think his theory of mind is informatively oriented with reference to these histories: they were his subject matter and his data. His work on the histories of science and philosophy is less an "application" of a developed theory of mind than they are bases for it. Recall his extended discussions of the romantics: Hegel, Fichte, Schelling, and the definitive essay of science.[6] If you will read Mead from this angle he is more understandable, and certain of his obvious inadequacies are explainable: particularly the naive view of the reactions of the individual thinker to "the community." Only if "community" is read to mean "scientific or intellectual community" do certain portions of Mead's work appear adequate. Of course, the theory of mind is also an immanent development from Wundt, Baldwin, Cooley, Dewey, and Watson (and long before Watson the behavioristics of C. S. Peirce.[7]) It is also informed by the Durkheim school.

In the present essay I wish to make concrete this sociologistic view of sociology of knowledge by showing it at work in Marcel Granet's *La Pensée Chinoise*. However, I shall concentrate on presenting an abstract, or condensed summary, of the main contours of Granet's study itself. It seems advisable to translate in paraphrase as much of the content of the book as space permits. For it, or nothing on it in any detail, is at present available in English.[8] Thus we are

[6] "Scientific Method and the Individual Thinker," in *Creative Intelligence,* edited by John Dewey.

[7] *The Collected Papers of C. S. Peirce,* vol. 5 (ed. by Charles Hartshorne and Paul Weiss).

[8] See, however, H. E. Barnes and Howard Becker, *Social Thought From Lore To Science,* vols. 1 and 2, index: "Granet;" and E. B. Smullyan's review of Granet, *American Sociological Review,* June 1936, pages 487-492, and Harvard Thesis *op. cit.*

interested in Chinese thinking and its connections with the culture of the ancient East. But underlying Granet's detailed examination are the contours of a perspective that we wish to grasp: the sociological approach to mind and knowledge, to intellectual history. There are several difficulties infecting Granet's theoretic orientation which we shall indicate and toward the more adequate solution of which we hope to contribute. And there is a new term I should like to introduce and make part of your working vocabulary.

## II

In *La Civilization Chinoise*,[9] Granet delineates the distinctive features of the societal and political system of the ancient Chinese. His framework is comprised of two major trends which he disengages from the drifts in ancient China's culture: "mastery over the soil and political unification." This work is complimentary to *La Pensée Chinoise*.[10] It sets forth political and cultural reconstructions, while the latter is concerned with Chinese thinking. The trends ascertained and reconstructed in each sphere support and are integrated with those in the other. "From the epoch of Han" there is a general movement in the intellectual life toward a scholasticism "which is a counterpart to the orthodox discipline of Chinese life."[11] In all spheres Chinese life during this period moved toward the reign of orthodoxy and formalism.[12]

*La Pensée Chinoise* is in no sense a manual of the literature or the philosophy of China. It is an attempt to set forth the "rules and symbols which govern the life of the mind in China." Of the four sections of the work, three are concerned with "common notions," notions which underly

[9] Translated as *Chinese Civilization,* by K. E. Innes and M. R. Brailsford.
[10] Both are concerned with the *ancient* period, concluding with the Han Dynasty.
[11] *Ibid.,* page 4.
[12] *Ibid.,* page 427.

and inform variant schools and sects.[13] Granet speaks of the "mental habits" and of "dispositions of mind." His concern is not with who thought what and when, nor with the minute connections between individual thinkers. He is attempting to lay ba¯e "the anonymous tradition" which "nobody, in effect . . . wrote" and the "institutional bases" (*"le fond institutionnel,"* 4) of the thought that it cradles.

He does not believe that one can undeistand the diverse sects and schools nor explain their *raison d'être* and variation without reference to these common and sociological factors. His aim is to analyze in a manner that he considers most objective several of the most influential and pervasive of Chinese conceptions and intellectualized attitudes. Above all, he is not concerned with judging these notions either as to their moral or intellectual worth. He is not trying to learn from these writings anything about the world. They are data, not pabulum. His primary concern is with the "parallelism" of ideas and social structures, the "origin" of conceptions from societal forms and drifts. This concern underlies and informs his entire examination of Chinese thought. It begins to be validated, as we shall see, from the first stroke of Granet's analysis of the language and particularly of the leading ideas themselves. He is able to show that the content of the leading categories is explainable by the structure of Chinese society and that the evolution of these ideas depend, in strict fashion, upon societal evolution. Names and dates are peripheral matters of Granet.[14] What is central and essential is the detailed marking of the "parallelism" between ideas and societal features. He does not appeal to a generalized "spirit of the times", or some such ghost, but attempts to explain ideas in terms of the concrete history of a social system.

*La Pensée Chinoise* is thoroughly consistent with the

[13] This paper will deal exclusively with these three sections, *i.e.,* from pages 1-419, and the brief conclusion.

[14] As a matter of fact he correctly indicates that the important dates in the histories of intellectual doctrines are not chronological ones, but the pivots and drifts that the society in question takes. (26) Such matters as these form the framework in which he writes, not a chronological system based on the movements of the stars and moon.

theory and research of Durkheim in sociology of knowledge. It "represents the most systematic and powerful attempt up to date to apply the fundamental conceptions of Durkheim's sociologistic theory of knowledge to a given body of facts.[15] But Granet correctly insists that he is, first of all, a Sinologist. Indeed, in his field, he is very eminent. He modestly disclaims knowledge of sociology, but explicitly states that the Durkheim-Mauss essay on "primitive classifications" contains remarks on China that "mark a date in the history of Sinological studies." He himself states that his work is consistent with and a test of Durkheim's theory of the categories.[16] However, he insists, justifiably, that he did not merely "apply" or illustrate the theory (28, 29). Neither my tendency to agree with this remark of Granet's or Smullyan's to question it,[17] are worth very much: only another able Sinologist is really competent to judge.

Granet's concern with the language and logic, with the "principles" of Chinese thinking, rather than with the sects, schools, and the individual thinkers, is due both to his sociologistic perspective and to the scantiness of firmly attested sources for the period in his focus. This concern is a striking departure from traditional intellectual histories. With reference to Sinology, it is new in aim and point of view, and it is significant that by it Granet claims he was enabled to isolate new relations and facts and to interpret the schools and individual thinker themselves.

His work shows clearly one important methodical consequence of sociology of knowledge. A notable feature of the book is the extreme caution and the informed manner in which Chinese sources are used. In order to control inferences from the ancient writings, Granet discounts and interprets their content in the light of the cultural contexts and the positions of their supposed authors, as well as the

[15] Smullyan microfilm, page 465.
[16] *Elementary Forms of the Religious Life,*—See first and last sections, but particularly page 630 ff.
[17] Review of Granet in *American Sociological Review,* June 1936, pages 487-92. On this point see also H. Berr's Preface to *La Pensée Chinoise.*

intellectual traditions which seem largely to have governed how and what they should write.

Many of those who wrote "histories" held high positions in the orthodoxy. They were inextricably attached to an aristocratic ruling stratum. The scholars were "learned counsellors of state." The intellectual continuum in which they worked contained an idealization of tradition as such: all historical writings were definitively inspired by a tenacious ideal of traditional piety. "In proportion as the editions (of a work) become perfect and as criticisms become more learned, the work becomes more perfectly in accord with ancient tradition." . . . Nothing is to contradict the official version. Such erudition makes "all research aiming at what a European historian would call truth almost impossible."[18]

By realizing these facts, Granet is able to control and shape his inferences, and properly to discount and evaluate the evidence before him. Not only does he do this in the usual manner of critical historiography.[19] He uses these traditional sources not as statements of historical fact, but as evidence from which to infer the sentiments and ideas of the Chinese writers as cultural units. Thus sociology of knowledge is used methodologically as an organon of historical reconstruction.[20] A concrete instance of this methodological control may be seen in connection with translation of the words, *jen* and *kien ngai*. Respectively they characterize the positions of Confucius and Motze. Western scholars have rendered them as "altruism" and "universal love." The error of such "translation" is corrected by sociological understanding of the Chinese language, which is simply not capable of expressing such abstract "conceptions." Even if this were not a linguistic fact, there is a further difficulty: no one can understand the ancient texts without reference to the glosses with which generations of men have endowed them. From the time of Han, these glosses are informed by a strict orthodoxy. They give the "correct interpretation,"

[18] *Chinese Civilization,* page 51.
[19] For an elementary statement, see A. W. Small, *Origins of Sociology,* Chapter 4-7.
[20] See C. Wright Mills, "Methodological Consequences of Sociology of Knowledge," *American Journal of Sociology,* Nov. 1940.

*i.e.,* the interpretation required of the candidates taking the examinations which gave access to official honors and a bureaucratic position. There is no "free reading" permitted. Academic guideposts, moral and political in purport, must be followed. If we wish to go beyond or beneath these commentaries we must have the aid of a "manual of semantics." The preparation of such a manual would require extensive sociological knowledge. Says Granet: "It is possible to ascertain the precise significance of an attitude or specific prescription only if one first endeavors to define the positions that the different sectarian groups occupied in the history of Chinese society." In discussing problems incident to a translation from Chinese to English, I. A. Richards says,

"One gets the impression that an unwritten and unelucidatable tradition accompanies and directs their interpretations. It is as though the text were only a bare fragmentary notation —to be supplemented out of a store of unrecorded knowledge—much as a music score may receive a special interpretation handed down in and through a school. And there is the further difficulty that this tradition is by no means uniform even for the best-trained scholars. Much of this applies of course, though with less force, to our own use of Western languages and it is by recognizing and analysing these esoteric determinants of meanings in our own speech that we can best approach the Chinese." [21]

## III

Granet begins his study of Chinese thought with an account of language because he considers language ". . . the most convenient point of departure in signalizing certain dispositions of Chinese mentality." Two "essential observations" emerge from this examination of the elements of language and of style: Chinese thought avoids all artifices which tend to utilize any verbal expressions of ideas in a manner to economize mental effort; and it disdains analytical forms of thought. All of the words and linguistic elements in the thinker's vocabulary glitter with those values

[21] *Mencius on the Mind,* page 12.

properly associated with *emblems*. Their intellectual traffic
does not convey ideas, or permit the smooth exchange of
conceptions; it simply evokes and invokes, stirs up vast
systems of attitudes destined to permit man to participate
in diverse aspects of *civilizing actions*.

This Sino-Tibetan language is shot through with emblems. It is heavy with judgments of value. It does not
conduce to an impersonal and objective expression.
Granet's analysis of the Chinese language discloses its
controlling function to be an ideal of moral, social, and
ritualistic *efficacy*. The language does not appear to be
organized in order to express abstract signs which are of
aid in specifying ideas. The symbols utilized are rich in
practical suggestions. Rather than definite meanings, these
possess an "indeterminate efficacy." This language does
not furnish an instrument for analysis, but rather channels
all thought into a sort of organon of conduct. The ideal
of efficacy definitely outruns the philosophical mentality
which would seek definite conceptions. It is not organized
for the purpose of noting concepts, analyzing ideas, or dis-
cursively exhibiting doctrines. It is fashioned entirely for
the communication of sentimental attitudes, the suggestion
of lines of conduct; to convince and convert. Rich in concrete values, this monosyllabic tongue is not apt for
medium for clear expression. It is a boundless repertoire
of "vocal emblems" of great effective power. It is practical[22] in its function and content.

The qualities of the Chinese language are very different
from those which Occidentals would choose in order to
insure a clear transmission of their thought. The words are
very brief. Their phonetic poverty makes it often difficult
to distinguish between them. A great majority of the words
may be used indifferently as nouns, verbs, or adjectives
without any sensible change in their form.

Now, only a language with a relatively rigid construction is able to carry clearly expressed "ideas" (Occidental

---

[22] It should be understood that the "practical" is always culturally
relative. To many strata of contemporary America the "practical"
is nearly equivalent to the pecuniary. This cultural content was of
course not present in the Chinese practicality. Compare T. Veblen,
*The Place of Science*.

ideas!).[23] The oral form of the order of words is determined by a succession of emotions and feelings. This order stresses the affective and practical importance attributed to different elements in a congeries of emotions. But it is not suitable for, indeed it obviates, the clear expression of abstract ideas.

Chinese is a really admirable force for communicating "a sentimental shock" for inviting one to take part in some action. Always it is concrete and tied closely to conduct. A word does not "correspond" to a concept. And it is not a simple sign neutrally denoting an object. It is not given its vivid life by grammatical or syntactical artifices. In its own immutable and monosyllabic form it contains all the imperative energy of the act of which it is the vocal correspondent and the emblem. This characterization is brought out forcibly in an article of Granet's, "Some Peculiarities of Chinese Thought and Language":[24]

> Almost all the words connote singular ideas, which are highly specialized. And what this vocabulary expresses is not the needs of a mentality that classifies, abstracts, and generalizes, and which aims at working upon clear-cut, distinct facts, prepared for logical organization: it shows, on the contrary, just the opposite tendency, the dominant desire for specification, particularization, the picturesque. . . . As they appear to us and as the Chinese explain them, the words of their vocabulary seem to correspond to conceptual images . . . united, on the one hand, to sounds that appear to be endowed with the power of evoking the characteristic details of an image, and, on the other hand, to signs that represent the gesture which is noted by the motor memory as essential.[11]

The word in Chinese is not a sign serving to note a concept. It does not fix in a definite manner a degree of abstraction and generality. It evokes and loosely fixes a very active and indefinite complex of particular images. For instance, there is no word which simply signifies "old man." There is on the other hand a great number of words which represent different *social* "aspects" of

[23] See Bloomfield, Linguistic Aspects of Science.
[24] *Revue Philosophique,* Jan.-Feb., and Mar.-April, 1920, pages 104-114.

old age: The aspect of those who have need of a very
rich food, the aspect of those old persons whose respira-
tion is suffocating them. Such concrete vocations lead the
mind to a crowd of other visions which are also very concrete. All the details, for example, of the mode of life
proper for those who are decrepit and require a nourish-
ing food, those whom one must exempt from military
service, those no longer obligated to go to "school," those
for whose death one must hold ready all the funeral materials, (for which one has prepared a long while), those
that have the right to carry a staff through the streets of
the village—such are a few of the images awakened by
the word *K'i* to which "corresponds" our quasi-singular
notion of old persons, sixty to seventy years. In ancient
China at seventy, one becomes specifically "old." One
merits then the appellation *Lao.* This word evokes a social
juncture of life. It does not "mean" merely a chronological
juncture. Its use leads to the evocation of a flock of images
which are not at all to be confused with an abstract idea.
If this wave of evocations is not stopped, the response
will spread to embrace all of the aspects which signify the
different categories of persons whose active period of
life is finished.

The emblematic function of words gives rise to what
Granet calls "descriptive auxiliaries." These are very important in the ancient poetry. Indeed, they play a considerable role in the Chinese poetry of all periods, and even
prose is not entirely without them. When a poet "paints"
(the term is used advisedly by Granet) the peformances of
two sorts of grasshoppers with the aid of the auxiliaries,
*yao-yao* and *t'i-t'i,* he does not intend to keep himself within
the bounds of description. He wishes to give counsel, to
order his audience to obey a set of rules of which the gestures of the grasshoppers are the *natural emblems* and of
which the auxiliaries, with which he paints them, are the
*vocal* emblems. These are specific rules of conduct giving
the obligation of marriage outside the family and residence
and the entrance into housekeeping after the agricultural
season. Implicit in these words is a certain discipline of
life.

Or again, there are the auxiliaries, *siu,* which paint the particular noise that a couple of wild geese make with their wings; the *yang,* which renders the cry of the same geese when the female responds to the call of the male. It suffices to invoke this vocal painting in order to be assured that one's spouse will impregnate herself with the virtues of a female goose, that she will follow, without ever passing beyond his command, the chief of the household, and henceforth she will be submissive to all his orders. And these are the types of words which even the wisest of the thinkers must use. For the language of the Chinese "philosophers" is not a bookish or intellectual formation; it proceeds, or is derived from, an ancient tradition of oral and practical teaching.

Nothing in their vocabulary or grammar even suggests that the Chinese ever felt the need of giving to each word a discrete and individual meaning. The meaning and syntactical function of words are vague; similar homophones awaken series of very dissimilar images and scenes. Often in certain words, reports Granet, one can detect a sort of imitative music. The language is, of course, quite isomorphic. It is not only that this language is powerfully evocative, but that merely to pronounce its elements is to constrain one's self and one's conduct. In each word there dwells, with a sort of efficacy, a latent and imperious value, a value-attitude and hence a sanctioned act. Each word in the language invites its users to feel that to speak is *to act or to react.* Woven through the language is a perennial drift toward magic.

The Chinese terms for life and destiny (ming) are not distinguishable from those which designate the vocal and graphic symbols. Thus, the names for two "concepts" resemble each other to the point whereat they are easily confused. And yet, each of these terms integrally expresses an individual essence. They are not mere terms. They are appellations which lead to the sensing of reality. To know the name, to say the word, is to possess the being itself or to create it. Suppose a lord is killed. This act would not exist if someone did not call the person who committed the crime an "assassin."

In the art of language one exalts himself and stresses the virtue of the *etiquette*. By language ranks are attributed and emblematic associations proper to them are drawn forth. Such words do not delimit an abstract class, but qualify, contaminate, lead to various destinies, and stir up real things. As emblematic realities words command the phenomena of man and of nature.

The "living, active" words are very numerous. By expressing an action or a state each word resuscitates an individual and singular essence. All of nature participates in the proper names. This swarm of singular words contrasts remarkably with the phonetic poverty of the language. In the abundant language of the Chinese there is not one expression which in a socially neutral manner conveys the general and abstract idea of "death." It cannot be spoken of without evoking (by the use of a single monosyllable) a set of intricate ritual, and an entire sector of societal action. By a single word one disposes of the defunct, assigns a mourning practice suitable to his rank, fixes his destiny in another life, classifies his family. If one is not circumspect in the appellation used, it will turn back upon him. The force of emblems is reciprocal, turns back upon him who knows not how to select and use the proper one. Each of many situations has its protocol and correct term.

The force of emblems realizes itself in an elaborate etiquette. This etiquette dominates Chinese life, and vocabularies are graded in order to permit each situation *the* protocol, the correct term. Only this term is endowed with the proper efficacy. Such vocabularies form a repertory of judgments of value, judgments singular in their persuasive power. The system of symbols is an instrument permitting the realization and the perpetuation of a reign of order by etiquette.

Each word, according to circumstance and mimicry, grasps in a determinate sense the preconceptions of the speakers and is endowed with its particular power of suggestion. This language is not concerned with conserving or enlarging its phonetic richness, or with developing its morphology. There is no tendency toward perfection of clear meanings. It is not at all modeled in a fashion conducive to the expression of "ideas." It remains in concrete values and above all does not decrease in the affective and practical power by which each word as an emblem is characterized. As Sumner said of preliterate language in general, so also of ancient Chinese: "They are overwhelmed by a flood of detail."[25] Thus if a poet employs in the right place the "single word" for "spring," not only will the usage suggest an enormous mass of images and acts properly to be performed at this time of year, but he will raise in his audience, in plain accord with the will of nature and the custom of his ancestors (the West says of its own similar terms: they are "self-evident"), a feeling or sentiment so active and efficacious that it is necessary to attribute to it the value of a vow, or of a sacred order. For the word is not a simple sign or a clear and distinct meaning, but an *emblem,* a pivot of life around which swings sacred constraints and solemn inducements. Condensed in it are all the values and virtues of prayer, orders, joy and poetic themes.

The graphic characters of Chinese correspond very closely to the oral symbols. They are figurative in the extreme. Chinese is a writing which conserves the original freshness and efficacy of its spoken words. And in these graphic symbols reside cues to the performance of a certain order of civilization. The literature which transmits and hence interprets the language, the "descriptions" of poets, the "narrations" of "historians," the historiettes, or "little moral tales" of the philosophers—these do not seek to be logical or original. Their construction depends upon formulae, upon thoroughly stereotyped themes. These thematic threads conserve the evocative power, the value-efficacy of the speech.

A certain *rhythm* almost completely replaces what is syntax in occidental languages. The role of this rhythm in the speech forms is quite prominent. Not only does it perform the ordinary functions of Western syntax, but it confers on the language formulations a further specific efficacy; it recalls to the reader something of the collective

[25] *Folkways,* page 137.

exaltation of the festival times with their songs and dances
and their living emotions. In these festivals and rites, man
has reaffirmed his intimate connections with all else in
the universe, his liaison with sound and with reality. And
the words, set forth in rhythm, recall those things and
sanctify them by the very act of utterance.

In their writing the Chinese seek above all to attain
the effects of action which seem more naturally reserved
for spoken language. Granet explains this, in part, by the
fact (a) of the importance so long accorded to the practice
of oral teaching in the Chinese intellectual tradition; and
(b) that the differences between the spoken and written
languages are due to the latter corresponding to the sort
of dead yet lively words characterizing the antique period.
This orientation of mind toward value-efficacy rather than
intellectual clarity explains, according to Granet, the fact
that writing in China has never ceased to be emblematic.

This writing is often qualified with ideograms because
a special *character* is attached to each word. These characters vary in complication. They are resolvable into a
certain number of graphic elements which are stripped
of signification and which simply correspond to certain
movements of the instrument used by writers. Thus, in
their form they are technologically and not socially determined. These several traits grouped in greater or lesser
number form small figures. These figures are endowed
as symbols with images. Only a few of them remain simple.
They are elaborated and in complex form exist in great
numbers. Thus, habit plus knife are equivalent to beginning. Even very complex figures are ideogrammatic. Each
figure is qualified with two "radicals," one to indicate its
meaning, and one serving as a phonetic index. The
radicals lead to the images of a concrete category of objects and to the specifying of objects belonging in one
class of pronunciation. Leibniz mistook this dissective
function of the radicals as indicative of a type of analytic
thought, but Granet finds its import to lie wholly in practice. The written language is phonetically complex, yet
with the aid of the radicals it can be utilized by widely
diffused populations speaking dialects. Thus, a word will

*mean* the same to different peoples yet be pronounced quite differently.

Granet does not make the point but it is possible that these radicals greatly and effectively reduced changes in the *meaning* of words due to contacts of variant cultures. For changes in pronunciations are completely separated from meaning. Thus, this particular language is an admirable organ of a traditional and sacred culture. By the very structure of each figure it conduces to the perpetuation of meanings. Also, by tolerating local pronunciations without selling out common meanings to them the language was the language of an entire civilization. Another factor involved in the latter point was the practice of inter-feudal reunions which fostered a common speech among the nobles of each district. But this structural separation of phonetics from meaning powerfully served in the diffusion of Chinese civilization in a way that phonetic script could not.

Yet at the same time that the figurative mode of writing is culturally "practical," it gravely limits the development of terminologies which could be used in procedures of thought removed from the cultural contacts from which the language was derived.

The language is firmly linked to governmental concerns. The first governmental obligation of a chief or lord is to furnish his subjects with emblems which permit them to domesticate nature. From the first time that a graphic symbol was used, write the ancient Chinese, the demons fled, complaining that men had destroyed their power. Graphic signs have this magical virtue. In utilizing them men gain power. By signalizing the essence of every object they signalize its personality, its rank, its proper location in the universe. Tradition has it that *Houang-ti,* an early chief, acquired great glory because he took care to give the correct designations to all things. By doing this he showed the people their utilizable resources. A prince must place in their proper order the objects of nature and the actions of men. By naming objects he adjusts actions to things. By pronunciations and written characters he performs these proper linkages, and thus orients his subjects to the proper lines of conduct. *Houang-ti,* who first founded the social order, commenced by designating each family, thus fixing its destiny and indicating its singular virtue.

Throughout the ancient epoch one of the chief duties of the sovereign was to survey and to "take care of" the systems of designations. He appointed a commission charged with constantly determining whether the visual or auditory emblems constituted a symbolic conformity with the "genius" of the dynasty. A group of scribes and the blind musicians composed the proper symbols. The correct meaning of words and consciousness of "etymological" values are identical, and they harbor the practices of an elaborate and ancient civilization.

The Chinese language "consists" of a realistic art of song and a graphic symbolization of the realistic art of design. The graphic symbols are highly stylized. Their usage evokes an attitude which characterizes or significantly judges a certain type of action or connection. Thus friendship is two hands united. The symbol of cold is composed of diverse elementary signs: men, straw, and house. This particular ensemble is suggestive of the initial conduct of the winter season. The Chinese countrymen at that time re-enter into village life, reliquished during the season of work in the fields and of the great rains. They commence by stopping up their clay walls with straw and the roofs of their hovels with thatch. Thus the idea, cold, is tied to a concrete matrix of action and in its graphic form it is "a sort of etymological reconstruction of notions." The Chinese language concerns itself very little with phonetic richness but it is enriched by the use of derivations in the writings. These serve to increase the vocabulary. Since the first combinations of signs began they learned to decompose into elements a complex figure and by recombining elements to create a limited number of characters. In order to obtain a new term with a definite pronunciation it suffices to combine with a radical each one of the ancient graphic emblems having this pronunciation. The taste for the *concrete*, joined to the passion for an *etiquette* governing each detail of life, lead to an extraordinary proliferation of graphic signs. In the course of their recital the poems graphically speak to the eyes. They set going a graphic memory which doubles the verbal memory. It is difficult for us to understand this procedure. But it is clear that it has had a decisive effect upon words never becoming simple signs. The figurative writing has for the most part aided in guarding the freshness of the character of the living words. They are always able to express in imagerial fashion the concrete. Such a language lends to the Chinese mind a disposition which is profoundly anti-abstract and consistently conservative. It appears suitable to a thinking which has never proposed to itself to economize mental operations.

The literary history of China is entirely given over to the constant reiterations of the same old themes. It remains dominated by the postulates of an indigenous orthodoxy. There are several reasons for supposing that the fashions of speaking and of literary prose do not differ from those utilized in the ancient poetry. The archaic prose which serves as a model for the learned prose is not a creation entirely due to the literary or learned men. This opinion of Granet's would be received as heretical among most Sinologists—Chinese and Occidental. The poetry of which the archaic prose drew its procedures is not a learned poetry, but simply the poetry of a sacred order. Only in this way, says Granet, can we account for the remarkable characteristics of the Chinese style. In speaking and writing the Chinese uniformly express themselves by employing *consecrated formula*. They compose their discourses with the aid of sentences that are enchained by certainty. These rhythms and sacred sentences provide authority for developments of certain phrases.

The Chinese literature is a literature of patch-work ("Centons"). When they wish to prove or to explain, relate or describe, even the most original authors fall into stereotyped historettes, suitable expressions borrowed from a common and traditional fund. This fund is not very abundant, and besides the writers do not seek to renovate it. A goodly portion of the themes which are favored are found in the productions of the most ancient and the most spontaneous of Chinese poetry. All of the poems of *Kouo fong* have been composed and sung on historical occasions. They all possess at these times a political and a sacred value, because they have for their objects the dictation of conduct to the princes in such a way as to make his conduct conform with the correct and customary canons. All the poetry has an essential sacred character. This character in part explains the conservation of these poems and the utilization which has been made of them in the course of Chinese history. The *Che king* of *Kuo fong* is a classic which inspires extreme respect. One finds there, more easily than in the rituals themselves, the principles of conduct. The ancient Chinese poetry appeared to be a gnomic type. It is adorned with all the wisdom and prestige of proverbs. It is less concerned with novelty of expression than with unpublished and "unedited" combinations, with original metaphor. The same images recur over and over again. They are all inspired by models and are drawn from a quite limited number of these models. The images which they evoke are not invented with a taste for new expression. They are dicta linked to the ancient seasonal rites and writings. They call upon, above all, the spring and the autumn with their societal concommitents. These are seasons of the great fetes. For generations the same ritualized landscape imperatively proposes the same images (see note section 3 below on "Social Factors in Perception"). Each re-invents them and believes himself to have improvised them. All the thinkers bring an efficacious collaboration to the common work from which they have refound by a free effort the formulas of which the ancestors verified the power. The old proverbs freely and newly recreated are chosen for their perfect suitability. They repeat and invent the exact nature of the fete. These adequate signs are valued because with them man revitalizes his traditional knowledge. They retain all the creative genius, the richness of effectiveness, which is the value of these emblems. In them live, with that essence of necessity which is the first virtue of all rite, the heart of spontaneity which is the moving force of all joy and play. None of these beloved emblems is definite, or the least abstract in its meaning. They are living emblems overflowing with affinities, bursting with evocative power and with symbolic omnivalence. The efficacy of the for-

mulas is also the first end of the poetry sung in the course
of sacred ceremonies. To declare the odes of *Che king*
banal because the themes have been repeated indefinitely
by sacred poetry is not to understand their real significance
and function. There are very few pieces of work which are
as rich in descriptive vigor and nuance of sentiment. To
the Chinese the poem loses in efficacy when it gains in
precision. The stereotyped formulas, of which the power
of concrete suggestion is infinite, have the force of signalizing by their nuances the most subtle of desires.

Those poems richest in consecrated expression are the
most admired. In these suitable formulas present themselves
for a sort of mystical meditation. The most profound
thought is that most strongly marked by "density."

The ancient forms of lyrical improvisation consists of
value emblems, poetic proverbs with great power of suggestion and description. The essential fact to note is that *the
role of such language and stylistic form is not less evident
and important in the prose than in the poetry, not less
evident and informing in the learned style than in the vulgar
language*.

The Chinese historians appear to have had for their task
the noting of singular facts. With names and dates they
situated events. But in order to do so the suitable forms had
to be used. And by their usage the historian has already
judged events when he began his recital. The consecrated
formula, the suite of value-judgments, are decisive elements
of his work. Confucius was a master in their use. It is so
evident that the narratives that are written in these Chinese
annals continually hesitate and ask: Am I being presented
with some set of particular facts, or am I being told what
it is proper to do and not to do?

This taste for formula is an aspect of the ubiquitous ad-
hesion to a moral conformism. The proverbial expressions
serve to delineate moral portraits of personages in terms of
their resemblance to this or that hero type. They serve to
relate events so that reading them the conduct of men will
always flow into proper ceremonial forms.

One of the most eulogized of biographies (that of *Kouan
Tze* by *Sseu-Ma Ts' ieu*) is only a "Chinese discourse," that
is a mosaic of proverbs. In this biography one finds the

first requisite of recited histories: they must promote value-attitudes. The philosophers have developed the greatest genius in the use of proverbs. Their writings are always within the tenets of the orthodoxy, yet they are masters of mystical thinking; they strive to express the ineffable. With the aid of their stereotyped emblems, they note the fugitive sentiments of ecstatic experience. But just like the annalists, the Chinese philosophers are always tellers of historiettes; little moral tales, we should probably call them. One finds in all their works the same anecdotes. But mark this: the same anecdote, told in the same terms, is able to serve in the defense of very diverse opinions. For instance, there is a certain tale about an indignant monkey which is cited by Li Tze in support of the dignity and pride of man and to place in evidence the profound analogy between man and animal. The same fable, without the least change, is used by another writer, Chuang Tze, to defend the thesis that all judgment is subjective. Thus each author, in order to "morally stiffen" his thoughts, draws from the common and proverbial tradition. It is something to which they are all tied. Yet identical proverbs and anecdotes serve to provoke various lines of "reasoning." The prestige of common fables are thus continually exploited. For they give the prestige of authority to ideas. They have the virtue not of defining or sharpening thought but of giving it in its entirety the aura of that which is sanctioned, sacred. Use of them disposes the mind to accept suggestions. They do not penetrate into the forms of thought in order to determine ideas in a logical way. They give an impulse to the imagination and render that impulse docile, traditional. They channel the directions it may take. These channels certainly do not lead to economical modes of thought. Nor to precise ones. They make thought come in "lumps:" the reader finds himself learning an entire system of notions in one stroke. For the anecdotal accompaniment makes it necessary that the thought be carried in immutable, ineffable packages.

The written literature is thus basically formed of schematic historiettes, which restrain its course and lend to each writer an invariable form. The mythical and literary themes and the works themselves have been able to conserve in all their freshness the omnivalent plasticity of emblems even though these do fall within the strict canons of the written literature. The most learned prose is sanctioned and guided by the same ideals as is the most archaic poetry.

Even in written prose, *rhythm* is all-essential. It is rhythm that links the elements of discourse and makes them understandable. Its position in the sentence is not important in the grasping of the meaning of a word. The elements of discourse seem intangible in their form and isolated in their composition. They are "jealously independent." The syntactical (*e.g.,* grammatical) value of the words are perceived only if the reader first knows the formulas which govern their meaning as a whole. Their meaning must be got all at once, in its entirety. But the formulas are brief. In certain cases, these "units" are conjoined and separated by terms which merit the name of oral punctuations. These denote different types of stoppages in thought, in the flow of images. They signalize the diverse modes of liaison and connection.

This language was taught, since antiquity, by the "scanned recitation" of discourse by a master. In order to learn meanings it was essential to know the "pronunciations." In the exercise of the mind that constitutes reading the object was not precision and economy of communication, but the gaining of admiration for and assent to the rich mass of formulas. In esoteric conferences and in simple "palavers" the first object of the teacher was to brighten up this mass; make it live. It was not important that the vulgar did not clearly see the precise meaning which lay under it all. His mind must first be awakened by the *suitable* utterances.

This is not, in the Chinese, a varied and precise syntax. Instead, there is the magic of consecrated rhythm. And it is with this, after his proper apprenticeship, that one expresses himself and in terms of which he composes. An example of what is meant by this rhythm is the obligatory use of a certain kind of sign. This is employed in a designated place in the recital of verse; it is part of that verse. The verse is not understandable without it. No one has ever felt the need of *defining* what that sign meant. One

learns it so that he may compose a verse of its order. It is
part of the particular rhythm and one must know the essential rhythms of each genus of verse. Perhaps it "stands for"
certain "mystical effusion" evoked by the verse. These
rhythms are not mere ornaments or diversification of discourse. They are always mingled "in an essential manner"
with the verse's power to inspire. They are components of
traditional wisdom.

By the term *Sociotics* I mean to demarcate for anlysis
(a) all the sociological phenomena that are involved in the
functioning of language; and (b) the ways by which
lingual phenomena channel, limit, and elicit thought. Sociotics is at once a portion of theory of language and a
division of sociology of knowledge.

Within the theory of language sociotics is a component
of the pragmatic dimensions of semiosis.[26] Within the sociology of knowledge, sociotics designates the attempt to
set forth linguistic mechanisms connective of mentality and
other cultural items. In this field a preliminary statement
from the standpoint of sociotics is to be found in my "Language, Logic, and Culture."[27] The reader will find in this
article a statement of the problem to which sociotical analysis in sociology of knowledge is addressed. He will also find
an initial attempt systematically to connect the sociological
theory of language with a linguistic theory of mind and to

[26] Whenever any item functions as a sign of another item, it is
said that semiosis occurs. There are then three sets of relations obtaining: the relations of signs to objects (semantics is the discipline
studying this relation); the relations of signs to other signs (syntactics, which embraces modern logic, grammar, and mathematics is
concerned with this type of relation); and the relations of signs to
their users, to persons (pragmatics). Sociotics isolates for study the
sociological components of pragmatics. Compare C. W. Morris,
*Foundations of the Theory of Signs* (Ency. of Unified Science).
The terms used in this footnote with the exception of sociotics are
Morris'. Mead and Dewey—indeed, the pragmatic movement as a
whole—concentrate on the pragmatic dimension; the logical posi-
tivists have focused on syntactics and semantics. Morris achieves in
his monograph an admirable synthesis of the two movements.

[27] *Am. Soc. Review*, October, 1939. The foregoing portions of the
present paper may be viewed as an extensive documentation of the
theoretical view outlined in "L.L.C."

set them both concretely within the categories of social interaction and social structure.

Among others, Karl Mannheim has given substantive notice to the type of analysis I have termed sociotic. In *Ideology and Utopia* (p. 244-247):

> Thought is a particularly sensitive index of social and cultural change. The variation in the meaning of words and the multiple connotations of every concept reflect polarities of mutually antagonistic schemes of life implicit in these nuances of meaning . . . For this reason, the sociological analysis of meaning will play a significant role in the following studies . . . Nowhere in the realm of social life, however, do we encounter such a clear traceable interdependence and sensitivity to change and varying emphasis as in the meaning of words. The word and the meaning that attaches to it is truly a collective reality. The slightest nuance in the total system of thought reverberates in the individual word and the shadow of meaning it carries. The word binds us to the whole of past history and at the same time mirrors the totality of the present. (p. 74)

In his "Das Konservative Denken[28] Mannheim shows how the members of various social positions discerned diverse meanings in the physically same word, and thus talked past one another. He also has given very brief notice to the manner in which "the absence of certain concepts," "the phenomenon of the counterconcept," "the level of abstraction," and "the structure of the categorical apparatus," may be utilized in analyses of the social dimensions of thought.

But it is the French school of sociologism that has given elaborate, if a little vague and certainly confused, theoretic articulation to sociotics. It is the members of this "school" who have employed this mode of analysis in monographic attacks on concrete materials. Among them Granet's work looms up as, on the whole, an admirable instance.

Now it must be clearly grasped that, as a theory and a technique of analysis, sociotics (under any name) involves a sociological theory of language and a social-lingual theory

---

[28] *Archv. fur Sozialwissenschaft und Sozialpolitik,* Vol. 57, p. 90 ff.

of mind. I question whether French sociology has been adequate in either of these connections.

Men like Meillet seem to have had a firm hold on the social influences on the functions of language. He brilliantly demonstrated the idea that vocabulary, registering changes in societal facts, is a sensitive instrument.

The principle involved in the majority of changes of meaning is to be sought in the division of speakers into various social groups and in the passage of the words from one social group to the other.[29]

Nevertheless, one misses the characterizaiton of the generic function of language which has been so brilliantly set forth by such American thinkers as Grace DeLaguna, Dewey, and Mead. The beginnings found in these works will, if carried on, enable a more precise formulation of a theory of sociotics and should open wider the gates to further monographic study in this field. Granet's excellent analysis would have been more penetrating and sound had he been fully and systematically aware of the sociological theory of language as set forth by DeLaguna, and the social-lingual theory of mind formulated in outline by Mead.[30] At the present writing I shall confine myself to a brief critique of Granet's conception of language.

In his summation of the features of the Chinese language, Granet writes:

> We are habituated to considering language as a set of symbols specially organized for the communication of ideas. (But) the Chinese do not place the art of language apart from other procedures of signaling and acting. It appears to them to be one with all the body of techniques serving to situate individuals in the system of civilization which forms society and the universe. These diverse techniques of attitude aim first of all to promote action. When they speak and write, they . . . are seeking to display and suggest lines of conduct. The thinkers have not pretended differently. They

[29] *L'Année Sociologique,* xi, p. 791 (also X, 600; VII, 676; IX, 15ff; XII, 850. Compare this with Morris' notion of the dual control of linguistic change, op. cit. See also Vendryes, *A Linguistic Introduction to History;* and: Cornejo, *Sociologie Generale,* p. 66.

[30] See references in C. Wright Mills' "Situated Actions and Vocabularies of Motive," *Am. Soc. Review,* December, 1940.

are perfectly content with a traditional system of symbols more powerful in the orientation of action than apt in formulating concepts, theories, or dogmas.

There are three things to be said of this:

(i) The characterization given is not adequate in setting off Chinese from other languages. It is now a guiding rule of sophisticated research and theory in the field of language that its generic function lies not in the "expression of antecedent ideas" but in the co-ordination of diverse social actions. This is as true of English and French as it appears to be of Sino-Tibetan tongues. Presumably all the languages have a pragmatic as well as a semantic and some sort of a syntactical dimension. Languages may be differentiated in terms of the emphasis and character given to one or to a combination of these dimensions. Differences between tongues which appear absolute will, if we employ an adequate theoretic frame for language study, be seen as relative emphases on certain characteristics of all tongues. So viewed, we may say that the Chinese language emphasizes the socio-pragmatic and the semantic dimension of language, that it is largely a *denotative language in which the denotata elicit consummatory responses.*[31] Such responses and concepts channel perception.

Why did the Chinese not look around them and see facts? We now know that perception itself is not a mirror-like operation. The eye of man is not only animal. It is an educated eye. The perceptual schemas in which men are involved are part of diverse frames of meaning. The eye is informed by a set of concepts. Sight is sensitized. Classifications lurk in every look. Latent in sight is selection of what one would see. Experience with the eye and thought are bound together in an institutionally based system of concepts.

Other languages have something of the features which Granet notes as Chinese. But in English, *e.g.,* they are not so widely evidenced by professional thinkers—or is it that we cannot become aware of them as easily? Yet sociological training, if it be thorough, must result in the ability to

[31] For the full import of these terms see John Dewey, *Experience and Nature,* first four chapters.

see the familiar in its societal significance. Do we not assume an entire social and economic order, and also the
limits of the solution to a problem when we call the men
lounging at the corner "unemployed?" And, do we not
have plenty of "Chinese emblems," words whose very syl-
lables give us the consummatory tinkle, *e.g.,* democracy,
peace? Until we know more concerning the differences between Chinese and Occidental languages in their relations
to conceptual thinking it had best be left a matter of emphasis and not absolute.

(ii) Besides the fact of relative emphasis on and the character of the generic dimensions of language, another differentiation is found in the apparent absence in Chinese
of a highly refined and specialized terminology for the intellectual elite. Or perhaps, I should say, in the direction
which the specialization of the elites' language has taken.
(See last two sentences in above quote.) No doubt the
character of the language was a factor in this matter. Certainly the relative absence of grammar or of any explicit
syntax influenced the logic of the Chinese. But it may also
be that the structure and position of the learned elite, its
distance from other cultural strata, and its close relation to
the conservative ruling clique—that such factors as these
have played their part. Granet is not too explicit on such
points.

(iii) It would also seem that the "low" position of the
crafts in Chinese life would be an influence working against
the development of a socially neutral vocabulary. In the
West, many words that can claim such a status have been
extracted and generalized from the material logic of physical manipulation. In this respect China is similar to ancient
Greece, but we all learned concepts filtered through to us
from Greece before we became in any sense critically self-
conscious. It is a blind spot.

Granet is given to explaining the persistence of several
mental bents (*e.g.,* the emblematic writing) by an appeal
to an "orientation of mind." This will not do. We must
go beneath all such phrases. Here the social-lingual
theory of mind is our key. With it we hope to explain mental action in non-mental language, by appeal to societal and
linguistic factors. Another name for this attempt is natural-

ism. An extreme and fascinating view on this matter has been suggested by I. A. Richards:

> The prime question is perhaps: How deep may differences between human minds go? If we grant that the general physiology and neurology of the Chinese and Western races are the same, might there not still be room for important psychological differences? Peoples who have lived for great periods of time in different cultural settings—developing different social structures and institutions—might they not really differ vastly in their mental constitution? Might not the differences be even more than differences in the interconnections of a common set of psychical functions and in the relative precedence or emphasis among them? Is it legitimate to conceive not only a different order among a set of common basic formations but further an actual difference among the basic formations themselves? . . . The Tripartite Division (Thinking, Feeling, Willing) might well be a scheme applicable usefully to minds that have grown up, taken form, and learnt to function within a given social and cultural framework (including language). Yet it might be applicable only to such minds and another scheme be more useful in considering minds which take shape under other conditions. Among such variable determining conditions popular psychology that is embodied in current speech might well take a chief place. It is a possible suggestion that we perhaps Think and Feel and Will because we have for so long been talking as though we did and that if language and tradition professed a different set of psychic functions we might be conducting our minds otherwise. This is an uncomfortable suggestion, since it would give to a change in popular psychological theory more consequence than we usually allow. If it is a nonsensical suggestion, as it may be, one may wish that some psychologist would reassure us with an argument, that would demolish it satisfactorily. (*Mencius on the Mind*, p. 80-82)

## V

Granet records three general characteristics of Chinese thought which are summarized by H. Berr.[32] (a) It is oriented towards the culture and not toward pure knowledge; it tends to be wisdom and not science, as the West under-

---

[32] In preface to Granet, *La Pensée Chinoise*, vii, viii.

stands these terms. Chinese wisdom ends politically, morally. (b) It binds man to the universe; "nature forms a
single order." This intimate unity of the world animates
Chinese thought in its naive manifestations and in all the
sects. There is nothing in Chinese literature which corresponds to the "spiritualism" of the West. The Chinese do
not oppose the subject of knowledge to its object as the
West has done. Subject and object are linked in unitary
fashion. The problems of epistemology which characterize
Western intellectual history are not found among the
Chinese. (c) There is nothing in the Chinese mentality suggestive of our proud *rationalism,* no discursive
reasoning, none of our "critical judgment." A unique order
presides over all life, organic and inorganic. This order
realizes itself concretely in meaningful knowledge which
does not take the form of abstract law. The wisdom of
man and the order of nature are in harmony. Society and
the world form a system of civilization.

These pervasive underpinnings find their detailed manifestations in the schools and sects. Already they have been
shown to be connected with the character of the language.
The second point will be detailed later. They are all evidenced in the basic categories of ancient China.
*Note on Technology and the Logic of the Craft-mind.*

There is one further characteristic that is important in
understanding Chinese mentality in its societal context.
It is particularly revealing to thinkers who are orientated
basically to Western thought, and especially to the intellectual currents in America:

> For thousands of years, there have been in China acute and
> learned men patiently devoting their lives to study. Having
> regard to the span of time, and to the population concerned,
> China forms the largest volume of civilization which the
> world has seen. There is no reason to doubt the intrinsic
> capacity of individual Chinamen for the pursuit of science.
> And yet Chinese science is practically negligible. There is no
> reason to believe that China if left to itself would have ever
> produced any progress in science. The same may be said
> of India.[33]

[33] A. N. Whitehead, *Science and the Modern World,* p. 8-9.

The reason for this is to be found in the fact that although the Chinese show a fine aptitude for the mechanical arts and crafts and for observation *this work is not accompanied by reflection* that is even close to what the West calls scientific. The "thinking elite" did not learn from the carpenters, the surveyors, the men who in the West combined eye and hand and tools and laid a basis for a logic of things: a material and tool logic that is at the heart of modern physical science. No progress in the crafts influence "the modern physical science." No progress in the crafts influenced "the thinkers." It is out of craft experience that Western minds have generalized the scientific type of logic and of mind with its canons of reality and opaque truth. The ethos of the Chinese community and thinkers did not allow such generalizations.[34] In America this type of generalization from laboratory and craft facts has gone further than anywhere else. American pragmatism from Pierce through Dewey, and the core of Veblen has been built squarely around the technological laboratory and industrial domain of the culture. The Chinese did not. Thus, although the means-ends, the physically technical logic, was no doubt implicit in the craft work of the Chinese (and everywhere over the world where tool and eye and hand inform and guide mind), this logic was not raised to form part of the circle of official canons of truth and reality. The thinking elite were concerned with other domains of culture: the moral, liturgical, and political. The conceptions and structure of Chinese thought cannot be explained in terms of technological domain and experiences. Such experiences were not had by the professional thinkers, definitely taken into account.

Certain ideas are directive of the operations of Chinese thought. They have the value of categories because they are basic. But they are *synthetic* and *concrete* categories. *Yin* and *Yang* and *Tao* are three such categories. Nothing in the West is comparable to these. They are not like the categories of time, space, number, cause, etc., so central to the West. They are not analytical but concrete notions. It is

---

[34] R. K. Merton has ably documented the Pietistic persuasions and permissives of Western science in seventeenth century England. *Science, Technology and Society in Seventeenth Century England.*

difficult to adapt these notions to the area of Western understanding. With Yin and Yang the elite of all "schools"
seek to translate a sentiment of rhythm which permits them
to conceive the connections of time and space as intimate,
as a duet. Tao is even more synthetic. Unlike our postulate of causality which is a principle, or a hope, of universal order, Tao invokes in its totality and unity an Order at
once ideal and active. Tao is the supreme category. Yin and
Yang are secondary. They are all active. And they encom-
pass all the world, all of mind. No one dreams of defining
them. They carry a putative quality of efficacy.

According to Granet, Occidental interpreters have gone
to their work with certain falsifying conceptions. In these
cardinal notions of the Chinese they have seen the products of this or that doctrine. They have treated these notions as academic conceptions, susceptible of being defined
and qualified in abstract fashion. They have begun by looking for their equivalents in the conceptual language of our
philosophers. They end by remarking on their curiosity
and their belief that these notions have no intellectual value.
Or perhaps they label the thought prelogical or mythical
and let it go at that.

Granet's approach is not limited by these kinds of pre-
conception. He respects and attempts to account for the
originality of the thought, its peculiarly synthetic, emblematic, and "efficacious" quality. Without attempting to define or qualify them, he tries to recognize the content of
the notions and to make their multiple usages apparent.
In the Chinese mind certain categories play the role
of principles of organization and intelligibility. These are
now to be exhibited and examined.

## VI

No Chinese philosopher dreamed of conceiving of time
as a monotonous duration constituted by succession, a
mere uniform movement of qualitatively similar moments.
No one has been interested in considering space as a simple extension resulting from the juxtaposition of homogeneous elements, as an extension of which all the parts would
be exchangeable. These thinkers see in time an ensemble

of eras, of seasons, and of epochs; and in space a complex of domains, of climates and of directions. In each direction space is singular and takes on the attributes peculiar to a climate or a domain. In similar fashion time is diversified into periods of various natures. Each is adorned with characteristics proper to a season or to an era. But while the two parts of space may differ radically from one another, and from the two parts of time, each period is solidly related to a climate, each direction is linked to a season.

To all discrete portions of space there corresponds a singular portion of time. The same nature appertains to them both and is signalized by an undivided set of attributes. They are indissolubly intertwined. "The Chinese thinker never separates considerations of time from those of space." Time and space are not conceived as two homogeneous milieus resident in abstract concepts. They are always imagined as "an ensemble of concrete and diverse groupings, of *sites* and *occasions*." They classify aspects of the world in view of action in it and by reason of the particular efficacies of object and events.

In section 3, above, I have summarized Granet's examination of the Chinese language. The "terms" for time and space follow the lines disclosed in that examination. They are not definite and distinct, but emblematic and rich in affinities. Time and space are not conceived as neutral, nonmoral, or abstract. *Fang* is applied not to space in itself, but to direction, to site (favorable or unfavorable to a certain action). *Che* is applied not to time in itself but to circumstance, to occasion. These are emblems which govern and elicit the correct action at the correct time and place. The actions which they thus control are governmental. They are the actions of a sovereign. But the terms are also the objects of "philosophic" speculation.

This speculation seeks to classify particular sites and occasions with the end in view of guiding the actions of the sovereign in terms of the particular nature of the sites and occasions. The philosophers are attachés of the ruling stratum. By thinking about these emblems they sought to discover the principles of a supreme art. The object of this art is to manage the universe and at the same time society as an intrinsic part of that universe. The collective representations of time and space are "deprived" . . . from the "principles" which preside over the partitions of human groupings: thus, a study of these representations cannot be carried on apart from a study of social morphology. That is the central thesis of Granet's chapter on time and space.

Time is round. Space is square. All surface is in itself square. If it be properly virtuous, time proceeds by revolution in great cyclical fashion. These are the "pure forms" of extension and duration. There are intermediary forms, such as the oblong, and these intermediary forms, combinations of the square and the circle, are symbols of particular interactions of space and time. For example, circles are symbols of particular interactions of space and time. For example, the convexity of mountains is linked with the temporal character of autumn. Each space is informed with a species of time. Together they make up an emblem.

The earth is square and is divided into smaller squares. The walls of the villages form a square. The fields and the camps are also square. Each side of the earth corresponds to a direction. Camps, buildings, towns must be oriented. The determination of these orientations is a task fulfilled by the chief in a religious assembly. The techniques of the division and management of space, such as carpentering, townbuilding, political geography, and the geometrical speculation which they presuppose, are connected with the practice of a public cult.

After a secular, egoistic time, monotonous and void of emotion, there occurs a time overflowing with sacred hope . . . and adds Granet, in characteristic Durkheimian vein, with "that creative activity proper to exercises accomplished in common." The faithful members arrange themselves in a square. The altar of the sun, a sacred mound, was their center. This mound was square and covered with a yellow earth which was the symbol of centerness. The sides of the mound are directed to the four directions and there covered with greenish earth. *The sacred square represented the totality of the empire.*

In times of impending disaster, for example an eclipse, the vassals from each portion of the dynasty run to the center and arrange themselves in their proper places

around the sacred square. Each of them wears a proper
badge or insignia which expresses the spatial nature of his
fief. By forming a square while wearing these insignia they
save the country, they reconstitute the space and time that
is thought to be deranged. They preserve the integrity of
space. By the arrangements of the vassals around and in
the sacred square, space is restored in all its dimensions.
This is thought to be accomplished by the sole force of the
emblems correctly arranged around the sacred place of
federal reunion. In this illustration is seen the idea of a
square earth and space linked to a set of social rules. These
rules of ordinance of the assemblies play a decisive role in
rendering sensible and imposing in all their detail the symbols which constitute the representations of space. According to Granet they explain the square form which he alleges
the idea of space to have for the ancient Chinese. This
social rule and collective practice also explains the heterogeneous character which the idea of space possesses: the
symbol of different species of space are linked with diverse
social groups which adhere to them.

Beyond the square sides of space and forming a sort of
fringe lie four vague regions which are named The Four
Seas. In or near these seas lives the animal-like barbarian.
Only the Chinese are human. And only the Chinese live in
"cultivated" space. Space that is uncultivated will support
only imperfect beings, the barbarians. Theirs is only a
diluted space and one that fades away and ends.

Full space only exists where extension is socialized. The
limits of the dynasty exhausts The Domain of Space. The
chief is charged with the care of this space—he manages
the world, keeps it in order. At his inauguration he promul-
gates his ordinances and they include a certain allotment
to the savage chiefs who are representative of the half-
spaces on the vague frontiers of the world which shade off
into nothing. The barbarians from the four seas must align
themselves behind the pregnant ritual which the faithful
undergo, for even they are part of constituted society.

The promulgations of the chief establishes a hierarchy
of extensions: different portions of space have different
values. At the center, space is most pure and dense, for
there congregate all the attributes of space as an integral

unity. This sacred place of federal unity is a closed world.
It is equivalent to an entire and total space. And it is here
that the social group knows its diversity, hierarchy, its
order. Here, where all diverse units of the society congregate, space is full, compact, concentrated, coherent. The
site for this sacred square is carefully chosen: it must be
near the celestial "palace;" it must be a place where the
convergence of rivers and climates authenticates its being
the true center of the world.

Space is complex: there is a hierarchy of spaces and there
are spaces which directly correspond to the seasons. In
order to keep space in order, to manage it, the chief must
spend certain allotted portions of his time residing in
various portions, or sections, of the dynasty. He must so
arrange these visits on which he receives in audience the
vassal from the sector so that he is at a certain place at a
certain season. Thus, while traveling with the sun from the
east, he connects time and space and preserves social and
universal harmony. It took five years to complete this
journey.

The circulation of the sovereign adapts time to space: it
also preserves a certain rhythm between the two. Every five
years this is helped along and space and time are reanimated and reordered by an assemblage and ritual around
the sacred square at the center of the earth. The order of
the society was feudal and this, according to Granet, is the
reason why the conception of space remained a hierarchical federation of heterogeneous extensions.

The ancient Chinese decompose time into periods, as
they do space into regions. But each of many times are defined by a set of attributes. Corresponding to each species
of time is a notion that is impersonal, but thoroughly concrete. Each period is marked by attributes which are proper
to a season of the year or to an hour of the day or something similar. But this is not to say that the conceptions of
time are astronomical. If seasons have been linked at all
with symbols of time it is because time appears to have
a cyclical nature and that the year with its seasons is the
image of a cycle and thus may properly furnish symbols
with which to characterize diverse cycles of time. The
Chinese representations of time are linked with a liturgical

order. The annual cycle of the seasons is not their prototype. Their order embraces a moment of history, a dynasty,
a reign, a portion of a reign, which is distinguished by a set
of rules or a formula of life which singularizes this or that
particular epoch of civilization.

The dynastic eras are signalized by the same set of emblems as the seasons and the directions. Are these cyclical
ideas and representations inspired directly by the seasonal,
astronomical rhythms? Granet's answer is: No. If the representations and the annual rituals seem to depend on astronomical, natural, sequences this is only so because the
society is above all agricultural. With an agrarian culture
as a base, these aspects of natural phenomena are selected
out for attention and linked with the representations for certain times and spaces. Nature offers the signal and furnishes
the occasion. But the need which implements the perception
of these particular signalizing aspects of nature has its
source firmly rooted in the social life of this agrarian
society. The Chinese have the conception of a space
and time which needed to be reordered in periodic "re-
pasts" or "rebuilding" because they themselves felt obliged
to reunite periodically in assemblies. As the fetes wherein
the human group retook life and social shape occurred at
the death of each season, so the participants imagined that
Time was remade, reanimated at the end of each year.[35]

Sometimes space is full. Sometimes it is diluted. It is
fullest during the time of the federal reunion. During this
time, some dozen days, each day takes on, ritually, the
aspects and characteristics of a full month. Time is concentrated then. In a chronologically short duration there is the
equivalent to the life of an entire year.

In a civilization where social activities never cease to be
close-knit and intense, continuity appears to be an essential
character of time. But when social life alternates with the
agrarian seasons there are times and spaces that are intense

[35] Granet's statement of the relative weight and the character of
the roles assigned to *natural events perceived* and *social events acted*
seems adequate to his task. However, a more adequate, adaptable
and rigorous statement is needed for a systematic sociology of
knowledge. There are excellent "leads" for such a statement in scattered literatures dealing with social factors involved in perception.

as well as those that are diluted and faint. Full spaces and strong times are linked only at the site and occurrence of the ritualistic assemblages. Between these fetes are weak times and empty spaces. A simple rhythm governs these conceptions, and it is a rhythm related to the life habitations of an agrarian life with agrarian liturgies. This rhythmical constitution, of which the principle is found in the antithesis of periods of dispersion and concentration, is expressed in the ideas of opposition and alternation and by the representations of time and space. Such is the source for the sentiment which invests different times and spaces with different values. And this latter idea is, of course, linked with the notion that time and space are of varied natures.

Enough has been said to show that the conceptions of time and space of these ancient peoples were not abstract and pure categories. In accord with the nature of Chinese language, they were concrete and always confounded with particular sites and occasions which were of social significance. Above all they are not understandable without reference to the social morphology, the economy, and the liturgy of the people who held them. The collective representations of time and space constituted a framework for the total art of ruling. They supported an art of managing, by symbol and ritual, the world and the society of humans at its center. There is nothing about them which even faintly suggests the employment of categories in the organization of abstract thought which has been among Western thinkers a predominant ideal.

## VII

Chinese philosophy from the ancient period is dominated by the notions of Yin and of Yang. These two "categories" are at various times, and always indistinctly, valued as forces, substances and genres. But strictly speaking, they are *not* comparable to any such Western categories. Their function is the "classification" and animation of all antithetical aspects of the universal order, which is Tao. Yin and Yang synthetically evoke, they stir up ("suscitement") globularly the rhythmic ordinance which presides over the lives of the world and the activities of mind.

All of Chinese thought proceeds under the joint persuasion of order, of totality and of rhythm.

There are many sources evidencing these notions; they occur in various types of literature and form a very early date. They appear in early *astronomical* writings, and in manuals of *divination*. The theorcticians of music never cease to use them. They constitute elements in *calendrical* and *geometric* lore: they are applied to sacred places by *theoreticians of orientation* and to the quasi-holy happenings proper to such places.

The book of *Che king* utilizes Yin and Yang as poetic prescriptions. In the language of this book, Yin evokes the idea of the times of coldness and of that which is cold; again, it may mean a wet, a rainy heaven or atmosphere, and it is applied to that which is interior. Yang awakens the idea of sunshine, of heat; it paints the male aspect of a dancer in full action, it is a word of the springtime and of that tenth month of the year in which begins the winter hibernation of man.

Yin and Yang signalize concrete and antithetical aspects of time and space. Yin is for the shady slope, Yang is for the sunlit hills and fields or for those who stand in the sunlight.

Yin and Yang are symbols which have been utilized by various technicians, magicians, and ritualists; but they are also words which are used in what is slightly akin to what the West calls the quest for knowledge. This quest takes the form of an "analysis" of the representations of time and space; this knowledge is closely connected with the ritualistic techniques of locating and utilizing sites and occasions. It ties in with liturgy and with ceremonial; with topographical and chronological arts. And on this knowledge depends the sets of divinatory techniques.

Yin and Yang evoke in a concrete fashion all the contrasts that are possible. In them concretely appear a résumé of all the other representatives used by men who think. This superantithesis is not of forces or of substances or of principles. They are simply two emblems which are the most powerfully suggestive, the richest in the vocabulary.

*No metaphysical dualism is implied by them.* The authority and the form of these master rubrics derive from the fact that together they make up a harmonious world. For in them are all contrasts and in their union in Tao is all the harmony of the universe, the cosmos, and man.

Such a concerted action of Yin and Yang are not attributes of them as intellectual principles. We shall see that its source, and that of the conceptions themselves, is clearly social. They do not "signify" in the first instance, two antagonistic Realities, but two rival groups. They are not to be defined as logical entities nor as simple cosmological principles. They are not substances or forces, nor genres. They are all these things, indistinctly; and various technicians have conceived of them in this or that dimension to the exclusion of what others have found in them. Compositely, as predominant features of the common, the communal, the anonymous intellectual tradition, they are groupings of "aspects" and of societal functions. They have their seat in the attributes of the two moieties which make up the social body.

To the ancient Chinese, a concrete space and time form the warp and woof of a universe that is finished. But Chinese thought seems dominated by the idea that the contrast of two concrete aspects characterizes this universe as well as each of its appearances. The thought is permeated by the domain of symbols of *correspondences* and *oppositions*. When one wishes to act or to understand, one sets these in operation. Yin and Yang have a managerial function over all things and they introduce into all things a rhythm.

The theory of Yin and Yang owes very much to the *musicians,* perhaps more than to the *astronomers* and *divinators*. But all three of these types of thinkers have worked from a common thought. It is out of this common thought that Yin and Yang arose to inform and channel diverse endeavors. This common thought is dominated by the notion of opposition, of dual contrast. For example, Yin and Yang have been utilized as directive principles by the wise men who organize the calendar. To the Chinese the calendar is a supreme "law." It appears to regulate the happenings of nature because within their social monism it also regulates the doings of the human world. These are symbols capable of evoking the rhythmical formula of the regime of life characteristic of ancient times.

Yin and Yang have been capable of organizing the calendar because they are able to evoke, with a peculiar power, the rhythmical conjugations of two concrete and antithetical "aspects." Conjugation by two is a central focus of this period of Chinese thought. Back of this focus is the cycle of the seasons which form the contours of Chinese life: the hibernation of the time of winter when the woman weaves and doors are closed in the huts (Yin); and spring when the men go out into the fields into the sunshine and the doors are open (Yang). During the winter hibernation Yin circumscribes Yang. Yin hides it, covers it in the subterranean springs under the ice. The changes in the habitat and in the types of animals (particularly birds) and the cracking of the ice—all these signalize the release of Yang. Yin and Yang denote all these natural signals. But the cradle of these conceptions, Granet traces to the semiannual fetes and to the occupational *divisions and cycles of the social structure* which proceeds along lines of sex. The changes in seasons overlap this sexual division of labor, so that the aspect of the social structure to which the conceptions are traced are the *division* of labor and the occupational *cycle* when the women and the men both shift their activities, the woman ceasing to weave at the death of the winter hibernation and the men coming out of hibernation and going to the sunlit fields to labor. These are alternating and contrasting societal segments, and the conceptions partake of their character.

The Chinese grammar is without the categories of gender. But Chinese thought is dominated by the idea of sex. All things may be classified under Yin or under Yang. All that is of feminine nature is covered by Yin; all that is of masculine nature, by Yang. If you would understand this sexual factor, do not think of sensual love. The "sex" here is of different content, function and form. I have said that Yin and Yang in certain combinations produce a harmony between human grouping and between man and nature. Now you are saying the same thing when you say that such harmony is produced and preserved by the sex life of the sovereign ruler. For that, too, is an interaction of Yin and

Yang. He must not be too chaste and he must not be debauched.

Not only is this true of the sovereign. It is true of sectors of the populace who have attained the status of a propitious age. I have mentioned the social division of labor and the occupational cycles of men and women which coincide with shift in season. There is a ritual, an orgy, a fete of ceremonial in which these societal factors are focalized and revivified. It occurs twice each solar year. The oppositions of the sexes is the cardinal rule of Chinese social organization. The category of sex is predominant. In this ritual the men line up on one side of a valley. The sun comes over the top of the hills and shines full upon them. In the shadows and opposite the men stand the women. Between these two groups has been divided the work during the year. Now they are to realize their complementary character in ritual form. Now they are to unite in copulation lying there upon the sacred square which marks the domain of their dynasty. Yin and Yang, these are the emblems they evoke and call back and forth. These are the two formulas which will unite and harmonize the world of man and nature. Yin and Yang are the emblems for the door. They are also the emblems for the sexual fete. Yang evokes the image of an open door, of generation, production, of forces that manifest themselves. It is of the spring. Yin is of the winter and the time of the women and the weaving, the closed door, of latent forces. But now they are all one. The boys have called. The daughters have answered. Now time blends perfectly with space. The site and the occasion are correct. There is harmony, there is order, and there is a unity between man and that cosmos of which he is a solid part. The two sexes have submitted to an antithetical discipline. And this is projected mythically: Yin and Yang are Tao.

Yin and Yang evoke in instantaneous fashion these dramatic spectacles in which solidified yet rival groupings communicate with emblem and deed and become complements of something larger than and embracive of all of life and time and place. They are two choruses singing of Yin and Yang. They are face to face and they dance antithetically. First one group dances and sings, then the other. They alternate. Then they interact. This rhythmical liaison of complementary, though diverse, social grouping explains the diversity of duration and extension and their close union under the domination of Yin and Yang. Here is a total and harmoniously related society focalized in a rite. The idea of the couplet so markedly evidenced in Chinese thinking has its origin in and owes its perpetuation to the aspects of social structure already noted. And the idea of the couplet, the antithetical, is perpetually connected to the idea of communion, an indissoluble ensemble.

If Yin and Yang form a *couplet* and seem to preside conjointly over the rhythm which underlies the universal order, it is because their conception was constructed in an age of history wherein the principle of rotation (rather than the ideal of single "authority") sufficed to regulate the social activity going on between two complementary groupings. The conception of Tao arose in a less archaic epoch. It was able to become explicit only at a time and place where the structure of society was more complicated and in a milieu where the authority of the chief justifies itself and is presented as the sole author of the order which rules the world of men and of things. Then, and then only, is the idea of a unique and central power of animation "set forth," and "accepted."

## VIII

The *idea of quantity* does not figure in the philosophic speculation of the Chinese, but *numbers* passionately interest these thinkers. The skills of the surveyor, carpenter, architect, musician, these might have led to arithmetical and geometrical knowledge. But no member of the professional thinking elite availed himself of these implicit materials. The aim was to manipulate numbers in the same manner as any other emblems are handled. If their image of the world is of numbers, then numbers cannot serve in measuring the world. Numbers are manifestations of the structure of reality. To the Chinese, numbers are remarkable by reason of their polyvalence, for this makes them eminently suitable for efficacious manipulation. This is the fundamental trait of this domain of intellectual life: *an extreme respect for numerical symbols combined with an extreme indifference for all quantitative conceptions.* To understand this conception is to disentangle and to grasp the curious blends that go to make up Chinese thought on this head.

The Chinese "knew" that the embryonic stage of man lasts 10 months. Now, heaven is emblematically valued at 1; the earth, 2; man counts to the score of 3. Three times three equals nine. Nine times nine equals eighty-one. One regulates the sun; the sun regulates man. And that is why man's embryonic stage lasts 10 months.

Things are classified by means of numerical symbols. Numerical classifications command the details of thought and life. They serve to express the *qualities* of certain groupings or in order to indicate an hierarchical ordinance. Over and above this classificatory function, numbers have the function of a protocol. Granet documents this fundamental thesis in minute detail and with close reference to a great number of the ancient writings. It is impossible to portray the character of his analysis within brief compass. Its value is in its detail. Hence, I sketch only the barest contours of his statement.

The distinction between ordinal, cardinal, and distributive employment of numbers is not, for the Chinese, an essential interest. One uses numbers in order to classify because they serve concretely to situate and figure. They remain emblems in all manipulations. They possess a great descriptive power. In order to describe numerically the Chinese arrange numerical signs in 3 series: in series of tens, twelves, and in decimals. One qualifies, in effect, numbers in these three manners.

The signs of the 10 and 12 series stir up groups of images and by so doing, are rubrics of concrete ensembles which they serve to *specify* by the sole fact that they *situate* in time and space.

The universe is closed. Space and time are finished. Numerical signs are also finished; they qualify in such a way as to be an etiquette for various sectors of space and time. Each of them corresponds to a time and a site and it orders them, orients action in the form of the cycle. The conception of a cycle of correct behavior is thus linked by numbers with a system of classification of time and place.

In order that the universe present itself as an ordered ensemble, it is necessary and sufficient that a calendar be officially promulgated. The world is recreated anew as soon as the chief exercises his right by setting up the numbers of the calendar.

The matrimonial system is under the authority of an exogamy of the name. Also if one wishes to wipe out the stain of a sacrilegious error, it is only necessary to discover the name of the genie which manifests it, and to fix the site of its appearance. The formulae for accomplishing these things is, in part, numerical.

The ontological and the logical order translates itself into a set of rhythmical and geometrical images. The two orders are so mingled that it is possible to classify and order the former by manipulation of numerical expressions. By reason of their descriptive power, numbers are called upon in the identification of real groups. Numbers signify diverse types of organization which impose themselves on things when their proper rank in the universe is realized.

Among these forms of organization the cycle is of the utmost importance. For this form is for the Chinese rich in geometrical and rhythmical representations. Richer than ordinary cyclical signs, numbers are better able to group relata, and identify them, to signalize their situation, and order, their form and composition.

The art of music is founded on the art of numbers. Numbers determine the lengths of the bamboo flutes. If the Chinese have founded their musical technique on an arithmetical principle, they have not found it necessary to apply it rigorously. This is because the reason for their discovery of the principle was a game played with numerical symbols (considered not as abstract signs, but as efficacious emblems). The end of this game was not the formulation of an exact theory which rigorously justified a technique, but to illustrate the technique in linking it to a fascinating image of the world.

Again it must be recorded that Granet's detailed exposition of the manner in which these numbers are linked with the musical notes, seasons, and sentiments proper to various tones and keys must here be omitted. In addition to these connections the role of numerical symbols in fixing architectural proportions and linking them to an image of the world is large. It received due attention from Granet. There remains one more point which must be mentioned: *the protocol function of numbers.*

This function is connected with their classificatory employment. The first usage of number, odd and even, lies in the distributing of all things within the categories, Yin and Yang. With the aid of numbers, the thinkers were able to represent the protocol order which rules the universal life. These are social rules. The order of the society was feudal. Hence, a logic of hierarchy inspires all the systems of numerical classification. The numbers have a logical function which is classificatory and protocol at the same time. They fix the etiquettes for diverse groups which they classify.

## IX

The sovereign lord manages the world and animates it. From the center of the confederation he holds it firmly to its course and then all the universe coexists and endures. The attribution of total authority to a person, the Unique Man, accompanies the Chinese conception of a powerful regularity. This power and regularity is envisaged under the aspect of a principle of order and supreme efficacy: Tao.

Of all the Chinese notions, that of Tao is the most obscure; its history is most difficult to establish, for there is great uncertainty about the chronology and authenticity of the documents which carry it. The idea cannot be considered as appertaining only to the school of Taoists. It belongs to the domain of common and anonymous thought. Conceptions of it vary, but at bottom all conceptions look to the notions of Order, Totality, of Responsibility, and Efficacy. Granet also connects it loosely to the notion of *mana*. And always the notion is tied to the consideration that the "total art" permits the Chief to regulate the world and the empire. It is the unique principle of all success and it is geared to the art of government.

Tao is also the virtue proper to "an honest man." This is modeled after the image of the prince who possesses in large degree this peculiar talent. Techniques are also thought to depend on the total knowledge that is Tao. Tao means "prescriptions, methods, rules." With Tao one can succeed in the astronomical and physical skills.

Historically, Tao, first meant "road" or "way." Granet ventures the hypothesis, and supports it with erudite detail, that Tao begins by evoking the image of the circulation of the sovereign which had for its aim the delimitation, by a series of roads, the sets or portions of reality (names, emblems, insignia) among the people. This act of royal circulation also signified the power of regulation and orderly efficacy vested in him. For in circulating on the earth the sovereign imitates the march of the sun and is considered by the Heavens as a Son.

Felicitous contact between the Earth and the Heavens is able to be set up only through the intermediation of the sovereign. He is the unique master of the public courts. He makes a tour of the Empire in the manner of the Sun; in this way he adjusts Directions to Seasons and proves that he is capable of making reign on the earth of man a Celestial Order (T'ien Tao). The Royal way (Wang Tao) invokes and is integrated with the Celestial Order. T'ien Tao and Wang Tao are two interrelated themes; they are different aspects of the same set of belief, emblem, and ritual. Only through the unique man is the sovereign heaven and is earth able to communicate and retain their fortunate harmony. He is the pivot of a great axis.

Hence there is much poetry and myth centering around this royal circulation, or imperial circuit. Its importance is magnified and sustained by this poetry, and by the emblems. If Tao has been able to take the meaning of efficacy, virtue, and authority, all of which in turn suggest a total order entirely conforming to a Celestial order, it is because the inauguration of a princely power accompanies the repartition of the things of the world between the groupings submissive to a new chief who partitions between them the sectors of the universe. Having distributed the insignia in circulating over the earth in the manner of the sun (T'ien Tao), he is worthy of being called the son of heaven and the unique man, and he has the right to become the axis of the world. In the sacred instant (in the reaffirmation of the celestial and heavenly spheres) the shadow and the light pivot around this man.

"All Yin, and all Yang, this is Tao." Tao is a total constituted by two aspects which are themselves totals, because they are mutually substitutable. Tao is not their *sum,* but their regulator (not the law) of their alternance. Like Yin and Yang, Tao is a concrete category; it is not in any sense an abstract or first principle.

The mythological thinking, and with it the different techniques which are employed in managing the world, is permeated with the belief that the realities are "stirred up" by emblems. The work of reflection carried on by the theoreticians of the divinatory art has contributed to this disposition of mind by their systematic modes of expression. Conceiving of Tao as an emblematic principle of o der which indistinctly regulates the mental activity and the life of the world, they uniformly admit that the changes which one sees in the course of things are to be identified with the substitution of symbols which are produced in the course of thought. There is in the Chinese record of mentation not the slightest trace of a search for efficient causes. Instead of considering the course of things as a sequence of phenomena susceptible of being measured, and firmly connected with one another, the Chinese see in sensible reality only a mass of concrete signals. The "history" of the analysts holds instead of physics. He who possesses the proper emblem is able to act effectively in reality, As such an emblem. Tao is supreme. It is a total efficacy, a center of responsibility or better, a responsible milieu. But it does not create the world. The sovereign, acting within the complex of emblems, and rituals that constitute Tao is responsible for this order of the world, but he is not its author. In order to give a rule to action and render the world intelligible, there is no need to distinguish between forces, substances, causes, and to look to the problems which lead to the ideas of matter, movement and work. The sentiment of the interdependence of emblematic reality and of its realization is sufficient in itself. It does away with the need to conceive of cause and to search for causes.

These dispositions of the Chinese mind have not prevented the ancient Chinese from realizing a great mechanical aptitude. The perfection of their bows and chariots are testimony to this. But their *conception* of the process of invention precludes the application of quantitive conceptions. When one of their philosophers wished to ex-

plain the invention of the wheel, he stated that the idea for
it had been furnished by flying seeds whirling through the
air. There is a constant tendency away from mechanical
explanations; Chinese thought does not exercise itself in a
domain which would accept opaque notions of movement
and of quantity. It is content in a world of emblems which
they do not differentiate from the "real" or physical world.

The principle of contradiction is not part of their operative minds. The principle which does, in fact, serve to order
their intellectual life is the principle of harmony of contrasts. The efficacious order that regulates their thinking
and action is the fact of *contrasts,* but they exclude the idea
of *contradiction* or even *contrarieties.* The ancient Chinese
built an order of civilization that endured for centuries,
and they did this without reference to the principle of
causation or to that of contradiction.

## X

The ideas of order, of Totality and of Efficacy, dominate
the thinking of the Chinese. They are not concerned with
"the laws of nature." All reality is in itself complete. Everything in the universe is like the universe. Matter and Spirit
are not two worlds that oppose one another. Man is not
given a place apart from the world or given a soul which
is of another essence than his body. Men perform their
differing functions in the social order, and by so doing col-
laborate in maintaining the social order which is founded
and modeled upon the universal order. There is a distinction
in the society between the crowd and the chiefs, the wise
men, the honest man. This idea is congruent with and sup-
portive of a representation of the world which is characterized not by anthropomorphism, but by the predominance
of the notion of *social authority.* The management of the
world is effected by princely virtue which must be informed
by the arts and the sciences of the wise men. The reign of
Etiquette is universal. It is not limited to the world of man
as something from an abstract "nature." The "natural" and
the "conventional" are not distinguished. All is subsumed
under the Etiquette: the natural world and the moral order.
Liberty is not distinguished from a determined order and
the idea of law is foreign to the Chinese thinkers.

"Politics" is given a central place in the Chinese scheme of things: for them the history of the world did not begin before the history of their civilization. They do not recite creation myths or cosmological speculation in the same grand manner as the West. Their myths and speculation along these lines is closely tied up with the biographies of heroes. All legend is linked to the pretended recital of human history and the "political" acts of heroes. One single prepossession inspires and governs these political philosophies and stories of origin: *All being and things exist and endure by reason of the harmony instituted by the sacred authors of the national civilization.* It is because of their wisdom that men and all other beings and things conform to their respective essences (Wou) and fully realize their destiny. This social harmony, which is due to the actions and the ascendency of the sages, leads to a perfect equilibrium of the macrocosm and this equilibrium is reflected in the organization of all microcosms. Thus the prominence of political preoccupation is linked in Chinese thought with a marked aversion for all creationist theory.

The conception of the world is entirely commanded by social representations. The universe is the carriage, or sometimes the house, of the chief. Explicit metaphors contain this idea. The liaison of all universal events with the history of man is the central fact and the principle of all observation. If the learned men have given vast proportions to the universe, they have not ceased to conceive of the world after the model created by their myth-making imaginations. Their knowledge increases in detail without any attempts toward the development of physical explanations. And the architects and the poets have enriched these ancient conceptions.

The universe has really existed only since the moment when the Sages instituted the national civilization. From that moment, too, man the microcosm corresponds in detail with the universe, the macrocosm: the feet of man are square in shape and they rest upon the earth; his head is round and is the image of the heavens. Human beings in their shape reproduce the architecture of the world and both are integrated with a social order. Harmony reigns, and Tao embraces all.

Contrary to Durkheimian expectations Granet finds that:

"The holy and the profane do not form (in China) two separated genres." For Chinese thought interests itself not in *contraries*, but in *contrasts*, in alternations and correlatives, in the hierarchical exchange of attributes.

Rather than trying to measure effects and causes the Chinese contrive to report "correspondences." The order of the universe in never distinguished from the order of the civilization. They do not dream of setting up necessary and unmodified sequences. To employ the traditional and the suitable is considered a more valuable art, and more subtle, and it is this that holds their interest. Knowledge is power. The wise sovereigns secrete, exude a civilization. They maintain and propagate it by extending to all the hierarchy of beings a coherent system of attitudes. There is no conception of constraint by law. The prestige of the traditional suffices. The men have need only of models and of things like them. They do not see in the physical world a necessitous reign and yet they do not claim liberty for the moral domain. The microcosm and macrocosm unite in conserving the venerable habits. The universe is a system of compartments, and the compartments of mind and spirit are not distinguished from those of matter. The distinction of mind and matter is not known. The idea of a soul, of an essence, entirely spiritual and opposed to the body as a material thing is unknown to the Chinese.

Unaware of all spiritual postulates, the Chinese psychology is psychology of conduct. It is part of the moral apparatus of their life.

I. A. Richards notes a decided ethical bent or purpose in Mencius' and his fellows' account of man which prevents their thinking from becoming self-critical. "What they are doing is not so much inquiring into the nature of man as giving an account of it which will conduce to the maintenance of these fixed, unquestionable observances." 'Mencius' psychology, *e.g.,* should be regarded as "an explanatory apology for a system of social practices whose sanction in the sense of compulsive authority is elsewhere than in the doctrine of the sages." It would be conceived as a construction designed to give intellectual support to a system of belief and thought having a definite social basis.

Even today, missionaries in distant areas of China, admit

that they are not able to teach the doctrine of the Fall or
of Original Sin. Man owes all to civilization and civilization owes to man harmonious equilibrium, a sanctity, the
quality of his being. The Chinese never consider man as
isolated from his society. And society is never thought of as
isolated from nature. They do not dream of placing underneath them some vulgar reality, nor above them a world of
purely spiritual essences. Nature forms a single realm. A
unique order presides over an universal life. And it is this
order which imprints itself upon civilization.

Their thought is always moral and social. Ideas serve to
justify the practices and attach to these practices a system
of common notions. No thinker would think of contesting
the concrete character of space and time. None would see
in numbers the symbols of quantity. The play of numerical
symbols, the alternations of Yin and Yang, these things
lend to nature, and to man as part of nature, a *regular
rhythm* and an *intelligible order*. All of the activties of
mind, the problems posed, and the answers suggested, at-
test to the fact that the intellectual life is determined by the
social crises of a feudal order.

There is no god. There is no law. In China religion is not a function differentiated clearly from the rest
of the social activity. The sentiment of "holiness" plays a
large role in many sectors of life; but in none of them is the
object of this veneration in the strict sense comparable to
any gods of the West. There is simply no tendency toward
a metaphysical spiritualism. Such beings as might be called
god are not transcendental, but only sacred. The Chinese
thinkers are independently wise. Always they are humanistic. And they owe nothing to the idea of God.

The ideal governing their reflective lives is not salvation,
but "fortunate agreement or understanding" between men
and between man and nature. These relations are not channeled by immutable laws or prescriptions. There is an
order, but it is not necessitous. All of their reflection is
caught, as well as it can be in one sentence: The principle
of a good and universal agreement is linked inextricably
with the principle of an universal intelligibility. That is
why Tao is the supreme category; and that is why the chiefs
must be sacred and learned. All Authority reposes upon
Reason.

# 6

## IDEOLOGY AND ECONOMICS

Many tracts of these times confuse ideology with social reality. This is not an unusual error. It is here displayed in a treatment of types of nationalism and especially in a portrayal of National Socialism.*

In his uncontrolled shuttling between conceptions of nationalism, presumably held by diverse "peoples," and the economic bases of nationalisms, de Sales manages an annoying ambivalance. What is important for social analysis is (a) the precise relations between the two; (b) the different conceptions of the nation which may be held by different social strata within each nation, and (c) the reasons for both these sets of differences in terms of the varying class and social backgrounds of peoples. No such discriminations are made by de Sales and, therefore, he cannot even ask, (d) to what extent does "nationalism" operate as an ideology—as a mask? and of what? to whom? and for whom?

Such questions are not answered by denouncing those who ask them as "debunkers." Unless we ask them, we cannot, for example, understand Hitler's speeches, no matter how many of them we have read. And we cannot answer them without knowledge of socio-economic history. Such differences as may exist between nationalism and imperialism cannot be grasped by considering different images of nationalism which various "peoples" are supposed to believe in. But such ambivalence may save *capitalism,* German and otherwise (from Book-of-the-Month-Clubbers) by shifting the guilt for war to "nationalism," Fascism, and Communism and these construed, not economically, but as patterns of bad ideas.

521

Just how inadequate de Sales' political economics are may be indicated by the fact that he sees "collectivism" as one of three major world trends (the other two are nationalism and opposition to war), defining it as "the tendency to integrate the individual into the complex organization of our modern industrial society to obtain more efficiency and—if possible—more security." Such a definition is merely a smudgy finger pointed at large scale industrialization and bureaucratization. It is so loose that what may be definitive of various nations or of specific stages in their development slip through, to be cursed or blessed without benefit of economic analysis. Those who operate with such definitions should not expect to locate the dynamic to war. The fact that the present world crisis is taking place in several dimensions does not give license for confusion by definition. The tap-root fallacy of this genre of reasoning is the confounding of the ideological with socio-economic fact.

The other side of an error in method is the distortion of the objects viewed with it. The empirical defects implicit in de Sales' method of thinking and style of observation come to flower in his statement of the situation in and of Germany. What does it mean to say that "the racial myth" is the "cornerstone of National Socialism"? The extent to which "racial nationalism" is the basis of the consciousness of Germany's ruled classes is seriously open to question; and the *Führerprinzip* is not "the natural outcome of the racial state," whatever that may be. What does it mean to say that "the Nazis have revived on a world plane some of the conflicts which were settled in America nearly 80 years ago"? It is also doubtful that Hitler "is God, for the Germans, at least," and "the mass man of our time," and that he has "expressed ideas that are characteristically German." Nor does reading "Hitler" back into Hermann vs. the Romans, Wotan vs. Charlemagne, *a la* Peter Viereck, help one iota in understanding Hitler, or Wotan. What is all this meta-historical foolishness *for?* And how does the war necessitate assertions about "anyone who has the unrewarded courage to read Fichte or Hegel"? and "a people,

---

* *"The Making of Tomorrow."* By Raoul de Russoy de Sales. Reynal & Hitchcock, New York. 1942.

the Germans, intent on bringing us all down to their level of barbarism"? In seeing Hitler as the "total incarnation of . . . the German Volk" and at the same time the "heir" of Frederick and Bismarck, and Hitlerism as "the last phase of an evolution toward total evil," de Sales not only confounds historical nonsense with old-fashioned cursing; he dignifies phenomena that are really not so grand. *He has read too many of Hitler's speeches without the necessary spectrum of economic history.* Such propaganda about "Germanism" will at no time be helpful to those Germans who are less easily duped by kitsch than Rauschning and de Sales.

Although the point that "capitalism" is in contradiction with "democracy" is not original, it is very well to point it out to the public this book will recruit; however, I doubt if its *de Salesian* statement will convince anyone. He can see capitalism as world-doomed only by isolating "capitalism" from monopoly capitalism. (Why does everyone do that?) Such strabismus does comfort those who believe that we are immersed in a "basic trend" which increases the "power of the people," and the consequent elimination of the rulers of the last 20 years and which enables one to speak seriously of "revolutionary England."

The inference that since war today necessitates the support of masses which demand democratic promises, the winning of the war will mean a "tangible victory for democracy" is invalid and, moreover, naive. Within the gambit of this logic the same can be said for Germany's winning of the war. And why will accumulations of surpluses in export countries necessarily lead to 'a "dwarfing" of the role private capital will play in setting up the peace?

Is it an ideological necessity to set forth the "meaning" and defense of democracy in such pure and splashy concepts as de Sales uses? And is there a morale necessity for circumlocution about British imperialism? If we do not face the facts, the peoples of Burma and India will let us know; and if we cannot see that far, let us look below the Caribbean to the rubber situation (despite Mr. Winkler's omission of the British point of view in his recent *New Leader* article, May 2, 1942, about that nasty old Italian corporation).

The account of American life and its world location is rooted, like the account of National Socialism, in ideologies uncontrolled by recognition of the situations out of which they came and into which they go. All of the American people do not agree with Mr. Luce. To confuse ideology with economics and politics is to misunderstand all three. Fortunately de Sales does not try to tell us what tomorrow will bring: the materials for finding out are not in this book, a tract too blurred and gentle for these times.

# 7

# THE PROFESSIONAL
# IDEOLOGY OF SOCIAL PATHOLOGISTS

An analysis of textbooks in the field of social disorganization reveals a common style of thought which is open to social imputation. By grasping the social orientation of this general perspective we can understand why thinkers in this field should select and handle problems in the manner in which they have.

By virtue of the mechanism of sales and distribution, textbooks tend to embody a content agreed upon by the academic group using them. In some cases texts have been written only after an informal poll was taken of professional opinion as to what should be included, and other texts are consulted in the writing of a new one. Since one test of their success is wide adoption, the very spread of the public for which they are written tends to insure a textbook tolerance of the commonplace. Although the conceptual framework of a pathologist's textbook is not usually significantly different from that of such monographs as he may write, this essay is not concerned with the "complete thought" or with the "intentions" of individual authors; it is a study of a professional ideology variously exhibited in a set of textbooks.[1] Yet because of its persistent importance in the development of American sociology and its supposed proximity to the social scene, "social pathology" seems an appropriate point of entry for the examination of the style of reflection and the social-historical basis of American sociology.

[1] No attempt has been made to trace specific concepts to their intellectual origins. Only elements admitted into the more stable textbook formulations have come within my view: the aim is to grasp typical perspectives and key concepts. Hence, no one of the texts to be quoted exemplifies *all* the concepts analyzed; certain

The level of abstraction which characterizes these texts is so low that often they seem to be empirically confused for lack of abstraction to knit them together.[2] They display bodies of meagerly connected facts, ranging from rape in rural districts to public housing, and intellectually sanction this low level of abstraction.[3] The "informational"

elements are not so visible in given texts as in others, and some elements are not evidenced in certain texts at all. In general, the documentary quotations which follow in footnotes are from the later editions of the following books: W. G. Beach and E. E. Walker, *American Social Problems* (1934); J. H. S. Bossard, (*a*) *Social Change and Social Problems* (1934) and (*b*) *Problems of Social Well-Being* (1927); C. H. Cooley, (*a*) *The Social Process* (1918), (*b*) *Human Nature and the Social Order* (1902, 1922), (*c*) *Social Organization* (1909); Edward T. Devine, (*a*) *The Normal Life* (1915, 1924), (*b*) *Progressive Social Action* (1933); R. C. Dexter, *Social Adjustment* (1927); G. S. Dow, *Society and Its Problems* (1920, 1929); M. A. Elliott and F. E. Merrill, *Social Disorganization* (1934, 1941); C. A. Ellwood, (*a*) *The Social Problem, a Constructive Analysis* (1915, 1919); *Sociology and Modern Social Problems* (1910-35); H. P. Fairchild, *Outline of Applied Sociology* (1916, 1921); M. P. Follet, *The New State* (1918), (*b*) *Creative Experience* (1924); James Ford, *Social Deviation* (1939); J. M. Gillette and J. M. Reinhardt, *Current Social Problems* (1933, 1937); J. L. Gillin, (*a*) *Poverty and Dependence* (1921, 1926, 1937), (*b*) *Social Pathology* (1933, 1939); J. L. Gillin, C. G. Dittmer, and R. J. Colbert, *Social Problems* (1928, 1932); E. C. Hayes, editor's introductions to texts in the "Lippincott Series"; W. J. Hayes and I. V. Shannon, *Visual Outline of Introductory Sociology* (1935); G. B. Mangold, *Social Pathology* (1932, 1934); H. A. Miller, *Races, Nations, and Classes* (1924); H. W. Odum, *Man's Quest for Social Guidance: The Study of Social Problems* (1927); Maurice Parmelee, *Poverty and Social Progress* (1916); H. A. Phelps, *Contemporary Social Problems* (1932, 1933, 1938); S. A. Queen and J. R. Gruener, *Social Pathology* (1940); S. A. Queen, W. B. Bodenhafer, and E. B. Harper, *Social Organization and Disorganization* (1935); C. M. Rosenquist, *Social Problems* (1940); U. G. Weatherly, *Social Progress* (1926).

[2] See Read Bain, "The Concept of Complexity," *Social Forces,* VIII, 222 and 369. K. Mannheim has called this type "isolating empiricism" ("German Sociology," *Politica,* February, 1934, p. 30).

[3] H. P. Fairchild, p. vii: "Dealing with applied sociology [this book] devotes itself to facts rather than to theories." James H. S. Bossard (*a*), p. xi: "In [*Problems of Social Well-being*] an effort was made to consider chiefly in a factual vein, certain elements which seemed of basic importance. . . ." G. B. Mangold, p. viii: "The author has tried to select that which [of factual material] best illustrates problems and practical situations."

character of social pathology is linked with a failure to consider total social structures. Collecting and dealing in a fragmentary way with scattered problems and facts of *milieux,* these books are not focused on larger stratifications or upon structured wholes. Such an omission may not be accounted for merely in terms of a general "theoretical weakness." Such structural analyses have been available; yet they have not been attended to or received into the tradition of this literature. American sociologists have often asserted an interest in the "correlation of the social sciences;" nevertheless, academic departmentalization may well have been instrumental in atomizing the problems which they have addressed.[4] Sociologists have always felt that "not many representatives of the older forms of social science are ready to admit that there is a function for sociology."[5] However, neither lack of theoretical ability nor restrictive channeling through departmentalization constitutes a full explanation of the low level of abstraction and the accompanying failure to consider larger problems of social structure.

If the members of an academic profession are recruited from similar social contexts and if their backgrounds and careers are relatively similar, there is a tendency for them to be uniformly set for some common perspective. The common conditions of their profession often seem more important in this connection than similarity of extraction. Within such a generally homogeneous group there tend to be fewer divergent points of view which would clash over the meaning of facts and thus give rise to interpretations on a more theoretical level.[6]

---

The quotations in the footnotes are merely indications of what is usual. The imputations presented must be held against the reader's total experience with the literature under purview.

[4] In Germany the academic division of specialties prior to the rise of sociology channeled sociological work into a formal emphasis. In America a somewhat comparable situation led to a fragmentalization of empirical attention and especially to a channeling of work into "practical problems."

[5] A. W. Small, *American Journal of Sociology,* May, 1916, p. 785, citing an editorial in the *American Journal of Sociology,* 1907.

[6] Such "homogeneity" is not, however, the only condition under which some common style of thought is taken on by a group of

The relatively homogeneous extraction and similar careers of American pathologists is a possible factor in the low level of abstraction characterizing their work. All the authors considered[7] (except one, who was foreign born) were born in small towns, or on farms near small towns, three fourths of which were in states not industrialized during the youth of the authors. The social circles and strata in which they have severally moved are quite homogeneous; all but five have participated in similar "reform" groups and "societies" of professional and business classes. By virtue of their being college professors (all but three are known to have the Ph.D.), of the similar type of temporary positions (other than academic) which they have held, of the sameness of the "societies" to which they have belonged and of the social positions of the persons whom they have married, the assertion as regards general similarity of social extraction, career and circles of contact seems justified.[8]

A further determinant of the level of abstraction and lack of explicit systematization (beyond which the mentality we are examining does not easily or typically go) is the immediate purpose and the type of public for which they have presumably written. They have been teachers and their specific public has been college students: this has influenced the content and direction of their intellectual en-

---

thinkers. Compare the formal conception of "points of coincidence" advanced by H. H. Gerth in *Die sozialgeschichtliche Lage der burgerlichen Intelligenz um die Wende des 18 Jahrhunderts* (diss., Frankfurt A.M.) (V.D.I-Verlag, G.m.b.H. Berlin, N.W. 7). The entire question of the grounding of imputations in terms of social extraction and career-lines is an unfinished set of methodological issues. In this paper the major imputations advanced do *not* proceed upon career data as much as upon the social orientation implied by general perspectives and specific concepts, and by the selection of "problems."

[7] Information concerning twenty-four of the thirty-two authors was full enough to be considered. Five of the eight not considered were junior authors collaborating with persons who are included.

[8] The order of their respective experience has not been systematically considered. All career data on contemporary persons should be held tentatively: open to revision by knowledge not now publicly available.

deavors.[9] Teaching is a task which requires a type of systematization to which the textbook answers. Most of the "systematic" or "theoretical" work in "social pathology" has been performed by teachers.[10] The fact that sociology often won its academic right to existence in opposition to other departments may have increased the necessity for *textbook* systematization. Such systematization occurs in a context of presentation and of justification rather than within a context of discovery.[11] The textbook-writing and the academic profession of the writers thus figure in the character and function of systematic theory within the field.[12] Systematization of facts for the purpose of making them accessible to collegiate minds is one thing; systematization which is oriented toward crucial growing-points in a research process is quite another. An attempt to systematize on the level of the textbook makes for a taxonomic gathering of facts and a systematization of them under con-

[9] See above. A. W. Small, p. 754: ". . . the mental experience of the teacher-explorer in the course of arriving at the present outlook of sociologists . . . has also been due to the fact that many of the advances in perception or expression have been in the course of attempts to meet students' minds at their precise point of outlook." See C. Wright Mills, "Language, Logic, and Culture," *American Sociological Review,* October, 1939, for mechanisms involved in such determinations of the thinker by his public.

[10] This statement, as is widely recognized, holds in a measure for all American sociology. Cf., *e.g.,* Pitirim Sorokin, "Some Contrasts in Contemporary European and American Sociology," *Social Forces,* September, 1929, pp. 57-58. "In America sociology has grown as a child nursed by the universities and colleges. . . . American literature in sociology has been composed largely out of textbooks."

[11] Cf. Hans Reichenbach, *Experience and Prediction,* chap. i. See P. Sorokin's comment, *op. cit.,* p. 59

[12] J. L. Gillin (*a*), p. v.: "My years of experience as a social worker and teacher have gone into the content and method of presentation." J. H. S. Bossard (*a*), p. 759: "In the preceding chapters, problems have been grouped on the basis of one underlying fact or condition. Obviously, this is an arbitrary procedure which can be justified only on the basis of pedagogical expedience"; p. xi: "The . . . is the method followed. . . . By way of defense, this seems simpler and pedagogically preferable"; p. xii: "The decision to omit them was made . . . second, because in an increasing number of colleges and universities, these particular fields are dealt with in separate courses.

cepts that have already been logically defined.[13] The research possibilities of concepts are not as important as is
the putting of the accumulated factual details into some
sort of order.

But, even though the perspectives of these texts are
usually not explicit, the facts selected for treatment are
not "random." One way to grasp the perspective within
which they do lie is to analyze the scope and character of
their problems. What, then, are the selecting and organizing
principles to be extracted from the range and content of
these texts? What types of fact come within their field of
attention?

The direction is definitely toward particular "practical
problems"—problems of "everyday life." [14] The ideal of

[13] Cf. Fritz Mauthner, *Aristotle,* for the pedagogic character of
the taxonomic logic of Aristotle. H. P. Fairchild, pp. 6-7: ". . . the
essential features of the scientific method . . . are three in number.
First, the accumulation of facts. . . . Second, the arrangement or
classification of these facts according to some predetermined logical
basis of classification. . . ." J. H. S. Bossard (*a*), p. 34: "It is the
present contention that the scientific study of social problems which
confines itself to mere descriptions and classification serves a useful
purpose."

[14] M. A. Elliott, *American Sociological Review,* June, 1941, p.
317. "The only problems which need concern the sociologists' theories and research are the real, practical problems of everyday living." Queen and Gruener, p. 42: "[In contradistinction to scientific
problems] social problems pertain directly to life. . . . Their concern
is usually 'practical,' and often personal." J. H. S. Bossard (*a*),
p. 32: "Frankly, applied sociology is utilitarian. It is concerned with
practical problems and purposes." Gillette and Reinhardt, p. 22:
"The study of social problems constitutes the heart of sociology as
a science. . . . Even so-called 'pure' sociology, or theoretical sociology, more and more devotes itself to these practical problems of
society."
On the other hand, such writers as Ellwood, rising to a *very*
high level of abstraction, conceive *formally* of "the social problem."
C. A. Ellwood (*a*), pp. 13-14: "Some of us, at least, are beginning
to perceive that the social problem is now, what it has been in all
ages, namely, *the problem of the relations of men to one another.*
It is the problem of human living together, and cannot be confined
to any statement in economic, eugenic or other one-sided terms
. . . it is as broad as humanity and human nature. . . . Such a
statement [in terms of one set of factors] obscures the real nature
of the problem, and may lead to dangerous, one-sided attempts at
its solution." In terms of social and intellectual orientation, both

practicality, of not being "utopian," operated, in conjunction with other factors, as a polemic against the "philosophy of history" brought into American sociology by men trained in Germany; this polemic implemented the drive to lower levels of abstraction. A view of isolated and immediate problems as the "real" problems may well be characteristic of a society rapidly growing and expanding, as America was in the nineteenth century and, ideologically, in the early twentieth century. The depictive mode of speech and the heavy journalistic "survey" are intellectual concomitants of an expanding society in which new routines are arising and cities are being built.[15] Such an approach is then sanctioned with canons of what constitutes real knowledge; the practice of the detailed and complete empiricism of the survey is justified by an epistemology of gross description. These norms of adequate knowledge linger in an academic tradition to mold the work of its bearers. The emphasis upon fragmentary,[16] practical problems tends to atomize social objectives. The studies so informed are not integrated into designs comprehensive enough to serve collective action, granted the power and intent to realize such action.

One of the pervasive ways of defining "problems" or of detecting "disorganization" is in terms of *deviation from*

---

ways of conceiving of "social problems" are similar in that neither is of a sort usable in collective action which proceeds against, rather than well within, more or less tolerated channels.

[15] See H. D. Lasswell, *Politics* (1936), p. 148; K. Mannheim, *op. cit.,* pp. 30-31; and *Ideology and Utopia,* pp. 228-29.

[16] Gillin, Dittmer, and Colbert, p. 44: "There are hundreds of social problems, big and little." Queen and Gruener, p. 171: "We present here some of the problems of day by day living encountered by diabetics and cardiacs." J. H. S. Bossard (a), p. 33: "Certain particular social problems are coming to be reserved for applied sociology. Their selection has been determined less by logic or principle than by accident and historical development;" p. 44: "The more one deals with life's problems at first hand, the more one is impressed with their concreteness, their specificity, and their infinite variety." Gillette and Reinhardt, p. 14: "From almost any point of view there must be a large number of social problems today;" p. 15: "This book is a treatise on a large number of social problems. It does not claim to consider them all. It repeatedly recognizes the plurality of problems in its treatment of the great problems."

*norms.* The "norms" so used are usually held to be the standards of "society." Later we shall see to what type of society they are oriented. In the absence of studies of specific norms themselves this mode of problematization shifts the responsibility of "taking a stand" away from the thinker and gives a "democratic" rationale to his work.[17] Rationally, it would seem that those who accept this approach to "disorganization" would immediately examine these norms themselves. It is significant that, given their interest in reforming society, which is usually avowed, these writers typically assume the norms which they use and often tacitly sanction them.[18] There are few attempts to explain deviations from norms in terms of the norms themselves, and no rigorous facing of the implications of the fact that social transformations would involve shifts *in them.*

The easy way to meet the question of why norms are violated is in terms of biological impulses which break through "societal restrictions." A paste-pot eclectic psychology provides a rationale for this facile analysis.[19] Thus, more comprehensive problematization is blocked by a biological theory of social deviation. And the "explanation" of

[17] C. M. Rosenquist, p. 19: ". . . popular recognition of any social condition or process as bad, followed by any attempt to eliminate or cure it, serves as a criterion for its inclusion in a study of social problems. The writer merely accepts the judgment of public opinion. This is the method to be followed in this book." E. T. Devine (*a*), in Note to the Second Edition: "The object of Social Economy is that each shall be able to live as nearly as possible a normal life according to the standard of the period and the community."

[18] C. M. Rosenquist, p. 19: "Perhaps we may be on solid ground through a recognition of the capitalist system and its accompaniments as normal. We may then deal with its several parts, treating as problems those which do not function smoothly. This, it seems, is what the more reputable sociologist actually does." H. P. Fairchild, p. 59: ". . . some of the social conditions which are the natural and consistent outcome of an individualistic-capitalistic organization of industry, and hence are to be considered as normal in modern societies." Examination of discussions of such items as poverty in most of the texts confirms this assertion. J. L. Gillin (*a*), p. 495: "For serious depressions carefully planned unemployment relief schemes should be formulated before the depression is felt."

[19] That is, an eclecticism that does not analyze in any adequate way the elements and theories which it seeks to combine. Cf. Reuter's critique, *American Journal of Sociology,* November, 1940, pp. 2939-304.

deviations can be put in terms of a requirement for more "socialization." "Socialization" is either undefined, used as a moral epithet, or implies norms which are themselves without definition. The focus on "the facts" takes no cognizance of the normative structures within which they lie.

The texts tend either to be "apolitical"[20] or to aspire to a "democratic" opportunism.[21] When the political sphere is discussed, its pathological phases are usually stated in terms of "the anti-social," or of "corruption," etc.[22] In another form the political is tacitly identified with the proper functioning of the current and unexamined political order; it is especially likely to be identified with a legal process or

[20] E. C. Hayes in the Introduction to H. A. Miller, p. x: "Not political action, the inadequacy of which Professor Eldridge (*Political Action*) has shown, nor revolution, the pathological character of which Professor Sorokin has demonstrated, but social interaction, the casual efficiency of human relationships, is the predominant factor in securing both order and progress."

[21] J. H. S. Bossard (a), pp. 14-15: "The constructive approach . . . may be summarized in one sentence: It is always possible to do something. . . . Such an approach represents in welfare work that hopelessly incurable optimism which in political life we call democracy." Gillette and Reinhardt, pp. 16-17: "There are no certain rules to be followed step by step in the discovery of the solution. Our best recourse is to employ scientific methods rigidly at every step . . . because of uncertain factors always present, we never can be sure that our conclusions are more than approximations of the truth. . . . Since we cannot completely control their activities . . . our cures must be partial and approximate." One type of link between democratic ideology and social pathology is shown in the following quotation, wherein a condition that deviates from the former is called pathological; the quotation also indicates a typical shying-away from all orders of domination other than that type legitimated traditionally, which is left open. H. A. Miller, p. 32: "When certain . . . psycho-pathological conditions are found, we may postulate an abnormal relationship as a cause . . . the particular form of pathology which is involved in our problem may be called the *oppression psychosis*. Oppression is the domination of one group by another." G. V. Price, reviewing Queen and Gruener, *Social Forces,* May, 1941, p. 566: "Without using the word democracy in the doctrinal sense the authors have shown what its utilities are in reducing pathologies."

[22] M. A. Elliott and F. Merrill, p. 28: "The pathological phases of the political process include such antisocial behavior as delinquency, crime, disorder, revolt, and revolution. Corrupt political activity is an important example of such malfunctioning."

the administration of laws.[23] If the "norms" were examined, the investigator would perhaps be carried to see total structures of norms and to relate these to distributions of power. Such a structural point of sight is not usually achieved. The level of abstraction does not rise to permit examination of these normative structures themselves, or of why they come to be transgressed, or of their political implications. Instead, this literature discusses many kinds of apparently unrelated "situations."

About the time W. I. Thomas stated the vocabulary of the situational approach, a social worker was finding it congenial and useful. In M. E. Richmond's influential *Social Diagnosis* (1917) we gain a clue as to why pathologists tend to slip past structure to focus on isolated situations, why there is a tendency for problems to be considered as problems of individuals,[24] and why sequences of situations were not seen as linked into structures:

> Social diagnosis . . . . may be described as the attempt to make as exact a definition as possible of the situation and personality of a human being in some social need—of his situation and personality, that is, in relation to the other human beings upon whom he in any way depends or who depend upon him, and in relation also to the social institutions of his community.[25]

This kind of formulation has been widely applied to isolated "problems" addressed by sociologists.[26] And the

[23] Note the identification of "political action" with legislation: Gillin, Dittmer, and Colbert, p. 94: "It is an American practice to attempt to solve any and every sort of social problem through political action. As a result, our statute-books are loaded with 'dead-letter' laws that are not enforced simply because public opinion does not respect them, nor does it feel responsible for them."

[24] J. L. Gillin (*a*), p.13: "Experience shows that rehabilitation is possible only when each case of poverty or dependency is taken separately and its difficulties handled with strict regard for all the attendant circumstances. . . . It must be done in terms of the individual, for . . . it cannot be done *en masse*."

[25] Richmond, p. 357; see also pp. 51 and 62.

[26] J. H. S. Bossard (*a*), p. 3: "Social problems consist of (*a*) a social situation, (*b*) which are. . . ." Gillette and Reinhardt, p. 15: "A social problem is a situation, confronting a group. . . ."

"situational approach" has an affinity with other elements which characterize their general perspective.[27]

Present institutions train several types of persons—such as judges and social workers—to think in terms of "situations."[28] Their activities and mental outlook are set within the existent norms of society; in their professional work they tend to have an occupationally trained incapacity to rise above series of "cases." It is in part through such concepts as "situation" and through such methods as "the case approach"[29] that social pathologists have been intellectually tied to social work with its occupational position and political limitations. And, again, the similarity of origin and the probable lack of any continuous "class experience" of the group of thinkers decrease their chances to see social structures rather than a scatter of situations. The mediums of experience and orientation through which they respectively view society are too similar, too homogeneous, to permit the clash of diverse angles which, through controversy, might lead to the construction of a whole.

The paramount fact of immigration in American culture, with each wave of immigrants displacing the lower-class position of former waves and raising the position of the earlier immigrants also tends to obscure structural and class positions.[30] Thus, instead of positional issues,

[27] J. H. S. Bossard (a), p. 57: ". . . the emphasis in our social thinking upon the situation as a unit of experience, as 'an aggregate of interactive and interdependent factors of personality and circumstance,' is in essence a recognition of the idea of the emergent. . . . Queen recognizes the implications of the situational approach very clearly in these words: 'For purposes of sociological analysis, a situation consists in relationships between persons viewed as a cross section of human experience, constantly changing. . . . Thus we make of the concept "situation" an intellectual tool' " (S. Queen, "Some Problems of the Situational Approach," Social Forces, June, 1931, p. 481).

[28] See K. Mannheim, Man and Society, p. 305.

[29] Queen, Bodenhafer, and Harper, p. viii: Editor's Note by S. Eldridge: "The present volume . . . features the case approach to social problems."

[30] Note the lack of structure in the conception of "class": Gillette and Reinhardt, p. 177: "Viewing the matter historically, then, it appears that the chief cause of rigid class systems of society with their attendant evils is the prolonged concentration of wealth in the hands of a relatively few persons.

pathologists typically see problems in terms of an individual, such as an immigrant, "adjusting" to a milieu[31] or being "assimilated" or Americanized. Instead of problems of class structure involving immigration, the tendency has been to institute problems in terms of immigration involving nationalist assimilation of individuals. The fact that some individuals have had opportunities to rise in the American hierarchy decreases the chances fully to see the ceilings of class. Under these conditions such structures are seen as fluctuating and unsubstantial and are likely to be explained not in terms of *class position* but in terms of *status attitudes*.[32]

Another element that tends to obviate an analytic view of structure is the emphasis upon the "processual" and "organic" character of society. In Cooley, whose influence on these books is decisive, one gets a highly formal, many-sided fluidity where "nothing is fixed or independent, everything is plastic and takes influence as well as gives it." [33] From the standpoint of political action, such a view may mean a reformism dealing with masses of detail and furthers a tendency to be apolitical. There can be no bases or points of entry for larger social action in a structureless flux. The view is buttressed epistemologically with an emotionalized animus against "particularism" and with the intense approval of the safe, of colorless, "multiple-factor" view of causation.[34] The liberal "multiple-factor" view does not lead to a conception of causation which would permit points of entry for broader types of action, especially political action.[35] No set of underlying structural shifts

[31] See below, the concept of "adjustment."

[32] Gillin, Dittmer, and Colbert, p. 59: "The most fundamental cause of class and group conflict is the attitude of superiority on the part of one class, or group, toward another."

[33] *The Social Process*, pp. 44-45.

[34] Elliott and Merrill, p. 38: "One of the most significant concepts in the understanding of social problems is the idea of multiple causation."

[35] See above comments on political relevance. C. A. Ellwood (*b*) p. 324: "We may, perhaps, sum up this chapter  by saying it is evident that the cure of poverty is not to be sought merely in certain economic rearrangements, but in scientific control of the whole life process of human society. This means that in order to get rid of poverty, the defects in education in government, in religion and

is given which might be open to manipulation, at key points, and which, like the fact of private property in a corporate economy, might be seen as efficacious in producing many "problems." If one fragmentalizes society into "factors," into elemental bits, naturally one will then need quite a few of them to account for something,[36] and one can never be sure they are all in. A formal emphasis upon "the whole" plus lack of total structural consideration plus a focus upon scattered situations does not make it easy to reform the status quo.

The "organic" orientation of liberalism has stressed all those social factors which tend to a harmonious balance of elements.[37] There is a minimization of chances for action in a social milieu where "there is always continuity with the past, and not only with any one element only of the past, but with the whole interacting organism of man."[38] In seeing everything social as continuous process, changes in pace and revolutionary dislocations are missed[39] or are taken as signs of the "pathological." The formality and the assumed unity implied by "the mores" also lower the chances to see social chasms and structural dislocations.

---

morality, in philanthropy, and even in physical heredity, must be got rid of. Of course, this can only be done when there is a scientific understanding of the conditions necessary for normal human social life."

[36] J. L. Gillin (a), pp. 51-128: ". . . the modern theory of the causes of poverty has passed beyond any one-sided explanation to a many-sided theory." The following conditions of poverty and independence are discussed: poor natural resources, adverse climate, adverse weather, insect pests, disasters, illness and diseases, physical inheritance, mental inheritance, adverse surroundings of children, death or disability of the earner, unemployment, lack of proper wages, traditions, customs, habits, advertising and installment buying, fluctuations between costs of living and income, inequitable distribution of wealth and income, family marital relations, political conditions, unwise philanthropy, etc. After these discussions, *family cases* are presented as ". . . studies in causation."

[37] Whereas many socialist theories have tended to overlook the elastic elements that do exist in a society. Cf. K. Mannheim, *Politica*, pp. 25-26.

[38] C. H. Cooley (a), p. 46.

[39] See Max Lerner, *It Is Later Than You Think*, pp. 14-15; and *Encyclopedia of the Social Sciences*, article "Social Process." See documentation and consequences below.

Typically, pathologists have not attempted to construst a structural whole. When, however, they do consider totalities, it is in terms of such concepts as "society," "the social order," or "the social organization," "the mores and institutions," and "American culture." Four things should be noted about their use of such terms: (*a*) The terms represent undifferential entities. Whatever they may indicate, it is systematically homogeneous. Uncritical use of such a term as "the" permits a writer the hidden assumption in politically crucial contexts of a homogeneous and harmonious whole.[40] The large texture of "the society" will take care of itself, it is somehow and in the long run harmonious,[41] it has a "strain toward consistency" running through it;[42] or, if not this, then only the co-operation of all is needed,[43] or perhaps even a right moral feeling is taken as a solution.[44] (*b*) In their formal emptiness these terms are commensurate with the low level of abstraction. Their *formality* facilitates the empirical concern with "everyday" problems of (community) milieu. (*c*) In addition to their "descriptive" use, such terms are used normatively. The "social" becomes a good term when it is used in ethical polemics against "individualism" or against such abstract moral qualities as "selfishness," lack of "altruism," or of "antisocial" senti-

[40] Gillin, Dittmer, and Colbert, p. 2: "All this group life is nicely woven into a system that we call society. . . ."

[41] *Ibid.*, p. 15: "But the aim of society is ever directed to the task of bringing uniform advantages to all." C. A. Ellwood (*b*), p. 395: "Social organization may refer to any condition or relation of the elements of a social group; but by social order we mean a settled and harmonious relation between the individuals or the parts of a society. The problem of social order is then the problem of harmonious adaptation among the individuals of the group. . . ."

[42] It is significant that it was Sumner, with his tacit belief in "natural" order, who set forth the phrase and what it implies.

[43] Gillin, Dittmer, and Colbert, p. 13: "Since a community is made up of a number of neighborhoods, it is necessary that all cooperate in order to secure better schools, improved. . . ."

[44] J. L. Gillin (*a*), p. 133: "Only as a passion for social righteousness takes the place of an imperative desire for selfish advantage . . . will society do away with the conditions that now depress some classes of the population and exalt others."

ments.[45] "Social is conceived as a "co-operative" "sharing" of something or as "conducive to the general welfare."[46] The late eighteenth-century use of "society" as against "state" by the rising bourgeoisie had already endowed "society" with a "democratic" tinge which this literature transmits. (*d*) There is a strong tendency for the term "society" to be practically assimiliated to, or conceived largely in terms of, primary groups and small homogeneous communities. Such a conception typically characterizes the litera-

[45] C. A. Ellwood (b), p. 84: ". . . increasing altruism is necessary for the success of those more and more complex forms of cooperation which characterize higher civilization and upon which it depends." G. B. Mangold, p. 17: "Without the spirit of altruism society would be but a sorry exhibition of the collective humanity that we believe has been made in the image of God." Conversely, the "antisocial" is held to include certain abstract, moral traits of individuals. Elliott and Merrill, p. 43: "An analysis of the disorganization process suggests two types of antisocial forces: (1) the consciously directed antisocial forces and (2) the impersonal organic forces which are an outgrowth of the formalism discussed above . . . to advance their own selfish ends. These men are thoroughly aware of their antisocial attitudes. Social values have no meaning for them. . . . There has often been no socializing influence in the lives of those men. . . . Co-operation, or 'mutual aid,' the implicit counterpart of effective social organization. . . . Vice areas . . . function because of human appetites, because individual desires are more deeply rooted than any sense of the social implications. . . . The prostitute exists only because she is a means to man's sensual pleasure and satiety"; p. 44: "Sin, vice, crime, corruption, all consciously directed antisocial forces, offer a primrose. . . ." G. M. Mangold, p. 59: "Unsocial habits lead to poverty; particularly do they degrade poverty into dependency. Chief among these vices is intemperance. Before the advent of prohibition it was. . . ." Queen, Bodenhafer, and Harper, p. 4: "When there is . . . characterized by harmony, teamwork, understanding, approval, and the like, we may speak of organization. When the opposite is true and there is a . . . marked by tension, conflict, or drifting apart, we may speak of disorganization."

[46] Gillin, Dittmer, and Colbert, p. 5: " 'The word [social] means conducive to the collective welfare, and thus becomes nearly equivalent to 'moral' [Cooley, *Human Nature and the Social Order*, p. 4] . . . it is this . . . meaning that comes closest to our interpretation . . . —'conducive to the collective welfare'—relationships, and products of relationships that are believed to foster and promote *group life,* and to insure *group survival.*"

ture within our purview.[47] In explaining it, we come upon an element that is highly important in understanding the total perspective.

The basis of "stability," "order," or "solidarity" is not typically analyzed in these books, but a conception of such a basis is implicitly used and sanctioned,[48] for some normative conception of a socially "healthy" and stable organization is involved in the determination of "pathological" conditions. "Pathological" behavior is not discerned in a *structural sense* (*i.e.,* as incommensurate with an existent structural type) or in a *statistical* sense (*i.e.,* as deviations from central tendencies). This is evidenced by the regular assertion that pathological conditions *abound* in the city.[49]

[47] J. L. Gillin (*b*), p. 313: ". . . personal relationships . . . are the most important ties in the social organization. . . ." C. A. Ellwood (*b*), pp. 3-4; "The tendency in the best sociological thinking is to emphasize the importance, for the understanding of our social life, of 'primary' or face-to-face groups"; p. 77: "Primary groups . . . are of most interest sociologically, because they exhibit social life at its maximum intensity, and because they are the bearers of the most vital elements in social life, especially the traditions of civilization"; pp. 79-80: "The chief importance of primary groups in our social life, however, is that they . . . furnish the 'patterns' which we attempt to realize in our social life in general"; pp. 84-85: "All human history has, from one point of view, been a struggle to transfer altruism and solidarity of the family to successively larger and larger groups of men"; pp. 90-91: "Primary, or face-to-face groups are the key to the understanding of our social life. . . ." Gillin, Dittmer, Colbert, p. 282: ". . . the home is probably our most fundamental social institution . . ." p. 285: "Anything that endangers the stability of the family endangers society." J. H. S. Bossard (*a*), p. 555: "Family life is the focal point of virtually all of our social problems."

[48] C. A. Ellwood (*b*), pp. 79-80: "The very ideal of social solidarity itself comes from the unity experienced in such [primary] groups." Elliott and Merrill, p. 581: "An ever-increasing number of persons living in the giant cities has become completely deracinated, cut off from all stable primary ties. They have lost not only their physical home, but often their spiritual home as well. Social disorganization breeds in these unattached masses of the urban proletariat. They furnish willing nuclei for robbery, brigandage, and revolution."

[49] J. L. Gillin (*b*), p. 411: "In the city we have a greater degree of disorganization in the sense in which we use that term;" p. 410: ". . . in the simple and well-organized ties of country life . . ."; p. 409: "Recreation in the country is largely home-made. . . . In

If they *"abound"* therein, they cannot be "abnormal" in the statistical sense and are not likely to prevail in the structural sense. It may be proposed that the norms in terms of which "pathological" conditions are detected are "humanitarian ideals." But we must then ask for the social orientation of such ideals.[50] In this literature the operating criteria of the pathological are typically *rural* in orientation and extraction.[51]

Most of the "problems" considered arise because of the

---

the city it is professional. . . . The patterns of behavior . . . are here again disorganized and new patterns have to be found." Gillette and Reinhardt, p. 116: "Cities exhibit all the social problems, save those peculiar to agricultural extractive pursuits." H. P. Fairchild, p. 304: "Since there are no *natural* facilities available to the majority of the *denizens* of cities for the gratification of the desire for dancing, it inevitably follows that provision is made on a commercial basis" (my italics). C. M. Rosenquist, p. 47: "The controls which were effective in the small, settled farm community no longer suffice in . . . the city. To this fact may be traced many of the conditions we speak of as social problems. . . ." W. G. Beach, and E. E. Walker, pp. 102-3: ". . . men find their life interests and values in group membership and participation. The most influential groups are those which provide intimate, face-to-face relationships, as the family, the playground, the club, the neighborhood, and the small community. . . . Any wholesome and satisfying life must provide for a continuation of such small groups and institutional forms. . . . One of the most elusive and challenging problems arising from the growth of cities is that of preventing the complete disorganization of essential social groups. In the rural community. . . ." J. H. S. Bossard (*a*), p. 113: "The marked trend of population to the city and the rapid rise of large urban centers, together with their reflex upon the rural regions, constitute the basis of virtually every problem to be discussed in this volume."

[50] This is what Waller does *not* do in his provocative discussion of "humanitarian" and "organizing mores" ("Social Problems and the Mores," *American Sociological Review*, December, 1936, pp. 922-33.

[51] J. L. Gillin (*b*), p. 407: The home "developing as . . . rural" is considered "disorganized" in the city; p. 409: "[In the city] it is only the rebel, unable and unwilling to adjust himself to machine and organization, who retains personal independence. . . . The farmer, conscious that he lives by his own thinking . . . responds to his environment with a feeling of independence—a normal response. The city worker has no keen perception of his dependence upon nature." Elliott and Merrill, p. 32: "However different their approach, the basic dilemma of civilization is the fundamental disparity of values and standards of universally accepted definitions of the situation."

urban deterioration of certain values which can live genuinely only in a relatively homogeneous and primary rural
milieu. The "problems" discussed typically concern urban
behavior. When "rural problems" are discussed, they are
considered as due to encroaching urbanization.[52] The notion of disorganization is quite often merely the absence of
that *type* of organization associated with the stuff of primary-group communities having Christian and Jeffersonian
legitimations.[53]

Cooley, the local colorist of American sociology, was the
chief publicist of this conception of normal organization.
He held "the great historical task of mankind" to be the
more effective and wider organization of that moral order
and pattern of virtues developed in primary groups and

[52] C. A. Ellwood (*b*), p. 281: "The reflex of the city problem is
the rural problem." J. L. Gillen (*b*), p. 429: "[Urbanization] which
has modified the solidarity of the rural family. . . ." W. J. Hayes
and I. V. Shannon, p. 22: "Contacts . . . emancipate individuals
from control of primary groups . . . this leads to setting up personal norms of behavior instead of conforming to group standards."
(Implies no conception of *urban* types of norms.)

[53] The intellectual consequences of the rural to urban drift are
much wider than the perspectives noted in the literature of pathology. In more general American sociology the writings of a man
like E. A. Ross are to be understood in terms of a reaction of those
oriented to a farmer's democracy against the growth of big business,
in its control of railroads, etc. Another division of American sociology in which America's rural past is *intellectually* evident is "rural
sociology" itself. This field shows the positive side of the matter, for
here the yearning for the values associated with rural simplicity and
neighborliness is even more noticeable. In this literature a primary,
rural heritage is taken as the source of "stability" and is conceived
as the reservoir of "values." Such straddling concepts as "urban"
function to limit recognition of the urban character of dominant
contemporary social structures. In a historical sense we need not
argue with these emphases: the underlying form of American democracy and religion, *e.g.* has drawn much from the dominance of
a rural society. And a rapid urbanization may well be only a veneer
upon masses of rurally oriented personalities. But the kind of structural stability in America which grew from rural patterns is historical. In the world today the kind of stability that can—indeed, in
part has—emerged from the hunger for those primary contacts
historically associated with ties of blood and closeness to soil is a
streamlined variety.

communities.[54] Cooley took the idealists' absolute[55] and gave it the characteristics of an organic village; all the world should be an enlarged, Christian-democratic version of a rural village. He practically assimilated "society" to this primary-group community, and he blessed it emotionally and conceptually.[56] "There is reflected here," says T. V. Smith of Cooley—an dwhat he says will hold for the typical social pathologist—"what is highly common in our culture, an ideal of intimacy short of which we do not rest satisfied where other people are concerned. Social distance is a dire fate, achieved with difficulty and lamented as highly unideal, not to say as immoral, in our Christian traditions. It is not enough to have saints; we must have "communion" of the saints. In order to have social relations, we must nuzzle one another."[57]

The aim to preserve rurally oriented values and stabilities is indicated by the implicit model which operates to detect urban disorganization; it is also shown by the stress upon *community* welfare. The community is taken as a major unit, and often it sets the scope of concern and problematization.[58] It is also within the framework of ideally

[54] *Social Organization,* chap. v.

[55] G. H. Mead, "Cooley's Contribution to American Social Thought," *American Journal of Sociology,* XXXV, 701: "Cooley was Emmersonian in finding the individual self in an oversoul." Cf. G. W. F. Hegel, *Lectures on the Philosophy of History* (London: Geo. Bell & Sons, 1884), especially pp. 39-44.

[56] Note the common association of urban "impersonality" and "formalism" and "formalism" with "disorganization." Elliott and Merrill, p. 16: ". . . lack of harmony between the various units of the social order is in a sense . . . exemplified by the impersonal nature of the social organization and the consequent process of social disorganization . . . [cf. C. H. Cooley, *Social Process,* pp. 3-29]"; p. 574: "There is a very close relationship between formalism and disorganization, although at first glance the two states appear to be opposite poles in the social process. They are in reality sequential steps in the same great movement of disorganization, which grows out of formalism. . . ."

[57] *Beyond Conscience,* p. 111.

[58] C. A. Ellwood (b), p. 12: "All forms of association are of interest to the sociologist, though not all are of equal importance. The natural, genetic social groups, which we may call 'communities,' serve best to exhibit sociological problems. Through the study of such simple and primary groups as the family and the neighborhood group, for example, the problems of sociology can be much better

democratic communities that proposed solutions are to be worked out.[59] It should be noted that sometimes, although not typically or exclusively, solutions are conceived as dependent upon abstract moral traits or democratic surrogates of them, such as a "unanimous public will."[60]

"Cultural lag' 'is considered by many pathologists to be the concept with which many scatered problems may be detected and systematized. Whereas the approach by deviation from norms is oriented "ideologically" toward a rural type of order and stability, the cultural-lag model is

---

attacked than through the study of society at large or association in general"; pp. 76-77: ". . . natural groupings, such as the family, the neighborhood, the city, the state or province, and the nation. They may be, and usually are, called *communities,* since they are composed of individuals who carry on all phases of a common life. Voluntary, purposive associations always exist within some community, whether large or small. Groups which we call 'communities' are, therefore, more embracing, more stable, less artificial and specialized than purely voluntary groups. For this reason communities are of more interest to the sociologist than specialized voluntary groups, and sociology is in a peculiar sense a study of the problems of community life." J. H. S. Bossard (*a*), pp. 49-50: "Acceptance of the community as a definite unit in social work and in social theory has become general during the past fifteen years. American participation in the World War was an important factor in bringing this about, first because the community constituted the basic expression of that democratic spirit which the war engendered, and second, the community was seized upon by the various war-time activities and drives as the most effective unit for the mobilization of the spirit and resources of the nation."

[59] Gillin, Dittmer, and Colbert, p. 15; " . . . . *social work,* which mean scientifically developing and adjusting human relations in a way that will secure normal life to individuals and communities and encourage individual and community progress"; p. 47: ". . . . it is important to keep in mind that the central problem is that of adjusting our social life and our social institutions, so that, as individuals and as communities, we may use and enjoy the largest measure of civilization possible, and promote farther progress." M. P. Follet (*a*), Part III, has suggested that neighborhood groups be organized into political units. This would permit the expression of daily life and bring to the surface live needs that they may become the substance of politics. The neighborhood as a political unit would make possible friendly acquaintance; it would socialize people and would make for "the realization of oneness."

[60] J. L. Gillin (*b*), p. 97: "The 'liquor problem' is as acute in the United States today as it ever was in the past, perhaps even more so;" p. 101: "The solution must spring from an aroused and unanimous public will."

tacitly oriented in a "utopian"[61] and progressive manner toward changing some areas of the culture or certain institutions so as to "integrate" them with the state of progressive technology.[62] We must analyze the use made by pathologists of "lag" rather than abstract formulations of it.[63]

Even though all the situations called "lags" *exist* in the present, their functional realities are refrred back, away from the present. Evaluations are thus translated into a time sequence; cultural lag is an assertion of unequal "progress." It tells us what changes are "called for," what changes "ought" to have come about and didn't. In terms of various spheres of society it says what progress is, tells us how much we have had, ought to have had, didn't have, and when and where we didn't have it. The imputation of "lag" is complicated by the historical judgment in whose guise it is advanced and by the programmatic content being shoved into pseudoobjective phrases, as, for example, "called for."

It is not enough to recognize that the stating of problems in terms of cultural lag involves evaluations, however disguised. One must find the general loci of this kind of evaluation and then explain why this form of evaluation has been so readily accepted and widely used by pathologists. The model in which institutions lag behind technology and science involves a positive evaluation of natural science and of orderly progressive change. Loosely, it derives from a liberal continuation of the enlightenment with its full rationalism, its messianic and now politically naive admiration of physical science as a kind of thinking and activity, and with its concept of time as progress. This notion of progress was carried into American colleges by the once prevalent Scottish moral philosophy. From after the Civil War through the first two or three decades of the twentieth

[61] Cf. K. Mannheim, *Ideology and Utopia,* for definitions of these terms.

[62] However, "lag" and "norms" are not unrelated: Queen, Bodenhafer, and Harper, p. 437: "Much of the discussion of cultural lags in the family assumes some kind of normal pattern which is commonly believed to have permanent validity because of the functions performed."

[63] See examples given in J. W. Woodard's "Critical Notes on the Cultural Lag Concept," *Social Forces,* March, 1934, p. 388.

century the expanding business and middle classes were taking over instruments of production, political power, and social prestige; and many of the academic men of the generation were recruited from these rising strata and/or actively mingled with them. Notions of progress are congenial to those who are rising in the scale of position and income.

Those sociologists who think in terms of this model have not typically focused upon the conditions and interest groups underlying variant "rates of change" in different spheres. One might say that in terms of the rates of change at which sectors of culture *could* move, it is technology that is "lagging," for the specific reason of the control of patents, etc., by entrenched interests.[64] In contrast to the pathologists' use, Veblen's use of "lag, leak, and friction" is a structural analysis of industry versus business enterprise.[65] He focused on where "the lag" seemed to pinch; he attempted to show how the trained incapacity of legitimate businessmen acting within entrepreneurial canons would result in a commercial sabotage of production and efficiency in order to augment profits within a system of price and ownership. He did not like this "unworkman-like result," and he detailed its mechanism. In the pathologists' usage the conception has lost this specific and structural anchorage: it has been generalized and applied to everything fragmentarily. This generalization occurs with the aid of such blanket terms as "adaptive culture" and "material culture."[66] There is no specific focus for a program of action embodied in the application of such terms.

Another model in terms of which disorganizations are instituted is that of "social change" itself.[67] This model is

[64] See, *e.g.*, B. J. Stern's article in *Annals of the American Academy of Political and Social Science,* November, 1938.
[65] *The Engineers and the Price System; The Theory of Business Enterprise.*
[66] J. H. S. Bossard (*a*), p. 5: ". . . . as Ogburn put it [W. F. Ogburn, *Social Change* (1922 )] to the extent that the adaptive culture has not kept pace with the material culture, the amount of social ill-being has increased relatively."
[67] J. L. Gillin (*b*), p. 416: "Social disorganization is a function of rapidly changing conditions in people's lives." W. J. Hayes and I. V. Shannon, p. 20: "Social disorganization is an abrupt break in the

not handled in any one typical way, but usually it carries the implicit assumption that human beings are "adjusted" satisfactorily to any social condition that has existed for a long time and that, when some aspect of social life changes, it may lead to a social problem.[68] The notion is oriented ideologically and yet participates in assumptions similar to those of cultural lag, which, indeed, might be considered a variant of it. Such a scheme for problematization buttresses and is buttressed by the idea of continuous process, commented on above; but here the slow, "evolutionary" pace of change is taken explicitly as normal and organized,[69] whereas "discontinuity" is taken as problematic.[70] The orientation to "rural" types of organization should be recalled. In line with the stress on continuous process, the point where sanctioned order meets advisable change is not

---

existing social arrangements or a serious alteration in the routine of group life causing maladjustment." H. W. Odum, p. 100: ". . . . if one reviews the general categories of social problems already listed in previous chapters, it must be clear that most of them or their present manifestations are due to or accentuated by the process of social change."

[68] The point is made and acutely discussed by Rosenquist, pp. 8-10.

[69] Gillin, Dittmer, and Colbert, p. 48: "Social life and its products require long periods of time to develop and ripen. . . . ." Gillette and Reinhardt, p. 13: "The larger proportion of social changes are small and simple, and resemble osmosis in the field of physics and organic life." This gradualism is related to the orientation to primary group relations and experiences and hence to the "sharing" conception of the social. E.g., Elliott and Merrill, p. 11: "Assimilation, on the other hand, is gradual and depends upon some degree of contact and communication, if there is to be any vital sharing of common experience (Cf. M. P. Follett, *Creative Experience*.) . . . ."

[70] Gillette and Reinhardt, p. 30: ". . . . the need for thought about discontinuity in industry or education, and about our dependence on proper training to keep society stabilized and progressive, should be emphasized"; p. 21: "The habitual, daily, routine, conventional activities of life fortunately make up the greater part of life, most of the time. Often, however, they are broken across by social breakdowns, disturbances, and dislocations and the appearance of troublesome classes of persons." C. A. Ellwood (a), p. 230: ". . . . revolution is not a *normal* method of social change; . . . . it marks the breakdown of the normal means of social development; . . . . it is not inevitable, but may easily be avoided by plasticity in social institutions and in the mental attitudes of classes and individuals. . . ."

typically or structurally drawn.[71] A conception of "balanc℈" is usual and sometimes is explicitly sanctioned.[72] The question, "Changes in what spheres induce disorganization?" is left open; the position taken is usually somewhere between extremes, both of which are held to be bad.[73] This comes out in the obvious fact that what a conservative calls *dis*organization, a radical might well call *re*organization. Without a construction of total social structures that are actually emerging, one remains caught between simple evaluations.

Besides deviation from norms, orientation to rural principles of stability, cultural lag, and social change, another conception in terms of which "problems" are typically discussed is that of adaptation or "adjustment" and their opposites.[74] The pathological or disorganized is the maladjusted. This concept, as well as that of the "normal," is

[71] The notion of temporal contingency, at times extended to the point of historical irrationality, plays into the processual, nonstructural characteristics of the perspective; notice also its commensurability with the apolitical and one-thing-at-a-time reformism. Elliott and Merrill, p. 3: "Life is dynamic. Life is ceaseless, bewildering change, and man, armed though he is with the experience of the past, can never be certain of the future. He must recognize that the immediate present is a constantly changing frame of reference and that future problems are a matter of chance for which the past offers no sure panacea."

[72] E. C. Hayes' Editor's Introduction to U. G. Weatherly, p. xii: "Realization that progressive change is not likely to be less in the generation next to come . . . . and determination . . . . to promote progress, is the normal attitude for every person who is animated by generous loyalty and. . . . ." Weatherly, p. 138: "Both innovation and conservatism have their value, and the balance between them, which is an ideal attitude . . . ."; p. 380: "Discipline and liberation are not two antagonistic processes; they are complimentary parts of the same process, which is social equilibration. They illustrate the law of physics . . . . stability is reached only by a balance of forces."

[73] A. Ellwood (*a*), p. vii: "The aim of the book is to indicate the direction which our social thinking must take if we are to avoid revolution, on the one hand, and reactions, on the other."

[74] H. P. Fairchild, p. 35: ". . . . . it can be safely said that maladjustments are among the most numerous and important of all forms of abnormality, frequently being so extensive as to include entire social groups or classes."

usually left empty of concrete, social content;[75] or its content, is in effect, a propaganda for conformity to those norms and traits ideally associated with small-town, middle-class *milieux*.[76] When it is an individual who is thought to be maladjusted, the "social type" within which he is maladjusted is not stated. Social and normal elements are masked by a quasi-biological meaning of the term "adaptation"[77] with an entourage of apparently socially bare terms like "existence" and "survival," which seem still to draw prestige from the vogue of evolutionism.[78] Both the quasi-biological and the structureless character of the con-

[75] Gillin, Dittmer, and Colbert, p. 536: "All social problems grow out of *the* social problem—the problem of the adjustment of man to his universe, and of the social universe to man. The maladjustments in these relationships give us all our social problems. . . . ." H. P. Fairchild, p. 16: "While the word 'normal' carries a fairly definite and, for the most part, accurate implication to the mind of any intelligent person, it is nevertheless extremely difficult to define in concrete terms. . . . . As commonly used to convey a definite idea, the word 'normal' means that which is in harmony with the general make-up and organization of the object under discussion—that which is consistent with other normal factors."

[76] Elliott and Merrill, p. 17, correctly assert that in "Edward T. Devine's discussion of 'the normal life' the norm is the healthy and uneventful life cycle of the average middle-class man or woman. These persons are never subjected to the temptations of great wealth. Neither do they come in contact with poverty, crime, vice, and other unpleasantly sordid aspects of life [*The Normal Life*, pp. 5-8]. His discussion is thus a consideration of the 'normal standards' for the several ages of the bourgeoisie. . . . ."

[77] When it is so hidden; but note the heavily sentimental endowment the term may receive: R. C. Dexter, p. 408: ". . . . few of the present generation of little ones, and fewer still of the next, will never see the sun or the green grass because of the sins of their parents or the carelessness of their physician; and thanks to our increasing provision for free public education, more and more adapted to the needs of the individual child, thousands of boys and girls will become intelligent, responsible citizens, worthy of a free nation, instead of pawns for unscrupulous politicians. All this and much more is due to social adjustments, made by the unceasing effort and sacrifice of men and women who. . . . ."

[78] J. L. Gillin (*b*), p. 4: "Social pathology . . . . is the study of the social patterns and processes involved in man's failure to adjust himself and his institutions to the necessities of existence to the end that he may survive and satisfy the felt needs of his nature."

cept "adjustment" tend, by formalization, to universalize the term, thus again obscuring specific social content. Use of "adjustment" accepts the goals and the means of smaller community *milieux*.[79] At the most, writers using these terms suggest techniques or means believed to be less disruptive than others to attain the goals that are given. They do not typically consider whether or not certain groups or individuals caught in economically underprivileged situations can possibly obtain the current goals without drastic shifts in the basic institutions which channel and promote them. The idea of adjustment seems to be most directly applicable to a social scene in which, on the one hand, there is a society and, on the other, an individual immigrant.[80] The immigrant then "adjusts" to the new environment. The "immigrant problem" was early in the path-

[79] J. L. Gillin (*b*), p. 8: "An individual who does not approximate these [socially approved] standards is said to be *unadjusted*. If he does not concern himself with living up to them, he is said to be demoralized or disorganized." R. C. Dexter, p. 407: "In this book the term Social Adjustment has been . . . . used as applying to . . . . the necessary task of smoothing-off the rough edges and softening the sledge-hammer blows of an indifferent social system. The term . . . . is practically synonymous with social adaptation— the fitting of man to his complete environment, physical and social alike. Until the present it has been the especially maladjusted individual or group who has received the service of 'straighteners.' " (Note *ideological* orientation of concept.)

[80] H. P. Fairchild, p. 34: "The other form of incompetence, which may be called 'maladjustment,' does not imply any lack on the part of the individual himself. . . . . The man is all right, but he is not in the right place. Our immigrants furnish abundant examples of this form of incompetence. . . . . But the foreigner is not by any means the sole example of maladjustment. Our modern life, particularly our modern city life, teems with cases of this sort." J. H. S. Bossard (*a*), p. 110 (under "The Immigrant's Problem of Adjustment"): "To most persons, life consists in large measure of habitual responses to the demands of a fairly fixed environment. When man changes his environment, new and perhaps untried responses are called for. New adjustments must be made, as we say." J. L. Gillin (*b*), p. 10: "Social pathology . . . . arises out of the maladjustment between the individual and the social structure." Elliott and Merrill, p. 22: "Just as an effective social organization implies a harmony between individual and social interests, so a disorganized social order must involve a conflict between individual and social points of view."

ologist's center of focus, and the concepts used in stating it may have been carried over as the bases for a model of experience and formulations of other "problems." *The Polish Peasant* (1918), which has had a very strong influence on the books under consideration, was empirically focused upon an immigrant group.

In approaching the notion of adjustment, one may analyze the specific illustrations of maladjustment that are given and from these instances infer a type of social person who in this literature is evaluated as "adjusted." The ideally adjusted man of the social pathologists is "socialized." This term seems to operate ethically as the opposite of "selfish;"[81] it implies that the adjusted man conforms to middle-class morality and motives and"participates" in the gradual progress of respectable institutions. If he is not a "joiner," he certainly gets around and into many community organizations.[82] If he is socialized, the individual thinks of others and is kindly toward them. He does not

[81] Gillin, Dittmer, and Colbert, pp. 16-17: "By *socialization* we mean the directing of human motives toward giving to 'even the least' of the members of the social whole the benefits of cultural development. Socialization is thus practically the opposite to *aloofness, selfishness, greed, exploitation,* and *profiteering.* It causes the individual and the group to *feel* their *oneness* with the social whole. . . . . In brief, what society regards as *moral, i.e.,* good for the whole, becomes the aim of socialized individuals and groups. This being true, the improvement of society rests to a very large extent upon *moral progress."*

[82] See Queen and Gruener, *Social Pathology: Obstacles to Social Participation.* These authors would deny this mode of statement, but such verbal denials must be tested against what they have done and the framework they have actually employed in defining pathologies. Their criterion of the pathological is correctly indicated in the subtitle of their book. Elliott and Merrill, p. 580: "There are various criteria by which the degree of individual participation may be measured roughly . . . . whether or not he votes at elections . . . . the individual's ownership of real or personal property . . . . the degree of specific interest in community activities may be roughly measured by the number and character of the institutions to which the individual belongs, as well as the voluntary community activities in which he participates. Communities in which there is a high percentage of individuals with a positive rating on the items listed above are logically those which are the most highly organized and efficient." (Note the character of the institutions, participation in which is defined as organized.)

brood or mope about but is somewhat extrovert, eagerly participating in his community's institutions. His mother and father were not divorced, nor was his home ever broken. He is "successful"—at least in a modest way— since he is ambitious; but he does not speculate about matters too far above his means, lest he become "a fantasy thinker," and the little men don't scramble after the big money. The less abstract the traits and fulfilled "needs" of "the adjusted man" are, the more they gravitate toward the norms of independent middle-class persons verbally living out Protestant ideals in the small towns of America.[83]

[83] See above documentation; notice the Protestant ethical accent on *utility* and what it will do for one, apparently irrespective of social fact: Gillin, Dittmer, and Colbert, p. 106: "People who are useful, no matter what happens to be their race or color, come to be liked and respected. Consequently, the central aim of a sound educational program should be to teach people ro be useful. (Hart, Hornell, *The Science of Social Relations,* 1927, pp. 521-524)" In the following, note the norm of competitiveness: Elliott and Merrill, pp. 29-30: "Often, however, the individual cannot or will not compete. We then have the following pathological manifestations: '. . . . the *dependent* . . . . who is unable to compete; *the defective* . . . . who is, if not unable, at least handicapped in his efforts to compete. The *criminal,* on the other hand, . . . . who is perhaps unable, but at any rate refuses, to compete according to the rules which society lays down." (Park and Burgess, *Introduction to the Science of Sociology,* p. 560). Among the traits thought to characterize "the good life from the standpoint of the individual," Odum, pp. 50-51, cites: "patience," "specialized knowledge of some particular thing," "skill," "optimism," "love of work," "dynamic personality," "moderation," "trained will power," etc. Cf., in this connection, K. Davis, "Mental Hygiene and the Class Structure," *Psychiatry: Journal of the Biology and Pathology of Interpersonal Relations,* February, 1938, pp. 55-65.

# 8

## TWO STYLES OF
## SOCIAL SCIENCE RESEARCH

When in the course of our work we are uncertain, we sometimes become more concerned with our methods than with the content of our problems. We then try to clarify our conceptions and tighten our procedures. And as we re-examine studies that we feel have turned out well, we create conscious models of inquiry with which we try to guide our own work-in-progress.

It is in terms of these models that we sometimes gain that sense of craftsmanship that is one subjective yield of work well done.

Modern men have generally been happier in their sense of craftsmanship when they have felt that they were at least approximating the generalized model of the laboratory. "Every step in science," Charles Peirce wrote, "has been a lesson in logic." In our search for a general model of inquiry, we have usually seized upon the supposed Method of Physical Science, and we have often fetishized it.

In the sociological disciplines, this grateful acceptance of "Science" is often more formal than operative and always more ambiguous than clear-cut. As a going concern, in the social studies, scientific empiricism means many things, and there is no one accepted version, much less any systematic use of any one model of science. The same work, admired by some as "great," is disparaged by another as "journalism." Professional expectations about method are quite confused, and our sense of craftsmanship may be realized in terms of quite different modes of inquiry.

There are, in fact, at least two working models of inquiry now available in current social studies, and accordingly two senses of craftsmanship in terms of which work is judged, and on the basis of which controversies over method occur.

I

The first of these two research-ways might be called the macroscopic. It has a venerable history, reaching notable heights, for example, in the work of Weber and Ostrogorski, Marx and Bryce, Michels, Simmel and Mannheim. These men like to deal with total social structures in a comparative way; their scope is that of the world historian; they attempt to generalize types of historical phenomena, and in a systematic way, to connect the various institutional spheres of a society, and then relate them to prevailing types of men and women. How did the Crusades come about? Are Protestantism and the rise of capitalism related? If so, how? Why is there no socialist movement in the U. S.?

The other way of sociological research might be called the molecular. It is, at first glance, characterized by its usually small-scale problems and by its generally statistical models of verification. Why are 40 per cent more of the women who give marketing advice to their neighbors during a given week on a lower income level than those who gave it during another week? Molecular work has no illustrious antecedents, but, by virtue of historical accident and the unfortunate facts of research finance, has been developed a great deal from studies of marketing and problems connected with media of mass communication. Shying away from social philosophy, it often appears as technique and little else.

Everyone involved in the social studies will recognize these two styles, and by now, a good many will readily agree that "we ought to get the two together." Sometimes this program is put in terms of the statement that the sociologist's ideal task during the next decades is to unite the larger problems and theoretical work of the nineteenth century, especially that of the Germans, with the research techniques predominant in the twentieth century, especially that of the Americans. Within this great dialectic, it is felt, signal and continuous advances in masterful conception and rigorous procedure will be made.

If we inquire more closely into just how the two research-ways differ, we find that there is sometimes a confusion of differences that are non-logical with those that are logical in character. This is revealed, for example, in statements of the difference between the two styles as a political and intellectual dilemma: the more socially or politically signifi-cant our problems and work (the more macroscopic), the less rigorous is our solution and the less certain our knowl-edge (the less molecular).

There is much social truth in such statements; as they have so far been used these two styles of thought do differ in their characteristic value-relevance and political orien-tation. But this does not mean that any political orientation is inherent in the logic of either style of thought. The evaluative choice of problems characteristic of each of the two methods has not been *necessarily* due to logical capa-bilities or limitations of either. Molecular work of great political relevance is logically possible; and macroscopic work is not necessarily of broad significance, as a glance at many "political science" monographs proves all too well. No, many of the differences between the two styles are not logical, but social:

From the standpoint of the individual researcher, the choice of problems in either style of work may be due to academic timidity, political disinterest, or even cowardice; but above all it is due to the institutional facts of the financial life of molecular research. Molecular work re-quires an organization of technicians and administrators, of equipment and money, and, as yet, of promoters. It can not proceed until agencies of research are sufficiently de-veloped to provide detailed materials. It has arisen in definite institutional centers: in business, since the twenties among marketing agencies, and since the thirties, in the polling agencies; in academic life at two or three research bureaus; and in research branches of government. Since World War II the pattern has spread, but these are still the centers.

This institutionalization of the molecular style has in-volved the applied focus, which has typically been upon specific problems, presented so as to make clear alternatives of practical—which is to say, pecuniary and administrative —action. It is *true* that only as general principles are discovered can social science offer "sound practical guidance"; often the administrator needs to know certain detailed facts and relations, and that is all he needs to know.

The sociologist in the applied focus no longer addresses "the public;" more usually he has specific clients with particular interests and perplexities. This shift, from public to client, clearly destroys the idea of objectivity as aloofness, which perhaps meant responsiveness to vague, unfocused pressures, and thus rested more on the individual interests of the researcher. In applied research of the molecular style, the client's social operations and economic interests have often supplied the sometimes tacit but always present moral meaning and use to the problem and to its solution. This has meant that most molecular work of any scale has been socially guided by the concerns and worries set by practical government and business interests and has been responsible to them. Accordingly, there is little doubt that the applied focus has tended to lower the intellectual initiative and to heighten the opportunism of the researcher. However technically free he may be, his initiative and interest are in fact usually subordinate to those of the client, whether it be the selling of pulp magazines or the administration of an army's morale.

Very little except his own individual limitations has stood between the individual worker and macroscopic work of the highest order. But the rise of the molecular style means that the unattached man cannot pursue such research on any scale, for such work is dependent upon organization and money. If we would "solve" the problem raised by the coexistence of these two styles we must pay attention to the design of work that is possible for the unattached men who still comprise the bulk of those claiming membership in the sociological community.

The rise of applied molecular work, as it is now being organized, makes questions of moral and political policy of the social studies all the more urgent. As a bureaucratization of reflection, the molecular style is quite in line with dominant trends of modern social structure and its characteristic types of thought. I do not wish to consider these problems here except to say that they should not be confused with any differences of a logical character between the two styles of inquiry.

## II

There are at least three relative differences of a logical sort between the macroscopic and the molecular styles of work as they are now practiced: the molecular is more objective; it is more open to cumulative development; and it is more open to statistical quantification.

Objectivity means that the work is so done and so presented that any other qualified person can repeat it, thus coming to the same results or showing that the results were mistaken. Subjectivity means the reverse, and thus that there is usually a persistent individual variation of procedure—and of solution. Under this difference lies the fact that when work is objective the procedures used are systematized or even codified and hence are available to any qualified operator; whereas in subjective work the procedures are often not systematized, much less standardized or codified.

This in turn means that in objective work there is a more distinct possibility of cumulation—or at least replication!—both in terms of empirical solutions and in terms of the procedures used. In the more subjective macroscopic work the sensitivity and talent of the individual worker weigh more heavily and although there may be those who "take up where he left off," this is usually a continuity of subject-matter, general ideas, and approach rather than an accumulation of procedure. It is possible within a few years to train competent persons to repeat a Sandusky job;[1] it is not so possible to train them to repeat a Middletown study. Another sample of soldiers in another war can be located on a morale scale and comparisons built up; Max Weber's analytic and historical essay on bureaucracy has not been repeated or checked in the same way, however

[1] Paul F. Lazarsfeld, *et al., The People's Choice* (New York: Duell, Sloan and Pearce, 1944).

much it has been criticized and "used." Macroscopic work
has not experienced the sort of cumulative development
that molecular work during the current generation of
sociologists has.

It is descriptively true that the molecular style has been
heavily statistical, whereas the macroscopic has not. This,
again, is an aspect of the greater codification and the lower
level of abstraction that molecular work entails. And it
can be confidently supposed that as macroscopic work is
made more systematic it will become more quantitative—
at least as a general form of thought. For example, Dar-
win's *Origin* as well as many of Freud's theories are quantitative models of reflection.

Each of these three points is underpinned by the fact
that molecular procedures can be, and have been, more
explicitly codified than those of the macroscopic style; and
by the fact that molecular terms are typically on a lower
level of abstraction than most macroscopic conceptions.

Insofar as the logical differences between the two styles
concern *procedures,* they are differences in the degree of
systematic codification. Insofar as they involve *conceptions,*
they are differences in level of abstraction.

### III

When we say that molecular terms are on *lower* levels
of abstraction we mean that they isolate from larger contexts a few precisely observed elements; in this sense they
are of course quite abstract. When we say that macroscopic
concepts are on *higher* levels of abstraction, we mean that
they are more generalized, that the number of single variables which they cover are more numerous. The molecular
term is narrow in scope, and specific in reference: it deals
with a few discrete variables; the macroscopic researcher
gains his broader scope by using concepts that cover, usually less specifically, a much larger number of variables.

There is no clear-cut variable, the presence or absence
of which allows application of the concept, "capitalism":
under such concepts there is likely to be a pattern of interrelated variables. Thus, such concepts are not only high-
level but their index structure is an elaborately compounded

affair. Put technically, most big macroscopic concepts already have under them rather elaborate, and often unsystematic, cross-tabulations of several variables; most molecular terms stand for single variables useful for the stubs of such tables.

We consider a term in its relation to some empirical item(s)—that is, its semantic dimension; and we can consider a term in its relation to other terms—that is, its syntactical dimension, or if you like, its conceptual implications.[2] It is characteristic of molecular terms that their semantic dimensions are pronounced, although syntactical relations may also be there. It is characteristic of macroscopic terms that their syntactical dimensions are pronounced, although semantical relations may also be available.

The higher macroscopic levels are more syntactically elaborate; semantically they involve a hierarchy of compounded indices pointing to whole *gestalts* of attributes. Macroscopic concepts are often sponge-like and unclarified in their semantic dimensions. Sometimes, in fact, they do not have any index structure that enables us to touch empirically observable facts or relations.[3] They have under them only a vague kind of many-dimensional indicator rather than an index. Yet, with all this, it may be that whether a statement is macroscopic or molecular is a mat-

[2] We can also consider it in relation to its users—the pragmatic dimension—which I am not here considering. These are the three dimensions of meaning which Charles M. Morris has systematized in his "Foundations of the Theory of Signs," International Encyclopedia of Unified Science, Volume I: Number 2. University of Chicago Press, 1938.

[3] To sort out the dimensions of a macroscopic concept requires us to elaborate it syntactically, while keeping our eyes open for semantic indices for each implication so elaborated. To translate each of these points into molecular terms requires us to trace the hierarchy of inference down to single, clear-cut variables. In assertions using macroscopic concepts, we must watch for whether or not the assertion (1) states a proposition, or (2) unlocks an implication. The guide-rule is whether the statement involves one empirical factor or at least two. If it involves only one factor, then it simply "spells out" or specifies one of the conceptual implications of that one factor; its meaning is syntactical. If the assertion involves two factors, it may be a proposition, a statement of a relation which can be true or false; its meaning is semantical.

ter of degree—a question of at what level we introduce
our syntactical elaboration.

## IV

Our choice of level of abstraction occurs, if I may
simplify the matter, in at least two distinct junctions of our
research act: The character and scope of the unit that we
take as problematic, the what-is-to-be-explained;[4] and the
model of explanation—the concepts we use in the solution
of the problem.[5]

The grand tradition in social studies has been to state
both problem and explanation in more or less macroscopic
terms. In contrast, the *pure* molecular student goes through
the whole research act on the molecular level. In the
simplest scheme of observation and explanation there are
four possibilities:

|  | OBSERVATIONS TO BE EXPLAINED: | |
| --- | --- | --- |
| EXPLANATIONS | Macroscopic | Molecular |
| Macroscopic | I | II |
| Molecular | III | IV |

I. Both what is to be explained and its explanation can
be on the macroscopic level. *E.g.:* Why do many people
follow Hitler? Answer: Because in the bureaucratization
of modern society, life-plans are taken over by centralized
bureaucracies in such a way that when crises occur, people
are disoriented and feel that they need guidance. Bu-

[4] In either style, one may of course start with a simple declaration of descriptive intent, finding more precisely-put problems as
one goes along. In either style, too, the assembly of stray facts without any general significance or interconnection may be found; the
new (molecular) ideography is no different in this respect from the
older macroscopic kind. Both are composed of details not connected
with any problem and entailing no evident syntactical implications.

[5] The difference here is not a difference in the general logic of
explanation: in both styles of work a third factor (or fourth or fifth
factor) is appealed to in the explanation of some relation observed.

The explanatory intent of the macroscopic style is to *locate* the
behavior to be explained within a structural totality or a cultural
milieu; it finds its explanation in this "meaningful location"—which
means that it seeks to interpret in the terms of a highly intricate,
interrelated complex of variables.

The explanatory intent of the molecular student is to break down
the behavior of the individuals involved into component parts and to
find the explanation in the association of further simplified attributes
of these individuals.

reaucracy has thus resulted in a trained incapacity of people to steer themselves. In crises the bureaucratic routine that trained them is gone: they therefore follow Hitler. Etc.

II. When the problematic observations are molecular, but the explanation macroscopic, the question is thought to be too general and figures on the vote, pro-Hitler sentiment, and urban residence, for example, are taken as what is to be explained. Then they are explained macroscopically, although usually in a more modest way because of the molecular problem-setting. *E.g.:* The urban people were more disoriented and thus in need of the image of a Father who would promise to plan their lives and take care of them. They therefore voted pro-Hitler. Etc.

III. The problematic observations may be macroscopic and the explanation molecular. Why do some people follow Hitler? Answer: We know that only 5 per cent of the population went to college: this is a fact pointing to social ignorance, which is further confirmed by the correlation of education and political information, revealed in all our polls. Ignorance, thus established, goes far to explain why some people follow Hitler. Etc.

IV. The question of procedure, both phases are held to the molecular level. *E.g.:* The question is too general to be appropriately answered, it must be rephrased: 30 per cent of the adult population voted for Hitler in a given election. Why? Answer: When we take into account the rural-urban distribution, the religious, and the income level of the population, we find that 80 per cent of the rural, Protestant, high income level voted pro-Hitler, only 15 per cent of the urban, Catholic, low income. These three factors in the combination indicated seem to explain something about why certain people voted pro-Hitler and others did not. Etc.[6]

Notice the following characteristics of these four models of thought:

The inadequacies of the purely macroscopic and the purely molecular (I & IV) are tied in with the fact that in both cases there is no shuttle between levels of abstraction.

---

[6] All illustrative facts and figures in this paper are products of the imagination.

Since rigorous proof only exists empirically on the molecular levels, in the pure macroscopic there is no proved connection between problematic observation and explanation;
when you are persuaded by such work, it is only because
"it makes so much sense," it is syntactically convincing.
On the purely molecular level there is a connection proved
between problematic observation and explanatory observation, yet here the larger implications and meaning of that
association are neither explored nor explained. When you
are unsatisfied with such work it is because, although it is
"neat" and "ingenious," you feel "there is more to it all."

In procedures II & III there is a shuttle between the
macroscopic and molecular levels but it does *not* occur
in the same phase of the total research act: we do not move
from macroscopic to molecular inside the problematic
phase, and we do not do this inside the explanatory phase.
This means that the problematic observation and the explanation are not logically connected.

When the problem is molecular and the explanation
macroscopic (II), there is an error of *falsely concretizing
a concept:* in explaining some molecular observation by
appealing, *ad hoc,* to a macroscopic concept, that tends to
be handled in discussion as if it were a definite variable
statistically related to the molecular observation.

When the problem is macroscopic and the solution molecular (III), the error might be called *unduly stretching
an index:* in explaining some macroscopic observation by
appealing to a molecular variable, that variable is unduly
generalized and handled in discussion as if it were a carefully built index. The molecular explanation is *imputed* to
explain the macroscopic observation, not connected.[7]

What all this (II and III) amounts to is the use of statistics to illustrate general points, and the use of general

[7] In some research shops, the term "bright" is frequently applied
when molecular facts or relations are cogently explained by macroscopic suppositions (II).

When further molecular variables, whose meaning is generalized
very far—*i.e.,* stretched—are brought in to explain, and they work,
the result may be referred to as a "cute" table (III).

I mention this only to indicate that there is slowly emerging a
shop language to cover the procedures I am trying to assert.

points to illustrate statistics. The general points are not tested, not necessarily enlarged; they are conveniently adapted to the figures, as the arrangement of figures are cleverly adapted to them. The general points and explanations can be used with other figures too; so can the figures be used with other points.

Perhaps there is nothing especially wrong in all this; it is almost respectable procedure in some circles. But it does fall short of what is coming to be our vision of what social inquiry might be.

## V

I have discussed these research-ways at length in order to be able to set forth an "ideal" procedure, which we can use as a sort of lordly measuring rod for any piece of work in current social studies. The inadequacies indicated above may be summarized in one positive statement: If our work is to be clarified, we must be able to shuttle between levels of abstraction *inside each phase* of our simplified two-step act of research. This, of course, is simply another way of referring to the problem of indices and their place in the research process. Examine this simplified chart:

|             | PROBLEMATIC | EXPLANATORY |
|-------------|:-----------:|:-----------:|
| Macroscopic | 1           | 2           |
| Molecular   | 3           | 4           |

Only by moving grandly on the macroscopic level can we satisfy our intellectual and human curiosities. But only by moving minutely on the molecular level can our observations and explanations be adequately connected. So, if we would have our cake and eat it too, we must shuttle between macroscopic and molecular levels in instituting the problem *and* in explaining it—developing the molecular index structure of general concepts and the general conceptual implications of molecular variables. We move from macroscopic to molecular in both problem and in solution phase (1 to 3 and 2 to 4); then we relate the two on the molecular level (3 and 4); then we go back to the macroscopic (3 to 1 and 4 to 2). After that we can speak cautiously (i.e., bearing in mind the shuttles made), of relations on the macroscopic level (1 and 2).

To illustrate these shuttles, we may now design one ideal way of asking and answering a general question: Why *do* some people follow Hitler?

First, we accept the question macroscopically, and without losing any of its intended meaning, break it into more manageable (molecular) parts; "following Hitler" means: Expressing pro-Hitler sentiments to an interviewer, consistently voting for him, going out on the street to demonstrate when he or his agents request it, urging others to follow Hitler. Etc.

Each individual in a cross-section of the population may be classified in terms of a table composed of such items, and the tables reduced to a scale of types. Thus we build an index for "following Hitler"; our observation of what-is-to-be-explained is molecularly translated: transparent and specific indices are available.

We also accept, as a rather complicated hypothesis, the macroscopic statements (A) that people follow Hitler because of an inability to plan their own life-ways, (B) that this inability has been trained into them by work and life in bureaucratic structures, (C) that it was the crises and collapse of these bureaucracies that precipitated their allegiance to Hitler, whom, (D) they see as the big planner of their little lives.

Now this is somewhat tangled, although ordering it into these four assertions helps some. We have set ourselves quite some work, in translating and interpreting molecularly each of the four parts of the hypothesis. To short-cut it: for (A) we develop an index of "inability to plan life-ways." Perhaps we ask each individual about details of his daily routine and his weekly and yearly cycle, scoring each detail as to its indication of ability or inability to plan. We also ask directly about the images or lack of them that they have about the future and their future, etc. Then we carefully relate these scores, and come out again with a scale of types: at one end are those most able to plan their life-ways, at the other end of those least able.

Then we go to segment (B) of the hypothesis, building indices to work and leisure within bureaucracies. And so on, with (C) and (D).

Finally, we interrelate our molecular indices to all four features of our hypothesis, reduce them, and emerge with a master scale: at its top are people who seem unable to plan their own lives, have been duly exposed to and "trained" by bureaucracies,[8] who began to be pro-Hitler in the major crises in Weimar society, and who have an image of Hitler as an omnipotent regulator and giver of satisfactory life-plans.

Given the crude state of our empirical technique and the clumsiness of our index building, we would probably finish with five cases in our extreme types, elaborate macroscopic explanation into molecular terms, and this must be done if we are serious about relating problematic observation to explanation. If we have other macroscopic explanations we must handle them in the same way; in our design we must think through their index structure.

Now we run our observations to be explained against our explanation, and this is what we obtain:

| OBSERVATION OF HITLER SENTIMENT | PREDISPOSITION ACCORDING TO BUREAUCRATIC HYPOTHESIS | | |
| --- | --- | --- | --- |
| | High | Intermediate | Low |
| Pro-Hitler | 80% | 20% | 5% |
| Intermediate | 15 | 60 | 15 |
| Anti-Hitler | 5 | 20 | 80 |
| Total | 100% | 100% | 100% |

Maybe, But if so—

After controlling all the possible other variables we can think of, the reader might agree that we have earned the right to discuss, on the macroscopic level, bureaucracy, dictatorship and the character traits of modern mass-man. That is, to shuttle between macroscopic observations and macroscopic explanations.[9]

[8] For simplicity of presentation, I skip here the casual links between, *e.g.,* B and A implied in the hypothesis.

[9] Of course, by the time we had gone through the three steps outlined, surely Hitler would have us in his clutches; but that is an irrelevant incident, and of no concern or consequence to the *designer* and methodologist of research, however inconvenient it might be to the research worker.

## VI

Even this brief discussion of this sketchy model suggests general rules of procedure for interpenetrating more neatly molecular terms and macroscopic concepts. We must build up molecular terms; we must break down macroscopic conceptions. For, as matters now stand, the propositional meaning of many macroscopic statements is ambiguous and unclear; the conceptual meaning of many molecular statements is often barren.

Any macroscopic statement that makes sense *can be* reduced to a set of molecular assertions—by untangling its dimensions and clarifying the index structure of each of them. Any molecular statement can presumably be built up to macroscopic levels of abstraction—by combining it with other molecular indices and elaborating it syntactically—although many of them are probably not worth it, except as a formal exercise in ingenuity.

Every macroscopic study runs the risk of being confused by the wealth of materials that come into its scope. In order to decrease the chance of ambiguity in the semantic dimension of macroscopic conceptions, we must strain towards a clarification of their index structure and, while making them as clear as possible, we must work towards an increased codification of how we are using them.

Every molecular study involves a series of guesses about the important variables that may characterize and explain a phenomenon. In order to increase the chance that our focus will be upon key variables, we must strain towards possible levels of macroscopic concepts in our molecular work, but not stretch indices of explanatory variables, or at least do so only with an awareness of our speculative posture.

The sociological enterprise requires macroscopic researchers to imagine more technically, as well as with scope and insight; it requires technicians to go about their work with more imaginative concern for macroscopic meaning, as well as with technical ingenuity. Perhaps we cannot hope, except in rare instances, to have combined in one man all the skills and capacities required. We must proceed by means of a division of labor that is self-guided, in each of its divisions, by an understanding of and a working agreement upon a grand model. When as individuals we specialize in one or the other phases of this model, we must do so with a clear consciousness of the place of that phase within the model, and thus perform our specialist role in a manner most likely to aid another specialist in the architectonic endeavor. The development of such clear consciousness, in fact, is the complete and healthy significance of discussions of the method of the social studies.

# 9

## IBM PLUS REALITY
## PLUS HUMANISM = SOCIOLOGY

Sociology, judging by the books of its practitioners, is a strange field of learning. In the libraries of its professors you will find books containing announcements like this: $p^1$ ($=p^2ij$). As well as books, also called sociology, full of mumblings like this: "Sociological theory, then, is for us that aspect of the theory of social systems which is concerned with the phenomena of the institutionalization of patterns of value-orientation in the social system, with the conditions of that institutionalization, and of changes in the patterns, with conditions of conformity with and deviance from a set of such patterns and with motivational processes in so far as they are involved in all of these." As well as (and this is the last sample) assertions of this kind: "Militarily, economically, and politically, there is going on a struggle for the world . . . this struggle has a portentous psychological meaning: we witness and we participate in an historic contest which will decide what types of men and women will flourish on the earth."

It is possible, I suppose, that the same mind might compose all three statements, but it is not very likely. And, in fact, the same mind did not do so; not even the same type of mind. All of which means that American sociology, as it is revealed in books, is now divided into three main camps. Some sociologists, after having drafted a dozen articles and a hundred memoranda to the foundations, believe themselves to be statesmen of social science, and claim to see just how each of the three fit into the orderly progress of a unified field of learning. But I am not one of them.

I hold that only one of the three camps is worthy of the name sociology, and accordingly, I am not even going to mention the names of the leading members of the other two. Some of my best friends are in those camps, but they will have to blow their own horns. This decision allows me to do all that I can honestly do: give growling summaries of the other two camps (exaggerating them slightly, in order the more clearly to reveal their tendencies); pleasantly elaborate the third, to which I belong; and then mention some key books from which one working sociologist has learned something.

The first camp is that of The Scientists, who are very much concerned to be known as such. Among them, I am sure, are those who would love to wear white coats with an I.B.M. symbol of some sort on the breast pocket. They are out to do with society and history what they believe physicists have done with nature. Such a view often seems to rest upon the hope that if only someone could invent for "the social sciences" some gadget like the atom bomb, all our human problems would suddenly come to an end. This rational and empty optimism reveals, it seems to me, a profound ignorance of (1) the role of ideas in human history, of (2) the nature of power and its relations to knowledge, and of (3) the meaning of moral action and the place of knowledge within it.

Among The Scientists, the most frequent type is The Higher Statistician, who breaks down truth and falsity into such fine particles that we cannot tell the difference between them. By the costly rigor of their methods, they succeed in trivializing men and society, and in the process, their own minds as well.

In fact, several men in the social studies now enjoy enormous reputations, but have not produced any enormous books, intellectually speaking, or in fact any contributions of note to the substantive knowledge of our time. Their academic reputations rest, quite largely, upon their academic power: they are the members of the committee; they are on the directing board; they can get you the job, the trip, the research grant. They are a strange new kind

of bureaucrat. They are executives of the mind, public relations men among foundations and universities for their
fields. For them, the memorandum is replacing the book.
They could set up a research project or even a school,
but I would be surprised if, now after twenty years of research and teaching and observing and thinking, they could
produce a book that told you what they thought was going
on in the world, what they thought were the major problems for men of this historical epoch; and I feel sure that
they would be embarrassed if you earnestly asked them to
suggest what ought to be done about it and by whom.
For the span of time in which The Scientists say they think
of their work is a billion man-hours of labor. And in the
meantime we should not expect much substantive knowledge; first there must be methodological inquiries into
methods and inquiry.

Many foundation administrators like to give money for
projects that are thought to be safe from political or public
attack, that are large-scale, hence easier "to administer"
than more numerous handicraft projects, and that are scientific with a capital S, which often only means made
"safe" by trivialization. Accordingly, the big money tends
to encourage the large-scale bureaucratic style of research
into small-scale problems as carried on by The Scientists.

In their practice, as in that of the Grand Theorists
which I will now describe, the social studies become an
elaborate method of insuring that no one learns too much
about man and society, the first by formal but empty
ingenuity; the second, by formal and cloudy obscurantism.

The Grand Theorists represent a partially organized
attempt to withdraw from the effort plainly to describe,
explain, and understand human conduct and society: in
turgid prose they set forth the disordered contents of their
reading of eminent nineteenth-century sociologists, and in
the process mistake their own beginnings for a finished
result.

To at least some of those who claim to understand their
work and who like it, Grand Theory is the greatest single
advance in the entire history of sociology.

To many of those who claim to understand it but who do not like it, it is a clumsy piece of irrelevant ponderosity.

To those who do not claim to understand it but who like it very much—and there are many of these—it is a wondrous maze, fascinating precisely because of its often splendid lack of intelligibility.

Those who do not claim to understand it and who do not like it—if they retain the courage of their convictions —will feel that indeed the emperor has no clothes.

And of course there are many who qualify their views, and many more who remain patiently neutral, waiting to see the professional outcome.

Serious differences among sociologists are not between those who would observe without thinking and those who would think without observing. The differences have rather to do with what kind of thinking, what kind of observing, and what kind of link, if any, there is between the two. The nerve of the Grand Theorists' difficulties lies in their initial choice of so general a level of thinking that one cannot logically get down to observation; and secondly, in the seemingly arbitrary elaboration of distinctions which do not enlarge one's understanding of recognizably human problems or experience. Moreover, almost any 500 laborious pages of theirs could be translated into seventy-five straightforward pages of English containing everything said in the 500. Too much of it is a getting ready to get ready, too much more a getting ready, and through it all, there are too many promises and not enough payoffs.

The line between profundity and verbal confusion is often delicate, and no one should deny the curious charm of those who, like Whitman, beginning their studies, are so pleased and awed by the first step that they hardly wish to go any further. Of itself, language does form a wonderful world.

Yet, isn't it time for sociologists, especially eminent ones, to stop thinking about thinking and begin directly to study *something*?

The third camp is composed of sociologists who are trying to perform three major tasks, which may be stated in this way:

Whatever else sociology may be, it is a result of consistently asking: (1) What is the meaning of this—whatever we are examining—for our society as a whole, and what is this social world like? (2) What is the meaning of this for the types of men and women that prevail in this society? And (3) how does this fit into the historical trend of our times, and in what direction does this main drift seem to be carrying us? No matter how small-scale what he is examining, the sociologist must ask such questions about it, or he has abdicated the classic sociological endeavor.

I know of no better way to become acquainted with this endeavor in a high form of modern expression than to read the periodical, *Studies in Philosophy and Social Sciences,* published by The Institute of Social Research. Unfortunately, it is available only in the morgues of university libraries, and to the great loss of American social studies, several of the Institute's leading members, among them Max Horkheimer and Theodore Adorno, have returned to Germany. That there is now *no* periodical that bears comparison with this one testifies to the ascendency of the Higher Statisticians and the Grand Theorists over the Sociologists. It is difficult to understand why some publisher does not get out a volume or two of selections from this great periodical.

What the endeavor of sociology looks like may also be seen in the many classics of sociology that have become available in English during the last decade. The most important, I believe, are the several works of Max Weber. Do you remember the big literary rush to Vilfredo Pareto during the thirties? Well, as the general inattention to him nowadays reveals, he wasn't worth it. Max Weber would be: his voice is that of the classic liberal in a world that seemed to him, back in the first quarter of the century, all set against liberalism, and at the same time he is the most sophisticated revisionist of classic Marxism.

Other important classics now available include: George

Simmel's *Conflict* and *The Sociology of George Simmel*, Emile Durkheim's *Suicide: A Study in Sociology* and *The Division of Labor in Society*. Gaetano Mosca's *The Ruling Class*, and Robert Michels' *Political Parties*.

The later volumes of Karl Mannheim do not have the general relevance of his first two—*Ideology and Utopia* and *Man and Society in an Age of Reconstruction*. There is now a paper-backed edition of Thorstein Veblen's *Theory of the Leisure Class*. (Someone ought to do his other books, especially *Absentee Ownership*.) H. Stuart Hughes has recently written an excellent critical estimate of *Oswald Spengler*. Francis Cornford, by his magnificent translation and editing, has given us a virtually new *Republic of Plato*.

The best attempt, since Weber, to organize key concepts and formulate hunches in a one-two-three manner is Harold D. Lasswell's and Abraham Kaplan's *Power and Society*, which draws upon Weber, Michels, and Mosca in a most intelligent way. Robert A. Dahl and Charles E. Lindblom, in their *Politics, Economics, and Welfare*, have recently produced an excellent statement of the integration of total societies.

Books on social structure or on the various institutional domains that compose it include Gunnar Myrdal's two-volume *An American Dilemma*, which deals primarily with the Negro, but is also valuable for much else. Franz Neumann's *Behemoth* and E. Herbert Norman's *Japan's Emergence as a Modern State* are models of excellence for any sociological studies of social structure.

Military institutions and their meaning for modern life have been explored by Hans Speier in several important essays, contained in *Social Order and the Risks of War*, which also contains excellent pieces on politics. The classic sociological account in English is Alfred Vagts' *A History of Militarism*. And there are good materials also in *Makers of Modern Strategy*, edited by E. M. Earle.

On the social and political meaning of the economic structure, Schumpeter and Galbraith are perhaps most significant, although Schumpeter—whose work is as much used as ideological material by the Eisenhower Administration as is any economist's—is the more solid and wide ranging. Henry Durant's *The Problem of Leisure* and J. Huizinga's *Homo Ludens* are fine statements about work and play in modern life. The best single volume on religious trends in America of which I know is Herbert W. Schneider's *Religion in Twentieth Century America,* and of educational practices, A. E. Bestor's *Educational Wastelands.* The best sociological statement of international relations is E. H. Carr's *The Twenty Years Crisis.*

William H. Whyte Jr., in *Is Anybody Listening?* does not seem to be aware of—or at any rate doesn't state— the full meaning of what he so penetratingly describes, but he represents the old-fashioned Man Who Goes Into The Field, rather than sending four dozen researchers there, and his work shows it. So does Floyd Hunter's *Community Power Structure,* which is the best book on an American community since the Lynds' studies of *Middletown.*

It is shameful that sociologists have not celebrated properly the two wonderful volumes of Arnold Hauser, *The Social History of Art.* And equally shameful that no American publisher has brought out George Lukács' *Studies in European Realism.*

Most recent books of sociological relevance dealing with the individual have been influenced by the psychoanalytic tradition. Harry Stack Sullivan and Karen Horney, with great sensibility, take into account the small group and the general cultural pattern, but neither has an adequate view of social structure. That is not true of Erich Fromm, who in his *Escape From Freedom* skillfully relates economic and religious institutions to the types of personality they select and form. One of the few books I know that really locates Freud's work in a more ample philosophical framework is the wonderful little volume by Paul Tillich, *The Courage To Be.*

Perhaps the most influential book of the last decade on types of individuals is *The Authoritarian Personality,* by T. W. Adorno, Else Frenkel-Brunswik, D. J. Levinson, and R. N. Sanford, which, although not well organized and subject to quite damaging criticisms of method, still remains of outstanding importance. In the same tradition is the neat monograph by Leo Lowenthal and N. Guterman, *Prophets of Deceit,* which ought to be read widely just now to understand something of what is involved in the Republican Party split. Many of the sociologically most interesting trends in psychiatric circles may conveniently be found in *A Study of Interpersonal Relations,* edited by Patrick Mullahy.

The main drift, the historic character of our time, has not been faced up to by many sociologists. Over-shadowing all such attempts in scope and in excellence of detail is Arnold J. Toynbee's six-volume *A Study of History,* which sociologists of the third camp will be studying for many years to come. It should be read along with Gilbert Murray's lovely little essay, *Hellenism and the Modern World,* Herbert J. Muller's criticism *The Uses of the Past,* and Pitrim Sorokin's comparisons, *Social Philosophies of an Age of Crisis.* Karl Löwith's *Meaning in History* and Paul Tillich's *The Protestant Era* are also key items for the historically grounded sociologist.

E. H. Carr, in his *The New Society*—his BBC Third Programme lectures—has produced an indispensable and commendably brief statement of major trends in modern society. David Riesman writes better essays than books, but his *Lonely Crowd* is within the third camp. A book selling in Germany much better than in America—to the loss of American readers—is Fritz Sternberg's *Capitalism and Socialism on Trial.*

All of these, of course, are samples of the kind of books from which one sociologist has learned something, and which sustain him against The Scientists—who during the decade have moved from marketing research to the foundations, and so from toothpaste and soap to higher mathematics—and against The Grand Theorists—who have moved from textual interpretation of sociological classics to careful thinking about their own possible thought.

In every intellectual age, some one field of study tends

to become a sort of common denominator of many other fields. In American intellectual life today sociology could become such a common denominator, and in fact, despite everything, it is slowly becoming that. But for such a salutary development to get fully under way, theorists are going to have to do their work with a sense of reality as well as with scope and insight. Research technicians are going to have to go about their work with more imaginative concern for its larger meanings, as well as with mathematical ingenuity. Both are going to have to drop their trivialization of subject matter and their pretensions about method. Both are going to have to face up to the realities of our time. And both are going to have to acquire the humanist concern—which some American historians have retained—for excellence of clear and meaningful expression.

# MASS MEDIA
# AND PUBLIC OPINION

The most dramatic event of U.S. public opinion in recent times, and a crucial proof of its independence and unpredictability, was the presidential election of Harry Truman in 1948. It was dramatic because it was almost universally unexpected; it was proof of the independent will of the electorate because the mass media of communication were largely against his election, and repeatedly said so; it indicated the unpredictability of public opinion because virtually all predictions, scientific and otherwise, collapsed before the event.

The 1948 election was not a stray happening. American politics over the last two decades has consistently displayed the fact of an overwhelmingly Republican press, and a Democratic party in power. And the tension and contradiction between public opinion and mass media holds not only for voting. It is also true for the largest mass movement in America: labor. The unions, almost always opposed by press and radio, rose from about three million to 15 million between 1933 and 1948, and since then have more than held their own.

No commentator of the American scene can be accurate unless his comment takes such facts into account, and, moreover, unless his general image of America and of American public opinion enables him to explain them. And no view of American public life can be realistic that assumes public opinion to be wholly controlled and entirely manipulated by the mass media. There are forces at work among the public that are independent of these media of communication, that can and do at times go directly against the opinions promulgated by them. The U.S. public has an au-

tonomy of judgment, and on many questions makes up its
own mind, without direction from any center and without
any authority but its own sovereignty. In the enormous flow
of words, signs, images, sounds, and entertainments there
is much that is openly controversial, much that is critical—
it does not add up to one, standardized, official image of
the world; it does not reiterate one standard set of norms
for reality; it contains various images and, to a considerable extent, they compete with one another.

Public opinion exists, as Hans Speier has remarked, when
people who are not in the government of a country claim
the right to express political opinions freely and publicly,
and the right that these opinions should influence or determine the policies, personnel, and actions of their government. In this sense there has been and there is a definite
public opinion in the United States. And yet, with the rise
of the mass media, it has often been thought, and correctly
so, that this formal right does not always mean what it once
did. For the world of pamphleteering open to a Tom Paine
is very different from the world of radio and motion pictures closed to those who do not have ready access to them.
But, again, the matter is not simple; the facts of public
opinion and of how the public makes up its mind, of the influences at work within it and upon it, are today quite complex. In fact, since the eighteenth century rise of democratic governments and liberal political theory, intellectuals
have more or less gone through three stages of thinking
about the role of independent public opinion in the body
politic.

I

The key feature of opinion which the rise of the democratic middle classes initiates is the free ebb and flow of
discussion going on between persons, as against the homogeneous inheritance and personal enforcement of traditional
opinion. Public opinion results from this ebb and flow, and
is seen by democratic theorists as the resolution of all these
discussions, which are transformed into action after opinion,
by public deliberation, has been formed.

In the simpler democratic society, powerful institutions

and public opinions interact in a two-way process: the public's opinion is expressed by operating institutions and the institution's operations affect opinion. The discussion, and the resulting public opinion, form the "general will" of the people, which parliament or Congress—the top and representative public—enacts into the law of the land, thus giving institutional force to public opinion. Parliament, as an institution, crowns all the primary publics; it is the archetype for each of the scattered little circles of face-to-face citizens discussing their public business.

This eighteenth-century idea of public opinion parallels the economic idea of the free market economy. Here is the public composed of discussing circles of opinion peers crowned by parliament; there is the market composed of freely competing entrepreneurs. As price is the result of anonymous, equally-weighted, bargaining individuals supplying and demanding of one another, so is the public of public opinion, with each man having thought things out for himself and contributing his weight to the great formation of the end result, public opinion. To be sure, some discussants might have more influence on the state of opinion than others, but no one man or group monopolizes the discussion, and although each may influence it, no one man or group sets the state of opinion that prevails.

In "the primary publics," of face-to-face groups, anyone is allowed to speak at will, and everyone interested does. The possibilities of answering back, of forming autonomous organs of public opinion, of realizing opinion in action, are automatically established by the institutional possibilities of democratic society.

The public, composed of innumerable discussion circles knit together by mobile people who carry opinions and struggle for powers of larger command, is organized into parties. Each party, representing a shifting viewpoint, which it pushes in discussion and expresses formally by vote, may in turn, with the circles composing it, acquire a place in parliament or congress, and there the discussion continues. It is a conception of authority by discussion, based formally on the theory that truth and justice will somehow come out of society as a great apparatus of free discussion.

The autonomy of these discussion circles is a crucial ele-

ment in the idea of public opinion as a democratic legitimation. The opinions formed are realized in action, within
the prevailing institutional framework of power by its
agents, who are made or broken by the prevailing opinions
of primary publics; or against the prevailing framework of
power by autonomous organs voluntarily developed as the
instrumentalities of discussing publics.

Insofar as public opinion is in line with the democratic
authority, it serves to legitimate that authority. It works out
the symbols of loyalty, the justifications of authority; and
at the same time, it sets up an undercurrent of more or less
continuous demands on this authority. Public opinion
forms and reforms about specific policy issues and events;
it judges the specific policies and actions of those in authority.

Insofar as the public is frustrated in realizing its demands
upon its agents, it may come to question the symbols of
authority to which it has been devoted. Such questioning is
of course of a deeper order than criticism of specific policies; now political parties, of left or right, may attempt in
their agitation to use the discussion of specific policies in
order to bring the legitimations themselves into question.
So, out of the little circles of people talking with one another, the big forces of social movements and political parties develop, and the discussion of opinion is one crucial
phase in a total act by which public affairs are conducted.

So conceived, the public is the loom of classic, eighteenth-
century democracy; discussion is at once the threads and
the shuttle binding discussion circles together. The people
are presented with problems and issues. They discuss them.
They decide on them. They formulate viewpoints. These
viewpoints compete. One viewpoint "wins out." Then the
people act out this viewpoint, or their representatives are
instructed to act it out, and this they promptly do.

## II

This classic view of course came under attack during the
nineteenth century, but it was with the rise of totalitarian
states in the twentieth century, in particular with the rise

of Naziism, that another view of the public and of public opinion was formed.

The rise of the mass media, especially radio and motion pictures, had already been accompanied by an immense enlargement of the scale of economic and political institutions, and by the apparent relegation of primary face-to-face relationships to secondary place. Institutions become centralized and authoritarian; and media markets gain ascendancy over primary publics. There is, again, an historical parallel between the commodity market in the economic sphere and the public of public opinion in the sphere of opinion. In brief, there is a movement from widely scattered little powers and laissez-faire, to concentrated powers and attempts at monopoly control from powerful centers. And in both centers, economic and opinion, power is partially hidden; they are centers of manipulation as well as of authority.

The small shop serving a small neighborhood is replaced by the anonymity of the national corporation; mass advertisement replaces the personal influence of opinion between merchant and customer. The political leader hooks up his speech to a national network and speaks, with appropriate personal touches, to a million people he never saw and never will see. Entire brackets of professions and industries are in the "opinion business," impersonally manipulating the public for hire.

In the simple democratic society of primary publics, competition of opinions and ideas goes on between people holding the various views which service their special interests and their reasoning. But in the mass society of media markets, competition goes on between the crowd of manipulators with their mass media on the one hand, and the people receiving their communications on the other. "Answering back" by the people is systematically unavailable.

Under such conditions, it is not surprising that a conception of public opinion as a mere impressment or as a reaction—we cannot say "response"—to the content of the mass media should arise. In this view, the public is merely the collectivity of individuals each rather passively exposed to the mass media and rather helplessly opened up to the

suggestions and manipulations that flow from these media.
The fact of manipulation from centralized points of control
constitutes, as it were, an expropriation of the information
and change of opinion participated in by the old multitude
of little opinion producers and consumers operating in a
free and balanced market.

Decisions are made by those in authority. These decisions are then set forth in the media of mass communication. They are impressed upon members of the media markets. They are acted out by official agents of the authorities,
but if it is needed to obtain action from others, that action,
too, is organized by the authorities in terms of their decision; crowds, selected out from the mass, organized by the
authorities, act as adjuncts of the official agents.

Technical conditions of the media make a selection of
speakers necessary and, by determining the low ratio of
speakers to hearers, limit the chances to answer back. In
addition, the authorities of the mass society, which is congruent with the predominance of media markets, attempt
to organize *all* communication processes. Public opinion
then consists of reactions to what is presented in the formal
media of communication; personal discussion does not affect the opinion formulated; each man is an isolated atom
reacting alone to the orders and suggestions of the monopolized mass media.

With centralized authority, opinion managers first
monopolize the formal means of communication, then
strive to set up enforced listening and reading groups.
They try to unite media markets and monopolized media
so as to insure a disciplined response from the people on
the media markets.

But the propagandist with authority is by no means content by his work in the media market. He would enter the
primary publics as well. In fact, he may use his authority
to terrorize it. He organizes and monopolizes the management of its voluntary organizations. Any institutions or
even informal situations which might become the forum of
a free discussion circle is broken up. He would atomize
those areas of it which are not amenable to his own organizational control. By terrorization and by rules enforced by threats and use of violence, he tries to frag-

ment the public, in order that each individual stands naked of social relations before the media of the authoritative propagandists. Enforce conformity, *Gleichshaltung,* bring them to heel; associate violent threats with standardized, simple symbols or emblems; then surround the individual with these emblems of menace—in this way act constantly on the mass and reinvoke in them the menace. Initiate in the media the menace of propaganda by the deed. This is the mechanism of intimidation, which is skillfully used by various media of communication, from radio to billboard, from movie to sidewalk chalking.

The aim of the regimenters of opinion is to keep the underlying population in continuous emotional subjection, this being more important than the inculcation of specific beliefs; for if the frame of the mind is set for docility in opinion, for obedience in will, the people will be ready to believe and to feel any number of specific beliefs. In this the regimenters work deeper than specific views and emotions; they are trying to modify the basic ideological predisposition of the person. And they want to do this on a mass scale: to make all the population alike in their ideological predisposition, in order that they will all think as it is desired that they think. So, the volume of assertion becomes "stunning;" from all sides and through all senses it converges upon the isolated individual. All power and all social initiative is exercised from above downward.

A mass society involves more than mass communications. The idea implies that multitudes of people participate in various public activities, but that they do so only formally and passively. Action and opinion are one again, and both are rigorously controlled by monopolized media. The authorities provide the opinions and the channels for their realization in activity. People on the media markets hold by mass, the lines of their action being parallel by virtue of their monogeneous opinion, homegeneously impressed by the media. More drastic action may occur when the mass becomes at selected points a temporary crowd, but in all cases public or collective action is guided by institutional authorities. The people, even as they act, are more like spectators than actors. The public of mass society acts, but only by acclamation, by plebiscite. It pas-

sively allows; it actively acclaims. Its activity does not
spring from its autonomous decision and initiative; it is
an implanted reaction to a controlled stimulus presented
by centralized management.

Since the public of a mass society is a media market and
an activated mass, the discussion phase of the process of
opinion formation is virtually eliminated. In it there is less
social or informal group cohesion; the institutionalized
means of free and informal discussion are fragmentalized;
individuals are atomized. There is an affinity between dispersed mass and contagiously juxtaposed crowd. In neither
are men joined; opinions, emotions, and drives to act con-
verge by virtue of the common denominator, the homogeneity of readiness to react planlessly to the exciting jerk
of symbols and slogans. With the destruction of primary
publics and voluntary associations, both the mass and the
crowd come into their own.

There are at least four things which taken together
characterize the mass ideal-type of "public" in a mass
society: (1) The role of mass media is increased and that
of discussion circles is decreased. In the extreme, the mass
communication industry, pumping opinions to huge media
markets, displaces the face-to-face communication systems
composed of a multiplicity of primary publics. (2) There
is thus a definitive centralization of the opinion process;
discussion circles are necessarily small and decentralized;
media markets are huge and centralized. (3) The way
opinions *change* is more authoritative and manipulative.
There is little or no self-regulation on the part of the public. The people in this media market are propagandized:
they cannot answer back to the print in the column, the
voice on the radio; they cannot even answer back to the
media in their immediate circle of co-listeners with ease
and without fear. (4) The use of physical and institutional
sanctions are involved in opinion process. As Kurt Riezler
has remarked: without Himmler's powerful grip, Goebbel's manipulations of opinion would have quickly failed.

Official opinion is thus monopolized by virtue of the
centralization and control of mass media, and by enforced
listening and reading by means of street mikes, radio jam-
ming, etc. Unofficial opinion is atomized by the fragmen-

talization of all institutions and occasions for discussion, by the infiltration of every block with opinion fixers, that is, agents of the central authority, and by the systems of "blackmailing" carried on by mutually fearful informers. Recall the headlines: "Nazi Plan of Terror Control of Public Revived in Berlin; Vicious Block System of Tyranny under 40,000 Quasi-Officials . . ." or: "Secret Societies in Japan Unmasked . . . Records Showing that Neighborhood Spies Controlled Thought . . ." Not only people as media markets, but also people as primary publics must be organized in order to make a mass out of a public, and to arrange an opinion process in full accord with such a mass conception.

Any modern society may be regimented into a total mass, or may drift into a mass-like set of performances. To paraphrase Goebbels, in the transition to mass society, the private formation of public opinion, as in the democratic image, is replaced by the public formation of even private opinion. The mass media, as it were, expropriate from individuals in discussion the formulation of opinion.

### III

So, the history of the idea of public opinion has gone through the classic democratic and the totalitarian phase. Today, a third phase is emerging in American intellectual circles. With it we arrive at a sort of synthesis, the whole dialectics of which has taken three stages:

(i) Two centuries ago, before the mass media as we know them today, it was thought that in a democracy the public of public opinion consisted only of small groups of people talking among themselves, electing spokesmen for their groups, who in turn talked among themselves. Problems occurred and were discussed until a public opinion was formed as to its popularly correct solution.

(ii) Then, in all industrialized countries, the mass media arose and grew to be large-scale in their coverage. When these were taken over by totalitarian parties and states, the idea arose among some students that the public of public opinion was merely the audience of these media, and public opinion merely the result of an impressment upon isolated individuals of the communications carried by radio and newspapers or movies which uphold the institutions of authority.

(iii) Today in the United States, a synthesis of these two stages of thought is coming about: both mass media and person-to-person discussion are important in changing public opinion. It is a question of which is the more important in different areas of opinion, at different times, and of just how the two, as forces causing opinion change, sometimes work together, and sometimes clash.

The American public is neither a sandheap of individuals each making up his own mind, nor a regimented mass manipulated by monopolized media of communication. The American public is a complex, informal net-work of persons and small groups interchanging, on all occupational and class levels, opinions and information, and variously exposed to the different types of mass media and their varying contents. There are many influences at work upon those publics and masses and within them, and there are many resistances and counter-forces to these various influences. But today it is still the case that the most effective and immediate context of changing opinion is people talking informally with people. "All conversation," Ralph Waldo Emerson once wrote, "is a magnetic experiment."

## I V

In American social science the careful objectivity and precise technique of physical and mechanical science are being carried over and applied to social, economic and political matters. Today, when few aspects of American reality are not being studied by U. S. social scientists, their work is slowly resulting in a wider awareness of how American society actually works. Private and public university groups, scientific foundations and commercial firms of various kinds have undertaken a great variety of investigations and experiments in the field of public opinion and the agencies of mass communications—radio and movies, magazines and newspapers, and now television.

Many technical problems have still to be worked out,

but social scientists are well on the way to solving them. Perhaps I can make clear how some of these problems are being solved, as well as a few of the results being achieved, by telling you something about one study of Decatur, Illinois, recently completed by Columbia University's social science laboratory in New York City.

Decatur, Illinois is a city of 60,000 population in the "corn belt." Its largest factory processes this corn, as well as soy beans, into many useful products; many of its workers are farmers part of the year. It is also, on a small scale, a railroad center and there is a good deal of retail business on its Main Street, the surrounding farmers driving their cars, filled with families, into town for shopping every Saturday. We selected this town on the basis of some thirty series of statistics as the most typical, or the average, American city of its size-group in the middle west. Anything we found out about the way its people make up their opinions, we figured would be typical of the people in any middle-sized American city.

We took a sample of its population, which gave us about 800 housholds, representing the whole 60,000 population of the city. We then got the help of 30 people—mainly housewives and young unmarried women—and in a short course trained them to interview. Early one summer, we began to interview the 800 women in our sample of households. We asked them their opinions on a great variety of topics—all sorts of political questions and topics of current public affairs in their town and in the nation; we also asked them about their fashion tastes and about their choices in movies, etc.

Now usually in public opinion research, the field work stops here. The answers are added up and interpreted and that is the end of the study. But we did not want to find out how many people held one opinion or another. *We wanted to find out how opinions change, how these people, as members of the public, actually made up their minds.*

So we waited after that first interview for two months; then we went back to these same people and interviewed them again. We ran a scientific test to make sure they had forgotten the exact answers they had first given our interviewers, and then we asked them, among other questions, about half of the original questions we had asked.

We did this in order to spot those people who had
*changed* their opinion during this two month period—
since the first interview. And we found that a good many
had changed. Here was a woman who in the first interview
had thought that business was stronger than labor in civic
affairs, but in the second interview felt that maybe labor
was stronger. Here was another who in the first interview
had been very enthusiastic about a new fashion of sleeve
in a dress, but in the second interview had changed her
fashion opinion, and now liked another kind of sleeve and
was, in fact, making it into a new dress on her sewing
machine for the fall season. Of course not everyone changed
her opinions between the two interviews, but enough did
change to allow us to study *how* they had changed—what
forces caused them to shift their opinions on one or another
of this variety of topics.

Here is how we tried to find this out: In every case of a
change of opinion, we asked a further series of questions.
We asked if they had read anything about it in a newspaper or a magazine, heard anything about it on some
radio program or seen it in the movies? And we asked
they had talked about it with anyone else, and if so, who
was the person, what was said, and so on.

This information gave us a list of all the possible influences at work in this sample of opinion changes. So we
began to analyze the figures, running six or seven thousand
tables over a period of months, some of them with as many
as 10 variables in them, which enabled us to answer rather
complicated questions on a statistical basis.

## V

It was clear from the beginning that two broad sets of
influences were at work in public opinion change: (1) the
media of mass communication and (2) person-to-person
discussion.

(i) One school, reflecting the second stage in our understanding of public opinion, believed that the newspapers and radio, magazines and movies were now so powerful and influential that they would be found to be the

chief cause of changes of opinion. This school pointed out that 60 percent of the people go to at least one movie a month, 25 per cent to four or more; that 50 per cent listen to the radio on an average week-day between one and three hours, and another 25 per cent listen three or more hours; that 60 per cent read at least one magazine regularly; and so on. The typical American is part of the audience for one or another of these mass media for several hours every day. With such wide coverage it seems only natural that the mass media would exert a great influence on opinion change.

(ii) The other school of thought admitted this, but they pointed out that after all not all people were very much exposed to the mass media, and moreover, that most people certainly spend more time talking with others than they do listening to radio or reading magazines. How do we know, they asked, that the mass media are *effective* in changing opinion. We should not forget what we said at the beginning: although most newspapers, for instance, are for the Republican party, most voters have for sometime voted for the Democratic party. However, they pointed out, the various mass media differ on many topics —despite the increased monopoly in newspapers, radio and movies, there is still considerable competition of ideas and opinions between the different radio commentators and magazine writers. One radio commentator is very much for President Truman's views, another is very much against them and says so to a million radio listeners a day.

Now, one thing that is well known about communication habits is that people of one or the other opinion tend to select the mass media with which they generally agree. Insofar as they can, Democratic party members listen to Democratic radio commentators, and Republican party members read Republican newspaper editorials. This self-selection of audiences means that the chief influence of the mass media is not really to *form* or to *change* opinion but to *reinforce* a line of opinion already held, or at least already well known.

Yet, here, in our sample were people who *did* change their opinions about various topics between our first and

our second interview. Therefore there must be other influences than the mass media at work in these changes.
There must, in fact, be some news of resistance to the contents of the mass media.

There were other arguments for the greater influence of
mass media, and other arguments for the greater influence
of person-to-person discussion. But nobody knew for sure.
You can only know for sure if you get your own facts together and study them carefully. Well, that is what we had
done in the Decatur study. Which of these schools of
thought turned out to be correct?

So far as our study goes, the second is more nearly correct than the first: in the last analysis, it is people talking
with people, more than people listening to, or reading, or
looking at, the mass media that really causes opinions to
change. Of course, the mass media do have an influence;
in fact, we were able in this study to measure the relative
influences of mass media versus talking to other people in
changes of opinion. In every topical area of opinion that
we studied, the personal conversations weighed a great
deal heavier and more effectively than the mass media in
the opinion change.

## V I

Now, it is an old sociological rule, supported by many
statistics, that social position exerts an influence on opinion, and this despite what goes on in the mass media and
despite what opinions are held by those in upper positions
of power. In spite of the attempt of those handling the
formal means of communication to manage opinion, there
exist many counter-opinions especially among the middle
and lower classes.

These tokens of resistance to media or counter symbols,
do not themselves depend upon any formal media. In fact,
they go precisely against the media, operating to guide the
further exposure to the media and to refract and even
reject its messages.

Now, it might seem, as both liberal and Marxian theory
holds, that a rational understanding of their position would
lead individuals to reflection, and hence to opinions ra-

tionally commensurate with their position. Yet from what we know of false consciousness, this is not the typical way social position comes to influence opinion. It is not by reflection and argument that opinions are adapted to interests, or at least that is not a major way. We also know that "interests" select the media contents to which people are exposed; and different opinions and slants are perpetuated and reinforced by this self-selection. Yet there are many opinions held that have never been carried by any formal media. So neither interests nor reflection fully explains class differences in opinion.

No doubt to some extent counter-opinions rest upon personal experience and deprivations, but for them to effect opinion they must be generalized at least on a rudimentary level; this work is done, and the counter-opinions sustained, by informal face-to-face publics, which thus act as a sort of legal underground to the formal communications system.

We have come to expect people in lower economic levels to hold different opinions, to vote somewhat differently, and to feel about local matters in a different way than do those on top. Underlying this fact is the further fact that in the American community there is a certain autonomy of opinion formation and change, a certain independence from those in charge of the key institutions of the political economy.

The range of social contact available to the individual is limited by his class and social position, and thus he is exposed to only one or two circles of opinion within his stratum. It is upon what is said and believed in these circles that his opinions feed. Such person-to-person influences, within delimited social contexts, form and sustain opinion. In every area of conduct and opinion, these pressures of social consensus, these minute daily influences of personal contact are at work.

## VII

Let us examine more systematically the available means of resistance to the mass media, from the standpoint of an individual on the receiving end. How can the single in-

dividual resist their media? or, what in his situation enables him to resist them?

(i) So long as the media are not completely monopolized, he can play one off against another; he can compare
them. The more competition there is among the media, the
more resistance the individual is able to command. But
do people play one media content off against another? (a)
We know that people select media which carry those contents with which they already agree. There is that kind of
selection from prior opinion. Very few seem to search out
counter-statements from alternative media offerings. Given
radio programs and magazines and newspapers often get
a rather consistent public; then they reinforce their messages in the minds of this public. (b) This idea of playing
one medium off against another assumes that the media
have varying contents; it assumes genuine competition. Although this is not always true, variations in media content
do provide the individual with a leverage by which to resist
media persuasions. Regardless of what the local paper says
about Decatur labor, the radio commentator in talking
about Detroit labor can provide food for the individual's
opposition to the paper. Nevertheless the trend of mass
communications is on the whole against its use.

(ii) The individual can compare what is said on the
media with his own personal experience and direct knowledge of events. This would seem a good democratic and
pragmatic way of resisting or rejecting or reinterpreting
media. But two things must be recognized: (a) Obviously
the individual cannot experience all the events and happenings that are discussed and displayed on the media. He
only has experience of an infinite fraction of them. That
is quite obvious in the case of international and national
and even local political events; but we have evidence that
in the field of consumer opinion, where direct experience
with the objects discussed is readily available that such
direct experience plays very little role in changes of opinion.
(b) At any rate, even if he has direct experience, it is not
primary, not raw, not really direct. It is mediated and organized in stereotypes. It takes very long and skillful training to so uproot an individual that he sees things freshly,
in an unstereotyped manner. One might suppose, for in-

stance, that if all the people went through a depression they would all "experience it," and in terms of this experience, that they could all debunk or reject or at least refract the media. But the experience of such a structural shift has to be organized, to be interpreted, if it is to count. The kind of experience that might serve as a basis for resistance to mass media is not experience of raw events, but experience of meanings. The fleck of interpretation must be there in the experience if we are to use the word seriously. Experience is socially organized; the capacity for it, socially implanted. Often the individual doesn't trust his own experience until it is confirmed by others or by the media. Canons of acceptability, standards of reality, are not gained by direct experience; for direct exposure to be accepted, it must not disturb beliefs that the individual already holds; and, it must relieve or justify the feelings that often lie in the back of his mind as key features of ideological predisposition.

(iii) There is a third kind of resistance operation: individuals may gain points of resistance against the mass media by the comparison of experience and of opinions among themselves. These discussions of the primary public are at once the spearhead and the master context against which resistances may develop. They give the individual support; they feed his assurance for his criticism. The undercover network of informal communication in the primary public may select and reflect, debunk or sanction what is said in the formal media. And everybody who talks with anybody is part of this network.

But it is reasonable to suppose that certain types of people having certain social positions and relations with others may be more important than others in channeling the flow of talk and mediating and shifting the impact of the formal media. The existence of these opinion leaders is one major reason why the flow of influence may go on within and between the structures of power, why opinion is not subject to its overweening dominance. For they rally those who by their informal discussions manufacture opinion. They are the radiant points, the foci of the primary public. This primary public is a resistor of media and the pressure upon the individual: at the same time it protects, it constantly molds. If there is any socially organized intelligence which is free to answer back and to give support to those who might answer back, it must somehow be this primary public.

No centralized agency of power effectively controls the informal discussions which go on among people in various sections and classes of the city. The network of discussion and the flow of influence which move through the streets and over the fences of the city are not formally organized by any centralized power. The ebb and flow of influence go on within the framework of power, with its organizational infiltrates and its control of communication agencies. But the informal flow of opinion is still autonomous and cannot be said to be weak. From the standpoint of the manipulator, as from that of the resisting individual, the primary public is crucial.

## VIII

But the primary public is a complicated affair. The people who make it up are, in the end, different individuals. Everyone knows, for example, that some individuals regardless of their class or social position, talk more than others, and that some talk to more people than do others. Also some people's expressions of opinion are listened to more and are more respected than others'. These common sense facts lead us to the idea that among the various publics, there may be "opinion leaders"—people who influence others more than others influence them.

We wanted to spot such opinion leaders among the people in our study. Now, we had asked every one we interviewed a set of questions like these: has anyone recently asked your advice about any political matter? Do you think, in general, that you are asked your opinion more or less frequently than other people you know? And so on. The answers to several such questions, scattered through the interview, were combined into an index, and with this index we were able to spot the people who were opinion leaders. Then we began to study these opinion leaders in order to see how they differed from those who were not opinion leaders.

One thing we found out that we think is important to

understanding how American public opinion changes is that opinion leaders are more exposed to the mass media of communication of all sorts than are the opinion followers. They listen more to various radio programs, and read more magazines, and so on. What seems to happen is that these opinion leaders pick up opinions from the mass media and pass them on to other people in face-to-face conversation. But that is by no means the end of the story.

You remember that people tend to select the radio programs and editorials and magazine articles with which they already generally agree. There is thus a self-selection of the audiences for these various media and their competing contents, which means that the media reinforce existing opinions more than they cause changes of opinions. Now, opinion leaders are no different than other members of the media's audience in this respect.

But listening or reading differs from talking with others in two very crucial respects: (1) you can turn off the radio, put down the magazine; if you don't like what it says, you can select another program or another magazine. But you can't do that so easily when you're talking with other people, or when you overhear them at your place of work or in a neighborhood store; very often you have to listen, at least for a while, even if you don't agree. There is less self-selection according to already agreed-to lines of opinion in personal conversation than there is in media exposure. (2) Formal media also differ from personal talk in that you can't answer back the media so easily as you can answer back another person with whom you are talking. You can, of course, write a letter to a magazine or call up a radio station on the telephone, but not so readily and not with the immediate result as you can tell another person you don't agree with what he says and why. There is a give and take about private conversation that just can't exist in mass media communication.

Now these two differences mean that even though opinion leaders—those unofficial concentration points of informal influence—are more exposed to media and try to pass on these opinions to others, these others are in

contact with other opinion leaders who in turn are exposed
to other selected programs and articles. So it is just here in
the give-and-take of persons talking with persons, brought
about by counter-influences, that differences and clashes of
opinion occur. And it is in these conversations, more than
in any other way, that opinions are actually changed.

So the media are influential, directly, and indirectly
through opinion leaders there is a clash of opinion occuring
in conversations between different opinion leaders and between all the people who are in contact with different
opinion leaders and different media offerings. For in these
conversations, these informal and unofficial relationships
of persons talking with persons, public opinion is most
effectively formed and changed.

## I X

But the matter has again to be qualified and rounded out.
Who are these people who give more influence than they
receive in personal conduct? So far we only know that they
are more exposed to the mass media of communication.
What else can we find out about them?

First of all, different people are opinion leaders for different topics of opinion. The housewife or the young white
collar woman who is an opinion leader for her circle in
fashion matters is not necessarily an opinion leader in
political affairs; and the advice of the informal leader in
public affairs is not usually taken up or even offered in the
choice of motion pictures to see, or what kinds of things
to buy. We have not yet explored this specialization in
much detail; but so far our evidence goes to show a definite
specialization of opinion leadership by areas or topics of
opinion.

Second, and more importantly, the opinion leaders are
pretty evenly scattered throughout the population, within
different classes and occupations and neighborhoods of the
American city. We had, frankly, expected that this would
not be the case; we had thought that people of higher class
position, people with more prestige, perhaps people who
belonged to specific organizations, or who were even
elected officials of organizations—that these would num-

ber more heavily among the opinion leaders. But that is not the case in this typical American city. Each class and prestige level, each neighborhood and section of the city, seems to have its own opinion leaders in the various areas of opinion we investigated. Informal leadership is horizontally, not vertically, distributed throughout the population.

The major reason for this is that people can influence others in personal discussion only if they are in more or less continuous personal contact with them. And people are in closer contact with other people who are like themselves, who live in the same neighborhood, work at the same place, go to the same entertainments. This fact of more frequent contact with others like themselves results in informal opinion circles, each with its one or more unofficial opinion leaders.

Of course, these hundreds of opinion circles over-lap at numerous points. One woman belongs to one circle and also to a second. Another woman who does not belong to the first belongs to the second and also to a third circle. We have not fully traced out the unofficial net-works of these opinion circles; but it is clear that they exist and that they are the most important context in which public opinions and their changes are anchored.

These circles with their opinion leaders can and do *reject* what the mass media contain; they can and do *refract* it, as well as *pass it on*. That is why you cannot understand the changing reality of American public opinion in terms merely of what the radio, newspapers, magazine and movies contain. They are only one force, and although at times they "express" public opinion they do not always do so, and what they say is subject at all times to rejection and interpretation at the hands of the opinion circles and unofficial opinion leaders with their many shades of opinion.

It is because of this fact that public opinion is still a popular fact to reckon with on the American scene.

It is because of this fact that if the mass media lie and distort, especially about things within the experience of the public, these media will come to be distrusted and subject, as it were, to popular editorial treatment and at times to plain rejection.

It is well to remember that no matter whose interests the press and radio try to serve—monopolists, or one party or another, or what not; no matter what "public opinion" the mass media may try to fabricate—their *effect* upon the opinions of various people is not dependent upon the interests it would serve or upon the content of the "opinions" it would fabricate. In the final analysis, the effective strength of any press or radio lies in its acceptability to informal opinion circles and their unofficial opinion leaders.

It is because of these facts of public opinion that American elections are often won against the pressure of the newspapers, and that America has a large and strong labor movement even though the mass media have been generally against it. And it is because some newspapers and some opinion leaders are openly against it and others are openly for it that the individual worker or farmer or businessman is subject to those cross-pressures that invite him to discuss it and give him the chance to make up his own mind in the unofficial context of personal discussion with others like himself.

Public opinion in America is not merely a slogan; it does not merely point to the formal right to speak up. It is a going fact of how the US as a people and as a state conduct their domestic and international affairs.

# ON KNOWLEDGE AND POWER*

## I

During the last few years I have often thought that American intellectuals are now rather deeply involved in what Freud once called "the miscarriage of American civilization." I do not know exactly what he meant by the phrase, although I suppose he intended to contrast the eighteenth-century ideals with which this nation was so hopefully proclaimed with their sorry condition in twentieth-century America.

Among these values none has been held higher than the grand role of reason in civilization and in the lives of its civilized members. And none has been more sullied and distorted by men of power in the mindless years we have been enduring. Given the caliber of the American elite, and the immorality of accomplishment in terms of which they are selected, perhaps we should have expected this. But political intellectuals too have been giving up the old ideal of the public relevance of knowledge. Among them a conservative mood—a mood that is quite appropriate for men living in a political vacuum—has come to prevail.

Perhaps nothing is of more immediate importance, both as cause and as effect of this mood, than the rhetorical ascendancy and the intellectual collapse of liberalism: As a proclamation of *ideals*, classic liberalism, like classic socialism, remains part of the secular tradition of the West. As a *theory* of society, liberalism has become irrelevant, and, in its optative way, misleading, for no revision of liberalism as a theory of the mechanics of modern social change has overcome the trade mark of the nineteenth century that is stamped upon its basic assumptions. As a political *rhetoric*, liberalism's key terms have become the common denominators of the political vocabulary, and hence have been stretched beyond any usefulness as a way of defining issues and stating positions.**

As the administrative liberalism of the Thirties has been swallowed up by economic boom and military fright, the noisier political initiative has been seized by a small group of petty conservatives, which, on the middle levels of power, has managed to set the tone of public life. Exploiting the American fright of the new international situation for their own purposes, these political primitives have attacked not only the ideas of the New and Fair Deals; they have attacked the history of those administrations, and the biographies of those who took part in them. And they have done so in a manner that reveals clearly the basis upon which their attractive power rests: they have attacked the symbols of status and the figures of established prestige. By their attack upon men and institutions of established status, the noisy right has appealed not at all to the economically discontented, but to the status-frustrated.* Their push has come from the *nouveau riche,* of small city as well as larger region, and, above all, from the fact of the rankling status-resentment felt by these newly prosperous classes who, having achieved considerable wealth during and after World War II, have not received the prestige nor gained the power that they have felt to be their due.

They have brought into dramatic focus the higher immorality as well as the mindlessness of the upper circles in America. On the one hand, we have seen a decayed and frightened liberalism, and on the other hand, the insecure and ruthless fury of political gangsters. A Secretary of the Army, also a man of older family wealth, is told off by upstarts, and in public brawl disgraced by unestablished nihilists. They have brought into focus a new conception

** Cf. Mills, "Liberal Values in the Modern World," *Anvil and Student Partisan,* Winter 1952.

* A modified version of this essay was presented to a joint meeting of the William A. White and the Harry S. Sullivan Societies in New York City, February 1955.

* Although this interpretation is now widely published, Paul Sweezy's and Leo Huberman's original article remains the most forthright account of it: "The Roots and Prospects of McCarthyism," *Monthly Review,* January 1954.

of national loyalty, which we came to understand as loyalty to individual gangs who placed themselves above the established legitimations of the state, and invited officers of the U. S. Army to do likewise. They have made plain the central place now achieved in the governmental process by secret police and secret "investigations," to the point where we must now speak of a shadow cabinet based in considerable part upon new ways of power which include the wire tap, the private eye, the widespread use and threat of blackmail. And they have dramatized one political result of the hollowing out and the banalizing of sensibility among a population which for a generation now has been steadily and increasingly subjected to the shrill trivialization of the mass means of entertainment and distraction.

As liberalism sat in these "hearings," liberals became aware, from time to time, of how close they were to the edge of the mindless abyss. The status edifice of bourgeois society was under attack, but since in America there is nothing from the past above that established edifice, and since those of once liberal and left persuasion see nothing in the future below it, they have become terribly frightened by the viciousness of the attack, and their political lives have been narrowed to the sharp edge of defensive anxiety.

Post-war liberalism has been organizationally impoverished: the pre-war years of liberalism-in-power devitalized independent liberal groups, drying up their grass roots, making older leaders dependent upon the federal center and not training new leaders round the country. The New Deal left no liberal organization to carry on any liberal program; rather than a new party, its instrument was a loose coalition inside an old one, which quickly fell apart so far as liberal ideas are concerned. Moreover, in using up, in one way or another, the heritage of liberal ideas, banalizing them as it put them into law, the New Deal turned liberalism into a set of administrative routines to defend rather than a program to fight for.

In their moral fright, post-war liberals have not defended any left-wing or even any militantly liberal position: their defensive posture has, first of all, concerned the civil liberties.

Many of the political intelligentsia have been so busy

celebrating formal civil liberties in America, by contrast with their absence from Soviet Communism, that they have often failed to defend them. But more importantly, most have been so busy defending civil liberties that they have had neither the time nor the inclination to *use* them. "In the old days," Archibald MacLeish has remarked, freedom "was something you used . . . [it] has now become something you save—something you put away and protect like your other possessions—like a deed or a bond in a bank." *

It is much safer to celebrate civil liberties than to defend them, and it is much safer to defend them as a formal right than to use them in a politically effective way: even those who would most willingly subvert these liberties, usually do so in their very name. It is easier still to defend someone else's right to have used them years ago than to have something yourself to say *now* and to say it now forcibly. The defense of civil liberties—even of their practice a decade ago—has become the major concern of many liberal and once leftward scholars. All of which is a safe way of diverting intellectual effort from the sphere of political reflection and demand.

The defensive posture, secondly, has concerned American Values in general, which, quite rightly it has been feared, the petty right seeks to destroy. Quite unwittingly, I am sure, the U. S. intelligentsia has found itself in the middle of the very nervous center of elite and plebeian anxieties about the position of America in the world today. What is at the root of these anxieties is not simply international tension and the terrible, helpless feeling of many that another war is surely in the works. There is also involved in them a specific worry with which many serious-minded Americans are seriously concerned.

The United States is now engaged with other nations, particularly Russia, in a full-scale competition for cultural prestige based on nationality. In this competition, what is at issue is American music and American literature and American art, and, in the somewhat higher meaning than is usually given to that term, The American Way of Life. For what America has got abroad is power; what it has

* *Atlantic Monthly,* August, 1949.

*not* got at home or abroad is cultural prestige. This simple fact has involved those of the new gentility in the curious American celebration, into which much scholarly and intellectual energy now goes. The celebration rests upon the felt need to defend themselves in nationalist terms against the petty right; and it rests upon the need, shared by many spokesmen and statesmen as urgent, to create and to uphold the cultural prestige of America abroad.*

The noisy conservatives, of course, have no more won political power than administrative liberals have retained it. While those two camps have been engaged in wordy battle, and while the intellectuals have been embraced by the new conservative gentility, the silent conservatives have assumed political power. Accordingly, in their imbroglio with the noisy right, liberal and once-left forces have, in effect, defended these established conservatives, if only because they have lost any initiative of attack, in fact, lost even any point of effective criticism. The silent conservatives of corporation, army and state have benefited politically and economically and militarily by the antics of the petty right, who have become, often unwittingly, their political shocktroops. And they have ridden into power on all those structural trends set into motion and accelerated by the organization of the nation for seemingly permanent war.

So, in this context of material prosperity, with the noisy little men of the petty right successfully determining the tone and level of public sensibility; the silent conservatives achieving established power in a mindless victory; with the

* Examples of The American Celebration are embarrassingly available. Unfortunately no one of them is really worth examining in detail: In order that the sort of thing I have in mind may be clear, by all means see Jacques Barzun, *God's Country and Mine* (Boston: Little Brown, 1954). Mr. Barzun believes that "the way to see America is from a lower berth about two in the morning," and so far as I can tell from his book, he really means it. For a less flamboyant example, done at least in dim daylight, see Daniel J. Boorstin, *The Genius of American Politics* (Chicago: University of Chicago Press, 1953); and for a scatter of celebrants, see *America and The Intellectuals* (New York: PR series, Number Four, 1953).

liberal rhetoric made official, then banalized by widespread and perhaps illicit use; with liberal hope carefully adjusted to mere rhetoric by thirty years of rhetorical victory; with radicalism deflated and radical hope stoned to death by thirty years of defeat—the political intellectuals have been embraced by the conservative mood. Among them there is no demand and no dissent, and no opposition to the monstrous decisions that are being made without deep or widespread debate, in fact with no debate at all. There is no opposition to the undemocratically impudent manner in which policies of high military and civilian authority are simply turned out as facts accomplished. There is no opposition to public mindlessness in all its forms nor to all those forces and men that would further it. But above all— among the men of knowledge, there is little or no opposition to the divorce of knowledge from power, of sensibilities from men of power, no opposition to the divorce of mind from reality.

## II

Once upon a time, at the beginning of the United States, men of affairs were also men of culture: to a considerable extent the elite of power and the elite of culture coincided, and where they did not coincide as persons they often overlapped as circles. Within the compass of a knowledgeable and effective public, knowledge and power were in effective touch; and, more than that, this classic public also decided much that was decided.

"Nothing is more revealing," James Reston has written, "than to read the debate in the House of Representatives in the Eighteen Thirties on Greece's fight with Turkey for independence and the Greek-Turkish debate in the Congress in 1947. The first is dignified and eloquent, the argument marching from principle through illustration to conclusion; the second is a dreary garble of debating points, full of irrelevancies and bad history."* George Washington in 1783 read Voltaire's "Letters" and Locke's "On Human

* *The New York Times,* January 31, 1954, editorial page.

Understanding"; Eisenhower, two hundred years later, reads cowboy tales and detective stories.** For such men as now typically arrive in the higher political, economic and military circles, the briefing and the memorandum seem to have pretty well replaced not only the serious book, but the newspaper as well. This is, perhaps, as it must be, given the immorality of accomplishment, but what is somewhat disconcerting about it is that these men are below the level on which they might feel a little bit ashamed of the uncultivated level of their relaxation and of their mental fare, and that no intellectual public, by its reactions, tries to educate them to such uneasiness.

By the middle of the twentieth century, the American elite have become an entirely different breed of men from those who could on any reasonable grounds be considered a cultural elite, or even for that matter, cultivated men of sensibility. Knowledge and power are not truly united inside the ruling circles; and when men of knowledge do come to a point of contact with the circles of powerful men, they come not as peers but as hired men. The elite of power, wealth and celebrity are not of the elite of culture, knowledge and sensibility. Moreover, they are not in contact with it, although the banalized and ostentatious fringes of the two worlds do overlap in the world of the celebrity.

Most men are encouraged to assume that, in general, the most powerful and the wealthiest are also the most knowledgeable or, as they might say, the smartest. Such ideas are propped up by many little slogans about those who "teach because they can't *do,*" and about "if you're so smart, why aren't you rich?" But all that such wisecracks mean is that those who use them assume that power and wealth are sovereign values for all men and especially for men "who are smart." They assume also that knowledge always pays off in such ways, or surely ought to, and that the test of genuine knowledge is just such pay-offs. The powerful and the wealthy *must* be the men of most knowledge; otherwise how could they be where they are? But to say that those who succeed to power must be "smart," is to say

** *The New York Times Book Review,* August 23, 1953.

that power *is* knowledge. To say that those who succeed
to wealth must be smart, is to say that wealth *is* knowledge.

These assumptions do reveal something that is true: that
ordinary men, even today, are prone to explain and to justify power and wealth in terms of knowledge or ability.
Such assumptions also reveal something of what has happened to the kind of experience that knowledge has come to
be. Knowledge is no longer widely felt as an ideal; it is seen
as an instrument. And in a society of power and wealth,
knowledge is valued as an instrument of power and wealth,
and also, of course, as an ornament in conversation, a tid-bit
in a quiz program.

What knowledge does to a man (in clarifying what he is,
and setting it free)—that is the personal ideal of knowledge. What knowledge does to a civilization (in revealing
its human meaning, and setting it free)—that is the social
ideal of knowledge. But today, the personal *and* the social
ideals of knowledge have coincided in what knowledge does
*for* the smart guy: it gets him ahead; and for the wise
nation: it lends cultural prestige, haloing power with
authority.

Knowledge seldom lends power to the man of knowledge. But the supposed, and secret, knowledge of some
men-on-the-powerful-make, and their very free use thereof,
has consequence for other men who have not the power of
defense. Knowledge, of course, is neither good nor bad, nor
is its use good or bad. "Bad men increase in knowledge as
fast as good men," John Adams wrote, "and science, arts,
taste, sense and letters, are employed for the purpose of
injustice as well as for virtue." That was in 1790; today we
have good reason to know that it is so.

The problem of knowledge and power is, and always has
been, the problem of the relations of men of knowledge
with men of power. Suppose we were to select the one
hundred most powerful men, from all fields of power, in
America today and line them up. And then, suppose we
selected the one hundred most knowledgeable men, from
all fields of social knowledge, and lined them up. How
many men would be in *both* our line-ups? Of course our
selection would depend upon what we mean by power and
what we mean by knowledge—especially what we mean by

knowledge. But, if we mean what the words seem to mean, surely we would find few if any men in America today who were in both groups, and surely we could find many more at the time this nation was founded than we could find today. For, in the eighteenth century, even in this colonial outpost, men of power pursued learning, and men of learning were often in positions of power. In these respects we have, I believe, suffered grievous decline.*

There is little union in the same persons of knowledge and power; but persons of power do surround themselves with men of some knowledge, or at least with men who are experienced in shrewd dealings. The man of knowledge has not become a philosopher king; but he has often become a consultant, and moreover a consultant to a man who is neither king-like nor philosophical. It is not natural in the course of their careers for men of knowledge to meet with those of power. The links between university and government are weak, and when they do occur, the man of knowledge appears as an "expert" which usually means as a hired technician. Like most others in this soicety, the man of knowledge is himself dependent for his livelihood upon the job, which nowadays is a prime sanction of thought control. Where getting ahead requires the good opinions of more powerful others, their judgments become prime objects of concern. Accordingly, in so far as intellectuals serve power directly—in a job hierarchy—they often do so unfreely.

The characteristic member of the higher circles today is an intellectual mediocrity, sometimes a conscientious one, but still a mediocrity. His intelligence is revealed only by his occasional realization that he is not up to the decisions

* In *Perspectives, USA,* No. 3, Mr. Lionel Trilling has written optimistically of "new intellectual classes," and has even referred to the Luce publications as samples of high "intellectual talent." What lends his view its optimistic tone, I believe, is less the rise of any new intellectual classes than (1) old intellectual groups becoming a little prosperous, even successful, in a minor way, on American terms, and, (2) of course, the confusion of knowledge as a goal with knowledge as a mere technique and instrument. For an informed account of new cultural strata by a brilliantly self-conscious insider, see Louis Kronenberger, *Company Manners* (Indianapolis: Bobbs Merrill, 1954).

he sometimes feels called upon to confront. But usually he keeps such feelings private, his public utterances being pious and sentimental, grim and brave, cheerful and empty in their universal generality. He is open only to abbreviated and vulgarized, pre-digested and slanted ideas. He is a commander of the age of the memo and the briefing. He is briefed, but not for longer than one page; he talks on the phone, rather than writes letters or holds conversations.

By the mindlessness and mediocrity of men of affairs, I do not, of course, mean that these men are not sometimes intelligent men, although that is by no means automatically the case. It is not, however, primarily a matter of the distribution of "intelligence"—as if intelligence were a homogeneous something of which there may be more or less. It is rather a matter of the quality of mind, a quality which requires the evaluation of substantive rationality as the key value in a man's life and character and conduct. That evaluation is what is lacking from the American power elite. In its place there is "weight" and judgment" which count for much more in their celebrated success than any subtely of mind or force of intellect.

All around, just below the weighty man of affairs, are his technical lieutenants of power who have been assigned the role of knowledge and even of speech: his public relations man, his ghost, his administrative assistants, his secretaries. And do not forget The Committee. With the increased means of decision, there is a crisis of understanding among the political directorate of the United States, and accordingly, there is often a commanding indecision.

The lack of knowledge as an experience and as a criterion among the elite ties in with the malign ascendancy of the expert, not only as fact but as a defense against public discourse and debate. When questioned recently about a criticism of defense policies made by the leader of the opposition party, the Secretary of Defense replied, "Do you think he is an expert in the matter?" When pressed further by reporters he asserted that the "military chiefs think it is sound, and I think it is sound," and later, when asked about specific cases, added: "In some cases, all you

can do is ask the Lord."* With such a large role so arro-
gantly given to God, to experts, and to Mr. Wilson, what
room is there for political leadership? Much less for public
debate of what is after all every bit as much a political and
a moral as a military issue?

Beyond the lack of intellectual cultivation by political
personnel and advisory circles, the absence of publicly
relevant minds has come to mean that powerful decisions
and important policies are not made in such a way as to
be justified and attacked, in short, debated in any intellectual form. Moreover, the attempt to so justify them is often
not even made. Public relations displace reasoned argument; manipulation and undebated decisions of power replace democratic authority. More and more, as administration has replaced politics, decisions of importance do
not carry even the panoply of reasonable discussion in
public, but are made by God, by experts, and by men
like Mr. Wilson.

And more and more the area of the official secret ex-
pands, as well as the area of the secret listening in on those
who might divulge in public what the public, not being
composed of experts with Q clearance, is not to know. The
entire series of decisions concerning the production and
the use of atomic weaponry has been made without any
genuine public debate, and the facts needed to engage in
that debate intelligently have been officially hidden, distorted, and lied about. As the decisions become more fateful, not only for Americans but literally for mankind, the
sources of information are closed up, and the relevant facts
needed for decision, and even of the decisions made, are,
as politically convenient "official secrets," withheld from
the heavily laden channels of information.

In the meantime, in those channels, political rhetoric
continues to slide lower and lower down the scale of cultivation and sensibility. The height of such mindless communications to masses, or what are thought to be masses,
is the commercial propaganda for toothpaste and soap and
cigarettes and automobiles. It is to such things, or rather
to Their Names, that this society sings its loudest praises

* Charles E. Wilson, Cf. *The New York Times,* March 10, 1954,
p. 1.

most frequently. What is important about this is that by implication and omission, by emphasis and sometimes by flat statement, this astounding volume of propaganda for commodities is often untruthful and misleading; and is addressed more often to the belly or to the groin than to the head or to the heart. And the point to be made about this is that public communications from those who make powerful decisions or who would have us vote them into such decision-making places, competes with it, and more and more takes on those qualities of mindlessness and myth which commercial propaganda or advertising have come to exemplify.

In America today, men of affairs are not so much dogmatic as they are mindless. For dogma has usually meant some more or less elaborated justification of ideas and values, and thus has had some features (however inflexible and closed) of mind, of intellect, of reason. Nowadays what we are up against is precisely the absence of mind of any sort as a public force; what we are up against is a lack of interest in and a fear of knowledge that might have liberating public relevance. And what this makes possible is the prevalence of the kindergarten chatter, as well as decisions having no rational justifications which the intellect could confront and engage in debate.

It is not the barbarous irrationality of uncouth, dour Senators that is the American danger; it is the respected judgments of Secretaries of State, the earnest platitudes of Presidents, the fearful self-righteousness of sincere young American politicians from sunny California, that is the main danger. For these men have replaced mind by the platitude, and the dogmas by which they are legitimated are so widely accepted that no counter-balance of mind prevails against them. Such men as these are crackpot realists, who, in the name of realism have constructed a paranoid reality all their own and in the name of practicality have projected a utopian image of capitalism. They have replaced the responsible interpretation of events by the disguise of meaning in a maze of public relations, respect for public debate by unshrewd notions of psychological warfare, intellectual ability by the agility of the sound and mediocre judgment, and the capacity to elaborate alternatives and to gauge their consequences by the executive stance.

## III

In our time, all forms of public mindlessness must expropriate the individual mind, and we now know that this is an entirely possible procedure.* We also know that ideas, beliefs, images—symbols in short—stand between men and the wider realities of their time, and that accordingly those who professionally create, destroy, elaborate these symbols are very much involved in all literate men's very images of reality. For now, of course, the live experience of men falls far short of the objects of their belief and action, and the maintenance of adequate definitions of reality is by no means an automatic process, if indeed it ever was. Today that maintenance requires intellectuals of quite some skill and persistence, for much reality is now officially defined by those who hold power.

As a type of social man, the intellectual does not have any one political direction, but the work of any man of knowledge, if he is the genuine article, does have a distinct kind of political relevance: his politics, in the first instance, are the politics of truth, for his job is the maintenance of an adequate definition of reality. In so far as he is politically adroit, the main tenet of his politics is to find out as much of the truth as he can, and to tell it to the right people, at the right time, and in the right way. Or, stated negatively: to deny publicly what he knows to be false, whenever it appears in the assertions of no matter whom; and whether it be a direct lie or a lie by omission, whether it be by virtue of official secret or an honest error. The intellectual ought to be the moral conscience of his society, at least with reference to the value of truth, for in the defining instance, that *is* his politics. And he ought also to be a man absorbed in the attempt to know what is real and what is unreal.

* See Czeslaw Milosz, *The Captive Mind* (New York: Knopf, 1953), which is surely one of the great documents of our time.

Power and authority involve the actual making of *decisions*. They also involve the *legitimation* of the power and of the decisions by means of doctrine, and they usually involve the pomp and the halo, the *representations* of the powerful.* It is in connection with the legitimations and the representations of power and decision that the intellectual—as well as the artist—becomes politically relevant.

Intellectual work is related to power in numerous ways, among them these: with ideas one can uphold or justify power, attempting to transform it into legitimate authority; with ideas one can also debunk authority, attempting to reduce it to mere power, to discredit it as arbitrary or as unjust. With ideas one can conceal or expose the holders of power. And with ideas of more hypnotic though frivolous shape, one can divert attention from problems of power and authority and social reality in general.

So the Romantic poets symbolize the French Revolution to an English public and elaborate one strain of its doctrinal legitimation; so Virgil as a member of the Roman ruling class writes his *Georgics;* so John Reed reports to America the early phase of Bolshevism; so Rousseau legitimates the French Revolution, Milton the regime of Cromwell, Marx—in vulgarized form—the Russian revolution.**

And so, in an intellectually petty way, do the U. S. intellectuals now embraced by the conservative mood—whether they know it or not—serve to legitimate the mindless image of the American ascendancy abroad, and the victory of the silent conservatives at home. And more important that that: by the work they do not do they uphold the official definitions of reality, and, by the work they do, even elaborate it.

Whatever else the intellectual may be, surely he is among those who ask serious questions, and, if he is a political intellectual, he asks his questions of those with power. If you ask to what the intellectual belongs, you must answer

* Cf. Gerth and Mills. *Character and Social Structure* (New York: Harcourt Brace, 1953), pp. 413 ff. for a further discussion of these three aspects of authority.
** Cf. Gerth and Mills, *op. cit.*

that he belongs first of all to that minority which has carried on the big discourse of the rational mind, the big discourse that has been going on—or off and on—since western society began some two thousand years ago in the small communities of Athens and Jerusalem.\*\*\* This big discourse is not a vague thing to which to belong—even if as lesser participants—and it is the beginning of any sense of belonging that is worthwhile, and it is the key to the only kind of belonging that free men in our time might have. But if we would belong to it, we ought to try to live up to what it demands of us. What it demands of us, first of all, is that we maintain our sense of it. And, just now, at this point in human history, that is quite difficult.

## IV

The democratic man assumes the existence of a public, and in his rhetoric asserts that this public is the very seat of sovereignty. We object to Mr. Wilson, with his God and his Experts, because in his assertion he explicitly denies two things needed in a democracy: articulate and knowledgeable publics, and political leaders who if not men of reason are at least reasonably responsible to such knowledgeable publics as exist. Only where publics and leaders are responsive and responsible, are human affairs in democratic order, and only when knowledge has public relevance is this order possible. Only when mind has an autonomous basis, independent of power, but powerfully related to it, can it exert its force in the shaping of human affairs. Such a position is democratically possible only when there exists a free and knowledgeable public, to which men of knowledge may address themselves, and to which men of power are truly responsible. Such a public and such men —either of power or of knowledge, do not now prevail, and accordingly, knowledge does not now have democratic relevance in America.

\*\*\* Cf. Joseph Wood Krutch, *The Measure of Man* (Indianapolis: Bobbs-Merrill, 1954).

# BIBLIOGRAPHY OF
# THE WRITINGS OF C. WRIGHT MILLS

Editor's Note:—This bibliography of the writings of C. Wright Mills, and studies made of his work, frankly aims at completeness. Fortunately, this is an ideal which cannot (at least for a long while to come) be realized, since Mills' writings continue to be translated, and unpublished manuscripts he left behind continue to be edited and published. Nonetheless, as far as possible, I have included all of his important writings, and most of his shorter essays, reviews and commentaries.

This bibliographical guide has been prepared primarily with the needs of the reader in mind. Far that reason, I have eschewed the traditional chronological listings, in favor of a division of the Mills corpus into various distinct categories: (1) Books and Pamphlets; (2) Introductions and Anthologies; (3) Translations; (4) Articles; (5) Review articles; (6) Reviews; (7) Miscellaneous commentaries; (8) Major lectures and addresses; (9) Monographs and essays on Mills; and (10) Reviews of Mills' work.

Each entry is given a separate number in addition to the conventional data concerning the place, date and circumstances of publication. This is to aid in cross-checking the entries. In the case of foreign language items the procedure used is as follows: when a study appeared for *the first time* in a foreign language, whether or not it subsequently appeared in English, it is given a separate number; but when a foreign language item is a direct translation from an English language original source, the English number is retained followed by a letter stipulating the precise relationship between original and translated items. In his later work, Mills used similar titles while modifying the contents of the text to meet the occasion. These entries are also given a separate number to distinguish direct republication or translation from actual modifications in the text.

I should like to thank Mrs. Yaraslava Mills for her great help in supplying me with whatever "archive" materials were available for examination. Without her understanding and generous assistance, this bibliography might have been done, but not nearly as well. And of course, Wright Mills' own impeccable sense of the *scholarly* imagination made the preparation of this extensive bibliography a difficult adventure rather than an impossible chore. For uncomplaining and knowledgeable typing and research assistance, I must record my appreciation to David Braun and William Sander, and above all to Ruth Horowitz.

IRVING LOUIS HOROWITZ

Hobart and William Smith Colleges
Geneva, New York (August 1, 1962)

## I. Books and Pamphlets

(1)   1942   *A Sociological Account of Pragmatism.* Unpublished Ph.D. dissertation. Copies on file at The University of Wisconsin Library.

(2)   1946   *Small Business and Civic Welfare* (with the assistance of Melville J. Ulmer). Washington, D.C.: Smaller War Plants Corporation, United States Senate. (p. 53)

(3)   1948   *The New Men of Power: America's Labor Leaders* (with the assistance of Helen Schneider). New York: Harcourt, Brace & Company. (p. 323)

(4)   1950   *The Puerto Rican Journey: New York's Newest Migrants* (with Clarence Senior and Rose K. Goldsen). New York: Oxford University Press. (p. 378)

(5)   1951   *White Collar: The American Middle Classes.* New York: Oxford University Press. (p. 378)

(5a)  1955   Translation. *Menschen im Büro: Ein Beitrag zur Soziologie der Angestellten* (translated into German by Paul Baudisch). Köln-Deutz: Bund Verlag GMBA, 1955. (p. 488)

(5b)  1956   Paperback edition. Galaxy Edition. New York: Oxford University Press, 1956. (p. 378)

(5c)  1957   Translation. *Las Clases Medias en Norteamerica* (translated into Spanish by Jose Bugeda Sanchez). Madrid: Aguilar, 1957. (p. 460)

(5d)  1960   Translation. Japanese language edition. Tokyo: Sogen:sha, 1960. (p. 345)

(6)   1953   *Character and Social Structure: The Psychology of Social Institutions* (with H. H. Gerth). New York: Harcourt, Brace & Company. (p. 490)

\*(7)      1954    *Mass Society and Liberal Education*. Chicago: Center for the Study of Liberal Education for Adults. (p. 17)

 (8)      1956    *The Power Elite*. New York: Oxford University Press. (p. 423)

 (8a)     1957    Translation. *La Elite del Poder* (translated into Spanish by Florentino M. Torner and Ernestina de Champourcin). Mexico D. F. and Buenos Aires: Fondo de Cultura Economica, 1957. (p. 388)

 (8b)     1959    Translation. *Vlastvuyuschchaye Elita* (translated into Russian by E. I. Rozenthal, L. G. Roshal; and V. L. Cohn). Moscow: Inostrannoy Literaturi—Foreign Languages Publishing House, 1959. (p. 542)

 (8c)     1959    Translation. *La elite del potere* (translated into Italian by Paolo Facchi). Milan: Feltrinelli Editore, 1959. (p. 431)

 (8d)     1959    Paperback edition. Galaxy Edition. New York: Oxford University Press, 1959. (p. 423)

 (8e)     1960    Translation. Japanese language edition. Tokyo: Sogen:sha, 1960. (2 volumes, p. 644)

 (8f)     1960    Paperback edition. Prometheus Paperback. New York: Liberty Book Club, 1960. (p. 423)

 (8g)     1961    Translation. *Elita Wladzy* (translated into Polish by Ignacy Rafelski). Warsaw: Ksiazka i Wiedza, 1961. (p. 536)

 (9)      1958    *The Causes of World War Three*. New York: Simon & Schuster. (p. 172)

 (9a)     1958    Paperback edition. Simon & Schuster. New York: Simon & Schuster, 1958. (p. 172)

 (9b)     1959    Translation. *Die Konsequenz: Politik ohne Verantwortung* (translated into German by Paul Baudisch). München: Kindler Verlag, 1959. (p. 238)

 (9c)     1959    Translation. *Le cause della terza guerra mondiale* (translated into Italian by Luciano Bianciardi). Milan: Feltrinelli Editore, 1959. (p. 206)

 (9d)     1959    English edition. London: Secker & Warburg, 1959. (p. 175)

 (9e)     1960    Translation. *Les causes de la 3ᵉ guerre mondiale* (translated into French by Dominique Guillet). Paris: Calmann-Levy, 1960. (p. 224)

 (9f)     1960    Second Paperback edition (with new materials on "Images of Russia" and "The Balance of Blame"). Ballantine Books. New York: Ballantine, 1960. (p. 187)

\* Asterisk indicates publication in the present volume.

(10)    1959    *The Sociological Imagination.* New York: Oxford University Press. (p. 234)

(10a)    1961    Translation. *La Imaginacion Sociologica* (translated into Spanish by Florentino M. Torner). Mexico D. F. and Buenos Aires: Fondo de Cultura Economica, 1961. (p. 236)

(10b)    1961    Paperback edition. Evergreen E-286. New York: Grove Press, 1961. (p. 234)

(10c)    1960    Extract. "On Reason and Freedom." *Identity and Anxiety: Survival of the Person in Mass Society,* ed. by M. R. Stein, A. J. Vidich, David M. White. Glencoe, Ill.: The Free Press, 1960. (pp. 110-19)

(11)    1960    *Listen Yankee: The Revolution in Cuba.* New York: McGraw Hill Book Company. (p. 192)

Simultaneous Paperback edition. Ballantine Books. New York: Ballantine Publishers, 1960. (p. 192)

(11a)    1960    English edition. *Castro's Cuba: The Revolution in Cuba.* London: Secker & Warburg, 1960. (p. 190)

(11b)    1961    Translation. *Escucha Yanqui* (translated into Spanish by Julieta Campos and Enrique Gonzales Pedrero). Mexico D. F. and Buenos Aires: Fondo de Cultura Economica, 1961. (p. 210)

(11c)    1961    Translation. Japanese language edition. Tokyo: Misuzu Shobo, 1961. (p. 316)

(11d)    1961    Translation. *Sluchajcie Jankes!* (translated into Polish by Jerzy Zbijewski). Warsaw: Ksiazka i Wiedza, 1961. (p. 269)

(12)    1962    *The Marxists.* New York: Dell Publishing Company. (p. 480)

*(13)    1963    *Power, Politics and People: The Collected Essays of C. Wright Mills* (edited by Irving L. Horowitz). New York: Oxford University Press. Simultaneous Paperback edition. Ballantine Books. New York: Ballantine Publishers, 1963.

## II. Introductions and Anthologies

(14)    1946    Introduction to *From Max Weber: Essays in Sociology* ("The Man and His Work" with H. H. Gerth). New York: Oxford University Press; London: Routledge & Kegan Paul Ltd. (p. 74)

(15)    1953    Introduction to the Mentor edition of Thorstein Veblen, *The Theory of the Leisure Class.* New York: New American Library. (p. 14)

(16)    1955    Introduction to W. E. H. Lecky, *History of the Rise and Influence of Rationalism in Europe,* and *History of European Morals.* New York: George Braziller. (p. 5)

(17)    1960    *Images of Man: The Classic Tradition in Sociological Thinking* (anthology with introduction).
New York: George Braziller, Inc. (p. 534)

## III. Translations

(18)    1944    *Class, Status, Party.* By Max Weber (translated and
edited from the German with H. H. Gerth). *Poli-
tics,* Vol. I, No. 3 (October, 1944), pp. 271-278.

(19)    1946    *From Max Weber: Essays in Sociology.* By Max
Weber (translated and edited from the German
with H. H. Gerth). New York: Oxford University
Press; London: Routledge & Kegan Paul Ltd.
(p. 490)

## IV. Articles

*(20)   1939    "Language, Logic, and Culture." *American Socio-
logical Review.* Vol. IV, No. 5 (October, 1939),
pp. 670-680.

*(21)   1940    "Methodological Consequences of the Sociology of
Knowledge." *American Journal of Sociology.* Vol.
XLVI, No. 3 (November, 1940), pp. 316-330.

*(22)   1940    "Situated Actions and Vocabularies of Motive."
*American Sociological Review.* Vol. V, No. 6 (December, 1940), pp. 904-913.

*(22a)  1940    Condensation of Item (22) in the *Bulletin of the
Society for Social Research.* (December, 1940), pp.
18-19.

*(23)   1940    "The Language and Ideas of Ancient China: Mar-
cel Granet's Contribution to the Sociology of
Knowledge." *University of Wisconsin, Department
of Sociology* (privately mimeographed and previously unpublished).

(24)    1941    "Guide to Sociological Specialties" (annotated bibliographical essay). *Contemporary Social Theories,*
edited by Harry Elmer Barnes and Howard Becker.
New York: D. C. Heath Company, 1941.

*(25)   1942    "A Marx for the Managers" (with H. H. Gerth).
*Ethics: An International Journal of Legal, Political
and Social Thought.* Vol. 52, No. 2 (January,
1942), pp. 200-215.

(25a)   1961    Reprint of Item (25) in part in *Basic Issues in Public Administration,* edited by Donald C. Rowat.
New York: The Macmillan Company, 1961. pp.
478-482.

*(26)   1942    "Collectivism and the Mixed-Up Economy." *The
New Leader* (December 19, 1942).

(27)    1943    "The Case for the Coal Miners." *The New Republic* (May 24, 1943).

(27a)   1943    Reprint of Item (27) in *The Unionist and Public Forum* (May 27, 1943).

(28)    1943    "The Sailor, The Sex Market, and the Mexican." *The New Leader* (June 26, 1943).

*(29)   1943    "The Professional Ideology of Social Pathologists." *American Journal of Sociology*. Vol. XLIX, No. 2 (September, 1943), pp. 165-180.

*(30)   1944    "The Powerless People: The Role of the Intellectual in Society." *Politics,* Vol. I, No. 3 (April, 1944).

*(30a)  1945    Reprint of Item (30) in *Bulletin of the American Association of University Professors.* (Summer, 1945), pp. 231-243.

(31)    1945    "The Conscription of America." *Common Sense.* (April, 1945), pp. 15-18.

*(32)   1945    "The Trade Union Leader: A Collective Portrait" (with the assistance of Mildred Atkinson). *Public Opinion Quarterly.* Vol. 9, No. 2. (Summer, 1945), pp. 158-175.

(33)    1945    "What Women Think of United States Highway 36 Plan." *Sunday Herald & Review—Decatur, Illinois.* (November 25, 1945).

*(34)   1945    "The American Business Elite: A Collective Portrait." *The Journal of Economic History.* Vol. 4, No. 4, Supplement V (December, 1945), pp. 20-44.

(35)    1945    "A Who's What of Union Leadership." *Labor and Nation.* Vol. I. (December, 1945), pp. 33-36.

(36)    1946    "Who Are Our Labor Leaders." *Read.* (February, 1946), pp. 9-14.

(37)    1946    "The Politics of Skill." *Labor and Nation.* Vol. II. (June-July, 1946), p. 35.

(38)    1946    "What Research Can Do For Labor." Vol. II. *Labor and Nation.* (June-July, 1946), pp. 17-20.

*(39)   1946    "The Competitive Personality." *Partisan Review.* Vol. 13, No. 4 (September-October, 1946), pp. 433-441.

*(40)   1946    "The Middle Classes in Middle-Sized Cities." *American Sociological Review.* Vol. 11, No. 5 (October, 1946), pp. 520-529.

(40a)   1953    Reprint of Item (40) in *Class, Status and Power: A Reader in Social Stratification,* edited by Reinhard Bendix and Seymour Martin Lipset. Glencoe, Ill.: The Free Press, 1953. pp. 203-212.

(40b)   1958   Translation of Item (40). "La clase media en las ciudades medias," in *Antologia sobre estratificacion social,* edited by Eduardo Hamuy. Santiago, Chile: Editorial Universitaria, S. A., 1958. pp. 239-262.

(41)    1946   "What the People Think: Review of Selected Opinion Polls" (with Hazel Gaudet). *Labor and Nation.* Vol. II (November-December, 1946), pp. 11-13.

(42)    1947   "The Theories of Edward Westermarck." *History of Social Thought,* edited by Harry Elmer Barnes. Chicago Press, 1947.

(43)    1947   "The People in the Unions" (with Thelma Ehrlich). *Labor and Nation.* Vol. III (January-February, 1947), pp. 28-31.

(44)    1947   "What the People Think: Anti-Labor Legislation" (with Hazel Gaudet Erskine). *Labor and Nation.* Vol. III (March-April, 1947), pp. 25-29.

(45)    1947   "Five Publics the Polls Don't Catch." *Labor and Nation.* Vol. III (May-June, 1947), pp. 17-19.

(46)    1947   "The Political Complexion of Union Leadership" (with Helen Schneider). *Labor and Nation.* Vol. III (July-August, 1947), pp. 11-15.

(47)    1947   "What Chances of Organic Trade Union Unity?" (with Helen Schneider). *Labor and Nation.* Vol. III (September-October, 1947), pp. 9-10.

(48)    1948   "Grass-Roots Union With Ideas: The Auto Workers—Something New in American Labor." *Commentary.* Vol. 20, No. 3 (March, 1948), pp. 240-247.

(49)    1948   "What Kind of Men Run Our Trade Unions Today?" *New York Star.* (September 5, 1948), Magazine Section.

(50)    1948   "Doctors and Workers." An unpublished report on the Health Problems and Medical Care of the United Automobile Workers Union, Congress of Industrial Organizations (*Cf.* report of study including its principal findings in *Fortune,* November, 1948).

(51)    1948   "The Contributions of Sociology to Industrial Relations." *Proceedings of the First Annual Conference of the Industrial Relations Research Association,* edited by Milton Derber. Urbana: The Association (December, 1948), pp. 199-222.

(51a)   1955   Translation of Item (51). "Note sur L'Ideologie des Relations Humaines dans L'Industrie." *La Revue Socialiste* (February, 1955). No. 84, pp. 192-201.

(52)   1949   "Notes on White Collar Unionism." *Labor and Nation.* Vol. V (March-April, 1949), pp. 17-21.

(53)   1949   "Dogmatic Indecision." (Reply to Mark Starr's review of N. M. of P.) *Labor Zionist* (April 15, 1949).

(54)   1949   "White Collar Unionism: Labor and Democracy." *Labor and Nation.* Vol. V (May-June, 1949), pp. 17-23.

*(55)   1950   "The Sociology of Mass Media and Public Opinion." An unpublished paper intended for publication in the Department of State Russian language journal *Amerika.* Publication prohibited by Soviet authorities. (Completed October 21, 1950)

(56)   1951   "Leaders of the Unions" (with Helen S. Dinnerman). *House of Labor,* edited by J. B. S. Hardman and Maurice Neufeld. New York: Prentice-Hall Publishers, 1951.

(57)   1951   "People in the Unions" (with Thelma E. Anderson). *House of Labor,* edited by J. B. S. Hardman and Maurice F. Neufeld, New York: Prentice-Hall Publishers, 1951.

(58)   1951   "No Mean-Sized Opportunity." *House of Labor,* edited by J. B. S. Hardman and Maurice F. Neufeld. New York: Prentice-Hall Publishers, 1951.

*(59)   1951   "The Sociology of Stratification." Mimeographed reading prepared for the course in "Culture, Personality and Society." *Contemporary Civilization B1,* Columbia College.

*(60)   1952   "Liberal Values in the Modern World: The Relevance of 19th Century Liberalism Today." *Anvil and Student Partisan.* (Winter, 1952), pp. 4-7.

*(61)   1952   "The American Political Elite." Previously unpublished.

*(62)   1952   "A Look at the White Collar." *Office Management Series* (Electronics in the Office: Problems and Prospects). Number 131. New York: American Management Association (1952), pp. 30-36.

(63)   1952   "Commentary on Our Culture and Our Country." *Partisan Review,* Vol. 19, No. 4 (July-August, 1952), pp. 446-450.

(63a)   1953   Reprint of Item (63) in *America and the Intellectuals,* edited by Partisan Review. PR Series No. 4 (1953), pp. 75-80.

(64)   1952   "Plain Talk on Fancy Sex: A Peek at Public Morality." *New York Journal American—International News Service Syndicate.* (August 31, 1952)

(65)    1952    "What Helps Most in Politics?" (materials drawn from an unpublished paper on "The American Political Elite: A Collective Portrait" with Ruth Harper Mills). *Pageant Magazine* (October-November, 1952), pp. 156-168.

(66)    1952    "La gauche Americaine: Savoir Attendre." *Esprit*. Vol. 20 (November, 1952), pp. 693-698.

*(67)    1952    "A Diagnosis of Our Moral Uneasiness." *New York Times Magazine* (November 23, 1952), pp. 10, 55-57. (Complete version previously unpublished.)

*(68)    1953    "Two Styles of Research in Current Social Studies." *Philosophy of Science*. Vol. 20, No. 4 (October, 1953), pp. 266-275.

*(69)    1953    "Leisure and the Whole Man" (speech to the New York Herald Tribune Forum). *New York Herald Tribune*. (October 25, 1953)

(69a)   1953    Reprint of Item (69). "The Business of Leisure." *International Ladies Garment Worker's Justice*. (November 15, 1953)

(70)    1954    "Introduction to White Collar." *The World of History*, edited by Courtland Canby and Nancy E. Gross. New York: The New American Library/ Mentor Books. 1954.

*(71)    1954    "The Labor Leaders and the Power Elite." *Roots of Industrial Conflict*, edited by Arthur Kornhauser, Robert Dubin and Arthur M. Ross. New York: McGraw Hill Book Company, 1954, pp. 144-152.

(72)    1954    "Work Milieu and Social Structure" (speech to the Asilomar Conference of the Mental Health Society of Northern California). *People at Work: A Symposium*. Proceedings of the Mental Health Society of Northern California.

*(73)    1954    "The Conservative Mood." *Dissent*. Vol. I, No. 1 (Winter, 1954), pp. 22-31.

*(74)    1954    "The Unity of Work and Leisure." *Journal of the National Association of Deans of Women* (January, 1954), pp. 58-61.

*(75)    1954    "IBM Plus Reality Plus Humanism = Sociology." *Saturday Review of Literature* (May 1, 1954), pp. 22-23, 54.

*(76)    1954    "Are We Losing Our Sense of Belonging?" *Food For Thought. Publication of the Canadian Association for Adult Education* (September-October), pp. 11-16.

*(77)    1955    "On Knowledge and Power." *Dissent*. Vol. II, No. 3 (Summer, 1955), pp. 201-212.

\*(78)    1956    "Amerika og Kampen om den europaeiske Kultur." *Berlingske Tidende* (Copenhagen, Denmark). (November 28, 1956)

(79)    1956    "Amerikanismen og de intellektuelles ansvar." *Berlingske Tidende* (Copenhagen, Denmark). (December 1, 1956)

(79a)    1956    "National Power and Cultural Prestige." English original copy of Items (78 and 79) in manuscript form only.

(80)    1957    "The Power Elite: Comment on Criticism." *Dissent*. Vol. V, No. 1 (Winter, 1957), pp. 22-34.

(81)    1957    "L'élite du pouvoir" (in two parts). *Les Temps Modernes*. Nos. 135, 136. (May-June, 1957), pp. 1704-1731; and (July-August, 1957), pp. 1943-1971.

(82)    1957    "Sobre Los Altos Circulos." *La Gaceta* (Mexico). October (1957).

(83)    1957    "Program for Peace." *The Nation* (December 7, 1957).

(84)    1957    "The Power Elite: Military, Economic, and Political." *Problems of Power in American Democracy*, edited by Arthur Kornhauser. Detroit: Wayne State University Press, 1957, pp. 145-183.

\*(85)    1958    "The Complacent Young Men: Reasons for Anger." *Anvil and Student Partisan*. Vol. IX, No. 1 (1958), pp. 13-15.

\*(86)    1958    "A Pagan Sermon to Christian Clergy." *The Nation* (March 8, 1958).

\*(87)    1958    "The Structure of Power in American Society." *The British Journal of Sociology*. Vol. IX, No. 1 (March, 1958), pp. 29-41.

(88)    1958    "Psychology and Social Science." *Monthly Review*. Vol. 10, No. 6 (October, 1958), pp. 204-209.

\*(89)    1958    "The Man in the Middle: The Designer." *Industrial Design* (November, 1958), pp. 72-76.

\*(90)    1958    "Characteristics of Our Times." Mimeographed *Proceedings of the Annual Assembly, Division of Home Missions, National Council of the Churches of Christ in the United States of America* (December 10-13, 1958).

(91)    1959    "On Intellectual Craftsmanship." *Symposium on Sociological Theory*, edited by Llewellyn Gross. Evanston, Ill.: Row, Peterson and Company, 1959.

(92)    1959    "Crackpot Realism." *Fellowship*. Vol. 25, No. 1 (January 1, 1959), pp. 3-8.

\*(93)    1959    "Culture and Politics: The Fourth Epoch." *The Listener*. Vol. LXI, No. 1563 (March 12, 1959).

\*(94)    1959    "The Cultural Apparatus." *The Listener.* Vol. LXI, No. 1565 (March 26, 1959).

\*(95)    1959    "The Decline of the Left." *The Listener.* Vol. LXI, No. 1566 (April 2, 1959).

(96)     1959    "The Intellectuals' Last Chance." *Esquire Magazine* (October, 1959).

(97)     1959    "The History Makers." Social Progress (October, 1959), pp. 5-16.

(98)     1959    "The Decline of the Left." *Contact.* No. 3 (1959), pp. 5-18.

\*(99)    1959    "The Big City: Private Troubles and Public Issues" (speech over the Canadian Broadcasting Company). Previously unpublished.

\*(100)   1960    "Remarks on the Problem of Industrial Development" (resistencias a Mudanca: Factores que impeden o Dificultan o Desenvolvimiento). *Centro Latinoamericano de Investigaciones en Ciencias Sociales.* Publication No. 10 (1960), pp. 281-287.

(101)    1960    "The Balance of Blame: Further Notes on the Strategic Causes of World War III." *The Nation.* Vol. 190, No. 25 (June 18, 1960), pp. 523-531.

(101a)   1960    Reprint of Item (101). *The Tribune* (London). (July 10, 1960).

(102)    1960    "The Theory of Balance." *Politics 1960,* edited by Francis M. Carney and H. Frank Way, Jr. San Francisco: Wadsworth Publishing Company. 1960 [reprinted from Item (8), pp. 265-268].

(103)    1960    "Letter to the New Left." *New Left Review.* No. 5 (September-October, 1960), pp. 18-23.

(104)    1960    "Den fjerde epoke." *Vindrosen: Gyldendal litteraere magasin.* Vol. 7, No. 6 (1960), pp. 443-466.

(105)    1960    "Listen, Yankee: The Cuban Case Against the United States." *Harper's Magazine.* Vol. 222, No. 1327 (December, 1960), pp. 31-37.

(106)    1960    "On Latin America, the Left and the U. S." *Evergreen Review.* No. 16 (January, 1961), pp. 110-122.

(107)    1960    "Las Celebridades." In *Sociología del Poder,* Santiago, Chile. Editorial Andres Bello (From *The Power Elite*), pp. 378-398.

(108)    1961    "On the New Left." *Studies on the Left.* Vol. II, No. 1 (1961), pp. 63-72.

(109)    1961    "Eschucha Otra Vez, Yanqui: 1961." Included as Appendix to the 3rd edition of *Eschucha Yanqui: La Revolucion en Cuba.* Mexico—Buenos Aires: Fondo de Cultura Economica, 1961. (pp. 211-259)

(110)   1961   "Modest Proposals for Patriotic Americans" (with Saul Landau). *The Tribune* (of London), May 19, 1961.

(111)   1961   "The Power Elite: The Higher Circles." *Readings in Sociology: Sources and Comment,* edited by John F. Cuber and Peggy B. Harroff. New York: Appleton-Century-Crofts, Inc., 1962. (Excerpt from Item 8, pp. 3-13.)

## V. Review Articles

(112)   1940   Karl Mannheim, MAN AND SOCIETY IN AN AGE OF RECONSTRUCTION. *American Sociological Review,* Vol. V, No. 6 (1940), pp. 965-969.

*(113)   1942   W. Lloyd Warner and Paul S. Lunt, THE SOCIAL LIFE OF A MODERN COMMUNITY. *American Sociological Review,* Vol. VII (April, 1942), pp. 263-271.

*(114)   1942   "Ideology, Economics, and Today." (Review of Raoul de Roussy de Sales' THE MAKING OF TOMORROW.) *The New Leader,* Saturday (June 26, 1942).

*(115)   1942   "Pragmatism, Politics and Religion." (Review of Charles Morris' PATHS OF LIFE: PREFACE TO A WORLD RELIGION.) *The New Leader,* (August, 1942 [Part I]; and *The New Leader,* September, 1942 [Part II]).

*(116)   1942   "Locating the Enemy: The Nazi Behemoth Dissected." (Review of Franz Neumann's BEHEMOTH: THE STRUCTURE AND PRACTICE OF NATIONAL SOCIALISM.) Vol. 4, *Partisan Review* (September-October, 1942), pp. 432-437.

(117)   1942   "Probing the Two-Party State." (Review of Wilfred E. Binkley's AMERICAN POLITICAL PARTIES, THEIR NATURAL HISTORY.) *The New Leader* (October 30, 1942).

(118)   1943   "The Political Gargoyles." (Review of Robert H. Brady's BUSINESS AS A SYSTEM OF POWER.) *The New Republic* (April 12, 1943).

(119)   1944   "Three Styles of Exhortation." (Review of Eric Johnston, AMERICA UNLIMITED; Alfred M. Bingham, THE PRACTICE OF IDEALISM; Norman Thomas, WHAT IS OUR DESTINY?) *Partisan Review,* Vol. 6 (Summer, 1944).

(120)   1952   "The Psychoanalysis of Truth and Culture." (Review of R. E. Money-Kyrle, PSYCHOANALYSIS AND POLITICS; and Paul Schilder, PSYCHOANALYSIS, MAN AND SOCIETY.) *The New Republic* (January 14, 1952), pp. 19-20.

(121)  1952  "The Fifty Years That Made Us What We Are To-day." (Review of Frederick Lewis Allen, THE BIG CHANGE.) *The New York Times Book Review* (November 2, 1952).

*(122)  1953  "Women: The Darling Little Slaves." (Review of Simone de Beauvoir, THE SECOND SEX.) (Previously unpublished.)

## VI. Reviews*

(123)  1940  Max Lerner, IDEAS ARE WEAPONS. *American Sociological Review* (April, 1940).

(124)  1940  Max Otto, THE HUMAN ENTERPRISE: AN ATTEMPT TO RELATE PHILOSOPHY TO DAILY LIFE. *American Sociological Review,* Vol. V, No. 4 (August, 1940).

(125)  1940  J. H. Woodger, THE TECHNIQUE OF THEORY CONSTRUCTION. *American Sociological Review,* Vol. V, No. 5 (October, 1940).

(126)  1941  Lewis A. Rohrbaugh, VECTORS IN GROUP CHANGE. *American Journal of Sociology,* Vol. 47, No. 1, 1941.

(127)  1942  Logan Wilson, THE ACADEMIC MAN. *American Sociological Review,* Vol. VII, No. 3 (June, 1942).

(128)  1942  Douglas Waples, Bernard Berelson, Franklin R. Bradshaw, WHAT READING DOES TO PEOPLE. *American Sociological Review,* Vol. VII, No. 2 (1942).

(129)  1943  John W. McConnell, THE EVOLUTION OF SOCIAL CLASSES. *American Sociological Review,* Vol. VIII, No. 1 (February, 1943).

(130)  1943  Virginia Thompson, POSTMORTEM ON MALAYA. *The New Leader* (February 20, 1943).

(131)  1943  Fred. C. Kelly, THE WRIGHT BROTHERS. *The New Republic* (May 31, 1943).

(132)  1943  Quincy Wright, A STUDY OF WAR. *Partisan Review,* Vol. 10 (May-June, 1943).

(133)  1943  Sidney Hook, THE HERO IN HISTORY: A STUDY IN LIMITATION AND POSSIBILITY. *The New Republic* (June 21, 1943).

(134)  1943  Isabel Paterson, THE GOD OF THE MACHINE. *The New Republic* (July 5, 1943).

(135)  1943  Kurt Singer, DUEL FOR THE NORTHLAND: THE WAR OF ENEMY AGENTS IN SCANDINAVIA. *The New Republic* (July 26, 1943).

* Unsigned reviews which Mills did for the *American Sociological Review* between 1939-1942 are not herein included. (I.L.H.)

(136) 1943 Gustavus Myers, HISTORY OF BIGOTRY IN THE UNITED STATES. *The New Republic* (September 6, 1943).

(137) 1943 Wilfred E. Binkley, AMERICAN POLITICAL PARTIES. *The New Leader* (October 30, 1943).

(138) 1943 P. Lamartine Yates and D. Warriner, FOOD AND FARMING IN POST-WAR EUROPE. *The New Republic* (November 22, 1943).

(139) 1943 Raymond Gram Swing, PREVIEW OF HISTORY, *The New Republic* (November 29, 1943).

(140) 1944 William Henry Chamberlain, THE RUSSIAN ENIGMA: AN INTERPRETATION. *Maryland Quarterly,* Vol. I, No. 2 (1944).

(141) 1944 J. F. Normano, THE SPIRIT OF AMERICAN ECONOMICS: A STUDY IN THE HISTORY OF ECONOMIC IDEAS IN THE UNITED STATES PRIOR TO THE GREAT DEPRESSION. *Journal of Legal and Political Sociology* (1944).

(142) 1944 Luther L. Bernard and Jessie Bernard, THE ORIGINS OF AMERICAN SOCIOLOGY (unpublished review).

(143) 1944 Eli Ginsberg, THE UNEMPLOYED. *The New Leader* (January 15, 1944).

(144) 1944 Hans Kelsen, SOCIETY AND NATURE: A SOCIOLOGICAL INQUIRY. *Political Science Quarterly,* Vol. LIX, No. 1 (March, 1944).

(145) 1944 Howard Selsam, SOCIALISM AND ETHICS. *Political Science Quarterly,* Vol. LIX, No. 1 (March, 1944).

(146) 1944 Arnold A. Nash, THE UNIVERSITY AND THE MODERN WORLD. *The New Leader* (April 29, 1944).

(147) 1944 Hadley Cantril (and associates), GAUGING PUBLIC OPINION. *The New Leader* (July 15, 1944).

(148) 1944 Marvin Farber (ed.), SYMPOSIUM ON THE SIGNIFICANCE OF MAX SCHELER FOR PHILOSOPHY AND SOCIAL SCIENCE. *American Journal of Sociology,* Vol. XLX, No. 2 (September, 1944).

(149) 1945 Joachim Wach, SOCIOLOGY OF RELIGION. *Political Science Quarterly,* Vol. LX, No. 1 (March, 1945).

(150) 1945 Felix Kaufmann, METHODOLOGY OF THE SOCIAL SCIENCES. *Political Science Quarterly,* Vol. LX, No. 2 (June, 1945).

(151) 1945 Otto Neurath, FOUNDATIONS OF THE SOCIAL SCIENCES. *American Journal of Sociology,* Vol. XLXI, No. 1 (July, 1945).

(152)   1946   Karen Horney, OUR INNER CONFLICTS. *Briar-cliffe Quarterly,* Vol. 3, No. 9 (April, 1946), pp. 84-85.

(153)   1950   Richard Centers, THE PSYCHOLOGY OF SO-CIAL CLASSES. *The Annals of the American Association of Political and Social Science* (March, 1950), pp. 241-42.

(154)   1952   Reinhard Bendix, HIGHER CIVIL SERVANTS IN AMERICAN SOCIETY. *American Journal of Sociology,* Vol. LVII, No. 5 (March, 1952).

(155)   1952   Morris L. Ernst, REPORT ON THE AMERICAN COMMUNIST. *The New York Times Book Review* (November 30, 1952).

(156)   1953   William Miller (ed.), MEN IN BUSINESS: ESSAYS IN THE HISTORY OF ENTREPRENEURSHIP. *American Sociological Review,* Vol. 18, No. 4 (1953), pp. 504-505.

(157)   1953   Philip Selznick, THE ORGANIZATION WEAPON: A STUDY OF BOLSHEVIK STRATEGY AND TACTICS. *The American Journal of Sociology,* Vol. LVIII, No. 5 (March, 1953).

(158)   1953   George Eaton Simpson and J. Milton Yinger, RACIAL AND CULTURAL MINORITIES: AN ANALYSIS OF PREJUDICE AND DISCRIMINATION. *New York Times Book Review* (April 26, 1953).

(159)   1953   Robert L. Heilbroner, THE WORLDLY PHILOSOPHERS. *Book Find News* (July, 1953).

(160)   1953   Floyd Hunter, COMMUNITY POWER STRUCTURE: A STUDY OF DECISION MAKERS. *Social Forces,* Vol. 30 (October, 1953), p. 92.

(161)   1953   Robert Straus and Selden D. Bacon, DRINKING IN COLLEGE. *New York Times Book Review* (October 4, 1953), p. 22.

(162)   1954   Robert A. Dahl and Charles E. Lindblom, POLITICS, ECONOMICS, AND WELFARE. *American Sociological Review,* Vol. 19 (August, 1954), pp. 495-496.

(163)   1954   Arthur Mann, YANKEE REFORMERS IN THE URBAN AGE. *The New York Times Book Review* (October 17, 1954).

(164)   1954   Roy Lewis, PROFESSIONAL PEOPLE IN ENGLAND. *Harvard Law Review,* Vol. 68 (November, 1954), pp. 198-199.

(165)   1955   Laurence Lader, THE MARGARET SANGER STORY: IN THE FIGHT FOR BIRTH CONTROL. *The New York Times Book Review* (April 17, 1955).

(166) 1955 David M. Potter, PEOPLE OF PLENTY: ECO-
NOMIC ABUNDANCE AND THE AMERICAN
CHARACTER. *Saturday Review* (July 16, 1955),
p. 19.

(167) 1955 A. C. Spectorsky, THE EXURBANITES. *Saturday
Review* (October 29, 1955), pp. 11-12.

(168) 1955 Albert P. Blaustein and Charles D. Porter, THE
AMERICAN LAWYER: A SUMMARY OF THE
SURVEY OF THE LEGAL PROFESSION. *Stan-
ford Law Review,* Vol. 8 (December, 1955), pp.
147-149.

(169) 1956 William H. Whyte Jr., THE ORGANIZATION
MAN. *The New York Times Book Review* (December 12, 1956).

(170) 1960 Reinhard Bendix, MAX WEBER: AN INTEL-
LECTUAL PORTRAIT. *The New York Times
Book Review* (January 7, 1960).

## VII. Miscellaneous Writings

(171) 1941 THE SOCIAL PSYCHOLOGY OF THE ME-
TROPOLIS. (Appendix to the mimeographed
translation of Georg Simmel's "The Metropolis
and Mental Life.") Unpublished, privately distributed, 1941-42. [With H. H. Gerth.]

(172) 1942 THE ERSATZ ABSOLUTE (Letter to the editor).
*Journal of Philosophy* (September 1942).

(173) 1943 CONVERSATION IN CAPETOWN—A DIA-
LOGUE (done in 1943, unpublished).

(174) 1945 THE BARRICADE AND THE BEDROOM. *Politics* (October, 1945), pp. 313-15. (A commentary
on Paul Goodman's "The Political Meaning of
Some Recent Revisions of Freud," July, 1945.)

(175) 1947 ALL THAT AND—A SURVEY OF THE LEFT.
(An editorial note.) *Labor and Nation* (March-
April, 1947).

(176) 1947 AUDIENCE RESEARCH IN THE MOVIE
FIELD. (By-line given to Paul F. Lazarsfeld, who
states at the conclusion of the article that "The
highlights here summarized are taken from a text
prepared by Dr. Mills.") *American Academy of
Political and Social Science,* Vol. 254 (1947), pp.
160-168.

(177) 1948 SOCIOLOGICAL POETRY. (A commentary on
James Agee published as a letter to Dwight Mac-
Donald.) *Politics* (Spring, 1948).

(178) 1951 HOPE FOR WHITE COLLAR WORKERS. (A
reply to a "White Collar Wife" in the form of a
letter.) *American Magazine* (May, 1951).

(179)  1952  HIGH CIVIL SERVANTS IN AMERICAN SOCIETY. (Reply to Reinhard Bendix' Letter to the editor.) *American Journal of Sociology*, Vol. LVIII, No. 3 (1952).

(180)  1954  WHO CONFORMS AND WHO DISSENTS? (Letter to the editor on Nathan Glazer's "Philistine Leftism.") *Commentary* (April, 1954), pp. 403-405.

(181)  1956  WHY I WROTE *THE POWER ELITE*. *Book Find News*, Issue 188 (1956).

(182)  1959  INTELLECTUALS AND RUSSIA. (Letter to Irving Howe.) *Dissent*, Vol. VI, No. 3 (Summer, 1959), pp. 295-298.

(183)  1961  C. WRIGHT MILLS ON KENNEDY. *Fair Play*, Vol. 2, No. 17 (August 26, 1961).

## VIII.  Major Lectures and Addresses

(184)  1940  SITUATED ACTIONS AND VOCABULARIES OF MOTIVES. Read to *The Society for Social Research,* University of Chicago, August 16-17, 1940.

(185)  1946  THE MIDDLE CLASSES IN MIDDLE-SIZED CITIES. Address given before the *American Sociological Society,* 40th Annual Meeting, Cleveland, March 1-3, 1946.

(186)  1947  THE NEW MIDDLE CLASS. Read to *The Labor Action School,* Hotel Diplomat, January 5, 1947.

(187)  1947  RECENT DEVELOPMENTS IN THE FIELD OF PERSONALITY STUDIES. Read to the *American Sociological Society,* December 29, 1947. (Previously unpublished.)

(188)  1949  HOW POWERFUL IS LABOR LEADERSHIP? (Radio discussion with Joel Seidman, Lee C. Shaw, N.B.C., text in: *Round Table,* May 8, 1949 [No. 58]).

(189)  1949  THE PATTERN OF HUMAN RELATIONS. Read to the Social Sciences Today Seminar, *Rand School of Social Science,* November 16, 1949.

(190)  1952  FREEDOM AND SECURITY IN OUR GARRISON STATE. Read at *Dean's Day Program,* Columbia College, March 22, 1952.

(191)  1953  LEISURE AND THE WHOLE MAN. Read at Twenty-Second Annual *Herald Tribune Forum,* October 20, 1953. [Printed in New York *Herald Tribune,* October 25, 1953.]

(192)  1954  GOVERNMENT AND MEN OF KNOWLEDGE. Read at *Dean's Day Program,* Columbia College, March 20, 1954.

(193) 1954  ARE WE LOSING OUR SENSE OF BELONG-ING? Read to the Twenty-Third Couchiching Conference, Toronto, Canada, August 15, 1954.

(194) 1954  ADMINISTRATIVE STRUCTURES AND THE MODERN STATE. Read to the Air War College, Maxwell Air Force Base, Alabama, August 25, 1954.

(195) 1955  THE POWER ELITE: MILITARY, ECONOMIC, AND POLITICAL, *Wayne State University,* Detroit Institute of Art Lecture Hall, April 25, 1955.

(196) 1958  WAR BECOMES TOTAL: A PAGAN SERMON FOR CHRISTIAN MINISTERS. Read to the *Board of Evangelism and Social Service of the United Church of Canada,* at Prince Arthur House, Toronto, Canada, February 27, 1958.

(197) 1958  THE CAUSES OF WORLD WAR THREE. Read at the *University of Illinois,* Urbana, Illinois, Friday, April 11, 1958.

(198) 1958  SOCIAL FORCES AND THE FRUSTRATIONS OF THE DESIGNER. *Read to the Aspen Conference—8th International Design Conference,* June 22, June 29, 1958, Aspen, Colorado.

(199) 1958  THE PROMISE OF SOCIOLOGY. Read to the Annual Meeting of the *American Political Science Association,* September 14, 1958, St. Louis, Missouri.

(200) 1958  WORLD WAR III AND UTOPIAN CAPITALISTS. Read to the *University of Texas* [series in honor of Wagner Gettys], October 24, 1958, Austin, Texas.

(201) 1958  CHARACTERISTICS OF OUR TIME. Read to *Annual Assembly, National Council of the Churches of Christ in the United States of America,* Atlantic City, New Jersey, December 10-13, 1958.

(202) 1958  CHARACTERISTICS OF OUR TIME. Read at the *University of Texas,* Townes Hall Auditorium, 1958.

(203) 1959  REMARKS ON THE PROBLEM OF INDUSTRIAL DEVELOPMENT. Read to *International Seminar on Resistances to Social Development,* Latin American Center of Investigations in the Social Sciences, Rio de Janeiro, Brazil.

(204) 1959  ON REASON AND FREEDOM. Read to the *London School of Economics and Politics,* and broadcast by the *British Broadcasting Corporation,* Third Programme, February, 1959.

(205)   1959    THE BIG CITY: PRIVATE TROUBLES AND
                PUBLIC ISSUES. Read to the *Fifth Annual Win-
                ter Conference of the Canadian Institute on Public
                Affairs,* February 7, 1959, Toronto, Canada.

## IX. Monographs and Essays on Mills' Work

(1)     1960    Abrams, Arnold: "C. Wright Mills: Controversial
                Figure In Conforming Society." *Columbia Daily
                Spectator* (November 29, 1960), p. 3.

(2)     1962    Albornoz, Orlando: "Wright Mills, Sociologo Mili-
                tante." *Critica Contemporanea* No. 8 (June-July
                1962), pp. 14-19.

(3)     1959    Alpert, Harry: "Revolt in the Social Sciences."
                *Northwest Review,* University of Oregon (Decem-
                ber 1959).

(4)     1958    Anderson, C. Arnold and Gracey, Harry L.:
                "C. Wright Mills' Power Elite: A Review Article."
                *Kentucky Law Journal,* Volume 46, No. 2 (Winter,
                1958), pp. 1-16.

(5)     1955    Andrieux and Lignon: "Une Étude Sur Les Nou-
                velles Classes Moyennes." *La Revue Socialiste,*
                Paris (November 1955).

(6)     1960    Aptheker, Herbert: *The World of C. Wright Mills.*
                New York, Marzani and Munsell, Inc., 1960.

(7)     1956    Aptheker, Herbert: "A Look at the Power Elite."
                *Mainstream* (September 1956), pp. 1-16.

(8)     1956    Bahsen, Poul: "Hvem Har Magten?" *Politiken
                Copenhagen* (July 27, 1956).

(9)     1958    Bell, Daniel: "The Power Elite Reconsidered."
                *American Journal Of Sociology,* LXIV No. 3
                (1958), pp. 238-250.

(10)    1960    Bottomore, Tom B.: "American Heretics." *Archive
                of European Sociology,* Vol. 1 (1960), pp. 289-
                296.

(11)    1959    Burgum, Edwin Berry: "American Society in Tran-
                sition." *Science and Society* (Fall, 1959), pp. 317-
                322.

(12)    1959    Cassill, R. V.: "Accusers and Pardoners." *The Na-
                tion* (November 14, 1959), pp. 354-360.

(13)    1960    Chamberlin, William Henry: "The Wild Talk Since
                Sputnik." *The New Leader* (January 20, 1960).

(14)    1956    Cochran, Bert: "Who Runs America." *American
                Socialist* (October, 1956), pp. 9-14.

(15)    1962    Dahrendorf, Ralf, "C. Wright Mills." Kölner *Zeit-
                schrift für Soziologie und Sozial-psychologie,* Vol.
                14, No. 3, pp. 603-605.

(16)  1961   Damish, Hubert: "L'Imagination Sociologique et la Perception de l'Histoire: Notes Sur L'Ouvre de C. Wright Mills." *Lettres Nouvelles,* Volume 9, Nos. 13, 16, 19 (1961), pp. 30-45, 128-139, 102-109.

(17)  1959   Davis, Arthur K.: "Sociology Without Clothes." *Monthly Review* (November 1959), pp. 256-263.

(18)  1959   Feuer, Lewis: "A Symposium on C. Wright Mills' *The Sociological Imagination." Berkeley Journal of Sociology,* Vol. 5, No. 1 (Fall, 1959), pp. 122-23.

(19)  1961   Friedenberg, Daniel M.: "Listen Yankee—A Review," *Dissent,* Vol. 8, No. 1, 1961. pp. 61-65.

(20)  1962   Gerth, Hans H.: "C. Wright Mills, 1916-1962." *Studies On The Left,* Vol. 2, No. 3 (1962), pp. 7-11.

(21)  1951   Haskell, Gordon: "The Middle Class in U. S. Society." *The New International* (September-October 1951).

(22)  1952   Hicks, Granville: "White Collar or Straight Jacket?" *New Leader* (January 28, 1952).

(23)  1962   Horowitz, Irving L.: "The Sociological Imagination of C. Wright Mills." *The American Journal of Sociology,* Vol. LXVIII, No. 1 (July 1962), pp. 105-107.

(24)  1962   Irving L. Horowitz, "C. Wright Mills: The Scientific Imagination of a Moral Man," *Our Generation Against Nuclear War,* Vol. I, No. 4. pp. 6-24.

(25)  1959   Hughes, H. Stuart: "A Politics of Peace." *Commentary* (February 1959).

(26)  1960   Kaufman, Arnold S.: "The Irresponsibility of American Social Scientists." *Inquiry: An Interdisciplinary Journal of Philosophy and the Social Sciences,* Vol. 3, No. 2 (1960), pp. 102-117.

(27)  1959   Lichtheim, George: "Rethinking World Politics." *Commentary* (September 1959), pp. 249-257.

(28)  1952   Macdonald, Dwight: "Abstractio Ad Absurdum." *Partisan Review,* Vol. 14, No. 1 (January-February 1952), pp. 110-114.

(29)  1960   Martinson, Robert: "The Critics of C. Wright Mills." *Anvil* (Winter, 1960), pp. 13-16.

(30)  1962   Miliband, Ralph: "C. Wright Mills." *New Left Review,* No. 15 (May-June 1962), pp. 15-20.

(31)  1960   Parsons, Talcott: "The Destruction of Power in American Society." *Structure and Process in Modern Societies.* Glencoe, Illinois: (1960), pp. 199-225.

(32)  1957   Rawick, George: "Who Rules in America; The Powerful." *Anvil* (Winter, 1957), pp. 7, 8.

(33)  1958   Record, Wilson: "Review of Power Elite." *Kentucky Law Journal,* Vol. 46, No. 4 (Summer, 1958), pp. 654-658.

(34)  1957   Rexroth, Kenneth: "The Boys Who Rule the World." *The Nation* (November 2, 1957), pp. 295-297.

(35)  1956   Rosenberg, Bernard; Walter, Eugene V.: "The Power Elite: Two Views." *Dissent* (Fall, 1956), pp. 390-398.

(36)  1959   Schuman, Frederick L.: "New World or No World: Two Spokesmen For Sanity." *The New Reasoner,* England (February 1959), pp. 401-406.

(37)  1961   Lipset, Seymour Martin and Neil Smelser: "Change and Controversy in Recent American Sociology." *The British Journal of Sociology,* Vol. XII, No. 1 (March 1961), pp. 41-51.

(38)  1960   Shark, G. B.: "Mills And Weber: Formalism and the Analysis of Social Structure." *Science And Society* (Spring 1960), pp. 113-133.

(39)  1952   Smythe, Dallas W.: "On Noticing Our White Collars." *A.E.B. Newsletter* (August 1952), pp. 13-15.

(40)  1956   Sweezy, Paul M.: "Power Elite or Ruling Class?" *Monthly Review* (September 1956), pp. 138-139.

(41)  1958   Toledo, Mario Monteforte: "Sociologia Del Poder En Estados Unidos." *El Universal* (February 16, 1958).

(42)  1959   Wisley, Charles: "World Without War." *Mainstream* (November 1959), pp. 1-12.

(43)  1962   Wolfe, Robert: "Intellectuals and Social Change," Vol. 2, No. 3 (1962), pp. 63-68.

(44)  1959   Wrong, Dennis H.: "Political Science And The Social Sciences." *Columbia University Forum* (Fall 1959).

(45)  1959   Anonymous: "Here, At Last, is the True Voice of American Radicalism." *London Tribune* (January 16, 1959).

(46)  1956   Anonymous: "Who Governs America." *Pravda* (December 21, 1956).

## X. Reviews of Mills' Work*

(47)  1959  Akerman, Johan: "Atomkrig Och Fornuft." *Syd-svenska Dagbladet* (February 11, 1959). (WWT)

(48)  1956  Berle, A. A.: "Are The Blind Leading The Blind." *New York Times Book Review* (April 22, 1956), (PE)

(49)  1951  Black, John S.: Review. *America* (October 27, 1951). (WC)

(50)  1959  Brogan, D. W.: "New Worlds." *The Spectator* (January 16, 1959). (WWT)

(51)  1951  Brogan, D. W.: "Rise And Decline Of A Class." *Saturday Review Of Literature* (September 15, 1951). (WC)

(52)  1951  Brunn, Robert R.: "Little Man In The White Collar." *Christian Science Monitor* (September 27, 1951). (WC)

(53)  1949  Bunzel, John H.: Review. *New Century* (Winter 1949), pp. 24-27. (NMP)

(54)  1956  Campion, Donald R.: "The Mindlessness of the Powerful." *America* (May 5, 1956). (PE)

(55)  1952  Cates, John: Review. *The Nation* (March 1, 1952). (WC)

(56)  1959  Chamberlain, John: "The Job And Jargon Of Sociology." *Wall Street Journal* (May 14, 1959). (SI)

(57)  1958  Chamberlin, William Henry: "Two Plans For Winning Peace Are Noteworthy For Their Lack Of Realism." *Wall Street Journal* (December 22, 1958). (WWT)

(58)  1960  Chapman, Dwight W.: "Anyone For Great Issues?" *Contemporary Psychology* (March 1960). (SI)

(59)  1958  Chartier, Richard A.: "Who Rules America?" *Fellowship* (May 1, 1958), p. 32. (PE)

(60)  1956  Chase, Stuart: "Do Rich Folks, Bosses And War Lords Run America?" *Herald Tribune Book Review* (July 1, 1956). (PE)

(61)  1959  Cliff, Terry: "A Sense Of Helplessness." *I. S. I. S.* (December 2, 1959). (SI)

(62)  1959  Cochran, Bert: "C. Wright Mills' Anti-War Manifesto." *American Sociologist* (May 1959), pp. 18-21. (WWT)

* The code used for the specific books being reviewed is as follows: (NMP) *The New Men of Power;* (PRJ) *The Puerto Rican Journey;* (WC) *White Collar;* (CSS) *Character and Social Structure;* (PE) *The Power Elite;* (WWT) *The Causes of World War Three;* (SI) *The Sociological Imagination;* (IM) *Images of Man;* (LY) *Listen Yankee;* (M) *The Marxists.* [I.L.H.]

(63)   1960   Coser, Lewis: "The Uses of Sociology." *Partisan Review,* Vol. 27, No. 1 (Winter 1960), pp. 166-173. (SI)

(64)   1956   Crossman, R. H. S.: "Grooming For Power." *The New Statesman* and *The Nation* (June 2, 1956). (PE)

(65)   1956   Cunliffe, Marcus: "American Trends." *Encounter* (July 1956). (PE)

(66)   1959   Das Gupta, Jyotirindra: "Sociology Of Brinkmanship." *Vigil,* New Delhi (June 6, 1959), pp. 317-319. (WWT)

(67)   1956   Davis, Lambert: "Power Without Knowledge." *Saturday Review* (May 19, 1956), p. 36. (PE)

(68)   1952   Denney, Reuel: "Not All Are Victims." *Yale Review* (Spring 1952). (WC)

(69)   1949   Dodd, Paul A.: Review. *Annals Of The American Academy Of Political And Social Sciences* (May 1949), pp. 249-250. (NMP)

(70)   1960   Dubois, Jules: "Apologia For Castro." *Saturday Review* (December 17, 1960), pp. 19, 36. (LY)

(71)   1959   Duffus, R. L.: "The Plan of Attack is on War Itself." *New York Times Book Section* (January 11, 1959), pp. 3, 16. (WWT)

(72)   1959   Dunn, Robert W.: Review. *New World Review* (February 1959). (WWT)

(73)   1956   Engler, Robert: "Power Without Accountability." *New Republic* (April 30, 1956). (PE)

(74)   1958   Evans, Stanton: "The Road To Millstown." *National Review* (December 20, 1958). (WWT)

(75)   1960   Fletcher, Ronald: (Review of *The Sociological Imagination.*) *The British Journal of Sociology,* Vol. 11, No. 2 (1960), pp. 169-170. (SI)

(76)   1959   Fitzgerald, Edward: "The Power Elite—A Resumé." *The Promethean Review* (January-February 1959). (PE)

(77)   1954   Gavin, Mortimer H.: Review. *Social Order* (September, 1954), pp. 329, 330. (WC)

(78)   1960   Gellner, Ernest: Review. *Nature* (May 14, 1960). (SI)

(79)   1960   Goldbloom, Maurice J.: "Spokesman For Castro." *New York Post* (November 27, 1960). (LY)

(80)   1959   Gore, Roy: "Pre-Mikoyan Pointer." *London Daily Worker* (January 29, 1959). (WWT)

(81)   1959   Gould, Julius: "A Self-Appointed Outsider." *Socialist Commentary* (November 1959). (SI)

(82)   1956   Grant, Laura: "C. Wright Mills Dissects the Rulers of America." *Labor Action* (July 30, 1956). (PE)

(83)   1957   Gross, Jesse: "Thought and Action in America." *Solidarity* (February 1957), p. 28. (PE)

(84)   1950   Grutzner, Charles: "They Live in Harlem." *New York Times* (September 24, 1950). (PRJ)

(85)   1958   Hacker, Andrew: "Realistic Pacifism." *Cornell Student Paper* (December 8, 1958). (WWT)

(86)   1948   Hall, Ben: "Labor's Leaders." *The New International* (November 1948). (NMP)

(87)   1960   Hallstrom, Anders: "Sociologisk Självkritik." *Kvälls Posten Malmö Moderat* (January 15, 1960). (SI)

(88)   1959   Halsey, A. H.: Review. *U. L. R.* (Autumn 1959), pp. 71-72. (SI)

(89)   1959   Hampshire, Stuart: "Power Elites Today." *London Sunday Times* (January 18, 1959). (WWT)

(90)   1961   Hansen, Joseph: "Theory of the Cuban Revolution." *International Socialist Review,* Vol. 22, No. 1 (Winter 1961), pp. 3-10, 29. (LY)

(91)   1952   Harrington, Lloyd: "America's New Middle Classes." *Canadian Forum* (February 1952). (WC)

(92)   1956   Harrington, Michael: "A Ruling Class." *Commonweal* (June 22, 1956). (PE)

(93)   1960   Haselden, Kyle: "Cuba: Two American Views." *The Christian Century* (December 21, 1960), pp. 1501-1502. (LY)

(94)   1957   Heard, Alexander: Review. *Annals of the American Academy of Political and Social Sciences* (May 1957). (PE)

(95)   1956   Henius, Bent: "Professor PAA Motorcykel." *Berlingske Tidende* (July 1, 1956), (Danish). (PE)

(96)   1948   Herrick, Elinore: "Labor Leaders of Today." *New York Herald Tribune* (October 17, 1948). (NMP)

(97)   1960   Herring, Hubert: "American Spokesman for Dr. Castro." *Herald Tribune* (November 27, 1960). (LY)

(98)   1962   Hodges, Donald Clark: "Review of *Images of Man*." *Science and Society,* Vol. 26, No. 1 (Winter 1962), pp. 77-81. (IM)

(99)   1959   Hoggart, Richard: "Nothing Like Leather." *Observer* (September 6, 1959). (SI)

(100)   1962   Horowitz, Irving L.: "C. Wright Mills and the Dragons of Marxism." *The American Scholar,* Vol. 31, No. 4 (Fall 1962), pp. 646-652. (M)

(101) 1958 Howard, Jack: "A Sociologist Tosses A Few Challenges to the Intellectuals." *San Francisco Chronicle* (December 14, 1958). (WWT)

(102) 1948 Howe, Irving: "Possibilities For Politics." *Partisan Review,* Vol. 15, No. 12 (December 1948), pp. 1356-1359. (NMP)

(103) 1951 Howe, Irving: "The New Middle Class." *The Nation* (October 13, 1951). (WC)

(104) 1959 Hughes, Everett: "Can History Be Made?" *New Republic* (June 22, 1959). (SI)

(105) 1951 Hughes, Everett: "The New Middle Classes." *Commentary* (November 1951), pp. 497-498. (WC)

(106) 1961 Huberman, Leo: "The Voice of Cuba." *Monthly Review* (February 1961), pp. 530-532. (LY)

(107) 1951 Hurwitz, Howard L.: Review. *Senior Scholastic* (November 28, 1951). (WC)

(108) 1961 Johnson, Gerald W.: "Latin Problem: Banana Republics or Banana Peels." *The New Republic* (January 1961). (LY)

(109) 1959 Johnson, Harry: "The Fourth Epoch." *Spectator* (London), (September 4, 1959). (SI)

(110) 1951 Kallen, H. M.: "The Hollow Men: A Portrayal to Ponder." *New York Times* (September 16, 1951). (WC)

(111) 1959 Kay, Ernest: "Slaves or Corpses." *Time and Tide* (London), (April 11, 1959). (WWT)

(112) 1958 Kirk, Russell: "Freely Given Advice on Saving the World." *Chicago Sunday Tribune* (December 28, 1958). (WWT)

(113) 1959 Kirk, Russell: "Shrewd Knocks at Sociological Theories." *Chicago Sunday Tribune* (May 24, 1959). (SI)

(114) 1948 Levenstein, Aaron: "Labor's Leaders." *The Progressive* (November 1948). (NMP)

(115) 1949 Lindblom, Charles E.: Review. *American Sociological Review* (June 1949), pp. 432-433. (NMP)

(116) 1948 Loftus, Joseph A.: "Labor Leaders and Trade Unions." *New York Times* (October 3, 1948). (NMP)

(117) 1956 Lynd, Robert S.: "Power In The United States." *The Nation,* Vol. 182, No. 19 (May 12, 1956), pp. 408-411. (PE)

(118) 1956 Macdonald, H. Malcolm: Review of *The Power Elite. American Political Science Review,* Vol. 50, No. 4 (1956), 1168. (PE)

(119) 1959 Madge, Charles: "The Politics of Truth." *The New Statesman* (September 5, 1959). (SI)

(120)  1959   Merriam, Charles E. (Review of *From Max Weber*.) *American Political Science Review*, Vol. 41, No. 1 (1947), pp. 150-151.

(121)  1956   Miller, William Lee: "Queen Ants and Cadillacs." *The Reporter* (May 31, 1956), p. 47. (PE)

(122)  1956   Miller, William: Review. *Book Find News*, Issue No. 188. (PE)

(123)  1960   Miller, William: Review. *Book Find News*, Issue No. 240. (SI)

(124)  1954   Mishler, Elliot G.: Review. *Public Opinion Quarterly*, Vol. 18, No. 3 (Fall 1954), pp. 323-326. (CSS)

(125)  1948   Morehead, Eleanor: "Two Views of American Labor Leaders." *New York Star* (October 3, 1948). (NMP)

(126)  1959   Muste, A. J.; Howe, Irving: "C. Wright Mills' Program: Two Views." *Dissent*, Vol. VI, No. 2 (Spring 1959), pp. 189-196. (WWT)

(127)  1959   Nathan, Otto: "On the Causes and Cure of War." *National Guardian* (January 26, 1959). (WWT)

(128)  1948   Nichols, Robert E.: "The Leaders of Labor." *The Nation* (October 2, 1948). (NMP)

(129)  1959   Neumann, William L.: "Program for Peace." *The Progressive* (February 1959). (WWT)

(130)  1959   Newman, James R.: "Four Approaches to the Problem of Preventing a Third World War." *Scientific American* (February 1959). (WWT)

(131)  1959   O'Donnell, Donat: "Distortions of Sociology." *Manchester Guardian* (September 8, 1959). (SI)

(132)  1951   Palyi, Melchior: "Sociologist's Bitter Study of the Middle Class." *Chicago Tribune* (November 25, 1951). (WC)

(133)  1959   Peck, Sidney M.: "Post Modern Sociology." *Studies on the Left*, Vol. I, No. 1 (Fall 1959), pp. 71-74. (SI)

(134)  1959   Pear, Richard H.: "Rationality Without Reason." *The New Reasoner* (Summer 1959). (WWT)

(135)  1959   Pickrel, Paul: "Images of Society." *Harpers* (June 1959). (SI)

(136)  1959   Pickrel, Paul: "The Olympians." *Harpers* (April 1956). (PE)

(137)  1956   Porter, R. E.: "Does a Power Elite Govern America?" *Brotherhood of Locomotive Fireman and Engineers' Magazine* (August 1956), pp. 94-95. (PE)

(138)  1951   Porter, Sylvia F.: "Review of White Collar." *The New York Post* (October 25, 1951). (WC)

(139) 1959   Record, Wilson C.: "Of History and Sociology." *American Quarterly*, Vol. 11, No. 3 (Fall 1959), pp. 425-429. (SI)

(140) 1956   Rieff, Philip: "Socialism and Sociology." *Partisan Review*, Vol. XXIII, No. 3 (Summer 1956), pp. 365-369. (PE)

(141) 1952   Riesman, David: "Review of White Collar." *American Journal of Sociology*, Vol. LVII, No. 5 (March, 1952), pp. 513-515. (WC)

(142) 1958   Roberts, Chalmers M.: "How Many Years to Go?" *Washington Post* (December 7, 1958). (WWT)

(143) 1956   Rodell, Fred and Dennis W. Brogan: "An American and a British View of *The Power Elite*." *Saturday Review* (April 28, 1956), pp. 9-10. (PE)

(144) 1960   Rogers, Edward: "The World We Live In." *Methodist Recorder* (January 7, 1960). (SI)

(145) 1956   Rossi, Peter H.: "Review of Power Elite." *American Journal of Sociology*, Vol. LXII, No. 2 (September 1956). (PE)

(146) 1956   Rovere, Richard H.: "The Interlocking Overlappers." *The Progressive* (June 1956). (PE)

(147) 1958   Schlesinger, Arthur Jr.: "This Isn't the Way." *New York Post* (December 7, 1958). (WWT)

(148) 1951   Seligman, Ben B.: "The Briefcase Man." *New Republic* (September 17, 1951). (WC)

(149) 1960   Shils, Edward: "Imaginary Sociology." *Encounter* (June, 1960), pp. 77-81. (SI)

(150) 1949   Shister, Joseph: "Important Study of Union Leaders." *Labor* and *Nation* (January-February 1949). (NMP)

(151) 1959   Skinner, J. Allen: "All Set for War." *Peace News*, England (March 6, 1959). (WWT)

(152) 1949   Starr, Mark: "Labor Through Polls." *The Labor Zionist* (March 18, 1949). (NMP)

(153) 1952   Stessin, Lawrence: Review. *The Management Review* (February 1952). (WC)

(154) 1948   Trott, Harlan: "American Leaders of Labor Today." *Christian Science Monitor* (September 23, 1948). (NMP)

(155) 1959   Vacha, Robert: "Is the U.S.A. Driving the World to War?" *Weekly Scotsman* (February 5, 1959). (WWT)

(156) 1962   Warde, William F.: "The Marxists." *International Socialist Review*, Vol. 23, No. 3 (Summer 1962), pp. 67-75, 95. (M)

Wheildon, Leonard: "World War Three, Can it be Stopped?" *Boston Herald* (December 8, 1958). (WWT)

(158) 1959 Wieck, David: "Private Troubles and Public Issues." *Liberation* (April 1959). (WWT)

(159) 1960 Willmott, Peter: Review. *Universities Quarterly* (January 1960), pp. 92-95. (SI)

(160) 1952 Wrong, Dennis H.: "Our Troubled Middle Classes." *American Mercury* (January 1952), pp. 107-113. (WC)

(161) 1956 Wrong, Dennis H.: "Power in America." *Commentary* (September 1956), pp. 278-280. (PE)

(162) 1959 Wrong, Dennis H.: "The Failure of Sociology." *Commentary* (November 1959), pp. 375-380. (SI)

(163) 1961 Young, Murray: Review. *New World Review* (March 1961), pp. 46, 47. (LY)

(164) 1959 Anonymous: "Cat Among Pundits." *London Times Literary Supplement* (January 16, 1959). (WWT)

(165) 1959 Anonymous: "He Examines Causes of W. W. III." *The Star,* Johannesburg (March 12, 1959). (WWT)

(166) 1954 Anonymous: "Man and Society." *The Economist* (October 2, 1954). (CSS)

(167) 1956 Anonymous: "Power and Morality." *King's Crown Essays* (Spring 1956), pp. 56-60. (PE)

(168) 1957 Anonymous: "The Challenge to the Individual." *Manas* (August 7, 1957), pp. 3, 4. (PE)

(169) 1956 Anonymous: "The New Oligarchy." *Atlantic Monthly* (June 1956). (PE)

(170) 1959 Anonymous: "War and Peace." *Weekly People* (January 17, 1959). (WWT)

(171) 1960 Anonymous: "Whither Sociology." *London Times* (January 29, 1960). (SI)

# SUBJECT INDEX

absentee ownership, 62-63
"abstracted empiricism," 3
abstraction; level of, 560-63
adjustment, 547-52
administration, 35, 53
administrator, 556
administrators; federal, 82
admirals, 204
advertisement, 581
affiliation, 49-50
affluent society, 8
Africa, 249
agencies of change, 18
agrarian revolt, 34
alienation, 233, 301; self, 161
American business elite, 110-39;
educational level of, 122, 125,
128; extraction by social level,
122, 128; and number of political offices, 130; and occupation of fathers, 124; place
of origin and success, 113,
115-16, 118
American celebration, 602-03
American Federation of Labor
(AFL), 77-96, 102-03, 281
American Labor Party (ALP),
90, 92n
American political elite, 196-207
American Revolution, 112
Ancient China; language and
ideas of, 469-520
anthropologists, social, 52
anthropomorphism, 517
anti-business, 281
anti-capitalist feeling; in anti-
Semitism, 177
anti-communists, 223-24, 226
anti-fascism, 222
anti-Semitism, 177, 223-24
Apollonian Way, 159
architect, 401
aristocracy, 12, 13, 211, 213-14;
authority of, 212; British, 63;
feudal, 312

army, 73, 297, 400-01
artisan (see also craftsmanship),
383
artist, 299, 401-02, 408, 412,
417-19
art; work and, 384
arts, 375, 417-19
Aryan, 177
Aryanization, 172
Asia, 5, 249
associations, 49-50, 318, 356-57;
trade, 72-75; voluntary, 254,
281-82, 360-61, 543n-44n,
584
Attorney Generals, 199
authority, 15, 23, 25, 193-94,
213-14, 345-59, 392, 410, 412,
416, 580-85; corporate, 34;
and culture, 409; institutions
of, 585; political, 172; and
power, 612; social, 517

balance, 32; image of, 30, 31;
of power, 33
Behemoth; Nazi, 170-78
big business, 185-86, 267-73,
277, 301-02, 545f
big cities, 333, 395-402
"biography," 15
biographical form; in social sciences, 5
biology; and woman question,
340
bourgeoisie, 309, 420-21, 539,
549n
brain-trusters, 68
Britain (see also England), 72-
73, 247, 258, 387-94; and
United States, 387
Buddhism, 159-62
bureaucracies, 65-69, 229, 237,
242, 269-71, 273, 298, 560-65;
twentieth century, 69

# NAME AND TITLE INDEX